```
FREQUENCIES VARIABLES= v58
FREQUENCIES VARIABLES= v58
     /STATISTICS= MODE MEDIAN
     /HBAR
MANOVA egal BY country(0,2) v50(1,2) WITH ses famsize
MEANS TABLES= egal BY countryr
     /STATISTICS= ANOVA
NONPAR CORR VARIABLES= v23, v24
     /PRINT= TWOTAIL
PLOT
     /SYMBOLS='*'
     /TITLE='prestige rating by education'
     /VERTICAL='prestige score'
     /HORIZONTAL='years of education'
     /PLOT=prestige WITH ed
REGRESSION DESCRIPTIVES
     /VARIABLES= prestige income TO ex
     /DEPENDENT= prestige
     /BACKWARD
RELIABILITY VARIABLES= v29 v30r to v33r
     /SCALE (sexatt)= v29 v30r to v33r
     /STATISTICS= DESC CORR
     /SUMMARY= MEANS CORR TOTAL
T-TEST PAIRS=time1 time2
T-TEST GROUPS=tire (1,2) / VARIABLES=time1
```

3. UTILITIES

```
COMPUTE newvar = (V16 + V28) / 2
IF (V15 LT 25) newvar = 1
LIST VARIABLES = id, v1, v17/CASES = 50
RECODE V33, V34 (1,2,3 = 1)(4 THRU 8 = 2) INTO V33R, V34R
SET WIDTH=80
SET LENGTH=59
SORT CASES BY dept,name
```

Methods

DOING SOCIAL RESEARCH

WINSTON JACKSON

ST. FRANCIS XAVIER UNIVERSITY

PRENTICE HALL CANADA INC., SCARBOROUGH, ONTARIO

Canadian Cataloguing in Publication Data

Jackson, Winston
    Methods: doing social research

Includes index.
ISBN 0-13-064031-X

1. Social science - Research - Methodology.
I. Title.

H62.J34   1995   300´.7   C94-931303-3

Prentice-Hall, Inc., Englewood Cliffs, New Jersey
Prentice-Hall International (UK) Limited, London
Prentice-Hall of Australia, Pty. Limited, Sydney
Prentice-Hall Hispanoamericana, S.A., Mexico City
Prentice-Hall of India Private Limited, New Delhi
Prentice-Hall of Japan, Inc., Tokyo
Simon & Schuster Asia Private Limited, Singapore
Editora Prentice-Hall do Brasil, Ltda., Rio de Janeiro

ISBN 0-13-064031-X

Acquisitions Editor: Marjorie Munroe
Developmental Editor: Maurice Esses
Production Editor: Norman Bernard
Production Coordinator: Sharon Houston
Art Director: Bruce Bond
Cover and Internal Design: Carole Giguère
Cover Image: Bert Klassen
Page Layout: Hermia Chung

1 2 3 4 5   RRD   99 98 97 96 95

Printed and bound in the United States of America.

Every reasonable effort has been made to obtain permissions for all
articles and data used in this edition. If errors or omissions have occurred,
they will be corrected in future editions provided written notification has
been received by the publisher.

 This book is printed on recycled paper.

To:
Marlies,
Janes, Kathleen, Danielle,
Jeremy, Paula

BRIEF TABLE OF CONTENTS

TABLE OF CONTENTS

PREFACE

Methods: Doing Social Research attempts to be inclusive. The underlying message is that while there are a variety of methodologies and theoretical orientations within the social science community, we should attempt to appreciate the value each has in furthering our knowledge of social behaviour. No one theory, research design, measurement procedure, or statistical approach can provide a satisfactory answer to all research questions. Simply put, we need to develop an appreciation of the diversity of approaches available to the social scientist.

Students are encouraged to do research projects. And to help them many rules, tips, and steps are presented in order to facilitate the completion of a project. When I meet up with students years after they have completed university studies, they sometimes will tell me about the project they did in research methods many years earlier. To me, this indicates that students learn most by doing projects. The task of the instructor is to help the student through the often intimidating task of doing a project.

While an effort has been made to cover the main contemporary methodological approaches, many had to be omitted. It is no longer possible to write a comprehensive social science methods text. Preparing a methodological encyclopedia would be the only approach to listing all the available methods. The text therefore has a bias towards featuring those methods that are most popular in contemporary usage. Many less frequently used techniques, or techniques that were considered too complex for the beginning researcher, simply did not survive the selection process.

The enormous expansion in the social sciences over the past three decades has seen an increase in the variety of theoretical, methodological, and pragmatic concerns of social science practitioners. And there appears to be confusion over the appropriate role of social scientists in bringing about social change, or in resisting it, and confusion over what kinds of evidence are appropriate for what kinds of questions. And there are competing ideological pressures to do one kind of social science or another, use one technique or another. Students will encounter much mystification in the areas of design, statistics, and measurement, and also about what constitutes appropriate kinds of questions to be researched by social scientists. This text tries to demystify these and other topics. Rules and steps are provided to help the student complete a first project in social science research. Only the basics are provided here, but the hope is that sufficient is provided to give the student an inclusive, generous view of the full range of social science approaches.

The order of the chapters follows the stages of the research process. Part 1 (Chapters 1 and 2) reviews the basic methodological approaches and discusses a variety of theoretical perspectives that social scientists use to explain human behaviour. Part 2 (Chapters 3 to 6) explores alternative research designs. Part 3 (Chapters 7 and 8) presents a review of elementary statistical procedures used by social science researchers. Part 4 (Chapters 9 to 14) begins by pointing out sources of bias and discusses ethical concerns in order to prepare the beginning researcher for designing a study. The following chapters deal with how to get a project started, and include discussions of measurement, questionnaire construction, and sampling. Part 5 (Chapters 15 to 18), deals with issues of data analysis, the testing of causal models, and a presentation of frequently used analysis procedures. Chapter 18 discusses the writing of a research report. Part 6 includes various appendices. Appendix A explains how to process data using SPSS (both mainframe and PC versions). This section walks the first-time user through the various steps in analyzing a project. Sample jobs are included which cover the basic procedures required to complete a project. The remaining appendices provide various statistical tables, a sample questionnaire, and the SSHRC ethics guide.

The chapters may be treated in any order. If the book is being used as a text in a course where research projects are required, it is recommended that the review of statistical matters be started early in the course, along with any computer labs (a set of training labs are included in the Instructor's Manual), so that by the time students have their studies designed and their data collected, they will be ready to commence analysis. Some instructors find it best to present the statistical chapters in every other lecture, using the other lectures for the discussion of the material included in the first six chapters.

Some of the features included in this text but not typically found in other Canadian methods texts are:

- an emphasis on practical, down-to-earth steps, rules, and procedures that help to guide students through a project from framing the question to designing the study, collecting the data, analyzing the data, and reporting the results;

- a de-mystification of the research process by explaining as simply as possible how research is done;

- a presentation of problems of bias in research early in the text to alert students to be strong critics of research and to recognize its limitations;

- a presentation of Milgram's (obedience to authority) and Humphreys' (observations of bi-sexual males in public washrooms) research, thus alerting students to two key studies which raised important ethical dilemmas and which helped shape the development of contemporary ethical guidelines;

- the use of computational methods that are kept as simple as possible and notations that can be followed easily;

- a section on analyzing data without using a computer for those researchers who do not have access to a computer or for problems that do not require computer analysis;

- the inclusion of an appendix providing instructions and illustrations for the use of SPSS^x and SPSS/PC+;
- the inclusion of Boxes to illustrate material in the text; over 50 percent of the authors cited in these boxes are Canadian;
- a presentation of original views in the areas of:
  - measurement, the problem of grouping data, and the impact grouping has on results;
  - encouraging the use of 9-point Likert-type items;
  - interpreting three variable relations. We present a *rule of thirds* which is easier to learn than the traditional approach;
  - techniques for visually estimating correlations and simple linear equations.

Relevant chapters include problems and suggested activities for the students to increase their involvement in the course materials. In addition, an international data set (an SPSS export file) is included which may be used in learning how to analyze data using SPSS. A number of training labs are included on the disk accompanying the Instructor's Manual.

Many individuals have freely given their advice on different aspects of this text as it was being developed. I would especially like to thank the many students who have challenged me with interesting research problems and have taught me so much. I also wish to acknowledge the help of Brian E. Butler, Linda Christiansen-Ruffman, Sandra Kirby, Michael Kompf, Murray Knuttila, Clayton Mosher, Chris Szafnicki, and Paul Wong and thank them for the invaluable suggestions they provided when reviewing the text. I hope they can spot the places where they improved the text, and perhaps not notice where I did not follow their counsel. Many people at St. Francis Xavier University helped in a variety of ways. In particular I would like to mention Sergei Aalto, Gary Brooks, Ann Louise Brookes, Moh Fiaz, Angela Gillis, Mary Gillis, Zoe Hayes, Marlies Jackson, Ron Johnson, Chris Jones, Jason Ryan MacLean, Marian MacLellan, Debbie Murphy, Barbara Phillips. I owe thanks to all of them.

I wish also to acknowledge the contribution of St. Francis Xavier University in providing the sabbatical leave which gave me the opportunity to work on the manuscript: the support of J.J. MacDonald, John Sears, and Ken den Heyer is most appreciated.

I am also particularly indebted to SPSS Inc. for permission to present the commands for SPSS^x and SPSS/PC+. As always, SPSS personnel have been most helpful and cooperative.

Finally I wish to acknowledge the Prentice Hall Canada Inc. staff whose professionalism and editorial and production work is much appreciated. In particular I would like to thank Patrick Ferrier, Maurice Esses, Norman Bernard, Carole Giguère, and Hermia Chung.

Winston Jackson
1995

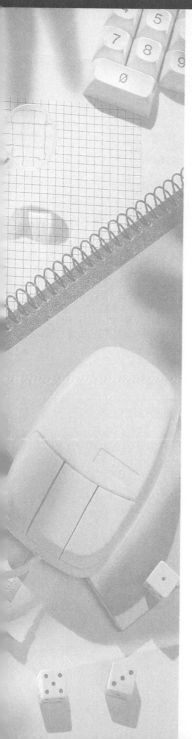

PRELIMINARIES

The first chapter introduces the reader to three basic approaches to social science methodology, distinguishes between qualitative and quantitative strategies in understanding human behaviour, and introduces some of the key terms used in talking about research methods. The second chapter introduces the reader to social science theories, arguing that theories are simply general explanations of social behaviour. Approaches to testing theories are presented along with the basic ideas of several social theories.

APPROACHES TO METHODS

Western cultures share a great confidence in and respect for science as the way to truth. Science is seen as a powerful tool—a tool which can help solve social problems. And contemporary societies have enormous problems: profound challenges posed by poverty, environmental degradation, uneven regional development, and inequalities in education, employment, and health care.

The challenge for social science is to live up to the expectations the larger society has of it. Social scientists are attempting to understand phenomena that are extremely complex and subject to many interpretations. While there are elements of human behaviour that may be simple, much of human behaviour cannot be understood satisfactorily with simple, mechanistic models. A *mechanistic model* is one which asserts that a particular behaviour is completely controlled by one or more external actions or events. In most cases, human behaviour is much more complicated. Many factors are usually involved, and involved differently, depending on the situation and on the culture. Social scientists come to know, to understand the complexity of human behaviour, by using a variety of methodologies. This text will introduce the key methodologies that contemporary social scientists use. Some of these methodologies are illustrated in Box 1.1.

BOX 1.1

Births and the Variety of Research Designs

To illustrate the range of available research techniques let us consider how information related to births in our society might be examined.

Secondary Data

Because of their impact on society, birth rates (along with other demographic patterns) are important to demographers, economists, and sociologists. For example, such researchers might want to find out if birth rates are lowered by structural constraints such as limited choice in housing (eg. few inexpensive apartment units that have more than two bedrooms) or limited opportunities in the labour market to earn sufficient income, or raised by family allowance programs such as those in Canada and France. Researchers who wish to monitor shifts in birth rates normally rely on the analysis of existing government statistics. They rely on **secondary data**, data collected by persons other than the researcher.

Survey

Changes in attitudes toward appropriate family size might be another factor a researcher should examine. A political scientist, historian, or sociologist might wish to explore why the province of Quebec went from having the second highest birth rate in Canada to the lowest within one generation. What factors influenced such a dramatic shift? If changing attitudes were a factor, what changed them? Here a sociologist would probably conduct a *survey* to represent people drawn from different age groups. The questions asked about "family size" would seek to measure those factors which the researcher identifies as probable causes of variation in family size. A political scientist might be particularly interested in the role of the church in the daily lives of Quebecers. The political scientist/historian might conduct a *historical-comparative* study to show how the influence of the Roman Catholic church in Quebec declined.

Experiment

A psychologist might be interested in examining the impact of a film on birth control on attitudes toward family size. In this case, the psychologist would probably use an *experimental design*. Two groups would be formed by random assignment and the attitudes of both groups on desired family size would be measured. One group (the experimental group) would then be shown a film about family planning, while the other (the control group) would be shown a film unrelated to the issue at hand. Finally the attitudes of both groups on desired family size would be remeasured. Here the experiment is designed to test whether a film has an impact on an attitude.

Quasi-Experiment

A nursing researcher might be interested in testing a program to increase the parenting confidence of new mothers. In such cases the researcher might monitor a group of new mothers over a period of time in an attempt to understand the importance of different support systems, education, and other factors in developing parenting confidence. Such an investigation represents a *quasi-experiment* designed to measure the response of new mothers to a training program.

Participant Observation

Another social researcher might want to examine how we have institutionalized the process of giving birth in our society. How do we organize the obstetrics ward? What are the rules of behaviour and rituals surrounding the birth of a child? In this case, the researcher might use a *participant observation* design, perhaps by working as a ward assistant, in an attempt to describe the various behaviours. Here the researcher would view the ward as a total social system where the needs of the mother and her new child are met within the ward. How are crises, such as the death of the child, managed? What are the unwritten tactics used by nurses to manage patients, newborns, doctors, hospital administrators, and visitors?

These approaches to studying aspects of births (see Box 1.1) indicate but a small number of those used to explore social science issues. The complexity of the questions we ask about human behaviour is truly humbling. In attempting to understand them, many theoretical perspectives have been developed, along with a diversity of research techniques. This text will introduce the beginning research methods student to some of the main methodological approaches and techniques used in the social sciences today. A single text cannot adequately cover all available methods, nor is it possible to provide sufficient detail for the more advanced student.

The goals of the social sciences vary from discipline to discipline and from researcher to researcher. Most would agree, however, that one goal is to produce an understanding of social behaviour. Why do we find regularities, or patterns, in human behaviour? Which patterns are unique to a particular culture and which are found in most cultures? We want not only to document these regularities, but also to understand the complexity of human perceptions, values, and motivations. An additional goal shared by many social scientists is to improve our quality of life through the application of the social sciences. All these goals are enormously challenging. There are many different paths we can take to try and attain them.

A. KEY METHODOLOGICAL APPROACHES IN THE SOCIAL SCIENCES

We can identify three important contemporary approaches in the social sciences: the positivist approach, the interpretive approach, and the critical approach. Let us investigate the assumptions that these approaches make about science, human behaviour, and values and also their preferred methodologies and possible weaknesses.

1. THE POSITIVIST APPROACH

A. THE NATURE OF THE POSITIVIST APPROACH

Most people will have some familiarity with the ***positivist approach***—for it is the approach used in the physical sciences. In the early development of the social sciences some theorists attempted to model the new disciplines on the physical sciences. The French scholars Auguste Comte (1798-1857) and Emile Durkheim (1858-1917) were leaders in encouraging positivist approaches to understanding social behaviour.

Often referred to as the father of sociology, Auguste Comte proposed that societies go through three stages in their development: the theological stage (dominated by religion), the metaphysical stage (dominated by abstract speculation), and the positive stage (dominated by scientific thinking). Comte argued that the social sciences should discover the laws that govern the shift from one stage to the next. The positive stage (which Comte thought was emerging in nineteenth-century France) is one where society is organized according to scientific observations and experiments. Comte also proposed a hierarchy of the sciences, with the social sciences at the top because of their greater complexity (reflected by the need to take many factors, such as plans and intentions, into account simultaneously). Ironically, although Comte began his academic writings as a positivist, stressing science over religion, in the latter part of his life he turned to a religion of humanity, advocating a strong role for the social scientists in directing the affairs of society and in defining appropriate goals for society (Comte, 1877).

In *The Rules of Sociological Method*, Emile Durkheim attempted to establish methodological principles to guide the new discipline of sociology. In his book, originally published in 1895, he argued that sociology should model itself on the physical sciences. Our knowledge comes from systematically codifying our experience of the social and the physical realities we encounter. Durkheim asserted that sociologists should study social facts. A *social fact* is any way of "...acting, thinking, and feeling, external to the individual [i.e., from society], and endowed with the power of coercion, [force toward conformity from society] by reason of which they control him [i.e., the individual]." According to Durkheim the social scientist should treat social facts "objectively"—just as the physical scientist treats data. Durkheim argued that social facts are expressed in society by way of patterns. These patterns or regularities (such as marriage rates or suicide rates) can be studied by means of statistics. Social patterns have an independent existence and cannot be understood adequately by studying individual psychology. (To understand why a particular individual committed suicide may not help in understanding the *pattern of suicides* should we find, for example, that in all Canadian provinces males are about four times more likely to commit suicide than females.)

A variety of labels is used to describe the positivist approach in various social science disciplines. Labels such as behaviourist, empiricist, and scientist, are attached to its practitioners, along, of course, with some less flattering labels, such as *abstracted empiricist,* as dubbed by C. Wright Mills (1959), or *number cruncher* as dubbed by others. These last two labels imply that too much attention is paid to the numbers themselves and not enough to the underlying reality that they reflect. Some critics of the positivist approach claim that positivist researchers have become overly impressed with the numbers and the tools used to process them and have lost sight of the goal of trying to understand human behaviour. But in any case positivism, in some or other form, is the predominant approach across the social science disciplines. But, as we shall see, the interpretive and the critical approaches represent strong alternatives.

Most positivists would agree with Carlo Lastrucci's definition of science and the postulates he outlines. In attempting to state a consensus on the essential attributes of science, he defines science as:

> *an objective, logical, and systematic method of analysis of phenomena, devised to permit the accumulation of reliable knowledge (1967, p. 6).*

An *objective* approach is designed to minimize bias, is impersonal, and seeks its authority in fact, not opinion. A logical approach uses deductive rules, and a systematic approach is consistently organized and makes use of such techniques as statistical analysis. Finally, *reliable knowledge* refers to knowledge one can count on, knowledge which allows one to predict outcomes accurately. "...reliable knowledge is that which is both objectively and empirically verifiable" (Lastrucci, 1967). Predictions are empirically verifiable if they can be tested for accuracy by making systematic observations.

B. POSITIVIST ASSUMPTIONS ABOUT SCIENCE AND HUMAN BEHAVIOUR

There are a number of basic postulates, or working assumptions, that positivist social scientists make in approaching their research. Again, following Lastrucci, we can summarize seven of the major postulates as follows: (1967, pp. 37-46)

i. All Behaviour Is Naturally Determined.

To understand human behaviour, we should look for causes in the natural world. This postulate emphasizes a mechanistic view of the world: each outcome is produced by one or more external causes.

ii. Humans Are Part of the Natural World.

Human beings are part of the natural world. Human behaviour can therefore be studied using the methods employed to study the behaviour of other species, although the study of human behaviour is made far more complex by the need to take language into account.

iii. Nature Is Orderly and Regular.

The natural world is orderly, predictable, and therefore knowable. The patterns of nature may be identified and observed. Those events which appear to be random may simply reflect our inability to comprehend fully the natural forces at work.

iv. All Objective Phenomena Are Eventually Knowable.

There are no intellectual limits on what we may eventually know about nature or about human behaviour.

v. Nothing Is Self-Evident.

Our knowledge of behaviour should be demonstrated objectively. And while we may wish to use folk wisdom or "common sense" as a starting point, ultimately we must test ideas systematically.

vi. Truth Is Relative.

What is regarded as a scientific truth today may be disproved or modified tomorrow. There is a dynamic element to what we know. Our knowledge is always on the road to some ultimate truth, but never quite reaching it.

vii. Knowledge Comes from Experience.

The belief that we need to test our understanding of the world systematically with knowledge gained through our senses is a fundamental principle of science.

Positivists are interested in understanding the patterns of human activity. An emphasis is placed on identifying, measuring, and expressing the relations among variables with mathematical precision. And since cause-effect relations are of central concern to the positivist, it is no surprise that emphasis is placed on prediction.

The positivist searches out ways of testing theories of human behaviour. Typically, this is accomplished by establishing *hypotheses* (predictions) about relationships, measuring the variables, and then analyzing the relationships to see if there is evidence to support or refute the prediction. Efforts are then made to replicate (repeat) the study to see if similar findings result when studying a different population.

A key indicator of an adequate explanation for the positivist is the ability to predict outcomes. Thus, the positivist wishes to identify the key causes in the variation of some variable. For example, the positivist may be interested in identifying the factors that contribute to the incidence of race riots, or illegal drug use, or job satisfaction, or the choice of non-traditional careers by female students. In each case, the researcher is interested in understanding what factors best predict the phenomenon under investigation. Thus a study is successful when most of the variation is accounted for, and when the causes can be linked to some general theory of social behaviour.

Unfortunately, the reputation of the social sciences is not impressive when it comes to accurate predictions. Generally it is thought that only the physical sciences are sufficiently well developed to predict with mathematical accuracy. Richard Henshel has examined this topic in some detail and notes that where the physical sciences deal with unaltered (natural) phenomena, they fare little better than the social sciences. For example, the ability of the geologist to predict when an earthquake is going to occur in a particular area is poor. Indeed most of the highly predictable outcomes in science are based not on natural, unaltered systems, but rather on engineered systems—systems designed to take into account various influencing factors (Henshel, 1976). For example, you can predict that no matter what the weather, the bridge you drive over every day to work will be there for you tomorrow. It will be there because it is designed to withstand weather and traffic conditions well beyond its normal loads. So unless something catastrophic happens, the bridge will be there. In contrast, the leaf that blew off the tree in your yard may or may not have moved since yesterday. To estimate its current location would be foolhardy since so many factors could influence where it has moved to since yesterday. Prediction for the positivist social scientist is akin to estimating the whereabouts of the leaf. Natural systems pose a tough challenge for the person keen on prediction.

C. POSITIVIST VIEW OF THE ROLE OF VALUES IN RESEARCH

Positivists argue that research should be value-free. Researchers should put their personal values to one side, so as to avoid influencing the outcomes of studies. Positivists maintain that science progresses when researchers systematically test alternative explanations of behaviour (attempting to rule them out) without trying to support some pet theory or favoured project.

D. RESEARCH DESIGNS ASSOCIATED WITH POSITIVISM

The positivist approach relies mainly (but by no means exclusively) on *experiments*, *surveys*, and *secondary data*, or data collected by others. Typically, positivist approaches rely on some form of numerical analysis rather than on verbal descriptions.

E. CRITICISMS OF POSITIVISM

Many criticisms have been levelled against the positivist approach to knowledge. Some of the major criticisms are:

- Some critics argue that value-free research is an unattainable goal. Some studies have shown that, despite the best intentions, it is extremely difficult for a researcher to prevent his or her biases or expectations from exerting some influence on the results of a study (see Chapter 9; also see Rosenthal, 1963).

- Some critics argue that the so-called value neutrality of positivism is itself a value.

- Other critics argue that, far from being value-free, positivists do research that helps to support the existing social order. For example, studies designed to help reduce the level of crime may be seen as research intended to help protect the property of the wealthy.

- Some scholars argue that the positivistic view ignores a crucial aspect of social reality—namely, that different people may experience and perceive the same events differently. The subjective experience of the social world is an alternate social *reality* that may be explored by the social scientist; it is the one emphasized particularly by those who employ the interpretive approach.

2. THE INTERPRETIVE APPROACH

A. THE NATURE OF THE INTERPRETIVE APPROACH

The German scholar, Max Weber (1864-1920), was particularly influential in developing methodological approaches which stressed the importance of the interpretation *individuals* put on their actions and on the actions and reactions of others. He emphasized **Versteben**, the empathetic understanding of behaviour. The researcher should try to imagine how a particular individual perceives social actions. How does the individual feel? What are the individual's motivations? What meaning does the individual attach to a particular event? Besides Weber, other figures important in the development of interpretive perspectives are Mead (1934), Blumer (1951), Schutz (1954), Becker (1961), Goffman (1962), and Glaser & Strauss (1967).

B. INTERPRETIVE ASSUMPTIONS ABOUT SCIENCE AND HUMAN BEHAVIOUR

Rather than confining itself to behaviour alone, the **interpretive approach** examines how people make sense of their lives, how they define their situation, and how their sense of self develops in interaction with others. Humans are always in a process of *becoming*: they are influenced by how they see themselves, by how others see them, and by what they want to become. Symbolic Interactionists, for example, would stress the idea of **role modelling**, that is, the extent to which an individual chooses to emulate someone else's attitudes and behaviours. Note that, in this view, the individual is actively choosing to be like someone else. In contrast, most theories that use the positivist or critical approaches emphasize the extent to which individuals are *shaped*, or moulded, by the institutions in their society.

Three major theoretical perspectives emerged from the interpretive approach: the *symbolic interactionist perspective*, the *ethnomethodological perspective*, and *grounded theory*. These perspectives all try to provide an adequate understanding of how people see and interpret the events of their everyday lives. How individuals reflect upon, and influence, one another are issues of concern to interpretive social scientists.

C. INTERPRETIVE VIEWS OF THE ROLE OF VALUES IN RESEARCH

Interpretive social scientists argue that values are relative. That is, they would argue that definitions of what constitutes appropriate or inappropriate behaviour depend on the socialization that one has received from one's society. These definitions will shift over time and across societies. Researchers should try to understand (empathetically) and to explain the values of the people being studied (i.e., the "actors").

D. RESEARCH DESIGNS ASSOCIATED WITH THE INTERPRETIVE APPROACH

The interpretive approach relies mainly on field studies, with an emphasis on *participant observation studies* (joining a group and participating in it), *in-depth interviews* with people, and on *ethnomethodology* (typically a detailed examination of a single event or case). Each of these studies typically involves a few cases which are described in detail. A key question for these researchers is: does the explanation offered make sense to the people whose behaviour is being explained? Communication of the results of such studies usually emphasizes verbal descriptions rather than numerical analyses.

E. CRITICISMS OF THE INTERPRETIVE APPROACH

As we have seen, the interpretive approach differs markedly from the positivist approach. Any proponent of the existence of general abstract laws would criticize the interpretive approach for its subjectivity. Moreover, some critics reject the interpretive theorists' assessment that all values are equally valid. Other critics argue that, with its emphasis on field studies, the interpretive approach does not enable the researcher to make clear generalizations. We cannot easily determine whether the findings of a case study are particular to it or more generally applicable. The difficulty is even more acute when studies cannot be replicated—an ethnomethodological study of individual understandings of events would be a good example. The emphasis on the single case gets us into an old dilemma of knowing more and more about less and less, although in fairness, this criticism can be levelled in varying degrees against all types of systematic inquiry. Finally, if emphasis is placed on the individual level of analysis, it seems to be difficult to understand social patterns: to what extent can we understand interrelations among social groups by studying interactions among individuals? But the response to this criticism may be that no social theory can hope to explain all of human behaviour.

3. THE CRITICAL APPROACH

A. THE NATURE OF THE CRITICAL APPROACH

There are numerous schools to be covered under this heading: the *conflict* schools and sub-schools would be included, such as Ralf Dahrendorf's *dialectical conflict theory* (1958), Lewis Coser's *conflict functionalism* (1956), Randall Collins' *exchange conflict theory* (1975), and Jurgen Habermas' *critical theory* (1984). In many ways *feminist* theory fits well with the critical approach; although, methodologically, feminism draws much of its inspiration from the interpretive approach. Proponents of the critical approach share a common desire to improve the condition of humanity. The classic theorists in developing this approach are Karl Marx (1818-1883) and Georg Simmel (1858-1918).

B. CRITICAL ASSUMPTIONS ABOUT SCIENCE AND HUMAN BEHAVIOUR

According to the ***critical approach*** human behaviour consists of different groups attempting to enhance their interests at the expense of less powerful groups. Whether it is the owners of factories exploiting labour, or males exercising dominance over females, this approach stresses that human relations are characterized by conflicting interests. Proponents of the critical approach argue that social scientists have an obligation to act as advocates working for changes in society, changes needed to bring social justice to all. The researcher helps bring about such changes by making us more sensitive to social problems. This knowledge in turn empowers citizens, helping them to become agents of social transformation (Fay, 1987, p. 27). The fundamental goal of the critical approach is to bring about a truly egalitarian society—one where there is an equality of opportunity *and* an equality of result.

C. CRITICAL VIEW OF THE ROLE OF VALUES IN RESEARCH

Critical social scientists forthrightly declare that certain values are correct while others are not. In short, the critical approach takes an absolutist view of values. Researchers working in the critical tradition would argue that the relativist position of mainstream social science has had the consequence of supporting the established order in society, and has had, therefore, little impact on reducing social inequities. Critical social scientists favour imposing moral absolutes in order to deal with inequalities.

D. RESEARCH METHODS ASSOCIATED WITH CRITICAL APPROACHES

The research methods associated with the critical approach span a broad range. But, given the interest in understanding the relations between groups in society and in understanding how social change occurs, it is no surprise that critical social scientists tend to work with historical materials, and thus pay particular attention to comparative studies and analyses of secondary data. This focus tends to emphasize ***macrovariables*** (properties of societies), as opposed to ***microvariables*** (properties of individuals).

Research and explanations are judged to be valid if they lead to an improvement in the social condition of humanity. The critical approach has a strong practical orientation. Social science analysis is seen as a means of achieving greater social justice for all.

E. CRITICISMS OF THE CRITICAL APPROACH

Like the positivist approach, the critical approach relies on general theories. But the positivist, as well the interpretive researcher, would reject the imposition of absolute values. The positivist critic would argue that the difficulty with adopting a value position in any scholarly discipline is that it enhances the likelihood of distorting research to promote one's personal values. Critical researchers may be too selective—reporting only those findings which are compatible with their values and ignoring all others. Critics maintain that critical researchers are unlikely to make a rigorous attempt to exclude competing explanations of behaviour or to find support for competing value systems. In fairness, however, this criticism could be levelled at all social science approaches. Turner (1981), in commenting on Dahrendorf's dialectical conflict theory, argues that insufficient attention has been paid to providing clear formal definitions of concepts that would render the various schemes empirically testable. The argument is that if concepts are loosely defined, then researchers will have little to guide them in developing measures of concepts and, as a result, will be unable to test theoretical formulations adequately.

Table 1.1 summarizes some of the main ideas of the three major contemporary

TABLE 1.1 SUMMARY OF THREE KEY METHODOLOGICAL APPROACHES IN THE SOCIAL SCIENCES

CRITERION	POSITIVIST	INTERPRETIVE	CRITICAL
Major figures	Comte, Durkheim, Skinner	Weber, Mead, Goffman, Becker, Schutz, Turner, Garfinkel	Malthus, Marx, Simmel, Dahrendorf, Coser, Collins, Habermas
Schools associated with	Operant and Classical Conditioning, Behaviourist, Exchange Theory, Functionalist	Symbolic Interactionist, Ethnomethodological, Grounded Theory	Conflict, Critical, Marxist, Segmentation, Feminist
View of science	A tool for uncovering general laws of cause and effect in social behaviour	A tool for understanding the reality experienced by people	A tool that should be used to improve the condition of the oppressed
View of human behaviour	Caused by forces acting on the individual; characterized by regularity and order	Determined by context and individual perception of meaning	Consists of groups attempting to exploit others for their own advantage
Goals of research	To predict behaviour; to test general theories of behaviour by testing of hypotheses	To provide an adequate reflection of peoples' experience of the social world; testing grounded theory	To improve the social conditions of the oppressed; to achieve a just society; advocacy
Role of values in research	Research should be value-free; relativistic	Research should be value-free; relativistic	Absolutist; research should impose moral absolutes derived from theory
Research designs associated with	Surveys, experiments, quasi-experiments, secondary data, historical analysis; (tends toward quantitative orientation)	In-depth interviews, participant observations, field studies, document analyses; (tends toward qualitative orientation)	Historical, comparative, interviews, advocacy research; (uses both qualitative and quantitative approaches)

methodological approaches. Each approach can increase our understanding of human behaviour. Rather than rejecting any one of them outright, we would do well to regard each approach as potentially valuable in our quest for knowledge about human behaviour.

B. QUANTITATIVE AND QUALITATIVE RESEARCH

Research techniques can be classified as either *quantitative* or *qualitative*. The distinction is based on the degree to which the analysis is done by converting observations to numbers. The distinction also reflects differences in the types of questions asked, the kinds of evidence considered appropriate for answering a question, and the methods used to process this evidence. It is probably best to think of the quantitative/qualitative distinction as a continuum.

1. QUANTITATIVE RESEARCH

Quantitative research seeks to quantify, or reflect with numbers, observations about human behaviour. It emphasizes precise measurement, the testing of hypotheses based on a sample of observations, and a statistical analysis of the data. The quantitative researcher attempts to describe relationships among variables mathematically, and to apply some form of numerical analysis to the social relations being examined. Quantitative researchers, like physical scientists, treat their subject matter like an object. Quantitative research is characteristic of the positivist approach. It is also used (to-

gether with qualitative research) in the critical approach. Box 1.2 presents the different levels in a quantitative project.

A. TYPES OF QUESTIONS ASKED

The types of questions asked in quantitative research often concern relationships among variables and patterns in social trends. Questions like the ones listed below would be typical:

- what is the relationship between gender and suicide?

- what factors are most important in determining the level of an individual's job satisfaction?

- is the popularity of a political leader rising or falling?

- what is the relationship between gender and conformity?

- is a stay-in-school intervention program effective in diminishing drop-out rates?

B. TYPES OF ANALYSIS

In quantitative research, findings are typically expressed in terms of relationships that are presented in tables and graphs. Variables are sometimes *cross-classified* to show how one variable changes as another variable changes. A table might be constructed, for example, showing how average levels of job satisfaction vary by educational achievement. This same finding could also be presented in the form of a graph. A great variety of statistical procedures are available to the quantitative researcher. It is important to learn which procedures are appropriate for a given research problem.

BOX 1.2

Levels in Quantitative Research

Quantitative research can be conceived of as having three levels: the theoretical, the conceptual, and the operational.

Theoretical Level

The **theoretical level** in a project is the most abstract, general conceptualization of the research problem. Theories propose explanations of phenomena—how things work, how parts are interconnected, and how things influence each other. In the social sciences, theories provide explanations to account for social patterns or for relationships. The more general the theory, the greater the number of predictions that can be derived from it. Indeed, the number of predictions that can be derived from a theory is also a measure of the theory's power. Theories may be viewed as lying on a continuum of explicitness. At one end of this continuum, we would place a theory in which there are detailed statements of the relations between the concepts of the theory and a specification of its underlying assumptions (in Chapter 2 we will refer to these as *formal theories*); at the other end, we would place those theories which offer an explanation of some particular relation (these will be identified as *partial theories*).

Social scientists use theories to predict behaviour. An important role of the methodologist is to try to refine them, to see if they hold true under all conditions. It is through efforts to *disconfirm* theories that we extend our general knowledge of human behaviour. One way to test a theory is to derive a prediction (or hypothesis) from it and then test that hypothesis. In Chapter 2 we will discuss the nature of theories and ways of testing them in greater detail.

Conceptual Level

The **conceptual level** defines the variables that are to be used in the research. A **conceptual variable** is an idea which has a dimension that can vary. Conceptual variables can be relatively simple or quite complex. Examples would include gender, weight, intelligence, peer approval, political orientation, anxiety. Derivations made at the theoretical level may be formed into conceptual hypotheses. A **conceptual hypothesis** is a statement of the relationship between two or more conceptual variables. Ordinarily, a hypothesis will take the form of *the greater X, the greater Y*. For example, "the higher one's socio-economic status, the higher one's educational aspirations."

The conceptual definitions of variables serve two important purposes. First, they should provide a clear statement of what is meant by the variables. Second, they should help us decide how each variable should be measured. For example, if we define the concept *socio-economic status* as a "differences in access to scarce resources," then we would try to measure the variable with *indicators* that reflect this definition as precisely as possible. This brings us to the operational level, which we will consider next.

Operational Level

Operationalization refers to the selection of indicators (measures) to reflect conceptual variables, and to the implementation of a research project. If socioeconomic status is defined as "differences in access to scarce resources," any measurement should attempt to reflect this definition. In this case, a measure of annual income might appropriately reflect the conceptual variable, as defined. And, in the study of program choice, the classification of programs into traditional and non-traditional would constitute a measure of the concept. The **operational level** consists of the measurement of variables as well as the collection and analysis of data. In Chapters 12 and 13 we will provide a number of suggestions for the measurement of variables. And in Chapters 7 and 8, and Chapters 15 through 17 we will discuss procedures for analysing data.

Linkages Between Levels

The theoretical, conceptual, and operational levels do not exist in isolation from one another. The three levels of research are connected by important linkages. Testing a theory properly entails documenting explicitly the connections between the theoretical and the conceptual levels, and between the conceptual and the operational levels.

Social researchers use two terms, *validity* and *reliability,* to refer to the connection between the conceptual and the operational levels. **Validity** refers to the extent to which a measure reflects a concept, reflecting neither more nor less than what is implied by the definition of the concept. It is not unusual for

researchers to use markedly different "indicators" for similar conceptual variables. While one might define socio-economic status as "differential access to scarce resources," another might define it as a "hierarchy of respect and prestige." Measures are valid to the extent that the chosen indicators reflect the concepts as defined.

Reliability refers to the extent to which, on repeated measures, an indicator will yield similar readings. One can think of reliability as the extent to which a measurement will produce similar readings for similar phenomena. A tire gauge that indicates 26 pounds of pressure now, but 29 pounds a moment earlier, suggests an unreliable gauge—either that or a bad leak in the tire. In survey research we sometimes repeat a question to test for reliability. Both responses to the question should be the same if the item is generating reliable responses. (The concepts of validity and reliability will be discussed in greater detail in Chapter 12.)

The figure below presents the three levels of research. Moving from top to bottom (from the theoretical to the operational), the researcher uses *deductive reasoning*. Deduction is used to derive testable conceptual hypotheses from theoretical propositions (representing movement from the theoretical level to the conceptual level). And deduction is used to choose the indicators to measure the conceptual variables (representing movement from the conceptual to the operational level). Moving from the bottom to the top of the figure, the researcher employs *inductive reasoning*. If the results

DEDUCTIVE AND INDUCTIVE REASONING IN RESEARCH DESIGN

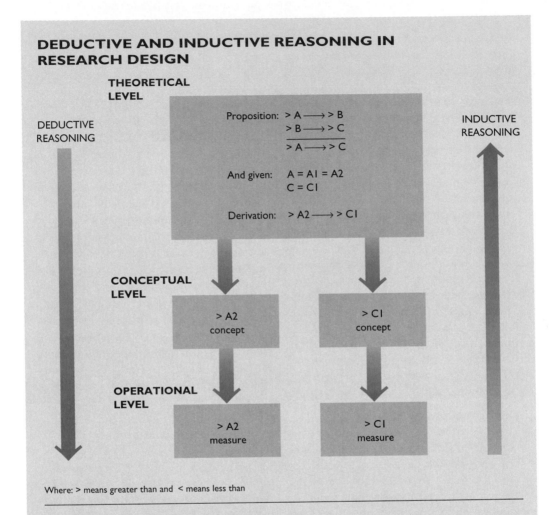

Where: > means greater than and < means less than

of the data analysis are consistent with the prediction of the conceptual hypothesis, then the researcher has inductive evidence to support the chosen operational methods, the derived conceptual hypothesis, and the theoretical propositions themselves. However, if the results of the data analysis do not accord with the prediction of the conceptual hypothesis, inductive reasoning does *not* enable the researcher to identify the cause of the inconsistency. The problem may lie in the theoretical propositions, the conceptual hypothesis, the operational methods, or even the technique used for selecting the sample, or for analysing the data.

But there are qualitative dimensions in quantitative research. In the process of turning observations into numbers there are typically a number of judgement calls, a number of qualitative decisions that must be made. So, whether the researcher wishes to decide how to design a question to find out how much self-esteem someone has, or how to classify student programs as gender-traditional (those typically taken by one gender or the other), or what is a women's magazine, a number of subjective judgements must be made. And, while these may be defined numerically, there is nonetheless a qualitative dimension to the research decision. Brett Silverstein, who designed a study to investigate the role of the mass media in promoting the belief that women must be thin to be attractive, classified a magazine as a women's magazine if 75 percent of its readers were women (Silverstein, 1986). Virtually all studies which claim to be quantitative have important qualitative dimensions to them.

2. QUALITATIVE RESEARCH

Qualitative research emphasizes verbal descriptions and explanations of human behaviour. Rather than concerning itself primarily with representative samples, qualitative research emphasizes careful and detailed descriptions of social practices in an attempt to understand how the participants experience and explain their own world. The tools for gaining information include participant observation, in-depth interviews, or an in-depth analysis of a single case. At the macro level, the qualitative researcher tends to look at whole institutions, or organizations; at the micro level, the qualitative researcher focuses on individual behaviours. Qualitative research is charac-

teristic of the interpretive approach. It is also used (together with quantitative research) in the critical approach.

A. TYPES OF QUESTIONS ASKED

The types of questions asked in qualitative research often concern how social systems operate, how individuals relate to one another, how individuals perceive one another, and how they interpret their own and others' behaviour. Questions like those listed below are typical:

- What is it like to be a prisoner?

- How do pool hustlers get their opponent to play?

- How do nurses handle patients who refuse to follow instructions?

- What is it like to be mentally ill?

B. TYPES OF ANALYSIS

In qualitative research, findings are typically expressed by quoting interviews or relating experiences the researcher has had in the field. Most final reports have few, if any, tables or graphs. Rose Weitz's article on living with the stigma of AIDS (see Box 5.2) is an illustration of this tradition. Since much qualitative research is based on a small number of participants, or on an in-depth examination of one group, it is often inappropriate even to attempt to quantify the results.

Various sections of Chapter 5 will elaborate on the procedures that may be used to conduct different types of qualitative studies and will also present an alternative view to that of quantitative researchers on such issues as the meaning of validity and the goals of research.

While there is considerable debate over the relative merits of quantitative and qualitative research strategies, to a large degree the issue is a false one. It is false because both approaches have their legitimate place in social science research. The choice of strategy is influenced by the following factors:

- The nature of the question asked: if the question has to do with a small number of observations, or a single case, then the use of quantitative techniques would be inappropriate; if the question has to do with patterns of social behaviour or descriptions of whole populations, the approach will be quantitative.

- The predisposition of the researcher: if the researcher has a preference for qualitative research strategies, the researcher will tend to ask questions best answered by using such methods.

Sometimes the author of a research report will use a qualitative reporting style in order to communicate effectively. Qualitative research uses language and presentations familiar to all educated members of a society.

C. SOME IMPORTANT DISTINCTIONS

1. DESCRIPTIVE VERSUS EXPLANATORY RESEARCH

Descriptive research emphasizes the accurate portrayal of a population. A study which is primarily descriptive has as its major concern the accurate description of some aspect of society. A researcher may wish, for example, to assess the current popularity of federal political parties. With the goal of gauging the general sentiments in a society toward each political party, the researcher tries to describe as precisely as possible what proportion of the population supports each party. Similarly, a census of the population is largely a descriptive project. Here, the attempt is to *count* a variety of attributes of the society, whether the count is of people, race tracks, or automobiles. In a sense, a census is a stock-taking of the objects, people, and resources available within a society. It seeks answers to *what* questions.

Fundamentally, the descriptive study is about *what* and how many of *what*. Since the goal is to describe, survey researchers will frequently draw a sample in order to make estimations about some *population*. As used by the researcher, the term *population* refers to that collection of individuals, communities, or nations about which one wishes to make a general statement. In order to save money and time, the researcher draws from the population a *sample* which will be representative of the population as a whole. While including the whole population would prove to be more accurate (as in a census), the costs may be prohibitive. Public opinion pollsters, market researchers, and census takers typically emphasize descriptive accuracy in their research. All explanatory studies will have descriptive dimensions, and some descriptive studies will have explanatory dimensions.

To explore the differences between female students who select gender non-traditional programs in university and female students who select traditional programs, a researcher would want to describe the characteristics of the two sets of students. Are rural students more likely to opt for traditional programs, such as education, nursing, or home economics? Are females from higher socio-economic levels more likely to choose non-traditional programs, such as engineering, business, or chemistry?

By contrast, the primary goal of ***explanatory research*** is to understand or to explain relationships. Why is it that females who pursue non-traditional occupations are more likely to be from higher socio-economic backgrounds than those who enrol in traditional programs of study? Here the issue is twofold. First, what is the relationship between background and type of program selected? Second, if there is a relationship, why does it exist? Explanatory studies ask *why* questions.

2. PURE VERSUS APPLIED RESEARCH

Social scientists who focus on understanding social relationships are engaging in ***pure research***; those who are interested in figuring out how to bring about specific changes in society are engaging in ***applied research***.

A. PURE RESEARCH

The social scientist engaged in pure research tries to understand the patterns of social behaviour. However, it is usually possible to devise many different explanations to account for any particular behaviour. A challenge of social science is to determine which, if any, of the possible explanations accounts for any given pattern. Patterns

may be understood through a variety of qualitative and quantitative techniques. But whatever the approach, the ultimate goal is to offer better descriptions and better explanations of human behaviour.

Frequently the social scientist is confronted with "interesting" findings which cry out for an explanation. Suppose, for example, that a project is being done which measures high school students' socio-economic backgrounds (SES) and their aspirations for higher education. And suppose, during data analysis, that a relatively strong relationship emerges indicating that the higher an individual's socio-economic origin, the greater the likelihood that the individual will aspire to post-secondary education. At this stage, the researcher may wonder what explains the pattern that has emerged. Possibilities such as the following might come to mind:

- peers of high SES students have high aspirations themselves and the students influence one another in planning to attend post-secondary institutions;

- parents of high SES students have greater expectations concerning the educational achievements of their children;

- high SES students know that they have the financial backing to attend a post-secondary institution and therefore plan on it;

- teachers encourage high SES students more because they have higher expectations of them;

- high SES students have been more exposed to high occupational achievers and are more likely to model themselves on such individuals.

We can identify three important goals of pure research:

- first, pure research aims to test existing theories of social behaviour;

- second, it attempts to explain observed patterns of behaviour;

- and third, it tries to document our knowledge of the emergence, modification, and persistence of patterned human behaviour.

B. APPLIED RESEARCH

Simply stated, what distinguishes the two types of researchers is that the pure researcher values knowledge for its own sake, whereas the applied researcher wishes to have an impact on some specific social behaviour. The applied researcher may want to maintain the enrolment in a music school, or eliminate deviance, or assess the popularity of a government, or change people's attitudes toward wearing seat belts, or persuade people to buy a new toothpaste.

On the one hand, pure researchers might be viewed as striving to be value-free by not promoting a particular theory, or view of the world. On the other hand, applied researchers might be viewed as striving to achieve particular social changes (which they may or may not believe in themselves). In many instances, the applied researcher rents his or her skills out. The service may be to monitor public responses to a new government policy or to measure the impact of an advertising campaign to discourage smoking. In such cases, the researcher wishes to further the goals of an employer. The applied researcher focuses on those variables which can be changed by intervention, so as to achieve the desired goals.

3. UNITS OF ANALYSIS: INDIVIDUALS AND AGGREGATIONS

Social scientists study nations, communities, groups, institutions, and individuals. Moreover, an institution such as the family may be studied either across cultures or within a culture. In doing research it is difficult to deal simultaneously with more than one level of analysis. At the outset of a project we should ask ourselves: "Am I studying individuals or aggregations?"

A. THE INDIVIDUAL AS THE UNIT OF ANALYSIS

If we are studying individuals, then we should pose questions that concern individual properties only. All the data collected should measure variations between individuals on a variety of subjects. And any analyses of the data will have individuals as the basic unit. Most surveys and experiments use the individual as the unit of analysis, although it is possible to have individuals report on data for other levels of analysis such as communities, companies, or groups. Furthermore, individuals may be counted and used to produce a measure for some aggregation: the proportion of university-educated people in a community would be an example of such a variable.

B. AN AGGREGATION AS THE UNIT OF ANALYSIS

Alternatively, if we are studying aggregations, then we should pose questions that concern properties of groups, institutions, communities, or nations. Individual characteristics, such as income, educational level, or ethnic background will have to be expressed as averages or proportions. If we begin a study using an individual level of analysis, then it is difficult, without careful advance planning, to switch to a different level, such as the community level. With computers it is easy enough to compute average scores. But it is unlikely that we will have sufficient cases to produce meaningful averages for all of the communities. (If you studied 300 people from 25 different communities, then to move from the individual to the community level you would have but 12 people from each community on which to base the average for the community.)

It is important, therefore, when we start designing a study to be absolutely clear about the level of analysis that we plan to use. If we want to use different levels in the same study, then we should think through how the analysis is to be done very carefully, in order to ensure that we will have a sufficient number of cases for the analysis. Table 1.2 summarizes the relation between the unit of analysis used and some of the tendencies related to the use of different levels.

In later chapters we will explore four research designs in more detail: experiments (Chapter 3), surveys (Chapter 4), field studies (Chapter 5), and non-reactive studies (Chapter 6). Each design is legitimate in its own way. The selection of a design should be guided by what is most appropriate for

TABLE 1.2   UNITS OF ANALYSIS AND RELATED TENDENCIES

	UNIT OF ANALYSIS			
	INDIVIDUAL		AGGREGATION	
DIMENSION	ONE	SEVERAL/MANY	ONE	SEVERAL/MANY
Tendency in orientation	Qualitative	Quantitative	Qualitative	Quantitative
Types of study	Case study	Survey Experiment Quasi-experiment Participant observation Non-reactive	Case study Participant observation Survey Non-reactive	Comparative Inter-nation Quasi-experiment Survey Non-reactive
Disciplines	Psychiatry Sociology-ethnomethodology	Psychology Sociology Political science Psychiatry Education	Anthropology Sociology Political science History Archaeology Education	Anthropology Sociology Political science Education Archaeology
Illustration	Explaining an individual suicide	Variations in suicide by gender, age	Explaining suicides in one community	Comparing suicide rates across countries/communities

the problem under investigation. No one design covers all problems. Each approach has its unique combination of strengths and weaknesses. We should choose the approach that is feasible and that optimizes our ability to solve the particular research problem under consideration.

D. TYPES OF VARIABLES

In designing, implementing, and evaluating studies, researchers distinguish various types of variables.

1. DEPENDENT VARIABLES

A *dependent variable* is a variable thought to be influenced by other variables. It is the "effect" in a cause-effect relationship. As its name suggests, it is "dependent" for its variation on other variables. Recall our example of investigating the factors that influence female students to choose gender-traditional programs rather than nontraditional programs. Here, "program choice" would be treated as the dependent variable. However, this would not preclude exploring the possibility that, in turn, variations in program choice have an impact on a variable such as income. In such a case, income would be treated as the dependent variable.

2. INDEPENDENT VARIABLES

An *independent variable* is a "cause" in a cause-effect relationship. It is a variable which has been selected as a possible influence on variations in a dependent variable. Typically, one finds a number of independent variables in a study. Once again, it is how the variable is treated—how it is thought of—that determines whether it is an independent or a dependent variable. The nature of the variable itself does not determine whether it is dependent or independent—it is how the researcher thinks about and uses the variable that counts.

In our example of university program choices by female students, many different factors might be treated as independent variables. We might well include such factors as rural/urban home community, subject preference and performance in high school, types of games and activities preferred in childhood, parental socio-economic status, measures of mothers' participation in the labour force, and the presence of role models who have opted for non-traditional female occupations.

In experimental designs, independent variables are referred to as *treatment variables*. A treatment is a variable whose effect on some dependent variable is being assessed in an experiment. There may be several treatments used simultaneously with their individual and joint effects being assessed.

In general, we should be careful to ensure that the variables we treat as independent are indeed different variables. For instance, if we measured the length of rooms in a building in inches and then repeated the measurements, but this time using centimetres, our two sets of measures would lack independence. In short, they would simply represent different measures of the same variable. The researcher must be careful not to fall into the trap of thinking that there is a powerful causal connection between two variables when the measures lack independence and thus represent two different measures of the same thing.

3. CONTROL VARIABLES

A *control variable* is a variable which is taken into account in exploring the relation between an independent variable and a dependent variable. There are three basic types of control variables: the intervening variable, the conditional variable, and the source of spuriousness (or confounding) variable.

A. INTERVENING VARIABLE

An *intervening variable (I)* is a variable that links an independent variable (X) to a dependent one (Y). An intervening variable represents an explanation of how the independent variable influences the dependent variable. It may be diagrammed as:

Let us return to our example of investigating the relation between socio-economic status and preference for a non-traditional program. A possible explanation of how socio-economic status (SES) influences the type of program preferred would be that high SES students are more likely to be exposed to people in non-traditional occupations. In other words, exposure to people in non-traditional occupations "intervenes" to account for the program preferred.

B. CONDITIONAL VARIABLE

A *conditional variable (C)* is a variable that accounts for a change in the relation-ship between an independent variable (X) and a dependent variable (Y) when the general conditions change. Suppose we are investigating the relationship between socio-economic status and attitudes toward capital punishment: we might want to find out whether that relationship is fundamentally altered (or is entirely different) for each gender. Accordingly, we might test males and females separately for a relationship between SES and attitudes. Here, gender would be the conditional variable, as in:

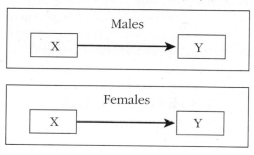

C. SOURCE OF SPURIOUSNESS VARIABLE

A *source of spuriousness variable (S/S)* is a variable which is viewed as a possible influence on both the independent (X) and the dependent variable (Y), in such a way that it accounts for the relationship between them. In other words, the relationship between X and Y is "spurious" because it is produced by the influence of S/S on each.

If we were exploring the relation between socio-economic background and choice of a non-traditional program by female students, we might consider the possibility that rural/urban background is a source of spuriousness. Here the idea is that it may be the type of community that the student comes from that influences the socio-economic achievement of her parents as well as influencing her own program preferences at university. The relation between socio-economic status and program choice might therefore be spurious. As in:

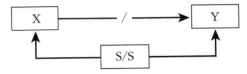

In experimental research a source of spuriousness variable is typically referred to as a confounding variable. A ***confounding variable*** is one which may be influencing the outcome of an experiment systematically and which, once recognized, is treated in the design and controlled.

E. DOING SOCIAL RESEARCH

1. STAGES OF A RESEARCH PROJECT

Most studies involve distinct stages. We will briefly introduce each of them now. In later chapters we will provide guidelines for getting through each one.

i. Problem Selection.

First, the researcher determines the purpose of the research project. Is a theory being tested, or is some known relationship being explored in detail, or some solution being sought to an applied problem?

ii. Design.

What kind of design is appropriate for the problem which is being researched? A thorough researcher will review the scientific literature to find out what has been discovered by other researchers working in the selected area. What variables are to be measured? What hypotheses are to be tested?

iii. Development of Procedural Instruments.

The researcher pretests the designed instruments, such as observational forms, questionnaires, and interview guides. This procedure affords the opportunity of refining the procedures and reducing the number of unanticipated problems.

iv. Sampling.

If a sample is to be used, the researcher determines the type of sampling procedure and the size of sample to be used. Any necessary permissions (such as those from a school system or from parents) are sought. In experimental research, one will often be concerned to determine how subjects are to be randomly assigned to different treatment groups.

v. Data Collection.

Using the procedures that have been developed for the particular study (which might be an experiment, a field study, a survey, in-depth interviews, or assembling secondary data) the researcher collects the data. Data verification procedures are used to ensure that the data were properly assembled.

vi. Data Coding.

The researcher then codes the data. If questionnaires or interview guides are used, they are numbered and sorted. All open-ended questions are coded. In content analysis studies, the researcher classifies the observations.

vii. Data Entry.

If a computer is being used, the collected and coded data are entered into it. If a computer is not being used, the researcher places the information on master sheets.

viii. Data Analysis.

The researcher checks the data for errors and makes any necessary corrections. When a computer is being used, the computer itself can assist with the error checking. In the absence of a computer the data should be carefully proofread. Field-study notes are copied and then classified into categories.

ix. Final Report.

The researcher writes a final report on the project.

2. USE OF COMPUTERS

Quantitative researchers rely on computers for two major reasons. First, research may entail collecting information about many variables from a large number of individuals. Since computers work quickly, they make it relatively easy to do calculations involving large numbers. Second, social researchers frequently build models involving many variables; computer technology makes it is possible to do the kinds of multivariate (many variable) analysis that is necessary to test such models. Qualitative researchers increasingly are relying on computers to assist in searching, sorting, and classifying non-numerical information.

SPSS (Statistical Package for the Social Sciences) is a collection of procedures for processing social science data. Versions of SPSS date back to the 1960s. Most universities and many research organizations have SPSS. While there are many statistical packages available, few can match the scope of SPSS. Appendix A of this book explains SPSS commands (mainframe and PC) that are used in computer analysis. Readers who have access to earlier versions of SPSS will find that, with a few modifications, the commands presented in this book will work. In addition, a special SPSS supplement is available for *Methods: Doing Social Research,* containing a series of computer assignments to familiarize the researcher with SPSS.

F. KEY TERMS

Applied research
Conceptual hypothesis
Conceptual level
Conceptual variable
Conditional variable
Confounding variable
Control variable
Critical approach
Dependent variable
Descriptive research

Explanatory research
Independent variable
Interpretive approach
Intervening variable
Macrovariables
Microvariables
Operational level
Operationalization
Positivist approach
Pure research

Qualitative research
Quantitative research
Reliability
Role modelling
Secondary data
Source of spuriousness variable
Theoretical level
Treatment variable
Validity
Verstehen

G. KEY POINTS

The *positivist approach* is modelled on the physical sciences, treats social behaviour as an object, sees behaviour as a result of forces acting on the individual or society, tries to describe and explain the patterns that characterize social behaviour, and tries to avoid allowing one's values to interfere with one's observations. Knowledge is to be based on testing one's ideas systematically by measuring variables and noting how they are related to one another. Positivists use the ability to predict accurately as a major criterion for judging the soundness of a theory. The research designs most associated with positivism include the use of experimental, survey, and secondary data.

Interpretive approaches ask questions about how people understand their everyday lives, how they define and react to situations. The job of the researcher is to develop an empathetic understanding of behaviour. The research designs most associated with an Interpretive approach include: participant observations studies, in-depth interviews, and the careful analysis of individual cases.

The *critical approach* views conflict as a basic characteristic of the human condition; groups attempt to exploit others for their own advantage. The practical job of critical work is to document social problems and use the knowledge gained in doing so to empower people so that they can become agents of social change. Researchers in this tradition take advocacy positions particularly with reference to assisting the weak and the powerless in society. The research techniques most associated with the critical approach would include comparative studies, historical analyses, secondary data analyses, and advocacy research.

Quantitative research seeks to quantify, or reflect with numbers, observations about human behaviour. Tables and graphs are incorporated in reports.

Qualitative research uses concepts and classifications in an attempt to interpret human behaviour in a way that rings true to both the analyst and the people whose behaviour is being described. Interview quotations and descriptions of events experienced during observations form key elements of reports written in this tradition.

Descriptive research is about what and how many of what; in polls and in descriptive survey research an emphasis is placed on estimating the extent to which a sample may be taken to represent the population from which the sample was selected.

Explanatory research seeks to provide answers to *why* questions.

Pure researchers attempt to understand human behaviour; the knowledge gained is viewed as important in its own right.

Applied researchers are interested in solving some social problem, in evaluating the extent to which some program is, or is not, effective in bringing about a desired change, or in using social science knowledge to further some goal set by others.

A *unit of analysis* is the element being studied in a research project. Some studies examine individuals, while others study aggregations such as families, communities, or societies. Measures taken reflect qualities of the unit being studied. Beginning researchers, when devising measures, should be careful to ensure that their measures reflect only properties of the unit of analysis they are studying.

Projects may be considered to have three levels. The *theoretical level* in a project is the most abstract, general conceptualization of the research problem. Theories propose general explanations of phenomena.

The *conceptual level* involves the definition of variables to be used in a project.

The *operational level* refers to the indicators (or measures) of the variables and to how the project is to be carried out.

Establishing *linkages* between the conceptual and operational levels of a research project is essential: *validity* is a measure of the extent to which an indicator reflects the concept, reflecting neither more nor less than what is implied by the conceptual definition; *reliability* refers to whether, on repeated measures, an indicator will yield similar readings.

A *dependent variable* is the effect in a cause-effect relation; it is the result, the variable one is trying to predict.

An *independent variable* is the cause in a cause-effect relation; it is one of the predictor variables.

A *control variable* is one taken into account in examining the relation between a given independent and dependent variable. There are three basic types of control variables:

(i) a *source of spuriousness* variable is one which may be influencing both the dependent and the independent variable, thus rendering any association between them false, only existing because of the common link to the source of spuriousness variable; in experimental research such variables are referred to as *confounding variables*;

(ii) an *intervening* variable links the independent to the dependent variable; and,

(iii) a *conditional* variable is one taken into account to see if the basic relation between the dependent and independent variable is altered under different values of the conditional variable.

H. EXERCISES

1. Examine one issue of a social science journal. For each article do the following:

(i) copy the title of each article;

(ii) classify each article by whether it is predominantly quantitative or qualitative orientation;

(iii) classify each by whether it is predominantly descriptive or explanatory;

(iv) classify each by whether its intent seems to be pure or applied;

(v) classify each by whether it falls most into a positivist, interpretive, or critical approach.

2. Identify five examples of research which fall predominantly into each of the Positivist, Interpretive, and Critical approaches in your major discipline. Did you encounter difficulties in coming up with examples for each approach in your discipline? Do you think there is a trend in your discipline toward one of these approaches? From your examination of various journals and books, estimate the percentage of research in your discipline that would fall into each of the approaches.

I. RECOMMENDED READINGS

EASTHOPE, GARY (1974). *History of Social Research Methods*. London: Longman Group Limited. This short book provides a brief history of the major methods used in social research.

LASTRUCCI, CARLO L. (1967). *The Scientific Approach*. Cambridge, Massachusetts: Schenkman Publishing, Inc. Lastrucci's lucid treatment of what the scientific approach is all about is particularly strong on the principles of scientific reasoning.

MILLS, C. WRIGHT (1959). *The Sociological Imagination*. New York: Oxford University Press. Mills argues for a more theoretically informed approach to social science research. Although it was published over thirty years ago, it still remains a "must read" for anyone considering graduate work.

MITCHELL, MARK, AND JANINA JOLLEY (1992). *Research Design Explained,* Second Edition. Orlando: Harcourt Brace Jovanovitch College Publishers. A favourite of students, this book is one of the most approachable methods texts in psychology. It contains lots of examples and helpful suggestions for the student.

NEUMAN, W. LAWRENCE (1991). *Social Research Methods*. Needham Heights, Massachusetts: Allyn and Bacon. This is a comprehensive text with an excellent discussion of different approaches in social science research.

PALYS, TED (1992). *Research Decisions: Quantitative and Qualitative Perspectives*. Toronto: Harcourt Brace Jovanovitch Canada Inc. This is an excellent, balanced treatment of various approaches in Sociology.

EXPLAINING

A. INTRODUCTION

Humans generalize. We are the generalizing species. In our efforts to understand one another, and to anticipate one another's behaviour, we learn rules, or we make them up, and apply them to our everyday activities. All cultures have phrases which attempt to offer general explanations of human behaviour. In English, these are variously referred to as adages, saws, old wives' tales, epigrams, maxims, proverbs, sayings, aphorisms, clichés, folk wisdom, platitudes, and truisms. All of them attempt to provide neat, commonly understood, explanations of behaviour.

We could probably not survive well without anticipating the behaviour of others. Smooth social functioning requires us to be able to anticipate the activity of others. We therefore rely on our everyday generalizations to guide much of our interaction. For example, in greeting your good friend, Sam, you anticipate that you will get an up-beat, positive response rather than a punch on the nose. You have generalized from your previous experiences with him when you conclude that you will be greeted warmly.

But there are problems with non-scientific explanations. Indeed, numerous pairs of contradictory aphorisms can be found: the first explains one result, and a parallel one the opposite outcome. No matter what happens, a ready explanation is available. This poses a difficulty for the social scientist: many of the conclusions arrived at, after painstaking research, can be dismissed as *obvious*. They seem obvious because there is some saying, some maxim, in our folk culture which anticipates the result. All too often, however, folk wisdom accounts for all outcomes. To illustrate the problem, the anecdote in Box 2.1 may help.

Folk wisdom is an important source of ideas for the social researcher. But one must always be careful to distinguish between ideas that have been scientifically tested and those which have not been

BOX 2.1

Charlie McMullin and Aunt Hazel

Charlie McMullin was in love. He had been dating Sally for seven months when she decided to take a trip to Europe. After two weeks, and four letters home to Charlie, the letters stopped. Charlie was in agony. It was then that his dear aunt, Aunt Hazel, explained the whole thing by saying, "Well that just proves once again, 'out of sight, out of mind'." But after six weeks Sally wrote, full of apologies, and suggesting that they get married on her return. Good old Aunt Hazel understood that too. "Oh," she exclaimed, "that's easy, 'absence makes the heart grow fonder!'" For a while Charlie thought that his aunt was a first-rate observer of the human scene until he realized that she had an answer for all outcomes.

tested. The social scientist might well ask "Under what conditions does 'Out of sight, out of mind' apply, and under what conditions are we more likely to feel that 'Absence makes the heart grow fonder'"? The most compelling predictions that the social scientist can make will be those which run counter to "common sense." If you are able to make a prediction which goes startlingly against common understandings, and it turns out to be true, you will have a powerfully convincing study. But it is sometimes difficult to find an outcome which is not covered by some cultural maxim. Box 2.2 lists a few contradictory proverbs. Can you think of other conflicting ones?

Social scientists are interested in understanding social behaviour. In their quest for understanding, they have de-voted energy to describing behaviour, and to developing and testing general explanations which try to account for the patterns of human behaviour. Perhaps because of its devilish complexity—or perhaps because of the tough standards we set for an adequate explanation—what we miss are well-confirmed, and widely accepted, explanations for behaviour. This chapter explores explanations—and insufficient explanations—for human behaviour. Attention will be paid to common errors in reasoning and to the role of theory in understanding human behaviour. This chapter also explores some simple theory-testing techniques that may be applied by the beginning researcher in attempting to understand the elusive patterns that characterize the social world.

BOX 2.2

A Few Contradictory Sayings

Absence makes the heart grow fonder./
Out of sight, out of mind.

Beauty is as good as ready money /
Beauty buys no beef.

Idleness is the mother of poverty./
It is well to lie fallow for a while.

A farthing saved is twice earned./
Frugality is misery in disguise.

Birds of a feather flock together./
Opposites attract.

Judge not a book by its cover./
Fine feathers make fine birds.

He who begins many things, finishes but few./
Whatever begins, also ends.

He will shoot higher who shoots at the sun than he who aims at a tree./
Hew not too high lest the chips fall in thine eye.

Better to have loved and lost than never to have loved at all./
Better safe than sorry.

SOURCE: Some found in Henry Davidoff, *A World Treasury of Proverbs*. London: Cassell & Company, 1953.

B. EXPLANATIONS

In order to survive in society, all of us need a shared understanding of human behaviour. We learn what a frown means, what a jaunty wave of the hand means, and we come to a common understanding of what a vast array of words and symbols mean in our culture. We learn about appropriate and inappropriate behaviour. As children we learn, for example, that it is okay to swear in front of our same-gender peers, but not okay to use the same words in front of our parents or in mixed company. We speculate on why others behave as they do and we think about our own behaviour. Depending on the role we are playing, each of us varies considerably in what we wish to understand, and what we accept as sufficient evidence. Suppose, for example, that we ask why Betty Podersky, the daughter of Elizabeth Peters-Podersky (who works full time as a vice-principal of a junior high school) and Alec Podersky (who works full time as the owner/manager of a local ski resort) went into engineering when she started university? How might people in the following roles explain Betty's decision and what kinds of evidence would they use?

- citizen

- novelist

- journalist

- quantitative social scientist

- qualitative social scientist

1. CITIZEN

The thoughtful citizen, if asked to speculate on why Betty chose engineering, might say something like "Well, Betty was always good at Math and she always seemed to be good at fixing toys and stuff." The citizen might also note that a neighbour's daughter, Lee Anne, also went into Engineering, now works as a supervisor of a highway construction crew, and has found that the job provides good, steady work. Additionally, the citizen reports that the high school principal has been saying that, by the turn of the century, job opportunities in engineering will increase.

A. COMMENT

In the citizen's explanation, note the reliance on **_anecdotal evidence_** concerning the neighbour's daughter. Note too that the citizen advances an explanation which has to do with Betty's ability in Mathematics and her skills at fixing things. Note that no evidence is presented beyond the ideas themselves or the anecdote. The reference to authority (the high school principal) is included in the citizen's construction of what has motivated Betty. In everyday life we frequently rely on explanations of this sort. For most people, the explanations offered by the citizen are plausible. In our everyday lives we routinely construct such explanations for our own and for others' behaviour; ordinarily we do not try to penetrate much behind the explanations offered. They are simply accepted as sufficient.

2. NOVELIST

The novelist might write a story about Betty who goes into engineering. Embedded in the story are lots of clues as to why she chose to take engineering. Her career choice would not be the main point of the novel but simply part of the portrayal. The story would develop a character with qualities that makes it seem reasonable that she would choose to take engineering. Betty perhaps had a fascination with trucks, loved playing hockey with the boys, and liked to operate the chair lift at the ski resort owned by her father.

A. COMMENT

Note that the treatment by the novelist is holistic; that is, the novelist attempts to provide a complete picture of the character and what motivates her. To the extent that the author creates a good character, her choice of engineering will appear to be reasonable, believable. The explanation given motivates one character's career choice and does not attempt to explain such choices in general. But to write a credible story, the author would have to have a keenly developed sense of our shared cultural understandings of what motivates people. Presumably the author employs these commonly understood explanations in constructing a character which will then be plausible to the reader. The use of the "Tom Boy" stereotype in the development of the character is such a device; in our culture, we often rely on such stereotypes to explain behaviour. Novelists use these; they make the story believable precisely because we share with the novelist these commonsensical understandings of the world. The novelist's genius is in using these shared visions to develop characters that ring true to the reader.

3. JOURNALIST

The journalist's response might be to write a story on women in engineering, perhaps by going to the local engineering school,

and establishing contact with three or four first-year female students, and spending some time talking with them individually. During these interviews the journalist would gather information on the background of the women, their hobbies, and ask about their reasons for going into engineering. An article would then be prepared, along with a picture of the women sitting in class, or working on computers, or perhaps a shot of them standing by a huge drill press. The article, researched and written over a four-day period, would then be submitted for inclusion in the "Life Styles" section of the local paper and would offer a sympathetic profile of the women who opted for engineering.

A. COMMENT

In contrast to the citizen and the novelist, the journalist goes out and collects information in the field. As an item in a "Life Styles" section of a newspaper, the article will be written with a light touch and will attempt to portray the women interviewed accurately. Note that the journalist would not claim to have demonstrated why middle-class women, in general, might be more likely to choose a non-traditional program than working-class women.

4. QUANTITATIVE SOCIAL SCIENTIST

A quantitative social scientist might proceed by identifying various hypotheses relating to non-traditional program choice. A survey might then be conducted among first-year female students enrolled in both traditional and non-traditional programs (including Engineering, Science, Mathematics, and Business), measuring factors which have been suggested in the literature related to choice of program. The study might involve an equal number of female students who have opted for non-traditional and traditional programs. The analysis would be completed by entering the survey results into a computer and determining which variables best distinguish the non-traditional from the traditional students. The various hypotheses established in advance of collecting the data, including various alternative explanations, would be tested to see which, if any, could be excluded as an appropriate explanation of why middle-class female students are more likely than those with working-class origins to choose a non-traditional program at college. The effort here is to see if any general statements can be advanced about how programs are selected.

A. COMMENT

Note that this study has been expanded to include those enrolled in traditional as well as in non-traditional programs. The non-traditional category is expanded to include not just engineering students but also students majoring in mathematics, science, and business. Since a survey is the research design that has been chosen, the variables examined had to be set up in advance of data collection. This means that once data collection has started, variables cannot be added as the study progresses. The study attempts to test various alternative explanations of why middle-class students, in contrast to working-class students, are more likely to opt for non-traditional programs. The study attempts to determine systematically which explanations of program selection are consistent in accounting for the

greater preponderance of women with middle-class origins in non-traditional programs.

5. QUALITATIVE SOCIAL SCIENTIST

The qualitative social scientist might choose to study the question by doing a participant observation study. Like the journalist, the qualitative researcher would make contact with the local engineering school, but instead of spending four days on the story, the researcher might arrange to spend several months as a participant observer in the lives of first-year engineering students. While the study would not start with any fixed hypotheses the researcher wished to test, considerable time would be spent with both the men and the women in the program: attending classes with them, and being with them in the evenings and on weekends. In short, the observer would move in with the students. Careful field notes would be recorded daily along with notes on the interviews conducted with the first-year students.

Having become familiar with the literature on non-traditional program choice, the researcher would be aware of explanations that have been suggested by other researchers. These possibilities, along with new ones which emerge during the observations, could then be tested in a variety of ways, to see how well they applied in the case of the nine female students enrolled in the program. It is likely that such a researcher would be particularly alert to the presence of non-traditional role models in the lives of the female students. There is a good possibility that this study would suggest some new reasons for the choice of engineering. After completing the observations, field and interview notes would be analyzed, and an extensive report would be written.

A. COMMENT

By comparison with the journalist, the qualitative social scientist spends considerably more time with the students, including the male students, and writes an in-depth analysis of the observations. While no hypotheses guided the study, the researcher would explore the motivations, ambitions, and values of both the male and the female students. The examination of both genders in the study provides a contrast group for the researcher so that the researcher can identify dimensions on which the female students appear to be different from the male students. In this way, the social scientist hopes to shed light not only on why Betty Podersky might opt for engineering but on the more general issue of why some females choose to enter what has been a traditionally male domain.

Table 2.1 presents a simplified view of how different categories of individuals attempt to understand the social world. While each of us may occupy more than one of these categories, we tend to ask different questions and to have different standards for the evidence that is taken to be acceptable, depending upon the category we occupy.

6. COMMENT ON THE QUESTIONS ASKED

The *individualistic questions* posed by the citizen and journalist focus on understanding a particular decision and attempt to come to grips with all the things that might have influenced Betty Podersky. To say a question is individualistic is to suggest that it asks about a particular person or event. Why did Aunt Martha move to the city? Why did the carnival stop coming to our town? Why did Betty go into engineering?

The journalist and the qualitative social scientist ask more holistic questions. To say that a *holistic question* is asked is to suggest that the researcher is attempting to understand an individual, a whole institution, or a situation. An attempt is made to understand the particular behaviour in the total context within which it is found.

TABLE 2.1   QUESTIONS AND EVIDENCE

CATEGORY	QUESTIONS ASKED	EVIDENCE USED	SYSTEMATIC TESTING
Citizen	Individualistic	Anecdotal, experience	No
Novelist	Holistic	Fictional, based on cultural myths	No
Journalist	Individualistic	Short study, interviews	No
Quantitative social scientist	Generalizing	Multiple cases, used to test hypotheses, models	Yes
Qualitative social scientist	Holistic and generalizing	Lengthy field study, intensive case analysis, in-depth interviews	Yes

The quantitative social scientist usually looks for a generalizing answer. The question might be expanded to ask why women from middle-class backgrounds are more likely than their working-class peers to opt for gender non-traditional programs in college. Here the attempt is to provide an answer in the form of a *generalization*: that is, the explanation identifies what most typically accounts for the differences in program selection for middle- versus working-class women.

7. COMMENT ON THE EVIDENCE USED

What is considered to be appropriate evidence varies across the categories outlined in the previous sections. In our everyday citizen role we might cite authority for our understandings of human behaviour. Or we might recount an anecdote which occurred recently to illustrate why Betty chose the Engineering Program.

A journalistic approach would involve serious effort to bring some evidence to bear upon the question (background statistical information on trends of women in Engineering, interviews with deans of engineering schools, and with women enrolled in the programs). Table 2.2 summarizes the types of evidence used.

What separates the social science approaches from the non-social science ones? A key difference is the pains taken to do the research. This is reflected in the greater care taken by the social scientist in collecting the information and in tracking down what other researchers have reported on the topic. In addition, the social scientist may attempt to rule out competing explanations for the phenomenon being investigated. Typically the social scientist begins a study with a commonsensical understanding of the behaviour in question. Citizen, novelist, and journalist might all provide important ideas for the social scientist. Ideas can be borrowed from them, defined carefully, measured, and then

TABLE 2.2	TYPES OF EVIDENCE	
TYPE OF EVIDENCE	DEFINITION	EXAMPLE
Assertion	A statement made without any apparent supporting evidence	Tall people are smarter than short people
Anecdote	A brief incident which is meant to demonstrate some principle	Lee Anne went into Engineering...she has found that it is good steady work
Authority	A statement is to be believed because some high-status person (an authority) says it is true	The principal says there will be an increased demand for engineers in the coming years
Scientific evidence	Evidence based on careful, controlled observations	The results indicate that among women there is no evidence to support the argument that differential role-modelling explains the link between class background and the likelihood of choosing a non-traditional program.

tested using appropriate statistical procedures. The social scientist simply tries to examine explanations more carefully and test them more rigorously than the citizen, novelist, or journalist.

Social scientists attempt to provide a disciplined understanding of human behaviour. To do this, a variety of methods are used. Since there is no one best method to cover all research questions, the beginning researcher must become familiar with the full range of methods so that appropriate choices can be made when a research question is posed. As social scientists, we attempt to provide convincing evidence for our explanations; sometimes the evidence is qualitative, sometimes it is quantitative, and sometimes a mixture of the two.

8. TYPES OF SOCIAL SCIENCE EXPLANATIONS

We can ask whether there are different kinds of social science explanations. Following the lead suggested by Ernest Nagel (1961) and Gwynn Nettler (1970), five types of explanations will be distinguished.

A. DEDUCTIVE EXPLANATION

When social scientists use **deductive explanations**, they try to show that the phenomenon to be explained is a logically necessary consequence of the explanatory premises. For example: if A = B, and B = C, then A = C. Emile Durkheim's analysis (1897), for example, of why the suicide rate in Spain will be low is based on the following set of interrelated propositions:

(i) In any social grouping, the suicide rate (SR) varies directly with the degree of individualism (I). > I ——→ > SR

(ii) The degree of individualism (I) varies with the incidence of Protestantism (P). (untested assumption) > P ——→ > I.

(iii) Therefore, the suicide rate (SR) varies with the incidence of Protestantism (P). > P ——→ > SR (Derivation)

(iv) The incidence of Protestantism in Spain is low. (Empirical observation.)

(v) Therefore, the suicide rate (SR) in Spain is low. (Empirically testable hypothesis.)

In the above illustration, by combining an untested, but stated assumption, (ii above) with a theoretical proposition (i), along with an empirical observation (iv), and a deductive step (iii), we get a testable hypothesis. If, indeed, the data prove to be consistent with the prediction, this would constitute one piece of evidence which is not inconsistent with the theory. We could not claim to have proven the theory correct because alternative theories might also make the prediction that suicide rates will be comparatively low in Spain.

For another illustration, which extends Durkheim's analysis, see the propositions used by Gibbs and Martin (1964). A brief excerpt from their work is featured in Box 2.6.

B. PROBABILISTIC EXPLANATION

Probabilistic explanation rests on linking a particular case to its general category. If asked to explain why Joe MacDonald (a college student) drinks excessively, and you respond by saying, "there's a lot of drinking on campus these days," you have given a probabilistic explanation. Joe drinks a lot because he is a member of a category of individuals who tend to drink a lot. The explanation suggests that an individual tends to be like others in the same category.

Another illustration of a probabilistic explanation would be the one offered by the neighbour who, in response to my complaint that "I've been buying 6/49 lottery tickets for years, but I never win the big prize," told me that the chances of winning the jackpot are about 1 in 14 million. In other words, he is telling me that the reason I never win is that the odds are against me.

C. FUNCTIONAL EXPLANATION

Functional explanations explain the presence of some phenomenon in terms of the role it plays in maintaining some system. For example, if the presence of the family unit in all cultures is explained in terms of its role in producing new members for each society, this would be a functional explanation: the family exists to propagate, in order to maintain the social system.

D. CAUSAL EXPLANATION

Here we have an event, or sequence of events, leading to something. In a **causal explanation**, an event is explained by making reference to preceding influencing events. The explanation traces the sequence of steps, each influencing the next, that has led to some event. Causal sequence thinking dominates the thinking of many researchers. Think of a line of dominos falling in sequence after one has been knocked over, and you have the idea of a causal sequence. Make a list of all the factors that you think might influence choosing a non-traditional college program: the list should include all the potential causes of those factors that influence program choice.

E. EMPATHETIC EXPLANATION

Empathetic explanations are those where the experience of coming to see, coming to understand, is stressed. At the core is the idea of an *imagined possibility*; the individual feels "Ah-ha, I've got it—I can see that I would do the same thing in similar circumstances." Everyday life is full of empathetic explanations and understandings: as Nettler points out, the "processes that makes human conduct understandable are usually amalgams of feelings, beliefs, and intentions that, from one's own life, seem to provide 'good reasons' for the behaviour" (Nettler, 1970, p. 34). Qualitative researchers pay much attention to empathetic explanations for, to social scientists working in this tradition, they are the key to adequate explanations. To come up with an explanation or a description of a behaviour that *rings true* to both the researcher and the person whose behaviour is being revealed, is a key element in judging the adequacy of the explanation.

9. THE NATURE OF SOCIAL SCIENCE EVIDENCE

Social science explanations serve the same function as proverbs, adages, and anecdotes: in all cases, they attempt to account for some behaviour, or to explain the behaviour. Does a generalization made by the social scientist substantially differ from that made by the non-scientist? To begin to come to grips with this question an examination will be made of quantitative and qualitative evidence and argument.

A. QUANTITATIVE EVIDENCE

For the quantitative social scientist an important goal is to arrive at general statements, statements which can be applied to a variety of situations. A *generalization* depicts the typical. The following statements constitute generalizations:

- among high school students, females achieve higher grades than males;

- tall people are paid more than short people;

- students who sit in the middle of the classroom get higher grades than those who sit in the back or to the sides of the classroom.

In contrast to the non-scientist, the evidence a quantitative social scientist would look for would be based on objective, verifiable, controlled observations, and communicated in a precise manner (Browne & Keeley, 1990, p. 67). By *objective*, reference is made to observations which are free from bias; by *verifiable*, we mean information which could be confirmed by tests conducted by others; by *controlled observations*, we mean those where other confounding factors are minimized or taken into account; and by *precise communication*, we mean that the information is unambiguous. In the social sciences many of our generalizations are probabilistic; this means that in most cases (but not all) the statement will be true. Certainly not all tall people are paid more than short people; not all high school females achieve higher grades than their male counterparts; and certainly not all students in the back row get lower grades than those sitting in the middle of the room. (Are you considering changing your seat in Methods?) Since the social scientist's argument must be based on evidence, information must be collected and then appropriately analyzed. The resulting conclusion is then an *informed*

opinion; that is, an opinion based on evidence which has been collected under controlled circumstances.

In making probabilistic generalizations, the social scientist has to indicate precisely how the information was collected, what kind of sampling procedures were used, and indicate how the data were analyzed. A probabilistic generalization (for example, women who choose non-traditional careers are more likely to have middle- rather than working-class backgrounds) should indicate the population about whom the generalization is being made (all women in the world, women in a particular country, region, community, or in the Arts Faculty at the University of Winnipeg). The researcher should also indicate the size and the method of selecting the sample upon which the generalization is based (convenience sample of 125 women in non-traditional and 125 women in traditional programs of study); and finally, the researcher should indicate the procedures used to measure the variables and to process the resulting data.

B. QUALITATIVE EVIDENCE

For the qualitative social scientist more emphasis is placed on the extent to which explanations and descriptions ring true to both the researcher and to the people who are being described. The evidence itself may be based on a painstaking analysis of documents (see section on Content analysis in Chapter 6), may be based on in-depth interviews (see Box 5.3 on Rose Weitz for an example), or may be based on lengthy participation in a group (see William Foote Whyte, Box 5.1 and Box 5.2 for examples). But in all cases, the evidence itself, and the interpretations placed on it, is judged in terms of how well it is perceived to deal with the matter at issue.

C. FLAWED EXPLANATIONS

The previous section illustrated some of the evidence that might be used in describing and explaining human behaviour. As a social scientist, one designs studies, makes observations, analyzes them, and then prepares a report on the results. During each stage one must be careful not to fall prey to errors in thinking or in argument. What are some of these errors? Following the arguments presented by Kahane (1988) and by Browne and Keeley (1990), a review will be made of common errors of particular relevance to the social science researcher.

i. Illegitimate Appeal to Authority.

Sometimes as researchers we may be tempted to argue that something is bad (for example, capital punishment) by using an **appeal to an authority**. For example, in this case, we could state that capital punishment is bad because Physics Nobel prize winner, Dr. X., claims that it is. In this case, the status of the person expressing the view should not influence our judgement. Legitimate authority, in contrast, is to be found in the literature of the various disciplines. Does the preponderance of evidence in the research literature point to one conclusion? Are the exceptional findings to be explained by quirks in methodology or in the samples studied? In any case, social science proceeds by testing and retesting old ideas under new conditions. And just as we should not be overly persuaded by the citizen's argument (see the Betty Poderski illustration used earlier) that the principal

thinks that there will be lots of jobs in engineering, we should avoid references to inappropriate authorities.

ii. Provincialism.

As researchers we carry with us the baggage of our culture. This makes us vulnerable to the danger of **provincialism**, of tending to see things as our culture sees them. Thus, if it is politically correct to view men and women as equally skilled at child rearing, then this may blind us from looking at areas in child rearing where this may not be true. Thus Kahane argues provincialism "tends to make us concentrate on our own society… to the exclusion of other cultures… and via *loyalty*, to influence our acceptance or rejection of alleged facts or theories, whatever the nature of the evidence" (1988, p. 47).

iii. False Dilemma.

A **false dilemma** is set up when the researcher argues that something is caused by either A or by B. Then, having provided some evidence that B is not responsible, the researcher falsely concludes that A must be the cause. The problem here is that there may be several other possibilities that have not been considered. Kahane cites an example from *Human Nature* (April, 1978) which argues that "Economics, not biology, may explain male domination." In this example, other possible explanations have been omitted, which then paves the way for the inappropriate conclusion that it is economics and not biology that explains male domination (Kahane, 1988, p. 56).

iv. Missing Evidence

When the reports of researchers are examined, read carefully to make a judgement as to the adequacy of the evidence for each point made. While it would be unrealistic to expect all assumptions to be identified and all statements to be demonstrated, watch out for signs of important **missing evidence** and be certain that evidence for key arguments is provided.

Frequently the social scientist is confronted with "interesting" findings for which an explanation should be offered. Suppose, for example, that a project is being done which measures high school students' socio-economic backgrounds (SES) and relates this variable to the age of first experiencing sexual intercourse. And suppose, during data analysis, that a strong relationship emerges indicating that the higher one's socio-economic origin, the older the average age of first intercourse. At this stage, the researcher may wonder what explains the pattern that has emerged. Possibilities such as the following might come to mind:

• peers of high SES students avoid early initiation into sex and influence their friends to do likewise;

• among high SES students, parental supervision is such that the opportunities to engage in pre marital sex are more limited; and

• high SES students have higher educational aspirations and avoid early initiation into sex because they think that to do so would impede their chances of going to university.

Unfortunately, the study may not have been designed to test, and possibly to rule out, competing explanations. Hence there may be no empirical evidence for the conclusion presented by the researcher. The problem here is that while much data may be presented documenting a variety of relationships, the reader of such a report may be convinced, inappropriately, that the researcher's numerous data, tables, and figures support the particular explanation being offered. Such explanations may sound good, appear reasonable, but lack evidence.

v. Insufficient Evidence.

Suppose an incident is cited (concerning a person on a day pass from prison who commits an armed robbery) in an attempt to justify the conclusion that the prison system is too lenient: what do you conclude? While this type of anecdotal evidence is commonly used, it is hardly sufficient to warrant the conclusion drawn. What are the overall rates of crime being committed by such persons? What are the social and human costs of lengthier sentences? Are lengthier sentences more likely to lead to rehabilitation, lead to decreases in crime rates, or provide greater protection, in the long run, to society? Be wary of anecdotal evidence.

Anecdotal evidence is the layperson's equivalent of arguments based on unrepresentative samples. When social scientists attempt to describe something (say the popularity of a political leader) they typically do so by working with samples. The conclusions should not go beyond the adequacy of the sample. A very small sample (like an anecdote where we have one case) should not be used to generalize about all of humankind. You can imagine how inappropriate it would be to generalize about Canadian attitudes toward a political leader based on a sample of 74 university students enrolled in a second-year political science class at The University of Western Ontario.

Since the sample appears to be one of convenience (students who were present when the questionnaire was administered), it is not only a small sample, but since the students were not selected using a strict sampling procedure, they could not be taken to represent even the students at Western. Avoid conclusions which state generalizations that go beyond those justified by the sampling procedure. (Details on sampling procedures will be discussed in Chapter 14.)

vi. Selected or Suppressed Evidence.

In citing evidence, researchers should attempt to represent the findings in the research literature and their own data fairly. We are all familiar with public debates that have gone on in recent years on such issues as pollution, the dangers of smoking, abortion, and capital punishment. In each case, expert researchers who claim to have special knowledge on these matters and claim also to represent the consensus in their discipline, have been called on to testify. The trouble is that each side seems to be able to produce an expert who supports its point of view. These experts are probably presenting **selected evidence**, choosing to report those studies that support a particular point of view, and ignoring the evidence that runs counter to what they are attempting to demonstrate. Advocacy is not science: both are legitimate enterprises, but do avoid confusing the two.

A similar situation exists with respect to researchers reporting their own data. Given the need to keep reports short, some information is not reported. Hence it is possible that researchers do not represent their own data fairly. Some information may be considered unreportable, or insufficiently interesting to merit inclusion. The reader cannot tell how much information has been omitted.

vii. Unwarranted Conclusions.

Sometimes in analysing data, a researcher will come to an unwarranted conclusion. Confusing *correlation* and *cause* is an example of this type of error in reasoning. Researchers take pains to measure variables and to investigate how they are related to one another. However, to show that as A goes up so does B, does not demonstrate that A causes B. While this issue will be explored in greater detail later (see Chapter 16, Testing Three and Four Variable Causal Models), let us illustrate this point by looking at Max Weber's argument concerning the connection between the Protestant Ethic and the Spirit of Capitalism (1904). He argued that there is a linkage between the emergence of the spirit of capitalism and the work ethic encouraged by the Protestant Reformation. Let us assume that such a correlation, in fact, exists (many would disagree): are we justified in concluding that the Protestant Reformation led to the emergence of work attitudes that helped develop modern capitalism? What are the possibilities when we have a correlation between the two variables?

- Religion has influenced $R \longrightarrow C$
  capitalism

- Religion has been $R \longleftarrow C$
  influenced by capitalism

- They influenced each other $R \longleftrightarrow C$

- Other factor(s) influenced $R \qquad C$
  both of them $\quad \underset{?}{\llcorner} \lrcorner$

Weber was interested in exploring the first possibility. In doing so, however, he failed to explore the other possibilities sufficiently. R.H. Tawney points out in *Religion and the Rise of Capitalism* (1926), that there was a general secularization going on in society, in politics, in economics, and in the church. Thus Tawney argues that a third factor—secularization—was the key, influencing both the emergence of capitalism and the Protestant Reformation itself.

Be careful not confuse association with cause.

D. THE EXPLANATORY ROLE OF THEORY

What is the function of theory in the social sciences—what is theory supposed to do? The major function of theory for social scientists is to explain the behaviour of humans, or of human institutions. A relationship may be said to be explained once someone has offered a satisfactory explanation for it—offered a satisfactory answer to a *why* question (Braithwaite, 1960). But what is satisfactory? For some, almost any answer might satisfy. For others, tough rules of evidence will have to be followed in order for the explanation to be considered adequate. The social scientist is more likely than the layperson to insist on considerable evidence before accepting an explanation. A simple opinion will not do. "What is your evidence?," is a question that will be asked. Skepticism and curiosity distinguish the scientist from non-scientist.

The function of theory is to explain patterns in the world. Theories may be more or less explicit. A theory may be highly detailed and explicit, in which case its underlying assumptions will be clearly specified and it will make many specific predictions. On the other hand, a theory may be entirely lacking in detail—it may be a simple explanatory variable. For example, we might include the variable, "variations in socialization patterns," as an explanation of why we get variations in educational aspirations as we move across the SES (socio-economic status) continuum. What we are proposing by this explanation is that as we move across the SES continuum, we get differences in socialization patterns, which, in turn, account for variations in aspirations. This is a partial theory because it fails to specify the underlying assumptions it makes about human behaviour; it does not tell us anything about how the explanatory variable (variations in socialization patterns) is connected to any other variables. A good deal of theorizing in the social sciences makes use of partial theories. The job of theory is to explain: to offer satisfactory, testable explanations for relationships. A testable explanation is one which can be disconfirmed—one which could turn out to be true or false.

Given the broad range of what may be considered a theoretical explanation, it is instructive to explore the properties of both formal and partial theoretical constructs.

E. FORMAL THEORY

What are the components of formal, explicit theory? According to George Homans (1964), a *formal theory* consists of three key elements. First, there is a set of concepts, or a conceptual scheme. Some of these concepts may be descriptive, serving to identify what the theory is about (in the

Durkheim suicide case, the terms *individualism, suicide,* and *Protestantism* are such terms); other concepts are operatives or properties of nature (such as: suicide rate, degree of individualism, incidence of Protestantism). These are the variables. But a conceptual scheme by itself does not constitute a theory. (Labelling types of deviance is not a theory of deviance; rather it is a classification of deviance.)

A theory consists, second, of a set of propositions, each stating a relationship (such as "inversely related to") between some of the concepts. Furthermore, the set of propositions must be interrelated so that one can derive new propositions by combining them deductively. When new propositions are derived they are said to be explained by the previous ones.

Third, Homans argues, some of the propositions must be contingent—that is they must be amenable to some form of empirical test. A theory, Homans argues, cannot be made up entirely of non-contingent propositions: some, but not necessarily all, must be testable. (E.g., Is the suicide rate in Spain relatively low?)

The power of a theory refers to the extent and number of propositions that may be derived from it; that is, the greater the number of predictive statements that can be derived from a theory, the more powerful the theory. Powerful theories are general theories. In the case of Durkheim's analysis of suicide, the theoretical formulation is not as general (and hence not as powerful) as it might be. By utilizing the highly specific variable, suicide, he has limited the generalizability of the theory. Had Durkheim used the term, deviance, then the theory would have been more powerful because one could not only have derived the suicide hypotheses, but could also

have derived all kinds of other predictions that would be worth testing.

Similar definitions of formal theory are to be found in the work of Braithwaite, Zetterberg, and Gibbs. Braithwaite defines theory as a "deductive system in which observable consequences logically follow from the conjunction of observed facts with the set of fundamental hypotheses of the system" (1960, p. 22). Or, from Zetterberg, theory is defined as a set of "systematically organized, law-like propositions about society that can be supported by evidence" (1965, p. 22). Gibbs defines theory as "a set of logically interrelated statements in the form of empirical assertions about properties of infinite classes of events or things" (1972, p. 5).

In summary, then, one does not have formal, explicit theory "until one has properties, and propositions stating the relations between them, and the propositions form a deductive system—not until one has all three does one have a theory" (Homans, 1964, p. 812). While Homans' minimum requirements for theory are stringent, they nonetheless provide a useful guideline. The essence of formal theories is the precision, and explicitness, with which they are stated. Assumptions are specified, as are statements of relationship.

However, as any satisfactory answer to a *why* question constitutes an explanation, there may be some advantage to viewing theory as a continuum, ranging from formal theory (such as that defined above by Homans, Braithwaite, or Zetterberg) through to partial theories, such as single intervening variable explanations. (Such as: "variations in socialization patterns explaining the connection between SES and educational aspirations.") And while these may not meet the requirements of the more formal constructions, they can sometimes be linked to existing formal theory, or lead to the development of new ones.

F. PARTIAL THEORY

A ***partial theory*** attempts to explain an assumed or known relationship by specifying a testable causal model. A good deal of the theoretical research in the social sciences employs partial theories. Their widespread use is explained perhaps by the notion that many researchers begin with a fascination for a relationship that has shown up in the literature. Researchers then wish to understand the pattern that the relationship seems to represent. Thus partial theories are often grounded in the findings of research and a further elaboration of the findings is sought by the researcher. An earlier illustration concerned the connection between socio-economic status and educational aspirations; a number of possible explanations were suggested which may account for the relationship. Each of these explanations represents possible answers to the *why* question about the connection between the two. As such, each is a theory. However, such theoretical formulations remain at an implicit level. As worded, they fail to specify what assumptions are being made, or articulate the underlying model of human behaviour implicit in the explanation. To illustrate, let us explore two of the explanations:

(i) that the reason high SES students are more likely to aspire to higher educational levels is to fulfil their parent's expectations of them; and

(ii) that high SES students have been more exposed to high achievers and more

likely, therefore, to model themselves after such individuals.

i. Fulfilling Parental Expectations.

This explanation contains two critical elements:

(i) high and low SES parents have different educational expectations of their children; and

(ii) students try to fulfil the expectations of their parents.

Theoretically, the idea is that people are influenced, or shaped, by the expectations of others. This type of explanation is most consistent with reinforcement theory in psychology (Thibaut & Kelley, 1959) or exchange theory in sociology (Homans, 1961). In this particular case, the child is seen as a rather passive object being shaped, or moulded, by the expectations of parents and reward systems controlled by parents. Students become what they are rewarded to become.

ii. Differential Exposure to Role Models.

The second explanation involves at least three assumptions:

(i) that there will be differences, correlated with students' SES levels, in the amount of exposure to people in elite occupations;

(ii) that students recognize the connection between educational and occupational achievement; and

(iii) that students recognize and desire the rewards that come to people who achieve higher occupational levels.

The implicit model of behaviour here is that the individual aspires to higher educational levels as a vehicle for moving into occupations similar to those whose lifestyles they admire. This view of human behaviour suggests that the individual is motivated more by the desire to achieve certain rewards than the expectations of others. In this case, education is the means used to attain these goals. Role models are copied. This view is most compatible with the ideas expressed by symbolic interactionists (Blumer, 1951) and with the concept of vicarious reinforcement (seeing others being rewarded) in psychology.

Other explanations for the connection between SES and educational aspirations could be developed and connected to existing theoretical perspectives. Frequently it is possible for the researcher to generate theoretical connections by carefully exploring the underlying theory of human behaviour that is being proposed in the research. In short, it is possible to make a backwards connection to theory—starting with a partial theory and moving backward to existing formal theories in the discipline. Carefully thought out, such research can lead to a general understanding of human behaviour.

But what is the use of theory? What do we gain by connecting research to new or existing theoretical perspectives? The answer has to do with power. Research that limits itself to the particular, to the unique, will not contribute to our general understanding of the human condition. General explanations allow research to have implications for our overall understanding of behaviour, as well as for increasing our knowledge of the particular variables involved in a project.

G. THEORY TESTING

As one might expect, there are many examples of theories and partial theories within the social sciences. There is considerable debate in the social sciences as to the proper role of theory and of methods. Most seem to agree that they are best viewed as partners in our attempts to extend our understanding of human behaviour. In that way *both* theory and methods should be regarded as tools. A theory may be thought of as a cluster of tentative ideas put forward to explain something; research methods are the means we use to test the adequacy of these ideas. Refinements in our theories are neither more nor less important than our refinements in techniques used to test theories. They are equal partners in the knowledge enterprise.

Hypothesis testing is a part of theory testing but, by itself, does not necessarily constitute a test of theory. The fundamental issue in theoretical research is to demonstrate the linkage between a set of theoretical propositions and the conceptual hypothesis that has been selected for examination. Only to the extent that this connection has been articulated successfully can we claim our research has bearing on theory. This next section will consider methods of testing partial theories followed by those used to test formal theories.

1. TESTING PARTIAL THEORIES

Previously the argument was made that the testing of alternative explanations is a primitive form of theory testing. This is the case because *theory* and *explanation* do the same thing—to answer some *why* question. The reason we identify the testing of alternative explanations as a primitive form of theory testing is that such formulations typically fail to identify fully the linkages to the model of human behaviour that is being used.

The first thing we need in order to test a partial theory is a relationship which, we feel, needs to be understood. Then we propose a series of alternative explanations for the relationship. After that, all we have to do is to measure the appropriate variables, and do the analysis.

For example, if we were to attempt to test an explanation of the connection between the age of initiation into sex and socio-economic background, we might wish to test:

- whether variations in socialization patterns accounted for conservative attitudes; or

- whether any such connection is simply spurious and conservative attitudes are due to differences in the rural versus urban background of the respondents.

Appropriate research would allow us to evaluate the adequacy of each of the two explanations. The idea here is that size of community (rural versus urban may be influencing both the SES achievement levels of the parents and the more conservative values found in the rural as opposed to the urban community. Hence it may be type of community and not SES level that is the key factor in the age of initiation into sex. Note however that, as stated, the first explanation is not well documented. It uses a socialization of values explanation (but connected to what general theory of human behaviour?). Nevertheless, since both ex-

planations are answers to a *why* question, each may be viewed as constituting a theory of human behaviour (albeit an implicit theory).

The advantage of the more formal constructions of social science theory is that we are forced to make explicit our core assumptions about human behaviour. Without such explicitness it is difficult to construct truly general, and therefore powerful, theories of human behaviour. When we seek to explain particular relationships with highly particularized explanations, we do not advance the general state of knowledge much. Hence, more formal approaches to theory construction are to be encouraged. Nonetheless, especially for the beginning researcher, important contributions to the discipline may be made by testing alternative explanations for relationships.

The basic requirements for the testing of alternative explanations are that:

- one has a relationship between two variables which one suspects will be strong (either positive or negative);

- one has a series of alternative explanations for the relationship;

- that it is possible to get measures for the appropriate variables; and

- that after data are collected suitable procedures are used for the analysis of the data so that an evaluation can be made of the adequacy of the competing explanations.

Box 2.3 illustrates a causal model used by Julian Tanner and Harvey Krahn (1991) in their study of the relationship between deviance and part-time work among high school seniors. Note the arrangement of the variables and how they are linked ultimately

Julian Tanner and Harvey Krahn: A Path Model of the Determinants of Self-Reported Illegal Activity Among High-School Seniors

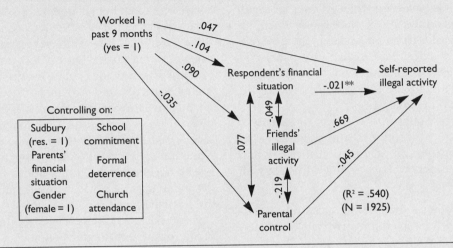

* The six control variables were included in the calculation of each of the four multiple regression equations, although the coefficients for these effects are not displayed. Equations for each of the intervening variables (respondent's financial situation; friend's illegal activity; parental control) did not include the other two intervening variables, because no particular causal order was specified. The bi-directional arrows linking these three intervening variables represent zero-order correlations.

** Path coefficient is *not* statistically significant (p > .01).

SOURCE: Tanner, Julian and Harvey Krahn (1991) "Part-Time Work and Deviance Among High School Seniors," *Canadian Journal of Sociology*, 16:3:296. Reprinted by permission of the publisher.

to the dependent variable, self-reported illegal activity. Models such as the Tanner/Krahn one are known as path analysis models. The arrows and lines represent the causal connections between the variables in the model. (Such models are analyzed using techniques in the correlation/regression family of statistical techniques; a preliminary discussion of these techniques will be introduced later in the text).

2. TESTING FORMAL THEORY

Formal theories involve a number of formally stated, interconnected propositions, contain clearly defined variables, and indicate the nature (direct or inverse) and the direction (what is causing what) of the relationships among the variables. The propositions normally take the form of the greater A, the greater B. Not all the concepts in the propositions need to be directly measurable. However, at some point, a connection to measurable variables must be made. It is this link, this connection, that must be specified in order for one's research to have bearing on a theoretical formulation. We will examine two methods used to demonstrate such connections: these are: (a) axiomatic derivations and (b) a replacement of terms.

A. AXIOMATIC DERIVATIONS

Doing **axiomatic derivations** refers to a method of logically deriving new statements of relationship from a given set of assumptions and propositions. Axiomatic derivations are illustrated in Box 2.4 and Box 2.5 using five statements from James Teevan (1992) and five from Peter Blau (1964).

Now let us extend Blau's propositions identified in Box 2.5 using axiomatic derivations. Suppose that the relationship between "a" and "f" and between "a" and "d" are reversible. This means that we are going to assume that there is a mutual causal link such that "a" influences "f" but also that "f" influences "a". This kind of relationship can be represented as:

Causally, the argument is that the greater a group's cohesion (a), the fewer members will deviate from the group's norms (f). The second argument is that the reverse is also assumed to be true; namely, that having fewer deviants in a group (f) will lead to a strengthening of group cohesion.

Since the original propositions indicated a number of variables to which cohesion is related, we can now suggest some new derived propositions which should be true if the original propositions and a reversibility assumption are correct. They are as follows:

(Derivation 1) The fewer the proportion of deviants from group norms (f), the greater the consensus on normative standards (b);

$$<f \longrightarrow >b$$

BOX 2.5 SOCIAL RESEARCHERS AT WORK

Peter Blau: Social Cohesion

The following five statements are contained in Chapter Two of his work:

(1) The greater the group cohesion (a), the greater the consensus on normative standards (b).

(2) The greater the group cohesion (a), the greater the effective enforcement of these shared norms (c).

(3) The greater the cohesion (a), the greater the significance of the informal sanctions of the group (d).

(4) The more the integrative bonds of social cohesion (a), the stronger the group in the pursuit of common goals (e).

(5) The greater the cohesion (a), the fewer the proportion of deviants from group norms (f). (Note that "f" is negative.)

Note that the wordings of the "a" variable vary somewhat from proposition to proposition. In doing a propositional inventory of any theoretical work, the student has to decide whether variations of this sort are intended to convey a different meaning, or whether the variations are simply for stylistic considerations.

SOURCE: Adapted from Peter Blau, *Exchange and Power in Social Life*. New York: John Wiley and Sons, Inc., 1964.

(Derivation 2) The fewer the proportion of deviants from group norms (f), the greater the effective enforcement of shared norms (c);

$$<f \longrightarrow >c$$

(Derivation 3) The fewer the proportion of deviants from group norms (f), the greater the significance of the informal sanctions of the group (d);

$$<f \longrightarrow >d$$

(Derivation 4) The fewer the proportion of deviants from group norms (f), the stronger the group in the pursuit of common goals (e).

$$<f \longrightarrow >e$$

How are these derivations made? As we have assumed that the "a" to "f" relation is reversible, we are able to argue that "f" leads to "a". And, as we were given the "a" to "b" relation in the original proposition, we can then conclude that "f" leads to "a" and this leads to "b". This may be represented as:

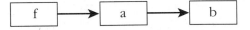

The remaining derivations are made in a similar fashion. In each case, the relationship can be simplified by leaving out the linking, or intervening, variable. Any time one has a situation such as the following, derivations may be made:

If, $> X \longrightarrow > Y$

and, $> Y \longrightarrow > Z$

therefore, $> X \longrightarrow > Y \longrightarrow > Z$

or simply, $> X \longrightarrow > Z$

The new derived propositions should be true if the assumptions, derivations, and original theoretical propositions are accurate. Derivations are made to locate testable

---

Jack P. Gibbs and W.T. Martin: Status Integration and Suicide: A Sociological Study

The following excerpts illustrate the axiomatic nature of the work done by Gibbs and Martin. In their work hundreds of predictions were made and then tested. The set of postulates that links status integration to variability in suicide rates is reviewed below:

- *Postulate 1:* The suicide rate of a population varies inversely with the stability and durability of social relationships within that population.

- *Postulate 2:* The stability and durability of social relationships within a population vary directly with the extent to which individuals in that population conform to the patterned and socially sanctioned demands and expectations placed upon them by others.

- *Postulate 3:* The extent to which individuals in a population conform to patterned and socially sanctioned demands and expectations placed upon them by others varies inversely with the extent to which individuals in that population are confronted with role conflicts.

- *Postulate 4:* The extent to which individuals in a population are confronted with role conflicts varies

directly with the extent to which individuals occupy incompatible statuses in that population.

- *Postulate 5:* The extent to which individuals occupy incompatible statuses in a population varies inversely with the degree of status integration in that population.

From the above postulates there follows the major theorem: The suicide rate of a population varies inversely with the degree of status integration in that population. This theorem is central to the present study...examples will be given of the type of hypotheses to be tested in line with the theorem...

Suicide rates by age groups vary inversely with measures of the integration of marital status with age.

In the United States, there will be an inverse relationship by age groups between suicide rates and measures of the integration of marital status with age.

There will be a direct relationship by age groups between the ratio of the suicide rate of widowed persons to married persons and the ratio of the measure of integration with age for the status of married to the status of widowed.

SOURCE: Jack P. Gibbs and W.T. Martin, *Status Integration and Suicide: A Sociological Study.* Eugene, Oregon: University of Oregon Press, 1964. Reprinted with permission, University of Oregon @ 1964.

hypotheses which then constitute a test of the theory. The reason one makes such derivations is to provide many different tests. The reason one wants to do different tests is that ideally one wishes to identify a theoretically predicted relationship, but one which is not obvious.

Box 2.6 identifies the major theoretical propositions, theorems, and a few of the derived hypotheses used by Gibbs and Martin (1964) in their comprehensive study of suicide. The researchers made a total of 676 predictions, of which 58.0 per cent were correct (1964, p. 197). And of 175 correlation coefficients examined, 91.4 per cent were in the predicted direction, thus lending considerable weight to their argument concerning the impact status integration has on suicide rates (1964, p. 198). Their study is a brilliant extension of Durkheim's (1897) original work.

Why would one want a counter-intuitive relationship? Here the answer is psychological rather than scientific. If an unexpected relationship is predicted, and if, indeed, the results of the study confirm it, the evidence is much more convincing. On the other hand, if the predicted relationship is commonsensical, even if it is confirmed, the critic will claim that the results only show what everyone already knew and certainly do not demonstrate any theory. The verification of Albert Einstein's simple but counter-intuitive prediction that a rapidly moving clock should run slower than a clock that is moving slowly provided powerfully convincing evidence for his theory of relativity.

B. REPLACEMENT OF TERMS

A further way of extending the number of predictions is to use a technique which will be called *replacement of terms*.

Replacement of terms refers to replacing general theoretical concepts by specific instances of these concepts. For example, if the general concept is deviance, such a concept could be replaced by a specific instance of deviance—perhaps shoplifting, or burglary, or drunk driving. To the extent that one is able to derive new predictions through such replacements, one can provide a virtually unlimited number of testable relationships. One can then select the better ones—choosing those that are counter-intuitive and those that permit one to refine and specify conditions under which the theory does, or does not, hold.

Using a combination of axiomatic derivations and replacement of terms provides powerful, yet simple, methods of deriving interesting testable hypotheses. The student would be well advised, however, to test directly the propositions of a theory and, if that is not possible, to restrict axiomatic steps to a minimum in locating testable hypotheses. As social relations are so complex, and given that few relations are extremely powerful, it is problematic to make a large number of axiomatic steps and still have an iron-clad connection to the original set of propositions. Many factors influence variables in our propositions and it therefore becomes problematic to predict even the sign (+ or −) of derived propositions. (See also: Costner and Leik, 1964; Gibbs, 1972; Blalock, 1969; and Bailey, 1970.)

H. FIVE PERSPECTIVES ON HUMAN BEHAVIOUR

A brief review, ordered alphabetically, will be made of some of the major social science perspectives. Detailed presentations of these perspectives are available in the items listed in the Suggested Readings section at the end of the chapter.

1. CONFLICT PERSPECTIVES

According to **conflict perspectives**, society is fundamentally characterized by conflict between interest groups: in the Marxist version, for example, these include owners of the means of production (factories, farms, businesses, etc.), the **bourgeoisie**, seek to exploit workers, the **proletarians**, whose labour is undervalued and underpaid. Marx argues that specialization (division of labour) results in different groups having unequal power. The difference in power occurs because of control of the means of production. Marx uses Hegel's view that social change is a cyclical process involving a *thesis, antithesis,* and a *synthesis.* The final synthesis becomes the new thesis for the next phase of development. In nineteenth-century Europe, capitalism is the thesis; the antithesis is a mode where the proletariate rules; the synthesis is a stage where there is a classless society.

Social change in Marx's view is brought about by material causes—primarily economic ones. His label as a conflict theorist fits because he views society as characterized by disharmony, competition, and conflict between groups. Fundamentally, society is characterized by disequilibrium.

Marx was concerned to produce not only a science of society but also a more equitable society.

Revolution is necessary because the bourgeoisie will not willingly give up power. The task, then, is to take over the means of production. (For Marx, class is defined in terms of ownership of the means of production.) State ownership leads to a classless society. Marx sees many social institutions as serving to keep the workers in their place; he declared that religion, for example, is the *opium of the masses,* as religion diverts the workers' attention away from their miserable conditions and leads them to dream of the good life in the hereafter. In essence, Marx views the individual as being at the mercy of powerful economic forces, a pawn in a game, where some players have a considerable advantage over others. Box 2.7 presents some of the key propositions found in Marx. The reader is reminded that conflict perspectives are far-reaching and contain many variants. (See Turner (1986) for a good review of various perspectives.)

BOX 2.7 SOCIAL RESEARCHERS AT WORK

Marx's Key Propositions[1]

I. The more unequal is the distribution of scarce resources in a system, the greater is the conflict of interest between dominant and subordinate segments in a system.

II. The more subordinate segments become aware of their true collective interests, the more likely they are to question the legitimacy of the existing pattern of distribution of scarce resources.

A. The more social changes wrought by dominant segments disrupt existing relations among subordinates, the more likely the latter are to become aware of their true interests.

B. The more practices of dominant segments create alienative dispositions among subordinates, the more likely the latter are to become aware of their true interests.

C. The more members of subordinate segments can communicate their grievances to each other, the more likely they are to become aware of their true collective interests.

    1. The more ecological concentration of members of subordinate groups, the more likely communication of grievances.

    2. The more the educational opportunities of subordinate group members, the more diverse the means of their communication, and the more likely they are to communicate their grievances.

D. The more subordinate segments can develop unifying ideologies, the more likely they are to become aware of their true collective interests.

    1. The greater the capacity to recruit or generate ideological spokespeople, the more likely ideological unification.

    2. The less the ability of dominant groups to regulate the socialization processes and communication networks in a system, the more likely ideological unification.

III. The more subordinate segments of a system are aware of their collective interests and the greater is their questioning of the legitimacy of the distribution of scarce resources, the more likely they are to join overt conflict against dominant segments of a system.

A. The less the ability of dominant groups to make manifest their collective interests, the more likely subordinate groups are to join in conflict.

B. The more the deprivations of subordinates move from an absolute to relative basis, the more likely they are to join in conflict.

C. The greater the ability of subordinate groups to develop a political leadership structure, the more likely they are to join in conflict.

IV. The greater is the ideological unification of members of subordinate segments of a system and the more developed is their political leadership structure, the more likely are dominant and subjugated segments of a system to become polarized.

V. The more polarized are the dominant and subjugated, the more violent is their conflict.

VI. The more violent is the conflict, the greater is the structural change of the system and the greater is the redistribution of scarce resources.

---

[1] SOURCE: Jonathan H. Turner, *The Structure of Sociological Theory,* Fourth Edition. Belmont, California: Wadsworth Publishing Company, 1986, p. 136. Reprinted by permission of the publisher.

At the level of the individual, the work of Sigmund Freud may be seen as fitting into the conflict perspective. In Freud's case stress is placed on the conflict between aspects of the self. Normal maturation involves resolving the conflicting urges of the id, ego, and superego.

2. EXCHANGE PERSPECTIVES

The **exchange perspective** emerged in the 1960s and incorporates principles and concepts drawn from economics, psychology, and sociology. In the behavioural psy-

chology/George Homans' variant, the basic premise is that social actors interact with one another so that both profit by the exchange. Interaction will persist to the extent that both parties are gaining more than they are losing. Indeed it has been argued that there is a *norm of reciprocity* according to which one is expected to reciprocate with another person—expected to return favours.

Box 2.8 presents an anecdote which uses an exchange perspective to explain the management of an interpersonal problem, the person who is always smoking your cigarettes and rarely seems to reciprocate the favour.

BOX 2.8

Escalating the Cost of Bumming Cigarettes

How do cigarette smokers increase the cost of others perpetually bumming from them? At first there is no problem so when you are having a cigarette you:

- offer a cigarette to others around, then take one yourself. After several such occasions, when you become aware that one of the people does not reciprocate by offering cigarettes, one tactic then might be to:

- not offer a cigarette, make the other person ask, increase the ante, in an effort to try to graciously encourage reciprocation, but if that is not successful:

- complain: "Why don't you ever buy some?", increase the ante some more, this is getting frustrating, so if this doesn't work, the ultimate test:

- carry two packs, one with only one cigarette; offer the bum a smoke from the one cigarette pack. Only the world's most evil person would take a smoker's last cigarette. If he takes this one, that will be his last cigarette! Since he doesn't, you have the *last* cigarette; bum gets none. Not even yet, but at least you've stopped the bleeding!

The general point is that we seek fairness in relations with others; we perform a kind of psychic calculus ensuring that our score sheet with each person balances. Reciprocations need not be in kind (the same things need not be exchanged) but can take other forms. In social life, we sometimes avoid becoming indebted to others because we don't want to have to reciprocate with them.

What are some of the key propositions of the exchange perspective? Sociologist George C. Homans, borrowing particularly from **operant conditioning theory** and using some economics principles, stated some propositions which argue that our behaviour is developed, sustained, and modified by the consequences that our behaviour produces (Homans, 1961). A simplified version of some of these propositions are listed in Box 2.9.

It should be noted that how the behaviour has been shaped has implications for extinguishing the behaviour. Where continuous reinforcement has been used to shape the behaviour, extinction (the behaviour is no longer emitted) will be most rapid. However, where various intermittent

---

BOX 2.9 SOCIAL RESEARCHERS AT WORK

Exchange Propositions[2]

I. Success Proposition
For all actions taken by persons, the more often a particular action of a person is rewarded, the more likely the person is to perform that action.

II. Stimulus Proposition
If in the past the occurrence of a particular stimulus or set of stimuli has been the occasion of which a person's actions have been rewarded, then the more similar the present stimuli are to the past ones, the more likely the person is to perform the action of some similar action now.

III. Value Proposition
The more valuable to a person is the result of his action, the more likely he is to perform the action.

IV. Deprivation-Satiation Proposition
The more often in the recent past a person has received a particular reward, the less valuable any further unit of that reward becomes for him.

V. Aggression-Approval Propositions
(a) When a person's action does not receive the reward he expected or receives punishment he did not expect, he will be angry and become more likely to perform aggressive behavior, and the results of such behavior become more valuable to him. (b) When a person's action receives the reward expected, especially greater reward than expected, or does not receive punishment he expected, he will be pleased and become more likely to perform approving behavior, and the results of such behavior become more valuable to him.

VI. Rationality Proposition
In choosing between alternative actions, a person will choose that one for which, as perceived by him or her at the time, the value of the result, multiplied by the probability of getting that result, is greater.

---

[2] SOURCE: Jonathan H. Turner, *The Structure of Sociological Theory*, Fourth Edition. Belmont, California: Wadsworth Publishing Company, 1986, p. 246. Reprinted by permission of the publisher.

schedules have been used, ***extinction*** will take longer.

The idea of ***inadvertent reinforcement*** describes a way in which we may unintentionally reinforce undesired behaviour. In dealing with others we may reinforce bad, unwanted behaviour by paying attention to it. For example, by paying attention to the bratty kid, we may be rewarding the very behaviour that we dislike. And, in so doing, encourage its repetition.

There have been many challenges to the exchange perspective; Skidmore claims that the role of a key element, *reward*, cannot be falsified (Skidmore, 1975, p. 114). Abrahamsson has noted contradictory statements in Homans who claims, in the same writing, that it is rewarding to be an egoist and be an altruist; conform to norms and deviate from norms; pay a low price and pay a high price. These contradictions are reminiscent of the pairs of contradictory everyday aphorisms noted at the beginning of this chapter. Both Skidmore (1975) and Turner (1986) have done a good job of presenting the basics of the exchange perspective and discussing various problems with it, and both should be consulted if one is anticipating doing research using this perspective.

3. FEMINIST PERSPECTIVES

Feminist researchers claim that one cannot adequately understand human societies without paying attention to the universal role of ***patriarchy***, which refers to the domination of social groups by males who have greater power and privilege than women and children. Some feminist researchers have argued that inequalities of the sexes emerged because of males' greater physical strength. The control this enabled men to exercise resulted in women playing socially subservient roles, and in stereotypes that portrayed women as inferior to men. Sexism is thus fostered and maintained through the transmission of an ideology justifying male domination (Saunders, 1988, pp. 159-160). ***Feminist perspectives*** stress the idea that inequalities suffered by women stem from an ingrained, systemic patriarchy in societies; this patriarchy pervades many institutions and practices, including, in particular, family socialization. Like researchers who subscribe to one or other of the critical perspectives, feminists see science as a tool that has largely been in the hands of the male oppressor. Feminists take a strong advocacy position in an effort to eliminate sexism from society.

Feminists display a tendency towards synthesizing various critical concepts, symbolic interactionist ideas, and qualitative research styles. Like critical theorists, feminists reject the relativistic stances of Positivism and the interpretive approaches. This stance can be explained by their interest in achieving gender equality. Instead they argue that science should be used to improve the conditions of the oppressed. Feminists wish to help eliminate sexism by understanding and documenting its sources. An emphasis on achieving gender equality is central. Box 2.10 summarizes some of the major propositions of feminist perspectives.

In *The Everyday World as Problematic: a Feminist Sociology*, Dorothy E. Smith argues that there is a invisible subtext of male domination in the institutions of government, business, the military, and the media. The academic world deals with abstractions while the world of women deals with the particular—with the particulars of child rear-

BOX 2.10 SOCIAL RESEARCHERS AT WORK

Key Feminist Ideas

In major cultural institutions (universities, media, advertising, the writing of history) men's standpoint is represented as universal. (Smith, 1987:19)

As one moves from elementary through to university educational institutions, the proportion of women on the staff declines; the proportion of women in administrative positions declines even more as one moves through the hierarchy of educational institutions.

Women have been systematically excluded from the making of cultural ideology.

An adequate social science must be grounded in the everyday experiences of both men and women.

An adequate social science must recognize the universal role of patriarchy—the domination of society by males who have greater power and privilege than women and children.

SOURCE: Dorothy E. Smith, *The Everyday World as Problematic: A Feminist Sociology.* Toronto: University of Toronto Press, 1987.

ing, of mothering, of household, and neighbourhood interactions. Smith wishes to construct a sociology which starts from the experience of women, to create a sociology that would "look back and talk back" from their unique perspective (1987, p. 8).

She is influenced by many theories developed by men but she is not enveloped by any one of these perspectives. Smith says that "...I am not symbolic interactionist, nor a phenomenologist sociologist, nor a Marxist sociologist, nor an ethnomethodologist" (1987, p. 9). Instead, she wishes to create a "way of seeing, from where we actually live, into the powers, processes, and relations that organize and determine the everyday context of that seeing" (1987, p. 9).

Smith focuses on how women have been excluded from making cultural ideology and excluded from forming the ideological apparatuses of society—the work done in universities, in the media, and in advertising. But women are subject to more

than simple exclusion. There is simply a non-presence of women. By this it is meant that women not only suffer from discrimination but that they are also simply ignored, treated as if they are not there. Although much work claims to present a genderless view of the relationship between inequality and education, Smith argues that when such issues have been explored, the approach has been to examine the issue by looking at men's occupations, and men's career patterns. Indeed, when one looks at inter-generational mobility literature, most of it presents the relation between the father's occupation and the son's.

Men are taken more seriously than women. Women are not viewed as being an autonomous source of knowledge, experience, or imagination. They are judged by criteria established and controlled by males. As an example, Smith cites work done by Jo Freeman who asked college women to judge a series of professional articles. While the articles were identical, the authorship was varied so that in some cases the author's name would be female, in others it would be male. The findings indicated that where the name indicated a male author, the students rated the article higher on value, profundity, writing style, and competence (cited in Smith, 1987, p. 30).

Smith argues that what is viewed as art has been defined by men. She points out, for example, that quilting remained defined as a folk art rather than a high art—relegated to a secondary status—although the level of excellence in design and execution merited inclusion as a serious art form. (1987, p. 23) The dominance of men in educational systems is illustrated by the declining proportion of female staff as one moves from elementary through university level institutions; similarly, the proportion of females in administrative positions declines as one moves across the spectrum of educational systems (Smith, 1987, pp. 27-28).

Smith argues for a sociology that is grounded in the everyday experiences of women. The explanations emerging from such a perspective would possibly ring more true to women than those of any traditional sociology founded in men's experiences and concerns.

Feminist social researchers adopt a wide range of quantitative and qualitative methodologies. Most emphasis seems to be on qualitative methods, particularly using in-depth interviews. Historical, comparative, and field study methods are also common.

4. FUNCTIONALIST PERSPECTIVES

Functionalism is a school of social thought that originated in the nineteenth century. The functionalists (Comte, Spencer, Durkheim, and later Parsons, Merton, Levi-Strauss, and Radcliffe Brown), using an organic analogy that compared societies to living organisms, emphasized the interrelationships of the various parts of a society and how they complement one another. Functionalists argue that there is a tendency for societies to move toward balance and harmony. Functionalists ask about how different cultural features contribute to balance, to the maintenance of the social system.

The interest of functionalists in such relationships is used to provide a point in time analysis of how components of society are interrelated. Functionalists are better at explaining how parts are interrelated than they are at explaining how changes occur. Table 2.3 summarizes some of the major ideas of functionalist perspectives.

TABLE 2.3   KEY ELEMENTS OF FUNCTIONALIST PERSPECTIVES

1. Societies are viewed as systems with needs and requisites required for survival.

2. Societies are viewed as being similar to living organisms.

3. The elements of societies are interrelated.

4. Societies tend toward balance, harmony.

5. Where imbalance occurs, mechanisms to re-establish balance will emerge.

While there is renewed interest in functionalist thought, as manifested in the neo-functionalist perspective of the nineties, functionalism itself, so important in American sociology in the first half of the twentieth century, lost its dominance during the 1960s. The following are some of the reasons for this decline in popularity:

i. Explanations Untestable.

Critics noted that functionalism was not stated in propositional form. This, together with the basic notion that social phenomena exist in the form that they do in order to maintain the social system meant, not surprisingly, that it was difficult to confirm or deny statements of function. To claim that something was either functional (contributing to the adjustment and maintenance of the social system) or dysfunctional (detracting from adjustment) was problematic because of the issue of long- versus short-term consequences. To illustrate the dilemma, one might argue that a small war is functional because it averts a larger scale war later; but then, in the longer term, overpopulation leads to mass starvation. So what is functional? If we cannot know the answer when we talk of war and starvation, the functionalist perspective is in serious trouble.

ii. Tends to be Descriptive Rather than Explanatory.

In the sixties when Functionalism declined in popularity, there was a movement toward formal theory construction (see Homans, 1964; Zetterberg, 1965; and Gibbs, 1972) in the hopes that sociology would become a discipline with more rigorous research designs and better tests of theoretical perspectives. Functionalism was seen as a perspective which was strong on description and on classifications but weak on testable hypotheses derived from formal propositions (Homans, 1964).

iii. Difficulty in Dealing with Conflict.

Skidmore (1975, p. 192) argues that explaining social change as a consequence of the use of power or open conflict is not well handled by the functionalist perspective.

iv. Tends to Be a Defence of the Status Quo: the Conservative Bias.

The gist of this criticism is that functionalists argued that things are the way they are because they are functional somehow for society. Since most social patterns end up being viewed as having some function (contributing to the maintenance of the social system) everything (deviance, inequality, etc.) is defended. Even such horrors as racial or gender inequalities are defended because both can be seen to have functions for society. Skidmore argues that there is nothing inherently conservative in the perspective itself, stating that "Theories are neither conservative nor radical, but men are" (1975, p. 194). Many scholars, however, sensed that functionalists were more sympathetic to the powerful than the underdog. Social scientists became convinced that a more adequate approach would have to acknowledge that the societies are characterized not only by balance and harmony, but that social change, power differences, and conflict would have to be a central part of a more realistic description of reality.

5. SYMBOLIC INTERACTIONIST PERSPECTIVES

Symbolic interactionist perspectives pay attention particularly to how one's *self-concept* is formed. People develop a sense of self that is influenced by how others see them or how others react to them. Charles Horton Cooley talked about the development of the self in terms of a ***looking glass self***. That is, our perception of self is reflected in how others see us—we come to see ourselves as others see us. Box 2.11 lists some key Symbolic Interactionist assumptions.

How we are labelled is important. If someone is labelled as stupid, the person may soon come to play out the *stupid* role; conversely, the child who is seen as *gifted*

may work very hard to maintain that image—becoming what she is seen to be. The self develops in interaction, particularly primary group interactions; self, then, is a social concept, formed in interaction with others.

For George Herbert Mead, the concept of *role,* and *role playing* is crucial. The model is that of the stage. We are all actors playing roles. When a famous athlete, movie star, or parent becomes the object of emotional involvement to the child, the model becomes a ***significant other***. Significant others define the world for children and serve as models for their attitudes and behaviour. Rewards and punishment doled out by the significant others shape the behaviour of the child. Because the child seeks approval and love from significant others, the child is motivated to think

BOX 2.11 SOCIAL RESEARCHERS AT WORK

Symbolic Interactionist Perspectives

The term symbolic interaction was coined by the American sociologist, Herbert Blumer. Those working within this general perspective stress the importance of:

1. the individual actor as the primary unit of analysis, hence these perspectives are strongly social psychological in nature;

2. the active involvement of the individual in the interpretation of events;

3. the interaction between the individual's internal thoughts and their relation to social behaviour;

4. individuals constructing, interpreting, and planning their actions; and

5. the individual act; rather than focusing on patterns of norms or rules of behaviour, the symbolic interactionist approaches stress the particular, stress the interpretation of each event as a unique one carried out by an individual.

SOURCE: Ruth A. Wallace and Alison Wolf (1991). *Contemporary Sociological Theory: Continuing the Classical Tradition.* Englewood Cliffs, New Jersey: Prentice Hall.

and behave like the model, learning mannerisms and cool ways of acting.

Mead argued that the development of the self-concept is necessary before role behaviour can emerge. An indication of when the self-concept has developed occurs when a person can be the object of his or her own activity—taking a position outside one's self and viewing one's self as an object.

The *definition of the situation* is a concept developed by W.I. Thomas. The symbolic interactionists argue that how things are perceived is critical. Each social situation is interpreted; the interpretation may or may not be correct but nonetheless people act on their interpretations. Thus, if you see a group as threatening, you will treat them in a special way. The greater the extent to which we share with others a common definition of the situation, the more consistent the patterns of social interaction that result. Thus if you see foreigners as threatening to your job, you may avoid interaction with them (your avoidance behaviour is consistent with your belief that they are threatening to your job). Or, to use another example, suppose that despite working hard and producing what you thought was a fine paper, you got a lower grade than your friend Petra, who wrote her paper in one night. You wili be angry. In this case your anger is a way of dealing with your frustration at feeling that you have been treated unfairly. Our sense of relative fairness is important.

In conclusion, the symbolic interactionist perspective is concerned with how people experience the social world, how they come to interpret their own behaviour and the behaviour of others. Qualitative research (participant observation, in-depth interviews, and detailed interpretations of individual behaviour) is often associated with this perspective in the social sciences.

I. CONCLUSION: POINTS OF AGREEMENT

Social scientists have many perspectives available to them, and there is a strong tendency for its practitioners to be identified with one school of thought, or one methodological approach. And even if people span a variety of approaches we tend to label them as members of one school or another. There are squabbles between the various schools over the kinds of evidence that should be used; and, indeed, serious arguments over what questions we should be asking as social scientists.

On occasion, such debate is carried on with a distinct lack of tolerance for differences. Perhaps it is a measure of the immaturity of our disciplines that we are divided up into warring camps. By the end of the first year of university, most students will witness at least one professor make an unrelenting attack on some theoretical or methodological perspective not shared by the instructor. While debates in the academy can be healthy and invigorating, so too can they be destructive and counterproductive if they fail to give the student a balanced view of the various approaches.

Are there points of agreement? Most social scientists would agree that we should:

i. Study the Full Range of Social Behaviour.

This is to acknowledge that it is equally legitimate to study both social constructions of reality (individual subjective perceptions of reality) and objective, measurable structural patterns found in any society. In short, both qualitative and quantitative methodologies have a contribution to make to understanding social behaviour.

ii. Use the Methodology Appropriate to the Questions Asked.

Everyone will agree that the methodology we apply should be appropriate to the question asked. And while we could never agree that either qualitative or quantitative methodologies are better, we could proba-

bly agree that both have their place in the various disciplines.

iii. Systematic Explanation.

Explanations offered by the social scientist should be based on a careful, painstaking analysis of the evidence.

iv. Peer Scrutiny.

Whatever our efforts, an important norm is that our scholarly work should be scrutinized by our peers. It is through circulating our analyses that others may criticize them, suggest alternatives, and ultimately, refine the product further.

J. KEY TERMS

Anecdotal evidence

Appeal to authority

Axiomatic derivation

Bourgeoisie

Causal explanation

Conflict perspectives

Controlled observations

Definition of the situation

Deductive explanation

Empathetic explanation

Exchange perspectives

Extinction

False dilemma

Feminist perspectives

Folk wisdom

Formal theory

Functional explanation

Functionalism

Generalization

Inadvertent reinforcement

Informed opinion

Insufficient evidence

Looking glass self

Missing evidence

Objective

Operant conditioning theory

Patriarchy

Partial theory

Precise communication

Probabilistic explanation

Proletarians

Provincialism

Replacement of terms

Selected evidence

Significant other

Symbolic interaction perspectives

Verifiable

K. KEY POINTS

A *key goal* of social science is to describe and explain human behaviour accurately.

Everyday explanations include the use of anecdotes, and any number of sayings and proverbs.

Qualitative social science explanations stress that the social scientist's descriptions of behaviour should be meaningful to the actors involved; while *quantitative explanations* emphasize reliable and valid observations, which are objective and verifiable.

A *deductive explanation* is a logically necessary consequence of the explanatory premises.

Probabilistic explanations convey the idea that people behave the way they do because they belong to a category of individuals who behave that way.

Functional explanations convey the idea that any given behaviour pattern exists in order to maintain the social system.

Causal explanations link a particular outcome to a sequence of preceding events.

Empathetic explanations stress the experience of how a person comes to know; these explanations "ring true" to the person who is describing the behaviour and to the person whose behaviour is being described.

Flawed explanations include improper appeals to authority, provincialism, setting up false dilemmas, missing key evidence, or suppressing evidence.

The *function of theory* is to answer *why* questions, to explain things.

Formal theories include concepts, interrelated propositions, some of which must be testable.

General theories are powerful because many predictions can be derived from them.

A *partial theory* is a testable causal model with three or more variables in it.

To *test a partial theory* one needs a relationship which is assumed to be true and two or more alternative explanations for why the relationship exists. The test attempts to measure the extent to which the data are or are not consistent with the explanations offered.

Testing derivations from *formal theory* involves deriving a testable hypothesis using axiomatic derivations and/or replacement of terms.

Replacement of terms involves replacing a general concept in a theory with a particular manifestation of that concept. An example would be to replace the term deviance with a particular manifestation of deviance, shoplifting.

Conflict perspectives argue that society is characterized fundamentally by conflict between interest groups, groups attempting to exploit others for their own advantage; social change is largely the result of economic factors. The role of the social scientist is to sensitize citizens to social problems and in that way encourage social change.

Exchange perspectives view behaviour in terms of reciprocal relations; interaction persists to the extent that parties in the exchange profit by the interaction. These perspectives share with operant conditioning a basic concern with how behaviours are moulded (through reinforcement).

Feminist perspectives stress the role of patriarchy in the development and maintenance of gender inequalities. And, in a manner similar to conflict theorists, feminist researchers favour social scientists playing an active role in attempting to bring about social change.

Functionalist perspectives are based on an organic analogy, stressing the interrelationship of parts of society, arguing that social patterns persist only if they have some value in maintaining the social system.

Symbolic interactionist perspectives are concerned with how people experience the social world, how they come to interpret their own and others' behaviours. Qualitative research methods (participant observation, in-depth interviews, and detailed interpretations of individual behaviour) are typically most associated with these perspectives in the social sciences.

Whatever theoretical or methodological perspectives are adopted, *most social scientists will agree that:*

* all social behaviour is appropriate for study;

* there are a variety of legitimate methodologies which allow us to explore human behaviour systematically; and,

* we have to communicate our results to our peers for scrutiny.

1. Choose a major theoretical work; do a propo-

L. EXERCISES

sitional inventory of a section of the work, selecting the major propositions involved. Label the concepts with letters, using the same letter for those you presume are intended to refer to the same variable. Attempt to derive new theoretical statements using axiomatic derivations and replacement of terms approaches. Be certain to specify assumptions you are making in doing the derivations. Identify testable propositions you think are not obvious on a common-sense basis.

2. Choose a relationship that you think would hold true and propose three alternative explanations for the relationship. Connect your proposed explanations to an existing social science perspective. Outline a study which would allow you to reject the various explanations.

3. Starting with the proposed explanations you

identified in question 2 above, use Jonathan H. Turner, *The Structure of Sociological Theory*, (Fifth Edition. Belmont, California: Wadsworth Publishing Company, 1991), to locate a theory that could be linked to each of your three explanations.

4. Identify one everyday activity (examples might include: greeting one another, terminating a conversation, trying to be the next to speak in a group setting); use Howard Schwartz and Jerry Jacobs, *Qualitative Sociology*, to develop suggestions as to how you might investigate how such everyday activities are carried out.

5. Examine the articles in one issue of a social science journal. Search for an illustration of each type of flawed reasoning discussed in the text. Describe why do you think each example is an illustration of flawed reasoning.

M. RECOMMENDED READINGS

BERGER, PETER L,. AND THOMAS LUCKMAN (1966). *The Social Construction of Reality*. Garden City, New York: Doubleday. A short book which is regarded as the classic statement of how reality is a social construction.

BROWNE, M. NEIL, AND STUART M. KEELEY (1990). *Asking the Right Questions: A Guide to Critical Thinking*. Englewood Cliffs, New Jersey: Prentice Hall, Third Edition. This small book is a useful guide to assist in developing clear, precise thinking. It contains many examples of common errors in argument.

HOMANS, GEORGE C. (1964). "Bringing Men Back In," *American Sociological Review*, 29, 809-818. This article is based on George Homans' presidential address to the American Sociological Association. It may be viewed as a turning point in twentieth-century sociology: it contains a strong critique of functionalism and important leads for a reconstruction of sociology along the lines of formal theory construction and testing.

SCHWARTZ, HOWARD, AND JERRY JACOBS (1979). *Qualitative Sociology: A Method to the Madness*.

New York: The Free Press. This is an comprehensive presentation of the rationales and methodologies of a variety of qualitative approaches.

SKIDMORE, WILLIAM (1975). *Theoretical Thinking in Sociology*. London: Cambridge University Press. This book covers exchange theory, functionalism, and symbolic interactionism.

SMITH, DOROTHY E. (1987). *The Everyday World as Problematic: a Feminist Sociology*. Toronto: University of Toronto Press. This book presents a spirited presentation of a feminist social science.

TURNER, JONATHAN H. (1991). *The Structure of Sociological Theory*, Fifth Edition. Belmont, California: Wadsworth Publishing Company. An advanced, comprehensive analysis of theoretical perspectives in sociology. It contains detailed propositional summaries of functionalism, conflict theory, exchange theory, interactionist, and structural theory.

WALLACE, RUTH A., AND ALISON WOLF (1991). *Contemporary Sociological Theory: Continuing the Classical Tradition*, Third Edition. Englewood Cliffs, New Jersey: Prentice Hall. This is a fine review of the major approaches to sociological theory.

ALTERNATE RESEARCH DESIGNS

Experiments, surveys, field studies, and non-reactive designs will be introduced in Part Two of this text. The experiment is a good starting point because it offers the most straightforward demonstration of causal links among variables. However, because of practical or ethical reasons, lots of things that social scientists want to study cannot be studied experimentally, so other designs have an important place in social science research. Non-experimental researchers need to understand the experiment in order to heighten awareness of factors that may be problematic in their own studies.

Chapter 3 introduces the student to the basic principles of experimental design and also presents examples of experiments and quasi-experiments. Chapter 4 presents survey designs, Chapter 5 field studies, and Chapter 6 various non-reactive designs. At the end of each chapter there are references to readings which will help the student come to a fuller understanding of how to implement these basic designs.

EXPERIMENTAL AND QUASI-EXPERIMENTAL DESIGNS

A. BASICS OF EXPERIMENTAL DESIGN

1. THE RATIONALE OF THE EXPERIMENT

John Stuart Mill (1806-1873), identified the *Method of Difference* (1925, pp. 255-56) as a key tool in understanding causal relations (see Box 3.1). And while Mill's presentation was the first to set out the logic of experimentation systematically, experiments,

in fact, go back much earlier. Palys reports that experimentation dates to at least 1648 when Blaise Pascal (1623-62) had his brother-in-law do an experiment testing for the presence of atmospheric pressure (Palys, 1992, pp. 241-44). A special container was taken up a mountain, and it was noted that the level of mercury in the container declined as it was moved higher. As a control, another mercury dish was not taken up the mountain and its level was monitored; its level remained unchanged throughout the observation period.

The positivist approach to knowledge (reviewed in Chapter 1) underpins experi-

---

BOX 3.1

John Stuart Mill: The Method of Difference

"...we require...two instances resembling one another in every other respect, but differing in the presence or absence of the phenomenon we wish to study. If our object be to discover the effects of agent A, we must procure A in some set of ascertained circumstances, as A B C, and having noted the effects produced, compare them with the effect of the remaining circumstances B C, when A is absent. If the effect of A B C is *a b c*, and the effect of B C, *b c*, it is evident that the effect of A is *a*. So again, if we begin at the other end, and desire to investigate the cause of an effect *a*, we must select an instance, as *a b c*, in which the remaining circumstances, *b c*, occur without *a*. If the antecedents, in that instance, are B C, we know that the cause of *a* must be A: either A alone, or A in conjunction with some of the other circumstances present.

It is scarcely necessary to give examples of a logical process to which we owe almost all the inductive conclusions we draw in early life. When a man is shot through the heart, it is by this method we know that it was the gunshot which killed him: for he was in the fullness of life immediately before, all circumstances being the same, except the wound.

The axioms implied in this method are evidently the following. Whatever antecedent cannot be excluded without preventing the phenomenon, is the cause, or a condition of that phenomenon: Whatever consequent can be excluded, with no other difference in the antecedents than the absence of a particular one, is the effect of that one. Instead of comparing different instances of a phenomenon, to discover in what ways they agree, this method compares an instance of its occurrence with an instance of its non-occurrence, to discover in what they differ. The cannon which is the regulating principle of the Method of Difference may be expressed as follows:—

If an instance in which the phenomenon under investigation occurs, and an instance in which it does not occur, have every circumstance in common save one, that one occurring only in the former; the circumstance in which alone the two instances differ is the effect, or the cause, or an indispensable part of the cause, of the phenomenon.

"Of these methods, that of Difference is more particularly a method of artificial experiment; while that of Agreement is more especially the resource employed where experimentation is impossible....

SOURCE: Mill, John Stuart, *A System of Logic*. London: Longmans, Green and Co., 8th Edition, 1925, pp. 255-56.

mental designs. These designs provide evidence for clear interpretations of cause-effect relations: a key feature of the experiment is that measures are taken at different points in time. A well-designed experiment should indicate whether or not a treatment (studying with the radio on) will bring about a change in some dependent measure (grade performance in Methods), *other things being equal.* The last phrase, other things being equal, is critical. It means that we must take into account any number of factors (hours of sleep, interest in the subject matter, previous performance) to make certain that it is our treatment and not some other factor that is influencing the dependent variable.

2. KEY ELEMENTS IN EXPERIMENTAL DESIGNS

Suppose you wish to assess the effectiveness of a film in promoting university attendance. Suppose that some students are exposed to a film about university attendance while others see a nature film. Will seeing the film about going to university increase the number of high school students wishing to attend university? You decide an experiment would be in order. There are a number of elements to such a study:

A. DEPENDENT VARIABLE

A *dependent variable* is the effect in a cause-effect relation; in this case, the dependent variable would be the subject's desire to attend university. In an experiment, the dependent variable is the phenomenon measured in order to determine if any change has taken place as a result of some experimental intervention.

B. INDEPENDENT VARIABLES

The *independent variables* include all the variables taken into account, or manipulated, by the researcher that may influence the dependent variable. Four types of independent variables may be distinguished:

i. Treatment Variable.

In an experiment, the independent variable whose effect is being studied is known as the **treatment variable**. In our example, the type of film shown—either about nature or about the university— is the treatment variable. An experiment attempts to detect the direct effect of the treatment on the dependent variable. In some experiments there will be more than one treatment variable. In such cases, the experimenter must determine the effects of each treatment used on the dependent variable. (We might consider being exposed to colour versus black-and-white films as an additional treatment variable.)

ii. Control Variables.

Control variables are those specifically taken into account in designing a study. In this case, they would include other major factors which may influence a student's plans to attend university such as gender, academic abilities, and whether the student comes from a family background where university attendance is expected. These variables need to be controlled, or taken into account, in designing the study.

iii. Confounding Variables.

Confounding variables are those which may unintentionally obscure or enhance a relationship. For example, one would not want to measure some students' attitudes toward university on Monday morning, and others on Friday afternoon, as it is possible that students' interest in attending university varies systematically during the week. If this possibility is not taken into account, it may confound the results of our study.

iv. Random Variables.

Since many variables may have an impact on our dependent variable, some may be treated as *random variables*. A **random variable** *varies without control but is taken into account by the way groups are set up for the study*—by, for example, randomly assigning some students to see the university film, and others to see a nature film.

C. LEVELS

Typically, various levels of treatment variables are identified. Often two or three **treatment levels** will be examined. In our example, a two-level study might compare the effect of seeing the university film with the effect of seeing the nature film. A study with three treatment levels might compare the effects of seeing a short, medium, or long film. The various control and confounding variables are also exposed to the subject at various levels. The simplest multiple-variable design would be a 2 × 2 one; this refers to a design where there are two levels of the treatment variable (the first two) and two levels in a control (or second treatment) variable. Thus, when experimentalists talk about designs they might talk of a 2 × 2 × 2 design. This means that the treatment has two categories; similarly the control variables each have two levels. A 2 × 3 × 2 design has two levels in the treatment, a three-level control variable, and a two-level control variable.

3. PRE-EXPERIMENTAL DESIGNS

In order to understand the factors that may inhibit a clear causal interpretation, we will examine some possible pre-experimental designs to explore the impact of the film on the desire to attend the university.

A. SAME GROUP: PRE-TEST/POST-TEST

Suppose that you decided that you would need a measure of the students' predispositions toward the university before seeing the film. Having completed this measure, the film could then be shown, and the difference between the pre-test and post-test scores could be used to measure the change in the desire to attend the university.

We could diagram the proposed design in the following way:

	TIME 1		TIME 2
Treatment group	0_1	University film	0_2

0_1 refers to observations made at Time 1;
0_2 refers to observations made at Time 2.

Could we conclude correctly that any change in attitude among the students occurred as a result of seeing the film? Suppose that at Time 1, 57.0 percent indicated that they wished to attend the university while at Time 2, after seeing the film, the percentage increased to 73.0. Could we argue that the film produced a 16.0 percentage point increase in those wishing to attend the university? (73 − 57 = 16) The answer is no. There are a number of factors that may render such an interpretation incorrect. Donald T. Campbell and Julian C. Stanley, in their book *Experimental and Quasi-Experimental Design for Research,* identify the factors that might confound interpretations (1966).

i. History.

Any number of events may have happened in addition to the film: a local university's basketball team may have won a championship; the university may have announced a new program; or a professor may have just won a Nobel prize. Many things other than the film may have influenced the desire to attend the university. In the context of experimental design, **history** refers to concurrent events that, along with the experimental manipulation, may be influencing variation in the dependent variable.

ii. Maturation.

People change over time: perhaps the students have become bored with school and, by the time the second measures are taken, systematic changes in attitude may have occurred. Such changes could, in part, be an influence causing the different responses at Time 1 and Time 2. By 3:00 pm on Friday afternoon, Grade 11 students may experience a profound drop in their motivation to attend university! **Maturation** refers to any changes that occur in an individual subject over the course of an experiment which may, along with experimental manipulation, influence the outcome of the experiment.

iii. Testing.

Even asking identical questions at both tests may influence the responses. Some respondents may want to appear consistent and, therefore, give the same responses in both tests. Others, suspecting that the study is meant to demonstrate how good the film is, might want to help the researcher and exhibit **response bias** by being more positive the second time.

iv. Instrument Decay.

Suppose we asked students to indicate their preferences by the strength with which they squeezed a hand dynameter. (A dynameter is a device with a calibrated dial that permits the researcher to read the indicated intensity.) If, for example, the spring in the device has weakened, the second set of readings will be slightly higher. **Instrument decay** refers to the fact that the dynameter no longer measures reliably.

v. Statistical Regression.

To explain this idea, we will need to alter the example slightly. Suppose, after our pre-test scores had been taken, that we decide to show the film just to those with the most negative attitudes toward attending university. Could we legitimately say that any gain in the scores of these students is a result of the film? The answer is no. The reason for this is that when a sample is selected on the basis of extreme scores, retesting will tend to show a **statistical regression** toward less extreme scores. Even without any film, the students' response

would, on average, be slightly more positive on the second testing. The explanation is that the measurement error at the time of the first measurement has tended to distort the data negatively. Box 3.2 presents another example of a regression effect.

B. EXPOSED/COMPARISON GROUP

After considering the flaws in the previous design, suppose you alter it to provide for a comparison group, as in the following diagram:

		TIME 2
Treatment	University film	0_1
Comparison group	Travel film	0_2

0_1 refers to observations on the Treatment Group;
0_2 refers to observations on the Comparison Group.

In the above design, one group is exposed to the film promoting the university, and the other is not. Can we legitimately conclude that the difference in attitude between the exposed group and the unex-

---

Regression Effect: Reading Scores

Suppose a reading specialist wants to try out a new reading program. If the specialist tests the reading ability of all students in a school and then selects the 10 percent of students with the lowest scores for the program, puts them through it, and then retests them, almost certainly

the scores will increase. However, the amount attributable to the program and the amount attributable to regression effects would remain uncertain. In short, the scores would increase, but how much of this increase would be due to the new program would be unclear.

posed group represents the impact of the film? (If 75 percent of the students exposed to the film expressed a desire to attend university and only 60 percent of those students who did not see the film wished to go to university, could we conclude that the film produced this 15 percentage point difference in measured attitudes?) Again there are problems. The major difficulty is that we do not know if the groups were the same to start with: any difference in test results may simply reflect initial differences, or differences which emerge during the study but which are unrelated to the impact of the film.

vi. Selection.

It is possible, for example, that the students most inclined to go to the university choose to go to see the film; thus if they score higher in the test, this result may simply reflect their initial predisposition to go to the university. **Selection** thus refers to subjects selecting themselves into a study.

vii. Mortality.

Just as people choose to belong to a group, they may choose not to. Some of those who see the film may withdraw from the study before their attitude toward attending the university has been measured. The effect of subjects withdrawing from the experiment may be that those who leave are less interested in higher education and hence the proportion for those who stay in the experiment will be more likely to indicate a desire to attend university. **Mortality** thus refers to subjects selecting themselves out of a study. Therefore, mortality may systematically distort the results of the study.

4. BETWEEN-SUBJECTS DESIGN

There are many variants of control group experimental design intended to deal with some of the above problems. Only the simplest one will be presented here:

	TIME 1		TIME 2
Treatment group	0_1	University film	0_2
Control group	0_3	Travel film	0_4

0_1 refers to observations on the treatment group at Time 1;
0_2 refers to observations on the treatment group Time 2;
0_3 refers to observations on the control group at Time 1;
0_4 refers to observations on the control group at Time 2.

A key point of a ***between-subjects design*** is that the treatment and the control groups (completely different groups) are to be as equivalent as possible before the treatment group is exposed to the experimental condition. There are three ways of achieving equivalence:

(i) through precision matching (possibly matching pairs according to gender, socio-economic status, and grades and assigning one person from each of the matched pairs to the control group, and the other person to the treatment group);

(ii) through randomization (where individuals are randomly assigned to either the treatment or to the control group); or

(iii) through a combination of the previous two techniques.

Randomization (if the numbers are large enough) will provide control over both known and unknown factors (the control and random variables). Note that we are randomizing if the process that we use to assign each person to a group results in an equal chance of that person being assigned to the control group or to the treatment group.

In the above design, to estimate the impact of the film we could do the following computation on the percent wanting to attend the university before and after seeing the film:

Table 3.1 indicates that at Time 1 57 percent of the treatment group planned to attend university, compared to 55 percent of the control group members. The Time 2 measures indicate that the treatment group (after seeing the film about attending university) now had 73 percent planning to attend university compared to a 61 percent figure for the control group (viewers of a neutral film). To estimate the impact of the university film on a person's desire to attend university, we subtract the Time 1 percentage from the Time 2 percentage. Here we note a 16 percentage point difference for those in the treatment group compared to a 6 percentage point difference among those in the control group. We subtract the control difference (6 percent) from the treatment difference (16 percent) and arrive at

an estimate of the impact of the film amounting to some 10 percentage points.

The seven factors (history, maturation, testing, instrument decay, statistical regression, selection, and mortality) identified by Campbell and Stanley (1966) discussed earlier are dealt with in experimental designs through:

- attempting to make certain that the groups are similar to begin with;

- by noting that the various factors should influence the treatment and the control groups equally.

Thus experimental designs rely on establishing pre-treatment similarity of control and treatment groups to minimize the effects of history, maturation, testing, instrument decay, statistical regression, selection, and mortality. Some form of randomization is a key tool in the experimenter's quest to establish unambiguous causal relationships.

A. HOW A CAUSAL RELATIONSHIP IS DEMONSTRATED

To show a causal relationship in any research, three conditions must be demonstrated:

TABLE 3.1	PERCENT WANTING TO ATTEND UNIVERSITY BY EXPOSURE AND NON-EXPOSURE TO FILM		
	PERCENT WANTING TO ATTEND UNIVERSITY		
GROUP	TIME I	TIME 2	DIFFERENCE
Treatment	57.0	73.0	73 − 57 = 16
Control	55.0	61.0	61 − 55 = 6
		Estimated impact of film:	10

i. Changes in the Treatment Variable Occur Prior to Changes in the Dependent Variable.

Because the control group design involves measures of both the treatment and the dependent variables at two points in time (Time 1, Time 2 measures), the procedure ensures that the measure at Time 1 precedes the one at Time 2. Second, as we introduce the treatment to the experimental group (the film about the university), but not to the control group (who see a nature film instead), and follow this by measuring the dependent variable at Time 2, it becomes possible to make an inference about the impact of seeing the university film (treatment variable) on the desire to attend university (the dependent variable). Thus, since the film was shown between the Time 1 and Time 2 measures, if there is a change in the attitudes toward university attendance among those seeing the university film, we will have made the first step in demonstrating that the film caused the change in attitude.

ii. The Variables are Associated; as Values on the Treatment Variable are Increased, the Dependent Measures Vary Systematically.

A variety of techniques might be used to illustrate that the variables are associated systematically. For example, we might show that those who saw the film are more likely to indicate that they are planning to attend university than those who did not see the film. To say that the dependent variable varies systematically indicates that either:

- the proportion of respondents saying that they plan to attend university is higher among those exposed to the university film; or

- the proportion of respondents saying that they plan to attend university is lower among those exposed to the university film; or

- the proportion of students saying that they plan to attend university increases as the length of the film increases. However, there appears to be a levelling off in the proportion of students planning on attendance when the film is longer than 23 minutes.

iii. Nothing but the Treatment Variable has Influenced the Dependent Variable.

To ensure that it is only the treatment variable that is causing variation in the dependent variable, steps must be taken to rule out various sources of contamination:

STEP 1

ENSURE THAT THE CONTEXT IN WHICH THE EXPERIMENT IS CARRIED OUT IS THE SAME FOR ALL SUBJECTS.

To guarantee the similarity of the experimental situation, researchers take great pains to ensure that physical conditions (temperature, humidity, lighting conditions) all remain the same; similarly, instructions to the subjects are standardized, even recorded, to be certain that each respondent gets the same information in the same manner. As much as possible, all subjects should have a similar experience in participating in the experiment.

STEP 2

BALANCE THE BACKGROUND CHARACTERISTICS OF THE SUBJECTS.

Typically this control is accomplished through some combination of precision matching (matching a female with a female; high IQ person with another high IQ person) or matching and then randomly assigning each person to the control or to the treatment groups. The goal is to try to populate both groups with similar kinds of people.

STEP 3

NEUTRALIZE ANY CONFOUNDING VARIABLES.

The researcher must be careful that the experience of the experiment is not having an impact on the results. For example, if you were testing the impact the intensity of light (treatment variable) has on the speed with which a fine motor task is completed (threading a needle), you should not simply move systematically from low lighting through to intense lighting. Subjects will probably learn to thread the needle more efficiently as they go through the trials, and you would therefore want to vary the presentation of different lighting conditions for each subject randomly. In this way, the order of presentation would not in itself systematically influence the speed of threading. If you do not deal with this potential confounding factor, you would not be able to tell how much of the increase of speed was due to increasing illumination and how much was due to a learning effect. Confounding variables of this sort are dealt with in varying the way the treatment is administered to the subjects: one strategy for doing this is known as **counterbalancing**. Here a treatment level is introduced, changed, maintained, and then returned to the first level to control for effects of learning on the subject's performance. (See the ABBA counterbalanced designs discussed below.)

STEP 4

DEAL WITH RANDOM VARIABLES.

Random variables include all those other factors that might be influencing the dependent variable, none of which you choose to control. Subjects are assumed to be different on all dimensions. Knowing this, experimenters do not let subjects choose which group they will go into (they might think it more fun to be in a treatment group than in a boring control group; or they might choose to be in the same group as their friends). Typically, assignment is done through a random process (using a table of random numbers, coin flips, or mixed slips of paper with Group A or Group B written on them). When sample sizes exceed 30 in each group, random assignment is likely to result in reasonable balancing of the groups on random factors.

Box 3.3 presents the design of one of the best known experiments in psychology, Stanley Milgram's obedience to authority study. This study is of interest for its design, for its unanticipated findings, and for the ethical issues which were subsequently raised about the study. The ethical issues will be discussed in detail in Chapter 10.

BOX 3.3 SOCIAL RESEARCHERS AT WORK

Stanley Milgram, Behavioral Study of Obedience

General Procedure

A procedure was devised which seems useful as a tool for studying obedience (Milgram, 1961). It consists of ordering a naive subject to administer electric shock to a victim. A simulated shock generator is used, with 30 clearly marked voltage levels that range from 15 to 450 volts. The instrument bears verbal designations that range from Slight Shock to Danger: Severe Shock. The responses of the victim, who is a trained confederate of the experimenter, are standardized. The orders to administer shocks are given to the naive subject in the context of a "learning experiment" ostensibly set up to study the effects of punishment on memory. As the experiment proceeds the naive subject is commanded to administer increasingly more intense shocks to the victim, even to the point of reaching the level marked Danger: Severe Shock. Internal resistances become stronger, and at a certain point the subject refuses to go on with the experiment. Behavior prior to this rupture is considered "obedience," in that the subject complies with the commands of the experimenter. The point of rupture is the act of disobedience. A quantitative value is assigned to the subject's performance based on the maximum intensity shock he is willing to administer before he refuses to participate further. Thus for any particular subject and for any particular experimental condition the degree of obedience may be specified with a nu-merical value. The crux of the study is to systematically vary the factors believed to alter the degree of obedience to the experimental commands.

The technique allows important variables to be manipulated at several points in the experiment. One may vary aspects of the source of command, content and form of command, instrumentalities for its execution, target object, general social setting, etc. The problem, therefore, is not one of designing increasingly more numerous experimental conditions, but of selecting those that best illuminate the *process* of obedience from the socio-psychological standpoint...

Method

SUBJECTS The subjects were 40 males between the ages of 20 and 50, drawn from New Haven and the surrounding communities. Subjects were obtained by a newspaper advertisement and direct mail solicitation. Those who responded to the appeal believed they were to participate in a study of memory and learning at Yale University. A wide range of occupations is represented in the sample. Typical subjects were postal clerks, high school teachers, salesmen, engineers, and labourers. Subjects ranged in

Distribution of Age And Occupational Types in the Experiment

OCCUPATIONS	20-29 YEARS N	30-39 YEARS N	40-50 YEARS N	PERCENTAGE OF TOTAL (OCCUPATIONS)
Workers, skilled and unskilled	4	5	6	37.5
Sales, business, and white-collar	3	6	7	40.0
Professional	1	5	3	22.5
Percentage of total	20	40	40	

educational level from one who had not finished elementary school, to those who had doctorate and other professional degrees. They were paid $4.50 for their participation in the experiment. However, subjects were told that payment was simply for coming to the laboratory, and that the money was theirs no matter what happened after they arrived. The table below shows the proportion of age and occupational types assigned to the experimental condition.

PERSONNEL AND LOCALE The experiment was conducted on the grounds of Yale University in the elegant interaction laboratory. (This detail is relevant to the perceived legitimacy of the experiment. In further variations, the experiment was dissociated from the university, with consequences for performance.) The role of experimenter was played by a 31-year-old high school teacher of biology. His manner was impassive, and his appearance somewhat stern throughout the experiment. He was dressed in a grey technician's coat. The victim was played by a 47-year-old accountant, trained for the role; he was of Irish-American stock, whom most observers found mild-mannered and likable.

PROCEDURE One naive subject and one victim (an accomplice) performed in each experiment. A pretext had to be devised that would justify the administration of electric shock by the naive subject. This was effectively accomplished by the cover story. After a general introduction on the presumed relation between punishment and learning, subjects were told:

But actually we know very little about the effect of punishment on learning, because almost no truly scientific studies have been made of it in human beings.

For instance, we don't know how much punishment is best for learning—and we don't know how much difference it makes as to who is giving the punishment, whether an adult learns best from a younger or an older person than himself—or many things of that sort.

So in this study we are bringing together a number of adults of different occupations and ages. And we're asking some of them to be teachers and some of them to be learners.

We want to find out just what effect different people have on each other as teachers and learners, and also what effect punishment will have on learning in this situation.

Therefore, I'm going to ask one of you to be the teacher here tonight and the other one to be the learner.

Does either of you have a preference?

Subjects then drew slips of paper from a hat to determine who would be the teacher and who would be the learner in the experiment. The drawing was rigged so that the naive subject was always the teacher and the accomplice always the learner. (Both slips contained the word "Teacher.") Immediately after the drawing, the teacher and learner were taken to an adjacent room and the learner was strapped into an "electric chair" apparatus.

The experimenter explained that the straps were to prevent excessive movement while the learner was being shocked. The effect was to make it impossible for him to escape from the situation. An electrode was attached to the learner's wrist) and electrode paste was applied "to avoid blisters and burns." Subjects were told that the electrode was attached to the shock generator in the adjoining room.

In order to improve credibility the experimenter declared, in response to a question by the learner: "Although the shocks can be extremely painful, they cause no permanent tissue damage."

Learning Task. The lesson administered by the subject was a paired-associate learning task. The subject read a series of word pairs to the learner, and then read the first word of the pair along with four terms. The learner was to indicate which of the four terms had originally been paired with the first word. He communicated his answer by pressing one of four switches in front of him, which in turn lit up one of four numbered quadrants in an answer box located atop the shock generator.

Shock Generator. The instrument panel consists of 30 lever switches set in a horizontal line. Each switch is clearly labeled with a voltage designation that ranges from 15 to 450 volts. There is a 15-volt increment from one switch to the next going from left to right. In addition, the following verbal designations are clearly indicated for groups of four switches going from left to right: Slight Shock, Moderate Shock, Strong Shock, Very Strong Shock, Intense Shock, Extreme Intensity Shock, Danger: Severe Shock. (Two switches after this last designation are simply marked XXX.)

Upon depressing a switch: a pilot light corresponding to each switch is illuminated in bright red; an electric buzzing is heard; an electric blue light, labeled "voltage energizer," flashes; the dial on the voltage meter swings to the right; various relay clicks are sounded.

The upper left-hand corner of the generator is labeled Shock Generator, Type ZLB, Dyson Instrument Company, Waltham, Mass. Output 15 Volts-450 Volts.

Details of the instrument were carefully handled to insure an appearance of authenticity. The panel was engraved by precision industrial engravers, and all components were of high quality. No subject in the experiment suspected that the instrument was merely a simulated shock generator.

Sample Shock. Each naive subject is given a sample shock on the shock generator, prior to beginning his run as teacher. This shock is always 45 volts, and is applied by pressing the third switch of the generator. The shock is applied to the wrist of the naive subject, and has its source in a 45-volt battery wired into the generator. This further convinces the subject of the authenticity of the generator.

Shock Instructions. The subject is told to administer a shock to the learner each time he gives a wrong response. Moreover—and this is the command—the subject is instructed to "move one level higher on the shock generator each time learner flashes a wrong answer." He is also instructed to announce the voltage level before administering a shock. This serves to continually remind subjects of the increasing intensity of shocks administered to the learner.

Preliminary and Regular Run. Pretests revealed that the procedure of reading words and administering shocks requires some practice before it can be handled smoothly. Therefore, immediately preceding the regular run, the teacher is given a preliminary series of 10 words to read to the learner. There are 3 neutral words in the practice series (i.e., words that the learner answers correctly), so that shocks are administered for 7 of the words, with the maximum shock at 105 volts (moderate shock). Almost all subjects master the procedure by the time the preliminary run is over.

Subjects are then presented with a second list, and are told that the procedure is the same as for the first list; the experimenter adds, however:

> *When you get to the bottom of the list, repeat it over again, and continue giving shocks, until the learner has learned all the pairs correctly.*

The experimenter instructs the subject to:

> *start from 15 volts and increase the shock level one step each time the learner gives a wrong answer.*

Feedback from the Victim. In all conditions the learner gives a predetermined set of responses to the word pair test, based on a schedule of approximately three wrong answers to one correct answer. In the present experimental condition no vocal response or other sign of protest is heard from the learner until Shock Level 300 is reached. When the 300-volt shock is administered, the learner pounds on the wall of the room in which he is bound to the electric chair. The pounding can be heard by the subject. From this point on, the learner's answers no longer appear on the four-way panel.

At this juncture, subjects ordinarily turn to the experimenter for guidance. The experimenter instructs the subject to treat the absence of a response as a wrong answer, and to shock the subject according to the usual schedule. He advises the subjects to allow 5-10 seconds before considering no response as a wrong answer, and to increase the shock level one step each time the learner fails to respond correctly. The learner's pounding is repeated after the 315-volt shock is administered; afterwards he is not heard from, nor do his answers reappear on the four-way signal box.

Experimenter Feedback. At various points in the experiment the subject may turn to the experimenter for advice on whether he should continue to administer shocks. Or he may indicate that he does not wish to go on. It was important to standardize the experimenter's responses to these inquiries and reactions.

If the subject indicated his unwillingness to go on, the experimenter responded with a sequence of "prods," using as many as necessary to bring the subject into line:

> *Prod 1: Please continue. or Please go on.*

> *Prod 2: The experiment requires that you continue.*
>
> *Prod 3: It is absolutely essential that you continue.*
>
> *Prod 4: You have no other choice, you must go on.*

The prods were always made in sequence: Only if Prod 1 had been unsuccessful, could Prod 2 be used. If the subject refused to obey the experimenter after Prod 4, the experiment was terminated. The experimenter's tone of voice was at all times firm, but not impolite. The sequence was begun anew on each occasion that the subject balked or showed reluctance to follow orders.

Special Prods. If the subject asked if the learner was liable to suffer permanent physical injury, the experimenter said:

> *Although the shocks may be painful, there is no permanent tissue damage, so please go on. [Followed by Prods 2, 3, and 4 if necessary.]*

If the subject said that the learner did not want to go on, the experimenter replied:

> *Whether the learner likes it or not, you must go on until he has learned all the word pairs correctly. So please go on. [Followed by Probe 2, 3, and 4 if necessary.]*

SOURCE: Milgram, Stanley, "Behavioural Study of Obedience" *Journal of Abnormal and Social Psychology,* 67 (1963): 371-78. Reprinted by permission.

5. WITHIN-SUBJECT DESIGN

An alternative to the between-subjects design is a ***within-subject design***. Sometimes these designs use a single subject, sometimes just a few subjects, and sometimes large samples. What is the idea behind this kind of design?

The previous section stressed the importance of controlling possible sources of contamination. Matching groups, or randomly assigning subjects to treatments, were noted as ways of ensuring pre-treatment similarity. Without such controls, it would be impossible to distinguish treatment effects from the effects of other factors.

Sometimes one can employ an alternative strategy which provides for the ultimate in control of extraneous factors:

suppose that instead of assigning people to different treatments, we instead expose one subject to the different treatments. Since the subject is the same person, background characteristics, attitudes, and intelligence are all perfectly controlled. In a control group design, on the other hand, the researcher counts on randomized assignment to groups (or precision matching) to adjust for known and unknown variations between the two groups. With large samples the assumption that sources of contamination have been satisfactorily addressed is reasonable; with smaller samples one has less faith in the ability of randomization to deal with such contamination.

Suppose we were interested in the relation between the frequency with which subjects win a video-poker game and the speed with which they play. Will the subjects play faster after being rewarded and then gradually play more slowly as they fail to win? This experiment could be set up by having a rigged poker video machine designed so that the frequency with which subjects won could be controlled by the experimenter. A subject would be introduced to the game, play for some time, and be allowed to win, on average, every tenth trial. The speed of play would be monitored and, after a stable speed-of-play baseline had been established, the conditions of the game would be changed so that the subjects won, on average, every fifth trial. These trials would go on for some time; finally, the experimenter would change the game again so that subjects won with the original frequency and the speed with which the game was played would be recorded again. This kind of experiment is known as a within-subject, ABBA (counterbalanced) design. The ABBA (counterbalanced) refers to four conditions: the first A refers to the reward condition (the subject, on average, wins every tenth trial) associated with the initial baseline speed; B refers to a period when the new reward condition is introduced; the second B refers to a continuation of the B reward condition; finally, reward condition A is repeated to see if the subjects play at a speed similar to that at which they played before the introduction of reward condition B. Suppose we measured the number of games played per minute in all conditions. The reference to counterbalance indicates that we revert to the original reward condition to ensure that it is the reward condition and not a confounding factor such as learning or boredom that influences the speed at which the game is played. If the confounding variables are having an effect, then the speed

of play will not return to the original condition. Figure 3.1 shows a graph of what we might expect for results.

Figure 3.1 shows considerable instability at the beginning of the experiment. The speed of play gradually increases and then levels off to a baseline. A baseline measure is taken once stability has been achieved in the dependent variable at the beginning of a set of observations; after a new experimental condition is introduced, measures of the dependent variable will be taken and compared to the baseline values. There will be some learning at the beginning and so play will be a little slower at the very start. After the reward condition is introduced, we expect that there will be a gradual increase in the speed of play which, again, will level off; the acid test comes at the end when we see if the speed of play declines when we revert to the original reward condition (subject wins one game in ten). The return to the original condition is important because we want to make certain that it is not learning, skill, or heightened interest that are controlling speed; we want to measure the impact of the frequency of reward on the speed of play. If the effect is not reversible, then we would have grounds for believing that other factors are influencing the speed of play.

When an effect is not reversible we may have what is known as a **_Hawthorne Effect_**: this effect refers to any variability in the dependent variable that is not the direct result of variations in the treatment variable. The effect is named after one of the experiments done in the Hawthorne Western Electric plants in Chicago by Roethlisberger and Dickson (1939). In their study workers' output was monitored under varying intensities of lighting. (The hypothesis was that worker productivity

FIGURE 3.1   PLOT OF PLAYS PER MINUTE AGAINST TRIAL NUMBER

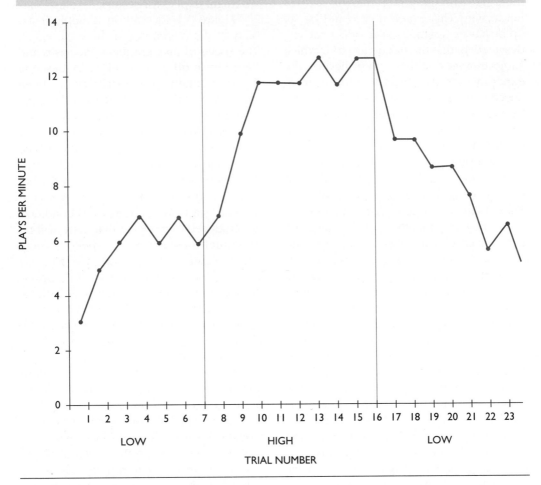

would increase with increasing levels of illumination.) The experimenters noted that as lighting intensity decreased, worker output increased. It looked as if simply dimming the lights in the workplace would be the way to increase productivity. However, when the experimenters then increased lighting intensities to the baseline levels, they noted that worker productivity con-

tinued to increase. Woops! Something other than the intensity of illumination was having an impact on the speed of work. A possible interpretation of this result is that the workers knew that they were being observed and that they tried hard to please the observers by increasing their productivity (Roethlisberger and Dickson, 1939). Whenever an effect cannot be reversed, you have to suspect that some factor(s) other than the treatment is influencing variations in the dependent variable, in this case, the speed of work. ABBA designs return to the baseline levels of the treatment variable in the final stage of the study to detect possible Hawthorne effects.

The key advantage of a within-subject design is that it provides convincing evidence for the impact of the treatment variable on the dependent variable. The evidence is all the more convincing, because, by using the same subject under different levels of the treatment variable, one can be confident that most of the possible extraneous influences, such as gender, age, socio-economic status, type of background, and values, have been controlled. Sometimes the control achieved in within-subject designs is called **control by constancy**. The term stems from the idea that, since the same subject experiences different levels of the treatment, the subject acts as his/her own control. In contrast, the between-subjects design has to try to control these differences by random assignment or precision matching. Especially in studies using relatively small samples, such controls are somewhat suspect, for there are always going to be some random fluctuations which may mask true effects.

Within-subject baseline studies permit the researcher to determine, for each subject, when baseline stability has been achieved; this permits the researcher to take into account different speeds with which subjects learn to do tasks, and to move to the next stage only when the experimenter is satisfied that a stable baseline has been achieved. Finally, there are circumstances, especially in working with special groups (blind students, students with IQ's above 150), when convincing tests can be done

using a within-subject design. When studying special groups, it may be impractical to find sufficient cases to permit a between-subjects design.

But these designs are not always possible. Frequently one cannot expect to be able to revert to the baseline level of the treatment and expect the dependent variable to fall to its baseline levels. Studies measuring memory skills, for example, cannot hope to return to baseline abilities because learning has occurred throughout the experimental session.

6. BETWEEN- AND WITHIN-SUBJECT DESIGNS FOR TESTING TIRES

Table 3.2 presents fictitious data modelled on David W. Martin's illustration of between-subjects and within-subject designs (1991, pp. 66-85). The example evaluates the efficacy of a new racing tire in improving lap times on an oval track.

A. TWO BETWEEN-SUBJECTS DESIGNS

The idea of a between-subjects design is that we want to establish two (or more) groups to allow us to compare different treatments. In this case, our task is to evaluate the effectiveness of the modified tire compared to the standard racing tire. Let us approach the question by looking at two between-subjects designs.

i. Ordinary Drivers Comparison: a Between-Subjects Design.

Suppose students in a methods class are asked to volunteer for an experiment. They are asked to meet at Riverside Speedway on Saturday afternoon. Students are given basic safety instructions and a chance to get the feel of the race cars by driving a few laps. The students are then randomly assigned to drive either a car equipped with standard tires or one with modified tires. Neither the students nor the person recording the lap times are aware of the type of tire on each car. This feature of the design is known as a **double blind** and is used to minimize the possible effects on the driver or timer of knowing which tire is being used. Each student drives three warm-up laps and then is timed on lap four. The results are shown in section i of Table 3.2. Note that there is considerable variation in the scores. Even though the average times were better on the modified tires, we are not comfortable in concluding that the modified tires were an improvement on the standard ones—there is simply too much variability in the scores. A change of one or two persons might alter the results substantially. (A test of significance confirms our suspicion, as the difference between the results achieved with standard tires and the results achieved with modified tires is not statistically significant: see Chapter 8 for a discussion of what these tests tell us.)

ii. Amateur Race Drivers: a Between-Subjects Design.

On Saturdays a number of amateur race drivers are available at Riverside. The second experiment is identical to the previous one, except we will use amateur race drivers. Using each driver's record permits us to rank-order all the drivers by skill level. Car assignment is done in pairs: using a coin flip the first- and second-ranked drivers are randomly assigned to drive either a car with the modified tires or one with the standard tires. The third- and fourth-

ranked drivers are randomly assigned to drive a car with either type of tire: this procedure is continued until 20 drivers have been assigned. Once again, three untimed practice laps are followed by a timed lap. Section ii of Table 3.2 shows much less variation than was apparent among the student drivers. Nonetheless, some of the variation between the amateur drivers may still be due to differences in driver skill, the cars, or the tires. The results indicate that the lap times of cars with the modified tires are somewhat lower than those of cars with the standard tires. The nagging problem, however, is whether differences in the cars may have been responsible for some of the differences in the times. As there is only a small sample of 10 drivers in each group, we are a little uncomfortable with the results. (The test of significance, however, does indicate a statistically significant difference in lap times for the two tire types.)

B. AMATEUR RACE DRIVERS: A WITHIN-SUBJECT DESIGN.

Given some uncertainty about the results, could we get even greater confidence in our results by changing our design? In the previous experiment, concern was expressed over the possibility that the differences could be the result of differences in the cars or in the skill of the drivers. However, some control over differences that may have resulted from differences among the drivers was achieved by ranking drivers by skill and then, for adjacent pairs, randomly assigning each driver to either a car with standard tires or a car with modified tires. Could we improve on this design?

Suppose we simply have *each driver run two trials* in the *same car,* once equipped

TABLE 3.2   RESULTS FROM THREE STUDIES TO TEST RACING TIRES

STANDARD TIRE	MODIFIED TIRE			
EXPERIMENT	NAME	TIME	NAME	TIME
i. Student drivers: between-subjects design; random assignment to groups	Kathleen	21.4	Paula	20.7
	Li	16.2	Marlies	19.0
	Danielle	18.0	Vanny	16.4
	Kim	16.1	Paul	16.7
	Kevin	15.9	Sandra	21.6
	Mary	20.3	Marius	20.1
	Yvonne	17.1	Chuck	14.4
	Tom	21.4	Andrea	16.3
	Ursula	17.7	Tony	15.7
	Stan	19.8	Carol	19.7
MEANS	18.39		18.06	
STANDARD DEVIATIONS	2.17		2.45	
MEAN DIFFERENCE		0.33		
ii. Amateur racers: between-subjects design; pairs matched on known skill level; random assignment to groups	Bob	14.1	Norm	14.0
	John	14.1	Ted	13.7
	Fred	14.2	Gary	13.9
	Charlie	13.9	Ron	13.7
	Jim	13.8	Moh	13.8
	Neil	13.3	Emily	13.4
	Hazel	13.7	Sara	13.8
	Iris	13.3	Edward	13.2
	Frank	13.8	Zoe	13.7
	Betty	13.5	Bruce	13.3
MEANS	13.77		13.65	
STANDARD DEVIATIONS	0.32		0.26	
MEAN DIFFERENCE		0.12		
iii. Amateur racers: within-subject design	James	13.1	James	13.0
	Peter	12.8	Peter	12.9
	Margaret	13.5	Margaret	13.4
	Jeremy	13.4	Jeremy	13.2
	Stefan	13.5	Stefan	13.5
	Don	13.6	Don	13.3
	Paul	13.5	Paul	13.3
	Tom	12.8	Tom	12.7
	Linda	12.9	Linda	12.9
	Melanie	13.5	Melanie	13.4
MEANS	13.26		13.17	
STANDARD DEVIATIONS	0.32		0.28	
MEAN DIFFERENCE		0.09		

with standard tires and once equipped with the modified tires? We now have control over the quality of the car as well as the skill of the driver. We have control by constancy—the driver and the car are the same for the test with the standard and with the modified tires. As before, the drivers and timer are not aware of which type of tire is on the car (double blind). The results, reported in section iii of Table 3.2, show about the same variability as the results of the previous experiment, but now we have greater confidence that we have controlled both car and driver variability. (The differences by tire type are statistically significant.) As a tire manufacturer, which of these tests would you trust more?

7. BETWEEN- AND WITHIN-SUBJECT DESIGNS COMPARED

The goal in experimental research is to isolate and measure treatment effects. To demonstrate an effect convincingly one wants clear differences in the dependent variable (mean lap speed) by treatment categories (standard versus modified tires). To make a study as convincing as possible we would want to have lots of variations between the categories (average lap times should vary consistently by type of tire) but little variation within the category (lap times for those drivers using the same type of tire). In the three designs presented above, note how the first design had a lot of within-group variation (the students varied considerably in their driving skills); the second and third designs had less within-group variation (all amateur race drivers).

While it is not always possible to use a within-subject design, the advantage of such a design over a between-subjects design is that you will need fewer subjects, require less time to train and run your experiment, and that you will exercise almost perfect control over extraneous influences on your dependent variable.

In designing experiments one attempts to reduce the within-group variation. In within-subject designs this is achieved by exposing the same person to different levels of the treatment; between-subjects designs achieve this by using precision matching and/or randomly assigning individuals to be exposed to different treatments. Another technique used in between-subjects designs to reduce within-group variations is ***blocking***. A blocked design refers to one where subjects have been grouped together on some variable that needs to be controlled, and subjects are then randomly assigned to treatment and control groups. For example, if you were testing for the effectiveness of a new instructional program, and you were working in an area with many immigrant children, you might want to use blocking in your experimental design. What you would do is assign immigrant children randomly to either the treatment group (new program) or to the control group (old program); you would then do the same for non-immigrant children. The blocking will not allow you to measure the influence of immigration status on learning, but it will increase your chances of detecting a significant effect on your new program. The reason for this is that you have reduced the variation between the treatment and the control groups.

8. CONCLUSIONS

Experimental designs produce the clearest view of causation. This is accomplished through the application of a treatment to subjects under conditions where extraneous variables are controlled. However, there are four special cautions to be taken in evaluating experimental results.

CAUTION 1

Few experiments are done on representative samples and therefore one cannot make extrapolations to the general population. This concern extends to questions about the accuracy of descriptive parameters and questions about whether the causal relationships in an experiment hold true in a larger population. In our racing tire test, even though we find significant differences in the performance of the tires, these differences may well hold true for younger drivers but not older ones (all of the drivers were under 40 in the test); thus we should not conclude that the tires perform better for all drivers.

CAUTION 2

The fact that experimental studies achieve higher explained variances (predictability) than surveys or secondary data analyses should not be misinterpreted. To illustrate: if a treatment variable X controls 10 percent of the variability in the dependent variable Y, then we should expect an experiment that controls all external factors to explain all variance except that which can be accounted for by measurement error or the application of inappropriate models (for example, using a linear models when the particular relationship to be explained is curvilinear: see Chapter 7). The explained variances of experimental and non-experimental designs are, therefore, not directly comparable. In principle, experiments should produce higher explained variances than those achieved by non-experimental designs using the same variables. A robust vari-

able in an experiment may be relatively impotent outside the laboratory setting.

CAUTION 3

The third major caution is that there is an element of artificiality in laboratory experiments that is difficult to detect, to interpret, or to control. A "good subject" may try to respond by giving the researcher what the subject thinks the researcher wants; the subject may also be intimidated and act atypically. These problems will be discussed in greater detail in Chapter 9.

CAUTION 4

For practical reasons, experimental designs can only deal with a few variables simultaneously (multiple-variable designs are possible, but with several treatment and control levels one would soon need far too many subjects to run the experiment: a $3 \times 3 \times 3 \times 3$ design produces 81 treatment conditions and, if there were 10 subjects per condition, would require 810 subjects). When a large number of variables require simultaneous analysis it is advisable either to use a different experimental design or to simplify the experiment by using fewer variables or fewer levels in each variable.

Despite some inherent weaknesses, experimental designs provide the greatest control and precision in testing causal models, and in dealing with many of the worrying sources of bias that plague other approaches. Moreover, through the use of *double blind* designs, where neither subjects nor researchers know which subjects are under what condition, there is considerable control over bias on the part of subjects and researchers.

It is neither practical nor ethical to experiment on all aspects of social behaviour and therefore other designs remain important tools for the social science researcher. The beginning researcher should have some understanding of experimental designs, as their great strength is their ability to control many of the confounding factors that influence outcomes. Where experimentation is not possible, it is more difficult to produce convincing inferences about causal relationships. The key strengths and weaknesses of each design will be discussed at the end of this chapter and also in subsequent chapters.

B. QUASI-EXPERIMENTAL DESIGNS

1. THE RATIONALE

Often we want the power of an experimental design in making causal inferences but find that it is not possible to conduct an experiment. Sometimes this happens because we cannot manipulate the required variables for ethical or for practical reasons; sometimes we cannot randomly assign people to different treatments. When these situations arise, researchers modify the experimental approach and design a quasi-experiment. A *quasi-experimental design* is one in which it has not been possible to do any or all of the following:

- randomly assign subjects to a treatment or control group; or
- control the timing or nature of the treatment.

The quasi-experimental design comes as close as possible to the experimental design in order to measure the impact of a treatment. To illustrate this approach, we will examine two studies using such designs.

2. FRANCES HENRY AND EFFIE GINZBERG: RACE DISCRIMINATION IN JOB SEARCH

In their imaginative study, Henry and Ginzberg wished to test whether racial discrimination in employment exists in Toronto. They wished to see if there were differences in the number of job offers to whites and blacks when similarly qualified applicants responded to the same job vacancy. Henry and Ginzberg also wished to examine if there would be differences in the treatment accorded to members of different racial groups. Two quasi-experimental designs were used in their study. In the first, similarly qualified white and black applicants applied in person for the same job. In the second approach, applicants using five different ethnic accents made phone inquiries about advertised job vacancies. The accents represented were: white-majority Canadian, Slavic, Italian, Jamaican, and Pakistani. Box 3.4 features a description of the in-person testing phase of the study.

The Henry and Ginzberg study is an important one both in terms of the design and for the findings that it produced. This study is convincing precisely because it was a quasi-experimental field study where the employers were not aware that their hiring behaviours were under scrutiny. The results almost certainly would have been different had a mailed survey been done on these same employers measuring their attitudes toward hiring minorities. The Henry and Ginzberg study also is convincing because they took great pains to design the study to test carefully whether employment hiring decisions were biased, while at the same time controlling for such things as the qualifications of the applicants and ensuring that a job vacancy existed with each potential employer. Furthermore, the number of cases was sufficient to provide confidence that the results were not the result of random fluctuations.

BOX 3.4 SOCIAL RESEARCHERS AT WORK

Frances Henry and Effie Ginzberg: Racial Discrimination in Employment

In the in-person testing, two job applicants, matched with respect to age, sex, education, experience, physical appearance (dress), and personality, were sent to apply for the same advertised job. The only major difference between our applicants was their race—*one was White and the other, Black.* We created four such teams: one junior male, one junior female, one senior male, and one senior female. The younger teams applied for semiskilled and unskilled jobs such as gas station attendant, bus boy, waitress, and clerk and sales help in youth-oriented stores. The senior teams applied for positions in retail management, sales positions in prestigious stores, and waiting and hosting positions in expensive restaurants. The senior team members were, in fact, professional actors. Applying for middle-class type jobs meant that they would be required not only to present a sophisticated image but also to participate in a fairly demanding job interview. Professional actors, we believed, would be more convincing in playing the many roles required for this project. The resumes of the team members were carefully constructed to be as alike as possible. In order to further control possible biases, the staff of testers was changed several times so that no individual personality could account for the results.

The younger teams were composed of high-school and university students who would normally be applying for the same types of job that they applied for in the testing situation. Since we were not testing for sex discrimination and did not want this type of discrimination to account for any of our results, the male teams were sent to traditionally male jobs and the women went to jobs traditionally associated with women's work. In some types of jobs, for example waiter/waitress, both men and women were acceptable. Men and women were sent to such jobs but never to the same job. Each tester had a different resume for the various types of positions that he or she was applying for, so each member of the senior female team, for example, carried several resumes, one for a secretary, another for a retail sales assistant, a third for a dental technician, etc. Each resume contained the names of references supplied by business people and friends who had agreed to support our research. Our applicants could thus be checked out by a potential employer who could obtain a reference for the applicant. In actuality, only two employers ever called for references.

Research Procedure

Each evening, a listing of jobs would be selected for the next day from among the classified advertisements. Some types of jobs were excluded such as those involving driving, where licences could be checked. Jobs which required highly technical skills were also excluded.

The testers were instructed either to go to a certain address or to phone for an appointment. They used standard Canadian accents when phoning since we did not want them to be screened out over the phone. The testers would arrive within approximately one half-hour of each other so that there was little chance that a job had been legitimately filled. In most cases the Black applicant went first. After their interviews the testers completed a summary data sheet especially designed for this project in which they wrote down the details of their treatment and the kinds of information they had been given. Their resumes listed telephone numbers which were in actuality lines connected to the research office. Call-backs for second interviews or with offers of employment were received and recorded by the researchers. On-the-spot offers to the field testers were accepted by them. In the case of call-backs and on-the-spot offers, employers were phoned back, usually within an hour and informed that another position had been accepted, in order to make sure that the employer could fill the vacancy as soon as possible.

Research Results: The In-Person Test

In three-and-one-half months of field testing, the testers were able to apply for 201 jobs for a total of 402 individual applications.

For our purposes, racial discrimination in employment was tested in two ways. First, was an offer of employment made to one of the applicants, both applicants, or neither applicant? Second, during the interview, were there any differences in the treatment of the two applicants? The following tables present the numerical results.

Blacks received fewer job offers than whites. Of a total of 37 valid job offers, 27 went to Whites, 9 to Blacks, and in one case both were offered the job (Table I). There were an additional 10 cases where both were offered jobs, but these were for commission sales which involved no cost to the employer. Our overall results therefore show that *offers to Whites outweigh offers to Blacks by a ratio of 3 to 1.*

We had thought that the nature of the job might influence whether Blacks or Whites would be hired. Only Whites received offers for managerial positions

TABLE I   Offer of a Job Versus no Offer

	NUMBER	%
Both offered job	10	5.0
White offered job; Black not	27	13.4
Black offered job; White not	9	4.5
No offer to either	155	77.1
Totals	201	100.0

or jobs as waiters and waitresses or hosts and hostesses in the restaurant trade. A Black was offered a job in the kitchen when he had applied for a waiter's job!

As noted above, the second measure of discrimination was whether differential treatment had occurred during the interview. Table II presents the results.

TABLE II   Treatment of Applicants

	NUMBER OF CASES
Treated the same	165
Treated differently	36

Blacks and Whites were treated differently 36 times and in all cases but one the White applicant was preferred to the Black. The ways in which differential treatment took place provide a great deal of insight into the nature of discrimination and its subtleties. Differences in treatment were sometimes very blatant, as the following examples show.

1. Mary, the young black tester, applied for a sales position in a retail clothing store and was told that the job had already been taken. Sylvia, our White tester, arrived a half-hour later and was given an application form to fill in and told that she would be contacted if they were interested in her.

2. In a coffee shop Mary was told that the job of cashier was taken. Sylvia walked in five minutes later and was offered the job on the spot.

   This pattern occurred five times. Another form of differential treatment was as follows: the Black was treated rudely or with hostility, whereas the White was treated politely. This occurred 15 times.

3. Paul, our White tester, applied for a job as a waiter. He was given an application form to fill out and an interview. He was told that he might be contacted in a week or so. Larry, the Black tester, was also given an application form and an interview. But as the Manager looked over Larry's resume, he asked Larry if he "wouldn't rather work in the kitchen."

4. Applying for a gas station job, the White tester was told that there were no jobs at present but that he could leave a resume. The Black tester was told that there were no jobs, but when he asked if he could leave a resume, he was sworn at: "Shit, I said no didn't I?"

Another form of differential treatment occurred when the wage offers to Blacks and Whites were different. There were two occasions where the Black tester was offered less money than the White tester for the same job. On a few occasions, derogatory comments were made about Blacks in the presence of our White testers. The Blacks being referred to were our own testers!

These results indicate that Black job seekers face not only discrimination in the sense of receiving fewer job offers than Whites but also a considerable amount of negative and abusive treatment while job hunting. The psychological effects of such experiences became evident in the feelings expressed by the research staff. The Black staff felt rejected and some doubted their own ability: "I was beginning to wonder what was wrong with me and why Jean [the White tester] was so much better than me."

In sum, the findings of the in-person test reveal that in 48 job contacts, or 23.8 per cent of the cases, some form of discrimination against Blacks took place. These findings indicate that Blacks and Whites do not have the same access to employment. *Racial discrimination in employment, either in the form of clearly favouring a White over a Black, even though their resumes were equivalent, or in the form of treating a White applicant better than a Black, took place in almost one-quarter of all job contacts tested in this study.*

SOURCE: Francis Henry and Effie Ginzberg, "Racial Discrimination in Employment" in James Curtis and Lorne Tepperman, *Images of Canada*. Scarborough, Ontario: Prentice-Hall Canada Inc., 1990, pp. 303-306. Reprinted by permission of the publisher.

3. DON CLAIRMONT AND WINSTON JACKSON: EFFECT OF EMPLOYER TYPE ON EMPLOYEES

The Clairmont and Jackson study of the impact of Marginal Work World (small companies with less secure and lowly paid employees) versus Central Work World (larger companies with more secure and highly paid employees) employment, used a quasi-experimental design to ensure as much similarity as possible in the characteristics of the employees used in the baseline phase of the study. Because of this, the impact of working for different types of employers could be gauged accurately in the follow-up study conducted two years after the baseline data were collected. The similarity was achieved by establishing matched pairs of employees, one who worked in the Marginal Work World, the other in the Central Work world. (See Box 3.5.)

BOX 3.5   SOCIAL RESEARCHERS AT WORK

Donald H. Clairmont and Winston Jackson: Segmentation of the Low Income Blue Collar Worker

Introduction

Does it matter much for the low-wage worker whether he/she works in a marginal or central work setting? Will people, otherwise similar in terms of human capital and occupation, develop differences in attitudes and behaviours as a result of working in a marginal or central work setting? Are the life chances of a 25 year-old typist affected by working for a city government rather than doing the same kind of work in a modest-sized wholesale operation? The Public Sector Comparison Project, from which the data in this report are drawn, was designed to make a tough test of a variety of segmentation hypotheses which suggest affirmative answers to these types of questions.

One of the problems which had to be faced in designing this project was that research coming from a variety of sources, including our own previous exploration, suggested that no matter how segmentation was operationalized, marginal and central work sectors would differ sharply in the composition of their workforces and the proportions with which certain jobs were represented within each sector. For example the marginal sector will overrepresent minorities, young people, women, part-timers, and have a larger percentage of purportedly low or semiskilled jobs. Such compositional variables may well have an important independent impact on attitudes, behaviours, and life chances and therefore must be taken into account in any adequate research design.

What would be an ideal design to test for the structural effects implied by the segmentation perspective? Perhaps the ideal situation would be one where it would be possible to conduct an experiment involving a number of identical twins, each having the same biological, social and even occupational training background. If it were then possible to make a random assignment so that one of the twins worked in the central segment, and the other in the marginal segment, we could then make systematic observations over time as to the impact work settings have upon each of the twins. Of course such an "ideal" design is impossible, but clear inferences may depend upon some fair approximation to it.

In order to deal with some of the sources of spuriousness that might influence the relationship between work place type (marginal or central) and a variety of possible consequences of that location, and to monitor expected developments, a longitudinal matched pair design was utilized. The criteria on which the matching was based included sex, occupation, age and ethnic origin. Besides using these major matching criteria we also matched workers, where possible, on their community of residence (e.g. urban core, urban fringe). It should be noted that by matching on the above criteria, we are, by implication, matching workers on a variety of additional characteristics. For example the age match means that we are picking up people at roughly the same points in their life cycles; the occupation match tends to build in similarity in terms of educational and training backgrounds; the ethnic match tends to build in cultural similarities, while the sex match builds in parallels in socialization. In general then, the procedure of matching means that one has also matched, in addition to the formal criteria, on a host of unmentioned and perhaps unknown criteria.

The research strategy was to ensure that the matched workers were as similar as possible. We wanted to examine the impact of type of work setting, controlling for other factors of demonstrable salience for attitudes, behaviours, and life chances, such as occupation, age, sex, and ethnicity. Other important factors such as human capital and work experience could not be built into the formal matching design conveniently, but it was hoped that our matching would entail similarities here as well. Indeed, given the fact that human capital and work experience are the key variables in the theoretical perspective which is the "bête noire" of segmentation researchers, the implicit matching on these variables is crucial. The entire matching effort was designed to facilitate the inference that it is reasonable to attribute differences between workers from the different segments to differences in the type of work setting in which they work. Caution has to be exercised, since the design cannot rule out selection effects—it can only hope to minimize them.

Work-Related Impacts

The segmentation perspective has led us to expect differences between the sectors in terms of working conditions and in employees' perceptions of their work environments. It suggests, for example, that while turnovers would be more common among the marginal sector respondents, on-the-job training and promotion would be more typical of the central work world scene....To what extent are the data consistent with these segmentation-generated expectations? ...Table I indicates the marginal sector respondents were more likely to report in 1976 that they had looked for a better job in the past six months. This potential job instability was realized subsequently

TABLE I   *Job Search, Turnover and Expectations of Continued Employment by Sex and Sector*

	MALE		FEMALE	
	PUBLIC	MARGINAL	PUBLIC	MARGINAL
% Who have looked for better job in past 6 months (1976)	7.4 (54)	27.8 (54)	0.0 (53)	15.7 (54)
Turnover (% who, in 1978, were no longer working for 1976 employer)	20.4 (54)	38.9 (54)	13.0 (54)	40.7 (54)
% Expecting to continue working for the same employer (those who, in 1978, were working for same employer as they were in 1976) over the next two years	93.0 (43)	71.9 (32)	95.6 (45)	80.6 (31)
% Who want to continue working for same employer (those who, in 1978, were working for same employer as they were in 1976) over the next two years	88.4 (43)	56.2 (32)	86. (44)	64.5 (31)

in the form of actual job turnovers. Those who were located in the marginal sector were much more likely to have left their 1976 job by the time of the second interview in 1978. While 38.9 percent of the marginal sector males had left during that time span, only half as many (some 20.4 percent) of those in the public sector had left their jobs. Among the females, perhaps not unexpectedly, the difference was even greater with figures of 40.7 and 13.0 percent respectively.

...So far the evidence presented appears to support the segmentation perspective. There is one area, however, where the evidence appears to be somewhat contrary to expectations. It is in the area of participation in on-the-job training programs and being given new responsibilities or promotions that the data seems either to show no difference between respondents from marginal and central work worlds, or to show differences that favour the marginal sector respondents. Table II presents these data.

TABLE II Participation in Training Programs and Promotions by Sex and Sector, Blue Collar Workers

OF THOSE WITH SAME EMPLOYER IN 1978 AS IN 1976	MALE		FEMALE	
	PUBLIC	MARGINAL	PUBLIC	MARGINAL
% Who took on-the-job training between 1976 and 1978	11.6	24.2	4.3	12.9
% given new responsibilities in job between 1976 and 1978	23.3	33.3	23.9	25.8
% who report 'definite' promotion between 1976 and 1978	7.0	11.6	2.2	12.1
% who report 'definite' or 'small' promotion between 1976 and 1978	25.6	25.6	10.9	22.6
Number of cases with same employer in 1978 as in 1976	(43)	(33)	(46)	(31)

SOURCE: Based on Donald H. Clairmont and Winston Jackson, "Segmentation of the Low Income Blue Collar Worker: A Canadian Test of Segmentation Theory." Halifax: Institute of Public Affairs, Dalhousie University, 1980.

4. CONCLUSIONS

An examination of the two examples shows how the researchers have attempted to model their studies on an experimental design. In the Henry and Ginzberg study, the important feature is the attempt to control the qualifications of the job applicants, only allowing their racial background to vary; the same employer was used for each pair of applicants, thus controlling for the employer. In the Clairmont and Jackson study the employees were matched (by type of work, ethnic background etc.), and measures were taken at different points in time to get an indication of the impact of type of employer on a number of dependent measures (rate of pay, promotion, job satisfaction etc.). In the Henry and Ginzberg study and in the Clairmont and Jackson study the results are more convincing in part because of the quasi-experimental designs employed by the researchers.

Table 3.3 outlines the advantages and disadvantages of experimental and quasi-experimental designs.

A. ADVANTAGES

The unmistakeable strength of experimental and quasi-experimental designs is their ability to clarify causal inferences.

B. DISADVANTAGES

As is true of surveys and interviews, experimental research makes it impossible to disguise the fact that an experiment is being carried out. To what extent do people modify their behaviour when they know that they are being studied? While more will be said about this topic in Chapter 9 (Bias), researchers need, and frequently do, take into account the effects of expectations on the response of subjects. Since subjects can manage their presentation-of-self to the experimenter, questions can be raised about the validity (are you measuring what you claim to measure?) of some experimental results. Experimentalists often use the terms internal and external validity. ***Internal validity*** may be taken to mean that the researcher has demonstrated that the treatment in fact produced the changes in the dependent variable. ***External validity*** has to do with the extent to which results

TABLE 3.3   ADVANTAGES AND DISADVANTAGES OF ALTERNATE DESIGNS

DATA COLLECTION TECHNIQUE	GENERAL	VALIDITY	CAUSAL INFERENCE	MULTI-VARIATE	PROBING
A EXPERIMENTAL STUDIES					
Experimental	–	–	+	–	–
Quasi-Experimental	+/–	–	+	–	–

In each category a + means that this is an advantage of the technique; a - means this is a disadvantage or problem.

- *General* refers to the extent to which extrapolations to larger populations may be made using each of the data collection procedures.
- *Validity* is the extent to which indicators clearly measure what they are intended to measure.
- *Causal Inference* refers to the ease with which inferences about causal relations among variables may be made.
- *Multi-Variate* refers to the ease with which information on many variables is collected, leading to the possibility of multi-variate analysis.
- *Probing* refers to the extent to which responses may be probed in depth.

may be extrapolated from the particular study to other groups in general.

As experiments are typically conducted on small, unrepresentative samples, their results cannot be generalized to larger populations. And while this is also a problem with many other designs, there is a sense that the bulk of experimental studies have used undergraduates as subjects. Quasi-experimental designs, often using panels who are interviewed over time, can more feasibly use representative samples.

The nature of experimental design makes it difficult to take into account a large number of variables at one time systematically. For example, in a $3 \times 3 \times 2$ between-subjects design, the researcher is facing 18 cells, and to run a modest 15 subjects per condition would take 270 subjects. Besides the treatment variable, we are only

dealing with three other variables simultaneously. And while there are experimental designs that make more efficient use of subjects, it is not easy to take even seven or eight variables into account simultaneously.

Given the nature of the experiment, probing into the details of individual behaviour during the course of an experiment is not typical. Participant observation studies and interviews are used when intensive probing is required.

Even though experiments provide the clearest view of causation, it is often not possible to experiment on all topics. As a result, other research designs—some incorporating different orientations to knowledge—have developed to enhance our understanding of the complexity of human behaviour.

C. KEY TERMS

Between-subjects design	External validity	Quasi-experimental design
Blocking	Independent variable	Random variable
Confounding variable	Instrument decay	Response bias
Control by constancy	Internal validity	Selection
Control variable	Hawthorne effect	Statistical regression
Counterbalancing	History	Treatment levels
Dependent variable	Maturation	Treatment variable
Double blind	Mortality	Within-subject design

D. KEY POINTS

Experimental designs provide the most convincing evidence for demonstrating causal relations among variables. There are two basic types of experiments: *between-subjects designs,* where each group of subjects is exposed to only one level of the treatment, and *within-subject designs,* where each subject is exposed to all levels of the treatment variable.

In an experiment, the independent variable whose effect is being studied is known as the *treatment variable*.

A *control variable* is a variable that is specifically taken into account in designing the study.

A *confounding variable* is one which may either obscure or enhance a relationship and must be taken into account in designing an experiment.

A *random variable* is allowed to vary without control but is taken into account by the way groups are set up for the study.

In a between-subjects design, *treatment and control groups are to be as equivalent as possible before the treatment begins*. There are three ways of achieving equivalence:

(i) through precision matching (possibly matching on sex, socio-economic status, and grades);

(ii) through randomization (where individuals are randomly assigned to either the treatment or to the control group); or

(iii) through a combination of the previous two techniques. Randomization (if the numbers are large enough) will provide control over both known and unknown factors (the control and random variables).

To show a causal relationship in any research, three conditions must be demonstrated:

(i) changes in the independent variable must occur prior to changes in the dependent variable;

(ii) the variables must be associated—as values on the independent variable are increased, the dependent measures vary systematically; and

(iii) nothing but the treatment variable must influence the dependent variable.

A *Hawthorne effect* refers to any variability in the dependent variable that is not the direct result of variations in the treatment variable.

In a *within-subject design* each subject is exposed to all levels of the treatment variable. Control over random and control variables is achieved by control by constancy—by having each subject act as his or her own control.

Experimental designs produce the clearest view of causation. This is accomplished through the application of a treatment to subjects under conditions where extraneous variables are controlled.

A *quasi-experiment* is one in which it has not been possible to do any or all of the following:

(i) randomly assign subjects to a treatment or control group; or

(ii) control the timing or nature of the treatment. The quasi-experiment comes as close as possible to experimental design in order to measure the impact of a treatment.

The particular *strength* of experimental and quasi-experimental designs is their ability to clarify causal inferences.

E. EXERCISES

1. Suppose you wished to investigate the impact of a guaranteed income scheme on the withdrawal of youth from the labour force. What research design(s) would be appropriate to deal with such a question? Outline the rationale for your choice.

2. Outline a within-subjects experimental project: be certain to identify all variables and the number of levels that will be employed; indicate how the dependent variable will be measured. Comment on the method by which controls will be achieved on possible contaminants.

3. Outline a between-subjects experimental project: be certain to identify all variables and the number of levels that will be employed; indicate how the dependent variable will be measured. How will control over possible sources of contamination be achieved?

4. Outline a quasi-experimental project: be certain to identify all variables; indicate how the dependent variable will be measured. How will control over possible sources of contamination be achieved?

F. RECOMMENDED READINGS

CAMPBELL, DONALD T., and Julian C. Stanley (1966). *Experimental and Quasi-Experimental Designs for Research*. Chicago: Rand McNally & Company. This is considered by many to be the classic statement on confounding variables in different types of research designs.

MARTIN, DAVID W. (1991). *Doing Psychology Experiments*. Pacific Grove: Brooks/Cole Publishing Company, Third Edition. Martin's approach is straightforward and entertaining.

MITCHELL, MARK, AND JANINA JOLLEY (1992). *Research Design Explained*, Second Edition. Orlando: Harcourt Brace Jovanovitch College Publishers. This is an excellent text which well explains experimental design and the analysis of results.

SURVEY DESIGNS

A. INTRODUCTION

In contrast to the experiment, the survey emphasizes making extrapolations from samples to whole populations. Also in contrast to an experiment, a survey typically measures many variables. Surveys include censuses, polls, and a whole range of situations where respondents are asked to provide answers to a set of fixed questions.

1. A SHORT HISTORY OF THE SURVEY

Surveys have been around for a long time—there are biblical references to the counts of the children of Israel, Napoleon did surveys, and censuses were taken of the population of ancient Egypt. However, the foundations of the modern survey were laid in nineteenth-century England by Charles Booth who conducted three major London surveys. He was the first to work out operational definitions (the indicators he used to measure poverty); the first to draw colour maps to reflect the social characteristics of an area; and the first to attempt to show how variables were related to one another, thus beginning efforts to understand the association between social variables. Booth was concerned with providing an accurate count and description of poor people living in London. The claim has been made that Booth was "the first empirical sociologist" (Easthope, 1974, p. 57). Booth's influence on North American sociology was particularly strong at the University of Chicago, where R.E. Park and E.W. Burgess extended his idea of using ecological maps to describe social patterns in urban areas.

The link between political interests and survey research is strong, and, just as

Booth's work in England had political relevance, so too did the work of another person who lived in England at the time. In 1880, Karl Marx attempted to survey some 25,000 French workers to gauge how badly they were being exploited. The questionnaire included 108 questions, many of which would take considerable time to answer. For example, questions 59 and 100 asked:

> 59. *Have you noticed that the delay in paying your wages makes it necessary for you to resort frequently to the pawnbroker, paying a high rate of interest, and depriving yourself of things which you need; or to fall into debt of shopkeepers, becoming their victim because you are their debtor? Do you know any instances in which workers have lost their wages through the bankruptcy of their employers? (Bottomore and Rubel, 1988, p. 215.)*

> 100. *What is the general physical, intellectual, and moral condition of the men and women workers employed in your trade? (Bottomore, 1988, p. 218.)*

It would take a thoughtful respondent, indeed, to respond adequately to these questions! The analysis of such responses would pose enormous difficulties and, judged by contemporary standards, some of Marx's questions seem to have a built-in bias:

> 56. *"If you are paid piece rates, how are the rates fixed? If you are employed in an industry in which the work performed is measured by quantity or weight, as in the case of the mines, does your employer or his representative resort to trickery in order to defraud you of your earnings?" (Bottomore, 1988, p. 215.)*

57. "If you are paid piece rates, is the quality of the article made a pretext for fraudulent deductions from your wages?" (Bottomore, 1988, p. 215.)

Apparently few questionnaires were returned (Bottomore, 1988, p. 211). And although the questions Marx raised were both interesting and important, it would have been difficult to do a meaningful analysis of the responses given the complexity of some of the questions and the likelihood that many questions would not receive complete answers from the respondents.

Survey research developed in this century partly through the efforts of pioneer pollsters George Gallup and Elmo Roper to provide an accurate profile of Americans, partly from efforts of market researchers to understand consumer behaviour better, and partly from the interests of journalists, government agencies, and political organizations, all of whom understood the advantages that could be gained if one could gauge public opinion accurately. Survey research was just too powerful a tool to be left to the scholars alone.

During the post-World War Two era, it was Samuel A. Stouffer and Paul F. Lazarsfeld who did much to make survey research a legitimate academic and practical pursuit. *The People's Choice* (Lazarsfeld, Berelson, & Gaudet, 1948) was a sophisticated analysis of voting intentions and behaviour. It was the first study to interview members of a panel several times leading up to an election. *The People's Choice* marks the beginning of voting studies in political science and it was the first study to take control variables into account systematically.

From the fifties onward, survey research became a key approach in several social science disciplines. Many universities support survey research centres. In the 1987 *Directory of Social Science Research Centres and Institutes at Canadian Universities* some 283 such organizations are listed. Table 4.1 lists those larger centres that do considerable survey research. Typically these centres offer consulting services and coordinate surveys being conducted by university scholars. The two which have had the highest profile in recent years are The Institute for Social Research, located at York University in Toronto, and the Population Research Laboratory at the University of Alberta in Edmonton.

As we near the end of the century, survey designs remain particularly important to sociologists, but they are also commonly used by academic researchers in many disciplines including psychology, political science, education, and nursing. Public opinion pollsters, community groups, and professionals doing evaluations of applied programs all make frequent use of survey methods.

This chapter will discuss the major types of surveys, and will provide practical guidelines for using them. Let us first examine the rationale of the survey to see how it contrasts with the experiment.

2. THE RATIONALE OF THE SURVEY

Surveys are a method of collecting information by having respondents complete a questionnaire. A **questionnaire** is made up of a series of set questions and either provides a space for an answer or offers a number of fixed alternatives from which the respondent makes a choice. Questionnaires

TABLE 4.1	SURVEY RESEARCH CENTRES IN CANADA	
NAME OF CENTRE	UNIVERSITY	LOCATION
Applied Research Unit	University of Saskatchewan	Saskatoon, Saskatchewan.
Canadian Plains Research Centre	University of Regina	Regina, Saskatchewan.
Centre de Recherche en Civilisation Canadienne-Francaise	Université d'Ottawa	Ottawa, Ontario.
Centre de Recherche en Études Quebecoises	Université de Québec a Trois-Rivières	Trois-Rivières, Quebec.
Centre de Recherche en Gestion	Université de Québec a Montréal	Montréal, Québec.
Centre de Recherche et Développement en Economique	Université de Montréal	Montréal, Québec.
Centre de Recherches en Aménagement et en Developpement (CRAD)	Université de Laval	Ste-Foy, Québec.
Centre for Urban and Community Studies	University of Toronto	Toronto, Ontario.
Centre Interuniversitaire de Recherches sur les Populations (SOREP)	Université de Québec à Chicoutimi	Chicoutimi, Québec.
Institute for Social Research	York University	Toronto, Ontario.
Institute of Urban Studies	University of Winnipeg	Winnipeg, Manitoba.
Laboratoire de Recherche en Écologie Humaine et Sociale (LAREHS)	Université du Québec à Montréal	Montréal, Québec.
Population Research Laboratory	University of Alberta	Edmonton, Alberta.
Sample Survey and Data Bank Unit	University of Regina	Regina, Saskatchewan.
Social Research Unit	University of Saskatchewan	Saskatoon, Saskatchewan.
Social Science Computing Laboratory	University of Western Ontario	London, Ont.
Survey Centre (part of Gorsebrook Research Institute)	Saint Mary's University	Halifax, Nova Scotia

SOURCE: Social Science Federation of Canada, *Directory of Social Science Research Centres and Institutes at Canadian Universities.* Ottawa: University of Ottawa Press, 1987. The research centres selected were those which have large budgets and which, judging from the description in the directory, seem to place an emphasis on survey research.

can be completed in group settings, mailed to respondents, or read to respondents by interviewers either over the phone or in person.

As indicated in Chapter 1, surveys are typically associated with the positivist approach to knowledge. But it is to be noted that both Marx (conflict approach) and Weber (interpretive approach) used surveys. Marx developed a questionnaire to measure French worker experiences (Bottomore, 1988, pp. 210-18), while Weber surveyed attitudes toward work.

Surveys can be a relatively inexpensive method of collecting much information from a large number of people. Survey researchers will frequently draw a sample in order to make estimations about some population. As used by the researcher, the term **population** refers to that collection of individuals, communities, or nations about which one wishes to make a general statement. In order to save time and money, the researcher draws a **sample** from the population which will be interpreted to represent the population. While including the whole population could prove to be more accurate (as in a census), the costs may be prohibitive. If the researcher wishes to make extrapolations from a sample to a larger population, then a fairly large sample will be required and hence it is likely that a survey design will be used. As social behaviour is often highly complex—subject to the simultaneous impact of many variables—a research strategy which measures many variables simultaneously may often be appropriate.

With both experimental and survey designs there can be difficulty in establishing the validity of the measures used. In the case of surveys, respondents are asked to report their own attitudes, behaviour, and backgrounds. Some of the data requested will require respondents to recall episodes from their past. ("How happy were you when you were first married?") And since questionnaires probe into sensitive areas, they permit respondents to manage their responses so as to appear in a favourable light. Suppose one was attempting to measure attitudes toward minorities: in such cases one has to understand that some people may try to appear tolerant—perhaps more tolerant than they actually are. There is not a one-to-one relationship between what people say they believe, and how they will actually behave when confronted with real situations. An initial field study

conducted by Richard T. LaPiere (1934) showed that only one establishment out of 251 would refuse accommodations to LaPiere and a Chinese couple. Yet when LaPiere asked the same businesses the same question some six months later in a mailed questionnaire, only one business indicated that it would accept members of the Chinese race as guests of the establishment. In his analysis, encapsulated in Box 4.1, Deutscher (1966) reminds us to consider the relation between attitudes expressed on a questionnaire and subsequent behaviour to be problematical. Sometimes there may be little relation between the two.

Nonetheless, surveys can produce reliable and valid responses on many issues. And, if one wishes to measure attitudes, there is no good alternative to asking people about them. One simply has to live with the problems of measurement if the variables are to be measured at all. According to conventional wisdom, surveys provide **point-in-time data** and are therefore poor at measuring changes over time. While it is no doubt risky to assume that people will recall their past reliably, most surveys in fact do ask questions about a variety of points in time, such as the year of the respondent's birth, the type of community the respondent grew up in, or how old the respondent was at the time of his or her first full-time job. Once again, while there are problems with recall data, sometimes there is no practical alternative to the survey for measuring some variables.

Questionnaires are restrictive because they can only be used with a literate population. The wording of questions must be straightforward so that all—or at least most—of the respondents will be able to handle the language. Also, the requirement that all respondents be able to understand

---

BOX 4.1   SOCIAL RESEARCHERS AT WORK

Irwin Deutscher: Words and Deeds

Deutscher argues that social policy analysts are concerned with altering social behaviour. Much of our work as social scientists indeed has to do with predicting behaviour. However, the predictions we make are derived from responses interviewed people have made, or from answers prompted by questionnaire items. The key issue is the extent to which we can rely on such responses to reflect behaviour accurately.

In his review of the relation between attitudes and behaviour Deutscher identifies considerable evidence showing that there is frequently an inverse relation between the two. Deutscher notes that:

...this discrepancy between what people say and what they do is not lim-ited to the area of racial or ethnic relations: it has been observed that trade union members talk one game and play another, that there is no relationship between college students' attitudes toward cheating and their actual cheating behavior, that urban teachers' descriptions of classroom behavior are sometimes unrelated to the way teachers behave in the classroom, that what rural Missourians say about their health behavior has little connection with their actual health practices, and that the moral and ethical beliefs of students do not conform to their behavior. (Deutscher, 1966:246)

SOURCE: Irwin Deutscher (1966). "Words and Deeds: Social Science and Social Policy," *Social Problems*, 13:235-54.

---

the questions prevents certain areas from being probed in depth. Everyone is given the same set of questions, and while it is advantageous to have all respondents reply to the same question, it does mean that interesting responses cannot be pursued. For in-depth probes, a personal interview is necessary.

This chapter will provide a general orientation to survey research. Anyone who wishes to know how to carry out a survey will need to consult two additional chapters in the book: Chapter 13 provides guidelines for developing a questionnaire and Chapter 14 talks about how one goes about selecting a sample and determining how large it should be.

B. GUIDELINES FOR THE ADMINISTRATION OF SURVEYS

In this section, general rules will be provided for administering questionnaires in a variety of ways. In all cases, the suggestions should be used with common sense, since there will be times when they should be violated.

As permission to distribute questionnaires will frequently be required, researchers will need to take this fact into account in planning a survey. Pursuing permissions takes time, and usually will require a statement of the problem under investigation and a copy of the proposed questionnaire. Plan for extra time.

1. GENERAL RULES FOR THE ADMINISTRATION OF SURVEYS

The following rules are intended to increase response rates for all types of surveys. Sections following this one will suggest approaches for particular types of surveys.

RULE 4.1

ESTABLISH LEGITIMACY.

Establish the legitimacy of the research by noting who is sponsoring it, noting why it is being done, and presenting it in such a way as to make it seem credible and competent. The covering letter and the questionnaire must look professional.

RULE 4.2

KEEP IT SIMPLE.

Keep questionnaires, interview guides, or phone interviews as simple and as non-threatening as possible. Questionnaires should be easy to respond to and should avoid asking questions which pry unnecessarily into the respondent's personal affairs. (Chapter 13 provides additional ideas for making questionnaires easy to complete.)

RULE 4.3

PROVIDE A REPORT TO THE RESPONDENT.

When individuals are to be interviewed more than once during the course of a study (as in a panel study), report findings to respondents. In all cases where a report has been promised to the respondents, it must be provided, otherwise the researcher makes it less likely that they will cooperate in future.

RULE 4.4

PAY RESPONDENTS.

Where reasonable, and financially possible, pay respondents for their time and cooperation. The fee helps establish the legitimacy of the study as well as a reciprocal relationship with the respondent. Such payments appear to have a modest impact on the willingness of respondents to participate (Heberlein & Baumgartner, 1978). Payments help establish reciprocity between researcher and respondents and help to avoid the respondents' perception that they have been "ripped off" for their data.

RULE 4.5

DO NOT PRESSURE RESPONDENTS TO PARTICIPATE.

Although the researcher has a powerful interest in getting everyone selected to complete the survey, it must be indicated that while cooperation in completing the questionnaire or interview is appreciated, it is, nonetheless, optional. Particularly in face-to-face encounters, considerable pressure may be placed on individuals to participate in the study. In the case of questionnaires administered to a gathering of individuals, there is considerable informal pressure on those present to cooperate by staying in the room and completing the survey. The researcher must exercise self-discipline and avoid putting undue pressure on individuals in an attempt to coax participation. (See the discussion on research ethics in Chapter 10.)

RULE 4.6

DO QUALITY CONTROL SPOT CHECKS.

It is critical to do spot checks to ensure that administrative procedures are being followed. Research directors are sometimes negligent on this point. Doing interviews, or even handing out questionnaires, is not many people's idea of fun. Research assistants will occasionally cut corners. These may range from ignoring the random sampling procedures which should be used to select which person in a household is to complete the questionnaire, to inventing respondents and their answers. Checks can be run on the representativeness of the sample (to see how well the respondents and their answers match known characteristics of the target population) or to see if the person who was supposed to have been interviewed actually was. However, by the time checks are run, field research funds may be expended and you may not be able to redo the work. And if any data have been faked, it will take a lot of time to distinguish the genuine data from the bad. Be cautious of interviewers who are doing much more than other interviewers. Watch out for systematic differences in response rates to sensitive questions. If an interviewer is missing data, try to go through the part of the questionnaire affected by this absence to see if the presentation can be improved. The quality of one's research can be no better than the quality of the data collected; monitor the process carefully.

There are many variants of the survey and we will only explore the major ap-proaches here. The main differences are determined by how the data are collected. Each method has a distinctive set of advantages and disadvantages. Let us begin with the questionnaire which is personally handed to a respondent.

2. INDIVIDUALLY-DELIVERED QUESTIONNAIRES

Individually delivered questionnaires are delivered to a respondent by a researcher. A brief explanation is offered, any questions are answered, and arrangements are made for the return of the completed questionnaire. This method of handing out questionnaires will typically be used in community surveys where the form is dropped off at selected houses, in campus dormitories, where questionnaires are handed to selected respondents (usually the researcher tries to obtain a systematic sample of campus dormitory rooms), and in studies of organizations (such as surveys of hospital staff, university faculty, or employees of a private firm) where the target respondents are approached individually.

In cases where a survey of a systematic sample of students in residence is being conducted, care should be taken to provide everyone with an equal chance of participating in the survey if there is a mixture of single and double rooms. This will mean that, in the case of double rooms, both residents should be asked to complete the questionnaire. In this way, all students will have an equal chance of being selected to participate in the survey. (See more details on the systematic sampling procedure in Chapter 14.)

RULE 4.7

MAKE PERSONAL CONTACT WITH THE RESPONDENT.

Where feasible, contact respondents in person to explain the survey to them and let them know when you will pick up the completed form. In a door-to-door survey, it should be possible to get over 80 percent to agree to complete the form. Avoid having third parties handing out your questionnaires: a member of the research team can explain the survey better and answer any questions that might be raised. In particular, avoid having teachers, workers' supervisors, or co-workers hand out questionnaires. The extra effort needed to have a member of the research team hand out the questionnaires will avoid many problems associated with a third-party delivery. In short, the greater the personal contact, the greater the response rate.

RULE 4.8

AVOID MAILED AND DROP-BOX RETURN METHOD.

Where possible, avoid mailed returns or having respondents drop their completed questionnaires into a box left in a dormitory or other convenient spot. If at all possible, completed forms should be picked up by the researcher at a time agreed to with the respondent. Such arrangements will encourage the respondent to complete the form by the pre-arranged time. Do not be tempted to violate this rule: if you do, you will pay a heavy price in lost and missing questionnaires.

RULE 4.9

RECORD PLACE AND TIME INFORMATION.

It is critical to record where questionnaires have been dropped off, and when they are to be picked up. Pick up the questionnaire on time: respondents will be annoyed if it is not picked up. A form for recording this information should be developed and then used faithfully. (See Table 4.2 below.) Besides information on place and time, the form should also have space to list dates when an attempt was made to contact the individual, and to record times when it would be convenient to return to meet the person. After the data have been collected these sheets will prove invaluable in calculating the response rate to the survey and in identifying what problems were encountered.

RULE 4.10

PROVIDE ENVELOPE TO HELP MAINTAIN PRIVACY.

Generally it is a good idea to provide respondents with an envelope into which they can seal their completed questionnaire. Sometimes questionnaires are left around waiting to be picked up and unwanted eyes may peruse the responses. A sealed envelope will foil most snoopers. In introducing the survey to the respondent, the researcher can indicate that the envelope is a means of protecting the confidentiality of the answers. This makes respondents feel safe.

RULE 4.11

USE A SLOTTED RETURN BOX.

In order to help convey the sense of anonymity, it is a good idea to use a box with a slot cut in one end (a box measuring 9" x 12" is a good size), and respondents' questionnaires can be slipped into the box as they are returned. In especially sensitive studies, this return procedure can be pointed out when the questionnaire is delivered to the respondent.

TABLE 4.2 SAMPLE DROP-OFF FORM

#	ADDRESS	TRY 1 DATE	TRY 2 DATE	TRY 3 DATE	PICK DATE	PICK TIME	DONE	NOTES
1								
2								
3								
4								
5								
6								
7								
8								
9								
10								
11								
12								
13								
14								
15								
16								
17								
18								
19								
20								

3. GROUP-ADMINISTERED QUESTIONNAIRES

Group-administered questionnaires almost always have good response rates. There is considerable informal pressure on individuals to cooperate with the researcher and, normally, between 90 and 100 percent of potential respondents will complete questionnaires in group settings.

RULE 4.12

INDICATE VOLUNTARY NATURE OF SURVEY.

Researchers should acknowledge this informal pressure and be sure to inform the potential respondents of their complete freedom to refuse to answer any or all questions; participation is voluntary. The person administering the questionnaire can briefly explain what it is about, and be available to answer any questions that may be raised.

RULE 4.13

ARRANGE WELL IN ADVANCE.

Frequently it will be necessary to gain permission to have a questionnaire administered, so it is a good idea to make arrangements well in advance. And just before the questionnaire is to be administered, it is also a good idea to remind the person concerned that you will be coming.

RULE 4.14

EXPLAIN SURVEY TO THOSE PRESENT.

Besides explaining who is doing the research and why it is being done, respondents should be encouraged to ask any questions about the survey in general or about particular questions.

RULE 4.15

ADMINISTER QUESTIONNAIRE AT THE END OF SESSION.

For practical reasons, it is usually best to administer questionnaires at the end of a meeting or class, rather than at the beginning. If, for example, one goes into a classroom with a questionnaire at the beginning of a class, problems will arise because not all the students will finish at the same time. Hence, from the teacher's point of view, valuable class time will be wasted as the researcher waits for the last forms to be completed. Similarly, at a meeting, avoid handing out a questionnaire before the meeting begins; administer it at the end, or before a break during the meeting. This will allow people who work at different speeds to complete the questionnaire without feeling rushed. However, in administering a questionnaire at the end of a meeting or class, we probably lose a little in terms of the quality of replies. At the end of sessions respondents may be tired or bored and wish to leave as soon as possible. But, given the researcher's desire to maintain cordial relations with those giving permission to administer the questionnaires, it is generally less disruptive to administer them at the end of the session.

RULE 4.16

TAKE STEPS TO IDENTIFY BAD QUESTIONNAIRES.

One hazard to watch out for is that a few within the room may decide to make a joke of the questionnaire and start making silly responses. This happens rarely, but watch out for such responses and discard any questionnaires that appear not to have been taken seriously.

Typically, when questionnaires are administered to groups, probability sampling procedures (see Chapter 14) are not employed and therefore the data collected cannot be used to extrapolate to some larger population.

4. MAILED QUESTIONNAIRES

Although researchers try to avoid doing so, often there is no choice but to use the mail system: long-distance phone interviews may be too expensive and travel costs would quickly eat up a research budget if the researcher attempted to deliver the questionnaires by hand.

Mail surveys are popular because they provide a relatively cheap way of contacting a large number of respondents. And despite the reputation mail surveys have for producing low *response rates,* it is possible to have the majority of questionnaires returned. The **response rate** measures the percentage of delivered questionnaires that are returned. In mail surveys we normally deduct from the total number of questionnaires sent out the number that are returned because respondents sent them to a wrong address. Therefore, the number of delivered questionnaires is equal to the number sent out, minus the number returned as undeliverable.

Since our major concern with the mail survey is the response rate, we will consider the factors that influence whether a questionnaire will be returned. John Goyder has done extensive work in examining survey research response rates. Using a regression-based method of analysis (see Chapter 17), he developed a nine-variable model for predicting final response rate (Goyder, 1982, 1985a, 1985b; Goyder and Leiper, 1985c; see Box 4.2). There are two factors involved: those largely beyond the control of the researcher, and those the researcher can control.

A. FACTORS BEYOND THE CONTROL OF THE RESEARCHER

These factors are of interest in trying to predict the likely response rate to a mailed questionnaire. The type of respondent receiving the questionnaire is important: as Heberlein and Baumgartner have noted (1978), students, employees, and military personnel are more inclined to return a mailed questionnaire than are members of the general public. The type of sponsoring agency also has an impact which favours government-sponsored research over market research. (Perhaps the response rates in government-sponsored projects are higher because some citizens may believe that they are legally required to participate

in the same way that they are required to participate in the census.) Finally, we need to consider the **salience of the topic** to the respondent; subjects which are important to the respondent are more likely to produce a positive response than those which are less important to the respondent.

B. FACTORS UNDER THE CONTROL OF THE RESEARCHER

While the quality of the questionnaire is not identified as a factor in the Goyder model, it should be noted that his research group was examining published studies which had passed various reviews before publication, so it would be reasonable to assume that all were highly professional. Common sense dictates that every effort be made to make the questionnaire look as professional as possible. For the convenience of the respondent, include a stamped return envelope. A cover letter should be included which explains the survey to the respondents. The legitimacy of the survey is enhanced if the questionnaire is well presented, the sponsoring agency identified, and the worthiness of the research established.

Among the variables examined, the evidence indicates that monetary incentives do increase response rates. Follow-up contacts in the form of letters, post card reminders, registered mail, and long distance phone calls all enhance the likelihood of a positive response. However, with each contact, one can expect slightly reduced effectiveness. Registered mail and long distance phone calls seem to impress on respondents the importance of the study and their role in it: using these approaches pays off well in increased participation. One of the follow-up contacts should contain a re-

BOX 4.2 SOCIAL RESEARCHERS AT WORK

Goyder Nine-Variable Model Predicting Final Response Rate

INDEPENDENT VARIABLE	REGRESSION COEFFICIENTS	
	UNSTANDARDIZED	STANDARDIZED
Data collection by interview	−0.206	0.157
Post-1970 field work	−0.059*	−0.045*
Interaction, interview by year	−0.143*	−0.068*
Number of contacts (logged)	0.856	0.436
Salience	0.272	0.338
Special third contact on questionnaire	0.130	0.193
Incentive on questionnaire	0.148	0.142
Government organization	0.260	0.188
General population	−0.099	−0.084
Constant	1.146	
R2	0.625	

* $p > .05$

SCORING: Response (proportion responding, after arcsine transformation); number of interview calls or questionnaire contacts (frequency count—logged); salience (0 = not salient, 1 = possibly salient, 2 = salient); form of data collection (interview = 1, questionnaire = 0); special third contact (0 = none, 1 = regular mail, 2 = special mail, 3 = telephone or personal contact); incentive on questionnaire (0 = none, 1 = less than 25¢, 2 = 25¢, 3 = 50¢, 4 = $1.00 or more); government organization, general population, post-1970 field work (dummy variables, scored 0,1).

Useful Figures: Since the log values of the number of contacts is used in the equation, it is useful to know the following logs   1   .000
                   2   .301
                   3   .477
                   4   .602

SOURCE: Adapted from John Goyder (1985). *Public Opinion Quarterly* 49:245 (Table 3). Reprinted by permission of the publisher.

placement copy of the questionnaire in case the first one has been "misplaced." Although follow-up contacts are worthwhile, one must always be careful not to harass potential respondents.

Given the many factors involved, it is difficult to estimate a response rate with precision before the survey is undertaken. However, a first-round response rate of about 50 percent should be considered average; three follow-up contacts can be expected to increase the response rate to about 75 percent (Dillman, 1974; Heberlein, 1978). Any response rate above 75 percent should be considered excellent. In Canada, Austria, and West Germany one can expect somewhat lower response rates (Eichner and Habermehl, 1981, Goyder, 1982). John Goyder has suggested that there may well be cultural factors working to lower response rates to mail questionnaires in

Canada. His research indicates that in Canadian studies the researcher should anticipate a response rate about 7 percent lower than is likely in the United States (Goyder, 1982; Goyder, 1985a).

It is useful for the researcher to estimate response rates by using John Goyder's formula presented in Box 4.3.

To illustrate the use of Goyder's formula, suppose a study is designed to survey graduates of a university in order to deter-

---

BOX 4.3   SOCIAL RESEARCHERS AT WORK

Estimating a Response Rate

It is useful for the researcher to estimate response rates by using John Goyder's formula presented in Box 4.3. To illustrate the use of Goyder's formula, suppose a study is designed to survey graduates of a university in order to determine their job experiences since graduation. The survey is sponsored by the

university, the subject is considered to be "possibly salient" to the respondents, and two follow-up contacts are planned. In this case, we estimate the response rate by simply plugging in the values we presented in Box 4.3. The predicted response rate is shown in the following table.

INDEPENDENT VARIABLE	COEFFICIENT UNSTANDARDIZED	VALUE	TOTAL
Data collection by interview	−0.206	0	0.000
Post-1970 field work	−0.059*	1	−0.059
Interaction, interview by year	−0.143*	0	0.000
Number of Contacts (logged)	0.856	2(0.301)	0.258
Salience	0.272	1	0.272
Special third contact on questionnaire	0.130	0	0.000
Incentive on questionnaire	0.148	2	0.296
Government Organization	0.260	0	0.000
General Population	−0.099	0	0.000
Constant	1.146	1	1.146
R^2	0.625		
Total			1.913

$$A = 2 \arcsin (\sqrt{p})$$
$$1.913 = 2 \arcsin (\sqrt{p})$$
$$\frac{1.913}{2} = \arcsin (\sqrt{p})$$
$$0.9565 = \arcsin (\sqrt{p})$$
$$\sin(0.9565) = \sqrt{p}$$
$$0.8172 = \sqrt{p}$$
$$0.67 = p$$

2. Divide by 2

3. Take sin of value (this removes the arcsine). [Put calculator in radian mode.]

4. Square both sides

5. The proportion expected to respond is the result

The use of the arcsine in computing the response rate prevents the predicted response rate from exceeding 100 percent. This can occur if the researcher does not take the diminishing returns of additional contacts with respondents into account. Heberlein and Baumgertner's (1978) regression estimate of response rate, for example, can lead to estimated returns of over 100 percent.

To calculate the estimated proportion responding, p, use the following equation (Goyder, 1985c:58): A = 2 arcsin ($\sqrt{p}$), where A is the total value calculated above.

USING A SCIENTIFIC CALCULATOR:

1. Use total value calculated above (in this case: 1.913)

mine their job experiences since graduation. The survey is sponsored by the university, the subject is regarded as "possibly salient" to the respondents, and two follow-up contacts are planned. In this case, we estimate the response rate by simply plugging in the values presented in Box 4.2. The predicted response rate is shown in Box 4.3.

Meeting the predicted response rate should be considered an excellent result. To be within 20 percent of the predicted response rate should be considered acceptable. If the researcher thinks that the estimated response rate will be insufficient, then additional steps should be taken to increase the likelihood of a response. An examination of the last column of Box 4.2 suggests that the two most important factors in determining response rate are:

- the number of contacts the researcher has with the respondents; and,

- the importance of the subject matter to the respondent.

One might wish to consider trying to make the questionnaire more salient for the respondents, or consider using phone call follow-ups, or include a 25 cent coin as a token of appreciation. While many researchers would feel uneasy (myself included) about sending money to try to encourage a positive response, because some potential respondents would be insulted by the gesture, it would, nonetheless, probably be effective in increasing the response rate. It has been shown, for example, that the use of incentives as small as ten cents will increase the response rate: in one study of top corporate executives,

40 percent of those receiving no incentive responded, 54 percent of those receiving 10 cents responded, while among those who received a 25 cent piece, 63 percent returned their questionnaires (Erdos, 1983, p. 97). Would you have guessed this result if you knew that the value of the token sent was all that differentiated the various surveys and that the respondents were among the highest-paid executives in North America?

Assuming that the questionnaire looks professional, and that the appropriate cover letter is prepared, the following tips are suggested as methods for increasing the likelihood of response to a mailed questionnaire:

TIP 1

The envelope should identify the sponsoring organization's name. By identifying the sponsor, an effort is made to increase the perceived legitimacy of the project.

TIP 2

The name should be typed, or even hand written, using the full name, rather than initials.

TIP 3

The mailing should be sent by first class mail, and should also use stamps rather than metered postage. The idea is to make the package seem as personal as possible. Avoid the mass produced look; do not use mailing labels.

TIP 4

Enclosed with the original material should be a stamped envelope for the return of the completed questionnaire.

TIP 5

If the questionnaires are to have identification codes placed on them, place them on the top right hand corner of the first page, and indicate in the accompanying letter that the number is there to assist in following up on those respondents who have not returned the questionnaire. Do not use secret codes.

TIP 6

If an incentive is being used, use new currency, enclosed in a plastic envelope.

TIP 7

You can follow up by sending a post card, thanking respondents if they have returned the questionnaire, and reminding them that returning the form would be much appreciated if this has not already been done.

TIP 8

A second follow-up, including a copy of the questionnaire, may be sent three weeks after the original has been mailed.

TIP 9

A third follow-up after six or seven weeks, using either registered mail or a phone call, is worthwhile and increases the response rate. Most researchers do not go beyond the third follow-up.

Generally, returns will be quicker at first and then slow down. After one week expect to get about 30 percent of those questionnaires that will be returned, and about 85 percent within two weeks. By the end of four weeks about 96 percent of those questionnaires that will be returned should have arrived (Erdos, 1983, p. 263).

5. PANEL STUDIES

Panel studies monitor specific organizations or individuals over time. Perhaps it is easiest to think of panel studies as a survey of a particular group supplemented by at least one follow-up interview.

Why would one choose to do a panel study rather than an experiment or a survey? The answer is that experimentation is frequently not possible, or judged not to be relevant, for the examination of some relationships. Surveys, on the other hand, might not provide a sufficient basis for making causal inferences.

Suppose, for example, that one was interested in studying the impact of working for large companies rather than small companies. In this case, the researcher needs to establish what the individuals are like at Time 1; next, the researcher will need to monitor changes that these individuals undergo over time. These are complex issues that require the individuals being compared to be roughly similar at the beginning of the study and also that the two groups compared over time be exposed to different types of employers. A carefully designed panel study such as the one described above provides a naturalistic experiment and may lead to a better understanding of the impact of the workplace on workers (Clairmont and Jackson, 1980).

A. ON KEEPING TRACK OF RESPONDENTS IN A PANEL STUDY

On occasion, respondents will be contacted at different points in time. When the time between contacts is a year or two, and the population being studied is fairly mobile, special problems are posed for the researcher. With an initial sample of 538,

Clairmont and Jackson (1980) were able to locate and interview 96.0 percent of respondents in the second wave of interviews, some two years after the initial interview. The following tips, based on the success of the follow-up, may be helpful in tracking down respondents:

TIP 1

At the time of the first interview, request that the name of a relative or friend who will always know how to get in touch with the respondent be provided. These names prove invaluable later in efforts to contact individuals.

TIP 2

Try the original phone number; even though the respondent has moved, the same phone number may have been maintained. If the phone has been disconnected, the operator may be able to provide the new number.

TIP 3

Phone directories for the original year and for the current one are helpful; check how the person was listed in the original directory. If the person is still in the area, the chances are that the name will be listed identically.

TIP 4

Contact the employer of the respondent. Also contact fellow workers in an effort to locate the individual.

TIP 5

Contact neighbours. Especially in smaller cities and towns, neighbours can be helpful in tracing respondents.

6. PHONE SURVEYS

Like all surveys, the ***phone survey*** relies on information reported by the respondent and is therefore vulnerable to image management. Questions and response categories must be kept simple since they are presented verbally. In-depth probes are difficult and, as with other surveys, it is always difficult to make causal inferences. The interviewer's expectations may inadvertently influence the responses that are recorded into the computer. Today most phone interviews employ computers to present the questions and to provide the response categories into which respondents' answers are to be fitted. Care must be taken, therefore, in monitoring response variations between interviewers.

Phone surveys are gaining in popularity. They are widely used by polling organizations, and academic and applied researchers, and represent a technique of data collection that will almost certainly increase in years to come. Phone surveys are a relatively cheap and quick way to collect data. Since there is no travel time, phone interviewers can do many more interviews in a day than would be possible if the interviewer had to travel to each respondent's home. Moreover, according to Sudman (1967, pp. 58-67), phone interviewing can provide cost-effective access to people with whom it is very difficult to arrange interviews (such as physicians), or those that

are not concentrated in one area (such as the blind). In national studies, Robert M. Groves and Robert L. Kahn have estimated that phone surveys cost about 45 percent as much as personal interviews (1979). Recently, there has been some troubling news regarding the willingness of people to participate in telephone interviews. In 1993, some 7 out of 10 respondents in the Toronto area were refusing to cooperate in pre-election polls. If these levels of non-participation become widespread it will be more difficult to justify using the phone for collecting such information. (Sheppard, 1993; Fisher, 1993).

But there are disadvantages to phone surveys. First, they are not the best means of gathering data if probing is required, or if complex response categories are to be presented. Second, the distribution of phones is uneven. The less well-off and the mobile are less likely to have a phone, or a phone listed. However, as phones become more universally available, there is less need to avoid phone surveys on principle so long as the researcher recognizes the possibility of sample distortions. Indeed, it is possible to weight samples to adjust for underrepresented categories in a survey. Respondents interviewed over the phone are slightly less at ease than respondents being interviewed in person. As a result, phone interviews will generally produce slightly higher refusal rates on sensitive issues, such as income or political preference (Groves, 1979, p. 98).

Phone interviews also have some special problems related to assessing response rates. It is not always easy to determine how many numbers called are connected to "live" phones; there will be a fair number (generally about 20 percent) of phones attached to businesses. Furthermore, phone interviews have lower completion rates than questionnaires: typically, the completion rate will not exceed 70 percent (Groves, 1979, p. 75). Studies based on rural populations generally have greater success in phone-book-based surveys since lower levels of mobility mean that fewer phones will be disconnected.

In conducting a phone survey, one will either be working with a list of potential respondents (such as a list of voters, members of a group or association, or from the names listed in the phone book). In such cases, one would usually proceed by using a systematic sampling procedure (see Chapter 14 for this sampling method).

It is also possible to create a sample by identifying the various residential phone exchanges in the area, and then using a table of random numbers to determine the numbers to be called. Typically phone numbers are assigned in five-digit blocks, the first three determining the exchange. The numbers might start 863-21xx. A table of random numbers may be used to determine the last two digits to be used. If it is possible to get the information from the phone company, one attempts to find out the percentage of phones in each block and then a sample is drawn to represent each block proportionally (Abrahamson, 1983, pp. 225-26).

Computer-assisted telephone interviewing is an important tool for polling organizations and market researchers. The computer dials a sample of respondents and then guides the interviewer through the data collection by presenting the questions on the screen and, depending on the response, it proceeds to show the next appropriate question. The answers are then recorded into the machine.

RULE 4.17

BEGIN WITH INTERESTING, SALIENT, AND YET SIMPLE QUESTIONS.

This is a tough rule to follow, but attempt to begin a phone interview with questions that are simple to answer, non-threatening, and that will be considered important. Since phone respondents are a little more likely than those interviewed in person to terminate the interview, it is especially important to ease them into the discussion. While phone interviews can last up to half an hour, they should be kept as short and as simple as possible.

RULE 4.18

SUPPLY PHONE INTERVIEWERS WITH RULES FOR DETERMINING WHO IS TO BE INTERVIEWED.

Procedures must be provided for determining who within the household contacted is to be interviewed. It is not acceptable to interview the person who happens to answer the phone. If this were done, the survey would overrepresent those who are most likely to answer the phone. The interviewer should not be making convenient decisions. Table 4.3 presents such a sample form.

RULE 4.19

MONITOR QUALITY.

A *quality control monitoring system* must be in place to ensure that interviewers are following established procedures for selecting respondents, asking questions, and entering the data. In particular, some interviewers find it difficult to resist the temptation to interview the person who answers the phone, or someone who is immediately available. Callbacks are the bane of the interviewer's life.

TABLE 4.3   CHOOSING PHONE RESPONDENT

#	PHONE #	LIST PEOPLE IN HOUSEHOLD[1]	SKIP[2]	INTER-VIEW NAMES[3]	NAME/ TIME[4]	DONE[5]	NAME/ TIME	DONE	NAME/ TIME	DONE
1										
2										
3										
4										
5										
6										
7										
8										
9										

[1]Get initials of members of household over the age of 19 who normally reside in the household, from oldest to youngest.

[2]Start with person X from this household; if skip interval is 3, do one, skip two, and do one. Carry over skip from interview to interview.

[3]Write down name of persons to be interviewed.

[4]Write down name of first person, and time interview to be done.

[5]Check when interview completed.

RULE 4.20

SIMPLIFY RESPONSE CATEGORIES.

Phone interviews must keep the response categories simple. While it is possible to conduct lengthy interviews by telephone, keep the questions simple, and if necessary, break complex questions into smaller simpler ones (Sudman & Bradburn, 1983). Respondents are slightly more likely to select a neutral response category and there is also a tendency to choose the last response category presented: hence researchers frequently vary the order of the response categories.

Phone interviews are relatively cheap and can be used to generate a representative sample. However, the representativeness of the sample has to be monitored carefully because phones are not evenly distributed among the population and, as mentioned earlier, there is a growing disinclination to agree to be interviewed over the phone.

7. INTERVIEWS

The final data collection procedure which we will consider is the interview. Generally there are two kinds of interviews:

(i) the structured interview which is a questionnaire that is read to the respondent; and

(ii) the interview schedule which outlines the areas that are to be probed by the interviewer.

A. STRUCTURED INTERVIEW

Structured interviews involve face-to-face interviews where questions are read to the respondents. Such interviews ordinarily will provide for in-depth probes on some of the questions. Interviews also allow the respondents to ask questions to help clarify any ambiguities. Basically, structured interviews are made up of set questionnaire items: the interviewer is expected to read the questions, exactly as worded.

B. INTERVIEW SCHEDULE

Interview schedules outline the major questions that are to be raised. The interviewer has greater autonomy in exploring questions in detail. Interviews require much skill on the part of the interviewer and care must be taken not to "lead" the respondent. Furthermore, the responses are filtered through the interviewer and therefore, if there are a number of interviewers, one must realize that some of the variations in response will be due to differences between interviewers and not solely to differences between the respondents. Interview schedules are used for in-depth interviews in field studies (see Chapter 5).

Since interviews are expensive, they are normally done when not too many are required and when in-depth information is needed. One major advantage is that good rapport is often built up between interviewers and respondents so that if repeated interviews are required, as in a panel study, it will be possible to maintain high response rates. A second major advantage of inter-views is that they permit the respondents to clarify any questions that they have about the interview. One of the disadvantages is that interview studies are expensive (more than double the cost of phone interviews) and time consuming (Groves, 1979, p. 211).

While it is beyond the scope of this book to discuss the selection and training of interviewers, some brief comments will be made on this subject. Research done by NORC (National Opinion Research Center) indicates that the quality of work done by interviewers is related to length of time spent working for NORC, high grade averages in high school, liking two or more science subjects, intelligence, and the completion of college. In addition, those who scored high on "need achievement" and manipulativeness (Machiavellianism scale) are more likely to do good interviewing. Of note is that happiness, financial need, religious behaviour, perfectionism, and size of home community were not found to be related to the quality of interviewing that a person does (Sudman, 1967, pp. 100-53).

Interviewers need to be trained. They will need to gain knowledge about ethical issues, the survey being conducted, appropriate dress, how to introduce themselves to the respondent, gaining rapport, organizing the interview setting, how to present questions, how to react to responses, which issues to probe, how to probe them, how to keep the respondent on topic, and how to end the interview gracefully. In addition to some of the above issues, research directors will need to provide potential interviewers with experience in a few simulated interviews (Weinberg, 1971).

Interviewers are frequently paid on a "per interview" basis. This method is often preferred since this allows the researcher to control costs. Also it seems to be the case that many interviewers will "burn out" after six or eight weeks. Interviewing is an especially challenging task, requiring great concentration, and it is not easy to remain alert after having walked many respondents through the interview. Expect high turnover among interviewing staff.

RULE 4.21

DO NOT INFORM INTERVIEWERS OF HYPOTHESES.

Generally, it is not advisable to inform interviewers fully about the hypotheses of the study: interviewer expectancy bias (see Chapter 9) may be reduced if the hypotheses are not known.

C. CONCLUSION

Surveys are the major tool in studies attempting to represent large populations. They often attempt to deal simultaneously with many variables and attempt to describe the complexity of human behaviour. Surveys also permit the researcher to construct new variables by combining a number of characteristics—status integration or status crystallization would be an example of such constructed variables. Despite the many advantages of survey research, it is difficult to make clear causal inferences from such data. Most of these difficulties derive from the nature of the data. Survey data are normally based on self-reports and frequently involve data based on recollection. While it is probably not difficult to recall factual information (such as reporting the community you were born in, or the salary of your first full-time job) it may be very difficult to recall how well you got along with your mother when you were six years old. Another fundamental issue has to do with the connection between words (what people say they will do) and deeds (what they actually do). There are therefore doubts about the extent to which surveys reflect ideal behaviour as opposed to real behaviour. To what extent, then, can we claim to reflect reality with survey data?

Table 4.4 summarizes the advantages and disadvantages of the first two approaches to research design that we have considered so far: the experiment and the survey. Causal inferences are clearest when experimental and, to a lesser degree, panel data are used. Generalizing about larger populations is the forte of survey designs.

While neither surveys nor experiments rate high on validity, this does not mean that they are, by nature, invalid. The negative sign simply means that this is a problem area in these designs. It is difficult to demonstrate that respondents have not altered their behaviour or their answers on a questionnaire in response to the fact that they know they are being studied. Both experimentalists and survey researchers take the problem of validity seriously and try to minimize distortions. The negative sign for group-administered questionnaires in the generalization column is there because such groups are typically selected in the most convenient way. Probability procedures have therefore not been followed in the way that would be necessary if one wished to make extrapolations to the general population. (See Chapter 14 for details on sampling.)

Whatever research design is selected, it is important to understand the strengths and weaknesses of each of the approaches.

TABLE 4.4 ADVANTAGES AND DISADVANTAGES OF ALTERNATE DESIGNS

DATA COLLECTION TECHNIQUE	GENERAL	VALIDITY	CAUSAL INFERENCE	MULTI-VARIATE	PROBING
A EXPERIMENTAL STUDIES					
Experimental	–	–	+	–	–
Quasi-Experimental	+/–	–	+	–	–
B SURVEY STUDIES					
Individual Questionnaire	+	–	–	+	–
Group-Administered	–	–	–	+	–
Mailed Questionnaire	+	–	–	+	–
Panel Study	+	–	+	+	–
Phone Survey	+	–	–	+	–
Interview	+	=	=	+	+

In each category a **+** means that this is an advantage of the technique; a **–** means this is a disadvantage or problem.

• *General* refers to the extent to which extrapolations to larger populations may be made using each of the data collection procedures.

• *Validity* is a measure of the extent to which indicators clearly measure what they are intended to measure.

• *Causal Inference* refers to the ease with which inferences about causal relations among variables may be made.

• *Multi-Variate* refers to the ease with which information on many variables is collected, leading to the possibility of multi-variate analysis.

•*Probing* refers to the extent to which responses may be probed in depth.

Such knowledge helps the researcher select an appropriate design and to try to deal with the weak points of each design. Where a decision has been made to use a survey design, Chapters 12, 13, and 14 contain information of particular relevance to the survey researcher (measurement, questionnaire construction, and sampling methods).

D. KEY TERMS

Interview schedule

Panel study

Phone survey

Point-in-time data

Population

Quality control monitoring system

Questionnaire

Response rate

Salience of topic

Sample

Structured interview

Survey

E. KEY POINTS

Survey designs are important in public opinion polling, census taking, market, and in academic research.

The strength of survey designs is that they offer a way of *estimating characteristics of a population* by studying a sample of that population.

A survey, in contrast to an experiment, typically includes measures of *many variables* and includes *many cases*.

Surveys are often the only *practical* means of measuring variables such as background characteristics of respondents and various attitudes that they express.

Surveys attempt to ensure *standardization* by asking all respondents the identical questions.

The *response rate* (percent of people who receive a questionnaire, complete, and return it) is influenced by: the type of organization doing the research, the length of the questionnaire, the method of delivery, the mode of retrieval, the type and number of follow-up contacts, incentives, and the salience of the topic to the respondent.

The greater the *salience* of the research to the respondent (interest in the topic by the respondent), the greater the response rate.

The greater the *personal contact*, the greater the response rate.

Quality control procedures must be in place to ensure that the questionnaire is being administered properly.

F. EXERCISES

1. Suppose you wished to understand what factors influence the grade performance of university students. What kind of design would you recommend for such a study? Outline the rationale for your choice.

2. Suppose you wished to investigate four alternative explanations for the relationship between socioeconomic status and attitudes toward minorities. What kind of design would you recommend? Outline the rationale for your choice.

3. Suppose you are interested in exploring gender differences in attitudes concerning the conditions when violence is acceptable. What design would you recommend to explore such a question? Outline the rationale for your choice.

4. Suppose you wished to explore the frequency and the intensity with which female undergraduates have experienced unwanted intimacy in their lives. What variables would you wish to measure in such a study?

G. RECOMMENDED READINGS

DILLMAN, DON A. (1978). *Mail and Telephone Surveys*. New York: John Wiley & Sons. This book by Dillman provides a good discussion of the various challenges in doing mail and telephone surveys.

EASTHOPE, GARY (1974). *History of Social Research Methods*. London: Longman Group Limited. This short book contains a good review of the history of survey research. See especially pp. 48-86.

ERDOS, PAUL L. (1983). *Professional Mail Surveys*. Malabar, Florida: Robert E. Krieger Publishing Company. This book contains a good presentation of mail surveys with numerous practical suggestions.

WEINBERG, EVE (1971). *Community Surveys with Local Talent*. Chicago: National Opinion Research Centre. This publication provides a number of basic suggestions for conducting a community survey.

FIELD STUDIES

Some of the most admired studies in the social sciences are field studies. ***Field studies*** include those investigations where the researcher observes and records the behaviour of individuals or groups in their natural settings. Part of the appeal of such studies is that humans are being directly observed in everyday situations; because of this these studies are more convincing—they ring true to the reader. While most field studies are associated with qualitative research methodologies, quantitative field research, in the form of experiments and some observational studies, is done in unaltered social environments. For the purpose of discussion, field studies will be subdivided into:

- participant observation studies;

- in-depth interviews;

- field experiments, and

- covert observational studies.

A. PARTICIPANT OBSERVATION STUDIES

A ***participant observation study*** ordinarily involves an intensive examination of some culture, community, organization, or group. Normally, such a study is based on a careful and complete study of one case and involves having the researcher join the group for an extended period. For example, in studying a pre-literate society by living with the group, the anthropologist is trying to study its customs and beliefs from within. Since the researcher is living with the group and is involved in the daily lives

of its members, such studies are called participant observation studies. The researcher is a participant in the lives of the group's members, sharing their joys and pains. Such studies frequently take much time to complete. This is not surprising given the need to learn the native language and to absorb the intricacies of the culture.

Erving Goffman's study on mental institutions, *Asylums* (1962), William F. Whyte's analysis of a street gang, *Street Corner Society* (1955), and Becker, Geer, Hughes, and Strauss's *Boys in White* (1961) are classic participant observation studies in sociology. Elliot Liebow, a graduate student in anthropology who was interested in understanding the world of marginalized blacks in an urban setting, wrote *Talley's Corner* (1967). In psychology perhaps the best known participant observation study is Festinger, Riechen, and Schachter's *When Prophesy Fails* (1964), a study of a quasi-religious group which had predicted the end of the world. Classical anthropology led the way in developing participant observation techniques: the names of Bronislaw Malinowski, Margaret Mead, and Oscar Lewis come immediately to mind. Working in this qualitative tradition, researchers have studied everything from exotic cultures to prisons (Gresham M. Sykes, 1968), hobos (Nels Anderson, 1929), and the world of the punker (Baron, 1989). Box 5.1 presents some of Whyte's thoughts on studying an Italian community.

1. THE RATIONALE FOR PARTICIPANT OBSERVATION STUDIES

The methods of participant observation studies can best be understood by com-

BOX 5.1 SOCIAL RESEARCHERS AT WORK

William Foote Whyte: Reflections on Field Research

As I carried through the Cornerville study, I was also learning how to do field research. I learned from the mistakes I made. The most important of these I have described fully. I learned from the successes that I had, but these were less spectacular and more difficult to describe. It may therefore be worth while to try to summarize the main characteristics of the research.

Of course, I am not claiming that there is a one best way to do field research. The methods used should depend upon the nature of the field situation and of the research problem. I am simply trying to fit together the findings of the study and the methods required to arrive at such findings.

In the first place, the study took a long time. This was due in part to the fact that I had no previous field experience and very little educational background that was directly relevant to my problem. But that was not all. It took a long time because the parts of the study that interest me most depended upon an intimate familiarity with people and situations. Furthermore, I learned to understand a group only through observing how it changed *through time*.

This familiarity gave rise to the basic ideas in this book. I did not develop these ideas by any strictly logical process. They dawned on me out of what I was seeing, hearing, doing—and feeling. They grew out of an effort to organize a confusing welter of experience.

I had to balance familiarity with detachment, or else no insights would have come. There were fallow periods when I seemed to be just marking time. Whenever life flowed so smoothly that I was taking it for granted, I had to try to get outside of my participating self and struggle again to explain the things that seemed obvious.

This explains why my research plans underwent such drastic changes in the course of the study. I was on an exploration into unknown territory. Worse than unknown, indeed, because the then existing literature on slum districts was highly misleading. It would have been impossible to map out at the beginning the sort of study I eventually found myself doing.

This is not an argument against initial planning of research. If his study grows out of a body of soundly executed research, then the student can and should plan much more rigorously than I did. But, even so, I suspect that he will miss important data unless he is flexible enough to modify his plans as he goes along. The apparent "tangent" often turns out to be the main line of future research.

Street Corner Society is about particular people and situations and events. I wanted to write about Cornerville. I found that I could not write about Cornerville in general without discarding most of the data I had upon individuals and groups. It was a long time before I realized that I could explain

Cornerville better through telling the stories of those individuals and groups than I could in any other way.

Instead of studying the general characteristics of classes of people, I was looking at Doc, Chick, Tony Cataldo, George Ravello, and others. Instead of getting a cross-sectional picture of the community at a particular point in time, I was dealing with a time sequence of interpersonal events.

Although I could not cover all Cornerville, I was building up the structure and functioning of the community through intensive examination of some of its parts—*in action*. I was relating the parts together through observing events between groups and between group leaders and the members of the larger institutional structures (of politics and the rackets). I was seeking to build a sociology based upon observed interpersonal events. That, to me, is the chief methodological and theoretical meaning of *Street Corner Society.*

SOURCE: William Foote Whyte, *Street Corner Society.* Chicago: The University of Chicago Press, 1955 (pp. 356-358). Reprinted by permission of the publisher.

paring such studies with different research approaches. We have seen (Chapter 3) that the experiment examines causal relations among a limited range of variables, and that it typically identifies treatment effects of one or two variables on some dependent variable. Surveys (see Chapter 4) focus on measuring a large number of variables and exploring the statistical relations among them. In contrast, participation observation studies try to understand institutions, gangs, groups, and even whole cultures. These studies are holistic because they attempt to understand the whole group. Typically, researchers using this approach do not begin with a limited number of variables, like survey researchers or experimentalists, but instead immerse themselves in the everyday life of the people they are studying, attempting to provide accurate descriptions and explanations of their activities. The important characteristics of these activities emerge during the course of field observations. Surveys and experiments begin with specific variables and proceed to analyze them; participant observers begin with the rather more ambitious goal of understanding how a whole group functions.

The rationale of such studies is that only through sharing in the daily lives of a group, can the researcher fully understand the behaviour that is manifested. Researchers doing participant observation studies try to minimize the effect of preconceived ideas by trying to see the world from the point of view of the members of the group they are studying. By spending a good deal of time within the community, the researcher gains first-hand knowledge of social behaviour as it unfolds over time. The fundamental point is that the conclusions of a participant observation study should be grounded in the data—that is, based on direct and careful observations of everyday life within the group. Indeed, Glaser and Strauss have referred to such research as **grounded theory** (1967).

Participant observation studies try to capture both the subjective and the objective complexity of human behaviour—try to penetrate the inner life of the people being analyzed. The argument in favour of such studies is that it is not possible to appreciate the complexity of human behaviour fully by studying it using techniques modelled on those developed in the natural sciences. As Schutz argued:

The world of nature, as explored by the natural scientist, does not 'mean' anything to the molecules, atoms, and electrons therein. The observational field of the social scientist, however, namely the social reality, has a specific meaning and relevance structure for the human beings living, acting, and thinking therein. By a series of commonsense constructs they have pre-selected and pre-interpreted this world which they experience as the reality of their daily lives (Schutz, 1954, pp. 266-67).

To the extent that we wish to study commonsense understandings—the social construction of reality—then it is clear that we have to try to understand the world from the point of view of the humans involved in these constructions (see Berger & Luckman, 1966). To do experiments on the people involved or to conduct a survey of them may well fail to document adequately the social construction created by them. As Burgess argues:

Although social scientists have a range of approaches for studying the social world—experimental methods, statistical measures and survey research—none of these methods can fully encapsulate the subjective elements of social life. Accordingly, researchers have turned to

observation and participant observation in order to get access to the meanings which participants assign to social situations (1984, pp. 78-79).

Indeed, the traditional methodologies of the physical scientists would have to be altered if they took as their subject matter what molecules think of one another, or how they make unwritten agreements about the nature of appropriate inter-molecular interactions. Social scientists challenge themselves when they attempt to understand the subjective dimensions of human activity. Doing participant observation studies is one of the ways in which social scientists attempt to meet this challenge.

2. STEPS IN CONDUCTING A PARTICIPANT OBSERVATION STUDY

Each participant observation study will be different. Special problems will require adaptations. Below is a list of some of the steps that will be necessary in most such studies.

A. GAINING ENTRY INTO THE GROUP

Gaining entry is sometimes a simple matter; at other times it is more difficult. For starters, the type of group has to be taken into account: if the researcher wishes to enter a formal organization (hospital, religious group, prison, bureaucracy, business organization, school) the entry methods will differ from those used when attempting to study an informal organization (community response to a crisis, gay and lesbian bar, hobo community, street gang, pool hustler, or business lunches of young executives). But no matter what the researcher studies, entry should be viewed as an ongoing and reciprocal relationship between the researcher and the population being studied. The researcher has to negotiate a relationship with each person in the study population (see particularly Schatzman and Strauss, 1973, pp. 18-34).

In entering a formal organization, it is probably best to begin by finding out as much as possible about the organization. Who are the key actors; are there any critical issues currently facing the organization (strike threatened, market disappearing, raw materials becoming increasingly expensive); what are the best times of the week or month to approach the leadership of the organization?

Having determined that the intended study would be appropriate, informal contact should be established with those persons whose permission will be required to gain entry. This initial contact should then be followed by a brief written statement which outlines the goals and methods of the proposed study. The preparation of this document will assist the researcher in defining the problem more clearly (in participant observation studies the precise problems studied emerge through the research process and are not necessarily present from the beginning of the project). The letter outlining the project should:

- establish the legitimacy of the project: this may be achieved by using the stationery of the sponsoring organization, and mentioning the sponsors of the project;

- indicate the goals and methods of the study: this provides the leadership of the target organization with a simple statement that can be used to communicate the project to others in the organization;

- specify the length of time that researchers will be on site: this provides the organization's leaders with important information as to how long the researchers will be present;

- indicate the amount of time that will be spent interviewing various members of the organization;

- indicate the extent to which anonymity and confidentiality will be possible for various participants;

- indicate the form in which feedback on the project will be provided to the organization: this may take the form of informal verbal reports, seminars, or formal reports.

Research reports typically mask the location of the site and the names of participants. However, the researcher should assume that published reports circulate among those studied. When studying a group it is difficult to disguise the identity of some of the individuals behind the pseudonyms—especially those whose role is occupied by only one person. The writer of a report must bear in mind that damage may be done to the reputations of those being studied. One must be careful, therefore, in promising anonymity before starting a study, for it may not be possible to mask everyone's identity adequately in the final report.

In studying informal organizations, it is usually not necessary to get an official's permission to enter the group; one simply has to establish cordial relations with the people being studied. For example, to do observations among the homeless one would simply need to establish a solid working relation with them. To keep things simple, one would probably just say that a book (or an article) is being written about the lives of the homeless, that the researcher would be talking to the homeless in the area, and that the identities of individuals will not be revealed in the publication.

William Foote Whyte's, *Street Corner Society,* illustrates some of the difficulties in gaining entry. After two false starts to gain entry to the Italian community, Whyte finally found success through Doc, a member of the Norton Street Gang. (See Box 5.2.) It was not until Whyte got Doc's sponsorship that he was able to gain admission to the community. To people in the community, Whyte was Doc's friend; when pressed, however, the academic outsider to the community felt awkward about his explanation of what he was doing in the community.

Whyte's description of how he explained his presence to the people of Cornerville, reflects three important points for those planning a participant observation study. First, it is probably wise to keep one's explanations simple (in Whyte's case the locals developed their own explanation); second, it is usual for a social gap to

---

BOX 5.2 SOCIAL RESEARCHERS AT WORK

William Foote Whyte, Explaining Presence in Cornerville

As I began hanging about Cornerville, I found that I needed an explanation for myself and for my study. As long as I was with Doc and vouched for by him, no one asked me who I was or what I was doing. When I circulated in other groups or even among the Nortons without him, it was obvious that they were curious about me.

I began with a rather elaborate explanation. I was studying the social history of Cornerville—but I had a new angle. Instead of working from the past to the present, I was seeking to get a thorough knowledge of present conditions and then work from present to past. I was quite pleased with this explanation at the time, but nobody else seemed to care for it. I gave the explanation on only two occasions, and each time, when I finished, there was an awkward silence. No one, myself included, knew what to say.

While this explanation had at least the virtue of covering everything that I might eventually want to do in the district, it was apparently too involved to mean anything to Cornerville people.

I soon found that people were developing their own explanation about me: I was writing a book about Cornerville. This might seem entirely too vague an explanation, and yet it sufficed...

SOURCE: William Foote Whyte, *Street Corner Society.* Chicago: The University of Chicago Press, 1955, p. 300. Reprinted by permission of the publisher.

exist between the researcher and the subjects being studied. (In *Street Corner Society* we have a Harvard graduate student studying a youth corner gang in an Italian community.) And while Whyte was not much older than the members of the corner gang, it is clear that, despite changes in his language and dress, he would always remain somewhat apart from the gang. Third, the importance of having local "sponsors" is illustrated in the crucial role that Doc and the Martini family played in legitimizing Whyte's presence in the community.

Although most participant observers are open about their studies, sometimes **covert entry** is used to become part of a group. While arguments have been advanced (see discussion of ethics in Chapter 10) that all research should be done openly, with the knowledge and consent of those being studied, there are times when this is not feasible. Festinger, Reiken, and Schachter, for example, wished to study a group predicting the end of the world (*When Prophecy Fails,* 1956). However, since the group initially avoided publicity, observers joined the group covertly to conduct the study.

The following are some of the advantages of covert entry:

- entry is gained in circumstances where it might have been denied;

- those being observed are less likely to alter their behaviour to please a researcher (as in overt entry studies), hence increasing the validity of the observations;

- if the people studied think they are dealing with a regular member of the group, they may be more open in sharing their thoughts and feelings than they would with someone known to be a researcher.

The following are among the disadvantages of covert entry:

- ethical reservations about doing research on individuals without having their consent. Indeed as research continues, and the observer develops a rapport with the group, considerable guilt may arise on the part of the researcher because of the deception involved;

- the researcher must play the role of a regular member and therefore may not have the freedom or time to roam about, ask questions, and collect data;

- by becoming more intimately involved it may be more difficult for the researcher to remain objective (Lofland, 1971, p. 94);

- the researcher has to find a way of leaving the group gracefully.

Where entry has been made without deception, the observer has the advantage of being able to ask questions, move about, and explore issues to a greater degree than might be appropriate in everyday social relations. Moreover, the observer need not expend effort to disguise the fact that research is being carried out.

The role of the observer is a marginal one: the researcher is in the group but not really part of it. There is always distance; the researcher is in the group temporarily, the regular participants are there longer, often for life. The commitment of the researcher in the eyes of the group is therefore suspect.

There are times when gaining entry is extremely difficult, taking weeks or even months to accomplish. In the case of anthropologist Gerald Berreman, who was studying a Himalayan village, it took four months to begin to have some success in overcoming the fear locals had of outsiders. Berreman provides an interesting account of the problems of gaining entry in an article published in an edited volume by Warwick and Osherson (1973).

B. RAPPORT

One challenge that the participant observation researcher faces is to develop good relationships with the people being studied. Maintaining these relationships is sometimes strained because the subjects may wish to "capture" the researcher to their points of view (Lofland, 1971). The researcher must be careful to not become overly attached to one faction since this would make it more difficult to get information from members of other factions. The researcher may also be blamed for difficulties that the group encounters. Furthermore, the researcher's objectivity may be strained if an unequal amount of time is spent with each side.

C. FIELD NOTES

Field notes attempt to capture, with as much accuracy as possible, descriptions and interpretations of individuals, interactions, and events. The exact time and location of observations should be recorded, along with other descriptions to help the researcher recall the events (weather conditions, other significant events going on in the community or in the world that day). Emphasis should be placed on reflecting exactly what people say, how they say it, and describing the reactions of others to what is said. As a practical suggestion, Anselm Strauss *et al.* (1964, p. 29) used the following method to distinguish types of quotations:

- Words recalled verbatim enclosed within "…"

- Where there is less certainty about the exact wording '…'

- Where meaning is clear but wording not exact: no quotation marks.

Field notes should also distinguish clearly between descriptions of events and people and interpretations of them. A suggestion for doing this is to organize field notes so that there is a wide column for descriptions and a narrow column for interpretations. Note, too, that there are two kinds of interpretations:

(i) the subjects' own interpretations of their behaviour and the behaviour of others, and

(ii) the interpretation that the observer places on these same activities.

The emphasis, particularly in the initial stages of research, should be on descriptive accuracy. Field research is a dynamic process where ideas develop, are refined, and are then tested and modified throughout the observational period. The writing of theoretical memos is encouraged to help the observer develop explanations systematically. These tentative interpretations emerge and are tested during the observational period. Indeed, participant observers do well to carry out both observations and theoretical reflection about these observations concurrently (Corbin and Strauss, 1990, pp. 6-10).

In order to make sense of field experiences, the researcher interprets the data continuously. For example, if the observer sees a person explaining something to another person, this may be thought to indicate the dominance of the person doing the explaining. Such dominance may be reflected in a variety of ways, and all of these may be thought to reflect dominance/submission behaviours. Grounded theories, Corbin and Strauss argue, are built out of conceptualizations of behaviour, not out of the actual incidents themselves; observations are generalized, and behaviours are interpreted as reflections of concepts (Corbin, 1990, p. 7).

In deciding what situations, or persons, are to be observed, Corbin and Strauss suggest that researchers should sample according to concepts and their properties, and not by trying to locate representative individuals. They argue that in grounded theory "representativeness of concepts, not of persons, is crucial" (1990, p. 9). Thus, if you want to study pool hustlers, you would go to where pool hustlers hang out and watch how they operate. Once at the pool hall, the observer would note events that occur, and begin classifying them according to some general principles. What techniques are used to initiate a game with a mark? How is the bet determined? How is the handicap negotiated? ("I'll play one-handed, make all the balls in the number 4 pocket...ten bucks a game, loser pays the table charge.") Perhaps the researcher would then try to observe some of the most highly skilled players, some of moderate skill, and some of the poorer players to note differences in how they operate. And since hustlers often hustle other hustlers, the technique of negotiating the bet is a crucial and complex process.

Field notes should be made as soon after field observations as possible, preferably the same day. At the very latest, notes should be made the morning after an evening's observations. Expect to spend as much time writing up field notes as you

spent in the field. Three hours of observation will usually be followed by three hours of writing up the observations. The use of a lap-top computer is most helpful in compiling field notes. It is also possible to tape field interviews and then have these interviews transcribed. Some researchers even prefer to dictate their observations and then have them transcribed. Field notes will tend to be lengthy. In the case of *When Prophecy Fails* field notes, combined with transcriptions of recorded information, came to well over 1,000 typewritten pages (Festinger, 1956, p. 251); *Boys in White* produced about 5,000 single-spaced typewritten pages of field notes and interview material (Becker, 1961, p. 30). When writing the report, the challenge will be to condense the field notes into a coherent document of reasonable length.

D. ANALYZING THE OBSERVATIONS

While it is recommended that field notes be entered on a computer, this may not always be feasible. Let us begin the discussion of data analysis by assuming that you are working with a typewritten field journal. A copy of the *master field file* should be placed in a binder and retained. The **master field file** is made up of the complete journal of the field notes. The first step in analysing the data will be to make several additional copies of the master field file. The copies are used as raw material for building up *analytic files*. **Analytic files** are files relating to a specific topic or relationship explored in the study. For example, you might wish to build up a subfile on interactions between status unequals. You would cut out all the field notes pertaining to such interactions. Frequently these will be ordered along some dimension (in this case perhaps along the degree of status difference between the two persons interacting). Each piece cut from the copy of the master file should have its original (master copy) page number on it. Various analytic files are made up in this way. There may also be files related to the methodology of the study and the history of the institution or area being studied. It may well be the case that not every part of the master file will make it into any of the subfiles which are created. The files typically will include:

- *Master Field File.* This is the original complete file of the field notes. Pages are numbered, and each entry is dated. This represents the raw data to be anaylzed.

- *Background, History File.* This subfile contains information drawn from the master field file as well as from other sources.

- *Analytic Files.* These files each deal with a particular type of observation or relationship (for example, descriptions of interactions between status unequals, interactions across gender lines, interactions of strangers).

- *Key Character Files.* Individual files may be established on key players in the organization or group being observed. These files attempt to reflect the personality, mannerisms, and typical behaviour of central characters.

If field notes are entered into a computer it will be possible to use special software packages to process the information. Currently a number of such packages are available. For an excellent review and description of some of these, the reader is referred to special issues of *Qualitative Sociology* on computers and qualitative data

(Vol. 14, Nos. 3 & 4, 1991). Keep an eye on this journal for updates on software packages of particular interest to the qualitative researcher.

If a word processor is used, it is possible to do much work simply by entering code words into the word processor's search capability to locate where instances of these code words appear. The paragraphs associated with the words may then be selected and moved to a separate file. Of course in doing this it is crucial to maintain a master copy of the original field notes. And, as always with computer files, be certain to have multiple printed copies and disk copies of the master file. Some word processors also have the ability to number paragraphs and lines; this facility is helpful in keeping track of one's records.

E. QUANTITATIVE ANALYSIS OF FIELD DATA

In addition to qualitative analysis of field data, there will be occasions when some quantitative analysis is appropriate. Where the analysis involves few variables and not too many cases, a quantitative analysis can be done by hand. Chapter 15 provides suggestions for how to proceed without the use of a computer and tips for how the data set should be prepared if computer processing is anticipated.

F. WRITING THE REPORT

The challenge in preparing a manuscript is to condense the field notes into a report that is readable and that increases the reader's understanding of the subject of the study. Suggestions for writing final reports are presented in Chapter 18.

B. IN-DEPTH INTERVIEWS

In-depth interviews are often used along with participant observations and provide a method of collecting respondents' perceptions of their world. In-depth interviews typically identify areas to be covered, but do not use standardized questions. Stephen Cole, in describing a study by Lee Rainwater, notes that:

> *The combination of in-depth interviews and field observation used by Rainwater and his research staff yields a detailed description of lower-class black subculture that would be difficult if not impossible to learn from quantitative research. In a quantitative survey the respondents would probably give answers that reflected their ideal values of family life rather than their real values and behaviour. (Cole, 1976, p. 207)*

Typically, in-depth interviews record people's descriptions and explanations of events in their world. These are then used to communicate this world to the social science reader. Quotations are selected from the interviews to illustrate the points the author wishes to make.

In-depth interviews also tend to be done by a senior member of a project. Because sensitive information is sought, the format must be flexible and the interviewer needs to be free to pursue leads suggested by the respondent. Typically such interviewing is done by highly experienced researchers.

In-depth interviews of people of high status are also used frequently. Here it is thought that people of high status (leaders of minority groups, churches, unions, and educational institutions and also individuals such as corporate executives, politicians, and doctors) would not respond well to a situation where a questionnaire is read to them (as in the case of a structured interview). Therefore a more open-ended strategy is adopted. Here the interviewer makes the interview more conversational, following up in detail on interesting points that the respondent makes.

Box 5.3 features the family section of Rose Weitz's study of how AIDS patients dealt with the stigma of their disease. Weitz conducted semistructured interviews with the 23 PWAs (Persons With AIDS) in the Arizona study. Multiple interviews were made, ranging in time from two to five hours (Weitz, 1990, p. 26). While Weitz began with a set list of questions, she probed into unexpected topics that seemed to warrant additional attention. Weitz expanded the topics covered in subsequent interviews to deal with new themes that were emerging in the research, as a researcher using grounded theory would have done. Note that the report of her study uses a series of illustrations drawn from her interviews, trying to summarize the experiences of the 23 men in her study population.

High-quality journalism and studies based on in-depth interviews are quite similar. While the social scientists typically are more concerned with how representative their respondents are of some social category, they share with the journalist a concern for accurate description. A report written by a journalist and one by a social scientist on the plight of the homeless, for example, might not be that different. However, one would expect that the social scientist would display greater care in arriving at conclusions and would spend much more time in exploring the theoretical and methodological issues in such a study.

BOX 5.3   SOCIAL RESEARCHERS AT WORK

Rose Weitz: Living with the Stigma of AIDS

All PWAs [Persons With AIDS] run a risk that their families will reject them, either because of their illness *per se* or because their illness exposes or emphasizes that they are gay or use drugs. One of the men I spoke with was a 27 year old computer operator whose parents lived in a small town in another state. He felt he had a good relationship with his parents, but had never told them of his sexual orientation. When asked how he thought his family would react to news of his diagnosis, he said:

> *You just can't predict. They might find it so disgusting that you'll basically lose them. They'll be gone. Or they'll go through the adjustment period and not mind. You really don't know.*

Virtually every respondent reported that at least one family member had ceased contact with him after learning of his illness. One source of this rejection is that diagnosis with AIDS can reinforce families' belief that homosexuality is immoral. Families who had always questioned the morality of homosexuality may interpret an individual's illness as divine punishment, regarding it as proof that homosexual behaviour should not be tolerated. For example, a 26 year old tailor from a fundamentalist Christian family, whose relatives had not known he was gay, described how AIDS forced him to reveal his sexual orientation and thus "put a wedge" between him and his family. His family considered homosexuality sinful and questioned whether they

should help him with his health problems if he would not change his behaviours. He was still in contact with his parents, even though his mother had told him that his homosexuality was an "embarrassment" to her. But he had stopped talking to his sister because he could not abide her constant admonitions "to repent" and "to confess sin." Even PWAs whose families have in the past appeared to accept their lifestyles may find that their families reject them once their diagnosis becomes known. When questioned about this, the PWAs suggested that somehow AIDS had made their homosexuality more real and salient to their families. Just as pregnancy forces parents to recognize that their daughters are not just living with men but having sex, diagnosis with AIDS apparently forces families to recognize that their sons or brothers are not simply gay in some abstract way, but actually engage or engaged in homosexual activities. As a result, families who have tolerated their relatives' homosexuality despite deep reservations about its morality find that they can no longer do so. A 38 year old business manager reported that when he first told his parents he was gay "their reaction while it wasn't initially effusive at least it was grudgingly accepting." Now, however, he felt that his parents had "used this whole AIDS thing against me" by telling him that AIDS was "just desserts for the homosexual community." Similarly, a 29 year old blue collar worker recounted how his mother, who previously had seemed to tolerate his lifestyle, responded to news of his diagnosis by telling him "I think your lifestyle is vulgar. I have never understood it, I've never accepted it…Your lifestyle repulses me." She subsequently refused to let him in her house or help him obtain medical insurance.

Even when families do not overtly reject ill relatives, their behaviour may still create a sense of stigma. This can happen when families either hide news of their relatives' illnesses from others altogether or tell others that their relatives have some less stigmatized disease. A 39 year old floral designer, whose Catholic family had all known he was gay before he became ill, reported that his mother refused to tell his brothers and sisters that he had AIDS, and ordered him not to tell them as well. When his siblings finally were told, they in turn would not tell their spouses. Such behaviour forces PWAs to recognize that, as one fundamentalist Christian said, "it was an embarrassment to [the family]…that I was gay and…that I have AIDS." This imposed secrecy places heavy burdens on individuals who subsequently must "live a lie."

Families may reinforce a sense of stigma by adopting extreme and medically unwarranted anti-contagion measures. One family brought their own sheets when visiting their ill son's home. Others refused to allow PWAs to touch any food, share their bathrooms, or come closer than an arm's length away. A 29 year old Mormon salesperson, whose family believed he deserved AIDS as punishment for his sins, reported that

initially his family "wouldn't come in the room unless they had gloves and a mask and they wouldn't touch me…[And] for a time I couldn't go over to somebody's house for dinner. And they still use paper plates [when I eat there]." Even PWAs who feel such precautions are necessary still miss the experience of physical warmth and intimacy. They report feeling stigmatized, isolated, and contaminated.

Although PWAs fear that their families will reject them once their illness becomes known, they also hope that news of their illness will bring their families closer together. A 38 year old store manager who had never had a particularly close relationship with his family described his fantasy "that something like this—an experience where you come this close to death or the reality of death—is when you realize what's really important and not who's right and who's wrong."

For the lucky ones, this fantasy materializes. The oldest man I interviewed, a 57 year old lawyer, had always considered his father a cold and selfish man, and had never been on good terms with him. This situation changed, at least partially, when he became ill. As he described it:

> We've gotten closer… There's the verbal "I love you," there's the letters. One of the nicest things that's ever happened to me…is my father sent me a personal card. In the inside he wrote "God bless you. I love you son"…It meant the world to me.

Another man described how, despite their disapproval of his lifestyle, his fundamentalist Christian family had provided him with housing, money, and emotional support once they learned of his illness. As he described it, in his family, when "little brother needed help...that took priority over all the other bullshit. They were right there."

Diagnosis can also bring families together by ending previous sources of conflict. Whether to preserve their own health, protect others from infection, or because they simply lose interest in sex once diagnosed with a deadly, sexually transmitted disease, PWAs may cease all sexual activity. For health reasons, PWAs may also stop smoking and drinking. As a result, families that previously had disapproved of PWAs' lifestyles may stop considering them "sick" or "sinful," even if the PWAs continue to consider themselves gay. Consequently, some PWAs achieve a new acceptance from relatives who attach less stigma to AIDS than to their former behaviours.

SOURCE: Rose Weitz, "Living with the Stigma of AIDS" *Qualitative Sociology*, Vol 13, No. 1 (1990), pp. 26-29. Reprinted by permission of the publisher.

C. FIELD EXPERIMENTS

There are some studies, *field experiments,* where the researcher intervenes in a natural setting and which, in contrast to most participant observation studies, can be simple and quickly completed. Suppose, for example, that a researcher greets a stranger while walking along a street and then records the type of response (if any) that results. In this case, the researcher is intervening in a natural environment and is interested in recording the response to a mild form of non-conformity (greeting a stranger). The kinds of observations that can be made in such studies are quite limited. However, as in most observational studies, fairly accurate measures may be recorded concerning the subject's age, sex, dress, and type of response. But the key point is that the observation is being made in a natural environment.

In Chapter 3 we pointed out that laboratory experiments attempt to maintain as much control as possible over the treatment variable(s) and over the conditions under which the experiment takes place. In field experiments, the researcher cannot exercise as much control. But what is given up in control may be compensated for by the fact that the subjects are probably not aware that they are part of an experiment and hence react normally. Both field and laboratory experiments attempt to understand the relationship between some treatment variable and some measurable outcome, exercising as much control over conditions as possible. A researcher conducting a field experiment simply takes conditions and events as they occur naturally, intervenes in some way, and observes the response to the intervention.

Box 5.4 features an early example of a social science field experiment in Canada. Sydney Wax reported on a study measuring the extent of anti-semitism in Canada. The study was conducted in 1948. It is of note both for its simplicity and for its striking findings.

BOX 5.4 SOCIAL RESEARCHERS AT WORK.

Sydney Wax: Anti-Semitism in Canada

In 1948 two Toronto newspapers carried about 100 resort advertisements. To each of the resorts Sydney Wax wrote two letters, mailed them within one day of each other, and asked for accommodations for the same date. One letter was signed "Mr. Greenberg," the other "Mr. Lockwood." The following table reports the results:

Nearly all the resorts welcomed "Mr. Lockwood" as a guest; over one-third failed to give "Mr. Greenberg" the courtesy of a response, and only 37.1 percent were prepared to have him as a guest. None of the resorts knew either of the fictitious gentlemen. For all they knew "Mr. Greenberg" might have been a quiet, orderly gentleman while "Mr. Lockwood" might have been be a rowdy drunk. The decision was made solely on supposed membership in an ethnic group.

Sydney Wax concluded his survey by noting:

This survey has shown that restrictive practices by summer resorts in *Ontario is a widespread occurrence. The statement that about 30% of the resorts discriminate appears to be borne out by actual investigation. The phrasing "RESTRICTED CLIENTELE" and others of a similar nature have been shown to limit the accommodation at summer resorts to certain racial types. The terminology used constitutes a violation of the Ontario Racial Discrimination Act. Subtle though the form may be, the discrimination is quite marked (1948:13).*

Wax perhaps was too quick to agree that 30 percent of the resorts discriminate. If we take the number offering accommodations to "Mr. Lockwood" minus the number offering accommodations to "Mr. Greenberg" as a measure of discrimination, we find that the difference is 57 (93 − 36 = 57). This calculation suggests that the percentage of resorts discriminating against the Jewish client is 58.8 percent ((57 ÷ 97) × 100).

Number of Ontario Resorts Responding, and Offering Accommodations, 1948

RESORT RESPONSE	MR. LOCKWOOD		MR. GREENBERG	
	N	%	N	%
No Reply	2	2.1	35	36.1
Reply	95	98.0	62	63.9
Total	97	100.1	97	100.0
Offering Accommodations	93	95.9	36	37.1

SOURCE: Sydney Lawrence Wax, "A Survey of Restrictive Advertising and Discrimination by Summer Resorts in the Province of Ontario," *Information and Comment*, Canadian Jewish Congress, 1948, 7, pp. 10-13.

Investigations of proxemics also illustrate field experiments. **Proxemics** refers to the norms surrounding personal space and the conditions under which such space will or will not be violated. For example, a researcher might position two confederates (people working with the researcher) facing one another, apparently discussing some issue, in a narrow corridor. Perhaps an 18" space is left behind the wall and the back of one of the confederates; the other confederate stands against the opposite wall. As people pass through the corridor, an observer will record information about the subjects: perhaps their age, sex, whether they are alone or with others, and whether they cut through between the confederates or squeeze through the 18" space. If the subjects cut through, do they acknowledge this by saying "excuse me" or bowing their heads slightly as a non-verbal apology? Following a number of observations of this sort, the distance between the confederates could be increased or decreased. As a control, the confederates could be replaced by large ash cans separated by the same distance as the experimenter's confederates (Cheyn, 1972). The above example illustrates a field experiment: an environment is set up under controlled conditions, and systematic observations are made of the people who pass through the space.

Field experiments can involve the violation of personal space. A student research group at St. Francis Xavier University did the following two studies. In the first, a confederate (a person who, unknown to the person under observation, is cooperating with the observers) sits right next to an opposite-sex student working in the library when many other spaces are available. This process is repeated a number of times. The responses of the target students vary, but many erect a barrier with books to mark off territory; only rarely do the "subjects" flee. In a related study, a female research student invades a group of male students, unknown to the female, who are standing in a public area chatting between classes. Once again, this intrusion is repeated with a number of all-male groups. Typically these violations produce a moment of silence: the males would look at one another in bewilderment, and then they would turn and flee! So far, no group of male students has volunteered to see if the same phenomenon occurs with female target groups.

The major advantage of the above studies is that behaviour undistorted by the artificiality of laboratory experiments is observed in natural settings. Such studies can be relatively inexpensive to do and, since conditions can be altered systematically by the researcher, some control can be maintained over the experimental conditions.

One of the disadvantages of these studies is that only a limited number of variables can be measured; the samples used are usually not representative and one cannot, therefore, generalize the findings.

The reader is asked to recall the field study conducted by Henry and Ginzberg (1990). In their study (featured in Box 3.1), the researchers examined racial discrimination in employment in Toronto. Their research is an excellent example of a quasi-experimental field study. Another well-known example of a field experiment is the series of such experiments done by Jane Allyn Piliavin and Irving M. Piliavin (1972). In this study, students faked various medical problems in a number of public locations and observed the conditions under which bystanders would assist the apparently stricken victim. In one of the studies, which compared trials when the victim was bloodied with trials when the victim did not bleed, the research had to be suspended when it was discovered that bystanders could create a major disruption by pulling an emergency cord on the subway car to alert others of the medical problem. Incidentally, Piliavin & Piliavin found that bystanders were more reluctant to assist someone who had blood coming from his mouth.

D. COVERT OBSERVATIONAL STUDIES

A *covert observational study* may be defined as a study where the people being studied are unaware that they are being observed. The goal is to observe and to record behaviour which occurs in natural settings. Unlike field experiments, covert observational studies do not attempt to alter the social environment in any way. The researcher observes and records behaviour which occurs in natural settings. Like field experiments, covert observational studies have high levels of validity (measuring what they claim to measure). However, with both field experiments and covert observational studies, sampling is almost always haphazard (based simply on who happens to walk by), making it problematic to generalize experimental findings to people other than those actually observed. Nonetheless, covert observational studies can reveal much about human behaviour.

Returning to the area of proxemics, a covert observational study could possibly observe pairs of individuals in conversation (standing position), and note the average toe-to-toe distance that they maintain over a 30-second observational period. The researcher would use a recording form to note information such as the type of interacting pair (male/male, male/female, female/female) and age and status differences (teacher/student, parent/child, employer/employee, peer/peer) between the two interactants. Studies such as the one suggested involve few variables and it is, therefore, possible to analyze them without the help of a computer—a decided advantage for those who do not have access to a computer.

Many daily activities can be observed and recorded without making subjects aware that their behaviour is being monitored. A few examples of this kind of study would include studies of:

- seat belt use

- jaywalking

- not stopping for stop signs

- car driver yielding to pedestrians in cross walks

- types of liquor purchased

- holding of a door for others

- smoking behaviour in public places

- distances between interacting pairs

- likelihood of obeying a superstition

- removal of dirty dishes to clean-up area in cafeteria

- elevator behaviour

In all of the above studies one would begin by defining the conditions under which the subjects would be observed. A review of the literature is necessary to determine if other researchers have reported on similar studies. Can the particular behaviour being observed be linked to some general category of behaviour? For example, can we view the failure to use a seat belt as an instance of a minor form of deviance? If the study were to be done, the variables would be carefully defined and cut-off points for the various categories would be determined. For example, if the age of the subject were to be estimated, the age categories might reflect those estimated to be:

(i)   under 25;

(ii) between 26 and 39; and,

(iii) over 40.

The observer would develop a **tally sheet** to record the observations (see Figure 5.1). After the necessary number of observations have been recorded, the information would be transferred from the tally sheets to a *master table* (see Figure 5.2). A **master table** records all the information so that all of the required tables can be derived from it without going back to the tally sheets. Appropriate tables are then constructed to show the relationships between each of the independent variables and the dependent variable.

1. STEPS IN CONDUCTING A COVERT OBSERVATIONAL STUDY: SEAT BELT USE

Suppose for example that you were doing the "use of seat belt" study, and that you wished to relate belt use to the independent variables of the driver's gender, the driver's age, and whether the driver is alone or with others. Let us go through the steps that would be involved in such a study, examining in greater detail how each step would be carried out.

STEP 1
RESTRICTIONS ON OBSERVATIONS.

Since this study concerns the use or non-use of seat belts, we would need to restrict observations to those cases where we can detect whether the driver and/or passengers in a passing vehicle are wearing seat belts. The first restriction, then, would be to limit the observations to recent models of automobiles, since trucks or older cars might be using lap belts which could not be seen as a vehicle passes by. Second, we would do the observations in a place where vehicles are moving fairly slowly so that the observer would have time both to see and record the information. Finally, a decision would have to be made as to whether observations will be limited to the driver (this will be easiest) or include other front seat passengers as well.

STEP 2
REVIEW OF LITERATURE.

At this point, a review should be undertaken of the literature to find out what studies, if any, have been done on seat belt use; furthermore if the failure to use a seat belt is viewed as a form of deviance, the literature on deviance could be reviewed to see what variables are related to deviance. For example, a researcher could check the literature to see if young males show higher levels of deviance for this minor infraction. If use of the seat belt is viewed as a form of conformity, a review could be done on the conformity literature to see what other researchers have found.

STEP 3

DEVELOPING HYPOTHESES.

At this stage, the researcher attempts to make predictions about expected outcomes. Such hypotheses may be derived from:
- common sense,
- what other researchers have found, or
- by relating the specific behaviour (seat belt use) to its general class (deviance) and then making predictions.

The following three hypotheses might be appropriate to the seat belt study:
(i) female drivers are more likely to use seat belts than male drivers;
(ii) older drivers are more likely to use seat belts than younger drivers; and,
(iii) drivers with others in the car would be more likely to use seat belts than drivers alone in the car.

By formulating hypotheses prior to collecting data one ensures that one is not inventing the hypotheses after the analysis has been done.

STEP 4

DEFINING TERMS.

Prior to collecting the data, a careful definition of each of the variables is required. Seat belt use (or non-use) refers to the apparent use (or non-use) of a shoulder seat belt by the driver (or others if they are included in the study). The observer also records the gender and age (in categories such as under 25, 25 to 49, 50 years of age and over) of the driver. The category "alone or with others" is added to classify those drivers who are alone and those drivers accompanied by one or more people.

STEP 5

DEVELOP A TALLY SHEET.

A tally sheet should be developed to record the observations. Generally the first variable listed is the dependent variable (wearing or not wearing a seat belt), followed by the independent variables, gender, age, and alone/with others. The sheet might look like the one listed in Figure 5.1. The tally sheet should be designed so that the observer can quickly tick off the categories the individual driver falls into. A check mark is easier than writing the estimated age or writing "female" for a female driver. If conditions or time of day are to be recorded, one can place a bracket around a set of observations done during a rainy, cloudy day, or a bracket around those done during rush hour traffic.

STEP 6

TRANSFERRING DATA TO THE MASTER TABLE.

Once observations have been completed, the tally sheet data are transferred to the master table. Typically, the dependent variable is arranged on the left side of the master table using the categories "wearing belt" and "not wearing belt." Categories of the independent variables are arranged across the top of the master table. In this case we have three independent variables: gender, age, and group size. Each observation ends up in one—and only one—cell of the master table. Thus a female driver under 25, who is alone in the car, and who does not appear to have her seat belt fastened, would end up in one cell only. Normally each observation is entered into the cell with a short line indicating one observation; these observations are grouped together

FIGURE 5.1 TALLY SHEET FOR RECORDING OBSERVATIONS

ID#	SEAT BELT		GENDER		AGE			GROUP STATUS	
	YES	NO	MALE	FEMALE	16-25	26-39	40+	ALONE	GROUP
1	✔		✔		✔			✔	
2	✔			✔	✔			✔	
3		✔		✔	✔				✔
4	✔		✔			✔			✔
5	✔			✔	✔				✔
6	✔			✔			✔	✔	
7		✔	✔				✔		
8		✔	✔			✔		✔	
9	✔			✔		✔		✔	
10	✔		✔			✔			✔
11	✔		✔			✔			✔
12	✔			✔		✔		✔	
13	✔			✔	✔				✔
14	✔			✔			✔	✔	
15	✔		✔			✔		✔	
16		✔		✔		✔		✔	
17	✔		✔		✔				✔
18		✔		✔	✔			✔	
19		✔	✔				✔		✔
20	✔		✔		✔				✔
21	✔			✔			✔		✔
22	✔			✔		✔		✔	
23		✔		✔		✔		✔	
24	✔		✔		✔			✔	

so that the fifth line entered into a cell has a line across the other four. Each group then reflects five observations falling into the cell. Later these can be counted and a total for each cell entered and circled at the bottom of the cell. Table 5.1 shows how the table could be designed.

STEP 7

CREATING THE INDIVIDUAL TABLES.

At minimum three tables would be created, each showing the relation between the use/non-use of the seat belt and gender, age,

TABLE 5.1   MASTER TABLE FOR SEAT BELT STUDY

	MALE						FEMALE					
	ALONE			GROUP			ALONE			GROUP		
Age/Belt use	Y	M	O	Y	M	O	Y	M	O	Y	M	O
Wearing belt												
Not wearing belt												

Age categories: Y = 16 – 25   M = 26 – 39   O = 40 +

and group size. Tables 5.2, 5.3, and 5.4 show the format of three of the tables. Note that the dependent variable is arranged on the left side of the page, and that the categories of the independent variable are arranged across the top of the page. Note also that the percentages are calculated on each of the columns. Details for the construction of such tables are presented in Chapter 15. More complex tables containing control variables may also be created from the master table. However, before constructing such tables, the student should examine the material in Chapter 16.

TABLE 5.2   SEAT BELT USE BY GENDER

	GENDER					
	MALE		FEMALE		TOTAL	
SEAT BELT USE	N	%	N	%	N	%
Using seat belt	244	75.8	138	79.8	282	77.7
Not using seat belt	46	24.2	35	20.2	81	22.3
Totals	190	100.0	173	100.0	363	100.0

TABLE 5.3   SEAT BELT USE WHEN DRIVER IS ALONE OR WITH OTHERS

	DRIVER ALONE OR WITH OTHERS					
	ALONE		GROUP		TOTAL	
SEAT BELT USE	N	%	N	%	N	%
Using seat belt	121	76.1	161	78.9	282	77.7
Not using seat belt	38	23.9	43	21.1	81	22.3
Totals	159	100.0	204	100.0	363	100.0

TABLE 5.4	SEAT BELT USE BY AGE							
	AGE CATEGORY							
	16-25		26-39		40+		TOTAL	
SEAT BELT USE	N	%	N	%	N	%	N	%
Using seat belt	87	71.3	110	78.6	85	84.2	282	77.7
Not using belt	35	28.7	30	21.4	16	15.8	81	22.3
Totals	122	100.0	140	100.0	101	100.0	363	100.0

STEP 8

WRITING A REPORT.

The final step would be to write a report on the research efforts. Chapter 18 presents additional information on report writing.

E. CONCLUSIONS

Table 5.5 summarizes the strengths and weaknesses of field study approaches. Overall, these studies are weak in clarifying causal inferences and in providing samples representative enough for the findings of a study to be generalizable; they are strong in the area of validity and, in the case of participant observation and in-depth interviews, in the ability to probe deeply into the behaviour being examined.

1. STRENGTHS

The advantages of participant observation studies are numerous. Such studies, for example, usually attempt to understand the total social system involved in the case. And since the observations are made over time, social processes can be observed (how friendships are formed and dissolved, for example). The relationships between individuals and between parts of the social system are of concern to the researcher. Emphasis is placed on obtaining careful, in-depth descriptions which can help to develop hypotheses worth testing with other research strategies. Furthermore, since observations are made of actual, real-life activities, there is increased validity in the measures: the researcher does not rely on artificial settings (as in the experiment) or on respondents' ability to report their behaviour (as in surveys) but, instead, records actual behaviour. The researcher may also probe deeply into a whole culture in order to come to a full understanding of how its various parts fit together. For the anthropologist, the major contribution of such studies is not just their ability to enable us to understand the world from the natives' point of view, but also their ability to describe a culture that may quickly be disappearing. Such descriptions are of historic significance since, if they are not made now, the phenomena described may be lost forever.

Participant observation studies can be done quite cheaply (one observer with a pencil and lots of paper and time) or be on the expensive side, with several paid observers, a secretarial transcription ser-

TABLE 5.5 ADVANTAGES AND DISADVANTAGES OF ALTERNATE DESIGNS

DATA COLLECTION TECHNIQUE	GENERAL	VALIDITY	CAUSAL INFERENCE	MULTI-VARIATE	PROBING
A EXPERIMENTAL STUDIES					
Experimental	–	–	+	–	–
Quasi-experimental	+/–	–	+	–	–
B SURVEY STUDIES					
Individual questionnaire	+	–	–	+	–
Group-administered	–	–	–	+	–
Mailed questionnaire	+	+	+	+	–
Panel study	+	–	+	+	–
Phone survey	+	–	–	+	–
Interview	+	–	–	+	+
C FIELD STUDIES					
Participant observation	–	+	–	–	+
In-depth interviews	–	+	–	+	+
Field experiments	–	+	+	–	–
Covert observation study	–	+	–	–	–

In each category a + means that this is an advantage of the technique; a – means this is a disadvantage or problem.

• *General* refers to the extent to which extrapolations to larger populations may be made using each of the data collection procedures.

• *Validity* is a measure of the extent to which indicators clearly measure what they are intended to measure.

• *Causal Inference* refers to the ease with which inferences about causal relations among variables may be made.

• *Multi-Variate* refers to the ease with which information on many variables is collected, leading to the possibility of multi-variate analysis.

• *Probing* refers to the extent to which responses may be probed in depth.

vice, a crew of coders, statisticians, editorial advisers, recording devices and computers being placed in the field for extended periods and at considerable cost. Most often, however, participant observation studies are of the cheaper variety. And although direct costs may not be that great, keep in mind that William Foote Whyte spent three and a half years living in Cornerville.

Field experiments facilitate making causal inferences, are strong on validity, and are often fairly inexpensive to complete. Covert observational studies, like field experiments, are inexpensive and have high validity since actual behaviour is being observed in a natural setting. In such studies, subjects are not even aware that they are being observed. In-depth interviews have the advantage of flexibility, as the interviewer can probe deeply into areas that seem to be particularly relevant.

2. WEAKNESSES

One of the weaknesses of participant observation studies is their inability to tell whether the patterns that emerge are representative or peculiar to the institution being studied. Nonetheless, such studies can provide important insights into how institutions work. An additional problem is that such studies are impossible to replicate, as any participant observation study involves examining a unique combination of individuals interacting with one institution at a particular time. While it would be possible for another observer to go into the same institution at a later time, a number of conditions probably will have changed. Moreover, the observers themselves may have rather different impacts on the organization. Thus, there are many factors which would confound an interpretation of any changes observed by different researchers. Making verifiable causal inferences is difficult, since only one case is being examined.

While they are usually time consuming, participant observation studies nonetheless have an important role in answering many research questions. Many examples of such research may be found in the social science literature.

In covert observational studies, the subjects are observed unobtrusively and are not aware that they are part of a study. A notable disadvantage of such studies is the limit on what can be observed. Since subjects are not asked questions, the variables observed are limited to gender, age, and other characteristics that are manifested during the time of observation. For example, a study that is examining the impact of group size on smoking would not know whether it is group size, or the fact that an observed subject is a non-smoker, that has inhibited smoking.

3. OVERVIEW

It is in the area of validity that field studies shine. For, by observing behaviour in natural settings, the researcher can have greater confidence that what is being observed is not influenced artificially by the respondents' knowledge that they are part of an experiment or by the image-management that may occur in studies based on questionnaires (Webb, Campbell, Schwartz, and Sechrest, 1966). And while there are problematic issues related to the researcher's interpretation of the behaviour being observed (perhaps simplifying assumptions that the same behaviour means the same thing to various actors or that the same person would react the same way the next time a similar situation arises are incorrect), there is little question that observing spontaneous social behaviour in everyday situations can provide convincing evidence that has not been manipulated by the researcher.

Researchers doing participant observation studies who emphasize a more qualitative approach to understanding behaviour should have their work judged by criteria different from those used to evaluate the studies of quantitative, positivist researchers. Many social scientists doing qualitative research try to understand the subjective meanings an action has for the person performing it; such research emphasizes how an individual interprets situations. Thus both the questions asked and the methodology used are different for qualitative and quantitative researchers. The validity of quantitative researchers' studies is determined by their ability to produce a description of, say, an individual's behaviour that rings true to the individual concerned. For the quantitative researcher, on the other hand, the issue may simply be whether or not a relationship is "statistically significant" (meaning that the covariation of variables is at a level unlikely to have been produced by chance factors: see Chapter 8 for more on this topic).

As this chapter illustrates, a range of qualitative and quantitative methodologies can be used in field studies. What distinguishes these approaches methodologically is their reliance on observations of people going about their everyday activities, thus minimizing the influence of the researcher on the behaviours that are being observed. Nonetheless, it must be recognized that it is the researcher who interprets the behaviours being observed. It is probable that any two observers will come to rather different conclusions. Furthermore, the researcher, particularly in participant observation studies, cannot avoid having an influence on how the group being observed works.

F. KEY TERMS

Analytic files

Covert entry

Covert observational study

Field experiment

Field notes

Field study

Grounded theory

In-depth interviews

Master field file

Master table

Participant observation study

Proxemics

Tally sheet

G. KEY POINTS

Some of the *most admired studies* in the social sciences are field studies: these include participant observation studies, in-depth interview studies, field experiments, and covert observational studies.

Participant observation studies typically require the researcher to gain entry into some group or institution, and involve recording the detailed interactions of members of the target group.

Participant observation studies typically examine *whole social systems* and are particularly sensitive to studying the processes of social change.

Field notes attempt to capture the essence of the group being studied: included are descriptions of events and people as well as the interpretations of the researcher and the participants of these events and people.

Because they are based on direct observations of everyday activities, participant observation studies have *high validity* when done carefully.

Chapter 5 • Field Studies **153**

Natural setting experiments can be done when every-day situations can be manipulated in such a way as to allow the researcher to observe the reactions of people to the intervention.

Covert observational studies are those where the researcher records observations without the subjects being aware that they are being observed, and where there is no experimental manipulation on the part of the researcher.

H. EXERCISES

1. As an exercise in taking field notes, two students might be asked to attend a meeting of a political party, religious group, or special interest group: working independently, the students are asked to record field notes on the same event. The field notes are put into a final draft in which descriptions and interpretations of events are carefully distinguished. The two versions are compared. What are the main points of difference between the two versions? What principles are illustrated by the exercise? Do most of the differences between the versions concern points of interpretation? How can the reliability of the observations be improved?

2. Try to think of some activity in your home community that you would like to investigate using participant observation techniques. Develop a proposal indicating what group or activity you wish to observe, what kinds of questions you think it might be interesting to pursue, and how you would propose to record the information gathered.

3. Try to come up with an idea for a field experiment or quasi-experiment. Outline what the variables would be and how they would be measured and recorded. Develop a linkage to a theory of human behaviour for your project.

4. Develop a covert observational project in which you attempt to do one of the following: find out who plays video gambling machines, who rents horror movies, or who buys lottery tickets in your home town. For your project indicate:

(i) what restrictions would be necessary;

(ii) what hypotheses could be investigated;

(iii) who would be observed and under what conditions;

(iv) what your tally sheet would look like; and

(v) how you would design two of your final results tables.

I. RECOMMENDED READINGS

BARON, STEPHEN W. (1989). "The Canadian West Coast Punk Subculture: A Field Study," *Canadian Journal of Sociology*, 14(3), 289-316. Based on observations done in Victoria, B.C., Baron's study illustrates a contemporary look at one aspect of pop culture.

BECKER, HOWARD S., BLANCHE GEER, EVERETT C. HUGHES, AND ANSELM L. STRAUSS (1961). *Boys in White*. Chicago: The University of Chicago Press. One of the classics: a painstaking analysis of the life of medical students and of their socialization into the role of doctor.

BECKER, HOWARD S. (1953). "Becoming a Marihuana User," *American Journal of Sociology*, (November), 224-235. A short study by one of the major figures in participant observations studies.

BERGER, PETER L., AND THOMAS LUCKMAN (1966). *The Social Construction of Reality*. Garden

City, New York: Doubleday. This short volume is one of the classics in qualitative social science.

BURGESS, ROBERT G. (1984). *In the Field: An Introduction to Field Research*. London: George Allen & Unwin. An excellent review of field research problems and methods.

CORBIN, JULIET, AND ANSELM STRAUSS (1990). "Grounded Theory Research: Procedures, Canons, and Evaluative Criteria," *Qualitative Sociology*, 13(1), 3-21. A recent article attempting to codify more precisely the grounded theory approach. A case is made for the use of different criteria in evaluating grounded theory studies.

FESTINGER, LEON, H.W. RIECKEN, AND S. SCHACHTER (1956). *When Prophecy Fails*. New York: Harper & Row. One of the classics, this book is rich in detailing the painstaking efforts that went into covertly recording a group as its doomsday prophesy came and passed.

GOFFMAN, ERVING (1961). *Asylums*, Garden City, N.Y.: Doubleday & Company. This is Goffman's classic study of a total institution. A fine illustration of qualitative research.

LIEBOW, ELLIOT M. (1967). *Tally's Corner: A Study of Negro Streetcorner Men*. Boston: Little, Brown and Company. This is a revision of Liebow's interesting doctoral dissertation; the methodological appendix is helpful.

LOFLAND, JOHN (1971). *Analysing Social Settings*. Belmont: Wadsworth Publishing Company, Inc. A short, readable guide to doing field research.

MINER, HORACE (1939). *St. Denis, A French-Canadian Parish*, Chicago: University of Chicago Press. A Canadian study using historical and participant observation techniques.

SCHATZMAN, LEONARD, AND ANSELEM L. STRAUSS (1971). *Field Research*. Englewood Cliffs: Prentice Hall Inc. A short guide to field research.

WHYTE, WILLIAM F. (1955). *Street Corner Society: The Structure of an Italian Slum*. Second Edition. Chicago: The University of Chicago Press. Probably the most-cited participant observation study.

WEITZ, ROSE (1990). "Living with the Stigma of AIDS." *Qualitative Sociology*, 13(1), 23-38. A study based on in-depth interviews with persons with AIDS. A good illustration of how to report interview material.

NON-REACTIVE STUDIES

A. AN INTRODUCTION TO NON-REACTIVE STUDIES

While experiments, surveys, and participant observation studies elicit responses from subjects, ***non-reactive studies*** involve indirect data collection. In such studies, there is no opportunity for the person being studied to react to the observations. Studies of this kind account for a large amount of the work done by social scientists. Indeed, any project contains a non-reactive element in its review of previous literature. Illustrations of non-reactive studies would include:

- the political scientist studying the relation between the percentage of people who vote Liberal and the percentage of immigrants in each polling station;

- the economist examining trends in unemployment statistics;

- the sociologist analysing sexual stereotyping in primary school readers;

- the sports psychologist studying the relation between violence in hockey games (as measured by penalty minutes) and audience size (as reported in game summaries in local newspapers);

- the nursing researcher studying trends in the length of time for which children are hospitalized;

- the historian comparing American and Canadian culture;

- or the social science student employed by the city's traffic safety department to observe how many drivers yield to pedestrians in marked cross walk zones.

The ability of subjects to modify their answers or reactions because they know that they are being studied is a problem frequently encountered in experiments, surveys, and interviews. A major confounding factor in social research is eliminated in non-reactive studies because the observed persons or groups are not able to react to the measurement process—not able to manage their presentation-of-self.

This chapter will briefly describe various non-reactive studies, using illustrations from comparative studies, secondary data analyses, and content analyses.

B. COMPARATIVE STUDIES

Most research is comparative. So whether we are doing an experiment comparing Time 1 measures with Time 2 measures, or whether we are trying to figure out why high socio-economic background females plan non-traditional careers areas, we make comparisons. Comparative research is not really a special type of research with its own methodology; it is the research process itself. However, when we think of comparative research, we think of cross-cultural studies or of historical studies. Comparative researchers use the full range of standard techniques, including surveys, interviews, field studies, and experiments, but, in particular, they use published information.

Looking at the similarities and differences between cultures, or within the same culture over time, is the essence of ***comparative studies*** (Warwick & Osherson, 1973, p. 8). Such studies began with the Greeks (Herodotus, 495-424 B.C.) and have persisted to the present. They are an important approach to the study of human cultures. When the modern social sciences were emerging in the nineteenth century, comparative studies were a central concern of social research. Many scholars pursued comparative studies by pursuing an evolutionary model of societal development. Comte examined the stages societies pass through in their development (1851); Durkheim analyzed religion among the aboriginals of Australia (1912); Weber compared religious systems (1964); and Marx analyzed stages in societal development (1867).

During the early years of the twentieth century, after arguments were advanced that a **unilineal model**, a model where the same patterns of development are followed by all societies, was inappropriate, comparative studies shifted to intensive studies of exotic cultures by anthropologists such as Bronislaw Malinowski (1925), Ruth Benedict (see Mead, 1966), and Margaret Mead (1935). More recently, the work of George Murdock (1960) emphasized the importance of cross-cultural comparative research. His work, coupled with the ethnographic information on over 500 cultures included in the *Human Relations Area File* at Yale University, has encouraged cross-cultural comparative analyses.

There is, then, a long comparative tradition in social science research. And while these studies do not have a distinct methodology associated with them—they use historical material, surveys, secondary data, experiments, and field studies—what they have in common is that they attempt to make comparisons between cultures or within cultures over time. Political scientists, historians, anthropologists, economists, sociologists, and psychologists all have contributed to our knowledge through comparative analyses. The Lipset debate on the differences between Americans and Canadians will be used to illustrate the approach.

1. CANADIAN-AMERICAN DIFFERENCES: THE LIPSET DEBATE

Seymour Martin Lipset continues to investigate cultural differences between the U.S. and Canada (1964, 1970, 1986, 1990). In describing the origins of the differences between Canadians and Americans, Seymour Martin Lipset says in *Continental Divide*:

> *One was Whig and classically liberal…doctrines that emphasize distrust of the state, egalitarianism, and populism—reinforced by a voluntaristic and congregational religious tradition. The other was Tory and conservative in the British and European sense—accepting of the need for a strong state, for respect for authority, for deference—and endorsed by hierarchically organized religions that supported and were supported by the state. (Lipset, 1990, p. 2)*

In 1964 Lipset presented an initial analysis of Canadian/American cultural differences. He began by noting the similarities in industrialization, ecology, level of urbanization, political, economic, and work conditions, immigration histories, and political stability. Some of the differences noted were as follows:

CANADA	UNITED STATES
Elitist	Egalitarian
Respect for law	Less respect for law
Collectively oriented	Individualistic
Ascriptive	Achievement
Traditional/conservative	Less traditional
Not assertive	Assertive

SOURCE: S. M. Lipset, 1964.

Lipset traces the differences to Canada's closer ties with Britain and the Anglican church; by contrast, the United States had an anti-British revolution. He notes two revealing phrases: in Canada's *British North America Act* reference is made to "Peace, order, and good government," whereas in the *American Declaration of Independence* reference is made to "Life, liberty, and the pursuit of happiness." Lipset quite correctly observes that these two phrases say a lot about the differences between the U.S.A. and Canada.

Lipset's writing reflects a thorough knowledge of North American history: his major concepts are drawn from functionalism, and his measures are gleaned from a diversity of published sources, especially government documents. Lipset argues that elitism (concept) in Canada is reflected by much lower participation rates in higher education (measure). Using 1960 data, he points out that among Americans aged 20-

24, 30.2 percent were attending university while in Canada the comparable figure was 9.2 percent. He also points to the paternalistic family pattern in Canada, the greater reverence/respect paid to the clergy, the deference shown to the old and to teachers by the young, and respect for politicians in Canada compared to the U.S.A. (Lipset, 1964).

The greater respect for the law is reflected by the fact that in Canada there is a third fewer police per capita; while one police officer was killed per annum in Canada in 1961 and in 1962, 37 police officers were killed in the U.S.A. in 1961 and 55 in 1962. Lipset therefore argues that Canadians use informal controls to a greater degree in controlling behaviour. Greater respect for the law also leads to more freedom for dissent. (See Table 6.1.)

The U.S.A. is a litigatious society in which the ratio of lawyers to the general population is twice as high as Canada.

TABLE 6.1   CANADIAN/AMERICAN DIFFERENCES ACCORDING TO LIPSET 1964

	CANADA	U.S.A.	RATIO
Percent 20-24 in university	9.2	30.2	3 ×
Police per 10,000	143.2	193.8	1/3
Police killed by criminals, 1961	1	37	37:1
Police killed by criminals, 1962	1	55	55:1
# Population/Lawyer	1630	868	2 ×
Crime rates 1960: (per 100,000)			
Burglary	46.4	126.7	3 ×
Criminal homicide	1.2	7.3	6 ×
Forgery	6.4	23.2	3 ×
Fraud	13.5	38.8	3 ×
Theft/Larceny	87.2	218.1	2 ×
Divorce rates 1960 (per 1,000)	53.5	257.5	5 ×

SOURCE: S.M. Lipset, 1964.

Crime rates in the United States are two to three times higher than the Canadian rates. In the U.S.A. everyone must be treated according to the same standard. Newcomers are seen as joining a "melting pot" in which everyone has the same rights and opportunities. (Americans, the argument goes, stress equality of opportunity, not equality of result.) Canadians celebrate a mosaic—the idea that individuals and groups should maintain their distinct identities. For Lipset it is Canada's counter-revolutionary beginnings that led to the continued emphasis on British ascriptive and elitist value patterns (1964). Thus, for example, Lipset would predict that Canadians would be more likely than Americans to make promotions based on whom you know (ascription) rather than what you know (achievement).

A. IRVING LOUIS HOROWITZ

Irving L. Horowitz, an American sociologist, challenged Lipset's position, arguing that Lipset used old data rather than looking at more recent trends. Horowitz argues that the differences perhaps reflect a "cultural lag." That is, the trends in Canada are in the American direction, just lagging behind a little. In the area of divorce rates, for example, there has been a massive shift toward higher, American level figures. (Note especially the change after 1968 when the grounds for divorce were extended.) Horowitz points to the boom in post-secondary education in Canada, pointing out that Canada has a higher number of science Ph.D.'s per capita than the U.S.A. Crime rates are going up in Canada as well (Horowitz, 1973). Like Lipset, Horowitz relies on public statistics to establish his points.

B. CRAIG CRAWFORD AND JAMES CURTIS

Surveys reported by Crawford and Curtis (1979) compare the U.S.A. and Canada in 1969 and 1970. The communities studied were in Oregon and Ontario. The findings indicated that Canadians were less collectively oriented than Americans, and were also less traditional. Americans attached more importance to achievement (Lipset agreement) and were less elitist. One interesting part of the analysis shows that among older respondents (61 years plus), the findings tend to support Lipset's predictions. Among the younger age groups, the survey's findings on tradition and collectivist orientation suggested the opposite of Lipset's prediction (1979). In this case, then, we have scholars pursuing comparative questions using survey methodology. (See also Curtis, 1971; Curtis, Lambert, Brown, and Kay, 1989.)

C. STEPHEN ARNOLD AND DOUGLAS TIGERT

Arnold and Tigert (1974) reported on surveys done in the U.S.A. and Canada in 1968 and 1970. The picture is mixed. Some findings support Lipset's analysis, others do not. In summary, their findings show Americans to be:

- higher on five of seven questions on achievement beliefs, such as a belief in equality of opportunity for all people (supporting Lipset);

- higher on all items concerning orientations to the collectivity through voluntary community work (not supporting Lipset);

- less supportive of big government and government income guarantees; (supporting Lipset);

- more traditional in their beliefs on moral issues (not supporting Lipset);

- more self-confident (supporting Lipset).

Their findings indicate that Americans are more assertive, self-confident, and optimistic than are Canadians. Americans hold more traditional views on moral issues; Americans are more likely to join organizations.

D. DOUG BAER, EDWARD GRABB, AND WILLIAM A. JOHNSTON

Baer, Grabb, and Johnston (1990) critically reviewed Lipset's work and, in particular, challenged him on a number of methodological issues. They argued that:

- there were inconsistencies in Lipset's characterization of national value differences;

- apparent contradictions between Lipset's earlier accounts and his most recent formulations;

- that Lipset shifts levels of analysis, when, for example, "structural differences in the two societies or possible differences in the values of elites in both countries are assumed to correspond precisely to value differences between individual citizens in the two nations" (Baer et al., 1990, p. 394);

- Lipset relies at times "on a selective and inconsistent reading of the available evidence in which data that are supportive of the thesis are mentioned but other data that are not supportive of the thesis are either interpreted differently or else placed in a different context" (Baer, et al., 1990, p. 694).

Baer, Grabb, and Johnston then go on to test many of Lipset's key arguments em-

pirically. When they do so they find little support for many of the arguments. In particular, and in direct opposition to Lipset, they find Canadians are *less* traditional than Americans about the role of women in society and note that English Canadians are less respectful of government leaders than Americans. Overall, they find little support for Lipset's arguments when the data from national surveys are examined (Baer et al., 1990, p. 708). And so the debate rages on.

E. SEYMOUR MARTIN LIPSET (1990)

To provide an additional example of the flavour of Lipset's writing, here is his speculation as to how the U.S.A. would be more like Canada had the American Revolution not succeeded:

> ...the continuing British North American polity would now be more leftist than the revolution's children, more statist, much more social democratic, more disposed to perceive equality in redistributionist rather than meritocratic terms. It would operate under a parliamentary system, more conducive to third parties. It would be less individualistic and more deferential to authority. That hypothetical polity would also be less protective of civil liberties, free speech, and a free press than the actual populist republic, less inclined to place restrictions on the police, less generally inhibitive of the power of government" (1990, pp. 226-27).

The debate between Lipset and his critics has been going on for over 30 years and promises to continue. Independent of the merits of the case, what are some of the key challenges in doing comparative studies?

2. CHALLENGES IN COMPARATIVE RESEARCH

Comparative research has additional challenges because it deals with different cultures and often a different language. Warwick and Osherson (1973, pp. 11-40) identify issues concerning equivalence in concepts, indicators, language, and sampling.

A. THE EQUIVALENCE OF CONCEPTS

While ideas such as incest or health are cultural universals, there is no precise agreement about what is meant by these concepts. What is incest in one culture may be defined as a preferred marriage partner in another; what is considered normal, healthy behaviour in one culture may be labelled as bizarre in another. So while we may have similar concepts, their content and meaning may vary considerably from culture to culture. Moveover, even within a culture there may be subtle variations in how concepts are defined.

TIP 6.1

DEFINE CONCEPTS CAREFULLY AND FULLY.

In all research, but particularly in comparative research, it is important to define concepts carefully, noting any variations between the cultures being studied. The search for appropriate indicators is facilitated by attention to the definition of the concepts. Only if a researcher is satisfied that there is an *equivalence of concepts*, can direct comparisons between cultures be drawn.

B. THE EQUIVALENCE OF INDICATORS

The evidence collected in different countries is rarely based on the identical definitions and collection procedures. For example, if the definitions and collection procedures used to measure unemployment are different, do we dare use the information to compare two societies? What about crime rates: given different definitions, recording methods, and, indeed, the different interests of the parties involved in the data collection (would they benefit by showing an increasing crime rate?), can we legitimately make comparisons across jurisdictions? For virtually every indicator suggested, there are problems with a lack of equivalence in measures.

TIP 6.2

USE TREND MEASURES RATHER THAN ABSOLUTE MEASURES.

How might we go about limiting the effects of such disparities? One suggestion is that we use data trends rather than absolute measures (like the rate of crime, the unemployment rate etc.). For example, if you are comparing the United States and Canada in unemployment statistics, minimize the effects of alternate measures by simply using the change-in-unemployment over periods of time. Then, even if definitions vary between the countries, at least they are comparable across time spans within the country (unless, of course, definitions or procedures have changed within the country). Just as we standardize data within a country by calculating rates and ratios to deal with units of unequal size, when between-country data are required, consider computing trend data. And while such trend data would not provide the absolute measures desired, at least one should be able to detect whether the rates are converging or diverging.

Most critics would argue that Lipset's use of higher American crime rates as evidence for attaching a greater importance to achievement is dubious. Does the fact that we have fewer police mean we respect the law more, as suggested by Lipset? What else might it mean? (Could such information indicate, among other things, that Canadians have less money for policing, have a less urbanized population, have less fear of crime?)

C. EQUIVALENCE OF LANGUAGE

Box 6.1 presents an anecdote concerning language problems in a project. Several years ago my colleague Don Clairmont and I were doing a study in Moncton, New Brunswick. We were comparing people who worked for large companies and government agencies (Central Work World in our jargon) with a matched sample of

workers in smaller companies (Marginal Work World). Since Moncton has a bilingual community, we hired a translator to develop a French version of our interview schedule. We then employed a number of bilingual interviewers to conduct the interviews with some 600 residents in Moncton.

D. SAMPLING

Warwick and Osherson (1973) point out that researchers are often rigorous in the sampling procedures they use within a country, but much more opportunistic when it comes to sampling countries themselves. However, it is reasonable for the selection of countries to be driven by pragmatic considerations such as the availability of data. And since a project's cost is often a fundamental issue, there is an understandable tendency for comparative research to be done on those countries where the fewest problems will be encountered in getting the information required. Moreover, since comparative studies typi-

---

BOX 6.1   SOCIAL RESEARCHERS AT WORK

Don Clairmont and Winston Jackson In the Field

There was, alas, some difficulty with the French version of the schedule. Some of our respondents seemed to be having difficulty with it. On checking, we discovered that our translator had done a fine job of converting our simple English version into a Parisian French schedule. Not good. Not Moncton. Our resourceful interviewers, when they found a respondent was having difficulty understanding a question, translated it into English. The respondent would reply (usually in English) and our interviewers would then dutifully translate the answer back into French. Ah, the pleasures and problems of data collection.

SOURCE: Memories of the Moncton Project.

cally involve two or three countries, there would be little point in using some form of random sampling to select them; to do so would be an abdication of reason! To compare radically diverse countries would not lead to much understanding, especially if the available data were not comparable. A random sample of two may sound scientific but such a sample would be seriously lacking in other regards.

The development of the *Human Relations Area Files* has been most helpful in providing researchers with inexpensive access to a file on the world's cultures that contains an enormous amount of information. This file is available at most universities.

In choosing to base much of his research on Canada and the U.S.A., Lipset minimized some of the problems that he would encounter. Statistical information is readily available in both countries and, while little comparative research had been done on the two countries prior to his work, a good deal of effort has since been expended, particularly by Canadian scholars attempting to test some of Lipset's hypotheses. And, one could identify few countries which would have as much in common as the U.S.A. and Canada, even though available measures are not exactly comparable.

E. THE PROBLEM OF SELECTING EVIDENCE

While the problem of researchers choosing among alternate indicators is relevant to all types of research projects, this is especially the case in comparative studies. (This argument will be treated more fully in Chapter 9.) Given the vast amount of information available, what is the best way,

for example, to measure elitism? (Lipset used the percentage of youth participating in post-secondary education in the two countries as one of his indicators.) The problem is that it is possible to demonstrate almost anything if you are free to search around for possible indicators. And while Lipset might well argue that the preponderance of evidence supports his position, his critics might not be so ready to agree (see Baer et al., 1990; Curtis et al., 1989). The general point here is that the selection of evidence is an especially problematic issue in comparative research. Not only can we question whether the indicators reflect what they are intended to, but we can also question whether the same variable will have the same meaning in different cultural contexts.

It would be difficult for most social scientists to avoid selecting indicators that produce results conforming to the researcher's preferred outcomes, ruling out those indicators not selected as insufficient in some way. There is no easy solution to this problem. One check is simply that researchers be public about which indicators were used and perhaps even public about which indicators were rejected and why they were rejected. It would not be practical to ask researchers to explain all of their decisions, or to list all the alternatives considered. To do so would be akin to asking a chess player to explain all the alternatives considered before making a move. The chess player's information processing is highly complex and the player, in fact, probably could not provide much useful information about how the choice was made. The same would be true of the researcher. But if we are public about what choices have been made, then critics can re-examine the issue using the same or alternate indicators.

TIP 6.4

INDICATORS, LIKE HYPOTHESES, SHOULD BE IDENTIFIED PRIOR TO COMMENCEMENT OF DATA EXAMINATION.

Social scientists have not always paid sufficient attention to identifying precise indicators before beginning data analysis. Such precision is required because otherwise the researcher may inadvertently bias the outcome of the study. Moreover, the exact cut-points that are to be used in collapsing categories should also be identified prior to beginning analysis. (For example, where will the line between large and small communities be drawn when looking at the relation between deviance and community size?) Once again, if commitments are not made, the researcher may inadvertently select cut-points which result in an analysis showing what the researcher anticipated, or wanted.

Realistically, these two suggestions are unlikely to be applied routinely by social scientists. It is sometimes a challenge to get researchers to state hypotheses formally, never mind provide details of exact operational procedures. However, even getting them to pay "lip service" would be a start. At present, there is little awareness that there is a problem in this area. Issues raised in Chapter 8 (Tests of Significance) and in Chapter 9 (Bias) are also related to the issue of committing oneself to operational procedures and operational hypotheses.

C. SECONDARY DATA ANALYSIS

Economists, political scientists, historians, and, to a lesser degree, sociologists, anthropologists, and psychologists frequently conduct research based on available material. These sources might include virtually any data—ranging from published statistical, census, or business data to the unpublished diaries of important historical figures. With the exception of those who record oral histories, historians rely on secondary data sources and the resulting studies are based entirely on ***secondary data analysis***.

Content analysis, which will be covered in the next section, is but one form of this approach, and involves analyses of messages conveyed by media such as radio, television, and film, or analyses of various written materials such as plays, poetry, psychiatric interview notes, songs, novels, newspapers, or textbooks.

The major limitation of research based on secondary data is that the necessary information is often unavailable or incomplete. But, with imagination, excellent work can be done. Economists are impressively adept, for example, at locating "indicators" in available data. And, as such data are frequently reported at different points in time, the economist is able to build, and test, elaborate causal models. So, whether they are attempting to understand the linkage between interest rates and unemployment, or between housing starts and the wage level of plumbers, economists make efforts to understand the world by using secondary data.

Secondary data analysis is cost-effective and, providing the data are relatively complete, can lead to sound general statements about the social world. Along with survey research, however, it has problems with demonstrating the validity of its indicators. For example, when evaluating Lipset's use of the proportion of people between the ages of 20 and 24 enrolled in university to reflect the degree of elitism in the United States as opposed to Canada, we need to consider what else such a measure could indicate. Is it possible that it also reflects the degree of industrialization and urbanization in the two countries? If the measure reflects things other than those we intend it to, we do not have a perfectly valid measure—one which reflects the concept, nothing more and nothing less. In this section we will illustrate three different data sources all used to investigate a social science issue.

1. DENNIS FORCESE AND JOHN DE VRIES: OCCUPATIONAL AND ELECTORAL SUCCESS

In the Forcese and De Vries study, the authors were able to record occupational information on candidates, including party affiliation, constituency, and region. All of this information was made available through the office of the chief electoral officer. While the number of variables that could be studied was limited to those made available by the electoral officer, it was possible to detect some important patterns determining who gets nominated as a candidate and who, among these nominees, is most likely to win. Similar studies could examine the occupational background of individuals appointed to the cabinet. (Such studies have in fact been done.) Given more detailed information, it would be possible to examine the extent to which other achieved or ascribed characteristics play a role in determining the selection of candidates and their success. Factors such as gender, ethnic origin, and age could be examined to

measure their relevance to electoral success, as shown in Box 6.2.

2. EDWARD WRIGHT, ET. AL.: HOME SITE DISADVANTAGE IN SPORTS

One of the clichés of sports is that the home team has an advantage. Baseball commentators, for example, refer to the home crowd as a "tenth man on the field," suggesting that playing in one's home stadium is a major advantage. Psychologists are not so sure. Research by Baumeister and Steinhilber (1984) suggests that in baseball and basketball the home setting is a disadvantage as one moves into the later games of a championship series. Since 1924, in baseball's world series, while the home team was more likely to win in the first two games (60.2 percent), in the final game only 40.8 percent of the home teams won (Wright, et al., 1991). The explanation for this effect is that there is increased self-awareness or anxiety, heightened by the pressure of performing in front of the home crowd. In the argot of baseball, the hitters begin to "press," the pitchers to "aim the ball," and the infielders to stiffen up their "soft hands."

Edward Wright wished to locate a sport which would not involve hostility toward the outsider, be supportive of the home player, and provide a scoring system that would allow analysis. Wright settled on an examination of the performance of the players in the British Open Golf Championship. The question was: would the scores of players from the British Isles deteriorate more than those of the foreign players? The Baumeister/Steinhilber's hypothesis would predict that the scores of the British golfers

BOX 6.2   SOCIAL RESEARCHERS AT WORK

Dennis Forcese and John De Vries: Occupation and Electoral Success

Forcese and De Vries were interested in examining the relative success of persons from different backgrounds in securing nominations and in winning in the 1974 federal election. The data for this study came from the Canada's chief electoral officer and indicated the occupations of all candidates; these were then grouped into high- and low-status groups. Comparisons were then made between the distribution of people in these occupations in the general population and the distribution of people in these occupations among the candidates. This comparison indicates that while 15.6 percent of the male labour force belonged to high-status occupations, some 60.0 percent of the candidates came from high-status occupational backgrounds. Not surprisingly lawyers were the single most overrepresented occupational group among the candidates.

Forcese and De Vries also examined the relation between occupational background and the winning of an election.

Here the authors report that a candidate with a high-status occupation is twice as likely (27.8 percent) to be elected than a candidate with a low-status occupation (12.8 percent).

Forcese and De Vries conclude as follows:

Data from the 1974 federal election confirm that higher occupational status persons are overrepresented in Parliament relative to the composition of the male labour force. Overwhelmingly, high status persons are more apt to be nominated, are more likely to be elected. Of all candidates, 60.5 per cent were high status, and of those elected, 76.9 were high status. It is apparent that the skills, financial resources, and leisure necessary to be interested in political candidacy, and sufficient to meet the risks and salary-earning displacement of such candidacy, remain the distinct privilege of a minority of Canadians.

SOURCE: Dennis Forcese and John De Vries, "Occupation and Electoral Success in Canada: the 1974 Federal Election," *Canadian Review of Sociology and Anthropology*, 14 (3) (1977), pp. 331-340.

would deteriorate more from round one to round four than those of foreign golfers. Wright's description of the methods and results of the study is featured in Box 6.3.

A key point to note about the Wright study is that all of the information was gleaned from secondary sources, in this case primarily from the *Royal and Ancient*

Championship Records 1860-1980 which listed the competitors and their scores on each round of the British Open.

Wright, Voyer, Wright, and Rooney (1994) have also examined the National Hockey League playoffs between 1961 and 1993 and show that while the home team wins 70.6 percent of games 1 and 3 in the play-offs, in the final games, the home team appears, as in other sports, to be at a disadvantage, winning only 41.2 percent of the games.

Wright's research, along with the work of Baumeister and Steinhilber, challenges popular notions that the home team has an advantage in championship matches.

Indeed, the evidence is just the opposite. And while conclusive evidence ruling out all competing explanations has not been provided, it seems reasonable tentatively to conclude that home players "tighten up" under the relentless pressure to perform well in front of their fans.

BOX 6.3   SOCIAL RESEARCHERS AT WORK

Edward Wright, et. al. Home Site Disadvantage in Sports

Method

SELECTION OF ARCHIVES The British Open Golf Championship was chosen for several reasons. First of all, it is arguably the most prestigious golf championship in the world. This claim can be supported by several facts. First, the British Open has been contested since 1860, and is therefore the world's oldest golf championship. Second, its official title, "The Open Championship", conveys that it is "open" to players of all countries, amateur or professional. The Open Champion can therefore be regarded as the champion golfer of the world (Williams, 1985). Our second reason for choosing the British Open was that it has a medal play as opposed to a match-play format (i.e., the champion is the player who records the lowest total score for the designated number of rounds). Third, the British Open has for several years been a 72-hole (or 4-round) contest. Thus, players' early and final-round performances can be compared. Fourth, careful records are kept of past British Open Championships. Finally, British golf fans are generally acknowledged to be highly supportive of British players and mildly supportive of foreign players.

...To study the effects of approaching the redefinition of self (claiming the new identity of champion) we compared first round and fourth (final) round scores for both British and foreign players (over the 35 championships). These differences were then compared. [We considered British golfers to be those players whose home courses were located in England, Scotland, Wales, and all of Ireland.] We used this data-analytic strategy rather than simply comparing first and final-round scores for British golfers for two reasons. First of all, as Baumeister and Steinhilber (1984) noted, competitors likely experience increasing amounts of pressure as championships progress. Secondly, the organizers of the British Open alter the level of difficulty of the golf links (i.e., golf course) from round to round. Moreover, they typically arrange for the course to be particularly difficult to play in the final round. They do so primarily by changing the location of the holes on the greens. For these reasons, then, the scores of all competitors should tend to increase from round one to round four, independent of other factors. To provide an appropriate test of our hypothesis, then, it is necessary to compare the performance of the British players to a relevant baseline—the performance of the foreign players.

It is also important to note that we restricted our analyses to rounds 1 and 4 for reasons pertaining to the fact that the British Open has both post-second-round and post-third-round cuts. That is, a number of players are eliminated or "cut" from further competition at the end of these rounds for failing to achieve a certain level of performance. To elaborate, "surviving a cut" in a major championship is a considerable achievement for some British and foreign golfers. If Baumeister and Steinhilber's (1984) reasoning is correct then the British players in this sub-group should experience greater pressure in rounds 2 and 3 than should the foreign players. Consequently, we felt that these middle rounds might be unsuitable for use as an index of early (and relatively unpressured) performance.

We also limited our analysis to the scores of players who had a reasonable chance to win the championship at the commencement of the final round of play. On the basis of a review of performance trends in this and other major golf championships, we decided to exclude the scores of players who were more than 9 strokes behind the leader at the

end of three rounds. The scores of past champions were also excluded from our analyses. Although a case could be made for including these scores—a two-time champion is indeed a desired identity—foreign past champions typically receive an extremely high degree of support from British golf galleries (Williams, 1985). [Note, too, that between the years 1952 and 1980 only one Briton captured the British Open Championship.]

To summarize, if Baumeister and Steinhilber's (1984) hypothesis has merit then the deterioration in scores from round one to round four should be greater for the British golfers than for the foreign golfers. If no such differences are found the alternative explanation would be supported.

RESULTS The relevant means appear in [the following Table]. A 2 x 2 repeated-measures analysis of variance conducted on these scores revealed a significant nationality main effect, $F(1,537) = 13.15$, $p > .0003$. This effect was qualified, however, by a significant Nationality x Round interaction effect, $F(1,537) = 4.47$, $p > .035$. The scores of contending British players, then, tend to increase (i.e., deteriorate) more than those of contending foreign golfers from round one to

Mean Scores of Contending British and Foreign Golfers in Opening and Final Rounds of the British Open Golf Championship (Years 1946-1980)

NATIONALITY	ROUND 1	ROUND 4
British	72.28	74.38
Foreign	71.72	73.35

Note: Includes all players within 9 strokes of leader at end of Round 3 except past champions.

round four. These findings, therefore, appear to refute the alternative explanation, and to support Baumeister and Steinhilber's (1984) account of their findings. [Because many golfers played in more than one championship the scores are not independent observations. Thus, the probabilities associated with our statistics may be slightly distorted.]

DISCUSSION The results of this study replicated Baumeister and Steinhilber's (1984) finding that athletes who play in front of a supportive audience perform less successfully than visiting players when they have the chance to capture a championship. Moreover, these findings lend further support to their view that these performance decrements are likely attributable to enhanced self-presentation concerns and heightened self-attention. Our findings seem to rule out one competing explanation of Baumeister and Steinhilber's effect—that hostile audiences facilitate the performance of visiting players in decisive games.

Because golf differs from baseball and basketball in many respects, our findings suggest that the home-venue disadvantage is a relatively pervasive phenomenon. This is important from a practical standpoint because extra home games are often accorded to teams or individual athletes in many sports as a reward for excellence in previous games. Moreover, fans, coaches, and players likely form unreasonably high expectations for success when having a home-venue "advantage." These findings, however, provide further support for the notion that the home venue may in fact be a disadvantage under certain circumstances.

It is also likely that these findings have some relevance to performances beyond the sports domain. As Baumeister and Steinhilber (1984) noted, supportive audiences can engender performance pressure and self-attention among students, courtroom lawyers, and others. There is, therefore, a clear need for more research on the impact of supportive audiences on performance.

SOURCE: Edward F. Wright, Winston Jackson, Scott D. Christie, Gregory R. McGuire, and Richard D. Wright, "The Home-Course Disadvantage in Golf Championships: Further Evidence for the Undermining Effect of Supportive Audiences on Performance Under Pressure." *Journal of Sport Behaviour*, Vol. 14, No. 1 (1991), pp. 51-60. Reprinted by permission.

3. FREDERICK J. DESROCHES, "TEAROOM TRADE: A RESEARCH UPDATE"

Chapter 10 on research ethics features Laud Humphreys' (1970) observational study on homosexual behaviour in public washrooms. That study became a classic, not only for its substantive observations, but

also for the ethical issues it raised. Frederick J. Desroches attempted to replicate the results of Humphreys' study in five Canadian communities. The study itself, however, was not a replication of Humphreys', since Desroches did not (like Humphreys) do the observations himself. Instead, Desroches relied on the reports of observations made by police. In three of the five cases, observations were recorded using video equipment, while in the remaining two communities direct observations were made through wall and ceiling air vents (Desroches, 1990, p. 41). The police surveillance resulted in some 190 arrests. No attempt was made by Desroches to interview any of the arrested men. Box 6.4 presents the concluding section of Desroches' study.

BOX 6.4   SOCIAL RESEARCHERS AT WORK

Frederick J. Desroches, "Tearoom Trade: A Research Update"

Conclusion

Like many studies of covert deviance, this paper is based upon a captive sample of persons who have come to the attention of law enforcement agencies. The existence of Laud Humphreys' research, however, makes possible a comparison of police generated data with data obtained through observations and interviews with "unapprehended" offenders. Because police observations were so detailed, a rare opportunity to replicate a qualitative study presented itself. This research largely substantiates the picture drawn by Humphreys in his classic study, *Tearoom Trade: Impersonal Sex in Public Places*. Consistent with his observations, most tearoom participants (a) communicate through non-verbal gestures and seldom speak, (b) do not associate outside the tearoom or attempt to learn one another's identity or exchange biographical information, (c) do not use force or coercion or attempt to involve youths or children, (d) are primarily heterosexual and married, (e) depart separately with the insertor leaving first, (f) commit their sex acts out of sight of the entrance and accidental exposure, (g) do not undress or engage in anal sex, (h) break off sex-

ual contact when someone enters the washroom, (i) rarely approach straight men, (j) read and write sexually explicit homosexual graffiti, and (k) linger inside and outside the washroom for someone to appear. In addition, (l) fellatio is generally not reciprocated and fellators are usually older men; (m) most offenders are neat in appearance; (n) some engage in series and simultaneous encounters; (o) encounters are brief, usually not exceeding twenty minutes; and (p) few have criminal records with the exception of those previously convicted of similar offenses.

The behavior of players reveals remarkable consistency over time, from community to community, and across national boundaries. Many men, the majority of them married and primarily heterosexual, continue to visit out-of-the-way public washrooms in search of fast, impersonal, and exciting sex despite the risk to family, friends, job, and reputation. Although shopping malls have usurped public parks as the favorite locale of tearoom participants, the basic rules of the game and profile of the players—as Humphreys contends—remain the same over time and place.

SOURCE: Frederick J. Desroches, "Tearoom Trade: A Research Update," *Qualitative Sociology*, Vol. 13, No. 1, 1990, pp. 59-60. Reprinted by permission of the publisher.

D. CONTENT ANALYSIS

As defined by Holsti and Stone, **content analysis** is "any technique for making inferences by objectively and systematically identifying specified characteristics of messages" (Holsti, 1969, p. 14). Social scientists frequently wish to examine the messages conveyed by various media. One might wish to understand the frequency with which "sexist" messages are communicated on television, or the extent to which traditional sex roles are portrayed in children's school books; or one might wish to compare the number of negative editorials on political officials now to the number 50 years ago. The chances are that if these are the kinds of research questions that are being asked, some form of content analysis will be used. Content analysis may involve examining a sample of films, books, newspapers, or television programs and attempting to categorize the messages that are being conveyed in them. In all cases, one is attempting to assess the "content" of the message that is being communicated.

Content analyses are appropriate for many questions, can be done relatively inexpensively, and, if the material is sampled appropriately, may be taken to represent the material that is available. Furthermore, the validity of the measures used may be fairly high since direct observations and classifications are being made. However, validity may also be limited because the material presented could be selected for its dramatic impact rather than its representativeness. For example, we cannot presume that the attitudes of a bigot reported in a story represent the views of the author or of the larger culture.

Content analysis is used in a variety of disciplines, and appears to be increasing in popularity (Holsti, 1969, p. 20). Fundamentally, the technique involves evaluating the content of communications—ranging from examining messages conveyed by various media to evaluating written, and even verbal, communications. Central to all researchers using the technique is a concern to analyze the content of the message. Sometimes emphasis is placed on understanding what factors influence the content of the message; in other cases, sometimes the researcher is concerned with the effects of the message; and in still others, the researcher is concerned with variations in the message itself. In all cases, however, the content of the message is part of what is analyzed.

1. BASIC DECISIONS IN CONTENT ANALYSIS

Typically content analysis, like most social science approaches, has both qualitative and quantitative dimensions. There may be some counting of the frequency with which some phenomena occur. But classifying messages into various categories may involve qualitative choices as to what categories are relevant. Since something about a message is analyzed, the analyst must make a number of fundamental decisions. Some of these are identified below.

A. UNIT OF ANALYSIS

In starting to do content analysis one must first decide on the ***unit of analysis***. Is it a speech, is it an issue of a magazine, a story, a book, or a scene in a film, or the whole film?

B. HOW ARE THE UNITS TO BE SELECTED?

Chapter 14 outlines the basic procedures for selecting samples and for deciding on sample size. Standard sampling procedures attempt to remove bias from the choice of materials selected. Since the analyst typically wishes to describe some phenomenon accurately, it is important that the procedures used represent all instances of the phenomenon fairly.

C. WHAT IS TO BE MEASURED AND HOW?

What is being measured? Is it a theme, the presence or absence of some phenomenon, or counting how often something is mentioned? And, having decided what is to be measured, how are the classification decisions made? What other pieces of information are to be recorded about the unit being measured? For example, it could be appropriate to record the gender of an author, the type of a magazine, or the name of a program. Suggested strategies for coding (placing into categories) information are discussed in Chapter 12. One of the key issues is to ensure that different people analysing the same content will agree on the categorization. This can be accomplished by having the coders work through the same items independently and then measure the extent of their agreement. A *coefficient of reliability* may be calculated as follows:

Coefficient of reliability =

$$\frac{\text{Number of units in identical category}}{\text{Total number of units coded}}$$

What the **coefficient of reliability** provides is a measure of agreement between the coders on the categorization of the items being analyzed. The proportion of times there is agreement is reflected in the coefficient. A rule of thumb would be to have a minimum coefficient of 0.6. Coders need to be trained to achieve this level. Much commonsense needs to be shown when adopting the 0.6 rule since the complexity and subtlety of the categories may influence the outcomes. To assess the gender of a person in an advertisement is one thing (where you would expect a coefficient close to 1.0!), but to decide whether a car is to be categorized as appealing to people in one of the following six categories (old man and old woman, middle-aged man and middle-aged woman, and young man and young woman) would produce less agreement among coders. If you could not get a 0.6 reliability coefficient here you would want to review your definition of the different categories to see if they could be refined further.

D. HOW IS INFORMATION TO BE RECORDED?

Before classifying data, a tally sheet should be developed for recording the information. A possible model for such a sheet would be the one used for recording field observations (see Figure 5.1). There should be space on the form to note all the variables, including the exact location of the item being measured.

E. HOW IS THE INFORMATION TO BE ANALYZED?

What techniques are to be used in presenting the information in a report? If the researcher is interested in showing what causes variation in the incidence of the phenomena, how is this analysis to be performed? If computer analysis is anticipated, be certain that coding is done so that transfer to the computer will be easy. If non-computer analysis is anticipated, follow the steps outlined in Chapter 5 (covert observational section) and in Chapter 15.

To illustrate content analysis, two studies in the general area of sex roles will be featured: the content of the diet messages in men's and women's magazines, and male domination in the English Canadian novel.

2. BRETT SILVERSTEIN, LAUREN PERDUE, BARBARA PETERSON, AND EILEEN KELLY: THE THIN STANDARD OF BODILY ATTRACTIVENESS FOR WOMEN

In 1986 Silverstein et. al. published an article examining the role of media in fostering the idea that women must be thin to be physically attractive. The article reports on four studies conducted by the researchers:

- **Study 1.** The weights of male versus female television characters: this study demonstrated that male characters are rated as fatter than female characters. This relationship persisted when age was taken into account.

- **Study 2.** This study presents a content analysis of the weight messages contained in a sample of men's and women's magazines for 1980. Box 6.5 presents the method and results of this study.

- **Study 3.** The body types portrayed by models in women's magazines during this

century: the researchers measured body types by calculating ratios between bust and waist size. The study demonstrated that thinness was fashionable during the twenties, and also emphasized again throughout the seventies.

- **Study 4.** The body types, measured in a manner similar to that used in Study 3, are examined by analysing photographs of the 38 top female film actors from 1932 to 1979. Again, the body types shown represented a trend towards thinness over the years.

The Silverstein et. al. studies are interesting because they illustrate the use of a variety of methodologies to see whether the media appears to have a role in defining female attractiveness. Taken together, the four studies provide rather convincing evidence that:

- the media promotes a thinner ideal weight for women as compared to men (Studies 1 and 2); and

- the standard for women is thinner now than it has been in the past (Studies 3 and 4).

The four studies represent a triangulation of the problem: **triangulation** is a term which refers to using a variety of techniques to test research questions. In all cases, the researchers relied on public information in order to test their ideas.

The content analysis aspect of the Study 2 was straightforward. The researchers carefully sampled issues of the male and female magazines from the first 80 years of this century, and then classified the advertisements and articles according to whether they dealt with body shape or size, dieting, or with cooking, drink, or foods.

BOX 6.5 SOCIAL RESEARCHERS AT WORK

Brett Silverstein, Lauren Perdue, Barbara Peterson, and Eileen Kelly

Method

The procedure entailed a content analysis of the most popular women's and men's magazines. A magazine was defined as a women's magazine if women make up at least 75% of its readership and was defined as a men's magazine if men make up at least 75% of its readership. The four women's magazines—*Family Circle, Ladies Home Journal, Redbook,* and *Woman's Day*—and the four men's magazines—*Field and Stream, Playboy, Popular Mechanics,* and *Sports Illustrated*—with the largest circulations were analyzed in this study.

For monthly magazines, the 12 issues from 1980 were analyzed. For weekly magazines, the 12 issues from the first week of each month of 1980 were analyzed. Each of the four raters analyzed the 12 issues of one women's magazines and the 12 issues of one men's magazine.

The content analysis focused on the advertisements and articles that dealt with body shape and size, and with dieting, and also on the ads and articles that dealt with food, drink, or cooking. An advertisement was defined as any pictorial or verbal description of a product that included a brand name prominently displayed. The size of the ad was irrelevant. Thus, the ads analyzed ranged from full-page ads to the smaller ads found at the back of magazines.

Advertisements for weight-loss products and for other products dealing with the size and shape of the body (e.g., diet pills and mechanical figure enhancers) were tabulated, as were articles concerning weight and body size (e.g., "Shape Up Now"). These ads and articles pertaining to weight, dieting, and body size were combined to form the category "Body" in the analysis.

Food advertisements were also analyzed. The food ads were classified according to the type of food advertised (e.g., diet foods, fruits and vegetables, dairy, sweets and snacks). In the event that an ad contained two foods labeled with brand names (e.g., Jell-O and Cool Whip) both foods were classified individually. Articles pertaining to food (e.g., "Souffles Made Simple"), dining (e.g., "Adventurous Eating in Exotic Lands Overseas"), and collections of recipes were placed in the category "Food Articles."

Results

The results of the content analysis provide strong support for the hypothesis that women receive more messages to be slim and stay in shape than do men. The total number of ads for diet foods found in the 48 issues of the women's magazines is 63. In the 48 issues of the men's magazines the total is 1. In the "Body" category—articles dealing with body shape or size, and advertisements for nonfood figure-enhancing products—the total in the women's magazines is 96 while the total in the men's magazines is 8 (see the Table below).

Ads and Articles in 48 Women's vs. 48 Men's Magazines

	TYPE OF AD OR ARTICLE				
	DIET FOODS	BODY ADS AND ARTICLES	TOTAL FOOD ADS	FOOD ARTICLES	ALCOHOLIC BEVERAGES
Women's magazines	63	96	1179	228	19
Men's magazines	1	12	15	10	624

At the same time, women receive many more messages about eating than do men. With one exception, discussed below, in every category of food and drink women's magazines contained many more advertisements than men's magazines. The ratio of food ads in women's magazines to food ads in men's magazines range from a low of 73:3 in the category "Meat, Fish, and Poultry" to 153:1 for "Starches," 359:1 for "Sweets and Snacks," and 150:0 for "Fats and Oils." The total number of ads for all foods in the women's magazines is 1179, compared to a total of 10 in the men's magazines. The women's magazines also contained 91 ads for nonalcoholic beverages compared to 15 in the men's magazines. The results of the analysis of articles pertaining to food, cooking, and dining are similar. The women's magazines contain a total of 228 of these articles while the men's magazines contain a total of 10.

The category "Alcoholic Beverages" is of interest because it is the only one in which men's magazines have more ads than do women's magazines. Men's magazines total 624 ads for alcoholic beverages while women's magazines total 19. This result indicates that women do not simply receive more information than do men in the magazines they read. The messages women receive and the aspects of life they must attend to are gender specific including the message to stay in shape and be slim while at the same time thinking about food and cooking.

SOURCE: Brett Silverstein, Lauren Perdue, Barbara Peterson, and Eileen Kelly, "The Role of the Mass Media in Promoting a Thin Standard of Bodily Attractiveness for Women," *Sex Roles*, Vol. 14, Nos. 9/10 (1986), pp. 519-532. Reprinted by permission of the publisher.

3. PAUL GRAYSON: MALE HEGEMONY IN THE ENGLISH CANADIAN NOVEL

The English Canadian novel is cited by Grayson as a cultural mechanism that reinforces male domination over women. This hegemony is reflected by writers' portrayal of male experiences and also by male control of publication institutions (Grayson, 1983, p. 3). Grayson's research examined 108 randomly selected Canadian novels. The novel is the unit of analysis and the analysis looks at the total message concerning male/female relations conveyed by the novels. The question posed for each novel is whether "it can accept, question or reject the subordination of women in society" (1983, p. 5). An examination was made of a number of variables, including when the novel was published, the period of the author's birth, the gender of the author, and the gender, age, and marital status of the main characters.

The analysis indicates that there has been no trend toward reducing male hegemony; indeed there is a slight trend in the opposite direction—slightly more pre-twentieth-century writers questioned or rejected the subordinate status of women. It was also noted that male authors are less likely to have a female main character than female authors are to have a male main character. Female authors were also more likely to portray younger main characters. In the twentieth-century novels, male authors were more likely than female authors to focus upon unmarried people. Box 6.6 presents some of the conclusions Grayson arrives at in his study.

BOX 6.6 SOCIAL RESEARCHERS AT WORK

Paul Grayson: Male Hegemony and the English Canadian Novel

Conclusion

The introduction mentioned that male hegemony was consistent with woman's role as a reproducer of labour and her prominence among the ranks of a reserve army of labour. It also pointed out that the apparatuses of state have worked, despite some changes, to maintain that status. This article has shown that one cultural medium, the English Canadian novel written by members of a Canadian literary elite, has been written to a large extent in accordance with notions of female subordination. As such, it both contributes to, and is a manifestation of, male hegemony.

The information analyzed also suggests that, at least with regard to an acceptance of woman's subordination, there has been little change over time. The twentieth century has seen the emergence of some works that question and reject woman's status, but their numbers are small. Moreover, the questioning is not confined to the twentieth-century Canadian novel. It was also evident prior to the turn of the century.

Despite a constant acceptance of woman's subordination, it could be argued that in some ways the twentieth-century novel is worse in this acceptance than its predecessors. For one thing, more works by twentieth-century female authors have centred on male characters than those of writers born prior to 1900. In this century, there may also be a greater female fixation on the twenties as an ideal age. It is certainly true that the works of twentieth-century female writers represent marriage or widowhood as the majority matrimonial state. Their predecessors in the nineteenth century, and contemporary male writers, are more concerned with unmarried heroes and heroines.

Last of all, it is clear that the novels of those born prior to 1900 that did not accept woman's position, were equally critical of the class structure. In the twentieth century, however, these factors are largely unconnected. A novel that expresses doubts about woman's position, in general, does not extend its criticisms to the class relations that sustain subordination. Conversely, works expressing a lack of contentment with the existing relations among classes do not usually embody dissatisfaction with women's position. It has been suggested that, in part, this twentieth-century phenomenon can be explained by the dominance of liberalism in advanced Canadian capitalist society.

As a final note it might be stressed that the English Canadian novel can be viewed as an effective weapon in the arsenal of the ideological state apparatus. Its reader is confronted with situations in which female subordination appears a natural condition. While women's subordinate status can be related to existing relations among classes, it is not possible, however, to automatically infer manipulation on the part of those who profit from a maintenance of the status quo. Rather, male hegemony is best seen as one of the taken-for-granted ideological conditions that, at the very least, is not inconsistent with, and, at the most, may be conducive to, the perpetuation of advanced Canadian capitalism. Nor should it be assumed that a change in class relations would necessarily deal a death blow to male hegemony. Certainly the Russian and Chinese cases point to the contrary. Unless one adopts a simplistic perspective, it is clear that under certain conditions many of the various aspects of hegemonies and ideologies have lives of their own (Althusser, 1971; Marx and Engels, 1976).

SOURCE: J. Paul Grayson, "Male Hegemony and the English Canadian Novel," *Canadian Review of Sociology and Anthropology*, 20(1) (1983), pp. 1-21. Reprinted by permission of the publisher.

E. A COMPARISON OF RESEARCH DESIGNS

Table 6.2 summarizes the advantages and disadvantages of the various research designs presented. And, while it is not possible to generalize about all the studies contained within any one type of design, we can conclude that experimental studies have an advantage over other research designs when we need to clarify ambiguous causal inferences. Surveys are particularly adept at representing populations with samples and such studies have become associated with complex multi-variate analyses. Field studies' strengths are in the area of validity, cost (in some cases), and in probing for depth. Non-reactive studies are often reasonably cheap to do, can lead to important general statements, and sometimes yield variables which permit the simultaneous treatment of many variables.

While the most common designs used in the social sciences have been reviewed in Chapters 3 through 6, others have been omitted. A discussion of evaluation research (evaluating the impact of a new social program on its target population, for example) is not presented in this book. Case studies are represented by the participant observation study. Various kinds of intervention, applied, polls, advocacy, and special interest approaches to research have also not been included.

TABLE 6.2   ADVANTAGES AND DISADVANTAGES OF ALTERNATE DESIGNS

DATA COLLECTION TECHNIQUE	GENERAL	VALIDITY	CAUSAL INFERENCE	MULTI-VARIATE	PROBING
A EXPERIMENTAL STUDIES					
Experimental	–	–	+	–	–
Quasi-experimental	+/–	–	+	–	–
B SURVEY STUDIES					
Individual questionnaire	+	–	–	+	–
Group-administered	–	–	–	+	–
Mailed questionnaire	+	+	+	+	–
Panel study	+	–	+	+	–
Phone survey	+	–	–	+	–
Interview	+	–	–	+	+
C FIELD STUDIES					
Participant observation	–	+	–	–	+
In-depth interviews	–	+	–	+	+
Field experiments	–	+	+	–	–
Covert observation study	–	+	–	–	–
D NON-REACTIVE STUDIES					
Comparative analysis	+	-	-	+	-
Secondary data	+	-	-	+	-
Content analysis	+	-	-	-	-

In each category a **+** means that this is an advantage of the technique; a **-** means this is a disadvantage or problem.

• *General* refers to the extent to which extrapolations to larger populations may be made using each of the data collection procedures.

• *Validity* is a measure of the extent to which indicators clearly measure what they are intended to measure.

• *Causal Inference* refers to the ease with which inferences about causal relations among variables may be made.

• *Multi-Variate* refers to the ease with which information on many variables is collected, leading to the possibility of multi-variate analysis.

• *Probing* refers to the extent to which responses may be probed in depth.

As you get ready to design a study, keep in mind that you should choose a design appropriate to the research question you are posing. On occasion, more than one type of design can be used to answer a research question. The question is the key concern. Try to decide precisely what it is you want to accomplish and then figure out the design that is best suited to your needs.

F. KEY TERMS

Coefficient of reliability

Comparative studies

Content analysis

Equivalence of concepts

Equivalence of indicators

Equivalence of language

Non-reactive study

Secondary data analysis

Triangulation

Unilineal model

Unit of analysis

G. KEY POINTS

Non-reactive studies are those in which there is no opportunity for the person (or group) being studied to react to the observations.

A problem encountered in experiments, surveys, and interviews is that *subjects may modify their behaviour* because they are aware that they are being studied. A major confounding factor in social research is eliminated in non-reactive studies because the observed person or group is not able to react to the measurement process—not able to manipulate presentation-of-self for the researcher.

Comparative research is not really a special type of research with its own methodology; it is the research process itself. Comparative research has additional challenges because it deals with different cultures, and often a different language.

The *evidence collected* in different countries is rarely based on identical definitions and collection procedures.

While the problem of researchers choosing among alternate indicators is relevant to all types of research projects, this is especially the case in comparative studies. The problem is that *it is possible to demonstrate almost anything if you are free to search around for possible indicators.*

Social scientists have not paid sufficient attention to *indicating the precise indicators* that will be used prior to beginning data analysis. Such precision is required because otherwise the researcher may inadvertently bias the outcome of the study.

Economists, political scientists, historians, and, to a lesser degree, sociologists, anthropologists, and psychologists often conduct *research based on available material.* These sources might include virtually any data—ranging from published statistical, census, or business data to the unpublished diaries of important historical figures.

As defined by Holsti and Stone, *content analysis* is "any technique for making inferences by objectively and systematically identifying specified characteristics of messages" (Holsti, 1969, p. 14).

The advantage of *experimental studies* is that they help researchers to make clear-cut causal inferences. *Surveys* are particularly adept at representing populations with samples, and such studies have become associated with complex multi-variate analyses. *Field studies'* strengths are in the area of validity and in probing for depth. *Non-reactive studies* are often reasonably cheap to do, can lead to important general statements, and sometimes yield variables which permit the simultaneous treatment of many variables.

H. EXERCISES

1. Choose one of the following studies, and identify the data sources that you would use. Write a proposal for how you will proceed with the analysis. How might:

• the political scientist study the relation between the percentage of people who voted Liberal and the percentage of immigrants in each polling station;

• the economist compare trends in American and Canadian unemployment statistics;

• the education student analyze the sexual stereotyping found in primary school readers;

• the sports psychologist study the relation between violence in hockey games (as measured by penalty minutes) to audience size (as reported in game summaries in local newspapers);

• the political science scholar compare the values of Americans to those of Canadians;

• a psychologist determine whether Canadian magazines reflect standards of attractiveness for women similar to those found in comparable magazines in the U.S.A., Britain, and France. How could the psychologist determine that the identified relation is always the same?

• the nursing researcher determine if there is a relation between physician status and the speed with which patients are admitted to hospital. Would it be possible to conduct such a study using non-reactive techniques?

2. Unemployment rate, crime rate, marriage breakdown, depression, self-esteem, left-wing support: using one of these concepts, identify problems which may occur in attempting to compare their values in the U.S.A. and in Canada. Can you recommend ways of minimizing the problems of using them in comparative studies?

I. RECOMMENDED READINGS

BAER, DOUG, EDWARD GRABB, AND WILLIAM A. JOHNSTON (1990). "The Values of Canadians and Americans: a Critical Analysis and Reassessment," *Social Forces*, 68(3):693-713. This is an excellent review and assessment of the Lipset debate over Canadian-American differences.

LIPSET, SEYMOUR MARTIN (1990). *Continental Divide*. New York: Routledge. A good illustration of comparative study which has generated a good deal of controversy.

SILVERSTEIN, BRETT, LAUREN PERDUE, BARBARA PETERSON, AND EILEEN KELLY (1986). "The Role of the Mass Media in Promoting a Thin Standard of Bodily Attractiveness for Women," *Sex Roles*, 14(9/10), 519-532. This is an imaginative but straightforward article reporting on four studies of the role of the media in promoting a thin standard of attractiveness for women.

WARWICK, DONALD P. AND SAMUEL OSHERSON (1973). *Comparative Research Methods*. Englewood Cliffs, N.J.: Prentice-Hall, Inc. This is an excellent collection of essays dealing with issues in cross-cultural research.

WEBB, EUGENE J., DONALD T. CAMPBELL, RICHARD SCHWARTZ, AND LEE SECHREST (1966). *Unobtrusive Measures: Nonreactive Research in the Social Sciences*. Chicago: Rank McNally. Still a classic in nonreactive approaches to research design and measurement.

STATISTICS

The two chapters in this section review the statistical concepts necessary for the beginning researcher. While the elementary view presented here will be helpful for the beginning student, a more profound understanding will be necessary for those students attempting more advanced work. (See Blalock, 1979; Siegel, 1956; Mitchell and Jolley, 1992.)

Those with a background in statistics can skip these chapters or review them quickly; those without such a background should work through the material carefully to acquire a foundation upon which they can build an understanding of advanced techniques. A reference to SPSS commands is included after each statistic is introduced so that the reader will be able to find the procedure in Appendix A quickly.

*Chapter 7 reviews elementary **descriptive statistics** (procedures for describing individual variables and for describing the relationship between variables). A second group of statistics is known as **inferential statistics** and deals with making extrapolations from a sample to the population from which it was drawn. Both types of statistics are of relevance to the social researcher. An introduction to inferential statistics will be presented in Chapter 8.*

A STATISTICS PRIMER

The social researcher asks questions about many kinds of phenomena: some of them are about individuals (age, type of job, income, job satisfaction, and attitudes toward minorities); some questions are about communities (how much deviance occurs, how many new houses have been built in the past year, has there been a change in the proportion of low-income people living in the community?); and some questions may be about nations (how many births and deaths were recorded, and have the incomes of the people increased or gone down over the past 10 years?).

Typifying a sample's characteristics may be achieved by a variety of *descriptive statistics*. Such statistics include various tools, conventions, and procedures for describing variables. (Means, standard deviations, normal distributions, and Z scores are of particular concern to the social researcher.) Besides describing individual variables, the social researcher is also interested in examining relationships between variables (is there a relationship between gender and income? Does this relationship persist when males and females in similar occupations are compared?). Once again, the researcher wishes to decide what relationship exists, and if it does, determine whether it holds in virtually all circumstances. There are a variety of conventions used to describe relationships. (Cross-classifications, means across categories, and correlations are important tools in describing relationships.)

Keep in mind that statistics are tools to help in describing and understanding social relationships. Be a master of these tools—but treat them as tools—they are no substitute for theory, and cannot make up for poorly designed studies or sloppy measurement.

A. LEVELS OF MEASUREMENT

An understanding of levels of measurement is necessary, since how one should go about analyzing a variable is constrained by the measurement level achieved in data collection. As a general rule, one attempts to achieve the most precise measurement possible.

One way to begin to understand levels of measurement is to ask if the variable being measured has an underlying continuum (does it vary from low to high?). If there is no underlying continuum, and the variable is made up of a number of discrete categories, then the measurement will be at the nominal level; if the variable has an underlying continuum, then the level of measurement will be either ordinal or ratio. This text will distinguish three levels of measurement: nominal, ordinal, and ratio. (See Box 7.1 for an explanation of what happened to the fourth level of measurement typically distinguished in social science texts).

i. Nominal Measurement.

Religious affiliation is a nominal variable. While there may be underlying continua related to religious affiliation (such as degree of religious commitment, or frequency of church attendance), by itself, the religious organization is a nominal category: it may be Baptist, Lutheran, Roman Catholic, or Jewish. When a respondent checks off which (if any) religious affiliations he or she was associated with while growing up, the measurement level attained is nominal. One category is neither higher

BOX 7.I TRADITIONAL LEVELS OF MEASUREMENT

What Ever Happened to Equal Interval Measures?

The conventional *equal interval* level of measurement (see S.S. Stevens, 1951) is not presented in this text for the sake of pedagogical simplicity. In most of those analyses requiring equal interval or ratio measurement, ratio level measurement will be used. Many texts in the social sciences use the temperature measures of Celsius versus Fahrenheit as examples of situations where the intervals between the points are equal but where the zero point is misplaced (absolute zero is about -273 degrees Celsius). The Table below shows the traditional measurement levels and their associated properties.

Arguably most social science measures that meet the equal interval assumption also meet the ratio measurement assumption of a correctly aligned zero point (see Blalock, 1979). Individual variables such as age, weight, height, income, years employed, number of magazines read last week, and the number of dates one had last month all would constitute ratio measures providing the data recorded reflect the characteristic being measured and are not placed in some pre-coded set of categories with uneven category sizes.

Similarly, those measures reflecting properties of communities or countries (or other groupings), such as the proportion of non-native-born members, the crime rate, and the number of motor vehicles per person in the community or country being studied are all ratio level measures.

While most textbook authors present the four types of measurement, some do not (see Levin and Fox, 1991; Rosenthal and Rosnow 1991; Jackson, 1988). For the sake of simplicity, equal interval measures will not be identified as such in this text. The reader then should be aware that, while the measurement assumptions of various statistics often call for interval level measurement, such measurements will be stated as ratio level measurements in this presentation. But, since virtually all the social science measures that meet interval level criteria are ratio level measures, this should rarely prove to be a difficulty.

Traditional Levels of Measurement

MEASUREMENT FEATURE	MEASUREMENT LEVEL			
	NOMINAL	ORDINAL	EQUAL INTERVAL	RATIO
Identifies categories?	Yes	Yes	Yes	Yes
Orders Observations?	No	Yes	Yes	Yes
Equal Intervals Between Points?	No	No	Yes	Yes
Properly Assigned Zero Point?	No	No	No	Yes

or lower than any other—they are simply different categories. ***Nominal measurement*** involves no underlying continuum and the numerical values assigned are arbitrary and have no arithmetical meaning. Other examples of nominal variables include gender, program of study, political party affiliation, and ethnic origin (see Table 7.1).

ii. Ordinal Measurement.

Ordinal measurement involves an underlying continuum in which the numerical values are ordered so that small numbers refer to lower levels on the continuum, and larger numbers to higher points; however, the distances between the assigned numbers and the underlying continuum are not in a one-to-one relation with each other. For example, suppose a statement like the following is presented to respondents:

The United Nations keeps the world safe.

Strongly 1 2 3 4 5 6 7 8 9 Strongly
Disagree   Agree

This kind of item provides ordinal measurement. While we know that high numbers indicate greater agreement with the statement, we do not know that the distances between the values are equal: the distance between 4 and 5 on the scale may

---

TABLE 7.1 EXAMPLES OF NOMINAL LEVEL MEASUREMENT*

TYPE OF RESEARCH DESIGN	VARIABLE	MEASURE
Experiment	Expectancy created?	Subject run under conditions where outcome is: Expected　— — — — 1( ) Not expected　— — — 2( )
Survey questionnaire	Place of residence?	The place where I live now is: Atlantic Canada— — — 1( ) Quebec　— — — — 2( ) Ontario　— — — — 3( ) Western Canada　— — 4( ) Other— — — — — 5( )
Participant observation	Suggests activity?	Decision event: George does: Initiate　— — — — 1( ) Support other　— — 2( ) Reject other— — — 3( )
Content analysis	Character plays traditional gender role?	Character X plays a gender role which is: Traditional　— — — 1( ) Non-Traditional　— — 2( )

* Nominal measurement involves no underlying continuum; numeric values assigned have no meaning; values cannot be added, subtracted, or multiplied.

not be the same as the distance between 8 and 9. Ordinal measurement orders values but does not assure equal gaps between the measurement points. Various examples of ordinal level measurement are provided in Table 7.2.

iii. Ratio Measurement.

Finally, there is ratio measurement. With **ratio measurement**, the zero point is aligned with true zero. For example, income is a variable whose nature makes it possible to represent an individual's income level exactly with a single number. In this case, it is also possible to use zero to reflect no income and other numerical values to reflect all other income levels. Here it is correct to say that an income of $50,000 is twice as much as an income of $25,000. With ratio level measurement it is possible to add and to subtract constants as well as to multiply or to divide by them, without changing the proportionality among the values.

If a researcher were to have respondents indicate with a check mark which of the magazines on a list they had scanned or read in the previous month, and a total were taken of the number ticked off, the result would be a variable that varies from 0 to the number required if a respondent checked off all the items listed: this measure would be a ratio level measure.

TABLE 7.2   EXAMPLES OF ORDINAL LEVEL MEASUREMENT*

TYPE OF RESEARCH DESIGN	VARIABLE	MEASURE
Experiment	Expectancy level created?	Subject run under conditions of: Low level— — — — — 1( ) Medium level — — — 2( ) High level — — — — 3( )
Survey questionnaire	Size of community?	The place where I live now is: Under 5,000 — — — — 1( ) 5,000 to 19,999 — — — 2( ) 20,000 to 99,999 — — 3( ) 100,000 to 999,999 — 4( ) Over 1 million — — — 5( )
Participant observation	Supportive behaviour?	Support of illegal activity: No support — — — — 1( ) Some support — — — 2( ) Strong support — — — 3( )
Content analysis	Degree of traditional gender role?	Character X plays a gender role which is: Non-traditional — — — 1( ) Neutral — — — — — 2( ) Traditional — — — — 3( )

* Ordinal measurement involves an underlying continuum; numeric values assigned are ordered but intervals are not equal; values may be added, or subtracted, but not multiplied.

TABLE 7.3	EXAMPLES OF RATIO LEVEL MEASUREMENT*	
TYPE OF RESEARCH DESIGN	VARIABLE	MEASURE
Experiment	Accuracy of recall	Number of correct answers in trial: _____ _____
Survey questionnaire	Weight?	My weight is: _____ _____ _____ Pounds or _____ _____ _____ Kilos
Participant observation	Community involvement	Number of people at bingo on January 15: _____ _____ _____
Content analysis	Conservative gender portrayals	Ratio of men portrayed in non-traditional gender roles to women portrayed in non-traditional gender roles: _____ : _____

* Ratio measurement involves an underlying continuum; numeric values assigned are ordered with equal intervals, the zero point is aligned with true zero; when different ratio measures are combined, the values may be added, subtracted, multiplied, or divided.

Similarly, where communities are being studied, measures such as the proportion of visible minorities, or the proportion of retired people in the population, and various rates and ratios (suicide rate, dependency ratio, sex ratio) are all ratio level measures (see Table 7.3 for additional examples).

B. DESCRIBING AN INDIVIDUAL VARIABLE

In this first section, we will consider how individual variables may be described. We will look at measures of central tendency, how variation within a variable is measured, and approaches to standardizing variables.

1. MEASURES OF CENTRAL TENDENCY

Measures of central tendency use one number to typify a set of values. Just as baseball fans cite the batting average to summarize a player's hitting ability, the social researcher uses various simple statistics to convey a sense of the data. There are three commonly used measures of central tendency.

A. THE MEAN

The *mean* is a measure which typifies a set of observations with a single value. Suppose, for example, we wished to examine grades in two first-year tests. The grades are listed in Table 7.4. Examine the grades. If you were asked to indicate the test on which students did best, what would you say? The task is a frustrating one. It is difficult to answer. The mass of detail is overwhelming. Quickly the need for some method of summarizing the grades becomes apparent. You need a way to compare the results in each of the two tests—a way to simplify the reporting of the numbers contained in Table 7.4. It is too inefficient to read an unordered listing of numbers; to do so would fail to convey to your reader any sense of the results. You would simply have a boring list of numbers. Your job as a data analyst is to put some order into the data, helping your reader to understand the results in the two tests. Presenting only the grades would not help the reader to detect if the performance in the two tests was very different.

Computing means might be a first step in comparing the grades in the two sections. The *mean* (more formally known as the *arithmetic mean*, less formally known as the *average*), is computed by summing

the values of a variable and dividing the result by the total number of cases. A mean is used on ratio level data. To find the mean grade in each test we would simply sum the grades and then divide by the number of students. This would result in a mean grade for each section of the course. Table 7.5 reports the means, showing that the average performance was somewhat higher in Test A. Students scored 2.0 points higher on the first test than on the second one. That difference is not easily apparent in looking at the raw scores.

B. THE MEDIAN

The *median* represents the mid-point of a distribution. One-half the cases fall above the median value, one-half below it. The median is used for ordinal level variables or in cases where the use of a mean would be problematic because a few extreme values would give an inappropriate impres-

TABLE 7.4		TWO SETS OF GRADES FOR A FIRST-YEAR CLASS										

TEST A. RESULTS

60	60	82	71	60	58	64	81	58	58	70	57	56
56	69	58	55	82	46	54	62	61	77	70	59	74
87	47	57	63	37	67	55	59	63	59	55	52	58
63	72	54	54	62	69	66	58	53	73	57	68	52
75	47	52	73	72	65	64	63	59	57			

TEST B. RESULTS

53	64	83	60	61	61	61	83	54	58	68	55	49
60	59	55	53	69	44	56	48	54	74	71	49	54
86	51	67	63	59	63	55	40	65	63	62	55	49
53	72	59	59	54	69	73	57	59	72	26	65	70
60	45	60	69	66	63	51	59	63	63			

TABLE 7.5	SUMMARY STATISTICS FOR STUDENT GRADES	
SUMMARY STATISTICS	TEST A GRADES	TEST B GRADES
Central Tendency		
Mean	62.02	60.02
Mode	58.00	59.00
Median	60.00	60.00
Variation		
Range	50.00	60.00
Standard deviation	9.53	10.13
Number of cases	62	62

sion of the typical case. The steps in determining the median are:

(i)   Arrange the cases in order from highest to lowest, or lowest to highest.

(ii) Number the values (ignoring no response or missing data).

(iii) If there is an odd number of cases, then the middle value is identified, and that value is the median for the distribution.

(iv) If, however, there is an even number of cases, then the mean of the middle two is calculated, and that value represents the median.

Table 7.6 illustrates medians on a 9-point attitude item for both odd and even numbered sample sizes. Note that the values have been ordered and the middlemost figure identified as the median.

Table 7.7 illustrates a situation where a median would be a better description of a sample than would a mean. Here the data list the annual incomes of 15 musicians in Montreal. When we compare the extremely high salary of $580,000 with the much more

TABLE 7.6	COMPUTING THE MEDIAN				
ODD NUMBER OF CASES			EVEN NUMBER OF CASES		
#	VALUE	MEDIAN	#	VALUE	MEDIAN
1.	1		1.	4	
2.	1		2.	4	
3.	1		3.	5	
4.	2		4.	6	
5.	3		5.	6	
6.	3		6.	7	
7.	4	← 4 is	7.	7	← 7.5 is
8.	4	median	8.	8	median
9.	5		9.	8	
10.	5		10.	8	
11.	6		11.	9	
12.	8		12.	9	
13.	9		13.	9	
			14.	9	

TABLE 7.7	MEDIAN FOR EXTREME VALUES	
CASE #	INCOME	
1.	5,400	
2.	6,600	
3.	7,700	
4.	10,200	
5.	13,400	
6.	16,400	
7.	16,700	
8.	18,300	← $18,300.
9.	19,000	median value
10.	20,000	
11.	20,500	
12.	22,900	
13.	24,600	
14.	31,500	$54,213.
15.	580,000	mean value

modest incomes of the other musicians surveyed, we realize that citing the mean would give the false impression that the incomes of musicians are quite high. The median value of $18,300 is a much better description of the income distribution than the mean of $54,213. When atypical values are present, the median may provide a better description of the data.

To perform this analysis using SPSS see the DESCRIPTIVES procedure in Appendix A.

C. THE MODE

The **mode** is the category of nominal variable with the most cases. If one wishes, for example, to describe "average" respondents in terms of their country, then the mode would be the appropriate statistic. In the case of country, it might be "Canada." This would simply mean that "Canada" was the most frequently occurring response to the question asking respondents to indicate their country. Table 7.8 presents a frequency distribution (simply reports the number of respondents who fall into each category) of respondents who report themselves to be from each of the three countries listed. From Table 7.8 one can identify the modal category by looking at the "Number" column, and picking out the category which has the highest frequency: in this case, the category is "Canada."

For nominal or ordinal variables it is appropriate to determine the mode and the median values as well as the distribution of the variable.

TABLE 7.8   DISTRIBUTION OF RESPONDENTS BY COUNTRY

COUNTRY	NUMBER	PERCENT	
Canada	65	34.9	← mode
New Zealand	58	31.2	
Australia	63	33.9	
TOTAL	186	100.0	

To perform this analysis using SPSS see the FREQUENCIES procedure in Appendix A.

2. MEASURES OF DISPERSION

Besides describing a variable in terms of central tendency, it is helpful to know something about the variability of the values. Are most of the values close to one another, or spread out? To illustrate, suppose we have two students, Mary and Beth. Their grades are indicated in Table 7.9. While both students have an identical 82 percent average, the distributions are quite different. Mary's grades vary little, Beth's vary considerably. We will explore three ways of describing the dispersion in the two students' grades.

A. RANGE

The **range** indicates the gap between the lowest and highest value in a distribution. It is computed by subtracting the lowest

TABLE 7.9 TWO GRADE DISTRIBUTIONS

SUBJECT	MARY	BETH
Sociology	78	66
Psychology	80	72
Political science	82	88
Anthropology	82	90
Philosophy	88	94
Mean[1]	82	82
Range[2]	10	28
Standard deviation[3]	3.7	12.2
Variance[4]	14.0	150.0

[1]Mean = Sum of values divided by
    number of cases
[2]Range = Highest value − lowest value
[3]See computation in Figure 7.10
[4]Variance = sd^2

value from the highest one. Table 7.9 indicates that the range of Beth's grades is 28, while for Mary the range is 10.

B. STANDARD DEVIATION

Researchers rely heavily on the ***standard deviation*** to give them a sense of how much dispersion there is in a distribution. Essentially, this measure reflects the average amount of deviation from the mean value of the variable. The formula is:

$$sd = \sqrt{\Sigma (X - \bar{X})^2}$$

Table 7.10 shows how the standard deviation for Beth's grades could be computed. An examination of Table 7.9 reveals that the standard deviation of Mary's grades is 3.7, considerably less than Beth's 12.2. An examination of the actual grades indicates that, indeed, there is much more variability in Beth's than in Mary's grades. The standard deviation reflects the variability in a set of values.

The beginning researcher should be familiar with how standard deviations are computed; this statistic is probably the sin-

TABLE 7.10 COMPUTATION OF STANDARD DEVIATION, BETH'S GRADES

SUBJECT	GRADE	$X - \bar{X}$	$(X - \bar{X})^2$
Sociology	66	66 − 82 − −16	256
Psychology	72	72 − 82 = −10	100
Political science	88	88 − 82 = 6	36
Anthropology	90	90 − 82 = 8	64
Philosophy	94	94 − 82 = 12	144
	MEAN 82.0		TOTAL 600

$$sd = \sqrt{\frac{\Sigma (X - \bar{X})^2}{N - 1}}$$

$$sd = \sqrt{\frac{600}{4}}$$

$$sd = 12.2$$

gle most important one that will be encountered. It will also be relevant for a number of other statistics. Once data have been entered into the computer, it will not be necessary to hand-compute standard deviations; nonetheless, it is crucial to understand what they measure.

C. VARIANCE

The third measure of dispersion is ***variance***, which is simply the standard deviation squared. Or:

$$\text{Variance} = sd^2 = \frac{\sum (X - \overline{X})^2}{N - 1}$$

In the illustration using Mary's and Beth's grades, the variances are 14.0 and 150.0 respectively (see Table 7.9).

To perform this analysis using SPSS see the DESCRIPTIVES procedure in Appendix A.

Table 7.11 summarizes the single-variable statistics that have been presented in this text. Note that it is possible to use all of the summarizing statistics when a ratio level of measurement has been achieved. Indeed, when there are unusual features in the data, such as a few extreme values, or a lot of identical scores, it sometimes makes sense to use a summary statistic other than the one highlighted in the table.

3. STANDARDIZING DATA

To standardize data is to make adjustments so that comparisons between units of different size may be made; data may also be standardized to create variables that have similar variability in them (Z scores).

A. PROPORTIONS

A ***proportion*** may be calculated to show, for example, how many females there are in a population compared to the total population. Suppose we wished to compute the proportion female in the community noted above:

TABLE 7.11   SUMMARY STATISTICS FOR SINGLE VARIABLES

LEVEL OF MEASUREMENT	MEASURES OF CENTRAL TENDENCY	MEASURES OF DISPERSION
Nominal	**Mode***	
Ordinal	Mode **Median**	**Range**
Ratio	Mode Median **Mean**	Range **Standard Deviation** **Variance**

* The statistic which is used under normal circumstances is indicated by bolding.

$$\text{Proportion female} = \frac{\text{Number females}}{\text{Total persons}}$$

$$\text{Proportion female} = \frac{31{,}216}{58{,}520}$$

Proportion female = 0.533

The females represent 0.53 of the population.

B. PERCENTAGES

If we wished to represent a proportion as a **percentage**, we would simply multiply the proportion by 100. In doing this, we note that females constitute 53.3 percent of the population.

Table 7.12 presents the relationship between size of home community and whether the respondent plans to attend university. It is not adequate simply to say that 69 rural students and 102 small-town students plan on attending university. We report percentages to adjust for the fact that there are different numbers of students involved in each of the categories. By computing the percentages, we are able to say that for every 100 rural students, 52.3 are planning to attend university, compared to 73.9 of every 100 high school students from towns over 5,000.

C. PERCENTAGE CHANGE

Often social scientists will compare numbers at one time to those at another one. For example, they might want to measure the percentage increase in the proportion of women in male-dominated professions from one period to the next. Table 7.13 illustrates a problem where social scientists might wish to calculate the percentage change between 1971 and 1981 in the number of women in pharmacy. The general form of the equation for calculating percentage change would be:

$$\text{Percent Change} = \frac{\text{Time 2 Number} - \text{Time 1 Number}}{\text{Time 1 Number}} \times 100$$

To calculate the percentage change use the following steps:

(i) Using the general equation, subtract the Time 1 number from the Time 2 number.

(ii) Divide the above total by the number at Time 1.

(iii) Multiply the above total by 100.

D. RATES

The incidence of a social phenomenon is often presented in the form of a *rate*. A

TABLE 7.12　PLANS TO ATTEND UNIVERSITY BY SIZE OF HOME COMMUNITY

UNIVERSITY PLANS?	RURAL		TOWN UP TO 5,000		TOWN OVER 5,000		TOTAL	
	N	%	N	%	N	%	N	%
Plans	69	52.3	44	48.9	102	73.9	215	59.7
No plans	63	47.7	46	51.1	36	26.1	145	40.3
TOTAL	132	100.0	90	100.0	138	100.0	360	100.0

* If appropriate, test of significance values entered here.

TABLE 7.13 CALCULATING PERCENTAGE CHANGE: PERCENTAGE CHANGE IN NUMBER OF WOMEN IN SELECTED OCCUPATIONS 1971 AND 1981

PROFESSION	NUMBER 1971	NUMBER 1981	PERCENT CHANGE 1971 TO 1981
Economists	640	2570	301.6
University teachers	5190	9785	88.5
Sociology and anthropology	170	540	217.6
Dentists	330	860	160.6
Physicians and surgeons	3150	7255	130.3
Lawyers and notaries	860	5390	526.7

SOURCE: Derived from Statistics Canada, Census of Canada.

Note the method of calculating percent change:

$$\text{Percent Change} = \frac{\text{Time 2 Number} - \text{Time 1 Number}}{\text{Time 1 Number}} \times 100$$

In the case of economists in the above table the calculation would be:

$$\text{Percent Change} = \frac{2{,}570 - 640}{640} \times 100$$

$$\text{Percent Change} = 301.6$$

rate indicates the frequency of some phenomenon for a standard-sized unit (such as incidence per 1,000 or per 100,000). This allows us to compare easily the incidence of a phenomenon in units of different size. To know, for example, that there were 27 suicides in a city of 250,000 (Middle City) in one year and 13 suicides in another city of 110,000 (Small City), does not allow quick comparison unless we compute a suicide rate. A suicide rate may be computed in the following manner:

$$\frac{\text{Suicide}}{\text{rate}} = \frac{\text{Number suicides per year}}{\text{Mid-year population}} \times 100{,}000$$

When calculated, we find that the suicide rate for Middle City is 10.8, while for Small City the rate is 11.8. This means that Middle City has 10.8 suicides in the year for every 100,000 people in the city; in

Small City the rate is 11.8 per 100,000. In this case, we see that the smaller of the two cities has a slightly higher suicide rate. Rates can also be computed for specific age categories, or on other bases; the only adjustment required is that we use the number of suicides in the category compared to its total size. Rates are computed for many things including births, marriages, divorces, deaths, and crime.

Table 7.14 presents provincial and state suicide rates for Canada and the United States. Note that rates permit easy comparisons between units of unequal size. The data are standardized, permitting comparison between the units. If the absolute number of suicides were presented, this would create the impression that suicide is a much more serious problem in the larger jurisdictions. This may not be the case. The rates adjust for the differences in size.

TABLE 7.14 SUICIDE RATES FOR CANADA (1985) AND THE UNITED STATES (1982)

	NUMBER OF SUICIDES	POPULATION	SUICIDE RATE[1]
A. CANADA			
Atlantic	189	2,307,400	8.19
Newfoundland	23	580,400	3.96
P.E.I.	3	127,100	2.36
Nova Scotia	90	880,700	10.21
New Brunswick	73	719,200	10.15
Quebec	879	6,580,700	13.35
Ontario	790	9,066,200	8.71
Western	708	7,404100	9.56
Manitoba	102	1,069,600	9.53
Saskatchewan	106	1,019,500	10.39
Alberta	243	2,348,800	10.34
British Columbia	238	2,892,500	8.22
Yukon & N.W.T.	19	73,700	25.78
CANADA	2,566	25,358,500	10.11

[1]The Canadian data were computed by drawing on data from: Statistics Canada, Mortality: Vital Statistics. Vol. 3, 1985. Statistics Canada, Postcensal Annual Estimates of Population by Marital Status, Age, Sex, and Components of Growth for Canada, Provinces and Territories, June 1, 1985. Vol. 3, Third Issue.

TABLE 7.14 SUICIDE RATES FOR CANADA (1985) AND THE UNITED STATES (1982) (CONTINUED)

AREA	SUICIDE RATE[2]	AREA	SUICIDE RATE[2]
B. United States:		Rhode Island	11.3
		Connecticut	7.7
Region			
Northeast	9.1	Middle Atlantic	8.8
Midwest	11.3	New York	7.6
South	12.9	New Jersey	7.8
West	15.4	Pennsylvania	11.3
New England	9.9	East North Central	11.2
Maine	13.0	Ohio	11.9
New Hampshire	11.7	Indiana	11.4
Vermont	16.0	Illinois	9.5
Massachusetts	9.4	Michigan	12.1

Wisconsin	12.3	Mississippi	8.7
West North Central	11.4	West South Central	12.5
Minnesota	11.4	Arkansas	12.0
Iowa	10.6	Louisiana	12.5
Missouri	11.8	Oklahoma	14.1
North Dakota	10.9	Texas	12.2
South Dakota	13.7	Mountain	17.4
Nebraska	10.3	Montana	15.7
Kansas	11.5	Idaho	14.1
South Atlantic	13.7	Wyoming	18.9
Delaware	12.7	Colorado	16.4
Maryland	10.1	New Mexico	19.8
District of Columbia	11.8	Arizona	17.6
Virginia	13.9	Utah	12.9
West Virginia	11.7	Nevada	29.0
North Carolina	13.3	Pacific	14.7
South Carolina	11.4	Washington	13.4
Georgia	13.2	Oregon	14.7
Florida	17.0	California	15.2
East South Central	11.7	Alaska	12.2
Kentucky	13.5	Hawaii	9.7
Tennessee	12.6		
Alabama	10.9	UNITED STATES	12.2

[2]The United States data were derived from Table 116, *Statistical Abstracts of the United States, 1986,* 106 Edition, U.S. Department of Commerce, Bureau of the Census, p. 75.

To perform this analysis using SPSS see the COMPUTE procedure in Appendix A.

$$\frac{\text{American/Canada}}{\text{burglary ratio}} = \frac{\text{U.S.A. burglary rate}}{\text{Canadian burglary rate}}$$

$$\frac{\text{American/Canada}}{\text{burglary ratio}} = \frac{200}{57}$$

$$\frac{\text{American/Canada}}{\text{burglary ratio}} = 3.51$$

E. RATIOS

Ratios are used to compare rates or other measures across categories. For example, suppose one wished to compare American and Canadian crime rates. The burglary rate in the U.S.A. is 200 per 100,000 while the comparable Canadian rate is 57 per 100,000. The American/Canadian burglary ratio could be represented as:

This ratio suggests that the American burglary rate is 3.51 times higher than the comparable Canadian rate. Many ratios can be computed which, like rates, facilitate comparison between categories.

Table 7.15 presents the ratio between male and female suicide rates for Canadian provinces. Note that, nationally, men commit suicide 3.79 times more frequently than

TABLE 7.15 MALE/FEMALE SUICIDE RATIOS BY PROVINCE, CANADA, 1985.

PROVINCE	SUICIDE RATE MALES	SUICIDE RATE FEMALES	RATIO MALE/FEMALE SUICIDES
Newfoundland	8.1	–	–
P.E.I.	4.4	2.6	1.69
Nova Scotia	18.6	3.2	5.81
New Brunswick	18.5	3.2	5.78
Quebec	23.8	6.4	3.72
Ontario	15.5	4.7	3.30
Manitoba	17.7	3.9	4.54
Saskatchewan	19.5	5.3	3.68
Alberta	19.0	4.2	4.52
British Columbia	14.7	3.9	3.77
CANADA	18.2	4.8	3.79

In this table the male/female suicide ratio is computed for each province by dividing the male suicide rate by the female rate. The result indicates how many male suicides there are for every female suicide.

women. The ratios facilitate comparison between the provinces.

In some cases, ratios are reported so that they are standardized to a base of 100. For example, if we had a community with 27,304 males and 31,216 females, we might compute a sex ratio. The ratio for the community could be calculated as follows:

$$\text{Sex ratio} = \frac{\text{Number of males}}{\text{Number of females}} \times 100$$

$$\text{Sex ratio} = \frac{27,304}{31,216} \times 100$$

$$\text{Sex ratio} = 87.5$$

This sex ratio would indicate that there are 87.5 males in the community for every 100 females. Such a ratio allows us to quickly compare the sex ratios of communities, nations, age groups, or any other category.

To perform this analysis using SPSS see the COMPUTE procedure in Appendix A.

4. THE NORMAL DISTRIBUTION

The normal distribution is another key concept used by researchers. Many of the observations we make on individual or group characteristics will approximate what is referred to as a ***normal distribution***. What does this mean?

If a graph is made showing the distribution, for example, of the weight of male university students, it would approximate a bell-shaped curve. There will be few cases on the extremes—the very light and

FIGURE 7.1 DISTRIBUTION OF NUMBER OF HEADS FLIPPED IN 10 ATTEMPTS, 1024 TRIALS

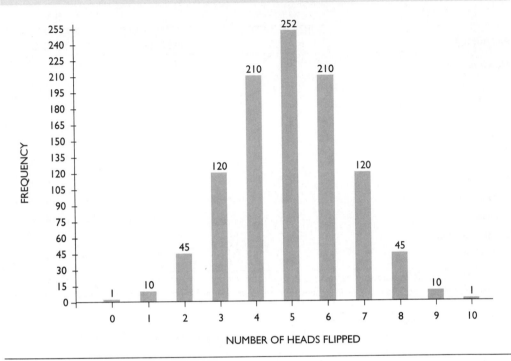

the very heavy; most of the cases will be found clustered toward the middle of the distribution.

Another way to illustrate the normal curve is to plot the outcomes of a series of 10 coin flips. Suppose we flip a coin 10 times, record the number of heads, repeat this operation 1,024 times, and then plot the number of times we got 0, 1, 2, ... 10 heads in the trials. The outcome will approximate that shown in Figure 7.1, which is a graph of the theoretical probabilities of getting each of the eleven possible outcomes. (I.e., 0 through 10 heads.) The result approximates that of a normal distribution.

A further characteristic of the normal distribution is its connection to the stan-

dard deviation. By definition, a fixed proportion of cases will fall within given standard deviations of the mean (see Figure 7.2). About two-thirds of the cases will fall within one standard deviation of the mean; just over 95 percent of the cases will fall within two standard deviations of the mean. More precisely, the following are some of the properties of a normal distribution:

- it will form a symmetrical, bell-shaped curve;

- the mean, mode, and median values will be the same; half the cases will fall below the mean, the other half above the mean;

- as the number of observations, and the number of measurement units become finer, the distribution curve will become smoother;

- 68.28 percent of the observations will be divided equally between the mean and one standard deviation to the right of the mean (34.14), and one standard deviation to the left of the mean (34.14);

- 95.46 percent of the observations will fall ± two standard deviations from the mean;

- 95 percent of the cases fall ± 1.96 standard deviation units from the mean;

- 99 percent of the cases fall ± 2.58 standard deviation units from the mean.

5. Z SCORES

Z Scores measure the distance, in standard deviation units, of any value in a distribution from the mean. Thus, if someone's income has a Z score of +1.43, it would indicate that the income is 1.43 standard deviation units above the mean of the distribution. Suppose that the mean income is $65,000 and the standard deviation $22,000: the Z score +1.43 would indicate an income of $96,460. How is this value computed? The formula for Z scores is as follows:

$$Z = \frac{X - \overline{X}}{sd}$$

where: X is the observation;

$\overline{X}$ is the mean of the distribution;

sd is the standard deviation of the distribution.

By plugging the values into the equation, and solving, the value $96,460 is obtained, as in:

$$1.43 = \frac{X - 65,000}{22,000}$$

X = (1.43 × 22,000) + 65,000

X = 96,460

One of the consequences of being able to report a value in terms of its Z score, is that we now have a powerful comparative tool. Suppose we wanted to compare individuals' relative income positions in two countries: we could simply report the incomes in Z score terms and this would tell us where each individual stands in terms of his or her country's income distribution. This would permit us to compare a British family's income of £24,000 pounds to a Canadian family's income of $90,000 dollars.

The student should recognize that whole sets of variables can be standardized by computing Z scores, and the resulting distributions will have means of 0 and standard deviations of 1. Thus, instead of just having variables with income scores, edu-

FIGURE 7.2 NORMAL DISTRIBUTION CURVE

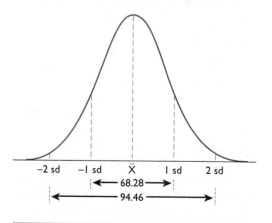

cational levels, and occupational prestige, we might have standardized variables containing the Z scores for each variable. Such standardization can be accomplished easily in SPSS.

> *To perform this analysis using SPSS see the DESCRIPTIVES procedure in Appendix A.*

Combining indicators to create an index is a major use of Z scores. Suppose, for example, that we have measures on income and years of education and that we wish to combine them to form a socio-economic index. It would not make sense simply to add a respondent's years of education to his or her annual income: the reason is that incomes might vary from $5,000 to $500,000, while years of education might vary from 0 to 20. By adding them together, the income component would totally dominate the index. Someone earning $50,000 with eight years of education would have a score of 50,008 while a person with a B.A. and $40,000 income would end up with a score of 40,016. Somehow, we need to weight the components so that income and education will equally influence the outcome. Using Z scores is an easy way to do this.

Table 7.16 shows the computation of socio-economic index scores using Z scores. Notice how either a lower-than-average income or a lower-than-average education leads to a reduction in the total socio-economic score. These indexes can be calculated quickly by a computer and the components weighted in any way the researcher likes. The Z scores, for example, may be added together, resulting in a value which can be taken to represent the relative socio-economic position of the various respondents, with income and education making equal contributions to the final score. Such computations can be done rapidly within SPSS.

> *To perform this analysis using SPSS see the DESCRIPTIVES and COMPUTE procedures in Appendix A.*

6. AREAS UNDER THE NORMAL CURVE

Another useful property of the normal distribution is that it is possible, with the help of a Table (see Appendix B), to work out what proportion of cases will fall between two values, or above or below a given value.

To illustrate, suppose we wished to know what percentage of incomes will fall above $100,000, given a population standard deviation of $22,000, and a mean of $65,000. The steps followed to solve this problem would be as follows:

STEP 1

Draw a normal curve, marking below it the mean and standard deviation values, and drawing a line through the curve at the point where you expect $100,000 to fall. Since the question asks about the percentage above this point, shade the curve to the right of the $100,000 mark.

STEP 2

Calculate the Z score to determine how many standard deviation units $100,000 is above the mean, as in:

$$Z = \frac{X - \overline{X}}{sd}$$

$$Z = \frac{100,000 - 65,000}{22,000}$$

$$Z = 1.59$$

STEP 3

Look up the value 1.59 (in Appendix B). Move down the Z score column until you come to the value 1.5, then read across to the column headed by 0.09, and read the value. You

should have found the number 4441. This number should be understood as "0.4441", a proportion.

STEP 4

By definition, we know that one-half of the cases will fall above the mean. Expressed as a proportion, this would indicate that 0.5 of the cases will fall above the mean. The question we are trying to answer is what proportion of the cases fall above $100,000? Looking at

---

TABLE 7.16 COMPUTING AN INDEX SCORE USING Z SCORE

	INCOME	YEARS EDUCATION
Given population values:		
Mean	65,000	11
Standard Deviation	22,000	4
Suppose five individuals:		
A.	55,000	7
B.	41,000	12
C.	30,000	8
D.	64,000	16
E.	86,000	9

Compute an Index equally weighting income and years of education. The general equation is:

$$Z = \frac{X - \overline{X}}{sd}$$

Case A.

Income: (55,000 – 65,000) ÷ 22,000	= –0.45
Education: (7 – 11) ÷ 4	= –1.00
Socio-economic index score	–1.45

Case D.

Income: (64,000 – 65,000) ÷ 22,000	= –0.05
Education: (16 – 11) ÷ 4	= 1.25
Socio-economic index score	1.20

Case B.

Income: (41,000 – 65,000) ÷ 22,000	= –1.09
Education: (12 – 11) ÷ 4	= 0.25
Socio-economic index score	–0.84

Case E.

Income: (86,000 – 65,000) ÷ 22,000	= 0.95
Education: (9 – 11) ÷ 4	= –0.50
Socio-economic index score	0.45

Case C.

Income: (30,000 – 65,000) ÷ 22,000	= –1.59
Education: (8 – 11) ÷ 4	= –0.75
Socio-economic index score	–2.34

the diagram we made in step one, we realize that if the right side of the curve contains 0.5 of all the cases, and, if the value $100,000 is 0.4441 above the mean, then the cases above $100,000 would have to be:

$$0.5000 - 0.4441 = 0.0559$$

STEP 5

As a proportion, 0.0559 of the cases will fall above $100,000. Or, another way of expressing the same thing, is to say that 5.6 percent of the cases will fall above $100,000 (multiply the proportion by 0.0559 by 100 to get 5.6 percent).

Suppose we wish to determine the proportion of cases that will fall between $40,000 and $70,000, given the same population mean and standard deviation. We should follow procedures similar to those used in the case above. This time, however, the diagram will show a shaded area between two points on either side of the mean. This time two Z scores will need to be computed, the values looked up in Appendix B, and the proportions between the mean and each cut-point will need to be determined, then added together to get the final answer. The computations may be done as follows:

STEP 1

(Proportion between the mean and $70,000:)

$$Z = \frac{X - \overline{X}}{sd}$$

$$Z = \frac{70,000 - 65,000}{22,000}$$

$$Z = 0.23$$

Proportion of normal curve included in Z score of 0.23 = 0.0910

STEP 2

(Proportion between $40,000 and the mean:)

$$Z = \frac{X - \overline{X}}{sd}$$

$$Z = \frac{40,000 - 65,000}{22,000}$$

$$Z = -1.14$$

Proportion of normal curve included in Z score of −1.14 = 0.3729

STEP 3

Adding the proportions together:

$$0.3729 + 0.0910 = 0.4639$$

The computation indicates that just under one-half of all the cases, 46.4 percent, fall between the incomes of $40,000 and $70,000. The proportion between the mean and the respective Z scores is shown in Figure 7.3. In this case, the values are added together to determine the proportion of cases that fall between $40,000 and $70,000.

FIGURE 7.3 AREAS UNDER THE NORMAL CURVE

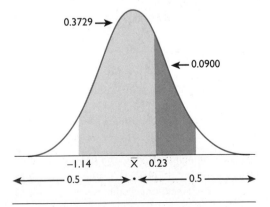

There are other types of normal curve problems that can be solved. Just keep in mind the above examples, draw a diagram shading in the area you need to determine, and remember that each side of the normal curve contains one-half, or 0.5, of the cases. With these things in mind, it should be possible to solve most normal curve problems.

7. OTHER DISTRIBUTIONS

Not all variables will be normally distributed. If, for example, we were to plot the weights of freshman students, we would almost certainly find that the result would be a ***bi-modal distribution***. The reason for this is that female students will have lower average weights than the males. Essentially we would end up combining two normally distributed plots, one for women and one for men, and one which would have two peaks, and considerable overlap between the male and female weights. (See Figure 7.4.)

If a set of values has little variability—a small standard deviation relative to the magnitude of the values—then the distribution will be peaked and it is said to be ***leptokurtic***; on the other hand, if the distribution has a great deal of variability, the

FIGURE 7.4 **OTHER DISTRIBUTIONS**

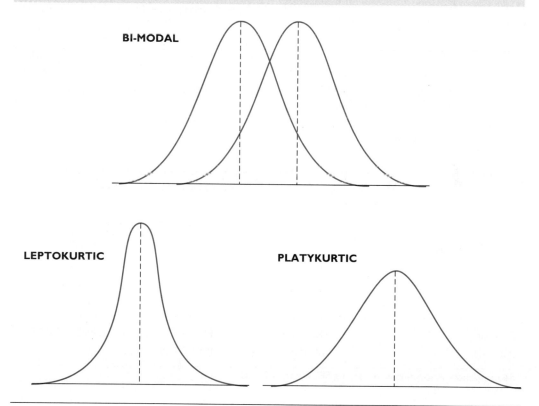

BI-MODAL

LEPTOKURTIC

PLATYKURTIC

distribution curve will tend to be flat and wide, and is called a ***platykurtic distribution***. The recognition that distributions can be quite different from one another will be important when the time comes to learn about sampling (Chapter 14) and tests of significance (Chapter 8).

As a review of this first section, before we go on to consider how we analyze relationships between variables, let us examine Table 7.17. Before we begin to analyse any variable, we need to appreciate its level of measurement so that appropriate analyses may be made. The level of measurement attained determines the best ways of summarizing a variable. Note the following points in Table 7.17.

- To provide a measure of central tendency use the mean (ratio measurement), median (ordinal measurement), or the mode (nominal measurement).

- A frequency distribution is used to reflect dispersion with nominal variables; the range is used as a measure of dispersion with ordinal variables; the standard deviation and variance are used to reflect dispersion of ratio level variables.

> *To perform this analysis usingSPSS see the DESCRIPTIVES/FREQUENCIES procedure in Appendix A.*

C. DESCRIBING RELATIONSHIPS BETWEEN VARIABLES

Researchers are concerned with describing the relationships among variables. In dealing with two-variable relationships, one of the variables will be treated as a dependent variable, and the other as an independent variable. Recall that the dependent variable is the effect, the independent variable the cause. If a control variable is used, it will either be an intervening, source of spuriousness, or conditional variable.

TABLE 7.17 LEVELS OF MEASUREMENT AND STATISTICS RELATED TO EXAMINING INDIVIDUAL VARIABLES

	LEVEL OF MEASUREMENT		
DESCRIPTIVE STATISTIC	NOMINAL	ORDINAL	RATIO
Central tendency	Mode	Median	Mean
Dispersion	Frequency	Range	Standard deviation variance
Commands[1]	FREQUENCIES	FREQUENCIES	DESCRIPTIVES
Options	RANGE MODE	RANGE MEDIAN	ALL

[1]See Appendix A for details in running SPSS^x and SPSS PC+

This section of the chapter will describe some of the major procedures used to examine relationships between variables. Three basic steps must be taken to begin analyzing any relationship:

- the first step is to decide which variable is to be treated as the dependent variable, and which one as the independent variable;

- the second is to decide on the appropriate procedure for examining the relationship; and

- finally, the analysis must be performed.

Since the researcher typically is trying to understand what causes variations in a dependent variable, commonsense alone can generally determine which variable should be designated as the dependent variable. However, there will be other cases where it is not obvious. In such cases, try to decide which variable occurs last in a temporal sequence. It is entirely possible that the two variables mutually influence one another. If this is the case, one will

nonetheless have to be designated as the "dependent" variable.

Having decided which variable is to be treated as the dependent variable, one must next identify the level of measurement of each of the variables. Now, using the information provided in Table 7.18, identify which procedure would be most appropriate for the analysis. Let us explore each of the procedures identified in Table 7.18.

1. CONTINGENCY TABLES: CROSSTABS

A ***contingency table*** presents information so that the relationship between a nominal-level dependent variable can be related to an independent variable. Table 7.19 presents findings on the relationship between the educational plans and the size of the home community for 360 high school students. We will examine this table in detail as it typifies the contingency table.

A contingency table cross-classifies cases on two or more variables. In this example, the data are first sorted into cate-

TABLE 7.18   SPSS PROCEDURES FOR BI-VARIATE ANALYSIS BY LEVELS OF MEASUREMENT

	INDEPENDENT VARIABLE		
Dependent	NOMINAL	ORDINAL	RATIO
Nominal	CROSSTABS	CROSSTABS	CROSSTABS MEANS*
Ordinal	CROSSTABS	CROSSTABS NONPAR CORR	CROSSTABS NONPAR CORR
Ratio	MEANS ANOVA	MEANS ANOVA	CORRELATION PLOT REGRESSION

*In SPSS for this case, run the independent variable as though it were the dependent variable (i.e., name it first); the interpretation of the test of significance would be standard.

TABLE 7.19 PLANS TO ATTEND UNIVERSITY BY SIZE OF HOME COMMUNITY

UNIVERSITY PLANS?	RURAL		TOWN UP TO 5,000		TOWN OVER 5,000		TOTAL	
	N	%	N	%	N	%	N	%
Plans	69	52.3	44	48.9	102	73.9	215	59.7
No Plans	63	47.7	46	51.1	36	26.1	145	40.3
TOTAL	132	100.0	90	100.0	138	100.0	360	100.0

If appropriate, test of significance values entered here.

gories representing community size; next, each of these categories is sorted into whether the person does, or does not, plan to attend university. This sorting allows us to see if those from rural areas are more likely to have university plans than their urban counterparts.

Let us now examine some of the rules for constructing and for interpreting cross-tabulation tables:

RULE 7.1

IN TABLE TITLES, NAME THE DEPENDENT VARIABLE FIRST.

Tables must be numbered and be given a title. In providing a title for a table, the dependent variable is named first, followed by the independent variable, followed by any control variables.

RULE 7.2

PLACE DEPENDENT VARIABLE ON VERTICAL PLANE.

Label the categories of the dependent variable and arrange these categories on the left side of the table. If the categories involve some cut-points, these should be specified. (For example: for income the first two categories might be: "Under 5,000," "5,000 to 19,999".)

RULE 7.3

PLACE INDEPENDENT VARIABLE ON HORIZONTAL PLANE.

Label the categories on the independent variable and arrange them across the top of the table. Again, if there are cut-points, be careful to specify these.

RULE 7.4

USE VARIABLE LABELS THAT ARE CLEAR.

Avoid the use of computer variable labels that have been designed to meet the space requirements of the statistical program. For example, FAED may have been used to refer to the variable, father's education. Use clear, easily understood labels, as in: "Father's Education."

RULE 7.5

RUN PERCENTAGES TOWARD THE INDEPENDENT VARIABLE

Percentages should be computed so that each column will total to 100 percent on each column. A percentage is computed by dividing the column total into the cell frequency. In the first cell, for example, the computation involves:

Cell percentage = $\frac{\text{Cell total}}{\text{Column total}} \times 100$

Cell percentage = $\frac{69}{132} \times 100 = 52.3$

RULE 7.6

REPORT PERCENTAGES TO ONE DECIMAL POINT.

Percentages should be reported to one significant decimal point. If the total is 99.9 or 100.1 percent, report it as such.

RULE 7.7

REPORT STATISTICAL TEST RESULTS BELOW TABLE.

Any special information and the results of statistical tests should be reported below the line under the table. (Tests of significance are discussed in Chapter 8.) The preferred method of presenting the probability or significance level is to report the exact value: such as p = .0037.

RULE 7.8

INTERPRET THE TABLE BY COMPARING CATEGORIES OF THE INDEPENDENT VARIABLE.

Since we are attempting to assess the impact of the independent variable on the dependent variable (size of community on educational plans), we are interested in the percentage of positive planners for each category of the independent variable. "While about one-half of the rural and small town students (52.3 and 48.9 percent respectively) plan on attending university, some 73.9 percent of those from communities over 5,000 have such plans." In short, compare percentages in each column. Usually it will be sufficient to use one row (in this case, just the row for those planning on university).

RULE 7.9

MINIMIZE CATEGORIES IN CONTROL TABLES.

Where control variables are used, it is necessary to minimize the number of categories in the independent and in the control variables. Generally, there should be no more than two or three categories within these variables. There are two major reasons for this limitation: first, the number of cases in each cell will become too small if there are many categories in either the independent or the control variable; second, the interpretation of the table is very difficult if simplicity is not maintained. Chapter 16 discusses interpretations of three-variable contingency tables.

Often it will be necessary to regroup data (code into fewer categories) before contingency tables are produced. This recoding may involve both the independent and the dependent variable. Indeed, some researchers will regroup the scores in a dependent variable measured at the ratio level and do a contingency table analysis. And while researchers generally favour using correlational or analysis of variance techniques (which makes more complete use of information that may be masked when variables are recoded), there are situations when researchers favour proceeding with contingency table analysis with a ratio level dependent variable. This will be done in the following circumstances:

• when the other analyses presented use contingency tables and the researcher does not wish to introduce into the research report a different analytical tool for presenting one or two relationships;

• when a researcher wishes to make comparisons with published reports which have reported the relationships in the form of contingency tables.

A. LAMBDA

Researchers are interested in how closely two variables are related. When analyzing a relation with a nominal dependent variable, a simple measure is *Lambda*. This statistic measures the *proportionate reduction in error* that occurs in estimating a dependent variable, given knowledge of the independent variable. If two variables are strongly associated, then errors in predicting variations in the dependent variable will be considerably reduced if information on the independent variable is taken into account.

The following example shows how Lambda is calculated. Suppose we wish to measure the strength of the association between gender and the ability to become pregnant. Table 7.20 reports the result of the appropriate medical examinations on 140 individuals.

TABLE 7.20	NUMBER OF CASES WHERE PREGNANCY IS POSSIBLE

ABLE TO BECOME PREGNANT	TOTAL NUMBER OF CASES
Yes	74
No	66
TOTAL	140

i. Guessing Who Can Become Pregnant.

If we were asked to guess whether a person could become pregnant, our best strategy would be to guess the category with the most cases. Each time a case is presented, our best guess is to say "Yes, can get pregnant". (There are more in the sample who can become pregnant than those who cannot become pregnant.) If we went through all the cases, guessing "yes" each time, we would be right 74 times and in error 66 times.

Table 7.21 supplements the material contained in Table 7.20 by adding information on gender. With this additional information, would we be able to make fewer errors?

This time, instead of using the "Total" column and always guessing "yes," we will use the gender information as a basis for our guess: if the case considered is male, we will guess "no, cannot become pregnant." If we do this, we will make 0 errors; if the case is female we will always guess "yes." By following this procedure we will make a total of 6 errors—the cases of females who are not able to conceive. Given the additional information on gender, we will now only make a total of 6 errors (0 + 6 = 6) in estimating whether a respondent could become pregnant.

ii. Proportionate Reduction in Error.

Lambda is based on how much error reduction occurs with the additional information provided by the independent variable (gender). Recall that we made 66 errors when we did not have the information on gender. Taking into account the information on gender, we make 6 errors—60 fewer than we made without the gender information.

In this case we have reduced the errors in our estimate by 0.909 (proportion) or 90.9 percent. Lambda varies from 0 to 1. The higher the value of Lambda, the more closely two variables are associated. A high

TABLE 7.21 RELATION BETWEEN ABILITY TO BECOME PREGNANT AND GENDER

ABLE TO BECOME PREGNANT?	GENDER		
	MALE NUMBER CASES	FEMALE NUMBER CASES	TOTAL NUMBER CASES
Yes	0	74	74
No	60	6	66
Total	60	80	140

$$\text{Lambda} = \frac{\text{Errors not knowing gender} - \text{Errors knowing gender}}{\text{Errors not knowing gender}}$$

$$\text{Lambda} = \frac{66 - 6}{66}$$

$$\text{Lambda} = 0.909$$

value on Lambda indicates that knowing the additional information about the independent variable (gender) greatly reduces the number of errors one would make in guessing the value of the dependent variable (ability to become pregnant). A value close to zero would indicate that the additional knowledge of the independent variable leads to a slight proportionate reduction in error. In most cases, the reduction in error will not be as dramatic as that found in the illustration used above.

B. GAMMA

Gamma is a measure of the strength of association between ordinal-level variables. This statistic takes advantage of the numerical order of the values and its values fall in the range from −1 to +1. (Later you will find that the correlation coefficient also varies from −1 through to +1.) A negative value indicates that the variables are in-

versely related: the greater X, the less Y. A positive value indicates a relation of the form the greater X, the greater Y. The higher the value, the stronger the association between the variables.

To illustrate the calculation of Gamma, Table 7.22 presents data showing the relation between alcohol and drug use. Note that drug use is taken as the dependent variable, alcohol use as the independent variable.

Is there an association between frequency of alcohol use and frequency of drug use? The data seem to be contrary to our expectations when we look at the category of people who use alcohol more frequently. Only two of the 19 frequent alcohol users use drugs once a month or more often. Indeed, of the 16 people who report rarely or never using alcohol, 10 of them indicate frequent drug use. If anything, then, there appears to be an inverse relation between alcohol and drug use. Gamma may be used to measure the strength of this association.

Gamma is based on two measures:

(i) a measure of a positive trend in the data; and

(ii) a measure of an inverse trend in the data.

TABLE 7.22 FREQUENCY OF DRUG USE BY FREQUENCY OF ALCOHOL USE

| | FREQUENCY OF ALCOHOL USE | | |
FREQUENCY OF DRUG USE	RARELY AND NEVER	ONCE A WEEK TO ONCE PER MONTH	EVERY FEW DAYS
Never	3	8	3
Less than once a month	3	25	14
Monthly or more often	10	15	2
TOTAL	16	48	19

A positive trend is one which shows that one variable increases as the other variable increases; an inverse measure shows that as one variable increases, the other variable decreases. The positive trend is reflected by multiplying the number of cases in each cell by a sum of all the cases that are *both below and to the right* of the cell. In the case of Table 7.22, this calculation would be done as follows:

Positive trend measure:

3(25 + 15 + 14 + 2) =	168
8(14 + 2) =	128
3(15 + 2) =	51
25(2) =	50
TOTAL POSITIVE TREND	397

The inverse trend is reflected by multiplying the number of cases in cells by the sum of the cases which are *both below and to the left* of the cell. The calculation would be done as follows:

Inverse trend measure:

3(25 + 15 + 3 + 10) =	159
8(3 + 10) =	104
14(15 + 10) =	350
25(10) =	250
TOTAL INVERSE TREND	863

Gamma is calculated according to the following formula:

$$\text{Gamma} = \frac{\text{Positive} - \text{Inverse}}{\text{Positive} + \text{Inverse}}$$

$$\text{Gamma} = \frac{397 - 863}{397 + 863}$$

$$\text{Gamma} = -0.3698$$

Note that the value is negative. The value indicates a modest inverse relation between alcohol use and drug use.

To perform this analysis using SPSS see the CROSSTABS procedure in Appendix A.

2. COMPARING MEANS: MEANS, T-TEST, ONEWAY, ANOVA, MANOVA

When one has a ratio level dependent variable, and either a nominal or ordinal independent variable, then it is appropriate to compute the mean values of the dependent variable for each category of the independent variable. Table 7.23 presents data that would be appropriate for this kind of analysis. Note that the dependent variable (income) is measured at the ratio level, while the independent variable is nominal (gender).

The following table presents a model for the presentation of a comparison of the mean values of a dependent variable (income) by categories of an independent variable (gender).

A. THE MEANS PROCEDURE (SPSS)

The MEANS procedure requires that the dependent variable be named first. This will cause the program to compute the mean value for the first variable (income) for each of the categories of the independent variable (gender). In cases where there are many categories in the independent variable, these will have to be regrouped into two or three categories before the analysis is run (RECODE procedure). The number of categories into which we arrange the variables will depend on the following criteria:

(i) a reasonable number of cases will appear in each category (often we try to have roughly equal numbers in the various categories); and

(ii) the categories used must make theoretical sense (we have to exercise caution to ensure that the categories remain as coherent as possible: thus, if we were recoding religious affiliation from eight categories to three, we would perhaps want to do the grouping so as to reflect the degree to which the religious categories we create either reflect or reject mainstream societal values).

In interpreting the outcome of an analysis, the mean values should be compared. In Table 7.23, for example, the average incomes of the males are compared to those of the females.

> *To perform this analysis using SPSS see the MEANS procedure in Appendix A.*

B. COMPARING MEANS USING THE T-TEST

When you are using samples under 30 and you wish to compare two groups on a ratio level dependent variable, the *t*-test is frequently used. The ***t-test*** is used to determine if the differences in the means may be regarded as statistically significant. These and related tests of significance will be discussed in greater detail in Chapter 8.

TABLE 7.23 MEAN INCOME BY GENDER

GENDER	MEAN INCOME	NUMBER OF CASES
Male	37,052	142
Female	34,706	37
COMBINED MEAN	$36,567	179

If appropriate, test of significance values entered here.

To perform this analysis using SPSS see the T-TEST GROUPS procedure in Appendix A.

C. ANALYSIS OF VARIANCE: ANOVA

Although used by many researchers, analysis of variance procedures are particularly important to experimenters. The procedures involved in doing an **analysis of variance (ANOVA)** require a measurement of two kinds of variation: variations within a column (for example, differences within the column for males), and variations between columns (differences that show up between the male and female columns). An analysis of variance involves computing a ratio which compares these two kinds of variability—within-column and between-column variability. In an experimental design, the treatment effect would be tapped in the measure of the between-column variabil-

ity; the random error is reflected in the within-column variability.

On examining the data within each column of Table 7.24, note that the variation within each column cannot be explained by a connection with the independent variable. (In the first column the male data are reported and, since all the cases are males, gender cannot explain variations within this column.) Differences between the columns, however, may be associated with the independent variable (gender). In the case under examination, perhaps recent hiring practices have favoured the appointment of female faculty and, therefore, the females will tend to be younger; or perhaps more women are attending graduate school and are now competing effectively for any new university positions.

In Chapter 8, the computations will be presented for doing a one-way analysis of variance. In this particular case, the estimates of variance indicate more variation within the columns than between them. Details for the computation and interpretation of ANOVAs will be presented in Chapter 8.

To perform this analysis using SPSS see the ANOVA procedure in Appendix A.

3. CORRELATIONAL ANALYSIS: CORRELATION

Correlation analysis is a procedure for measuring how closely two ratio level variables co-vary together. Once the fundamentals of this family of statistical techniques are understood, the beginning researcher is in a position to grasp such

TABLE 7.24 FACULTY AGES BY GENDER

	MALE AGES	FEMALE AGES	TOTAL
	24	24	
	26	27	
	30	30	
	35	31	
	36	33	
	40	38	
	42	40	
	45	42	
	48	42	
	51	44	
Sums	377	351	728
Means	37.7	35.1	36.4
Number of Cases	10	10	20

procedures as partial correlations, multiple correlations, multiple regression, factor analysis, path analysis, and canonical correlations.

A major advantage of using correlational techniques is that many variables can be analyzed simultaneously without running out of cases. Multi-variate (many variable) analysis, whose computations have been made easier through the use of computers, relies heavily on correlational techniques. But the cost of utilizing these powerful statistical tools is that more attention must be paid to measurement. Correlational techniques assume measurement at the ratio level. While this assumption may be relaxed, the cost of doing so is that the strength of the relationships between variables will tend to be underestimated. (See Chapter 12 on this point.)

Given the importance of correlational techniques, it is crucial that the beginning researcher understands the fundamentals of these procedures. Once understood, the more sophisticated procedures are extensions of the simple ones.

We have two basic concerns:

• What is the equation that describes the relation between the variables?; and,

• What is the strength of the relation between the two?

An attempt will be made to show how each may be visually estimated; in addition, a simple, intuitively obvious, approach to each computation will be presented in Boxes 7.2 and 7.3.

A. THE LINEAR EQUATION: A VISUAL ESTIMATION PROCEDURE

Our first concern will be to determine the equation that describes the relation between two variables. The general form of the equation is:

$$Y = a + bX$$

The components of the equation are Y, the dependent variable (starting salary to the nearest 10,000 dollars), and X, the independent variable (years of post-secondary education); a is a constant which identifies the point at which the regression line crosses the Y axis; b refers to the slope of the regression line which describes the relation between the variables. The terms "Y axis," and "regression line" are discussed below.

For purposes of illustration we will use the data shown in Table 7.25.

STEP I

The first step in visually estimating the equation that describes the relation between the variables, would be to plot the relation on graph paper. To have fairly accurate estimates, it is necessary to plot carefully and to ensure that units of measurement of the same size are used on both dimensions of the graph. Figure 7.5 shows what such a graph would look like. Note that the dependent variable (Y) is plotted on the vertical axis, and the independent variable (X) on the horizontal axis.

TABLE 7.25 **SAMPLE DATA SET**

X	Y
2	3
3	4
5	4
7	6
8	8

FIGURE 7.5 SCATTERPLOT OF SAMPLE DATA

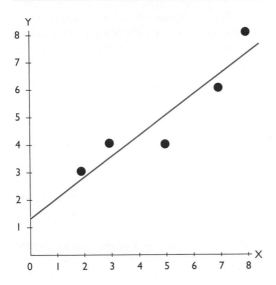

STEP 3

Observe where the regression line crosses the Y axis; this point represents the constant, or the *a* value, in the regression equation. Note that on Figure 7.6 we have estimated that it crosses the Y axis at 1.33.

STEP 4

Draw a line parallel to the X axis and one parallel to the Y axis to form a right-angled triangle with the regression line, similar to that shown in Figure 7.7. Measure the lines in millimetres. (In Figure 7.7, the vertical measures 72 mm, the horizontal 91 mm.) Divide the horizontal distance into the vertical distance: this computation will provide our estimated *b* value. (In our figure, 72 ÷ 91 = 0.79.)

STEP 2

Insert a straight **regression line** such that the vertical deviations of the points above the line are equal to the vertical deviations below the line. There need not be the same number of points above and below the line, nor need any of the points necessarily fall right on the line. The regression line offers the best linear description of the relation between the two variables. From the regression line one can estimate how much one has to change the independent variable in order to produce a unit of change in the dependent variable. The following is a hint to locate where the regression line should be drawn. Turn a ruler on its edge; then move the ruler to achieve both minimal deviations from it and equal deviations on both sides of the ruler. (See Figure 7.6).

FIGURE 7.6 SCATTERPLOT OF SAMPLE DATA

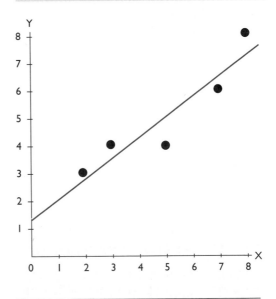

STEP 5

If the slope of the regression line is such that it is lower on the right-hand side, the *b* coefficient is negative, meaning the more X, the less Y. If the slope is negative, use a minus sign in your equation.

STEP 6

The visual estimation of the equation describing the relation between the variables is determined by simply adding the *a* and *b* values to the general equation:

$$Y = a + bX$$

In our illustration the values would be as follows:

$$Y = 1.33 + 0.79(X)$$

The above formula is our *visually estimated equation* of the relation between

the two variables. Box 7.2 presents a calculation of the actual equation. After the calculations have been made we can compare the results to those we got using the visual estimation procedure.

Note that we have come fairly close to the computed figures. In a research project we would have the computer generate the *a* and the *b* values using the REGRESSION procedure.

> *To perform this analysis using SPSS see the REGRESSION procedure in Appendix A.*

Estimating equations is a good exercise to become familiar with the different elements involved in regression analysis.

In some cases, the *a* value will turn out to be negative; this simply means that the regression line crosses the *Y* axis below the *X* axis. It should be noted as well that, as the *b* value increases, the regression line is steeper. Thus smaller increments in the *X* variable lead to increments in the *Y* variable. A negative value on the *b* indicates a negative slope, a situation in which the data are indicating a relationship where the greater *X*, the less *Y*.

The beginning researcher should recognize that, with a linear equation, it is possible to *predict* the value of a dependent variable given a value of the independent variable. When social scientists speak of **prediction** this is usually the sense in which they are using the term. Figure 7.8 shows how one could visually estimate the predicted value of Y (income), given a value of X (years of post-secondary education). The procedure simply involves locating the X value on the X axis, moving vertically to the regression line, then moving horizontally to the Y axis. The point at

FIGURE 7.7 ESTIMATING THE EQUATION

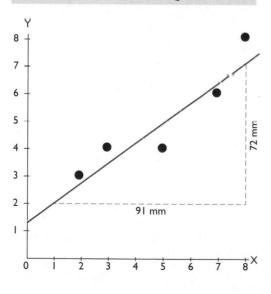

which the Y axis is intersected represents the visual estimate of the Y variable.

A predicted value is computed using an equation where values of the independent variable(s) is(are) plugged into the equation. Suppose, for example, that we attempted to predict the values of Y given X values of 1, 4, and 6. To solve the problem we would simply use the equation computed above and then determine the predicted values of Y, as in:

Computed equation: $Y = 1.35 + 0.73(X)$

	Y_p
With X value of 1: $Y = 1.35 + 0.73(1) = 2.08$	
With X value of 4: $Y = 1.35 + 0.73(4) = 4.27$	
With X value of 6: $Y = 1.35 + 0.73(6) = 5.73$	

BOX 7.2   CALCULATING A LINEAR EQUATION

The Linear Equation: A Simple Computational Procedure

Having estimated the equation describing the relation between the variables, let us now compute the actual equation. The following table presents the data and the computations necessary to determine the equation. The following steps are required:

STEP 1. Determine the mean value for the X and Y variables. This can be done by summing the values and dividing by the number of cases.

STEP 2. Subtract each value of X from the mean of X.

STEP 3. Square the values determined in the previous step.

STEP 4. Subtract each value of Y from the mean of Y.

STEP 5. Multiply the value determined in Step 2 by those values determined in Step 4.

STEP 6. Sum all columns.

STEP 7. To determine the b value: divide the column total determined in Step 5 by the column total in Step 3. As in:

$$b = \frac{\sum (X - \overline{X})(Y - \overline{Y})}{\sum (X - \overline{X})^2}$$
$$b = 19 \div 26$$
$$b = 0.73$$

STEP 8. Inspect the regression line: if it slopes upward (highest on the right side) the sign of the b will be positive (+); if it slopes downward (lowest on the right side), then the b value will be negative (–).

STEP 9. To determine the a value apply the formula:

$$a = \overline{Y} - b\overline{X}$$
$$a = 5 - 0.73(5)$$
$$a = 1.35$$

STEP 10. The values may now be applied and the final equation determined. The calculated equation is:

$$Y = 1.35 + 0.73X$$

Recall that the visual estimation of the formula was:

$$Y = 1.33 + 0.79X$$

Computing a Linear Equation

STEP 1		STEP 2	STEP 3	STEP 4	STEP 5
X	Y	$X - \bar{X}$	$(X - \bar{X})2$	$Y - \bar{Y}$	$(X - \bar{X})(Y - \bar{Y})$
2	3	−3	9	−2	6
3	4	−2	4	−1	2
5	4	0	0	−1	0
7	6	2	4	1	2
8	8	3	9	3	9
25	25	0	26	0	19

$\bar{X} = 5$

$\bar{Y} = 5$

General equation: $Y = a + b(X)$ where:

$$b = \frac{\Sigma (X - \bar{X})(Y - \bar{Y})}{\Sigma (X - \bar{X})^2} = \frac{19}{26} = 0.73$$

$a = \bar{Y} - b\bar{X}$

$a = 5 - 0.73(5)$

$a = 1.35$

Hence, $Y = 1.35 + 0.73(X)$

NOTE: that the sign of the *b* coefficient is determined by inspection. If the slope of the regression line is positive (highest on the right side), then the *b* coefficient is positive (+); if it is negative (lowest on the right side), then the *b* coefficient is negative.

We use the same procedures in situations where there are multiple independent variables determining the predicted values of a dependent variable, except that there are more values to be plugged into the equation.

B. CORRELATION COEFFICIENT: A VISUAL ESTIMATION PROCEDURE

In learning to estimate a correlation visually, it is important to develop some sense of what correlations of different magnitude look like. Figure 7.9 presents graphs of eight relationships. In the first four, the correlation coefficients vary from 0.99 to 0.36. Note that if the correlation dropped below the 0.36 level, it would become difficult to determine where the regression line should be drawn. At the other end of the continuum, note that correlations drop fairly slowly as the scatter around the regression line increases. Plot 5 shows a **curvilinear** relationship where the plot goes in one di-

FIGURE 7.8 VISUALLY ESTIMATING Y FROM X

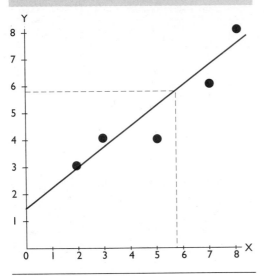

tween two variables. The correlation may vary from +1 to -1. Perfect correlations are rare, except when a variable is correlated with itself; hence almost all of the correlations will be represented by values preceded by a decimal point, as in: .98, .37, or -.56. Negative correlations mean that there is a negative slope in the relation.

Let us now develop an intuitively simple way of estimating the strength of the relation between two variables. Examine the first four plots shown in Figure 7.9. Note that the closer the plotted points are to the regression line, the higher the correlation. Conversely, the more points diverge from the regression line, the lower the correlation. In estimating the correlation coefficient, there are two kinds of variability that we have to be concerned with:

- variations around the regression line; and

- variations around the mean of Y.

We can determine the ratio between these two types of variability. In essence, the correlation coefficient (r) reflects this ratio so that the higher the ratio, the higher the correlation. Indeed, we can represent the relation as follows:

$$r^2 = 1 - \frac{\text{Variations around regression}}{\text{Variations around mean of Y}}$$

As an exercise in trying to visually estimate the strength of a correlation, the following steps may be taken:

STEP I

Plot the data on graph paper, and draw in an estimated regression line. Again, remember that the same units of measurement must be used on both dimensions of your graph.

rection and then switches to another one. Plot 6 shows a case where the linear correlation is zero, but where there is a fairly strong association between the variables. Plots 7 and 8 show situations to be wary of—namely those where a few deviant cases can radically shifts the slope of the regression line. The change of two points in the two plots shifts the sign of the correlation from a positive one (Plot 7) to a negative one (Plot 8).

One reason that it is important to plot out relationships is to permit a visual inspection of the results. If there are extreme values, or if the plot indicates a non-linear relationship, then a linear correlation analysis would be inappropriate.

The **correlation coefficient (r)** is a measure of the strength of association be-

FIGURE 7.9 EIGHT LINEAR CORRELATIONS

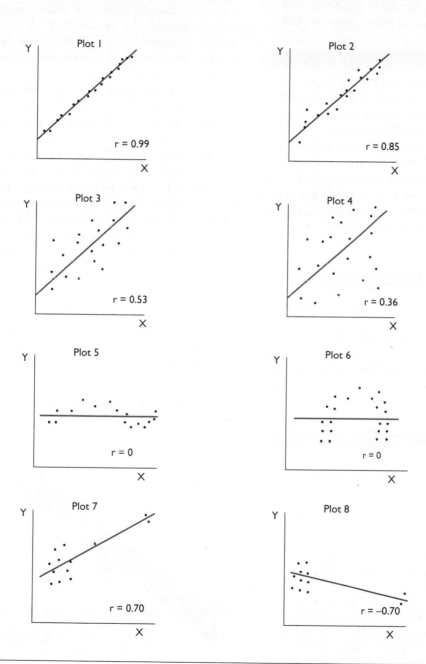

STEP 2

Draw in a line, parallel to the X axis, that will cut through the estimated mean value of Y.

STEP 3

To estimate the deviations around the regression line, draw in an additional regression line, parallel to the original one, for the points on or above the existing regression line. (You may want to cover the points below the regression line to avoid confusion.) Now draw in yet another regression line, parallel to the other two, for those points below the original regression line. Measure, and record, the perpendicular distance between the two new regression lines.

STEP 4

To estimate the deviations around the mean of Y, two additional lines parallel to the mean of Y line must be drawn, the first for those points above the line, the second for those points below the line. Once again, the perpendicular distance between these new lines should be measured and recorded.

STEP 5

At this point you should have drawn a graph similar to the one shown in Figure 7.10.

To estimate the correlation simply enter the values from your graph into the following equation:

$$r^2 = 1 - \frac{\text{Variations around regression}}{\text{Variations around mean of Y}}$$

$$r^2 = 1 - \frac{8}{44}$$

$$r^2 = .82$$

$$r = .91$$

Your estimation is based on the idea that the correlation reflects the ratio of *variations around the regression line* to *variations around the mean of Y*. As the variations around the regression line become relatively smaller, the correlation rises. Conversely, as the two measures of variation approach equality, the correlation approaches zero. Although visually estimated correlations are never reported because they are not exact, the exercise is an excellent one for becoming familiar with the meaning of the correlation coefficient. If you have few cases, it is easy to hand-compute the exact correlation using the steps outlined in Box 7.3. However, with more than 15 or 20 cases you would probably want to have the computations done by a computer.

Note that the computations in Box 7.3 have led to results roughly similar to those achieved using the visual estimation procedures. (Usually the results will not be so close.) Having done a few visual estimations, and a few hand calculations of correlations, you should have a good understanding of

FIGURE 7.10 ESTIMATING A CORRELATION

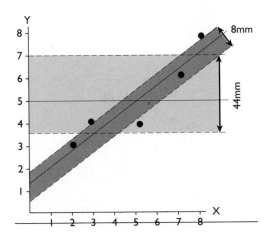

BOX 7.3   CALCULATING A CORRELATION

Correlation Coefficient: A Simple Computational Procedure

The following table presents the information needed to hand-compute a correlation using a method which parallels the estimation procedure outlined earlier. The steps are simple and can be performed quickly if there are only a few observations.

Computing the Correlation Coefficient

X	Y	$(Y - \overline{Y})^2$	Y_p	$Y - Y_p$	$(Y - Y_p)^2$
2	3	4	2.81	0.19	0.0361
3	4	1	3.54	0.46	0.2116
5	4	1	5.00	−1.00	1.0000
7	6	1	6.46	−0.46	0.2116
8	8	9	7.19	0.81	0.6561
		16			2.1154

The Y_p value is computed by substituting each value of X into the equation determined in the Table in Box 7.2. In the first observation the computation would be: $Y_p = 1.35 + 0.73(2) = 2.81$. The procedure for performing the calculation is given below:

STEP 1. The first step is to determine the variation around the regression line. For each observation of X, we will need to compute the predicted value for Y. To do this, we simply go to the equation determined in Box 7.2, plug in the value for X, and solve. The first observation would be done as follows:

$$Y_p = 1.35 + 0.73(X)$$
$$Y_p = 1.35 + 0.73(2)$$
$$Y_p = 2.81$$

The predicted values for Y are determined for each case in the manner described for the first observation.

STEP 2. The second step is to compute how much each observation deviates from its "predicted" value. $(Y - Y_p)$

STEP 3. The third step is to square the results of the previous step. After this is completed, this column should be summed. $(Y - Y_p)^2$

STEP 4. The previous three steps provide us with a measure of the variations around the regression line. To get an estimate of the deviations around the mean of Y, we need only look at the sum for the column:

$$(Y - \overline{Y})^2$$

STEP 5. We are now able to plug the values into the formula:

$$r^2 = 1 - \frac{\text{Variations around regression}}{\text{Variations around mean of Y}}$$

$$r^2 = 1 - \frac{\sum (Y - Y_p)^2 \div N}{\sum (Y - \overline{Y})^2 \div N}$$

$$r^2 = 1 - \frac{0.423}{3.2}$$

$r^2 = 1 - 0.13$
$r^2 = .87$
$r = .93$

NOTE: that if the regression line is highest on the right side, the *r* value will be positive; if it is lowest on the right side of the plot, the *r* value will be negative.

simple correlations. There are many statistical techniques that are extensions of correlational techniques. Once the basics are understood, then the drudgery of computation may be turned over to a computer.

To perform this analysis using SPSS see the CORRELATION procedure in Appendix A.

4. PLOTTING THE DATA: PLOT

It is a good idea to produce a scatterplot of important relationships in your study. A plot will alert you to problems such as:

- a few extreme cases, which may be influencing the correlation between the variables (see Figure 7.9: Plots 7 and 8);

- a strong relationship exists, but it is not linear, and the correlation does not reflect the true strength of the relation (see Figure 7.9: Plots 5 and 6);

- there are a lot of data points with the same value; this lack of variation may alert you to a problem in the measurement of one of the ratio variables involved in the plot.

Many computer programs can produce such plots quickly.

To perform this analysis using SPSS see the PLOT procedure in Appendix A.

5. COMPUTING SPEARMAN CORRELATIONS: NONPAR CORR

Sometimes researchers may wish to run a correlation on ordinal data without violating the measurement assumptions of correlation. In cases where one or both of one's variables are ordinal, then a ***Spearman Correlation*** is the appropriate measure of association. The details of such computations may be checked in any elementary statistics text and will not be presented here. Think of them as being similar to the correlation procedures just discussed.

To perform this analysis using SPSS see the NONPAR CORR procedure in Appendix A.

6. COMPUTING PARTIAL CORRELATIONS: PARTIAL CORR

A ***partial correlation*** is a special type of correlation which may be used with ratio level variables. It measures the strength of association between two variables while simultaneously controlling for the effects of one or more additional variables. In partial correlations we adjust the values of the dependent and independent variables in order to take into account the influence of other independent variables. The advantage of partial correlations over contingency table analysis is that:

(i) we make use of all of the data (by not recoding variables into two or three categories as would be done in a contingency table analysis (CROSSTABS); and

(ii) we can work with fewer cases without running into cell-size problems as happens frequently with contingency table analysis.

Like ordinary correlations, partial correlations take on values from +1.0 through to -1.0. Partial correlations control one or more independent variables. The number of controls determines the order of the partial. A correlation with one control variable is a *first-order partial correlation*; one with two controls is a *second-order partial correlation*, and so forth. Incidentally, ordinary correlations are sometimes referred to as *zero-order correlations*, which simply means that there are no control variables in the analysis.

The strategy involved in partial correlations is that regression equations can be used to express the relation between each pair of variables in the equation. For any value of an independent variable, it is possible to predict the value of the dependent variable, while adjusting for the influence of the control variables.

The idea of residuals is also useful in understanding partial correlations. In the three-variable case, if the possible combinations (X-Y, Z-Y, and X-Z) are plotted, and a regression line is entered for the X-Y relation, we could argue that the deviations from the line are the result of the influence of factor Z plus that of other known, and unknown, factors. These deviations are *residuals*. They arise when we allow one variable to explain all the variation that it can in another variable; what is left unexplained (deviations from the regression line) are the residuals. By correlating residuals, we can get a measure of the amount of influence a third variable has on the first relationship (X-Y), independent of the second relationship (X-Z).

The notational convention that we use in referring to partial correlations shows the numbers of the two major variables and these are separated from the numbers of the control variables by a "." as in:

$$r_{12.3} = .56$$

In this case, we have a first-order partial reported, with a value of 0.56. This value represents a measure of the strength of association between variables 1 and 2, controlling for variable 3. A third-order partial simply designates three control variables, as in:

$$r_{12.345} = .28$$

Partial correlations will be used in testing causal models where the variables involved are measured at the ratio level of measurement (see Chapter 16).

Since it is easy to hand-compute a first-order partial, the formula is presented here. It may be used if the researcher has the zero-order correlation matrix.

$$r_{12.3} = \frac{r_{12} - (r_{13})(r_{23})}{\sqrt{1 - r_{13}^2}\ \sqrt{1 - r_{23}^2}}$$

To perform this analysis using SPSS see the PARTIAL CORR procedure in Appendix A.

D. KEY TERMS

Analysis of variance (ANOVA)	Measures of central tendency	Range
Bi-modal distribution	Median	Rate
Contingency table	Mode	Ratio measurement
Correlation analysis	Nominal measurement	Ratios
Correlation coefficient (*r*)	Normal distribution	Regression analysis
Curvilinear	Ordinal measurement	Regression line
Descriptive statistics	Partial correlation	Spearman correlation
Gamma	Percentage	Standard Deviation
Inferential statistics	Platykurtic distribution	t-test
Lambda	Prediction	Variance
Leptokurtic distribution	Proportion	Z scores
Mean	Proportionate reduction in error	

E. KEY POINTS

Researchers use a variety of statistics to present their findings. These may be grouped into *descriptive statistics*, which include methods for typifying samples in terms of central tendency and dispersion. Often it is necessary to standardize data so that comparisons between groups of different size may be made: thus rates and ratios are calculated along with proportions and percentages.

Many distributions may be described as *normally distributed*. This kind of distribution is bell-shaped, which means that there are fewer observations of extreme values, and more as the middle-range values are examined. A *Z score* expresses an observation's location within a normal distribution.

Relationships between variables are analyzed using contingency tables, by comparing means across categories, and by calculating correlations and regression equations.

F. EXERCISES

1. As an exercise in learning to identify different levels of measurement, go through a sample questionnaire (there is one included in Appendix J), and for each question identify the level of measurement achieved.

2. Calculate the mode, median, mean, range, standard deviations, and variance for the grades in the table below.

STUDENT GRADES IN A TEST

STUDENT	GRADE	STUDENT	GRADE
A	80	N	53
B	57	O	63
C	67	P	50
D	63	Q	73
E	67	R	57
F	77	S	53
G	73	T	80
H	60	U	50
I	70	V	70
J	80	W	57
K	50	X	67
L	70	Y	53
M	57	Z	57

3. Using the mean and standard deviation calculated above, use Z scores to estimate the percentage of the students you would expect to score 58 percent or below. What percentage would you expect to score over 65 percent? What percentage between 70 and 80 percent?

4. Equally weighting income and education, use Z scores to calculate each person's socio-economic status from the following data set:

SUBJECT	$ INCOME	YEARS OF EDUCATION
1	80,000	14
2	70,000	10
3	91,000	19
4	56,000	8
5	60,000	12
6	66,000	12
7	77.000	16
8	82,000	18
9	70.000	11
10	72,000	14

Assume that the mean for the population on income is $72,000 with a standard deviation of $18,000; assume a mean of 11 years for education with a standard deviation of four years.

5. Using the data given in the next column on a respondent's, father's, mother's, and sister's years of education, plot the data (treating the respondent's education as dependent) and go through the procedures to estimate visually the correlation and the equation that describes the relationship between the respondent's education levels and the father's educational levels.

SAMPLE DATA FOR YEARS OF EDUCATION

RESPONDENT	FATHER	MOTHER	SISTER
1	3	1	4
2	3	4	3
3	4	3	5
9	7	6	6
10	10	10	8
12	11	9	14
14	13	15	8
5	4	7	2
6	7	5	8
8	8	10	12

6. Compute the *r* and the equation. How close were your estimates to the actual value?

7. Using the formula computed in question 5, what would you predict the respondent's education to be if the father received 9, 11, or 15 years of education?

8. Using visual estimation procedures, estimate the correlation between mother's and sister's educational levels.

9. Using visual estimation procedures, estimate the linear equation that describes the relation between respondent's (dependent) and the mother's educational level.

10. Is a batting average an average? From what you have learned in this chapter, how might the batting average be described better?

G. RECOMMENDED READINGS

BLALOCK, HUBERT M. JR. (1979). *Social Statistics*. New York: McGraw-Hill Inc. This remainsone of the finest social science statistics texts.

IVERSEN, GUDMUND R., AND HELMUT NORPOTH (1976). *Analysis of Variance*. Beverly Hills: Sage Publications. This short book provides a clear description of analysis of variance.

MITCHELL, MARK, AND JANINA JOLLEY (1992). *Research Design Explained*, Second Edition. Orlando: Harcourt Brace Jovanovitch College Publishers. This text prepared by two psychologists is highly readable and even entertaining at times!

THREE TESTS OF SIGNIFICANCE

A. WHAT DOES STATISTICALLY SIGNIFICANT MEAN?

Beneath most tables a number of values are reported. Almost certainly one of these will indicate whether the differences reported in the table are statistically significant. What does this mean? A **test of significance** reports the probability that an observed association or difference is the result of sampling fluctuations, and not reflective of some "real" difference in the population from which the sample has been taken.

This chapter will explore three tests of statistical significance. Other such tests are based on similar principles and, therefore, need not be explored in detail by the beginning researcher. The three that will be presented include the Chi-Square test, the *t* test, and the *F* test. Since tests of significance are often misunderstood, this chapter will also review the conditions under which such tests are not appropriate.

1. THE RESEARCH AND THE NULL HYPOTHESIS

Tests of significance are used to test hypotheses. These are set up in a "research" and in a "null" form. The **research hypothesis** (also commonly known as the **alternative hypothesis**) is simply a prediction of the relation between variables; the **null hypothesis** states that there will be no relation between the variables. The following statements illustrate research and null hypotheses:

• Research Hypothesis 1: "The greater the participation, the higher the self-esteem."

• Null Hypothesis 1: "There is no relation between levels of participation and levels of self-esteem."

• Research Hypothesis 2: "Controlling for qualifications, achievements, and experience, male university faculty members are paid more than their female counterparts."

• Null Hypothesis 2: "Controlling for qualifications, achievements, and experience there is no difference in the earnings of male and female faculty members."

It is the null hypothesis that is tested—the proposition that there is no relation between the variables. The test will lead us either to accept or to reject the null hypothesis. If the null hypothesis is accepted, we conclude that the association or the difference may simply be the result of sampling fluctuations and may not reflect an association or difference in the population being studied. The implication is that if we accept the null hypothesis, then the research hypothesis is false. If the null hypothesis is rejected, then we argue that there is an association between the variables in the population and that this association is of a magnitude that probably has not occurred because of chance fluctuations in sampling. If the null hypothesis is rejected, the data are examined to see if the association is in the predicted direction; if it is, then this is one piece of evidence which is consistent with the research hypothesis. (The finding may be in the opposite direction predicted, in which case the evidence is not consistent with the prediction.)

Positivist social scientists typically avoid expressions such as "proof," or "conclusively conclude." Instead they prefer a more tentative phrasing such as: "the evidence supports the view that...," or "the data are consistent with the research hypothesis." The reason for the cautious wording is that scientists are well aware that future research may well disconfirm, or qualify in important ways, the findings of any research. Hence, when the results of a study lead to the rejection of a null hypothesis, this only means that there is *probably* a relationship between the variables under examination. Simply put, the possibility that the hypothesis is correct has not been ruled out. The point is that empirical scientists can never provide absolute proof of the accuracy of a research hypothesis. It is always possible that some other theory might make the same prediction. That is why the language of science is tentative.

When a null hypothesis is accepted, however, this is taken to mean that the predicted relationship in the research hypothesis is false. And even this conclusion must remain tentative because of the pos-

sibility that luck or error may have played a role in the results. Nonetheless, the way the positivist proceeds is to test null hypotheses. When the evidence leads to the acceptance of the null hypothesis, this indicates that the research hypothesis is probably in error.

Often new researchers think that they have somehow failed if they do a project and find out that they have to accept the null hypothesis. Such should not be the case. To accept the null hypothesis is: (i) a research finding; and (ii) it may well be just as important to find out that two variables are not associated as it is to find out that they are. It might be extremely important to discover, for example, that among people under 25, there is no significant difference between Catholics and Protestants in their attitude toward the use of birth control; perhaps among those over 50 there is less inclination among Catholics, in comparison to Protestants, to support the use of birth control.

BOX 8.1

Terminology conundrum: do you accept a null hypothesis or do you fail to reject a null hypothesis?

There appears to be some variation in usage here. Psychologists usually prefer to say that they *fail to reject the null hypothesis.* And while this is probably the most accurate phrasing, it does have an unfortunate, unintended implication. It conveys the idea that the researcher has somehow failed if a statistically significant association is not found.

For pedagogical reasons, I prefer to say that we *accept the null hypothesis,* which does not imply that the researcher has failed if no significant association is found. Thus it is easier to convince students that it is acceptable to have findings which are not statistically significant. Sociologists and political scientists appear to follow the terminological usage adopted here.

Tests of significance report whether an observed relationship could be the result of sample fluctuations or reflect a "real" difference in the population from which the sample has been taken.

2. THE SAMPLING DISTRIBUTION

Perhaps the best way to begin understanding tests of significance is to recognize that in drawing one sample (containing 50 individuals, for example), we are getting a unique collection of respondents who are assumed to represent the larger population from which the sample was selected. If another sample is drawn from that same population, we would have another unique collection of individuals, slightly different from the first sample. If 1,000 such samples were drawn and the means of the same variable for each of the samples were plotted, a normal distribution curve would result, albeit a peaked, or leptokurtic, one. (See Chapter 14 for more details.)

Suppose, for example, the means of the weights of respondents are plotted. While these weights might range from 159 to 169 pounds for the males, the majority of the samples would cluster around the true mean of 164 pounds. Note that we are not plotting the weights of the respondents— we are plotting the mean weight of the respondents in each of the 1,000 samples drawn. The distribution is quite peaked because we are plotting the *mean weight for each sample*. To measure the dispersion of the means of these samples, we use a statistic known as the ***standard error of the means***. If the standard deviation of the population was 14 pounds, with repeated samples of size 50, the standard error of the means would be given by the following formula:

$$\text{Standard error of means} = \frac{\text{Sd population}}{\sqrt{N}}$$

$$\text{Standard error of means} = \frac{14}{\sqrt{50}}$$

$$\text{Standard error of means} = 2$$

FIGURE 8.1 DISTRIBUTION OF RAW DATA VERSUS MEANS OF SAMPLES

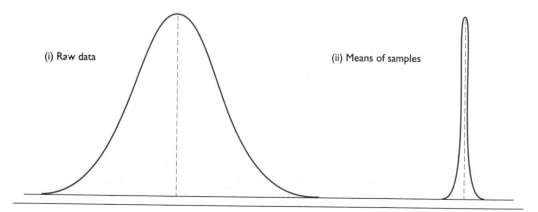

(i) Raw data

(ii) Means of samples

FIGURE 8.2 SAMPLE SIZE AND THE NORMAL DISTRIBUTION

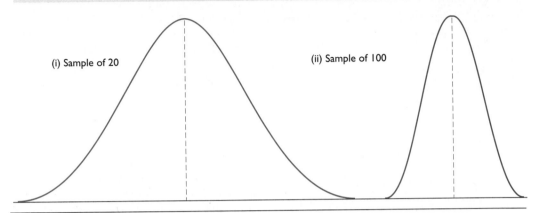

(i) Sample of 20

(ii) Sample of 100

When a sample is drawn, the sample mean will fall somewhere within a normal distribution curve. In doing tests of significance, we are assessing whether the results of one sample fall within the null hypothesis acceptance zone (usually 95% of the distribution) or outside this zone, in which case we will reject the null hypothesis.

Although the beginning researcher is not likely to be doing methodological research and selecting repeated samples, it is necessary to understand such distributions in order to understand sampling and related tests of significance. There are four key points that can be made about probability sampling procedures where repeated samples are taken:

- Point 1. Plotting the means of repeated samples will produce a normal distribution. Note that this distribution, however, will be more peaked than that achieved when raw data are plotted. (See Figure 8.1.)
- Point 2. The larger the sample sizes, the more peaked the distribution, and the

closer the means of the samples to the population mean, as shown in Figure 8.2.

- Point 3. The greater the variability in the population, the greater the variation in the samples.
- Point 4. Where sample sizes are above 100, even if a variable in the population is not normally distributed, the means will be normally distributed when repeated sample means are plotted. For example, weights of a population of males and females will be bi-modal but if we did repeated samples, the means of sample weights would be normally distributed.

3. ONE- AND TWO-TAILED TESTS OF SIGNIFICANCE

An understanding of tests of significance requires knowledge of the difference between one- and two-tailed tests. If the direction of the relation is predicted in the research hypothesis then the appropriate test will be one-tailed; in such cases we speak of a ***one-tailed test*** because we are predicting which particular tail of the normal distribution the result will fall into if the null hypothesis is to be rejected. If no prediction about the direction of the relationship is made, then a ***two-tailed test*** is in order. For example:

- A one-tailed research hypothesis: "Females are less approving of physical conflict than males." (Note that the prediction indicates which gender will be less approving.)

- A two-tailed research hypothesis: "There is a difference between males and females in their approval of physical conflict." (Note that there is no prediction here about which gender will be more approving.)

A test of significance measures the likelihood that an observed difference (for example the difference in "approval of conflict" scores between males and females) falls within normal sampling fluctuations, and therefore does not reflect a real differ-ence between the males and the females in the population. This means that if there is less than a 5 percent chance that the magnitude of the observed relationship is the result of sampling fluctuations, then the null hypothesis is rejected: we are con-cluding that there is *probably* a real differ-ence between the male and female tolerance of conflict. If we predict the "tail" of the normal distribution curve that the difference will fall into, then we have made a one-tailed prediction; if we simply pre-dict a difference without specifying into which tail the difference will fall, then we would do a two-tailed test.

Figure 8.3 shows two normal distribu-tion curves; the first one has the 5 percent rejection area split between the two tails—this would be a two-tailed test; the second one has the 5 percent rejection area all in one tail, indicating a one-tailed test. The same principle applies to tests at the 1 per-cent level—only now the difference be-tween the males and the females would have to be greater in order to fall into the null-hypothesis-rejection-area.

FIGURE 8.3 FIVE PERCENT PROBABILITY REJECTION AREA: ONE- AND TWO-TAILED TESTS

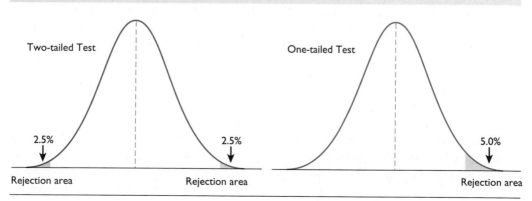

4. A SIMPLE PROBLEM: ARE THERE MORE RED BALLS IN THE CONTAINER?

Suppose that we have a huge container filled with a mixture containing thousands of red and white balls. Now suppose that we draw a sample of 200 balls from the container and that we get 114 red ones and 86 white ones. Can we safely conclude that there are more red balls in the container than white ones? Perhaps if we drew another sample we would find more white than red balls. Let us introduce the Chi-Square test to try to answer to this question.

B. THE CHI-SQUARE TEST OF SIGNIFICANCE (X^2)

The *Chi-Square test* is used primarily in contingency table analysis, where the dependent variable is a nominal one. Essentially, the Chi-Square is based on a comparison of **observed frequencies** that show up in the sample to **expected frequencies** which would occur if there were no difference between the categories in the population.

The null hypothesis we wish to test is that there is no difference in the proportion of red and white balls in the container; here we are testing whether the sample selected could have come from a population (total contents of container in this case) containing 50 percent red balls and 50 percent white ones. The **Chi-Square test** (also known as X^2) is defined by the following equation:

$$X^2 = \frac{\Sigma\,(f_0 - f_e)^2}{f_e}$$

Where f_0 is the frequency observed; f_e is the frequency expected. Note that the formula reflects the amount of deviation from the expected values, in relation to the magnitude of the expected values.

1. HAND-COMPUTING A CHI-SQUARE OF RED/WHITE BALL EXAMPLE

Let us now analyze the red/white ball example using the Chi-Square test. Normally, Chi-Squares will be computed by the computer; in the particular example under consideration it is quite simple to hand-compute the required value. The computations are shown in Box 8.2.

The results reported in Box 8.2 would lead us to *reject the null hypothesis* since the difference observed would occur by chance less than 5 percent of the time. We can then conclude that there are more red balls than white balls in the container. The risk we take in making that conclusion is that we may, by chance, just happen to have over-selected red balls. A difference of that magnitude, however, would occur in fewer than 5 percent of the samples we draw. Another way to think about it is to say that we can be confident that we will make the correct decision 19 out of 20 times.

In attempting to understand tests of significance more clearly, one might note that if repeated samples were taken and the results plotted (say, the percentage of red balls), the plot would resemble a normal distribution curve. As sample sizes become larger, a more peaked (leptokurtic) distribution would result. Most times we draw one sample and have no way of knowing if it is a truly representative sample. Perhaps our sample is atypical—we just happened to draw one with a preponderance of red balls and we might, therefore, wrongly conclude that there are more red balls in the container. But since we cannot easily observe all the cases, we simply take the chance of being wrong. We can reduce that risk by changing the probability level at which we will reject the null hypothesis

from 0.05 to 0.01 or even to 0.001. That would reduce, but not eliminate, the chance of coming to an incorrect conclusion. If we reject a null hypothesis when it should be accepted, we have made what is referred to as a ***Type I error***. If we accept a null hypothesis that should be rejected, we have made a ***Type II error***. The probability of making a Type I error is referred to as the significance level of the test (Blalock, 1979, p. 158).

BOX 8.2

A Sample Chi-Square Computation: Red Ball / White Ball Example

COLOUR	STEP 1 f_o	STEP 2 f_e	STEP 3 $f_o - f_e$	STEP 4 $(f_o - f_e)^2$	STEP 5 $\dfrac{(f_o - f_e)^2}{f_e}$
Red	114	100	14	196	1.96
White	86	100	-14	196	1.96
				TOTAL	3.92

Chi-Square = 3.92   df =   Significant at the 0.05 level

The critical value required to reject the null hypothesis is 3.841 (two-tailed test, 1 degree of freedom, at 0.05 level; see Appendix B). Since the Chi-Square value is 3.92, and this exceeds the critical value, the null hypothesis is rejected. The steps needed to do the calculation are as follows:

STEP 1. Create a calculation table which contains the relevant headings, as shown in the above Table. Enter the observations that have been made for each of

the cells. The convention for naming cells is to label them by starting in the top left corner of the table, naming them a, b, c, etc. across the table, then continuing at the beginning of the next line.

STEP 2. Compute the frequency expected (f_e) for each of the cells. There are four basic techniques for doing this:

(i)   determine what the expected frequency would be if the null hypothesis is correct (in the red/white ball example, the theoretical expectation would be that one-half would be red, the other half, white;

(ii) in a contingency table, a cell's expected frequency can be determined by multiplying the row marginal by the column marginal and dividing this result by the total number of cases;

(iii) alternatively, in a contingency table, the expected frequency would have the same number corresponding to the percentage distribution of the margin column; and

(iv) having computed the expected frequency in some columns, it is possible to compute the remaining ones by subtraction, knowing that the margin totals for expected and observed frequencies must be identical.

STEP 3. Subtract the expected from the frequency observed (f_o) for each of the cells.

STEP 4. Square the values determined in Step 3.

STEP 5. Divide the result of Step 4 by the frequency expected.

STEP 6. Sum the column of values determined in Step 5. This is the Chi-Square value.

STEP 7. Determine the degrees of freedom. The number of cells where the expected frequency would have to be computed before the remaining cells could be determined by subtraction, given that the total expected must equal the total observed. In the red ball/white ball example, once we determine that

we would expect 100 red balls (50% of all balls selected is implied by the null hypothesis), and since there were 200 balls selected in all, then 100 would be expected to be white).

In contingency tables with two or more categories in both the dependent and independent variables, the degrees of freedom may be determined by the following formula:

$$\text{Degrees of freedom} = (\# \text{ rows} - 1) \times (\# \text{ columns} - 1)$$

STEP 8. Decide the "level" of risk you wish to take; usually you will choose either the .01 or .05 level. This means that you are willing to accept that a difference is statistically significant with a 1 percent or 5 percent chance of being wrong.

STEP 9. Determine whether you are doing a one- or a two-tailed test of significance. Remember that if the direction of the relation is predicted, then the appropriate test will be one-tailed; one-tailed because we are predicting which particular tail of the normal distribution the result will fall into if the null hypothesis is to be rejected. If no prediction about the direction of the relationship is made, then a two-tailed test is required.

STEP 10. Look up the raw Chi-Square value found in Appendix C to determine if the difference between the expected and the observed frequencies is statistically significant. But note:

• For a two-tailed test, at the .05 level, use the value as indicated in Appendix C. (For example, with 1 degree of freedom, the value must exceed 3.841 to be statistically significant.)

- For a one-tailed test, at the .05 level, use the value printed under the proability level 0.10 (with 1 degree of freedom, the value must exceed 2.706 to be regarded as statistically significant). The switch to the 0.10 probability is made because a prediction has been made about into which tail the difference will fall. The Chi-Square values were originally calculated in the table above by assuming that a two-tailed test had been done; using a 0.10 probability would simply convert these values for use in a one-tailed test.

STEP 11. Below the table report the raw Chi-Square value, degrees of freedom, and whether the difference observed is statistically significant, and at what level (.05 or .01 generally).

STEP 12. If the null hypothesis is rejected, the data must then be inspected to see if the data are consistent with the research hypothesis. (It is possible, of course, that the difference could be statistically significant, but in the opposite direction predicted by the research hypothesis.) If the difference is not statistically significant, then the null hypothesis is accepted.

2. A ONE SAMPLE CHI-SQUARE TEST: A SOCIAL SCIENCE EXAMPLE

There are situations where one wishes to compare a cohort of respondents to some known distribution. Table 8.1 reports the family incomes of university students along with the income distribution of all families in the vicinity of the university.

TABLE 8.1 SAMPLE STUDENT AND GENERAL POPULATION FAMILY INCOMES

INCOME	STUDENT SAMPLE		GENERAL POPULATION
	N	%	%
Over $50,000	30	15.0	7.8
$20,000 to $49,999	160	80.0	68.9
Under $20,000	10	5.0	23.3
TOTAL	200	100.0	100.0

The research hypothesis tested in Table 8.1 is that "university students come from the wealthier families in the region." Note that this hypothesis predicts which group (the wealthy as opposed to the non-wealthy) would be overrepresented, and we therefore use a one-tailed test. The null form of this hypothesis would be that there is no difference between the income distribution of university students' families and that of other families in the region served by the university. Box 8.3 presents the steps in computing the Chi-Square value for this example.

The critical value that must be exceeded in order to reject the null hypothesis is 4.605 (see Appendix B: note that we look up the value for 2 *degrees of freedom*, under the .10 column, since we are predicting the direction of the relationship). Since the observed X^2 value is 45.61, we reject the null hypothesis and, after inspecting the data, conclude that university students come from the wealthier families in the region.

3. TYPICAL CHI-SQUARE ILLUSTRATION

Box 8.4 will present a two-variable contingency table showing the relationship between frequency of drug use by gender. Beneath the table, the computational procedures are presented for the computation of the Chi-Square. But, before proceeding to Box 8.4, note especially the following calculations:

A. CALCULATING EXPECTED FREQUENCIES

There are four basic techniques for calculating expected frequencies:

(i) determine what the expected frequency would be if the null hypothesis is correct (in the red/white ball example, the theoretical expectation would be that one-half would be red, the other half, white); this

---

BOX 8.3

Computing Chi-Square for Student Family Income Data

INCOME CATEGORY	f_o	f_e	$f_o - f_e$	$(f_o - f_e)^2$	$\dfrac{(f_o - f_e)^2}{f_e}$
Over $100,000	30	15.6*	14.4	207.36	13.29
$40,000-$99,999	160	137.8	22.2	492.84	3.57
Under $40,000	10	46.6	−36.6	1,339.56	<u>28.75</u>
TOTALS	200	200			45.61

*The expected frequencies are computed on the assumption that if there is no difference between the general population and the families of university students, that the income distribution would have similar proportions in the various categories. In the first cell, where there were 30 students, we would have expected 15.6: (200 x 0.078 = 15.6). In the general population 7.8 percent of the families had incomes above $100,000. The following list outlines the degrees of freedom, the critical value required to reject the null hypothesis, and the decision based on the calculation:

- Degrees of freedom = 2 (two cells would have to be computed before the final one could be calculated by subtraction.

- Required critical value to reject the null hypothesis is 4.605 (one-tailed test, 2 degrees of freedom, at the .05 level); see Appendix B.

- Decision: Since the Chi-Square value is 45.61, and this exceeds the critical value, the null hypothesis is rejected.

technique would also be used in the example concerning the proportion of students drawn from wealthy families;

(ii) in a contingency table, a cell's expected frequency can be determined by multiplying the row marginal by the column marginal and dividing this result by the total number of cases; for cell *a* (males, no experience) the computation would be as follows: (110 × 135) ÷ 263 = 56.5

(iii) alternatively, in a contingency table, the expected frequency would have the number corresponding to the *proportion* (percentage ÷ 100) distribution in the total margin column; for cell *a* (males, no experience) the computation would be as follows: (0.418 × 135) = 56.4

(iv) having computed the expected frequency in some columns, it is possible to compute the remaining ones by subtraction, knowing that the margin totals for expected and observed frequencies must be identical. In cell *a* of Box 8.4 (males, no experience with drugs), by using either method ii above [(110 × 135) / 263 = 56.5] or iii above [135 × 0.418 = 56.4], it is possible to compute the expected value for cell *b* (females, no experience with drugs) by subtracting the expected frequency of cell *a* from the marginal total [110 − 56.5 = 53.5]. Rounding errors result in a slightly different answer if the other expected frequency is used: [110 − 56.4 = 53.6].

B. CALCULATING DEGREES OF FREEDOM

To determine the degrees of freedom in the examples used so far, several approaches may be used:

(i) Counting the number of cells where the expected frequency would have to be computed before the remaining cells could be determined by subtraction provides one method of determining the degrees of freedom in a table. The total expected must equal the total observed. In the red ball/white ball example, once we determine that we would expect 100 red balls (50% of all balls selected is implied by the null hypothesis), we would also expect 100 white balls, since 200 balls were selected in all. This method of computing degrees of freedom is used when there is only one column in the table (as in the case of the red ball/white ball example, or the example of the proportion of students from wealthy families).

(ii) In contingency tables with two or more categories in both the dependent and independent variables, the degrees of freedom may be determined by the following formula:

Degrees of freedom
$$= \frac{(\text{number of}}{\text{rows} - 1)} \times \frac{(\text{number of}}{\text{columns} - 1)}$$

It should be noted that there are two degrees of freedom in Box 8.4. In determining the number of rows and columns, the marginal total column and total row are not counted. In Table 8.4 there are two degrees of freedom because:

Degrees of freedom
    = (rows – 1) × (columns – 1)
Degrees of freedom
    = (3 – 1) × (2 – 1)
Degrees of freedom = 2

Note that if there are no "response categories", these are excluded from the computations.

In Box 8.4, since the critical value is not exceeded, the decision is to accept the null hypothesis. (Note, however, that had we been doing a one-tailed test, we would reject the null hypothesis.) The data indicate that there is not a statistically significant association between gender and frequency of drug use. There is a greater than 5 percent probability that the differences observed in drug use between the genders are the result of chance fluctuations in sampling (assuming the null hypothesis of no difference by gender in drug use in the population).

BOX 8.4

Frequency of Drug Use, by Gender

| FREQUENCY OF DRUG | GENDER | | | | TOTAL | |
| USE IN LIFETIME | MALE | | FEMALE | | | |
	NO.	%	NO.	%	NO.	%
No experience	47	34.8	63	49.2	110	41.8
Once or twice	51	37.8	39	30.5	90	34.2
Three or more times	37	27.4	26	20.3	63	24.0
TOTALS	135	100.0	128	100.0	263	100.0

Chi-Square = 5.689   df = 2 Not significant at 0.05 level

The Chi-Square could be hand-computed in the following manner:

CELL	f_o	f_e	$(f_o - f_e)$	$(f_o - f_e)^2$	$\dfrac{(f_o - f_e)^2}{f_e}$
a	47	56.5	–9.5	90.25	1.597
b	63	53.5	9.5	90.25	1.68
c	51	46.2	4.8	23.06	0.499
d	39	43.8	–4.8	23.06	0.526
e	37	32.3	4.7	21.72	0.673
f	26	30.7	–4.7	21.72	0.707
					Σ

5.689

- Required critical value to reject the null hypothesis is 5.991 (two-tailed test, 2 degrees of freedom, at the .05 level; see Appendix B).

- Decision: Since the Chi-Square value is 5.689 and this does not equal or exceed the critical value, the null hypothesis is accepted.

To perform this analysis using SPSS see the CROSSTABS procedure in Appendix A.

The next two sections will introduce tests which involve the comparison of means between categories. Each test assumes that the dependent variable is measured at the ratio level. We will begin with two versions of the *t*-test.

C. THE *T* DISTRIBUTION: *T*-TEST GROUPS, *T*-TEST PAIRS

Suppose that an experimental/control group design has been used to measure the acquisition of mathematical skills (measured at the ratio level) and that the study involves the comparison of 20 students, ten taught in the conventional manner and ten using a new methodology. What test would be appropriate here? We could collapse the mathematical scores into high and low scores and then run a Chi-square. But this would not make full use of our data. In effect, we would be throwing out all the variability within the two grade categories. Instead, it would make more sense to compare the means of the mathematics scores of students exposed to the different teaching techniques. And, as we have a small sample, a *t*-test would do what we want.

The *t*-test is used most often in cases where:

- sample sizes are small (under 30 typically);

- the dependent variable is measured at the ratio level;

- assignment to groups has been done independently and randomly;

- the treatment variable has two levels: presence or absence;

- the population from which the sample was drawn is normally distributed and where, therefore, the distribution of sample means would be normally distributed;

- the researcher wants to find out if there are statistically significant differences between the groups.

Two commonly used variants of the *t*-test will be presented in this section: the first is appropriate for a between-subjects experimental design, the second for a within-subject design.

The **t-test** represents the ratio between the difference in means between two groups and the standard error of the difference. Thus:

$$t = \frac{\text{Difference between means}}{\text{Standard error of the difference}}$$

1. BETWEEN-SUBJECTS T-TEST

Box 8.5 shows how one could compute the *t* score in a between-subjects design for differences in the tires being used at the Riverside Speedway reported in Chapter 3.

While the student drivers with the modified tires were able to get around the track slightly faster (on average 0.33 of a second) there was a lot of variation within the two groups. The test of significance leads us to accept the null hypothesis: there is simply not enough between-group variation compared to within-group variation to reject the null hypothesis.

2. A WITHIN-SUBJECT T-TEST

A variation of the *t*-test is available for dependent samples (where the comparison groups are not selected independently). The steps for hand-computing a dependent *t*-test are reported for the within-subject design Riverside Speedway data originally reported in Chapter 3. (See Box 8.6.)

BOX 8.5

Between-Subjects t-Test for Equal Sized Groups

In Chapter 3 data were reported comparing a modified versus standard racing tire. The means and standard deviations were reported for the speeds of drivers using each type of tire. The data were as follows:

	STANDARD TIRE DRIVER	TIME	MODIFIED TIRE DRIVER	TIME
i. Student Drivers:	Kathleen	21.4	Paula	20.7
between-subjects	Li	16.2	Marlies	19.0
design; random	Danielle	18.0	Vanny	16.4
assignment to groups	Kim	16.1	Paul	16.7
	Kevin	15.9	Sandra	21.6
	Mary	20.3	Marius	20.1
	Yvonne	17.1	Chuck	14.4
	Tom	21.4	Andrea	16.3
	Ursula	17.7	Tony	15.7
	Stan	19.8	Carol	19.7

MEANS	18.39		18.06
STANDARD DEVIATIONS	2.17		2.45
MEAN DIFFERENCE		0.33	

Using the following formula we can quickly compute the t-test:

$$t = \frac{\overline{X}_1 - \overline{X}_2}{\text{Standard error of the difference}}$$

The standard error of the difference may be computed using the following formula:

$$\sqrt{\frac{sd_1^2}{N_1} + \frac{sd_2^2}{N_2}}$$

In the above formula, sd_1^2 is the variance for group 1; sd_2^2 is the variance for group 2. N_1 refers to the number of subjects in group 1; N_2 refers to the number of subjects in group 2.

STEP 1. Subtract the mean speed of the modified tires test from the mean speed for the standard tires test: ($18.39 - 18.06$ = 0.33). This is the value we will use in the numerator (the value above the line in the equation).

STEP 2. For the denominator (below the line in the equation) we require the variance for each type of tire, and since we have the standard deviations reported in the table, all we have to do is square the standard deviations to get the variances. Hence:

Variance Standard Tire:
$$sd^2 = 2.17^2 = 4.71$$
Variance Modified Tire:
$$sd^2 = 2.45^2 = 6.00$$

STEP 3. The N (number of cases) for Standard Tires is 10; the N for Modified Tires is also 10.

STEP 4. Calculate the values for the denominator by using the values calculated in Step 2, using the equation given above.

$$\frac{\text{Standard error}}{\text{of difference}} = \sqrt{\frac{sd_1^2}{N_1} + \frac{sd_2^2}{N_2}}$$

$$\frac{\text{Standard error}}{\text{of difference}} = \sqrt{\frac{4.71}{10} + \frac{6.00}{10}}$$

$$\frac{\text{Standard error}}{\text{of difference}} = 1.03$$

STEP 5. Plug the values into the equation for the t-test, as in:

$$t\text{-test score} = \frac{0.33}{1.03}$$
$$t\text{-test score} = 0.320$$

STEP 6. Determine the degrees of freedom by subtracting number of groups from number of cases ($20 - 2 = 18$).

STEP 7. Decision: Since the t value does not exceed the one shown in Appendix D, we accept the null hypothesis. The differences in the speeds may simply be the result of sampling fluctuations.

SPSS Commands to do the Above Calculation.
T-TEST GROUPS=TIRE (1,2)/ VARIABLES=SPEED. See Appendix A.

BOX 8.6

Testing Tires: a Within-Subject Design

	STANDARD TIRE		MODIFIED TIRE	
	DRIVER	TIME	DRIVER	TIME
iii. Amateur racers:	James	13.1	James	13.0
within-subject	Peter	12.8	Peter	12.9
design	Margaret	13.5	Margaret	13.4
	Jeremy	13.4	Jeremy	13.2
	Stefan	13.5	Stefan	13.5
	Don	13.6	Don	13.3
	Paul	13.5	Paul	13.3
	Tom	12.8	Tom	12.7
	Linda	12.9	Linda	12.9
	Melanie	13.5	Melanie	13.4

MEANS	13.26	13.17
STANDARD DEVIATIONS	0.32	0.28
MEAN DIFFERENCE	0.09	

Calculating a Within-Subject (Dependent Groups) t-Test

SUBJECT	TIME 1 STANDARD	TIME 2 MODIFIED	DIFFERENCE T1-T2 (D)	AVERAGE DIFFERENCE (AD)	AD − D	$(AD − D)^2$
			Step 1	Step 2	Step 3	Step 4
James	13.1	13.0	0.1	0.1	0.0	0.00
Peter	12.8	12.9	−0.1	0.1	−0.2	0.04
Margaret	13.5	13.4	0.1	0.1	0.0	0.00
Jeremy	13.4	13.2	0.2	0.1	−0.1	0.01
Stefan	13.5	13.5	0.0	0.1	0.1	0.01
Don	13.6	13.3	0.3	0.1	−0.2	0.04
Paul	13.5	13.3	0.2	0.1	−0.1	0.01
Tom	12.8	12.7	0.1	0.1	0.0	0.00
Linda	12.9	12.9	0.0	0.1	0.1	0.01
Melanie	13.5	13.4	0.1	0.1	0.0	0.00
Totals			1.0			0.12

Average difference	= 1.0 ÷ 10
	= 0.1
Variances of differences	= 0.12 ÷ 9
	= 0.013

STEP 1. Subtract Time 2 measure from Time 1 measure to get the difference score (D): (in the case of James: 13.1 − 13.0 = 0.1).

STEP 2.. Calculate the average difference score (AD): sum the values for the 10 subjects (0.1 − 0.1 + 0.1 + 0.2 + 0.0 + 0.3 + 0.2 + 0.1 + 0.0 + 0.1 = 1.0); divide sum by number of subject (1.0 ÷ 10 = 0.1).

STEP 3. Subtract the Difference Score (D), calculated in Step 1, from the Average Difference Score (AD) calculated in Step 2: (in the case of James: 0.1 − 0.1 = 0).

STEP 4. Square each value calculated in Step 3.

STEP 5. Sum the squared values in Step 4 and divide by the number of subjects minus 1 (10 − 1) = 9. The measure of the variance of the differences is 0.12 ÷ 9 = 0.013.

STEP 6.. To get the standard deviation of the differences, calculate the square root of the variance of the differences. As in:

Standard deviation = $\sqrt{0.013}$ = 0.115
  of differences

STEP 7. Calculate the standard error of the difference by dividing the standard deviation of the differences by the square root of the number of pairs of scores. As in:

Standard error of = 0.115 ÷ $\sqrt{10}$ = 0.037
the eifferences

STEP 8. Compute the *t*-ratio by dividing the average difference (AD) by the standard error of the difference. As in:

t = 0.1 ÷ 0.037

t = 2.74

STEP 9. Determine the degrees of freedom by subtracting 1 from the number of pairs of scores (10 − 1 = 9). Look up the *t* value in Appendix D. The two-tailed value with 9 df = 2.262.

STEP 10. Decision: since the *t* value exceeds that in Appendix D, we reject the null hypothesis.

SPSS Commands to do the Above Calculation.
T-TEST PAIRS TIME1,TIME2.
See Appendix A.

In the case of the within-subject design to test the efficacy of the different racing tires, we are led to reject the null hypothesis, and conclude that, indeed, the modified tires do seem to make a difference. Note that the differences in the speeds achieved on the two different types of tires is slight (0.09 of a second), yet the difference in this case is found to be statistically significant (we reject the null hypothesis). In

comparison to the student drivers (see Box 8.5), the amateur drivers show much less variation in lap times (ranging from 12.8 seconds to 13.6 seconds compared to a range of 8.4 to 20.7 seconds for the student drivers).

Where a test of significance is required for a study with a more complex experimental design, such as those with several independent variables, or more than two different levels in the treatment or control variable, the researcher typically uses *analysis of variance* techniques. These will now be introduced.

D. THE
F DISTRIBUTION:
MEANS, ANOVA

A second test of significance associated with comparing means involves an *analysis of variance*. The distribution associated with this test is the ***F distribution*** and it is used to test whether there is a significant difference in the means of various categories. Some of this material will not seem to be new, since similar ideas were presented when discussing both the Chi-Square test and correlation analyses. ***Analysis of variance*** will typically be used when:

- the dependent variable is measured at the ratio level;

- the treatment variable has two or more levels;

- in cases where two or more treatments are used simultaneously;

- it is assumed that the population from which the sample was drawn is normally distributed and, therefore, that the distribution of sample means would be normally distributed;

- the researcher wants to find out if there are statistically significant differences between the groups;

- the researcher wants to check to see if the various treatments may be interacting with one another.

1. ONE-WAY ANALYSIS OF VARIANCE: EGALITARIANISM SCORES BY COUNTRY

Data on egalitarianism scores have been collected and the researcher wishes to examine whether they vary significantly from country to country. Egalitarianism was measured using six items which reflect how equally respondents think the wealth of society should be spread among its members. The sample involves a total of 182 respondents from Canada, New Zealand, and Australia. Our research hypothesis is that egalitarianism scores will vary by country. The null hypothesis is that there is no difference in egalitarianism scores across national boundaries.

The procedures used to answer the above question involve:

- determining the appropriate test to run;

- stating the null hypothesis;

- deciding the probability level we wish to employ (normally specifying whether we risk being wrong 5 percent or 1 percent of the time);

- determining whether the observed difference is, or is not, within the range of normal sampling fluctuations; and

- deciding whether we accept or reject the null hypothesis.

Box 8.7 presents the results from our study of egalitarianism. Various computations are made and the resulting test of significance, the *F* test, indicates that the null hypothesis should be rejected. The differences in the mean scores on egalitarianism (27.35 in New Zealand, 30.60 in Canada,

BOX 8.7

Analysis of Variance of Egalitarianism by Country

	EGALITARIANISM SCORES			
	CANADA	NEW ZEALAND	AUSTRALIA	TOTAL
	34	36	37	
	28	49	34	
	24	38	33	
	31	33	24	
	30	27	31	
	...	...	...	
	30	34	43	
Sums	1,989	1,559	2,061	5,609
Means	30.60	27.35	34.35	30.82
Number of cases	65	57	60	182

Steps in Computing a Simple Analysis of Variance

Three measures of variation are required to compute the analysis of variance. These are total variation, between variation, and within variation:

$$\frac{\text{Total}}{\text{variation}} = \frac{\text{Between}}{\text{variation}} + \frac{\text{Within}}{\text{variation}}$$

The *total variation* may be computed by summing the squares of all the egalitarian scores and subtracting from that result the square of the sum divided by the total number of cases. As in:

STEP 1. $34^2 + 28^2 + \ldots + 43^2 = 186,677$

minus

STEP 2. $5,609^2 \div 182 = 172,862$

equals

STEP 3. $186,677 - 172,862 = 13,815$

Total variation $= 13,815$

STEP 4. The *between variation* may be computed by squaring the column totals, dividing this value by the number of cases, then summing the result, and finally subtracting the value in step 2 above. As in:

$((1,989^2 \div 65) + (1,559^2 \div 57) + (2,061^2 \div 60)) - 172,862 = 1,437$

STEP 5. The *within variation* may be determined by simply subtracting the between variation from the total variation. As in:

$13,815 - 1,437 = 12,378$

STEP 6. An *F* ratio table may be computed as follows:

	SUMS OF SQUARES	DEGREES OF FREEDOM	MEAN OF SQUARES	F	F. PROB.
Total variation	13,815	N – 1 = 181			
Between variation	1,437	k – 1 = 2	718.4	10.39	0.0001
Within variation	12,378	N – k = 179	69.2		

Where k = number of categories in the independent variable.

STEP 7. To estimate the mean squares (population variance) for the between and within rows, divide the sums of squares for the row by the degrees of freedom for the row, as in:

(i) Between estimate of mean squares: 1,437 ÷ 2 = 718.5

(ii) Within estimate of mean squares: 12,378 ÷ 179 = 69.2

STEP 8. To calculate the F ratio, divide the *within variation* (69.2) into the *between variation* (718.4):

718.4 ÷ 69.2 = 10.39

STEP 9. If the probability is not calculated for you (in cases when the values are hand calculated, or when using some software packages) we will need to determine the value which has to be exceeded in order to reject the null hypothesis by looking up the value on the F table (Appendix E). The F table requires the use of two values for degrees of freedom: the *between variation df* value is placed across the top of the table (in the sample case df = 2); the *within variation df* value is arranged along the vertical column (in our table df = 179). We will test the hypothesis at the 0.05 level. The critical value given in the table is 3.07. The F ratio must equal or exceed this value in order to reject the null hypothesis.

STEP 10. Since the F ratio for the sample data is 10.39 (exceeding the critical value), the null hypothesis is rejected. Variability of the magnitude reported in the egalitarianism scores is considered to be statistically significant. If the differences between the countries had been smaller, and we were led to accept the null hypothesis, we would argue that the differences observed simply reflect sampling fluctuations and that we could not reasonably conclude that there is a "real" difference in the egalitarian scores of the respondents from each of the three countries. (In most software packages the exact probabilities are provided for the researcher, which allows the researcher to skip steps 9 and 10.)

and 34.35 in Australia) are more than one would expect from normal sample fluctuations. We conclude, therefore, that there is a statistically significant difference in egalitarianism scores of samples drawn from the three countries.

The test of significance is based on the idea that, when a sample is drawn, there will be fluctuations in the mean egalitarian scores. What the test is doing is assessing the chance, if the true difference between the countries in egalitarianism is zero, of getting a sample fluctuation of the magnitude shown in the sample data. In the case under examination, the differences range from a low of 27.35 in New Zealand to a high of 34.35 in Australia on the egalitarianism index. The test of significance reveals that the observed fluctuation is greater than a fluctuation that would probably be due to normal sample variability. In other words, if there was no "real" egalitarianism difference between the countries, a sample would reveal a difference ± 7.0 points less than 5 percent of the time simply because of sampling fluctuations. On the other hand, if the observed difference could occur more than 5 percent of the time, we would accept the null hypothesis, and conclude that there are no statistically significant differences in egalitarianism in the populations studied.

To repeat, a statistically significant relationship is one where the observed difference would occur by chance less than 5 percent of the time. If the test were set at the 1 percent level, it would simply be more difficult to reject the null hypothesis; here the difference would be statistically significant only if it could occur by chance less than 1 percent of the time.

2. COMPUTATIONAL DETAILS FOR A SIMPLE ANALYSIS OF VARIANCE

Like the computational procedure involved in determining the correlation between two variables, the procedures for an analysis of variance require a measurement of two kinds of variation: variations within a column (for example, differences within each country), and variations between columns (differences that show up between Canada, New Zealand, and Australia). An analysis of variance involves computing a ratio which compares these two kinds of variability—within-column and between-column variability.

On examining the data within column one (Canada data) of Box 8.7, note that country of origin cannot explain variations *within* this column (all cases are Canadian). Differences in egalitarian scores *between* the columns, however, may be explained by the association with the independent variable (country).

Box 8.7 goes through the computation of a one-way analysis of variance for the sample data. In this particular case, the estimates of variance indicate more variation between the columns than within them; as a result, the F ratio is more than one. After the F ratio is computed, and the critical value is looked up in Appendix C, the decision is made to reject the null hypothesis, since the computed F ratio is more than the value looked up in the Appendix.

A. MEANS: COMPARING A DEPENDENT VARIABLE ACROSS CATEGORIES OF INDEPENDENT VARIABLE(S)

Frequently researchers use multiple independent variables to show how the means on the dependent variable vary across the categories of the independent variables. Survey designs often use this procedure to compute results.

To perform this analysis using SPSS see the MEANS, procedure in Appendix A.

3. ANALYSIS OF VARIANCE WITH ADDITIONAL VARIABLES

A. ANOVA

Experimental researchers use **analysis of variance (ANOVA)** when their design has more than one independent variable or multiple treatment levels. The inclusion of additional complexity is relatively simple and provides an opportunity to explore the interaction of treatment variables (where effects change for different combinations of treatment variables) in influencing the dependent variable. Note that the variations which are compared in an analysis of vari-ance are composed of two elements: random error and possible treatment effects. The test which is done compares the ratio in the following way:

$$F = \frac{\text{Random error} + \text{Possible treatment effects}}{\text{Random error}}$$

The interpretation of the results of an ANOVA test is split between a concern for:

- the main effect of treatment variable A;

- the main effect of treatment variable B;

- an interaction of the treatment variables (A x B);

- an error term (within groups).

Box 8.8 presents the results of an analysis of variance test. To interpret such a table one normally begins with an examination of the main effects, and if there are significant main effects, one would then examine whether there are significant interactions.

BOX 8.8

Sample ANOVA Results

Suppose we had run an experiment with one dependent variable, two treatments, and that we wished to test for possible interactions between the treatments. In such cases, we would perform a two-way analysis of variance, with a test for interaction (ANOVA).

The output might be summarized in the following way:

SOURCE OF VARIANCE	SUM OF SQUARES	DF	MEAN SQUARE	F	SIG. OF F
Main effect (A)	1,449.393	2	724.697	10.421	.000
Main effect (B)	12.652	1	12.652	0.182	.670
Interaction (A x B)	125.990	2	62.995	0.906	.406
Error term-within groups	12,239.591	176	69.543		
Total	13,815.016	181	76.326		

Understanding the Values in the Summary Table

The steps outlined below should be followed to understand the above table:

(i) The degrees of freedom are calculated as follows:

- main effect (A): df = 1 less than number of levels in that factor. (In this case: $3 - 1 = 2$)

- main effect (B): df = 1 less than number of levels in that factor. (In this case: $2 - 1 = 1$)

- interaction effect (A × B): df = product of the dfs making up the interaction. (In this case: $2 \times 1 = 2$)

- error term: df = total number of cases minus the product of number of levels of A and B. (In this case, $182 - (3 \times 2) = 176$.)

- Total df = N − 1 (In this case $182 - 1 = 181$)

(ii) To compute the mean square for an effect, divide the sum of squares for the effect by its df.

(iii) To compute the F value for each effect, divide the mean square by the mean square error term.

2. Interpreting the Results

In inspecting your results, you will want to examine two issues as you begin to interpret them. First you will want to know if your treatment variables had a significant effect; and, if either or both did, you will want to see if there is any interaction between the treatments.

A. MAIN EFFECTS To decide if a treatment was statistically significant, you will need to compare the F value to the values found in Appendix E using the appropriate degrees of freedom. If the value you obtained is larger than the one reported in Appendix E, you have a statistically significant effect. To use Appendix E you will need values for the required degrees of freedom: use the smaller value across the top of the table, and the larger one on the vertical axis.

B. INTERACTION EFFECTS If you have a significant main effect, you will then want to inspect your results for any interactions between the effects.

Your job is simple if there is no significant interaction effect: you simply report that none was present. It is more complicated with an interaction. In this case, the effect of a treatment is not independent of the other treatment; it may be that under the high condition of Treatment A, we find that treatment B does not enhance the impact on the dependent variable.

See the figures in Box 17.7 for an illustration of how plots can be used to show relationships with and without significant interactions.

Analysis of variance is a major analytical tool, used particularly by experimental researchers. Normally, all such computations will be made by computers. The re-

To perform this analysis using SPSS see the ANOVA procedure in Appendix A.

searcher will encounter *F* distributions in using the MEANS, ANOVA, MANOVA, and REGRESSION procedures.

E. WHEN TESTS OF SIGNIFICANCE ARE NOT APPROPRIATE

Tests of significance are often inapplicable. Yet they are widely used, often improperly (Selvin, 1957; Gold, 1958; Beshers, 1958; McGinnis, 1958; Morrison and Henkel, 1970; Skipper, Guenther, & Nass, 1967). Why is this the case?

Performing tests of significance is, no doubt, often motivated by the desire to be scientific, or appear to be scientific. If one's data turn out to be "statistically significant," then that is taken to demonstrate the importance of the finding, and to confer scientific legitimacy on one's work. Such tests help to create the impression that the God of science—that independent, unbiased arbiter of truth—has blessed one's research with approval.

A second motivation perhaps has to do with the fact that such tests are routinely—even if inappropriately—reported in the literature. Hence, to produce a report that meets the standards of the discipline, tests of significance are expected.

A third possibility is that tests of significance are poorly understood by social scientists, and that they are inappropriately used because of such misunderstandings.

For a variety of reasons, many studies should not be using tests of significance. The following rules indicate when such tests are inappropriate.

RULE 8.1

Tests of significance are not applicable when total populations are studied. If a study is being done on the wage differences between male and female faculty members and data relating to all faculty members are analysed, then a test of significance would not be in order. If a $1,500 difference is observed after the appropriate controls are introduced, this difference is absolute. The researcher must decide whether the difference is to be characterized as substantial, modest, or trivial. To say that it is statistically significant is simply wrong!

Arguments have been advanced that a study like the one above represents a sample out of a universe of possible samples that might be taken. The problem with this argument is that not all institutions were given an equal chance to be included; second, if you wish to make the argument that this is but one case among many, then you have shifted the unit of analysis to the institutional level (a university) and now have one case represented by one difference. Here you would be left with a difference of $1,500, but with no knowledge of what differences are present in other institutions.

RULE 8.2

Tests of significance are not appropriate when non-probability sampling procedures are employed. Data gathered using convenience or quota samples are not properly analysed using tests of significance. Since tests of significance only provide a measure of the probability of a given difference being the result of sampling fluctuations, assuming that probability sampling procedures have been used, such tests are not appropriate if those methods are not used. If an experimenter asked people to volunteer to be in a treatment group and then wished to compare these individuals to others who agreed to serve as controls, any test of significance on the differences between the groups would be meaningless.

In experimental designs where volunteers have been sought for participation (convenience sample), but where subjects have been assigned to treatment and control groups using random sampling techniques, it is appropriate to use tests of significance to compare the treatment and control groups. However, in such instances the population should be regarded as those who volunteered for participation.

RULE 8.3

Tests of significance are to be considered suspect when there is a substantial non-participation rate. If substantial numbers of respondents have refused to participate (for argument's sake, let's say 40 percent), then tests of significance become problematic, for it is difficult to assume that non-participants are similar to those who agree to participate in the study. Hence the extent to which such data can be considered representative can be called into question.

RULE 8.4

In *non-experimental research*, if one is exploring a relationship which has been shown to be statistically significant, it is inappropriate to employ a test of significance once again when controls have been applied to check for spuriousness or an intervening variable. The issue in evaluating models is to assess the impact of the control on the original relationship, and to observe whether the differences have remained the same, increased, decreased, or disappeared. Frequently, they may change from being statistically significant to being statisti-

cally insignificant, but this change may simply represent the fact that the data have been partitioned (perhaps cut in half). Therefore, if fewer cases are involved, the switch from significance to non-significance may simply reflect that change.

The researcher should note how much the original relationship has shifted, not simply note whether the relationship is still statistically significant. To avoid confusion, do not employ tests of significance when causal models are being evaluated beyond the stage of the initial relationship. For example if the relationship between *X* and *Y* is being explored, and if sampling and other conditions are appropriate, then a test of significance for the relation between *X* and *Y* is legitimate. However, having established that there is a statistically significant relation between *X* and *Y*, a further test of significance would not be appropriate when one is testing to ensure that the relationship is not spurious because of its connection to some third variable. (This point is discussed in Chapter 16.)

RULE 8.5

Tests of significance may not be applied to relationships which were not formulated as hypotheses prior to the collection of data for the study. Researchers routinely collect data on many variables—it is not unusual in a survey, for example, to collect data on 100 or more variables. If we run every variable against every other one, we will not only generate enormous piles of computer output, but we will also generate results for many hundreds of theoretically meaningless relationships, and will also generate many "statistically significant" relationships. Indeed, one would expect that one-in-twenty tables will prove to be significant, providing one is using the 0.05 level for one's tests. Unfortunately, researchers rarely report how many relationships were analyzed, what confounding data have been discarded, and which causal models were not fully developed prior to data collection.

An exception to the above rule has to be made for those analysing secondary data. In such cases, hypotheses need to be formulated prior to data analysis. In addition, while not reporting the results of the tests, some researchers find it useful to run tests of significance even in inappropriate situations to help shed light on the relationships explored.

Researchers must use tests of significance only with great care. Above all, the beginning researcher must appreciate what such tests really measure. All too often it is not recognized that a finding may be equally important whether the relationship is statistically significant or not. Social scientists are in the business of trying to understand and to describe the social world, and to have discovered that there is no relationship between *A* and *B* is as important as it is to discover that there is a relation between *A* and *B*. And, if one is testing a theory, it is especially important to find that a predicted relationship does not hold, for this will cast doubt on the theory and, perhaps, lead to a refinement or refutation of it. In short, do not despair if your study does not yield statistically significant results. Science proceeds through disconfirmation, through ruling out alternatives, through rejecting, modifying, and continually re-thinking theoretical formulations.

F. KEY TERMS

Accept the null hypothesis	Null hypothesis	Statistical significance
Analysis of variance (ANOVA)	One-tailed test	*t*-test
Chi-square test (X^2)	Reject the null hypothesis	Test of significance
Covariates	Research hypothesis	Two-tailed test
Degrees of freedom	Sampling distribution	Type I error
F distribution	Standard error of the means	Type II error

G. KEY POINTS

A *test of significance* reports the probability that an observed association or difference is the result of sampling fluctuations, and does not reflect of some "real" difference in the population from which the sample has been taken.

It is the *null (no relationship) hypothesis* that is tested in a test of significance. The test will lead the researcher to one of two conclusions: either to *reject* the null hypothesis or to *accept* it.

If the nature of the relationship has been specified in the research hypothesis (e.g., "females are less accepting of physical violence than males"), then a one-tailed test is performed to test the null hypothesis. If the nature of the relationship has not been specified (e.g., "there is a relationship between gender and the acceptance of physical violence"), then a two-tailed test of the null hypothesis is performed.

When researchers talk about sampling distributions, they are talking about how, by drawing repeated samples from the same population, and plotting the mean values of some measured variable, the plot of the means from the many samples would result in a normal curve. The *standard error of the means* is a measure of variability in the means of repeated samples.

In doing tests of significance, we are assessing whether the results of one sample fall within or outside the null hypothesis acceptance zone (usually 95% of the distribution). A *chi-square test* is a test of significance used with nominal or ordinal data which compares expected frequencies (if there are no differences between categories) and observed frequencies.

T-tests and analysis of variance tests of significance compare variability of a ratio-level dependent measure within categories of a treatment variable(s) to the variability between the categories.

Tests of significance are not used when:

• total populations are measured;

• when non-probability sampling procedures have been employed;

• when testing for spurious, intervening, or conditional relationships;

• when hypotheses have not been formulated prior to data analysis.

H. EXERCISES

1. Test the null hypothesis that there is no difference in parental identification by those women enrolled in sex-traditional versus non-traditional university programs. Test the hypothesis at the 0.05 level. The data are shown in the table below.

GENDER TRADITIONAL OR NON-TRADITIONAL PROGRAM ENROLMENT BY GENDER OF PARENT IDENTIFIED WITH, FEMALE STUDENTS

PROGRAM TYPE	IDENTIFY MOTHER		IDENTIFY FATHER		TOTAL	
	N	%	N	%	N	%
Traditional	31	47.0	21	34.4	52	40.9
Non-traditional	35	53.0	40	65.5	75	59.9
TOTAL	66	100.0	61	99.9	127	100.0

2. You have examined the salaries of all the staff working in a department store. What is the appropriate test to determine if there is a statistically significant difference between male and female salaries? (Caution: this is a trick question!) The data are shown in the table below.

INCOME LIST BY GENDER, BIGTOWN DEPARTMENT STORE

Males	Females
26,200	26,600
27,300	26,800
18,800	29,100
30,200	28,700
29,600	17,700
28,800	28,600
27,900	37,700
31,100	30,400

I. RECOMMENDED READINGS

BLALOCK, HUBERT M., JR. (1979). *Social Statistics* (Second Edition). Toronto: McGraw-Hill Book Company. This classic is widely used in both undergraduate and graduate courses in social science statistics courses.

MITCHELL, MARK, AND JANINA JOLLEY (1992). *Research Design Explained* (Second Edition). Orlando: Harcourt Brace Jovanovitch College Publishers. This is an exceptionally fine text with excellent research examples and it explains analysis of variance well.

SIEGEL, SIDNEY (1956). *Nonparametric Statistics for the Behavioral Sciences*. New York: McGraw-Hill. This book remains a basic reference for behavioral scientists. It pulls together a variety of tests which require fewer assumptions about the sample studied.

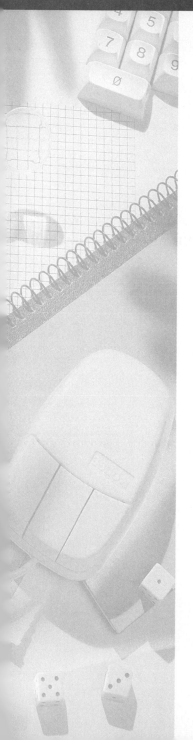

BEGINNING THE PROJECT

Part Four of the book begins with issues that need to be thought about carefully as you commence a research project: these issues have to do with the problem of bias (Chapter 9) and with ethical questions (Chapter 10). The remaining chapters in Part Four deal with taking the first steps in designing a project (Chapter 11), thinking about measurement issues (Chapter 12), designing questionnaires (Chapter 13), and how to go about sampling (Chapter 14). How relevant each of these chapters is will depend upon the type of research design that you are working with; if you are doing a content analysis, for example, you will be able to skip Chapter 13. If you are doing a participant observation study in a hospital, chapters 13 and 14 will not be of much relevance to your study.

BIAS

Chapter 2 argued that humans like to generalize—always trying to come up with rules to understand behaviour. These general rules set up expectations about how things work. These shared understandings may be thought of as biases or sets of predispositions and expectations. If social research is to produce reliable generalizations about human behaviour, we need unbiased evidence—evidence not influenced by what the researcher would like to find. But the tendency to bias conclusions in the direction of expectations—or preferences—is a danger in all research. This chapter will explore the nature of bias and illustrate that, at all stages of the research process, the danger of bias needs to be recognized. The chapter will conclude with some rules for detecting and minimizing bias.

A. THE NATURE OF BIAS

A **bias** may be thought of as a preference—or predisposition—to favour a particular conclusion. **Research bias** may be defined as the systematic distortion of research conclusions. Typically these distortions are inadvertent, but they can also be intentional. They no doubt occur in all disciplines, and can influence most phases of a project: from problem selection, to the identification of variables, to developing measurements, to collecting and analysing data, and to interpreting the results of the research.

To suggest that there is bias, or distortion, implies that there is an underlying truth waiting to be described accurately. For the social scientist this stable, unwavering truth is not so easily described. The reality we study varies according to many conditions and varies also across individuals, groups, and cultures. Indeed the questions we ask about social issues are difficult. And the results of any study depend not only on who is studied, but also on subtle cues that we provide in asking questions. So the results social scientists get are highly dependent on a whole host of factors. We can only hope to minimize the effects of these factors.

To illustrate this point, recall the experimental work by Stanley Milgram (1963) on obedience to authority. (See Box 3.3 for an excerpt from one of his studies.) His research program involved testing how many subjects would be willing to apply electric shocks to a fellow volunteer in an experiment. (See Chapter 10 for more details on Milgram's studies.) Milgram's research program was an extensive one, involving some 19 different experimental conditions and 616 subjects (Reynolds, 1982 pp. 25-26). By changing the conditions of the study slightly, the percentage of subjects who were prepared to administer strong shocks to fellow participants varied from zero to 92.5 percent. The variation depended on the instructions, who gave the instructions, the location of the experiment, and so forth. In other words, many factors influenced the level of compliance showed by subjects when ordered to administer electric shocks. So what is the underlying truth? It depends. Many factors seem to be at play here. Indeed, the Milgram research indicates that variations in the results of studies should not be surprising, since relatively small changes in the design of a study can make enormous differences to its results. Each set of conditions has its own truth.

Bias is just one of many factors that may be influencing the outcome of a study.

How important bias itself is will vary across many conditions. When we fail to replicate a study (fail to get the same finding as another researcher), we cannot assume that the difference in results is due to bias alone. Many factors, including bias, may have been responsible.

In everyday life we have our likes and dislikes. Often interpretations of our experiences serve to confirm for us what we already knew or thought. In short, bias helps to organize our interpretation of events and make sense of a complex world. So when our good friend John messes up and fails to submit his term paper on time, he interprets this as a sign that he is under a lot of pressure, and, on top of that, his girlfriend just walked out on him. An acquaintance of John sees his failure to submit his work on time as just another indication that John will never amount to much, with all his drinking and womanizing. The point is that we often find corroborative evidence for our predispositions. John himself finds a justification for his behaviour; the John-basher finds yet another reason why John should be shunned. Sometimes it takes quite powerful contrary evidence to change our minds; and when we must change our minds, we do so unwillingly, with much moaning and groaning.

In theory at least, social research systematically challenges our predispositions. The trouble is that we also take these same predispositions with us to our social research laboratories. Furthermore, as researchers, we tend to incorporate some research findings into our predispositions, and these too may become difficult to change. Science itself is part of the lore of the culture, but it also has a lore all of its own. In a sense, then, the social scientist has a double load of biasing predisposi-

tions: one acquired as a member of society, and another heaped on by the experience and knowledge acquired as a participant in an academic discipline. Both sources of bias need to be recognized as potential blinders to a clear view of social behaviour, unfettered by expectations or preferences.

The view of women in the development of psychology is an excellent illustration of the problem of bias in a discipline. Shields (1988) argues that much of nineteenth- and early twentieth-century psychology was severely limited because it assumed female intellectual inferiority. Research was devoted not to questioning this assumption but rather to various attempts to understand this inferiority. Thus efforts were made to:

(i) identify those parts of the brain which were more poorly developed in women than in men;

(ii) understand how the greater variability in male skills leads to a higher proportion of male geniuses;

(iii) understand the role of the maternal instinct in maintaining women in passive, subservient roles.

Shields concludes her article by noting:

Graves (1968, p. v) included among the functions of mythologizing that of the justification of existing social systems. This function was clearly operative throughout the evolutionist-functionalist treatment of the psychology of women: the 'discovery' of sex differences in brain structure to correspond to 'appropriate' sex differences in brain function; the biological justification (via the variability hypothesis) for the enforcement of women's subordinate social status; the

Victorian weakness and gentility associated with maternity; and pervading each of these themes, the assumption of an innate emotional, sexless, unimaginative female character that played the perfect foil to the Darwin male. That science played handmaiden to social values cannot be denied. Whether a parallel situation exists in today's study of sex differences is open to question (Shields, 1988, p. 55).

While there may be dangers in the researcher becoming overly self-conscious about research procedures and unwarranted assumptions, nonetheless he or she should be aware of the way in which bias may affect the conclusions of a social science report. The danger of becoming overly concerned is that the researcher may spend far too much time contemplating the difficulties of research, and, as a result, not get the job done.

B. SOURCES OF BIAS IN THE RESEARCH PROCESS

Frequently the social researcher is confronted with "interesting" findings for which an explanation should be offered. Suppose, for example, that a project measures high school students' socio-economic backgrounds (SES) and their aspirations for higher education. And suppose, during data analysis, that a robust relationship emerges indicating that the higher a student's socio-economic origin, the greater the likelihood that the student will aspire to post-secondary education. At this stage, the researcher may wonder what explains the pattern that has emerged. Possibilities such as the following might come to mind:

- peers of high SES students have high aspirations themselves and influence their friends in such a way that they plan to attend post-secondary institutions;

- the parents of high SES students have higher expectations concerning their children's educational achievements;

- high SES students know that they have the financial backing to attend a post-secondary institution and therefore plan to do so;

- teachers encourage high SES students more;

- high SES students have been exposed more frequently to high occupational achievers and are therefore more likely to model themselves on such individuals.

Unfortunately, the study may not have been designed to test, and possibly to rule out, competing explanations. The problem here is that while much data documenting a variety of relationships may have been presented, the reader of the report may be convinced, inappropriately, that the researcher has provided evidence for the particular explanation offered: "after all, look at all the tables that are presented." There may, however, be little or no such evidence, even though the explanation may sound good and appear reasonable. We need to design studies which systematically test a variety of possible explanations for the relationship under examination. At times the social scientist may feel pressured to provide an explanation even though there is little or no evidence available to check it.

We are, in short, contending that much of what is said about social science research methods describes ideal practices and is not always a good description of what is actually done. Much is not reported. Indeed, a term, researcher affect, has been used to characterize this phenomenon. **Researcher affect** refers to the danger of researchers falling in love with a particular explanation for some relationship, or some view of the world, and inadvertently using procedures that lead to conclusions supporting the preferred explanation or world view. All stages of the research process may be affected adversely by bias. In this chapter, we shall examine how bias can affect the initial selection of the problem to be researched, the sample design, funding decisions, data collection, data analysis, and the reporting and use of research findings.

1. SELECTION OF THE PROBLEM

The issue in problem selection is that some phenomena are judged to be more important than others—some are considered worthy of exploration, others not. Because of this, the choice of subject matter provides a clue as to the values held by the researcher. Within North American culture, researchers are more likely to study armed robbery than the incidence of friendly greetings on a street corner. The former is viewed as a social problem, the latter not. The researcher is likely to see robbery as a problem which has negative consequences, and also as one which should be controlled or eliminated. It could be argued that identifying the most effective variables in reducing robberies can be done without bias. But there is

probably no value-free, culture-independent way of choosing variables for a study. Bias will result in the selection of those variables conventionally considered important and the exclusion of those conventionally considered unimportant.

2. SAMPLING DESIGN

Whether one opts for a survey, panel study, case study, or experimental design, there are potential sources of bias in the sample selected for study. For example, by choosing to survey attitudes toward capital punishment in a community containing a maximum security prison, a researcher will probably produce a study that shows fairly high levels of support for capital punishment. To pursue the example further, a researcher might do a case study of the attitudes of police officers in a rural community on public policy issues. Once again, attitudes favouring capital punishment will probably emerge. Choosing both a rural community and a police organization increases the likelihood that the attitudes expressed will favour capital punishment more than would be the case in most other areas, or with many other work groups. The experienced researcher, knowing how different variables usually work out, can choose a research design, sets of variables, and ways of wording questions so as to bias results.

A problem that has plagued social science research is that of sexism. At all stages of research, but especially at the design stage, care must be taken to avoid sexism. Margrit Eichler's *Nonsexist Research Methods* (1988) identifies several types of sexism in research. The major types she identifies include:

A. ANDROCENTRICITY

If someone presents the world from an exclusively male perspective as if this perspective were universal, that person is guilty of *androcentricity*. Eichler uses the example of "intergroup warfare" as a "means of gaining women and slaves." Eichler points out that the real group here is males, since what is gained is women. Here women are seen as passive objects that are acted upon, not as part of the group being discussed. (Eichler, 1988, p. 5).

B. OVERGENERALIZATION

If a study claims to study all people but, in fact, samples only, or largely, males, we have an example of an *overgeneralization*. Eichler uses the example of a sample of males to study social class; she also points out that when one uses the term "parents" to refer to mothers, one is guilty of overgeneralization, since one is ignoring fathers. A parallel problem is *overspecificity*, when single-sex terms are used to describe situations applicable to both sexes: for example "the doctor...he"; "the nurse...she" (Eichler, 1988, p. 6).

C. GENDER INSENSITIVITY

To ignore gender as an important variable is to display *gender insensitivity*. Researchers should identify the gender composition of their samples and be sensitive to the different impacts social policies have on men and women (Eichler, 1988, pp. 6-7).

Familism is a special case of gender insensitivity and involves treating the family as the unit of analysis when, in fact, it is individuals within the family unit that engage in a particular activity or hold a certain attitude. Familism is also a problem when we assume that some phenomenon has an equal impact on all members of the family when, in fact, it may affect different family members in different ways.

D. DOUBLE STANDARDS

If a researcher uses different means of measuring identical behaviours, attitudes, or situations for each gender, that researcher would be guilty of using a *double standard*. But note that some qualities may only exist in one gender category (Eichler, 1988, p. 7).

Sex appropriateness is a special case of the double standard and refers to a situation where "attributes are assigned only to one sex or the other and are treated as more important for the sex to which they have been assigned" (Eichler, 1988, p. 8).

If a researcher treats the sexes as discrete social, as well as biological, cohorts rather than two cohorts with shared characteristics, then the researcher is guilty of *sexual dichotomism* (Eichler, 1988, p. 9).

3. FUNDING

Granting agencies, although they may claim to fund projects on the basis of merit, are themselves subject to bias. In Canada, for example, the Social Sciences and Humanities Research Council (SSHRC), has funds targeted to encourage research in specified areas. The federal government, which provides the funding for SSHRC, may wish to promote scholarly inquiry into some areas. These are designated, and funds are set aside for projects in that area. Projects in such areas are then favoured over other projects.

In addition, scholars in the traditional disciplines are more readily funded than those in newer areas. Indeed, in recent years, the SSHRC has set up a special committee to deal with applications for people working in inter-disciplinary programs or in newly developing areas. The establishment of the new review committee was a response to the perception that scholars in some areas were at a disadvantage when competing with scholars in traditional disciplines.

The value society places on different kinds of research is also reflected in the relative amounts of research funds made available. The NSERC (Natural Sciences and Engineering Research Council) and the MRC (Medical Research Council) are relatively well funded in comparison to the SSHRC.

Project funding decisions are adjudicated by peer review committees. University scholars are appointed to discipline committees and make recommendations on funding. SSHRC committees have an especially difficult time given the high demand for funds and the severely limited resources available to each committee. These committees more or less represent the collective wisdom of each discipline. They reflect current research trends and views as to what kinds of research should be funded.

Research operates in a social context. The researcher is constrained by peers and granting agencies from engaging in "trivial" research and required to tackle issues that are considered "important." Research is not free of social constraints.

4. DATA COLLECTION

There is an extensive literature in psychology dealing with the influence the experimenter may have on the results of a study.

Robert Rosenthal and K.L. Fode (1963, pp. 183-89), for example, did a series of important ***experimenter effect*** studies where student researchers were asked to collect data on the number of trials it took rats to learn a maze. The student researchers were informed that a new breed of laboratory rat was being developed and that it had been bred for intelligence; the observations were to see if, in fact, there was any difference between the specially bred "smart" rats and ordinary laboratory rats. And so the students set to work, running the two types of rats through the maze.

It turned out that, indeed, the "smart" rats took fewer trials to learn the maze than the "ordinary" ones. Apparently the breeding program was working. There was just one problem. Dr. Rosenthal did not have any smart rats. The rats were simply assigned randomly to the "smart" and the "ordinary" categories. It was the students who were the "real" subjects of this study. Somehow their expectations about the outcome of the trials had an impact on the results of the study. If the experimenter expects a rat to learn fast, somehow the data will come out that way. Thus Rosenthal and Fode's findings indicate that there is a tendency to produce findings which are consistent with the experimenter's expectations. The explanation of the so-called experimenter effect has been more difficult to identify.

Did the students "fudge" the data to please the professor? Did they perceive "errors" differently for the two groups, perhaps being less likely to note an error made by the "smart" rats? Did they handle the rats differently? The generally accepted view is that experimenter effect occurs because of both the influence of behaviour by expectations and slight, but systematic recording errors by the observer (Johnson and Adair, 1970, pp. 270-75). But no matter what the explanation, Rosenthal's research is of critical importance to the experimentalist as well as to all social science researchers.

Before discussing the implications of Rosenthal's research, one other illustration is pertinent. A German mathematics teacher had a horse with unusual talents (Rosenthal, 1966). The amazing horse, known as Clever Hans, could solve simple mathematical problems by stamping his foot to indicate his answer. At first, skeptics thought that Clever Hans' trainer was signalling to the horse, thus accounting for the horse's unusual ability. However, it turned out that even when the trainer was removed from the room, the horse could still do the trick for other people posing the same questions.

The horse was, indeed, very smart. It turned out that Clever Hans' mathematical skills declined dramatically when the audience did not know the answer, or when he was blindfolded. Apparently he was watching the audience. If the answer was three, the audience would gaze intently at the hoof of the horse clumping out the answer; after three stomps, members of the audience would raise their heads slightly, focusing their gaze on the horse's head. The horse simply watched the audience— they cued him when to stop. A pretty smart horse. Not much at mathematics, but a good observer of body language.

How is Clever Hans relevant to the social scientist? Or, for that matter, what can we learn from Robert Rosenthal's experiments? Suppose you are conducting an interview. And suppose you have just asked the respondent how often she goes to church. The respondent replies: "I don't go to church." You say, raising your eyebrows

slightly, "Oh, so you don't go to church?" In all likelihood, your respondent now feels slightly uncomfortable—your eyebrow movement and your comment have communicated a message. After this, future questions about religious issues may well encourage the respondent to express more interest in religion than she actually has. It is as if the interviewer is demanding a pro-religion response. Respondents are often interested in figuring out what the survey is "really" all about. They will therefore be looking for cues, and may be influenced by them. If a Clever Hans notes a slight raising of heads in the audience, it is probable that most human subjects will be sensitive to a raised eyebrow, a change in voice tone, or a shift in the body position of the interviewer.

Box 9.1 presents one of a series of studies done by Johnson and Ryan (1976), demonstrating that while experimenters could not intentionally influence a subject's behaviour by using nonverbal cues, the experimenters did err in recording the subjects' responses. In this study the experimenters were to follow instructions carefully and were specifically told not to tell subjects how to respond. The study shows that while a subject's responses were not significantly altered by the experimenter, the results (because of the recording errors) were nonetheless biased in the direction of the experimenter's preferences.

Given the issue of **_expectancy_** raised by Rosenthal and the results of the Johnson and Ryan studies, the social researcher should avoid specifying the hypotheses of the study either to the respondents or the research assistants. Sometimes it is difficult, however, to withhold such information from one's research assistants. As a principal investigator, you want to make them feel that

BOX 9.1 SOCIAL RESEARCHERS AT WORK

Ronald W. Johnson and Brenda Ryan, Recording Errors and Expectancy: Excerpts from Experiment III

...It was hypothesized that experimenters would be unable to bias their subjects' responses in a positive direction (i.e., in the direction of their intended influence) and that any effects would be negative. Second, it was hypothesized that these experimenters would err in a positive direction when observing and/or recording their data.

Method

SUBJECTS AND EXPERIMENTERS Nine male and nine female paid volunteers from undergraduate courses served as experimenters, and were randomly assigned to conditions with the provision that equal numbers from each sex were represented. Their subjects were 144 paid respondents to newspaper and radio advertisements. All subjects had reached the age of 14 and the vast majority were either high school or university students. Experimenters were told that they were participating in an experiment on experimenter expectancy, and were given a brief history of research on that phenomenon. They were told that the investigators wished to determine whether or not experimenters could manipulate subjects' responses if they tried. Experimenters were asked to attempt such manipulation in any fashion they wished, with one exception. They were specifically directed not to tell subjects how to respond nor to tell subjects anything beyond the specific instructions. They were thus, more or less, restricted to nonverbal and/or to paralinguistic cues. Those experimenters who recorded data were cautioned as to the necessity for accuracy. Subjects were randomly assigned without regard to sex to the eight cells of a 3 × 2 × 2 factorial representing three levels of task, two levels of expectancy, and two sexes of experimenter.

TASKS Three different tasks were used. The first task was a marble-dropping task previously used by Johnson (1973). Subjects picked marbles, one at a time, from a cache and dropped them through holes drilled in a table top. They were instructed to drop as many as possible during a 6-min time period. Experimenters attempted to have half their subjects increase their rate during the sixth minute. Responses were recorded automatically by means of an event recorder [thus controlling for recorder errors]. A single score was derived for each subject by subtracting the number for the first minute from the number for the sixth minute.

Two other tasks were used besides the marble-dropping task with which a negative effect had previously been demonstrated (Johnson, 1973). The person-perception task and the latency-of-word-association task were selected. Subjects taking the person-perception task recorded their own responses so that observer/recorder error was controlled. The latency-of-word-association task was administered in the same fashion as in the first two studies; a digital timer was used. The experimenters were given lists of names indicating which subjects should be influenced to respond slowly to experimental words...

Results

In order to test the effects of the first hypothesis, that is, experimenters would be unable to influence their subjects' performance in the direction of their attempts and that any effects would be negative, a randomized-design analysis of variance was performed on scores derived for each subject. Observer/recorder error had been controlled for with the marble-dropping and with the person-perception tasks. For the latency-of-word-association task scores derived from the independent observer's recordings were used rather than the experimenters' observations. No main effects nor interactions are statistically significant. Thus, the first hypothesis is supported; that is, experimenters do not appear to have influenced positively their subjects' performance. However, neither was there any negative influence.

In order to test the hypothesis that experimenters would err in observing/recording their data in the direction of their attempted influence, an analysis of variance was performed on estimates of observer error for the latency-of-word-association task. A score was derived for each subject by subtracting the D-score derived from the experimenters' observations. Means for conditions are presented in the table below. The main effect for expectancy is statistically significant ($F(1,4) = 7.04$, $p < .02$). The effect of sex of experimenter and the Sex of Experimenter x Expectancy Interaction are not statistically significant. This supports the second hypothesis that experimenters will show systematic observer/recorder error. The significant main effect was further analyzed in order to ascertain whether all of the experimenters systematically erred in their observations. Randomization tests of independent samples (Siegel, 1956) indicated that two of the six experimenters significantly ($p < .05$) erred in the direction of their expectations.

Mean Estimates of Observer Error for the Word Association Test (Experiment III)[a]

	MALE EXPERIMENTER	FEMALE EXPERIMENTER
Expected high scorers	0.34	0.52
Expected low scorers	−0.07	−0.55

[a] N for each cell = 12.

Discussion

...In sum, these four studies demonstrated systematic observer bias whenever, but only when, observers intentionally tried to manipulate subjects' responses on the word association task it is more probable that the successful inducement of an expectancy is a necessary precondition for the demonstration of systematic bias. ...it would appear that systematic observer bias is task specific.

...The phenomenon of experimenter expectancy is demonstrated in something less than half of the studies testing expectancy hypotheses. That researchers can, only sometimes, replicate the Rosenthal effect may be indicative of a weak effect, perhaps of relatively little importance to psychology.

In light of the present data, where negative results were observed in the two experiments in which the major manipulation appeared to have been unsuccessful, and where some positive results coincided with successful manipulations in the third and fourth experiments, an interpretation of negative expectancy studies as a result of inadequate expectancy inducements should not be discounted. It is possible that, with more attention paid to the major inducement manipulation, more consistent results across studies will emerge. It may be that observer error, as well as expectancy affecting subjects' responses, occurs only with successful expectancy inducement.

Observer error in line with induced expectancies has again been demonstrated. Unlike the two previous reports (Johnson and Adair, 1970, 1972) this followed intentional inducement manipulations, rather than the standard expectancy inducement. Thus, observer error appears to play an important, although not nec-

essarily the entire, role in the demonstration of experimenter bias. It is particularly interesting to note, however, that observer error was demonstrated for one experimental task but not for a second task. It should be especially noted that this interaction between Task and Observer Error was demonstrated with the same experimenters testing subjects on both tasks. It would appear on the basis of these and earlier studies that the latency-of-word-association task is particularly susceptible to observer error following an expectancy inducement. It would also appear that at least one other task may be less susceptible to this artifact. It seems important, at this point, to measure expectancy-induced observer/recorder error with other experimental tasks.

It also seems clear from studies three and four that not all observers are equally susceptible to biasing their data. Tested individually, only 5 of the 14 observers in the two studies combined, demonstrated significant bias. As these tests were based on very small comparisons it may be that 5 of 14 is a low estimate of the ratio of observers susceptible to bias. Nonetheless, it is probable that individual differences are important. Future studies should include attempts at determining personality correlates of this susceptibility.

SOURCE: Johnson, Ronald W. and Brenda J. Ryan, "Observer Recorder Error as Affected by Different Tasks and Different Expectancy Inducements," *Journal of Research in Personality*, 10, (1976), pp. 201-214. Reprinted by permission of the publisher.

they are a part of the study and, therefore, feel that they should know what the study

is "really" about. However, if you tell the research assistants what the hypotheses are, they may inadvertently bias results either toward the hypothesis (if they are friendly), or away from it (if they are hostile).

Questionnaires or interview guides may also provide cues to the respondent and, unless one is careful, these may distort responses in the direction that the respondent thinks the researcher prefers. Such distortions are labelled **demand characteristics**. In such situations, test results are distorted because people respond in the way they think they are expected to respond. The term "demand characteristic" was coined by psychiatrist Martin T. Orne, who noted that subjects in experiments will sometimes play the role of "helpful subject" and produce the results they think the researcher desires (Orne, 1962). An illustration drawn from survey research would be the rather obvious attempt by Marx to elicit negative comments from workers when he posed the following question:

> *"If you are paid piece rates, is the quality of the article made a pretext for fraudulent deductions from your wages?"* (Bottomore, 1988, p. 215).

During the data collection phase, a research director must ensure that when a selected respondent refuses to participate, or is unavailable, that the replacement is selected on a equal probability basis (see Chapter 14). If this is not done, there is a danger that the data collection personnel will simply choose the most convenient replacement, and this will tend to bias the study by overrepresenting those people who spend more time at home.

5. DATA ANALYSIS

At the beginning of an analysis in surveys, interview studies, and participant observa-

tion studies, researchers go through a process of coding the information. What this means is that if data are collected in an open-ended format (questions without fixed-response categories), then the information will have to be placed into categories before analysis begins. The process of coding is subject to two kinds of error: random and systematic.

Random error refers to inconsistencies which enter into the coding process but which display no systematic pattern. For example, suppose that you are coding people into the following educational categories: (1) eight or fewer years of formal education, (2) nine to twelve years of formal education, (3) some post-secondary training, or (4) college or university graduation. If you accidentally coded a person with five years of education into category (2), you would have made an accidental or random error. In processing data, one often enters the information twice, comparing the first version with the second in order to locate such random errors. Occasionally, entry errors will include values that are not within the range of possible values: in the above example, entering a 6 would be an example of such an error. These errors are easiest to spot because, once data analysis begins, an out-of-range value will become apparent as soon as one runs a frequency distribution of the variable. And, since these errors simply represent "noise" in one's data, they are not as threatening to the conclusions of a study as systematic errors.

Systematic errors are especially problematic. These errors are in danger of biasing a study because they are systematic—they distort the data in one particular direction. For example, suppose that any person who does not answer the question on education is assigned to the lowest category, the category representing those people with eight or fewer years of education. In such cases, we would be biasing the data systematically for those who refuse to answer the question by always coding them as if they should fall into the lowest educational category. (Normally those who do not answer a question are assigned a missing value code for the question.) Another kind of systematic error could occur if we discovered, after having developed code categories and starting our work, that another and uncategorized kind of response is occurring halfway through the analysis. If, to save time, we do not go back to the beginning and reexamine all of our cases to see if some of the codings have been inappropriately forced into certain categories, we will have decreased the number of cases that fall into the newly discovered category systematically. This kind of difficulty is likely to pop up in studies which have many open-ended questions. (This is one reason, incidentally, why many social researchers avoid using a lot of open-ended questions.)

Particularly in survey and in non-reactive research, a great amount of information is collected on a large number of variables. This data may be treated in a variety of ways—many of which may be viewed as alternative modes of analysis. The researcher may analyze the data in a number of different ways, discarding those results which are "less interesting," and keeping those which make "the most sense." If cross-tabulations are being done, a variety of cut-points may be tried; some will be retained, and others will be discarded. (If you had measured respondents' education by years of formal school completed, and you now wished to group them

into two categories, low-and high-education, where would you draw the line between the two groups?) Frequently the data are worked with until the analysis producing the strongest association is identified and retained. Such procedures violate the principles of objectivity but are, nonetheless, practised in all disciplines. Each discipline has a range of approved methods of analysis. Thus playing with the data seems perfectly legitimate. After all, you want to produce the "best" analysis of the data. For some, the "best analysis" may include only statistically significant, publishable results. In massaging the data, the bias will be to find evidence supporting expected or preferred outcomes. Such ***data massaging*** is often done, but rarely reported, in formal presentations of the research.

Given the modern computer, it is now possible to run tests for many different relationships. There may be four or five different operationalizations of a concept (such as socio-economic status, for example) available to the researcher in a data set; perhaps the various hypothesized relationships are run using each of these possibilities. Finally, the one which is most congruent with the researcher's expectations gets reported. A rationale for throwing out some of the results can readily be found by arguing that they represent a "poor measurement" of the relevant variable. Most researchers have, from time to time, engaged in some "selective" use of data. If the researcher "hunts" through a data set long enough, an acceptable—even interesting—finding will surely emerge. At that point, the hunt stops.

In the physical and the social sciences "hunting" is common (Selvin and Stuart, 1966). What student in a chemistry or a physics laboratory has not checked the results obtained by other students? If unexpected results occur, then the procedure is rerun on the grounds that something must have been done wrong. In short, if anticipated results are not obtained, the results are discarded. Even the mature researcher has a tendency to work with the data until the "right" finding is obtained. The search for "reportable" findings is a continuous process in all science. Yet few papers acknowledge this search. Reading research papers leaves the impression that most projects are easy and straightforward. Few are.

For the survey researcher there is a special problem. Given many variables and observations, it is possible to run any variable against every other variable in a search for "significant findings." If we use the .05 level of significance (see Chapter 8), then we would expect one in twenty of the relationships examined to be statistically significant. Unless the researcher reports the "hunting" that has occurred, the reader of a report will be in no position to regard the conclusions with the skepticism they deserve.

Finally, it should be pointed out that there is nothing inherently wrong with "exploring" data, looking at relationships which have not been hypothesized. But such analyses should not be reported unless it is made clear that no hypothesis has guided the search. At least then, the reader has been cautioned.

6. REPORTING OF FINDINGS

In 1959 T.D. Sterling published an interesting paper which suggested that much of what is being published in learned journals may represent fluke results (Sterling, 1959, pp. 30-34). His argument is that there are a lot of researchers, and many may be working on a similar problem at any time. If the .05 level of significance has been used, one study in twenty will, on average, produce a statistically significant relationship purely by chance, and such studies may even get published (journals ordinarily do not publish papers reporting "no relationship" findings). The obvious question is: what proportion of journal articles are based on these fluke studies? While Sterling's point is an interesting one, it no doubt overstates the problem (Rosenthal, 1979, pp. 638-41). Nonetheless, the argument needs to be kept in mind as one possible source of bias in published studies.

Sterling's argument can be extended into another area. There is a selection process which finds certain findings reportable and others unreportable. Indeed, it is unusual for one's first analysis of the data to make it through to the final report. While there are many good reasons for analyzing data in different ways, the process of deciding which findings to report may have more to do with aesthetics than science.

The key issue is this: what scientific principle determines when analysis is finished? Do we stop analysis when we get a reportable, respectable finding? If we stop analysis when we get the results we like, the bias will be toward confirming expectations. While some of the data may be consistent with expectations, some may not be. Frequently, inconsistencies are not reported.

The difficulty is that some non-scientific considerations come into play when reports are written. Are the findings culturally acceptable? Are the findings acceptable to one's peers? Since there is pressure to keep papers reasonably short, only the "major" finding is reported: this "major" finding, however, may not be representative of the findings of the whole research project.

The point here is that not only does the choice of subject matter reflect values, but the researcher's theoretical predispositions may influence the conclusions of the study as much as any data collected. Marxists come to Marxist conclusions, functionalists to functionalist ones.

Chapter 2 outlined some types of flawed arguments that may find their way into the final report of a study. Included among these were: inappropriate appeals to authority; provincialism; setting up a false dilemma; missing, insufficient, or suppressed evidence; and unwarranted conclusions. The reader should be alert to these flaws in reading a final report on a research project.

In addition to being evident in theoretical predispositions and improper argument, bias can also be reflected by insensitivity to minorities, sexism, or in tendencies to go beyond the limits of one's data when interpreting them. And, while scholars are trained to be cautious in their interpretations, it is difficult to avoid suggesting extrapolations beyond those justified by the data. For example, any suggestion, made only on the basis of a study of 63 first-year students in political science at the University of Victoria, that there is a relation between social class and political party preference among Canadians would read far more than is justified into such data. Some of these issues will be explored more fully in Chapter 18, which deals with report writing.

7. THE USE OF FINDINGS

Given the enormous confidence that western culture has in science, it is no surprise that the findings of science are powerful tools. Courts, politicians, the media, and the general public seem to respect science. Increasingly social scientists are interviewed on radio and television, appear as expert witnesses in courts, and, indeed, provide evidence taken into account when legal and public-policy decisions are made. Scientific evidence is taken seriously.

Unfortunately, the research literature is easily misrepresented. The fact that the research literature contains many findings, some of which support a particular view and others which do not, is itself a potential source of biased reviews of that literature. The social scientist who is committed to some social cause, or to a particular theoretical perspective, may select evidence which helps establish a particular position—like a debater seeking support for a particular conclusion. Because of a desire to support a particular position, the debater is not interested in contrary evidence—only preferred evidence is reported. The problem with using the debater's approach is that many people may think that the findings are objective and impartial, that they reflect a dispassionate, scientific view. But they may simply be a conclusion seeking corroborating evidence. Debaters enjoy the credibility of social science while violating the principle of impartiality. When social scientists slip inadvertently into advocacy roles, they compromise their credibility as "impartial social scientists."

An impartial approach would try to disconfirm a theory, try to rule out alternatives, and continually press any given theory hard in an effort to discover the limits under which it is applicable. While this can never be achieved perfectly, those who attempt to follow this approach are, nonetheless, trying to eliminate as much bias as possible in their research or in their reviews of the literature.

Peter W. Huber has explored the problem of the scientist-for-hire as it relates to the American court system in his book *Galileo's Revenge: Junk Science in the Courtroom* (1991). Numerous court cases in which huge sums of money are at stake involve the use of expert scientific witnesses. Huber argues that the system is at fault because it seems unable to distinguish good scientific testimony from that of the science charlatans who make careers out of court appearances. American courts are faulted for setting insufficient standards as to who may testify. Frequently lawyers consider many scientists, settling finally on the ones who are willing to make "appropriate" testimony and to be coached. As personal injury lawyer, Dennis Roberts notes:

> *You get a professor who earns $60,000 a year and give him the opportunity to make a couple of hundred thousand dollars in his spare time and he will jump at the chance . . . They are like a bunch of hookers in June" (quoted in Huber, 1991, p. 19).*

While Huber is concerned primarily with the problem of testimony from practitioners of the medical and the physical sciences, it will be even more difficult to establish the legitimacy of evidence from the social scientists who may be asked to testify on such matters as community standards of morality, or on whether there is evidence that our legal and commercial institutions display bias against the poor, minorities, immigrants, or women.

In any case, Huber would argue that courts would do well to:

- pay more attention to establishing the consensus on a topic in the research community and rely less on the personal opinion of some expert who has been selected and groomed by a lawyer seeking a favourable outcome;

- note whether the findings reported have been peer-reviewed (articles judged by a panel of professional scientists);

- note whether the findings have been replicated (repeated by others);

- seek out their own independent experts who can testify objectively and impartially (Huber, 1991) .

So long as lawyers are doing the hiring, they are likely to stack the deck to improve their chances of winning their cases. This practice fails to represent the findings of science objectively and, thus, may compromise the ability of the courts to come to reasonable conclusions.

A Carnegie Commission report suggests that junk science testimony typically does not win in court. The commission recommends that courts ask three questions.

(i) can the scientific claim be tested;

(ii) has the test been done; and

(iii) was an appropriate scientific methodology used? (Begley, 1993, p. 64).

C. A PERSPECTIVE

As citizens, social scientists belong to a culture, but they are also members of the social science community and of sub-units within that community. And, just as membership in a culture predisposes one to favour certain beliefs, values, and behaviours, so, too, does membership in the social science community. There are many written and unwritten rules and understandings about what we should believe and how we should go about our work as social scientists.

1. UNDERSTANDING BIAS

Not only do we take the predispositions, or biases, of our culture to our research, but we also bring those acquired as members of various social science sub-groups. So, regardless of whether we are positivist, interpretive, or critical, in our basic perspective, we bring a set of assumptions, beliefs, theoretical orientations, and expectations to our research. Indeed, a text on methods provides sets of techniques for conducting research and attempts to socialize the student into an understanding and acceptance of the latest approaches to research. In their education, research methods students are provided with a set of dispositions, a set of rules not only for doing research but for judging the work of other scholars. In short, the norms of research are being communicated.

But the ideas conveyed in a methods text focus on the formal system of social science. You learn how to do research "properly." You learn what techniques are appropriate in any given circumstance. And most methods texts will urge you not to fall prey to bias, urge you to be fair and objective, and urge you to exercise great care so that you will do *good*, impartial research. Are there any problems with this?

The problem is that an important part of social research is missed. While most presentations of research sound straightforward, there is much that happens in the course of the research process that never gets reported. In short, the research act itself can be the subject of research. A careful examination of most social science research projects would reveal how bias inadvertently plays a role in research outcomes. There is, then, a formal system of science—somewhat mythical—and there is the real world of social science. The gap between myth and reality exists in all academic disciplines.

Research is social behaviour. There are expectations of others to be met, norms of behaviour to be followed, and findings which are anticipated. This social component of science is frequently at odds with the fundamental canons of science. Science as practised is neither value-free nor wholly objective. If actual research practices are observed, a whole host of non-scientific factors enter the picture. While the achievements of science have, indeed, been impressive, it is nonetheless true that there is a gap between the ideal and actual practices of science. An awareness of this gap, and of the sources of bias in research, can only benefit the beginning research methods student. Just as the good scientist is portrayed as a skeptic, so should we be skeptical of the methods of social science itself. Table 9.1 provides a few examples of gaps between actual and ideal practices in the social sciences.

Projects are rarely as straightforward as the final report on the project implies. Take sampling. It is a rare project that does not run into some difficulties here. First there are problems with refusals and lost questionnaires. Some of the responses may not be clear; when comparisons between the sample and the known parameters of the

TABLE 9.1 MYTHS AND REALITIES OF THE SOCIAL SCIENCES

CATEGORY	SOCIAL SCIENCE MYTHS	SOCIAL SCIENCE REALITIES
Value free?	Research is objective and value neutral	There are significant subjective elements in all research
Stereotype: Psychology	Psychologists primarily use experimental data	They also do field studies, surveys
Stereotype: Sociology	Sociologists primarily use survey data	They also do field studies, content analysis, experiments
Stereotype: Anthropology	Anthropologists study exotic cultures	They also study many contemporary western societies
Stereotype: Political Science	Political scientists study formal political organization and voting behaviour	They also study many other things, using a variety of techniques
Sampling	Most studies involve representative samples	Most studies are based on non-representative samples
Refusals	Most people are willing to participate in studies	Refusals run from 0% to 95%; commercial market researchers have highest non-participation rates
Funding	Open to all; based on peer review and an evaluation of the quality of the proposal and the research record of the applicant	Researchers who are not part of the university system have little chance of receiving funding; there are fads that determine what kinds of projects are funded
Measurement	Agreement on appropriate way to measure most variables	Little standardization or agreement on measures
Report writing	Final reports summarize the results of the observations	Evidence is selectively reported; some facts ignored, not reported
Tests of significance	They assess the extent to which results may be the result of chance sampling fluctuations	Often inappropriately used when non-probability sampling is used, or when whole populations studied

population are compared, there are often uncomfortable disparities. Interviewers may have cut corners in the interest of completing the project (such tactics may range from faking interviews to avoiding the normal random respondent-selection process, even going so far as to include whomever happens to be available in a sample). In short, research is inevitably more messy than our reports of it.

In our exploration of sources of bias in the various stages of research, we have noted how the outcomes of research may be distorted inadvertently. Findings tend to move in the direction of the culturally acceptable, in the direction of our expectations, and in the direction of our preferences. And, if the pervasive attitudes of both the relevant scholarly disciplines and the larger society are liberal, inclusive, and stress tolerance, then the research outcomes will tend to reflect these views. On the other hand, a more conservative, exclusive, and intolerant society will encourage research outcomes that are supportive of these views. Funding agencies and their selection processes will particularly encourage "mainstream" researchers—those whom referees think meet the standards governing "good" research. A similar argument can be advanced about the publication decisions of journal editors.

In recent decades a blurring of the line between ***advocacy research*** on the one hand, and ***pure/descriptive research*** on the other seems to have occurred. One possible explanation is that social science practitioners have become increasingly aware that all research carries cultural baggage with it. So, whether we talk of research design bias, funding decisions, data collection, analysis, interpretation, or publication decisions, research tends to reflect its sociocultural milieux. This realization perhaps helped to legitimize the use of social research to advocate changes or advance the personal or collective agendas of its practitioners. Box 9.2 contains a tongue-in-cheek classification of various diseases found in the social science community.

The challenge to create an impartial social science has been enormous: some would deny its possibility; others would claim that it is difficult, though not impossible; while still others would claim that all we can do is try to minimize bias in social research. Realizing that there are many difficulties in doing research should not lead the student to despair. The social sciences deal with an extremely difficult subject matter. So difficult, in fact, that some would argue that a scientific social science is impossible. However, all disciplines have their

difficulties and challenges. A major problem for the social scientist, in addition to the inherent complexity of the subject matter of the social sciences, is that we are part of the subject matter we are trying to study. We are dealing with a subject where the researcher has to deal continually with strongly held beliefs not only about how society works, but about how it ought to work. A science of society is a challenge, indeed.

The degree of bias reflected in research reports ranges across a continuum. On the one hand, there are research reports specifically designed to study bias; the psychology experiments exploring experimenter effects fall into this category (see Rosenthal, 1963, 1966; Johnson and Adair, 1970; Johnson and Ryan, 1976 for examples). While there may well be some inadvertent bias to find bias in these studies, great pains are taken to measure the sources and extent of distortions. At the other end of the continuum are the social activists and advocates whose research leaves little doubt as to its underpinning assumptions and preferences. So, whether we are dealing with a community group doing research to block a school closure, or a research project to oppose the location of a landfill site, there is no question as to the stance that will be taken in the study. Bias will almost certainly take the form of overstating both the size and social importance of the problem. In between these extremes fall those studies whose distortions are subtle, but almost certainly present.

Social scientists' increasing awareness of the problems of bias in all research has, in some ways, helped to legitimate those who openly devote their research to advocacy. Critics of mainstream social research believe it supports the interests of the established order in society. Thus, those who consider crime worthy of investiga-

BOX 9.2

Social Science Afflictions

As an exercise in understanding bias better, social science afflictions are classified. All researchers are afflicted to some degree with at least one of these biases. (Let the innocent cast the first stone.) The following diagnostic categories and treatments are offered for your consideration:

Theoretical Rigor Mortis

Characterized by a quest to do research that will support a favoured theory, those suffering from this affliction, when asked about it, protest their health, and continue to do research that is rigidly interpreted as evidence for a particular theory. The patient appears to be interested not in testing the theory's limits but in finding additional support for it. *Cure*: Do a project which puts the favoured theory at risk. Publish the results. Use your real name.

Methodological Paralysis

An inability to move to different research designs, measurement procedures, or analytical techniques. People who suffer from this affliction spend their time locating problems that can be done using familiar design and measurement procedures. *Cure*: Conduct a study using a design, measurements, and statistical procedures never used before. Enjoy it. Understand it.

True Believer Fever

These are the people always in search of evidence to support their particular view of the world or some pet hypothesis or finding; they strongly challenge

tion, are considered to be responding to middle-class concerns about the security of property; those who study declines in government funding for higher education are perhaps responding to middle-class parents' concerns about the cost of educating their children. Those supporting such advocacy research would argue that if mainstream research has supported the established order in society, there should also be support for those who openly advance the interests of the underclasses. Why should researchers not try to advance the interests of minorities, women, people with disabilities, the working poor, the homeless, or third-world countries? Why should

social science not apply knowledge to alleviate suffering? Should the pure researcher stop at describing and explaining the incidence of suffering? Should the applied question, the question of alleviating suffering, be addressed directly by the social scientist? Increasingly, social scientists seem to be coming to the view that pure research, while it has its place, does not go far enough; if the social researcher does not press for the applied changes suggested by social research, who will? Thus the role of the social scientist has broadened to include an applied dimension. But this broadening has led to confusion as to the line between pure research and advocacy.

competing evidence, ruling it out as irrelevant. *Cure*: Write a paper enumerating the flaws in your perspective. Mean it.

Good Cause Syndrome

These are the researchers with a cause: social science is used where its findings can be made to support the preferred view. Evidence to the contrary is dismissed as methodologically or theoretically flawed. These are the researchers who inevitably show up to help the underdog. Or the overdog. They may also suffer from terminal liberalism, terminal political correctness, or terminal conservatism. All for a good cause, all in the name of virtue, all in the name of social science. *Cure*: Write an essay defending cannibalism. Try to believe it.

Guerilla Raiders' Syndrome

These patients typically do not do original research. Instead they fashion a career out of attacking a particular theoretical or methodological approach. This syndrome is often jointly found in those who suffer from *True Believer Syndrome*. *Cure*: Do a primary research project. High cure rate.

Scientism Ailment

The belief that, if we follow the models of the physical sciences, we will even-

tually understand social behaviour and that it will become as predictable as relations in engineered physical systems. *Cure*: For each day during the next month, predict the weather 10 days in advance. Check performance.

Anti-Science Fever

Characterized by the belief that social behaviour cannot be understood using orientations borrowed from the physical sciences. Anger is directed at the science practitioners who are favoured in our culture. *Cure*: Marriage to someone with the *Scientism Ailment* is recommended. Check frequently: there is a danger of a double murder.

Replicationitis

The researcher in this condition of terminal boredom is characterized by the need to keep replicating the same study—with minor variation in samples, or in the variables involved. This is the person who makes a career out of studying the same set of variables. Incessantly. *Cure*: Cut off funds. Get a hobby.

No Affliction Affliction

These are the social scientists who think that their research is unbiased—untainted by brushes with their socio-cultural milieux. *Cure*: Not treatable since the patient is in strong denial. Pray.

2. RULES FOR MINIMIZING BIAS

The following sections provide some tentative suggestions for dealing with research

bias. There are no easy answers here. These rules are intended to provoke discussion and, since some of them would not be acceptable to all social scientists, they should be considered tentative.

RULE 9.1

ALERT KEY PLAYERS TO THE PROBLEM OF BIAS.

We need to alert our society to the idea that much research, in the end, tends to support some interest or interest group. Education about bias needs to be directed to students, research practitioners, public policy personnel, courts, governments, and to the general public. To the extent that research supports some interest or interest group, research activities may have an underlying structural bias which favours doing work on certain types of research questions and arriving at socially acceptable conclusions.

RULE 9.2

AVOID SEXISM.

In all phases of research, avoid sexism.

RULE 9.3

IDENTIFY ROLES PLAYED BY THE RESEARCH PROCESS.

As researchers we need to be honest about the role we are playing. Advocacy research should be identified as such as this will avoid confusion. In many cases, our role shifts several times while doing a project. For example, the choice of subject matter may be influenced by advocacy interests, the interpretation of the descriptive and pure aspects of the research may be largely impartial and value-neutral, and the policy recommendations may be directed toward bringing about changes meant to benefit a particular social group. Try to be clear about what hat you are wearing and alert the reader to when you switch hats. Have the standards of evidence altered as you move from one phase to another?

RULE 9.4

ELIMINATE BIAS IN DESCRIPTIVE PHASE OF RESEARCH.

In the descriptive phase of research, efforts should be made to ensure that the description is not biased by the way questions are asked and to ensure that proper sampling procedures have been followed rigidly. While subjective elements will influence choices about what should be described and how questions should be posed, once such decisions have been made, the collection, analysis, and interpretation of data should be as free of distortion as possible.

RULE 9.5

IN EXPLANATORY RESEARCH, LET DISCONFIRMATION BE YOUR GUIDE.

In pure research, be certain that competing explanations are given a fair chance. Efforts should be made to disconfirm relations, not support them.

RULE 9.6

POLICY RECOMMENDATIONS IDENTIFIED AS VALUE-BASED.

In the policy recommendation phase, it should be made clear that the evaluations and recommendations of the researcher are intended to achieve some end; given this assumption, we should ask if there is any connection between the conclusions of the research and the researcher's assessment of the likely success of the proposed intervention strategy. In some cases, the research has specifically evaluated competing intervention strategies; in other cases, the intervention strategy proposed is purely commonsensical and has not been evaluated. In both cases, the extent to which the research has assessed intervention alternatives should be made clear to the reader. In short, has the research actually tested the likely response to both intervention strategy A and intervention strategy B?

RULE 9.7

BE SKEPTICAL OF RESEARCH FINDINGS.

Be skeptical of all reported research findings, given the many sources of bias that may have influenced the conclusions. A healthy, questioning attitude toward one's own and others' findings is appropriate, particularly in those disciplines where there is so much room for interpretation.

RULE 9.8

READ LITERATURE CAUTIOUSLY.

In reviewing literature, try to distinguish between those conclusions which appear to be demonstrated logically and/or empirically from those which are speculative. To avoid bias is also to recognize it. One must distinguish between conclusions that appear to have a sound basis and those which are speculative and untested.

RULE 9.9

DISTINGUISH ADVOCACY FROM PURE RESEARCH.

Try to identify those researchers who are engaged in advocacy. By being able to identify someone who is mounting evidence to support a position, whether on theoretical or public policy issues, one can recognize a debater at work. There is nothing inherently

wrong with advocacy, but it must be recognized that its conclusions are not impartial. Where it is clear that a case is being mounted, the question to ask is: "But, Sir, what experiment could disprove your hypothesis?" (Platt, 1964, p. 352.)

RULE 9.10

ORIENT RESEARCH TO DISCONFIRMATION.

If studies are designed to rule out alternatives, to disconfirm theories, then one is on the road to minimizing bias.

RULE 9.11

USE THEORY TO GENERATE TESTABLE HYPOTHESES.

Use theory as a guide, as a tool for generating testable hypotheses. Theories should be regarded as efficient summaries of findings and as tools for deriving predictions about relationships between variables. Theories are attempts to make general, summary statements, and are to be revised continually. Remember, theories are for testing, not supporting.

RULE 9.12

BE SENSITIVE TO YOUR OWN OUTCOME PREFERENCES.

Contemplate your own values. Recognizing your own preferences concerning the kind of society you would like to live in will help to alert you to potential biases that you may bring to a research project. Being sensitive to your own biases enables you to design studies which are more value-neutral rather than studies predisposed to generate results favouring your personal preferences.

RULE 9.13

DO NOT DISCLOSE HYPOTHESES TO SUBJECTS OR ASSISTANTS.

Do not reveal hypotheses to research subjects or assistants. It seems safest to follow this rule if expectancy bias is to be reduced. It may, however, be necessary to provide some general idea of what the study is about, but it is best not to provide either research assistants or subjects with the details.

RULE 9.14

COVER THE ATTITUDINAL CONTINUUM.

Where possible, avoid showing your hand by presenting a variety of views. This will give the respondent a sense that all responses are acceptable. Be certain to offer a full range of attitudinal response categories so that no respondent is always forced to the extreme of the continuum.

RULE 9.15

BE ACCEPTING OF ALL RESPONSES.

Interviewers must be trained to appear to ask questions neutrally and to respond in the same way to all respondents' answers. Ideally, the interviewer should convey an impression of neutrality, yet have a keen interest in respondents' answers. Interviewers should avoid coaching responses.

RULE 9.16

SPECIFY DATA ANALYSIS PROCEDURES IN ADVANCE

Just as hypotheses must be specified in advance, so must data analysis procedures. To avoid bias or playing with the data, analytical procedures must be specified in advance of data collection. While this may be viewed as a restrictive rule, if followed, it prevents unwarranted massaging of the data.

RULE 9.17

CHECK FOR RANDOM AND SYSTEMATIC ERRORS.

Researchers need to be aware of both random and systematic errors and put into place procedures to minimize both types of errors.

RULE 9.18

REPORT EXTENT OF DATA MASSAGING.

Report the number of relationships that have been explored in the course of data analysis. Researchers should clarify the number of relationships that have been examined, and the reasons why certain findings have not been reported.

The above section is intended to suggest that we need to be more sensitive to bias and to its role in both different types of research projects and different phases of a research project. Predispositions to favour certain outcomes will always be present in human activities, including social research. To appreciate that simple idea is a good start.

D. KEY TERMS

Advocacy research

Androcentricity

Bias

Data massaging

Demand characteristic

Double standard

Expectancy

Experimenter effect

Familism

Gender insensitivity

Overgeneralization

Overspecificity

Pure/descriptive research

Random error

Research bias

Researcher affect

Sexual dichotomism

Systematic error

E. KEY POINTS

A bias may be thought of as a preference—or pre-disposition—to favour a particular conclusion. *Research bias may be defined as the systematic distortion of research outcomes.* Such distortions occur in all disciplines and in all phases of the research operation: from selecting the problem and the variables to be studied, to developing measurements of the relevant variables, to collecting and analysing data, right through to reporting the results of the research. There are worrying sources of bias in all research, and in all disciplines.

Researchers must be careful to avoid bias in the design, execution, and reporting of research.

The term *researcher affect* refers to the tendency of researchers to fall in love with a particular explanation of some relationship or a particular view of the world in a way that inadvertently leads them to use procedures that generate conclusions supporting the preferred explanation or world view.

The term *experimenter effect* refers to a tendency to produce findings which are consistent with the experimenter's expectations.

F. EXERCISES

1. What is meant by "researcher affect" and how might it influence the conclusions of a study?

2. What are the fundamental differences between a debater approach to research and an impartial approach? What cues might alert the student to the type of researcher being encountered?

3. Identify a research problem that interests you. Describe the problem briefly. List a minimum of five predispositions that you have concerning this research problem, indicating your expectations in each case. Propose a way of managing your expectations so as to minimize their effect on your research.

G. RECOMMENDED READINGS

EICHLER, MARGRIT (1988). *Nonsexist Research Methods*. Boston: Allen & Unwin. Eichler identifies many examples of sexism in research and proposes a number of solutions.

ROSENTHAL, ROBERT, AND RALPH L. ROSNOW (1991). *Essentials of Behavioural Research*. New York: McGraw-Hill, Inc., Second Edition. Chapter 6 of this book is an excellent discussion of experimenter effect bias as well as proposed ways of minimizing the effect.

ETHICAL ISSUES

A. TWO STUDIES ILLUSTRATING ETHICAL DILEMMAS

The decade of the sixties was a time of enormous growth in the social sciences. University enrolments expanded and the number of social science practitioners grew correspondingly. There were few rules governing research in the burgeoning disciplines.

Several studies conducted in the sixties raised key ethical issues for social scientists. By the nineties, many professional associations, all universities, colleges, hospitals, and most government agencies had in place codes of ethics to guide social researchers. Researchers have obligations to their subjects, to themselves, to their disciplines, and to their society; researchers need to recognize their different roles and role obligations.

Conflicting pressures often emerge in designing studies, as the researcher may be torn between the desire to use the "ideal" design for a study and the desire to use a less effective design that does not entail activities and techniques that go beyond what is "ethically possible" when studying human subjects. What is convenient for research may be unacceptable ethically. This chapter outlines two studies which illustrate some of the ethical dilemmas faced by the social researcher. Following this review, a series of rules will be presented to guide the researcher in resolving ethical problems which may emerge.

There are a number of studies which have become landmarks in the discussion of research ethics. Two major studies are Stanley Milgram's research on compliance with authority, which had subjects administer electric shocks to victims, and Laud Humphreys' research observing homosexual contacts in a public washroom. Both of these studies had an impact on the development of regulations governing social research. While many studies do not pose serious ethical dilemmas for the social researcher, it is important for the beginning researcher to understand the impetus behind the development of the codes of ethics adopted by various professional and governmental agencies.

1. LAUD HUMPHREYS: *TEAROOM TRADE*

Let us begin this section by examining a study which has been important because of both its subject matter and the ethical issues it raises. Humphreys' classic study, emerging from his doctoral dissertation at Washington University in St. Louis, was based on observations of homosexuals meeting in public washrooms. An excerpt from the methodology section of Humphreys' work is included in Box 10.1.

The publication of Humphreys' book provoked both critical comment and support. Many have opposed Humphreys' research on ethical grounds; the statements of Nicholas Von Hoffman (1970) and by Donald P. Warwick are particularly incisive. The following quotation provides a sense of journalist Von Hoffman's position:

We're so preoccupied with defending our privacy against insurance investigators, dope sleuths, counterespionage men, divorce detectives and credit checkers, that we overlook the social scientists behind the hunting blinds who're also peeping into what we thought were our most private and secret lives. But they are there, studying us, taking notes, getting to know us, as indifferent as everybody else to the feeling that to be a complete human involves having an aspect of ourselves that's unknown...No information is valuable enough to obtain *by nipping away at personal liberty, and that is true no matter who's doing the gnawing, John Mitchell and the conservatives over at the Justice Department or Laud Humphreys and the liberals over at the Sociology Department (Von Hoffman, 1970, pp. 4-6).*

BOX 10.1   SOCIAL RESEARCHERS AT WORK

Laud Humphreys: Tearoom Trade

The Sociologist as Voyeur

For several months, I had noted fluctuations in the number of automobiles that remained more than fifteen minutes in front of the sampled tearooms. My observations had indicated that, with the sole exception of police cars, autos that parked in front of these public restrooms (which, as has been mentioned, are usually isolated from other park facilities) for a quarter of an hour or more invariably belonged to participants in the homosexual encounters. The same is true for cars that appeared in front of two or more such facilities in the course of an hour.

...I also noted, whenever possible, a brief description of both the car and its driver. By means of frequent sorties into the tearooms for observation, each recorded license number was verified as belonging to a man actually observed in homosexual activity inside the facilities...

...The original sample thus gained was of 134 license numbers, carefully linked to persons involved in the homosexual encounters, gathered from the environs of ten public restrooms in four different parks of a metropolitan area of two million people.

...The tearooms are challenging, not only because they present unusual problems for the researcher but because they provide an extraordinary opportunity for detailed observation. Due to the lack of verbal communication and the consistency of the physical settings, a type of laboratory is provided by these facilities—one in which human behavior may be observed with the control of a number of variables.

...A sociologist without verbal communication is like a doctor without a stethoscope. The silence of these sexual encounters confounded such research problems as legitimation of the observer and identification of roles...the patterns of behavior themselves acquire meaning independent of verbalization.

...Despite the almost inviolate silence within the restroom setting, tearoom participants are neither mute nor particularly taciturn. Away from the scenes where their sexual deviance is exposed—outside what I shall later discuss as the "interaction membrane"—

conversation is again possible. Once my car and face had become familiar, I was able to enter into verbal relationships with twelve of the participants...

After the initial contacts with this intensive dozen, I told them of my research, disclosing my real purpose for being in the tearooms. With the help of some meals together and a number of drinks, all agreed to cooperate in subsequent interviewing sessions...Apart from the systematic observations themselves, these conversations constitute the richest source of data in the study.

Some may ask why, if nine of these cooperating respondents were obtained without the formal interviews, I bothered with the seemingly endless task of acquiring a sample and administering questionnaires—particularly when interviews with the intensive dozen provided such depth to the data. The answer is simple: these men are not representative of the tearoom population. I could engage them in conversation only because they are more overt, less defensive, and better educated than the average participant.

This suggests a problem for all research that relies on willing respondents. Their very willingness to cooperate sets them apart from those they are meant to represent. *Tally's Corner* and *Street Corner Society* stand high among the classics of social science—and rightly so—but I wonder sometimes how well Tally and Doc represent the apathetic, alienated, uninvolved men of the street corners. When authors such as Liebow and Whyte strive to compensate for this by extending their research throughout the friendship networks, great ethnogra-

phy results. But the saddest works in the name of social science are those that barrage the reader with endless individual case studies and small samples from private psychiatric practices, few of which can be representative of the vast numbers of human beings who are supposed to be "understood" in terms of these deviant deviants.

...Identification of the sample was made by using the automobile license registers of the states in which my respondents lived. Fortunately, friendly policemen gave me access to the license registers, without asking to see the numbers or becoming too inquisitive about the type of "market research" in which I was engaged. These registers provided the names and addresses of those in the sample, as well as the brand name and year of the automobiles thus registered. The make of the car, as recorded in the registers, was checked against my transcribed description of each car... Names and addresses were then checked in the directories of the metropolitan area, from which volumes I also acquired marital and occupational data for most of the sample...

Like archives, park restrooms, and automobiles, the streets of our cities are subject to public regulation and scrutiny. They are thus good places for nonreactive research (nonreactive in that it requires no response from the research subjects)...The first purpose of this survey of homes was to acquire descriptions of the house types and dwelling areas...As physical evidence, however, homes provide a source of data about a population that outweighs any failure they may have as a status index. Swing sets and bicycles in the yards indicate that a family is not childless. A shrine to Saint Mary suggests that the resident is Roman Catholic in religious identification. Christmas decorations bespeak at least a nominal Christian preference. A boat or trailer in the driveway suggests love of the outdoor life. "For Rent" signs may indicate the size of an average apartment and, in some cases, the price. The most important sign, however, was the relative "neatness" of the house and grounds...

Realizing that the majority of my participant sample were married—and nearly all of them quite secretive about their deviant activity—I was faced with the problem of how to interview more than the nine willing respondents. Formal interviews of the sample were part of the original research design. The little I knew about these covert deviants made me want to know a great deal more. Here was a unique population just waiting to be studied—but I had no way to approach them. Clearly, I could not knock on the door of a suburban residence and say, "Excuse me, I saw you engaging in a homosexual act in a tearoom last year, and I wonder if I might ask you a few questions." Having already been jailed, locked in a restroom, and attacked by a group of ruffians, I had no desire to conclude my research with a series of beatings...

About this time, fortunately, I was asked to develop a questionnaire for a social health survey of men in the community, which was being conducted by a research center with which I had been a research associate. Based on such interview schedules already in use in Michigan and New York, the product would provide nearly all the information I would want on the men in my sample: family background, socioeconomic factors, personal health and social histories, religious and employment data, a few questions on social and political attitudes, a survey of friendship networks, and information on marital relationships and sex.

With the permission of the director of the research project, I added my deviant sample to the over-all sample of the survey, making certain that only one trusted, mature graduate student and I make all the interviews of my respondents. Using a table of random numbers, I randomized my sample, so that its representativeness would not be lost in the event that we should be unable to complete all 100 interviews.

...My master list was kept in a safe-deposit box. Each interview card, kept under lock and key, was destroyed with completion of the schedule. No names or other identifying tags were allowed to appear on the questionnaires. Although I recognized each of the men interviewed from observation of them in the tearooms, there was no indication that they remembered me. I was careful to change my appearance, dress, and automobile from the days when I had passed as deviant. I also allowed at least a year's time to lapse between the original sampling procedures and the interviews.

This strategy was most important—both from the standpoint of research validity and ethics—because it enabled me to approach my respondents as normal people, answering normal questions, as part of a normal survey...they were not interviewed as deviants.

...Once these interviews were completed, preparations could be made for the final step of the research design. From names appearing in the randomly selected sample of the over-all social health survey, fifty men were selected, matched with the completed questionnaires...

...These last fifty interviews, then, enabled me to compare characteristics of two samples—one deviant, one control—matched on the basis of certain socioeconomic characteristics, race, and marital status.

From a methodological standpoint, the value of this research is that it has employed a variety of methods, each testing a different outcropping of the research population and their sexual encounters. It has united the systematic use of participant observation strategies with other nonreactive measures such as physical traces and archives. The exigencies of research in a socially sensitive area demanded such approaches; and the application of unobtrusive measures yielded data that call, in turn, for reactive methods.

Research strategies...they are the outgrowth of the researcher's basic assumptions. Special conditions of the research problem itself also exercise a determining influence upon the methods used. This chapter has been an attempt to indicate how my ethnographic assumptions, coupled with the difficulties inhering in the study of covert deviants and their behavior, have given rise to a set of strategies.

With the help of "oddball" measures, the outlines of the portrait of participants in the homosexual encounters of the tearooms appeared. Reactive strategies were needed to fill in the distinguishing features. They are human, socially patterned features; and it is doubtful that any one method could have given them the expressive description they deserve.

SOURCE: Laud Humphreys. *Tearoom Trade.* Chicago: Aldine de Gruyter Press, 1970, pp. 28-44. Reprinted by permission of the publisher.

Irving Louis Horowitz and Lee Rainwater (1970) wrote a spirited response to Von Hoffman's article by pointing out that Humphreys was perfectly entitled to be in a public washroom and that the tactics Humphreys used to gain interviews with the participants were necessary if the project was to be completed. Furthermore, they point out that no one has demonstrated that the subjects' right to privacy was violated. Their concluding argument is as follows:

Laud Humphreys has gone beyond the existing literature in sexual behavior and has proven once again, if indeed proof were ever needed, that ethnographic research is a powerful tool for social understanding and policy making. And these are the criteria by which the research should finally be evaluated professionally...In other words, the issue is not liberalism vs. conservatism or privacy vs. publicity, but much more simply and to the point, the right of scientists to conduct their work as against the right of journalists to defend social mystery and private agony (1970, p. 8).

Donald P. Warwick indicates three ethical objections to Humphreys' research. These include:

(i) taking advantage of a powerless group of men to pursue the study;

(ii) the method used to follow up on the tearoom participants reinforces the image that social researchers are "sly tricksters who are not to be trusted" and;

(iii) by using deception, Humphreys encourages others in society to follow his lead (1973, p. 37).

Warwick goes on to argue that:

Social research involving deception and manipulation ultimately helps produce a society of cynics, liars and manipulators, and undermines the trust which is essential to a just social order (1973, p. 38).

There appear to be four key points in Humphreys' procedures that raise ethical issues:

(i) the researcher acted as a lookout, alerting participants engaged in an illegal activity of any impending danger;

(ii) unknown to the subjects, the researcher noted the licence numbers of their cars;

(iii) licence numbers were traced to reveal the name and address of each car owner;

(iv) traced participants were interviewed as part of a larger public health survey.

i. Aiding in Crime

Tearoom Trade raises the issue of a social scientist aiding in crime, acting as a lookout to alert people engaged in an illegal activity; when this study was done homosexual activity in Missouri was punishable by a sentence of not less than two years upon conviction (Humphreys, 1970, p. 26). Technically, then, Humphreys was assisting in committing a crime. Should the social scientist ever engage in such activities? Under what conditions does the importance of a project justify an illegal activity?

ii. Withholding Information

On two occasions, Humphreys withheld information from the police. The first occurred when he was arrested for loitering after refusing to give police officers his name. Humphreys did not give the police the reason for his presence at the public lavatory. In fairness, he did not lie to the police: he just did not tell them what he was doing. Humphreys felt that the police were harassing him, and he also wished to protect the identity of the people he was observing. After all, his field notes could have been subpoenaed. (Social researchers' sources are not protected by law in the United States or Canada.) He then would have compromised not only his project, but would also have exposed those being observed to possible harassment, arrest, or public humiliation. Should Humphreys have told the police what he was doing?

On another occasion, Humphreys got names and addresses (traced from the licence numbers of participants' cars) from the police department under the guise of doing market research. The ease with which Humphreys was able to get the information might lead one to fault the police department for laxness. Humphreys was careful to make certain that the police did not record the licence numbers or the names he was getting. Indeed, Humphreys took great care to protect the identity of respondents by having the names and addresses locked in a safety deposit box in another state. Should Humphreys have misrepresented his reasons for tracing the licence numbers to get the names and addresses?

iii. Informed Consent

Humphreys did not inform respondents how they had been selected for participation in a health survey. Here Humphreys admits that he was less than candid with his respondents (1970, p. 171). To further ensure that the respondents would not identify the researcher as the lookout, the interviews took place some 18 months after the tearoom observations, and the researcher wore a disguise. None of the respondents indicated that they recognized the researcher. Had the respondents known how they were selected for the health survey, many would have refused participation. These men were most secretive about their clandestine tearoom liaisons, and the thought that someone had recorded information about them would have been scary. Was Humphreys justified in not revealing how the respondents were selected for participation in the study?

iv. Endangering a Respondent

Humphreys was extremely careful to protect the identity of his respondents. His use of the safety deposit box for storing the names and addresses, his refusal to tell the police when he was arrested that he was a social researcher, and his use of a disguise were all used to reduce the real or perceived dangers of subjects being identified publicly as homosexuals. Nonetheless,

there were risks. Was the project justified given the slight possibility that the respondents' names could inadvertently have been revealed, thus exposing the subjects to a heightened risk of arrest or harassment? Could the publication of the book lead morality squads to put even greater pressure on the gay community?

Perhaps all researchers need to try and anticipate possible dangers and then either abandon the project, or rethink it, in light of its potentially harmful effects. Humphreys was sensitive to the difficult ethical issues involved in his project; indeed, even before much of the furore over his project erupted (see postscript below), he had written a chapter on his view of the issues involved. Box 10.2 excerpts Humphreys' comments on the ethical issues in his study.

As a postscript to the discussion of Humphreys' research, we should note that his work had a positive influence in the development of the gay rights movement in the United States (Reynolds, 1982, p. 69). Nonetheless, his work raised agonizing ethical issues, and also had an unfortunate impact on Washington University's sociology program. Ethical questions concerning his research resulted in an attempt to prevent Humphreys from receiving his Ph.D. The resulting battle created problems in the department, placed significant federal funding in jeopardy, led to the departure of several senior faculty members and, ultimately, was one of the factors that led to the demise of sociology courses at the university. To this day, Washington University does not have a sociology program; this is unfortunate as, in the sixties, Washington University's sociology program was considered to be in the top twenty in the United States.

BOX 10.2   SOCIAL RESEARCHERS AT WORK

Laud Humphreys, Postscript: A Question of Ethics

So long as we suspect that a method we use has at least some potential for harming others, we are in the extremely awkward position of having to weigh the scientific and social benefits of that procedure against its possible costs in human discomfort…

…Are there, perhaps, some areas of human behavior that are not fit for social scientific study at all? Should sex, religion, suicide, or other socially sensitive concerns be omitted from the catalogue of possible fields of sociological research?

…I believe that preventing harm to his respondents should be the primary interest of the scientist. We are not, however, protecting a harassed population of deviants by refusing to look at them. At this very moment, my writing has been interrupted by a long-distance call, telling me of a man who has been discharged from his position and whose career has been destroyed because he was "caught" in a public restroom. This man, who protests his innocence, has suffered a nervous breakdown since his arrest. Even if acquitted, his personal identity has been damaged, perhaps irreparably, by the professional spy who apprehended him. The greatest harm a social scientist could do to this man would be to ignore him. Our concern about possible research consequences for our fellow "professionals" should take a secondary place to concern for those who may benefit from our research.

Situation Ethics

If it be granted, then, that the sociologist may commit a grave ethical violation by ignoring a problem area, we may consider the methods that should be used in such studies. Let it be noted that any conceivable method employable in the study of human behavior has at least some potential for harming others. Even the antiseptic strategies involved in studying public archives may harm others if they distort rather than contribute to, the understanding of social behavior. Criminologists may study arrest statistics, as filtered to us through the FBI, without stirring from the safety of their study chairs, but such research methods may result in the creation of a fictitious "crime wave," a tide of public reaction, and the eventual production of a police state—all because the methods may distort reality.

…The problems facing researchers, then, are of which methods may result in more or less misrepresentation of purposes and identity, more or less betrayal of confidence, and more or less positive or negative consequences for the subjects. Those who engage in the study of deviant behavior—or any behavior, for that matter—must become accustomed to the process of weighing possible social benefits against possible cost in human discomfort… The ethics of social science are situation ethics.

Problems of Misrepresentation

At the conclusion of his article, Erikson proposes two rules regarding misrepresentation of the researcher's identity and purposes:

- It is unethical for a sociologist to deliberately misrepresent his identity for the purpose of entering a private domain to which he is not otherwise eligible.

- It is unethical for a sociologist to deliberately misrepresent the character of the research in which he is engaged.

Since one's identity within the interaction membrane of the tearoom is represented only in terms of the participant role he assumes, there was no misrepresentation of my part as an observer: I was indeed a "voyeur," though in the sociological and not the sexual sense. My role was primarily that of watchqueen, and that role I played well and faithfully. In that setting, then, I misrepresented my identity no more than anyone else. Furthermore, my activities were intended to gain entrance not to "a private domain" but to a public restroom. The only sign on its door said "Men," which makes me quite eligible for entering. It should be clear, then, that I have not violated Erikson's first canon. Although passing as deviant to avoid disrupting the behavior I wished to observe, I did not do so to achieve copresence in a private domain.

The second rule may be applied to the reactive part of my research, when I interviewed persons I had observed in the tearooms under the pretext of a so-cial health survey. Here it should be noted that all interviews were in fact made as part of a larger social health survey, and abstracted data from my interviews are already in use in that study. The problem then may be viewed in two ways: First, I gave less than full representation of what I was doing, though without giving false representation. I wore only one of two possible hats, rather than going in disguise. Second, I made multiple use of my data. Is it unethical to use data that someone has gathered for purposes one of which is unknown to the respondent? With the employment of proper security precautions, I think such multiple use is quite ethical; it is frequently employed by anyone using such data banks as the records of the Bureau of Census.

Problems of Confidentiality

...I have taken every possible precaution to protect the identities of my respondents and the confidential nature of their communication with me...I have guarded the names and addresses in my sample and used only strategies that would safeguard all identities. I even allowed myself to be jailed rather than alert the police to the nature of my research, thus avoiding the incrimination of respondents through their possible association with a man under surveillance.

Problems of Consequentiality

Finally, I must weigh the possible results of this research. It is not enough to plead that I am no seer, for I am a sociologist and should have some ability for prediction. If I have been honest enough in my analyses and convincing enough in their presentation, there should be no negative reaction from the forces of social control. I should hope they would have learned something. Perhaps some will move to construct and situate restrooms in such a way as to discourage the tearoom trade. Except where such activity constitutes an obvious public nuisance, I hope there will be no change in the tearoom locale. There is no need to drive this harmless activity underground. Those who deal in the sex market are resourceful, however and I doubt that anything short of a total police state could erase the search for sex without commitment!

...I doubt that this work will have any effect in either increasing or decreasing the volume of homosexual activity in park restrooms. I do hope it will give readers a better understanding of the activity that is already there. I have no moral or intellectual objection to what goes on in the tearooms, and only a mild aesthetic one. I do have a moral objection to the way in which society reacts to those who take part in that action. As a scientist, I must believe that any addition to knowledge, which has suffered as little distortion as possible from the methods used, will help correct the superstition and cruelty that have marked such reaction in

SOURCE: Laud Humphreys. *Tearoom Trade*. Chicago: Aldine de Gruyter Press, 1970, pp.167-173. Reprinted by permission of the publisher.

Laud Humphreys (1930-1988) did receive his degree, and went on to a distinguished research and teaching career at the State University of New York at Albany, School of Criminal Justice.

2. STANLEY MILGRAM: *BEHAVIORAL STUDY OF OBEDIENCE*

In 1963 Stanley Milgram published "Behavioral Study of Obedience." The study was important for a number of reasons:

- its findings were disturbing to many readers because no one anticipated the extent to which subjects would comply with the request to continue administering electric shocks to fellow participants in an experiment;

- its findings illustrate vividly the need to take into account the authority of the researcher as a possible confounding variable in a social experiment; and

- the study raised difficult ethical issues concerning the treatment of experimental subjects.

The ethical issues raised will be of particular concern in this chapter. The Milgram experiment has become, like Humphreys' research, a touchstone when questions of ethics are raised in connection with social research. Virtually all introductory textbooks in psychology use the Milgram study as an illustration when discussing research ethics (see Box 3.3, which presents the design of the Milgram study).

Box 3.3 reports on the procedures used in the original study. Briefly, subjects were fooled into believing that they are administering increasingly powerful shocks to a another subject (who was actually a confederate working with the experimenter, faking increasing pain as the intensity of the "shocks" increased). If the subject asked for permission to stop, the experimenter told him to continue. About two-thirds of the subjects administered shocks that were labelled as dangerous to the victim. Following the experimental session, the subject met with the confederate and was then debriefed by the experimenter. In addition, a follow-up survey was made of the various participants in the studies, which indicated that they felt good about their involvement in the experiment (Milgram, 1964).

Diana Baumrind led off the questioning of Milgram's research. Her questions focused on two central points: first she questioned whether the design of the study was appropriate for the study of obedience given the "special quality of trust and obedience with which the subject appropriately regards the experimenter" (1964, p. 421). In short, Baumrind wondered whether the results showed strong compliance because the experiment took place in a laboratory setting in which the subject may have been particularly sensitive to the cues offered by the researcher. The second major point Baumrind raised is the issue of whether it is appropriate to entrap a subject into committing acts which, on later reflection, may lead to a loss of self-esteem and dignity. Could the subject be saying, "My God, on the instructions of another person, I was willing to inflict a dangerous electric shock to someone else participating in a social psychology experiment...what a jerk I am."

Does the social researcher have the right to do experiments which may lead to such devastating self-knowledge? (Holden, 1979, p. 538) Should we be in the business of showing people how awful they really are? And, since the study produced a lot of discomfort for the subjects, was Milgram justified in continuing with the work once this became apparent? How much subject discomfort is permissible in social research? (See Kaufmann, 1967; Kelman cited in Holden, 1979, p. 538.) How do we balance important gains in knowledge of human behaviour against the damage we may be doing to the self-esteem of our respondents? On the other hand, perhaps making experimental subjects recognize their flaws is no bad thing, as this may lead them to think more carefully about their own values (Kaufmann, 1967). Indeed, as the psychiatrist Milton Erickson argues in defending Milgram's research, it is important to study undesirable behaviour so that, as a society, we may be able to control the "ugly realities that have characterized human history since its beginning..." (1968, p. 278). And, while challenging Milgram about the legitimacy of trying to make inferences about relations among nations from the study of interactions between a researcher and a subject, Amitai Etzioni recommends extending Milgram's research to take up related questions, such as the impact of a liberal education on the likelihood of obeying evil orders, or the effect that seeing a film on a war crimes trial would have on the likelihood of obeying such orders. (Etzioni, 1968, pp. 279-80).

The one point which should not be overlooked, and which is taken up by Milgram in later trials, is the effect of different pressure techniques on the likelihood of subjects continuing with the shocks. The way in which subjects are encouraged to continue, or given an "easy out," seems to be critical in determining the percentage of subjects who continue administering shocks to victims.

Milgram responded to Baumrind's arguments by making clear that great care was taken in the post-experiment phase of the study to **debrief** the subjects. The experimenter pointed out to them that the confederate was not really receiving electric shocks, that their behaviour was entirely normal, and that their feelings of tension were also experienced by others. Milgram also provides information on two follow-up studies of the participants. The first was a questionnaire asking about their reaction to the study, which indicated a high level of approval for the study (about 84 percent claimed to be glad to have participated in the study). The second follow-up was conducted by an impartial medical examiner who concluded that among the 40 experimental subjects "no evidence was found of any traumatic reactions" (Milgram, 1964, p. 850). Unfortunately, in his response, Milgram did not provide a separate breakdown for how the original 40 subjects responded to the questionnaire on their experience with the study.

Milgram also suggests that had fewer subjects complied with the experimenter's request, there would have been much less reaction to his research. Milgram seems to suggest that his critics hated the findings, hated to learn that two-thirds of Americans would provide a lethal electric shock to an innocent participant simply on the instruction of an authority figure. Had most subjects refused to apply the electric shock to the confederate, would there have been much debate about the research?

Milgram's research was extended to include 18 additional experimental conditions. These have been neatly summarized by Reynolds, and his table is reproduced in Box 10.3. Note that the percentage of subjects administering the maximum shock varied from zero percent to 92.5 percent (Reynolds, 1982, pp. 25-26).

B. CRITERIA FOR ASSESSING ETHICAL ACCEPTABILITY

The studies cited above illustrate a range of ethical dilemmas. What criteria can be used to identify possible problems with a research design? Two approaches to this question have been noted: the *consequentialist* and the *deontological*.

1. THE CONSEQUENTIALIST VIEW

The consequentialist view is that ethical judgements about a research project should be made by evaluating its consequences for the subject, for the academic discipline, and for society. A cost-benefit analysis might reveal that the advantages gained because of the resulting advancement of our knowledge justify the violation of some rules: deception may be acceptable if it does not do any long-term damage. In Warwick's view (1973), Humphreys' research procedures do not justify the project because of the negative consequences to the discipline and to society.

The **consequentialist** view emphasizes anticipating the possibly unfortunate consequences of the research. Thus, one would want to assess the possible dangers to the subjects. (What would happen if the identity of Humphreys' tearoom participants become public or get into the hands of the police?) Will participation in the study be in any way degrading, dangerous, or expose

BOX 10.3 SOCIAL RESEARCHERS AT WORK

Major Results of the Obedience to Authority Research Program

PERCENTAGE ADMINISTERING MAXIMUM SHOCK[1]	MEAN SHOCK LEVEL[2]	EXPERIMENT NO.[3]	EXPERIMENTAL CONDITION
Original Condition			
30.00	17.88	4	Touch-proximity (n=40) "Teacher" must hold "pupil's" hand on metal plate to complete circuit and operate equipment simultaneously
40.00	20.80	3	Proximity (n=40) "Teacher" and "pupil" in same room
62.50	24.53	2	Voice-feedback (n=40) "Teacher" hears "pupil" protest over intercom
65.00	27.0	1	Remote (n=40) "Teacher hears "pupil" bang on wall in protest
Revised Procedure			
.00	10.00	12	"Pupil" demands to be shocked (n=20) Experimenter instructs "teacher" not to go on
.00	10.00	14	Experimenter serves as "pupil" (n=20) Ordinary man instructs "teacher" to go on
.00	10.00	15	Two experimenters give conflicting instructions (n=20) Ordinary man serves as "pupil"
2.5	5.50	11	"Teacher" chooses shock level (n=40) "pupil" protests coordinated to shock level
10.00	16.45	17	Two peers rebel (n=40) "Teacher" task subdivided into three activities, subject "shocks"

20.00	16.25	13	Ordinary man gives orders (n=40) Experimenter leaves; "ordinary man," an accomplice, suggests increasing shock levels as own idea
20.50	18.2	7	Experimenter absent (n=40) Orders to "teacher" received over telephone
40.00	21.4	9	"Pupil" does not give full informed consent (n=40) Insists on right to terminate at will prior to becoming involved
47.50	20.95	10	Research conducted in commercial building (n=40) All other conditions on campus of major university
50.00	22.20	6	Variation in personal (n=40) Different experimenter–"pupil" team
65.00	24.55	5	Voice-feedback condition: male subjects (n=40)
65.00	24.73	8	Voice-feedback condition: female subjects (n=40)
65.00	23.50	16	Two experimenters (n=20) One served as "pupil"
65.75	24.90	13a	Subjects as bystander (n=16) "Ordinary man" assumes right to administer shocks on own initiative
92.50	26.65	18	Peer administers shock (n=40) Subject maintains records on "pupil's" performance

[1] Refers to the percentage that administer shocks at the 450-volt level (Danger, "severe shock," and "XXX" labels of equipment). In all but one condition, Ex. No. 12, this reflects obedience to terminate the study; he is always compliant.

[2] Equipment involved 30 levels of shock, labelled from 15 to 450 volts at 15-volt intervals. The shock level, in volts, can be computed by multiplying the level by 15; for example, level 10 was 150 volts.

[3] Indicated the number of the experiment as described in Milgram (1974).

Source: Descriptions based on Milgram (1974). Numbers in parentheses indicate the number of participants in each condition, a total of 636. Except in Exp. No. 8, all participants were male, chosen to represent different ages in the following proportions: 20-29, 20 percent; 30-39, 40 percent; and 40-49, 40 percent. Occupational categories were represented as follows: skilled and unskilled workers; 40 percent; white color, sales, and business, 40 percent; and professionals, 20 percent.

Source: Paul Davidson Reynolds, *Ethics and Social Science Research*, ©1982, pp. 25-26. Reprinted by permission of Prentice-Hall, Englewood Cliffs, New Jersey.

the subject to undue levels of stress? Can these adverse experiences be justified by the study's contributions to our knowledge of human behaviour? Are we in any way entrapping individuals so that they do things that they otherwise might not do? Are we forcing them to take a position on some issue that they have never thought about? Would subjects' participation in the study reveal unpleasant, unsavoury things about them that might otherwise remain hidden? Should research be imposing unpleasant and perhaps unwanted self-knowledge on subjects? And, if this is sometimes the consequence, can it be justified by other pay-offs? The consequentialist would permit projects so long as reasonable precautions are taken and subjects are debriefed so that no long-term negative consequences result.

In the biomedical area, permission to use unproven therapies on dying patients is now more readily available. There is pressure to permit the use of unproven drugs or therapies on such patients. In the area of AIDS and cancer treatments we permit the use of experimental therapies because of the imminent death of the patient.

2. THE DEONTOLOGICAL VIEW

The **deontological** approach to research ethics proposes absolute moral strictures that must never be violated. Absolutes like never using deception, always masking the identity of respondents, and never putting any pressure on respondents to participate in a study might be proposed by someone taking the deontological view. Rather than assessing the consequences of a given social science procedure, the deontological approach might propose, in its most extreme form, that deception in social psy-

chological experiments is never justified, no matter what the positive contributions to our knowledge might be. Alasdair MacIntyre (cited by Holden, 1979, p. 538) argued that one can distinguish between types of harm to a human subject. He distinguishes between:

- harm to a subject's interests (such as reporting a case of venereal disease)

- wrongdoing (for example, lying to someone, which may not cause any damage)

- a moral harm (doing something to make the subject less good, such as encouraging the person to tell a lie)

MacIntyre argues that harms can be compensated for whereas wrongs cannot be; hence, the argument is that if doing a wrong is essential to conducting a research project, then the project should be banned (cited in Holden, 1979, p. 538). According to this view, neither Milgram's research (because of the deception), nor Humphreys' research (because the health survey was misrepresented) could be condoned as ethically acceptable. Both would be barred, no matter what their importance for increasing our understanding of human behaviour.

C. RULES FOR RESOLVING ETHICAL ISSUES

The following ethical rules are presented as guidelines and are organized around two themes:

(i) the researcher's ethical responsibility to respondents; and

(ii) the social researcher's responsibility to his or her discipline and society.

1. RULES FOR THE TREATMENT OF RESPONDENTS

RULE 10.1

PROTECT THE CONFIDENTIALITY OF RESPONDENTS.

The researcher's promise to respect the confidentiality of responses to a questionnaire, an interview, or the identity of a subject in an experiment or field study is to be treated as a sacred trust. Most surveys, interviews, experiments, and field studies are completed on the understanding that individual responses, or information which would permit the identification of the individual, will never be released. Researchers have not only an ethical responsibility to preserve the anonymity of respondents, but have also a practical interest in doing so: their ability to collect accurate information would be impaired if the public believed that responses were not kept in confidence.

Where it is necessary to identify individual names with particular questionnaires (as in panel studies, for example) number codes should be used, not names. The questionnaires and a master list listing names and identification numbers can then be stored separately. Such master lists should be destroyed after the study has been completed. In Humphreys' case, the identifying information was stored in a safety deposit box in another state.

The location of the research project is frequently masked to further protect the identity of subjects. When Humphreys did his research over a quarter of a century ago, neither his research location (St. Louis) nor the locations of the tearooms were revealed. Social scientists cooperated in the masking, although any vice-squad member would certainly have been able to identify this information quickly had he or she taken a little time. (The supervising professor, Lee Rainwater, was thanked in the Preface and he was, during the period of the study, a prominent professor at Washington University in St. Louis.) In any case, vice-squad members were well aware of the activities in the public restrooms.

If data are released to other researchers, steps should be taken to mask the individual identities of respondents. This can be achieved by removing highly specific identifiers such as area of residence, specific job, or employer identifications.

RULE 10.2

DO NOT PLACE PRESSURE ON RESPONDENTS.

No pressure should be placed on the respondent to cooperate in a study. Respondents must feel free to refuse participation, withdraw at any time, or refuse to answer any particular question. Researchers should not put pressure on respondents or cajole or harass them in an effort to coax cooperation with the study. While it is appropriate in a mail survey to follow up on those who do not respond with a letter or phone call, these contacts should seek information and provide prospective respondents an opportunity to seek additional information themselves.

The original Milgram study appeared to place a lot of pressure on respondents to continue with administering the electric shocks; indeed, as many as four prods were used to "bring the subject into line."

Prod 1: *Please continue;* or *Please go on.*

Prod 2: *The experiment requires that you continue.*

Prod 3: *It is absolutely essential that you continue.*

Prod 4: *You have no other choice, you must go on (Milgram, 1963, p. 374).*

In subsequent experiments, which used weaker prods or gave the subject an easy out, subjects were much less likely to administer the maximum shock. (Reynolds, 1982, p. 25).

RULE 10.3

MAKE THE SUBJECT'S PARTICIPATION PAINLESS.

Completing a questionnaire, interview, or participating as a subject in an experiment should be a painless experience for the subject. Researchers must not expose subjects to needlessly long experimental trials, questionnaires, or ask questions which pry unnecessarily into personal matters. This constraint is not meant to suggest that the researcher should not examine certain areas of social behaviour, but suggests that only relevant information be collected. (Often when people are working on their first project, they will suggest many variables; however, when asked what they would do with the information, they are unable to articulate a meaningful analysis.) Moreover, consideration should be given to using alternate, or indirect indicators, for those questions which may offend respondents.

Maintaining the comfort and self-esteem of the subject should be a central concern of the researcher.

The Milgram research has been faulted for its possibly adverse effects on the subjects' self-esteem. We cannot reasonably expect Milgram to have anticipated the high proportion of subjects who would willingly administer the maximum shock (he took steps to estimate how many would do this by asking various students and colleagues); nor can Milgram be faulted for not anticipating the stress subjects would experience. But should the experiment have been aborted once the high stress experienced by the subjects was recognized? Other researchers have decided to abort projects when it was clear that the study had potential dangers.

Piliavin and Piliavin (1972), for example, aborted trials on the bystander intervention studies once it was clear that there were dangers involved in staging phoney emergencies. The researchers stopped one study when it was observed that bystanders, seeing a person fall with blood trickling from his mouth, activated an emergency stop alarm. It was simply too dangerous and disruptive to continue. Should Milgram have aborted his study?

RULE 10.4

IDENTIFY SPONSORS.

There should be no deception concerning the sponsorship of a project. Respondents must be informed about who is doing the study. On this basis alone, they may choose not to participate in the study.

Many people have opened their doors to a person claiming to be doing a survey on educational matters, only to discover that they are not dealing with a reputable social scientist but rather with a door-to-door encyclopedia salesperson. Feel free to encourage the "researcher" to leave rapidly!

Similarly, you might choose not to participate in a study conducted by an organization whose aims and objectives you find unacceptable; but, for you to refuse, you will need to know who is sponsoring the study. Full disclosure about the project is required.

RULE 10.5

DISCLOSE THE BASIS ON WHICH RESPONDENTS HAVE BEEN SELECTED.

The consensus in the social science community is that the respondent has the right to know how he or she was selected for participation in a study. Has the selection been made by means of a probability sampling procedure, or has it been based on special characteristics (membership in a particular organization, the job one has, or any other qualities). The prospective respondent should be given a reasonable amount of information upon which a decision to participate can be made.

This criterion is an interesting one in the case of Humphreys' research: in the "tearoom" observation phase of the research, the participants were engaging in an activity in a public lavatory. So, while they did not agree to participate in a research project, they did engage in an activity with others present. They clearly made the assumption that the observer was a "safe" person—a lookout. In the interview phase of his research, there was a lack of forthrightness in telling respondents how they were selected. The fifty who were interviewed were selected because they agreed to the interview. However, the respondents did not know that they had been seen using a "tearoom" for sexual purposes.

Since their tearoom activity was clandestine, it is clear that few of the respondents would have agreed to the interview had they known how they had been selected. The dilemma is that the researcher could not have completed the comparison with the "straight" sample without the interviews; and obtaining a sufficient number of interviews was possible only if the researcher did not fully disclose the basis on which the respondents had been selected. Catch 22? Recall that addresses were identified by tracing car licence numbers; Humphreys was also less than candid about how respondents were selected for the health survey (1970, p. 171). Does the anticipated pay-off of the research warrant the failure to disclose fully the basis on which the respondent was selected?

RULE 10.6

PLACE NO HIDDEN IDENTIFICATION CODES ON QUESTIONNAIRES.

Researchers should not use hidden codes on questionnaires to assist in the identification of those who have or have not returned questionnaires. Such codes are sometimes used to enable the researcher to find out who has not returned a questionnaire: such subjects may be sent another request. While such codes may save the researcher much time and money, they are unethical. If individuals are to be identified, this information should be placed directly on the questionnaire itself and discussed in a covering letter.

RULE 10.7

HONOUR PROMISES TO PROVIDE RESPONDENTS RESEARCH REPORTS.

Where an offer to provide a research report to respondents has been given, the promise must be fulfilled. The relation between researcher and respondent/subject should be reciprocal. In practice, it is to the advantage of the researcher to fulfil such obligations because doing so will encourage the continued cooperation of respondents in long-term projects.

Where individuals are offered the opportunity of receiving a report on the study, a separate, stamped envelope and request form should be provided for the respondent. The separate return envelope not only keeps the respondent's name disassociated from the questionnaire, but also conveys to the respondent that the researcher takes a promise of confidentiality seriously.

While there may be no ethical responsibility to pay respondents who volunteer their cooperation, such payments are to be encouraged in order to reinforce the idea of a reciprocal contract between researcher and respondent. Participant observation studies frequently involve rather long periods of observation, and it is particularly important to reciprocate by providing a payment or a report on the research project.

RULE 10.8

INFORMED CONSENT IS A KEY CONCERN.

In dealing with competent adults, participation should be based on *informed consent*—that is, potential respondents must be informed about the nature of the study, what kinds of issues will be explored, how respondents were selected, and who is sponsoring the research.

Moreover, prospective respondents should be informed that they should feel free to withdraw from the study at any time if they wish to do so. In surveys, respondents should be told to feel free to skip any questions that they consider inappropriate.

When studies involving children, the infirm, or incompetent adults are done, the organization or individual responsible for the prospective respondents should provide consent in writing.

The issue of informed consent may be a problem for researchers doing participant observation studies. It would not be reasonable to insist that all members being observed would have to consent to being observed. The test in such cases perhaps should be:

- whether sufficient steps are taken to protect the anonymity of those who are observed; and

- that no negative consequences could reasonably be seen to result from the activity of the research project.

To put a blanket prohibition on such studies would mean that works such as Erving Goffman's *Asylums* or Margaret Mead's *Sex and Temperament in Three Primitive Societies* could not have been done.

Covert observational studies, such as those observing whether the drivers of automobiles have their shoulder belts fastened, can be performed so long as there is no apparent danger to the subject being observed or to the observer. In such cases it is not practical to attempt to gain the permission of the person being observed. When deciding if the study should be undertaken, the best test the researcher can make is an attempt to balance any good that may come out of the project against its potentially negative consequences.

In experimental studies, particularly those involving some deception, there is a problem concerning informed consent. If the experimental manipulation requires deception, it is not possible to inform the subject fully, in advance, of the deception: to do so would spoil the study. In such cases, Rule 10.9 needs to be applied.

RULE 10.9
DEBRIEF SUBJECTS.

Where experiments or field studies involve deception, subjects should have the study explained to them after the session. The researcher should note what deception was used, why it was necessary, and the subjects should be reassured that their participation was appreciated and helpful.

2. ETHICS AND THE SOCIAL RESEARCHER

The social researcher has two special difficulties, not experienced to the same degree by researchers in other areas:

(i) the researcher frequently has a theoretical and practical "vested interest" in the outcome of a study; and

(ii) the social scientist, particularly the survey researcher, typically works with a large number of indicators, providing many opportunities for alternative interpretations.

And, given the special difficulties involved in replicating social research, we often have to trust the findings reported by the social researcher. This situation places an even greater ethical responsibility on the social researcher to conduct unbiased studies.

RULE 10.10
RESEARCHERS SHOULD DISTINGUISH BETWEEN SCIENCE AND ADVOCACY.

In your role as social scientist, do not work on projects where you are asked to develop a "scientific case" for a conclusion. Given the legitimacy of science in Western culture, it should be no surprise that both scientists and non-scientists will be tempted to utilize this legitimacy to achieve personal or group goals. Evidence which is viewed as scientific carries a lot of weight in argument, and hence, when a presentation is being prepared, collecting or referring to scientific evidence is tempting and sensible.

If you are hired to "develop a scientific case for..." then you have an ethical problem. You are being asked to provide scientific evidence to convince others of some position. You are, in this case, being asked to make others believe that you have scientific evidence for some position. Such research should not be presented as science: to do so would be unethical.

As a citizen-advocate it is perfectly legitimate to comment on the evidence of others and to produce evidence that is appropriate to the issue under dispute. It should be noted, however, that the information is being presented from the perspective of a citizen-advocate, not from that of the expert social scientist. We would be well advised to maintain a distinction between citizen-advocate roles and social science roles. Too often the line between them is blurred.

RULE 10.11

DO NOT HUNT THROUGH DATA LOOKING FOR PLEASING FINDINGS.

The surest way to be guilty of misrepresentation is to search for support for your own views. To do so would be both bad science and unethical behaviour. If data are being scanned for interesting findings, these cannot be reported unless the process by which they have emerged is made absolutely clear.

RULE 10.12

BE AWARE OF POTENTIAL SOURCES OF BIAS.

Becoming aware of the sources of bias may help you avoid bias in your own work and spot it in the research reports of others. Researchers have an ethical responsibility to report their work fairly, attempting to avoid bias as much as possible. Review the discussion of sources of bias in Chapter 9.

RULE 10.13

REPRESENT RESEARCH LITERATURE FAIRLY.

In the interest of objectivity and ethics, researchers must attempt to portray accurately the body of literature in their area of research. Reporting findings selectively is not acceptable.

RULE 10.14

DO THE BEST RESEARCH YOU CAN.

Research must strive to be competent and impartial, and its results must be reported objectively. Use qualified personnel and consultants. Keep up with developments in your field, and use the best techniques of data collection and analysis. Seek always to do the best research you can; do research with care.

RULE 10.15

ACKNOWLEDGE ALL YOUR SOURCES.

Acknowledge people who have played a role in your research and acknowledge all literature sources that have directly influenced your study. Excluding the respondents (who have been assured of anonymity), all other people who have assisted in the project should be acknowledged by way of a footnote. Similarly, when literature has been used in developing the project, each source should be cited.

RULE 10.16

SEEK ADVICE ON ETHICAL ISSUES.

If ethical issues arise, seek the advice of appropriate professional bodies or institutions involved in the project. Most studies will not pose difficult ethical issues. However, when the research team identifies an ethical dilemma, outside consultations are appropriate. Such consultations would weigh the benefits of the research to society against the costs that bending ethical guidelines may entail. Before any study begins, all such ethical dilemmas should be resolved by appropriate adjustments to the project (for good discussions on these matters see Nachmias, 1981; and Reynolds, 1982).

A code of ethics applied to much social research in Canada is included in Appendix H. It is the Social Sciences and Humanities Research Council (SSHRC): "Ethical Guidelines for Research With Human Subjects." Various professional associations have developed their own codes of ethics. In addition, universities, colleges, and hospitals are required by granting agencies to have a committee to review the ethical suitability of proposed research projects. You should familiarize yourself with

the applicable code for your discipline or place of work.

D. KEY TERMS

Consequentialist

Deontological

Informed consent

Debriefing

E. KEY POINTS

The *consequentialist view* is that ethical judgements about a research project should be made in the light of its consequences for the subject, for the academic discipline, and for society. A cost-benefit analysis might reveal that the advantages gained by the advancement of our knowledge justify the violation of some rules: in this view, deception is okay if it does not do any long-term damage to the subject.

The *deontological view* of research ethics proposes absolute moral strictures that must never be violated.

Maintaining the *comfort and self-esteem* of the subject should be a central concern of the researcher.

Respondents should feel free to refuse participation, withdraw at any time, or to refuse to answer any particular question.

The respondent has a right to know how he or she was *selected for participation* in a study.

There should be *no deception concerning the sponsorship* of a project.

Researchers should *not use hidden codes* to assist in the identification of those who have or have not returned questionnaires.

In dealing with competent adults, participation should be based on *informed consent*—that is, the potential respondents must be informed about the nature of the study, what kinds of issues will be explored, how the respondents were selected, and who is sponsoring the research. Where studies are done involving children, the infirm, or incompetent adults, the organization or individual responsible for the prospective respondents should provide consent in writing.

When experiments or field studies involve deception, following the session, subjects should be *debriefed*—that is, they should have the study explained to them, any deceptions should be noted, their necessity explained, and the subjects should be reassured that their participation was appreciated and helpful.

If you are hired to "develop a scientific case for..." then you have an ethical problem.

The surest way to be guilty of misrepresentation is to *search for support for your own views*; to do so would be both bad science and unethical behaviour.

If ethical issues arise, *seek the advice* of appropriate professional bodies or institutions involved in the project.

F. EXERCISES

1. If you were designing a survey dealing with the sexual behaviour of university students, what would you see as the major ethical problems in such a study? What steps would you recommend be taken before data collection begins?

2. Examine the SSHRC code of ethics. In view of this code, what changes would you recommend if you were proposing to replicate Milgram's original study on obedience?

3. Suppose you were considering replicating Laud Humphreys *Tearoom Trade* in your home community: what changes would you make to Humphreys' methodology to satisfy ethical questions? What do you give up because of the alterations you propose?

4. Suppose you were planning a study of substance abuse in a small native community. What ethical dilemmas might you face in doing such a study? What procedures would you recommend to be followed?

G. RECOMMENDED READINGS

DESROCHES, FREDERICK J. (1990). "Tearoom Trade: A Research Update." *Qualitative Sociology,* 13 (1), 39-61. This study uses police records to examine tearoom trade activities in selected Canadian cities.

HUMPHREYS, LAUD (1970). *Tearoom Trade.* Chicago: Aldine Publishing Co. This is a classic study in the study of deviance which, at the same time, raises many thorny ethical issues.

MILGRAM, STANLEY (1964). "Behavioral Study of Obedience."*Journal of Abnormal and Social Psychology,* 67(4), 371-378. This is the report of the original Milgram study. Reynolds (1982) provides an overview of the many additional studies carried out by Milgram.

NACHMIAS, DAVID, AND CHAVA NACHMIAS (1981). "Ethical Concerns in Social Science Research," in *Research Methods in the Social Sciences,* Second Edition. New York: St. Martin's Press. This is a good discussion of ethical concerns in social research.

REYNOLDS, PAUL DAVIDSON (1982). *Ethics and Social Science Research.* Englewood Cliffs: Prentice-Hall Inc. This a short book but one which does a fine job in reviewing ethical issues; it includes an evaluation of the ethical issues involved in the studies reviewed in this chapter.

GETTING THE PROJECT STARTED

Getting started is sometimes the most difficult part of a project. But care taken during the beginning stages will pay off handsomely. A carefully designed study which enables the researcher to come to conclusions about some social behaviour, which includes some theory-testing dimensions, and which is informed by the existing literature, will provide the basis for an excellent project.

A. CHOOSING A PROBLEM, A DESIGN, AND VARIABLES

An enormous variety of topics can be studied using social science techniques. To provide some sense of the range of topics that can be treated, a listing of some projects carried out by my students is found in Box 11.1.

BOX 11.1 STUDENT RESEARCHERS AT WORK

Typically, these projects were designed by groups of students and carried out during a year-long methods course. The students were primarily drawn from sociology or nursing, with a few from business, political science, and anthropology. The students determined the subject matter and the faculty member assisted them in completing their projects. Traditionally, the course emphasized survey research methods so most, but not all, fit into that type of design.

Territorial Invasions among Students

Summer Employment and Economic Need

Community Size and Prejudice Level

Territorial Imperatives: the Elevator

Religiosity and Morality

Conformity Among University Students

Status Crystallization and its Application to Nurses, CNA's, Orderlies, and Aides

Professor-Student Exchange Relations

Energy Crisis: Attitudes and Concerns

Errors in the Self-Administration of Drugs

Desired Family Size

Factors Contributing to Alcohol Consumption

Cigarette Smoking: Patterns of High School and University Students' Use

Religious Participation at Two Universities

Attitudes Toward Campus Medical Facilities

Residence Satisfaction: A Comparison of Two Residences

Factors Influencing Academic Achievement

Social Class and Educational Aspirations of Female Students

Spatial Invasion as a Function of Interaction Intensity

The Effect of Threat Upon Distance in an Interacting Dyad

University Students and Involvement in Voluntary Associations

Attitudes Toward Women and Faculty

Classroom Seating Location and Grade Performance

Satisfaction with the Nursing Program

Dress and Day of the Week

Patterns of Soap Opera Viewing

Attitudes Toward Separation of Quebec from Canada

Patterns of Superstitions

Survey of University Graduates

Pre-Marital Sexual Patterns

Academic Performance and On- or Off-Campus Residence

Attitudes Toward Open Housing

Factors Influencing Liberalism

Grade Performance: What Causes Variation?

Factors Influencing Mother's Satisfaction with Birth Experience

Weight Gain Among Female University Students

Attitudes Toward the Police

Factors Influencing Program Selection Among Females Enrolled in Nursing and Physical Education Programs

Leadership Among University and Hospital Trained Nursing Students

Attitudes Toward Abortion, Euthanasia, and Invitro Fertilization

Relative Status of University Departments

Attitudes Toward Campus Police

Class Attendance and Grade Performance

Factors Influencing Professional versus Traditional Career Orientations

Participation and Self Esteem

Effects of Contact and Attitudes Toward the Handicapped

Attitudes Toward Capital Punishment

High School Students' Attitudes Toward Alcohol Consumption

Attitudes Toward Abortion

Relation Between Sexual Knowledge and Sexual Behaviour

Retirement and Life Satisfaction: A Study of Senior Citizens in Small-Town Nova Scotia

Attitudes Toward Pre-Marital Sex Among High School Students

Attitudes Toward the Elderly

Drug Use Among First Year University Students

Contraception Use: A Study of Female University Students

Factors Influencing Social Adjustment and Academic Achievement

Attitudes of Nurses Toward Student Nurses

Delinquent Compared to Non-Delinquent Females

Attitudes Toward Sex Roles

An Analytical Comparison of Attitudes Toward Capital Punishment and Abortion

Choice of Non-Traditional University Programs by Females

Wage Discrimination: Comparing Salaries of Male and Female Professors

Attitudes Toward the Male Nurse

Male Attitudes Toward Homosexuality

Factors Influencing Addictive Behaviour

Fertility Expectations and Intended Labour Force Participation of Nursing Students

Factors Influencing Expected Age of Marriage

Attitudes Toward Primary Care Nursing

Comparing the Occupational Aspirations of High School Students in Antigonish and Dartmouth

Factors Influencing Maternal Confidence

Attitudes Toward Euthanasia

Suicidal Thoughts Among University Students

Attitudes Toward Homosexuality

Traditional and Non-Traditional Program Choices

A Survey of Nursing Graduates of the Eighties

Liberal Attitudes Toward Pre-Marital Sex

Shifts Between Freshmen and Seniors' Perceived Role of the Nurse

Attitudes Toward AIDS

Factors Influencing Academic Performance

The Effect of Talkativeness on Group Dynamics

Sexual Harassment on Campus

Male Perceptions of Aggression and Date Rape

A Study of Stress

Analysis of Residence Satisfaction

Cross-Cultural and Sex Role Comparisons

Factors that Influence the Degree of University Student Self-Support

Factors Affecting R.N.'s Shift Preference

The Status of Programs

Attitudes Toward the Ordination of Gay Clergy

A Study of Basal-Infusion Patient Controlled Intravenous Analgesic Versus Intramuscular Injection of Women in Labour

Fear Among Female Students Living on Campus

Males' Attitudes Toward Dating Relationships

PMS as it is experienced by Female Students

Nurses' Perceptions of Job Satisfaction

Factors Influencing Deviant Behaviour in Adolescents

Unwanted Intimacy

Male Attitudes Toward Non-Traditional Roles of Women

Evaluation of the Distance Nursing Program

Attitudes Toward the Elderly

Heavy Drinking at University

Fear Among Female University Students of Being Attacked

Effects of Eating Breakfast on Grade Performance

Attitudes Toward Authority

Diploma Students' Attitudes Toward Degree Nursing Students

Attitudes Toward Contraceptive Use

1. CHOOSING A PROBLEM

Given the considerable effort required to complete a project, the single most important consideration in choosing the topic is genuine interest. Some suggestions of how to go about choosing a project are presented below.

A. CURRENT ISSUE

One method of selecting a project is to choose one which is the subject of public debate. Such topics might include capital punishment, abortion, environmental degradation, free trade, religious cults, race prejudice, gender inequities, population growth, poverty, attitudes toward people with AIDS, date rape, unemployment, or the popularity of a political leader.

B. VARIATION IN A DEPENDENT VARIABLE

Another approach is to try to understand variations in some dependent variable. What factors influence grade performance? What influences the popularity of a teacher? What variables influence the choice of a non-traditional program among female students? How do people communicate non-verbally to indicate that they wish to terminate an interaction? Here the goal is to understand the factors influencing the dependent variable.

C. TESTING A THEORY

Those researchers who have theoretical inclination, may wish to test a current theory of human behaviour. Chapter 2 outlined methods for generating testable theoretical hypotheses. The challenge is to examine a relationship between variables that is predicted by a theory but which, at the same time, is not obvious to commonsense. The most convincing theory-testing projects will be those that will make a counter-intuitive (against common sense) prediction which, if it turns out to be true, will be a convincing demonstration of the theory. (See Chapter 2 for some examples.)

D. TESTING PARTIAL THEORIES

A review of the literature may reveal a consistent relationship between two variables, but alternative explanations for this relationship may not have been carefully tested. In such cases, it is reasonable to propose alternative explanations for the relationship, design a study, and then test which, if any, of the proposed explanations best accounts for the relationship. (See Chapter 2 for some examples.)

E. TESTING FOLK WISDOM

Interesting projects can often be designed to test the accuracy of some taken-for-granted wisdom systematically. To provide a few examples, consider the following:

- In romance, do opposites attract?

- Among 10-year-olds, are males better than females in solving mathematical puzzles?

- Among 10-year-olds, are females better than males in solving crossword puzzles?

- In a classroom setting, do the strongest friendships occur among those who have the most in common: in short, do "Birds of a feather flock together?"

- In sports, does playing in front of a home audience provide any advantage? (See Box 6.3.)

Spend some time thinking about commonly accepted views of how things work and then try to think of some way in which the idea could be tested systematically. Ask yourself how experimental, field, survey, or non-reactive designs might be used to study the problem. Which design would be ideal and which one most practical?

F. APPLIED RESEARCH

Another source of projects is to look at some "applied" problem. Perhaps through research the identified problem will be understood better, or even resolved. Typically the problem is defined by the sponsor. The rescarcher must decide, if the project is ethically acceptable (and the fee is right!), how to do the project. The applied rescarcher might be asked to figure out how to attract more students to a university program; to describe the public's attitude toward some current issue; or to help a political candidate figure out what issues are of concern to voters in a constituency.

Social scientists are frequently called upon to provide an evaluation of some social intervention. Evaluations are often required for social programs. A solid understanding of experimental design, and a good deal of imagination, and flexibility, are qualities well suited to doing evaluations. There is a demand for people who know how to do evaluation work.

G. REPLICATION STUDY

Finally, one can choose to replicate, or repeat, some earlier study. But even if a replication is attempted, the researcher should attempt to add a new dimension to the study and try to answer some question that was left open by the previous project.

2. CHOOSING A DESIGN

Many factors influence the choice of research design. Primarily the nature of the question being asked determines which design would be most appropriate. But there are pragmatic considerations too: such as the amount of time and research funds available, or the kind of respondents that are available to the researcher.

Assuming you have a rough idea of the problem you wish to investigate, what steps might you take to decide on the appropriate research strategy? Remember, there may be constraints imposed by funding, time, availability of research assistants, ethical issues, computer resources, and technical competence. The following summarizes some steps you might wish to take to decide which research strategy will be followed.

STEP 1

WHAT HAVE OTHERS DONE?

Do a preliminary review of the literature to get some sense of what has been written about the subject you wish to explore. What research designs were employed in these studies? Can you locate any articles that reflect the use of different designs to explore the problem? Tips for locating such articles will be discussed later in this chapter in the Review of Literature section.

STEP 2

CONSIDER ALTERNATIVES.

Consider alternatives when faced with difficulties such as those listed below:

- time ("Rats, the project report is due in 3 months!");
- ethical issues ("The Ethics Review Board probably would not approve of the decep-

tion involved in the study.");

- computer resources ("Our institution does not have the programs that we need to do the analysis.");
- technical competence ("Regression analysis is beyond me, and to replicate the study, I would need to do understand it.");
- availability of research assistants ("To do this project properly we would need assistance and there are not enough sufficient qualified people available to do the interviewing and observations.");
- funding ("We just don't have enough money to do the project properly.").

Given difficulties such as these, are there alternative strategies that might be employed? It may be possible to:

- Use data that have been generated by other researchers; you will need to get the data and permission to use them; you will also have to live with someone else's operationalizations.
- Use publicly available data: (i) university and college social science departments often maintain data banks; (ii) government agencies sometimes make data of interest available to social scientists; and (iii) other publicly available data sources exist such as the Human Relations Area Files (see discussion in Chapter 5). Typically data sets are available in the form of computer files.
- Use information published in newspapers or books; much secondary data can be gleaned from regularly published information. For example, if you were interested in examining the relation between final score difference and the likelihood of violence in hockey, you could study one N.H.L. hockey season and, from daily newspaper game summaries, record the final score gap and relate this to the total number of penalty minutes.

STEP 3

REVIEW THE CHAPTER THAT INTRODUCES THE TYPE OF DESIGN TENTATIVELY SELECTED.

The following chapters introduce different types of research designs:

- Chapter 3. Experimental and Quasi-Experimental Designs
- Chapter 4. Survey Designs
- Chapter 5. Field Studies
- Chapter 6. Non-Reactive Studies

There are recommended readings in each of the chapters and these may be helpful in gaining additional insights for the design of your study. Those students opting for a qualitative approach will want to review Chapter 5 in detail. A section called "Steps in Conducting a Participant Observation Study" may be relevant to your research.

STEP 4

BE PREPARED TO RECONSIDER THE RESEARCH DESIGN USED.

Continue developing the project but be prepared to reopen the research design question. As various factors are considered, it may be necessary to consider alternative approaches to the research question. As you review the literature in detail, different questions may come to seem more relevant to the goals of your project. If this happens, be prepared to reconsider the type of research design to be used in the study.

3. DETERMINING THE PRECISE QUESTIONS

Having selected the general area of research and a tentative research design, the next step is to articulate precisely what you wish to investigate. To illustrate the point further, suppose you wished to do a project on capital punishment. As you start to think about the project, determine whether you wish to examine:

- public attitudes toward capital punishment;

- compare the types of people who support capital punishment with those who do not;

- the relationship between other social attitudes (poverty, abortion, people in authority) and capital punishment;

- whether there is a sex difference in support for capital punishment;

- whether women are less inclined to support capital punishment, and if so, determine what accounts for this tendency.

The list of issues you might wish to tackle could be extended. Once a problem has been selected, the work of pinning down the precise questions begins. Suppose that you decided to focus on the last question (understanding gender differences in attitudes toward capital punishment); a thorough review of the literature should be undertaken to find out what other researchers have discovered. The review will also help you determine more precisely what is to be investigated.

As projects are developed it is normal for the first ideas to be fuzzy and to require a project of a rather grand scale. As the researcher becomes more familiar with the literature and sensitive to practical considerations, the project will become more focused, specific, and move to something that can be accomplished with the resources available. It is necessary to go through a process of "pinning down the project," "focusing the project," and "specifying the hypotheses." It is normal to begin with rather grand plans: with time, the project will gradually take shape.

4. REVIEWING THE LITERATURE

In reviewing the literature, you are trying to get a sense of the state of scientific knowledge about the topic. The first question is "Where do I start?"

- If you are part of a university or college, ask instructors who work in the area for any ideas they might have on where to get information.

- Check with a reference librarian for sources that may lead you to research done on your topic.

- Check text books for a lead.

- Check the appropriate discipline's Abstracts, as they provide brief descriptions of published papers dealing with a variety of topics. Box 11.2 lists some of the relevant Abstracts and Indexes available in many libraries.

- Check journals that are likely to publish work in the area. It is advisable to begin by checking through the most recent issues: once you have found an article that is close to your topic in either the particular variables treated or the general concepts presented, check it for references to other articles. By starting with the most recent issues, you will identify the latest research; and if an article published in the 1950s is referenced in many

BOX 11.2

Abstracts and Indexes of Periodicals of Relevance to Anthropology, Education, Nursing, Political Science, Psychology, and Sociology

General Listing (Relevant to Several Disciplines)
Canadian Periodical Index (Canadian content)
Infotrac (Academic Index) CD-ROM

Social Sciences Citation Index
Social Sciences Index
Public Affairs Information Science Bulletin (PAIS)
Newspaper Indexes
Canadian News Index
Canadian Press Newsfiles
Index de l'actualite
The National Newspaper Index
New York Times Index
The Times Index

Anthropology
Abstracts in Anthropology
Anthropological Literature: Index to Periodical Articles
International Bibliography of Social and Cultural Anthropology

Education
British Education Index
Canadian Education Index
Education Index
ERIC CD-ROM

Nursing
Cumulative Index to Nursing and Allied Health Lit. (CINAHL)
Index Medicus
Medline CD-ROM

Political Science
ABC Pol Sci
International Bibliography of Political Science
International Political Sciences Abstract
Political Science Abstracts

Psychology
Child Development Abstracts and Bibliography
Psyclit CD-ROM
Psychological Abstracts

Sociology
Human Resources Abstracts
International Bibliography of Sociology
Social Work Research and Abstracts
Sociological Abstracts
Sociofile CD-ROM

of the articles, you will want to read it, since it is still considered to be one of the classics.

• You may not be able to find published results on the specific relationship, or category of individuals, you wish to study. If this is the case, focus on variables that researchers have found to be related to the major dependent variable you propose to examine.

• In many cases, it will be appropriate to review research which uses similar methodologies or theories.

The goals of a review include:

• identifying areas where there seems to be consensus among researchers;

• noting where there are inconsistencies in research findings;

• identifying variables that others have found to be relevant to the problem at hand;

• identifying areas which, if explored, could lead to important new understandings of the phenomenon under examination;

• seeing how other researchers have made connections to theory; and,

• seeing how other researchers have measured variables and analyzed their data.

Generally, when reviews are presented in a report, they should try to summarize briefly the areas of agreement and disagreement in the literature. Article summaries may be useful to the researcher but are generally not appropriate in a final report. What is required is a sense of the current state of knowledge on the topic under investigation. Table 11.1 shows one method of summarizing articles: by using such a grid system, you can make additions to the list, and also provide a quick summary of areas of agreement and disagreement among researchers.

In preparing a discussion of the literature reviewed, it generally seems best to report the findings on one variable at a time. Thus, if you were studying attitudes toward the availability of abortions, you might begin by talking about how such attitudes are related to gender, then to age categories, then to rural versus urban residence, and so forth. In each case, you would want to summarize the consensus (or lack of it) in the research literature. And, if you have provided a summary grid for the literature, your reader will be able to review the findings quickly.

TABLE 11.1 ALCOHOL CONSUMPTION AND CORRELATES: A SUMMARY OF FINDINGS

PROBLEMS	RESEARCH AUTHORS						
	1	2	3	4	5	6	7
Illness	+	+	+	−	+	+	−
School	+	+	+	−	+		−
Legal	+	−	+	+	+	+	+
Forgetting	−	+	−	−	−	−	+
Vandalism	+	+	+	−	+	−	−
Fighting	−	+	+	−	+	−	−
Binge problem	+	−	+	+	+	−	−
Job problem	+	−		+	−	−	
Financial	−	−	−	+	−	−	+
Year of report	1988	1986	1984	1976	1977	1984	1981
Number of subjects	410	4607	489	582	1300	140	10500
Place of study	University of Arkansas	University of California	Oklahoma State University	University of California	Indiana	Auburn	Boston

Legend: + indicates problem was covered in the study and was found to be correlated with alcohol consumption;

– indicates problem not correlated with alcohol consumption;

Blank: indicates variables not reported in study.

1/Werch, C.E. and D.R. Gorman (1988); 2/Temple, M. (1986); 3/Hughes, S.P. and R.A. Dodder (1984); 4/Clark W.B. (1976); 5/Engs, R.C. (1977); 6/Ratliff, K.G. and B.R. Burnhart (1984); 7/Wechsler, H. & M. Rohman (1981).

SOURCE: Adapted from Terrance O'Callaghan, (1991). "Alcohol Consumption and Its Correlates at St. F.X.U." Antigonish: St. Francis Xavier University, Research Methods Paper.

RULE 11.1

PROVIDE BIBLIOGRAPHICAL REFERENCES.

Record full bibliographic details of each article or book used. When the final report is being prepared, all the sources will be cited in the bibliography. If you have not recorded this information in full, you will waste a lot of time retracing your steps to recover the information.

5. CHOOSING VARIABLES

Variables may be defined simply as concepts which we intend to measure. Variables may be identified by:

- reviewing the research literature and identifying what variables other researchers have used in doing similar research;

- applying relevant theoretical models and identifying the variables that are implied by the theories;

- examining questionnaires for ideas concerning what variables should be measured if a survey is to be conducted;

- developing causal models and figuring out what sources of spuriousness, intervening, or control variables may be relevant for the project; and

- simply thinking about what variables may influence the dependent variable.

At the beginning of the project the researcher should not worry too much about whether the identified variables can be measured. Simply identify relevant variables. The issue of measurement can be confronted later.

B. DEVELOPING CAUSAL MODELS

Clarity and precision are at the core of successful research. A ***causal model*** is a graphic representation of proposed causal interconnections between variables. In quantitative research, one way to force accuracy is to draw a diagram of the causal connections between variables. The advantage of a diagram is that it forces clear thinking about what you are doing. Thus, drawing a diagram with causal arrows forces you to indicate which variable is causally prior to other variables. You are forced to be specific. Such diagrams can also replace stating formal hypotheses; each hypothesis should be reflected in a properly drawn diagram.

We will begin with the simplest models and gradually move toward the more complex ones. What all models have in common is that each of them can be represented by a diagram: each such diagram shows either a causal direction, a hypothesis, or a set of hypotheses. We begin with the two-variable model. Chapters 15 and Appendix A present procedures for analyzing these models.

1. TWO-VARIABLE MODELS

In Chapter 1 the distinction between a dependent and an independent variable was made: the dependent variable is the "effect" in a cause-effect relationship, or the result of the influence of an independent variable. Conventionally, we refer to the dependent variable as the *Y* variable, and the independent variable as the *X* variable. The relationship can be described simply with a diagram:

What does the diagram tell us? First, it describes a relationship between two variables known as *X* and *Y*. Note that there is an arrow pointing from *X* to *Y*: this tells us that *X* is the independent variable, and that *Y* is the dependent variable. The hypothesis reflected by this diagram argues that *X* influences *Y*. Next, note the > symbol before the *X* box. This symbol means "the greater;" the opposite symbol, <, means "the less." Putting all these elements together, the hypothesis can be stated as: "The greater *X*, the greater *Y*." Had we wished to express a negative relationship, the first symbol could be reversed. In this case, the hypothesis would be stated as: "The less *X*, the greater *Y*."

If the *X* and *Y* were replaced with variable names, we might, for example, be talking about the relationship between participation in social activities and self-esteem, suggesting that "The greater the participation in social activities, the greater the self-esteem" (Brennan, 1985). The wording of the hypothesis indicates that participation is the independent variable, self-esteem the dependent variable.

The advantage of drawing a diagram to represent the relationship is that the researcher is forced to:

- indicate causal direction (arrow points to dependent variable); and,

- indicate if the relationship is positive (note use of > symbol) or negative (< symbol).

Drawing a picture forces precision. There may be times when you cannot formulate a problem in such a way that you are able to say whether the relation is positive or negative. In these cases one cannot speak in "greater than," "less than" terms. Where you are unable to specify the nature of the relationship use a '?' to indicate that no prediction is being made.

Occasionally, you will not be in a position to set out a causal order: here you may be faced with a situation where variables exist together and influence one another simultaneously. In this event, you can indicate reciprocal causation by placing arrows at each end of the line linking the two variables.

2. THREE-VARIABLE MODELS

Now let us turn our attention to various three-variable models. Some terms need to be reviewed. Besides independent and dependent variables, there are three additional types of variables that will need to be un-

derstood: intervening, source of spuriousness, and conditional variables.

A. AN INTERVENING VARIABLE MODEL

An ***intervening variable*** (I) is a variable that links an independent variable (X) to a dependent variable (Y). An intervening variable represents an explanation of how the independent variable influences the dependent variable. The interest here is in understanding the relationship between *X* and *Y*—understanding the mechanism by which *X* is connected to *Y*. Frequently the researcher will be testing a number of alternative explanations of how *X* influences *Y*. In the case of one intervening variable, the relationship could be diagrammed as follows:

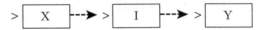

In this diagram, *I* is the intervening variable, or the linking variable between *X* and *Y*. The hypothesis is that variations in *X* cause variations in *I*, which, in turn, influences *Y*. Typically, one would propose a number of possible intervening variables, so the following diagram would be more appropriate:

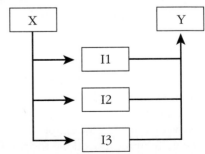

In this diagram, three alternative explanations are suggested for the connection between *X* and *Y*. The researcher would collect data that measures each of the variables involved, and conduct the appropriate statistical tests to determine, which, if any, of the proposed alternative explanations or intervening variables explains the connection between *X* and *Y*. These matters will be examined further in Chapter 16.

B. A SOURCE OF SPURIOUSNESS MODEL

A ***source of spuriousness model*** is one in which a variable is identified as a possible influence on both the independent variable (X) and the dependent variable (Y) in such a way that it accounts for the relationship between them. In other words, the relationship between X and Y may be "spurious" because it is produced by the influence of S/S on each of them. Here the researcher proposes that, while there is a statistically significant relation between the variables *X* and *Y*, this relationship may be non-causal, only existing because some third variable is influencing both *X* and *Y*. The argument is that *X* and *Y* are only related to one another because a third factor is influencing both of them. Having observed a statistically significant relation, the researcher will want to ensure that the relationship is not spurious and, therefore, will run a number of spuriousness checks. The source of spuriousness model may be diagrammed as follows:

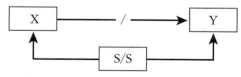

In the source of spuriousness model, the researcher is suggesting that the rela-

tion between *X* and *Y* may be spurious. The techniques for examining such relations is examined in Chapter 16.

C. AN ANTECEDENT VARIABLE MODEL

An ***antecedent variable model*** is a causal model which proposes a variable which causes variation in an independent variable which, in turn, influences the dependent variable in the model. Thus the antecedent variable is one which precedes the main independent and dependent variables. This variable may be having an impact on the independent variable which, in turn, may be influencing the dependent variable. An antecedent variable may be diagrammed as follows:

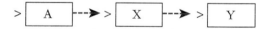

In a sense, an antecedent variable combines one idea from the source of spuriousness model and one from an intervening variable model:

- it is causally prior to both the independent and the dependent variable (as in a source of spuriousness model);

- it converts the independent variable into one which intervenes between the antecedent variable and the dependent variable.

D. EXTENDING THE NUMBER OF VARIABLES

It is possible to add variables to three-variable models. In *Causal Inferences in Nonexperimental Research*, Hubert M. Blalock Jr. (1964) outlined partial correlation methods for analysing relationships where two intervening variables are being evaluated simultaneously. However, it does seem that most researchers have moved toward using regression-based approaches when analysing such relations rather than using partial correlations, as suggested in Blalock's presentation. A four-variable model such as that suggested by Blalock is shown in the following diagram:

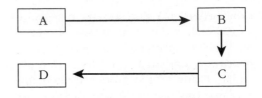

3. MULTI-VARIATE MODELS

Models that use numerous variables are known as ***multi-variate models***. The first

---

FIGURE 11.1   PREDICTING POSITIVE ATTITUDES TOWARDS THE ELDERLY*

INDEPENDENT VARIABLES   DEPENDENT VARIABLE

Education variables:
> B.A. program
> Years at institution
> Average

Contact with the elderly:
> Worked with elderly
> Lived with elderly
> Involvement with elderly

Attitudes and knowledge:
> Positive attitude toward minorities
> Knowledge about elderly

Gender:
> Females

Self:
> Self-esteem

Background:
> Size of community
> Parental marital status (married)
> Mother/father education
> Grandparents living
> Number of brothers and sisters
> Birth order
> Parental occupational prestige

> Positive attitudes towards the elderly

SOURCE: Lara MacDonald (1991). "Attitudes Towards the Elderly." Research Methods Paper. Antigonish: St. Francis Xavier University.

we will consider is the candidate variable model.

A. CANDIDATE VARIABLE MODEL

A *candidate variable model* is one which proposes several independent variables as possible causes of variation in a dependent variable. Here the researcher is proposing a number of independent variables that may be influencing the dependent variable. This type of model is illustrated in Figure 11.1.

The variables on the left side of the diagram are the independent variables and are viewed as potential causes of variations in the dependent variable, positive attitudes toward the elderly (MacDonald, 1991). Note that the model uses the symbols > and < to indicate whether the independent variables are positively or negatively associ-

ated with the dependent variable. The independent variables will be related to the dependent variable either one at a time or simultaneously, through procedures that are outlined in Chapter 17.

B. PATH MODELS

A *path model* is a graphic representation of a complex set of proposed interrelationships among variables. A model of this type is shown below in Figure 11.2 (Jackson and Poushinsky, 1971). (See also Box 2.3 which features Julian Tanner and Harvey Krahn's model of self-reported deviance among high school seniors.)

All the models we have discussed reflect the causal thinking of the researcher in such a way that this reasoning can then be tested in later stages of the project.

FIGURE 11.2 INTERRELATIONSHIP OF MAJOR DEPENDENT VARIABLES

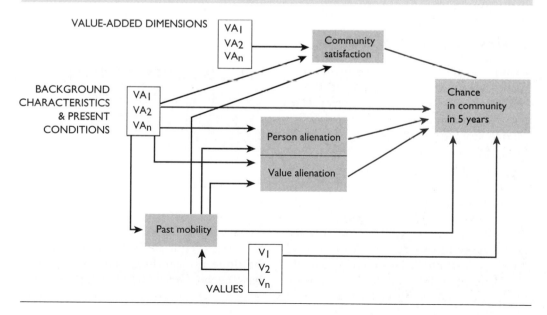

C. SPECIFYING HYPOTHESES, PROCEDURES OF ANALYSIS

Having developed diagrams for the various relationships that are to be investigated (which imply the hypotheses to be tested), it is now time to indicate formally how the analyses of the data will be done. Proposed methods of analysis are specified in advance to help prevent the researcher from manipulating the data until it conforms to expectations.

We state hypotheses (or diagram them) prior to data analysis to ensure that the researcher is not inventing them after the data have been analyzed. As noted in Chapter 8, developing hypotheses after data are analyzed would render tests of significance meaningless; we would not be able to make judgements about the statistical significance of findings if we do not specify hypotheses in advance of data analysis.

1. STATING HYPOTHESES

Good diagrams can replace formal hypotheses statements. By using > and < symbols it is possible to indicate "greater than" and "less than" relations; arrows may be used to indicate causal direction. Particularly in candidate variable models, which include a large number of variables, it is easier to diagram the hypotheses than to present a written version of each one. Similarly, where many alternative explanations are being tested for a particular relationship, a good diagram clearly shows the causal model and the implied research hypotheses.

In theory-testing projects, it is important not only to state the derived hypotheses but also to indicate the steps that were taken in making the derivation(s). Only to the extent that such derivations can be traced, can one claim to have tested a theory.

2. SPECIFYING METHODS OF ANALYSIS

Specifying methods of analysis in advance forces the researcher to be committed to particular procedures. Selecting these procedures also has implications for the way in which variables will be measured. Thus, if contingency tables are to be used exclusively, it will not be necessary to get ratio level measures on the variables. It is probably unreasonable to require a researcher to specify "cut-points" for contingency tables because of the large number of variables that may be involved. However, it is reasonable to indicate the number of categories that will be used, and the principle which was used in making the cut-points. (Perhaps splitting the sample into thirds, or at the mid-point. See Rule 7.16.)

D. HOW TO KNOW WHEN YOU ARE READY TO START THE PROJECT

Table 11.2 provides a check list for items that need to be attended to before beginning a project. Not all items will be relevant to your study. But it is worth going through the list to see if all the things that should be done prior to beginning your project have been completed. Research projects frequently get behind schedule for all sorts of

TABLE 11.2   PROJECT INITIATION CHECK LIST

ITEMS TO CHECK	NOT RELEVANT	INITIATED DATE	TARGET DATE	COMPLETED DATE
Preparation of research proposal:				
Statement of problem	[ ]	_____	_____	_____
Literature review complete	[ ]	_____	_____	_____
Methodology statement	[ ]	_____	_____	_____
Written formal hypotheses	[ ]	_____	_____	_____
Diagrammed formal hypotheses	[ ]	_____	_____	_____
Ethics review committee submission	[ ]	_____	_____	_____
Funding application	[ ]	_____	_____	_____
Permissions				
From subjects or guardians	[ ]	_____	_____	_____
For use of copyright material	[ ]	_____	_____	_____
For entry into country/group	[ ]	_____	_____	_____
For office/lab space	[ ]	_____	_____	_____
Project staff hired	[ ]	_____	_____	_____
Subjects:				
Method of contact established	[ ]	_____	_____	_____
Instruments completed				
Letters to respondents/others	[ ]	_____	_____	_____
Questionnaires	[ ]	_____	_____	_____
Pre-testing	[ ]	_____	_____	_____
Pilot study	[ ]	_____	_____	_____
Recording forms	[ ]	_____	_____	_____
Other (list)	[ ]	_____	_____	_____
Equipment				
Tape recorders	[ ]	_____	_____	_____
Computers & programs	[ ]	_____	_____	_____
Other (list)	[ ]	_____	_____	_____
Sampling procedures determined	[ ]	_____	_____	_____
Scheduling, provision for:				
Training of staff	[ ]	_____	_____	_____
Holidays, bad weather days	[ ]	_____	_____	_____
Data collection period	[ ]	_____	_____	_____
Time to get last few cases	[ ]	_____	_____	_____
Data entry time	[ ]	_____	_____	_____
Data analysis time	[ ]	_____	_____	_____
Report-writing time	[ ]	_____	_____	_____

unanticipated reasons. The check list may help anticipate some of the problems.

The first section deals with the development of a research proposal. Researchers preparing theses will have been told by their supervisor that it is possible to develop a draft of the first three chapters of a thesis before any data are collected. These chapters would include:

- a problem statement,
- a literature review, and
- a methodology section.

RULE 11.2

COMPLETE A RESEARCH PROPOSAL.

The proposal should include: a problem statement, a literature review, and a methodology section. These sections should be completed (at least in draft form) before data collection begins.

An exception to this rule would be made for researchers embarking on field studies where the project will only take shape in the field. Nonetheless, the proposals for such projects can develop the rationale behind the study, and discuss the relevance of the location chosen for the study.

In using Table 11.2, the researcher is encouraged to make realistic estimates of the amount of time it will take to complete various elements. Experienced researchers know that unanticipated delays will often occur, and plan for them by adding in some extra time. The more people involved in the project (either subjects, respondents, or informants), the greater the number of delays that may be anticipated. But even projects which involve few others (such as a content analysis of children's books) may be delayed because getting some of the material on inter-library loan may take longer than anticipated. Try to avoid delays, but it is good advice to assume that they will occur.

So how do you know when you are ready to start the data collection phase of your research? A rule to follow would be:

RULE 11.3

You are ready to commence data collection when all the relevant items noted in Table 11.2 have been realistically planned, and when all the necessary written materials, permissions, instruments, and equipment are in place.

E. KEY TERMS

Antecedent variable model	Intervening variable	Source of spuriousness model
Candidate variable model	Multi-variate models	Variables
Causal model	Path model	

F. KEY POINTS

There are researchable problems galore. Some cues to help select one: consider doing something that is currently the subject of public debate; or identify some dependent variable and attempt to understand what factors influence it; or test some aspect of folk wisdom; or perhaps tackle some applied issue (how to reduce shoplifting at the local mall); or one might wish to replicate a piece of research that someone else has done elsewhere.

Selecting an appropriate design requires some knowledge of what the possibilities are; an awareness of how other researchers have tackled similar problems; and a host of practical issues related to what kind of design is feasible.

Reviewing the literature is important to help identify where there are gaps in our knowledge and to find out how other researchers designed their studies, and noting what their findings were.

Many studies can benefit if the *proposed relationships among variables are diagrammed*, indicating: (i) causal direction (which variable is influencing which); and (ii) noting whether the relations are positive or negative. That is, are we saying "the greater A, the greater B" or "the less A, the greater B."

An *intervening variable model* suggests possible variables that link an independent and a dependent variable.

A *source of spuriousness model* identifies variables that may be creating a non-causal relation between a dependent and independent variable.

Candidate variable models simply list a number of independent variables that may be influencing a dependent variable. Normally when such models are tested, a number of variables essentially compete with one another to see which ones best account for variations in the dependent variable.

Path models typically propose an interconnected set of variables, with interaction effects, in an attempt to understand a system of variables.

G. EXERCISES

1. From a current issue, identify some relationship, or set of relationships, that are relevant to the issue, and draw a diagram(s) indicating the proposed relationships that are to be tested.

2. Choose some dependent variable that is of interest to you, and draw a diagram showing what variables may be influencing variations in the dependent variable.

3. Drawing on propositions of a social theory, derive a testable hypothesis, and draw a diagram of the proposed relationship. You may combine axiomatic and replacement of terms approaches in your derivations. Try for a counter-intuitive prediction.

4. Propose and diagram a series of at least three alternative explanations for a proposed relationship.

5. Choose some "applied" problem and diagram relationships that you would explore to solve the applied problem.

6. Diagram the relationship(s) that would be explored if you were to replicate an existing study, and indicate and diagram one additional relationship you would explore in the replication.

7. Complete the relevant sections of Table 11.2 for a project which you wish to conduct.

H. RECOMMENDED READINGS

BART, P., AND L. FRANKEL. (1986). *The Student Sociologist's Handbook*, Fourth Edition. New York: Random House. This handbook provides a detailed review of the methods for doing library research, identifying a variety of journals and indexes.

MARTIN, DAVID W. (1991). *Doing Psychology Experiments*. Pacific Grove: Brooks/Cole Publishing Company, Third Edition. Martin includes a useful chapter on knowing when you are ready to commence an experiment.

MEASUREMENT

A. THEORETICAL, CONCEPTUAL, AND OPERATIONAL LEVELS

Measurement takes many forms: from unobtrusively observing students and recording which of them remove their dirty plates from dining hall tables, to getting information on suicides from public statistics, to observing levels of aggression in people who are frustrated as part of an experiment, to classifying television ads according to whether they use sex to sell soap, to having individuals complete questionnaires or undergo personal interviews. Most methods of data collection involve an attempt to measure variables.

We measure things because we wish to describe objects accurately. We wish, for example, to know how popular the Prime Minister is now as opposed to six months ago, or to describe the Prime Minister's popularity in various parts of the country, or to see if the Prime Minister's popularity varies with the gender of the person doing the rating, or to understand what factors explain gender differences in the ratings the Prime Minister receives. If we pose such questions, we will need to measure the appropriate variables and analyze them. We could guess about the answer, but we would not have much confidence in our answer unless the question is tackled seriously and systematically.

As Carmines and Zeller (1979, p. 10) indicate, **measurement** is the "process of linking abstract concepts to empirical indicants." Typically, researchers work from the general to the specific: for each general concept, an indicator is identified. To look for a way of reflecting the idea of social

prestige is to ask a measurement question. How might we best measure, or indicate, a person's social prestige? We refer to concepts we intend to measure as *variables*.

Figure 12.1 presents the levels of a research project. To move down the figure is to move from the general to the specific—from the *theoretical level* to the *operational level*. At the theoretical level there are a number of interconnected propositions, assumptions, and statements of relationship between concepts. By employing axiomatic derivations and replacement of terms (see Chapter 2), it is possible to derive *conceptual hypotheses*. Such hypotheses may also be identified by reviewing the research literature, or by an insightful analysis of the problem. A **conceptual hypothesis** is a statement of the relationship between two or more conceptual variables. An example would be: "the greater the integration into campus life, the less the unemployment experienced after graduation." Having stated the conceptual hypothesis, the researcher would proceed to the operational level, deciding how each of the concepts would be measured, and what procedures would be used to collect and analyze the information.

In some approaches the process is reversed and, after doing some observations, the researcher may ask, "well, what concept does this reflect?" In this case, the researcher begins with observations and then tries to link them to more general ideas. This is the approach recommended by the grounded theory (Glaser & Strauss, 1967). This approach involves a process of discovery in which the researcher begins with observations and tries to make sense of them, to identify the concepts the data seem to reflect. As observations are made, the concepts are continuously identified

FIGURE 12.1   LEVELS IN RESEARCH DESIGN

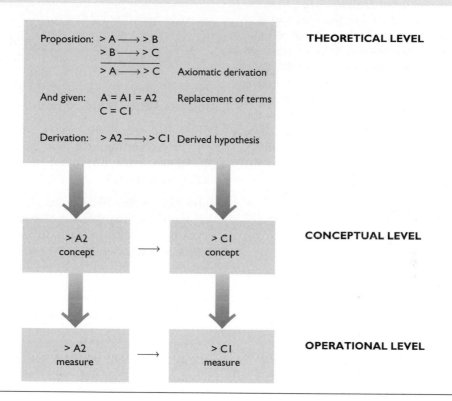

Proposition:	$> A \longrightarrow > B$		THEORETICAL LEVEL
	$> B \longrightarrow > C$		
	$> A \longrightarrow > C$	Axiomatic derivation	
And given:	$A = A1 = A2$	Replacement of terms	
	$C = C1$		
Derivation:	$> A2 \longrightarrow > C1$	Derived hypothesis	

> A2 concept $\longrightarrow$ > C1 concept   **CONCEPTUAL LEVEL**

> A2 measure $\longrightarrow$ > C1 measure   **OPERATIONAL LEVEL**

and refined. Concepts become the basic units of analysis:

> *In grounded theory, representativeness of concepts, not of persons, is crucial. The aim is ultimately to build a theoretical explanation by specifying phenomena in terms of conditions that give rise to them, how they are expressed through action/interaction, the consequences that result from them, and variations of these qualifiers...For instance, one might want to know how representative 'comfort work' is of the total amount of work that nurses do...Do nurses engage in it all of the time or some of the time? What are the conditions that enable them to do it or prevent their doing it? (Corbin & Strauss, 1990, p. 9).*

Measurement refers to the process by which categories or numbers are used to reflect, or indicate, concepts. A ***concept*** is a general idea referring to a characteristic of an individual, a group, or a nation. Concepts help us to organize our thinking about the world. Social scientists use such concepts as socio-economic status, alienation, job satisfaction, conformity, organizational effectiveness, age, gender, poverty, and political efficacy. There are hundreds of such concepts. It is important that the researcher define precisely what is meant by each concept used. Precision helps to make clear what is included in the idea and also provides a guide as to how it should be measured. The **operational level** of research refers to the indicators used to reflect the concepts as well as to the procedures used to collect and analyze data. *Measurement*, in essence, refers to the linkage between the conceptual and the operational levels. There are two key issues in this linkage: validity and reliability.

1. VALIDITY

In Chapter 1 **validity** was defined as the extent to which a measure reflects a concept, reflecting neither more nor less than what is implied by the conceptual definition. Validity has to do, then, with the congruence of concept and indicator.

A. THE IDEA OF VALIDITY IN QUANTITATIVE RESEARCH

To illustrate, let us examine one possible conceptual definition of socio-economic status. If SES is defined as a "hierarchical continuum of respect and prestige," and we then choose to operationalize the concept by measuring the annual salary of each individual we study, we will most certainly have problems convincing others of the validity of our measure.

On inspection, it becomes clear that annual salary would not adequately reflect an individual's place on a continuum of respect and prestige. Such inspections are generally referred to as *face validity*. The following are reasons why you might doubt the validity of the proposed measures:

- you think of the local drug dealer who is making a fortune but enjoys little respect in the community;

- the best poker player in town always seems to have lots of money, takes expensive trips, and many people admire his worldliness even though his salary at the legion hall is little above the minimum wage;

- the Protestant minister is looked up to by almost everyone even though his salary is a pittance;

- and there is Mrs. Bell Corden, the widow of good Dr. Corden who served the community with dedication for many years, and who left his wife a substantial estate. Although she has no salary, she, along with the owner of the hardware store, probably has more prestige than anyone else in the community.

The problem here is that salary does not always capture the concept of social prestige adequately, and even if you could get a measure of annual income rather than salary, you would still not have a valid measure of the concept as defined. (Think of your own home community: can you think of cases where annual income might not reflect prestige?)

When measuring SES, most social researchers in Canada rely on occupational rating scales which have been based on either:

- the average levels of income and education for people in any given occupation in Canada (see Blishen, 1976; Blishen and McRoberts, 1976); or

- the subjective assessment of the prestige of different occupations in Canada (see

Pineo and Porter, 1967; this index is included in Appendix H.)

Both of the above approaches lead to quite similar rankings of the different occupations in Canada. A major advantage of using such indexes is that it is quite easy to find out a person's occupation and then simply use the score supplied in one of the above indexes to reflect the SES of the individual.

However, one of the problems of using prestige indexes is that such indexes may not reflect the complexity of the organization of the modern household. For example, such indexes traditionally did not produce a prestige score for "housewife" (researchers would assign a missing value code, or separate special code, to housewives), and researchers simply tended to use the father's occupational prestige as a measure of the family's socio-economic level. Given the participation of women in the labour force, this is no longer a satisfactory solution for gauging household socio-economic status. To avoid the inherent sexism of using the father's occupational prestige rating as a measure of a household's socio-economic status, in recent years my students have been basing ratings of a household's socio-economic status on the *higher* of the two occupational prestige scores in those households where parents are living together and both are employed outside the household. When only one of the parents is employed outside the household, the occupational prestige of that person is used. Simply adding the prestige scores together would result in a prestige score that would not be in line with public perceptions. (For example, the combined prestige scores of parents who are both teachers would be about one and a half times that of a single-earner physician household.) It would be possible to add the values together but weight the lower of the two at a reduced level, perhaps using only one-quarter of its value. These calculations are easily done in SPSS, but they are a little tricky (because of the housewife problem). An example will be shown in Appendix A.

To perform this analysis using SPSS see the Index Construction section of Appendix A.

Clearly, however, a definition of socio-economic status that stresses the relative respect and prestige of members of a community begs for a measure that would get at the extent to which different individuals in the community are looked up to. In a community study, perhaps a panel of local informants could estimate the relative prestige of known members of the community.

When choosing indicators one should, ideally, not select causes, consequences, or correlates of the variable but, instead, get a direct measure of the phenomenon itself. As annual income may be one of several important causes of variation in prestige, one must not simply measure prestige by income. To do so would be to choose a correlate as one's only measure. Similarly, to measure the prestige of Mrs. Bell Corden by the success of her children would be to look at a consequence of her position, and may not adequately reflect her prestige itself. Again the resulting measure may be correlated with her prestige, but not reflect it adequately. It is not always feasible, however, to get a direct measure of the concept being studied, and one may therefore be forced to use indicators that are causes or consequences of it. David Heise and George Bohrnstedt note that:

> ...*validity is defined as the correlation between a measure and the true underlying variable. A high validity coefficient does not imply that one has measured that which he set out to measure. It means only that whatever the items are measuring, the composite constructed is highly correlated to it" (Heise and Bohrnstedt, 1970, p. 123; see also Bohrnstedt, 1969).*

Researchers must ensure that measures developed to reflect an independent variable are indeed independent of those used to reflect the dependent variable. If care is not taken a researcher may end up with two different measures of the same phenomenon and may inappropriately conclude that there is a strong causal relationship between the two variables; instead there may only be a correlation between two measures of the same underlying phenomenon.

For example, suppose we measured the length of all the classrooms of a college building in inches; suppose we then measured the classrooms again, this time in centimetres. We would then have two measures, highly correlated, and which reflect the same underlying reality. But we would err if we concluded that the length in inches *causes* length in centimetres. These measures lack independence—they both reflect the same underlying variable (the lengths of the rooms). The example is a simple one and few researchers would be in danger of concluding that variation in inches influences length in centimetres.

But in social science research things are not always so easy. Suppose that you were measuring factors that influence job satisfaction and that you included the following among the measures of job satisfaction:

INDEPENDENT VARIABLES (CAUSES OF VARIATION IN JOB SATISFACTION)	DEPENDENT VARIABLE (JOB SATISFACTION)
Employee benefits such as retirement benefits	Income
	Satisfaction with income
Hours of work	Satisfaction with being paid the right amount given the contributions you make to the company
Rate of Pay	
	Satisfaction, compared to how much others are paid

Clearly there is some overlap between measures of the independent and dependent variables: note that "income" is one of the measures used for dependent variables and that "rate of pay" is one of the measures used for independent variables. You would need to review these indicators to ensure that they are measuring different variables and not simply reflecting the same underlying reality. If you are not careful you may inadvertently inflate the relationship and come to an inappropriate conclusion. Thus, we can formulate the following rule:

RULE 12.1

MAKE CERTAIN THAT THE INDICATORS OR YOUR INDEPENDENT AND DEPENDENT VARIABLES DO NOT OVERLAP.

This means that the researcher must be careful to ensure that the strength of the association between the independent and dependent variable is not inflated by failing to use measures that reflect different concepts.

Another issue, not typically discussed in methods texts, is the problem of inflating the apparent validity of a measure by choosing a conceptual definition after considering what the most convenient measure would be. What does this mean? In the discussion so far, we have assumed that the researcher is working down from the theoretical to the conceptual and, finally, to the operational level of research. In fact, much research does not follow such a simple path. Before researchers offer conceptual definitions of variables, they often will have given thought to how they will measure the variable. One way to increase the apparent validity of a measure is to select a conceptual definition that is most congruent with the proposed measure. To go back to the earlier example of measuring socio-economic status: SES was defined as a "hierarchical continuum of respect and prestige." If the design of the study was to be a door-to-door questionnaire in a community, then the researcher might well reconsider the conceptual definition of SES, since it would be difficult to measure it easily in this way using a questionnaire. It is easier to ask about educational level, occupation, or even income. Knowing this, the researcher might decide that a definition of SES along the lines of "differential

access to scarce resources" would be more appropriate: now the researcher can achieve greater face validity by using some combination of education, occupation, or income to reflect SES. Ultimately, in quantitative research, analysis proceeds by examining relationships between indicators. And one must be careful when evaluating such research because, even though two studies may examine socio-economic status, the measures used to determine socio-economic status may differ enormously. Is this a shell game? To the extent that conceptual definitions are selected to enhance validity, one could argue that something of a slight-of-hand is going on. Thus, even with clearly defined concepts and an indication of the measures used, the research consumer must always be alert to tautologies lurking beneath the surface of a research report.

While techniques for assessing the validity of measures are beyond the scope of this book, the beginning social researcher should, at minimum, be convinced that selected measures have *face validity*. A measure has ***face validity*** if, on inspection, it appears to reflect the concept that you wish to measure. Researchers use the term ***criterion validity*** to refer to the extent to which a measure is able to predict accurately. Thus if you were attempting to develop a measure to predict success in university studies, you could assess the validity of your measure by correlating it with grades achieved in university. A high correlation would indicate high criterion validity. Moreover, *if a theoretically derived hypothesis turns out as predicted, this would constitute one piece of evidence for the validity of the measures.* This latter type of validity is known as ***construct validity.*** Another way to think about construct validity is to recognize that it is based on inductive evidence. If one finds evidence to support a theoretically derived hypothesis, then this would indicate that one's measures have construct validity. Finally, **content validity** refers to the extent to which a measure reflects the dimension(s) implied by the concept.

Experimentalists in particular distinguish between internal and external validity. **Internal validity** may be taken to mean that the researcher has demonstrated that the treatment in fact produced the changes in the dependent variable. **External validity** has to do with the extent to which results may be extrapolated from the particular study to other groups in general.

B. THE IDEA OF VALIDITY IN QUALITATIVE RESEARCH

In qualitative research the issue of external validity perhaps needs to be thought about in a slightly different way. Given the small number of cases typically studied in qualitative projects, the issue of validity is perhaps better thought about in terms of **credibility**. As Margarete Sandelowski has argued, citing Guba and Lincoln (1981) and George Psathas (1973):

> *A qualitative study is credible when it presents such faithful descriptions or interpretations of a human experience that the people having that experience would immediately recognize it from those descriptions or interpretations as their own. A study is also credible when other people (other researchers or readers) can recognize the experience when confronted with it after having only·read about it in a study" (Sandelowski, 1986, p. 30).*

In qualitative studies, the degree to which a description "rings true" to the subjects of the study, to other readers, or to other researchers is an indication of whether you have, in fact, measured what you wished to measure. Furthermore, it has been argued that the closeness of the researcher and the subject being studied should be encouraged rather than discouraged; only through such closeness can the researcher truly penetrate and understand the experiences of the subject (Sandelowski, 1986, pp. 30-31).

In terms of external validity, the very act of controlling so many extraneous factors (as in an experiment) actually serves to reduce the generalizability of such studies; in qualitative studies such artificiality is reduced given that studies are done in natural settings even though the limited sample sizes mitigate against extrapolations to other populations.

In distinguishing qualitative from quantitative research traditions, Margarete Sandelowski notes:

> *the artistic approach to qualitative inquiry emphasizes the irreplicability of the research process and product. Every human experience is viewed as unique, and truth is viewed as relative. The artistic integrity, rather than the scientific objectivity, of the research is achieved when the researcher communicates the richness and diversity of human experience in an engaging and even poetic manner...qualitative methods such as historical inquiry may employ the methods of science but the presentation or reporting style of art" (Sandelowski, 1986, p. 29).*

In order to maximize rigor in qualitative research, Sandelowski makes several suggestions. Note, also, that these suggestions are relevant to the quantitative researcher:

i Keep Careful Records

The researcher should keep a detailed record of all decisions that have been made, and how they were made. If details are recorded, years later another researcher may be able to repeat the study. Thus details on how the subject matter was selected, how data were collected, what evidence was deemed unimportant, and the ways in which categories were developed should all be noted. (See Sandelowski, 1986.)

ii Avoid Holistic Fallacy

This fallacy would make the results of the study look more patterned than they actually are; the researcher should attempt to establish how typical the observations of the study are. Be careful not to report only those events and behaviours that are patterned and consistent; report the exceptions as well (Sandelowski, 1986).

iii Guard Against an Elite Bias

Elite bias is a danger because informants are more likely to be drawn from the more articulate, high-status elements in a society. Hence, unless care is taken, there is a tendency to represent the views of the elite in one's research (Sandelowski, 1986, p. 32).

iv Be Wary of Being taken Over by the Respondent

If the researcher identifies completely with the views of a respondent, it may be difficult to maintain a clear distinction between the researcher's experiences and those of the subject. This may be a problem unless the researcher attempts to record how the respondent and the researcher have mutually influenced one another. If this is done, the report will recognize the reciprocal influence of the respondent on the researcher (Sandelowski, 1986).

The issue of generalizability (external validity) poses difficulties in many research designs, but it presents special challenges in ethnographic studies. Conventional sampling procedures are usually not relevant to ethnographic studies, as such studies depend so extensively on case studies. However, it may be possible to argue that the circumstances studied in a particular ethnographic case study are comparable to other situations and that the conclusions of the study may therefore be applied to them. One solution is to carry out research on numerous sites. But as LeCompte points out (1982, pp. 50-53) there are four factors that may influence the credibility of such cross-group comparisons:

v Selection Effects

The researcher may select sites in which some factors may not be present. A study based on such a site may, therefore, not allow testing of certain ideas.

vi Setting Effects

Studying a social situation may itself influence the results derived. The impact of the researcher's intrusion may vary from setting to setting, distorting the results more in some settings than in others. Hence it is difficult to compare the degree to which the researcher influenced the results of different studies conducted at different sites.

vii History Effects

Each group studied is subject to unique historical influences. When sites are studied at different times, some of the variations between the sites may be explained by history rather than the interaction of factors within the site.

viii Construct Effects

Concepts may be regarded differently by both observers in different settings and those being observed.

2. RELIABILITY

Reliability was defined in Chapter 1 as the extent to which, on repeated measures, an indicator yields similar readings. Reliability issues emerge in both "single-indicator" questions, and in those where a number of indicators are used to reflect a variable.

A. THE IDEA OF RELIABILITY IN QUANTITATIVE RESEARCH

There are both simple and complex ways of assessing reliability. Perhaps the easiest of all is to repeat a question that has been posed. The idea of a *retest procedure* is that if the same question is posed twice, and the respondent understands the question identically on both occasions, the response should be identical on both occasions. A second simple approach, though often not feasible, is to verify the answers independently. Occasionally, for example, it may be possible to compare a student's self-reported grade to that "actually" received by the student. Here the issue is the extent to which students systematically over- or under-report grades.

When you are assessing the reliability of the items being used to construct an index (an index represents the combination of several items into a single score), you can randomly split the items into two groups, compute the indexes, and then correlate the resulting scores. Internal reliability would be indicated by a high correlation. This method is known as a ***split-half method*** for testing reliability. Another procedure is to compare an individual item's correlation to the total index score: if an item is consistent with the total score, it will correlate with it. This technique, known as the ***internal consistency approach*** to reliability, will be described when index construction is discussed.

> *To perform this analysis using SPSS see the RELIABILITY procedure in Appendix A.*

No matter what indicators are used, the researcher is always trying to reflect both a concept(s) and the reality that is being described precisely.

B. THE IDEA OF RELIABILITY IN QUALITATIVE RESEARCH

When a particular group is studied, there are problems with replication because the circumstances and the individuals can never be the same at some later time.

> *...what observers see and report is a function of the position they occupy within participant groups, the status accorded them, and the role behaviour expected of them. Direct observer effects may occur when informants become dependent on the ethnographer for status enhancement... (LeCompte and Goetz, 1982, p. 46).*

Social settings where questions are asked can also be important. So unless the ethnographer fully reports how and where the observations were made, there is little chance of replicating a study.

To increase the chances of replicating a study, LeCompte (1982) has suggested the use of five strategies:

(i) focus on verbatim reports—sticking to the facts;

(ii) use multiple researchers, as this allows the results of the researchers to be compared;

(iii) use participant researchers: this involves training individuals in observational techniques;

(iv) use peer examination: when careful descriptions have been made, researchers can check their results against the observations and experiences of fellow researchers;

(v) use mechanical recording devices such as tapes and videos to allow others to check your observations independently at a later date.

Avoiding incorrect conclusions, such as identifying a causal variable incorrectly, is a challenge for the ethnographic researcher. There are three issues that must be handled:

(i) The qualitative researcher must establish that the causal variable precedes the effect; since qualitative researchers make observations over time, establishing the causal ordering of variables is usually not problematical. The researcher is present on the research site over time and is able to observe actions and reactions.

(ii) The researcher must establish that the variables are related to one another (vary together); the researcher depends, to some degree, on the occurrence of social events which permit him to see whether the variables are varying together. In contrast, the experimentalist creates a situation which systematically varies the intensity of the treatment and observes the reaction to the treatment.

(iii) The researcher must eliminate rival hypotheses. All researchers who attempt to eliminate rival hypotheses face a challenge, since new hypotheses can always be suggested. The qualitative researcher has to test alternative hypotheses continually as observations are being made. Since observations are made over time, there are opportunities to explore such hypotheses as the study unfolds.

B. MEASUREMENT ERROR

Typically we begin with the assumption that the manifestations of the object we wish to measure have:

(i) two or more values inherent in them (i.e. we are dealing with a variable, not a constant); and

(ii) that any manifestation has a *true value*.

A ***true value*** is the underlying exact quantity of the variable at any given time. In measurement, we attempt to reflect this true value as precisely as we can. By specifying "at any given time," we acknowledge that variables change over time, and that any measure will vary from day to day. Just like our weight, such measures vary slightly from one day to the next. And while some variables, like our gender or religious affiliation remain quite stable, it is possible nevertheless that a change may occur. Sex-change operations and religious conversions are not unknown.

Measurement error will always occur because our instruments are imperfect, because our subjects do not always pay sufficient attention to our instructions, or because we are not careful enough in coding data. **Measurement error** is any deviation from the true value.

Measures are made up from the following components:

$$MEASURE = TV \pm (RE \pm SE)$$

The above equation contains four elements:

- *Measure* This refers to the value that the researcher assigns to the variable in the process of recording the information.
- *TV* The *True Value* is the underlying exact quantity of the variable.
- *RE Random Error* is fluctuation around the "true" value, where higher or lower scores are equally likely.
- *SE Systematic Error* is non-random error representing systematic under- or overestimation of the value (Carmines & Zeller, 1979).

An Example: Suppose a male respondent is asked to indicate his weight on a questionnaire. The respondent writes in "70 kilograms." Providing the information is correctly transcribed when entering the data into the computer, the MEASURE is recorded as 70.0 kilograms. Suppose, however, that the TV, or true value, is 73.367132 kilograms (rounded!). If the person usually under-reports his weight by two kilograms, two kilograms at the discrepancy between actual and reported weight will be due *SE*, or systematic error. The remaining 1.367132 kilograms at the discrepancy is due to random error (*RE*).

$$MEASURE = TV \pm (RE \pm SE)$$
or
$$70.0 = 73.367132 - (2.0 + 1.367132)$$

The adequacy of a measure is the extent to which the indicator reflects the true value of the variable. All of the above components vary over time and through the various stages of data collection in a research project. Usually we think that measurement errors are made by the subject. But actually the situation is more complex. First, the *true value* of variables changes over time. If we repeat a measure several times to make certain that we have an accurate reflection of the variable, differences will be due to variations in the true value, random error, and systematic error. (Respondents may change their attitudes over time, hence the true value itself may shift; theoretically, it is fixed only at the time measured.)

1. TIPS FOR REDUCING RANDOM AND SYSTEMATIC ERROR

Researchers can do several things to reduce random and systematic error. Random error refers to those fluctuations that are unsystematic: the respondent who cannot decide whether to rate the quality of lectures in the methods course as a 6 or a 7 on a 9-point scale, and finally decides on a 6, may have made a random choice. Systematic error is error in one direction. For example, if you tell respondents what you expect to find, they may bias their responses to confirm the expectation. Where feasible, consider using some of the following ways of reducing error:

TIP 12.1

TAKE THE AVERAGE OF SEVERAL MEASURES.

Sometimes it is possible to repeat a measure several times and then use the average of these measures to reflect the variable. A subject could be weighed on three different scales and the average used. In this way, the researcher hopes to average out random measurement error.

TIP 12.2

USE SEVERAL DIFFERENT INDICATORS.

In measuring a variable such as attitudes toward abortion, the researcher typically would pose several questions and then combine the responses to form an index. By combining the responses to several questions the researcher hopes to minimize the effect of any one question.

TIP 12.3

USE RANDOM SAMPLING PROCEDURES.

By giving all people an equal chance of being included in your study, it is possible to minimize distortions that occur when people select themselves. If the goal, for example, was to estimate the popularity of the leader of a coun-try, one would want to reflect the views of the whole country, not special groups within it. By reporting on what the average person thinks about the leader you will minimize the random fluctuations that might occur if you talked to very few, unsystematically selected respondents. By not oversampling those who spend more time at home, you will have avoided systematically biasing the study by overrepresenting the views of people with that characteristic.

TIP 12.4

USE SENSITIVE MEASURES.

In asking questions, provide respondents with as broad a range of response categories as possible so as not to constrain them. In questions used to create indexes, provide many response categories; in asking respondents to estimate the population of their community, provide many categories. By providing many response alternatives (or indeed allowing the respondent simply to respond without using any categories at all) the researcher can decrease the amount of random error in measurement. However, you can go overboard in suggesting increased numbers of response categories: if there are too many response categories, a respondent's ability to make distinctions may be exceeded. To ask someone to report their weight to two-decimal point accuracy would be silly: few people know their weight with such accuracy.

TIP 12.5

AVOID CONFUSION IN WORDING QUESTIONS OR INSTRUCTIONS.

Respondents' varied misunderstandings of what is being asked of them is one source of random error. Thus variation in response may simply be the result of these different understandings. Attempt to develop instructions and questions that are clear and have but one interpretation.

ERROR CHECKING DATA.

Both systematic and random errors can occur easily. These should be eliminated by conducting error checks on the data. If data are being coded (the process of assigning categories to responses) by several people, interrating reliability checks should be carried out in training the individuals to do the work. Only

when high levels of inter-rater reliability are achieved should the coding proceed (see Chapter 6). The use of video-recording equipment has permitted those doing observational studies to confirm their data by having other experts examine the work.

REDUCE SUBJECT AND EXPERIMENTER EXPECTATIONS.

As discussed in Chapter 9, subject and experimenter expectations can systematically alter the measures achieved in a research project. Attempt to control these expectations as much as possible.

TABLE 12.1   SOURCES OF MEASUREMENT ERROR BY STAGES OF RESEARCH, BY RESEARCH DESIGN

	SOURCES OF MEASUREMENT VARIATION	
TYPE OF RESEARCH DESIGN	RANDOM ERROR	SYSTEMATIC ERROR
Experimental designs:		
Subject responses	X	X
Recording responses	X	X
Coding of responses	X	X
Data entry	X	X
Data presentation	X	X
Survey designs:		
Question design	X	X
Respondent's responses	X	X
Coding of responses	X	X
Data entry	X	X
Data presentation	X	X
Field study designs (participant observation):		
Subject responses	X	X
Recording behaviour	X	X
Coding behaviour	X	X
Data presentation	X	X
Non-reactive designs (content analysis):		
Coding the information	X	X
Data entry	X	X
Data presentation	X	X

Table 12.1 presents the possible sources of variation in measures in experiments, surveys, and field studies. In the interests of simplicity, variation in the true value (TV) as a source of variation in measurements, is not included in Table 12.1. Do recall, however, that it may vary over time. As various stages of research projects are considered, note that there are possibilities of both random and systematic measurement error.

Precise measurement is indeed a challenge. Anytime a measurement is taken, there will be error. The error may be slight or substantial. Measurement should be seen as a matter of probability: most of the time your measurements will fall within a given margin of error. This implies that, some of the time, your measurements will not fall within a given (and acceptable) margin of error. Researchers attempt to estimate the amount of error that is likely in their measurements. The specific procedures for doing this were explained in Chapter 8.

Figure 12.2 presents a target shooting analogy to help show the relation between reliability, true value, and validity. In measurement, we attempt to consistently (reliability) hit the bull's eye (the true value) and if we do so, we have measured what we intended to (validity).

An inspection of Figure 12.2 illustrates that a measure may be reliable but lack validity; however, a measure that is valid is also reliable, since measures that hit the bull's eye are closely grouped and, therefore, must be reliable. The three diagrams illustrate the point.

- Diagram 1 depicts measurements that are neither reliable nor valid; the measurements have missed the true value (bull's eye) and produced a lot of scatter.

- Diagram 2 displays a reliable measure, but one which lacks validity. Note that the shots are closely grouped together (hence reliable), but that they are not right on the bull's eye which represents the true value.

- Diagram 3 displays a valid and reliable measure where the shots are nicely grouped on the bull's eye.

FIGURE 12.2   BULL'S EYE: TRUE VALUE, RELIABILITY, AND VALIDITY

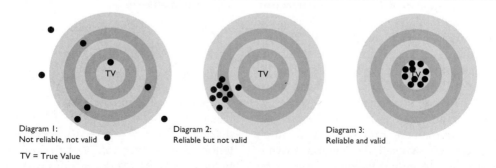

Diagram 1:
Not reliable, not valid

Diagram 2:
Reliable but not valid

Diagram 3:
Reliable and valid

TV = True Value

SOURCE: Modelled after Babbie (1992: 134). The idea of true value is added to Babbie's original drawing; a different interpretation is put on Diagram 1.

C. LEVELS OF MEASUREMENT

Three levels of measurement were presented in Chapter 7. We will briefly review that discussion to refresh the reader's mind on this important topic. An understanding of levels of measurement is necessary since the ways in which one should go about analysing a variable are constrained by the measurement level achieved in data collection. As a general rule, one should attempt to achieve the most precise measurement possible.

One way to begin to understand levels of measurement is to ask if the variable being measured has an underlying continuum (does it vary from low to high?). If there is no underlying continuum, with the variable being made up of a number of discrete categories, then the measurement will be at the nominal level; if the variable has an underlying continuum, then the level of measurement will be either ordinal, or ratio. This text will distinguish three levels of measurement: nominal, ordinal, and ratio.

1. NOMINAL MEASUREMENT

Examples of ***nominal measurement*** (those with an arbitrary assignment of numbers to categories) would include measurements of such variables as religious affiliation, gender, program of study, political party affiliation, and ethnic origin. While there may be underlying continua related to religious affiliation (such as degree of religious commitment, or frequency of church attendance), by itself, the religious organization is a nominal category: it may be Baptist, Lutheran, Roman Catholic, or Jewish. When a respondent checks off which (if any) religious affiliations he or she was associated with while growing up, the measurement level attained is nominal. One category is neither higher or lower than any other—the categories are simply different. Nominal measurement involves no underlying continuum and the numerical values assigned are arbitrary and have no arithmetic meaning. Such values cannot be added, subtracted, multiplied, or divided.

2. ORDINAL MEASUREMENT

Ordinal measurement involves an underlying continuum with the numerical values ordered so that small numbers refer to lower levels on the continuum, larger numbers to higher points; however, the distances between the assigned numbers and the underlying continuum are not in a one-to-one relation with each other. Note the following questionnaire item asking about the size of a respondent's current home community:

The place where I live now has a population of:

Under 5,000 - - - - - - - - - - - 1( )

5,000 to 19,999 - - - - - - - - - 2( )

20,000 to 99,999 - - - - - - - 3( )

100,000 to 999,999 - - - - - - - 4( )

Over 1 million - - - - - - - - 5( )

Note that the numbers assigned by the researcher (1 through 5) are arranged so that higher numbers refer to larger population centres; but note that the intervals between the numbers are not equal (the second category spans a population range of 15,000, while the fourth category spans a range of 900,000).

Another frequently used type of question would ask respondents to assess their degree of agreement with a statement like the following one:

The United Nations keeps the world safe.

Strongly Disagree 1 2 3 4 5 6 7 8 9 Strongly Agree

This kind of item provides ordinal measurement. While we know that high numbers indicate a greater degree of agreement with the statement, we do not know whether the distances between the values are equal: the distance between 4 and 5 on the scale may not be the same size as the distance between 8 and 9. Ordinal measurement orders values but does not assure equal gaps between the measurement points. Additional examples of ordinal level measurement are provided in Table 7.2 (Chapter 7).

In conclusion, ordinal measurement involves an underlying continuum; numerical values assigned are ordered but intervals are not equal. When ordinal measures are combined, the values may be added, or subtracted, but not multiplied.

3. RATIO MEASUREMENT

Finally, there is ***ratio measurement***. With this level, the intervals between the measurement points are equal and the zero point is aligned with true zero. For example, in the case of income, the nature of the variable is such that it is possible to represent income with a number that reflects the income of a person exactly. In this case, it is

also possible to use zero to reflect no income and other numerical values to reflect all other income levels. Here it is correct to say that an income of $50,000 is twice as much as an income of $25,000. With ratio-level measurement, it is possible to add and subtract constants as well as to multiply or divide by them without changing the proportionality among the values.

If a researcher were to have respondents indicate with a check mark which of the magazines on a list that they had scanned or read in the previous month, and a total was taken of the number ticked off, the result would be a variable that varies from 0 to the number required if a respondent checked off all the items listed: this number would be a ratio measurement. Note that a 0 in this example refers to no exposure to any of the magazines listed, and other values simply provide a count of the number of the listed magazines that the respondent has scanned or read in the past month. There is a one-to-one relationship between the value assigned by the researcher and the number of listed magazines identified by the respondent.

Similarly, where communities are being studied, measures such as the proportion of visible minorities, or the proportion of retired people in the population, and various rates and ratios (suicide rate, dependency ratio, sex ratio) are all ratio level measures (see Table 7.3 for additional examples).

In conclusion, ratio measurement involves an underlying continuum: the numerical values assigned are ordered with equal intervals, the zero point is aligned with true zero, and when different ratio measures are combined, the values may be added, subtracted, multiplied, or divided.

D. THE EFFECT OF REDUCED LEVELS OF MEASUREMENT

This chapter has encouraged researchers to achieve the most precise measurements that are practical. To explore the consequences of reducing the level of measurement, the author examined what would happen if a ratio level variable (student's high school average grade) was regrouped, using random numbers to establish cutpoints, into 9, 7, 5, and 3 categories. The new variables were then correlated with unchanged ratio variables (high school English grade and first-year university grade). As anticipated, the correlations declined further with each succeeding grouping into fewer categories (see Box 12.1).

BOX 12.1

The Effects of Reduced Level of Measurement

An attempt to examine the consequences of reduced levels of measurement was carried out.

The Hypotheses
The hypotheses which guided this investigation were as follows (hypotheses 2, 3, 4, and 5 are relevant for a regression analysis):

- *Hypothesis 1.* The greater the number of categories in a Likert-type variable, the less reduction there will be in the correlation between the variable and other variables.

- *Hypothesis 2.* A ratio variable that is measured using a Likert-type question will result in an analysis that explains less variation than would have been the case had a ratio level measurement been used;

- *Hypothesis 3.* The beta weights of Likert-type items will be reduced by comparison with those using raw scores;

- *Hypothesis 4.* The above effects will be greater for those variables having fewer categories.

- *Hypothesis 5.* Beta weights of variables not categorized will be enhanced by comparison with those where categorization has been done.

A data set containing 3,617 cases was used in this investigation. The variables included university students' high school average, high school English grade, and average at the end of the first year of university study. Correlations were calculated (see Table I) for the relation between these variables. The correlation between university average and the English grade high school average was .464 and .573 respectively; the high school English grade and the average high school grade correlated at .662.

A regression analysis was done taking first year university average as the dependent variable and high school English grade and the high school aver-

Table I Correlations Between First Year University Average, Average High School Grade, and English High School Grade (N = 3617)

CORRELATIONS	FIRST YEAR UNIVERSITY AVERAGE	AVERAGE HIGH SCHOOL GRADE	ENGLISH HIGH SCHOOL GRADE
First year university average	1.000		
Average high school grade	.573	1.000	
English high school grade	.464	.662	1.000

age grade (excluding the English mark) as independent variables. The results of this analysis are shown in Table II. The R^2 was .341 (34.1 per cent of the variance explained); the beta weight for the English grade was .152 while for high school average it was .472. The impact of high school average was about 3 times as great as the English grade alone.

In an attempt to test the hypotheses, a series of trials was done on the data testing the effect of regrouping the high school average variable. We wished to compare what would happen if it were collapsed into 3, 5, 7, and 9 categories; we wished also to observe the impact of such collapsing on the R^2 and the beta weights. A table of random numbers was used to determine the cut-points; a total of 40 variables was created in this way (10 for 9- category variables, 10 for 7-category variables, 10 for 5-category variables and 10 for 3-category variables). In all cases, the new variables were used as independent variables in each trial along with the English grade and in all

Table II Regression Analysis Predicting First Year Average Grade (N = 3617)

VARIABLE	B COEFFICIENT	BETA WEIGHT	PERCENT EXPLAINED
High school English grade	.16290	.15195	8.30
High school average*	.54188	.47203	25.78
		% Explained	34.08
CONSTANT	11.08264		
Multiple R	.58383		
R Square	.34085		

*The high school average was calculated excluding the high school English grade.

cases the university average was used as the dependent variable. The results of the correlational analyses are summa-rized in Table III; Table IV summarizes the results of the 40 regression analyses.

Table III Average Change in Correlations Between High School Average Grade and First Year University Grade When Data Are Grouped Into 9, 7, 5, and 3 Categories

NUMBER OF CATEGORIES	AVERAGE DECLINE IN CORRELATION	STANDARD DEVIATION	NUMBER OF RECODINGS
9	−0.03810	0.03151	10
7	−0.05790	0.03208	10
5	−0.11260	0.09623	10
3	−0.18240	0.16038	10

*The raw data, based on 3617 cases (St. Francis Xavier University), was used for this analysis. The high school average grade was recoded into 9, 7, 5, or 3 categories; ten recodings for each category. For each, the new variable was then correlated with the first year university average. The above table summarizes the results. For example, when the data were recoded into 3 categories, the average drop in correlation (for the 10 randomly determined cut-points) was 0.18.

Table IV Summary of Changes in R^2, and Betas when One Variable Is Grouped into 9, 7, 5, and 3 Categories, Regression Analyses

NUMBER OF CATEGORIES IN RECODED VARIABLE	MEAN CHANGE IN R^2	MEAN CHANGE IN BETA HS[*]	MEAN CHANGE IN BETA ENG[**]
9 Categories	−0.025	−0.067	0.059
7 Categories	−0.033	−0.099	0.094
5 Categories	−0.055	−0.162	0.135
3 Categories	−0.069	−0.217	0.179
Probability	0.0059	0.0039	0.0001

[*]HS refers to high school average grade; this is the variable that was recoded.

[**]ENG refers to high school English grade; this variable was left in its raw form for the analysis.

This analysis summarizes the results of 40 separate regression analyses, 10 for the recoding of each of the four categories. The total N for each analysis is 3617. Table II presents the results when the high school average is used in its raw form.

SOURCE: Winston Jackson. The author wishes to thank Dr. Bernard Liengme, Registrar, St. Francis Xavier University, for providing the data for the analysis.

The analysis suggests that, where reduced levels of measurement are achieved, the result will underestimate the strength of association between variables. Furthermore, in doing analyses which permit a comparison of the relative effects of independent variables on a dependent variable, (see Regression Analysis, Chapter 17) the effect of an independent variable that has a reduced level of measurement will be underestimated. The research suggests the following general principles:

PRINCIPLE 12.1

The greater the reduction of measurement precision, the greater the drop in the correlation between the variables.

PRINCIPLE 12.2

In analyses comparing relative effects of variables, the effects of those variables with reduced levels of measurement are underestimated by comparison with those whose measurement is more precise.

PRINCIPLE 12.3

Conversely, variables whose measurement is more precise will have their effects overestimated relative to those whose measurement is less precise.

These three principles suggest that we should attempt to reflect the underlying concepts as precisely as possible. But there are constraints. It is foolish to ask people to give us exact answers when there is little likelihood that they will be in a position to make precise estimates. For example, asking anyone on campus to estimate the weight of a school bus would invite highly variable and inaccurate answers. Furthermore,

it is sometimes inappropriate to ask for extremely precise information if such information will be considered too personal by a respondent: in some populations, asking someone his or her exact annual income would fall into that category. Sometimes, in order to soften a question, to make it less threatening, we reduce its precision. In asking about age, for example, we sometimes ask people to indicate into which age category they fall, rather than their exact age. So the rule to be followed is:

RULE 12.2

ACHIEVE AS PRECISE MEASUREMENT AS IS PRACTICAL.

Researchers recognize that weaker measurement will typically result in underestimating the importance of a poorly measured variable relative to other, more precisely measured variables.

E. INDEXES, SCALES, AND SPECIAL MEASUREMENT PROCEDURES

Readers will be familiar with some indexes in common use. For example, indexes are used to summarize stock market trends: the Toronto Stock Exchange 300-Composite Index, the Dow-Jones 30 Average, and the Nikkei Stock 225 Average each report the value of stocks from a sample of companies drawn to represent different sectors of the economy. Social researchers also use composite measures. Blishen and McRoberts (1976) occupational rating index and Pineo and Porter's (1976) occupational prestige scale are important examples of widely used Canadian indexes.

Combining several indicators into one score results in an index or scale. While these terms are often used interchangeably, where a distinction is made, an ***index*** refers to the combination of two or more indicators. A ***scale*** refers to a more complex combination of indicators where the pattern of the responses is taken into account.

Indexes are routinely constructed to reflect variables such as socio-economic status, job satisfaction, group dynamics, or an attitude toward some social issue. (For details of many indexes and scales, see Miller, 1977.) Frequently, the researcher will construct sub-indexes which may be treated alone or combined with other sub-indexes to form a composite measure. For example, a researcher measuring attitudes toward abortion might construct a sub-index for "soft reasons" (economically inconvenient, preference for having a baby later, etc.) and "hard reasons" (pregnancy as a result of rape, severely handicapped, etc.). These sub-indexes might also be combined to form an overall index. In each case, however, the researcher will have to ensure that appropriate items are included in each sub-index.

1. ITEM ANALYSIS

It is important that the components of an index discriminate. That is, various elements must discriminate between high scorers and lower scorers. To illustrate, suppose that you are attempting to develop a set of multiple-choice questions to measure students' knowledge of the material covered in an Introductory course, and that you wish to identify those items which best measure

mastery of the subject matter. Let us suppose that you have 100 questions on the test and that you wish to identify the best 50 questions for a future test. The issue is to select those items which best discriminate between high and low performance on the test. Let us suppose that we have given the preliminary test to 200 students enrolled in an Introductory course.

We could proceed by grading the test and computing the total correct responses for each student. If the "marking" was done with a computer program, we would have a matrix which has students and questions on the dimensions. Each cell would identify a correct or an incorrect response to each question for a particular student. Now we could order the students by the number of correct responses, and then choose the top and bottom quartiles. Table 12.2 shows the percent from each quartile getting each question correct.

The next step would be to select those items in which the performance of top and bottom students differs most. We assume here that, overall, the questions measure knowledge of the subject matter and that we are simply choosing those items which discriminate best.

The first two questions discriminate well—the high scorers do considerably better on those items than the low scorers. The third question would be rejected: while 55 percent of the students in the top quartile gave the right answer, so did 60 percent of the bottom group. Similarly, question 4 would be dropped because a similar proportion of top and bottom students answered correctly.

Similar procedures may be used to select high discrimination items for indexes. Suppose, for example, that we had 15 items

TABLE 12.2 DISCRIMINATION ABILITY OF 100 ITEMS: PERCENT CORRECT FOR EACH ITEM, BY QUARTILE

QUESTION#	PERCENT CORRECT BOTTOM 25%	EACH ITEM TOP 25%
1	40.0	80.0
2	5.0	95.0
3	60.0	55.0
4	80.0	80.0
5	10.0	40.0
6	20.0	60.0
...	...	...
100	30.0	20.0

for an index measuring job satisfaction, and we wished to determine which items to include in the index. We want items that do two things:

(i) validly reflect the dimension of the concept they are supposed to; and,

(ii) discriminate between high and low scorers.

What we might do is:

• include those items which have face validity;

• add them together, coming up with a total score for each individual;

• split the sample into the top and bottom quartiles in job satisfaction scores;

• test each item's ability to discriminate between high and low job satisfaction; and,

• select those items which best differentiate high scorers from low scorers.

2. SELECTING INDEX ITEMS

Indexes are constructed by combining several individual questions and represent an attempt to summarize, in one score, a measure of a variable. Indexes are constructed in situations where we have a single-dimension variable, but where one question might not adequately measure the variable. Indexes can be constructed by combining a number of similarly formatted questions, or combinations of questions with different formats. In all cases, the indicators are combined, and possibly weighted, to sum to a single index score. The steps involved in developing an index are identified below.

STEP 1

REVIEW CONCEPTUAL DEFINITION.

As in developing other measures, the first step is to review the conceptual definition of the variable. Some sense of the "range," or the dimensions, involved in the variable should be developed. The chances are that several questions can then be designed to measure the variable, reflecting each of the dimensions in the conceptual definition.

STEP 2

DEVELOP MEASURES FOR EACH DIMENSION.

Here the same principles apply as for the development of individual measures. For example, in measuring attitudes toward capital punishment, one might identify which, if any, offences would lead a respondent to favour capital punishment. Items may initially be selected on the basis of face validity. That is, if the item appears, on the face of it, to represent a part of the theoretical continuum being measured, then an effort should be made to get a measure of that item. Three capital punishment items which could be part of an index might be:

I support capital punishment for convicted child molesters.

Strongly
Disagree   1 2 3 4 5 6 7 8 9   Strongly
Agree

I support capital punishment for a murderer of a police officer.

Strongly
Disagree   1 2 3 4 5 6 7 8 9   Strongly
Agree

I support capital punishment for drug smugglers.

Strongly
Disagree   1 2 3 4 5 6 7 8 9   Strongly
Agree

STEP 3

PRE-TEST INDEX.

Index items should always be pre-tested. A pre-test is simple; all you have to do is:
• complete the index yourself;
• sit beside individuals who are within the population being studied and have several complete the index items.

Encourage these pre-test respondents to ask questions, telling them in advance that you are trying to find out if all the questions are clear. Reword questions to achieve clarity.

Pre-tests almost always lead to revisions in the wording of index items.

STEP 4

PILOT TEST INDEX.

If time permits, indexes should be pilot tested. A pilot study involves having a number of respondents complete a questionnaire containing the proposed index items. In a pilot study you take what you consider to be the final version of the index to a sample of respondents. The results are analyzed to see if the index items discriminate, and if they are internally consistent. Items may be dropped or altered on the basis of a pilot study.

If time is not available to do a pilot test, at least ensure that a full range of possible variability is represented by the index items. When the data are being analyzed, the various items can be evaluated using the SPSS procedure, RELIABILITY. This procedure provides a method of checking the internal consistency of index items. Items may be dropped if they do not prove to be internally consistent.

3. THE RATIONALE FOR USING SEVERAL ITEMS IN AN INDEX

Suppose we are interested in measuring people's attitudes toward abortion. Would it be better to use one question or several questions in our measure? The general consensus among social researchers is that measures with multiple items have an advantage over single-item measures in attaining precise measurement. John McIver and Edward G. Carmines (1981, p. 15) summarize the arguments in favour of using multiple items in measurement:

- an attitude toward abortion would almost certainly be complex, and one would want to reflect this complexity in any measurement; (would people have the same attitude toward abortion if the pregnancy threatened the life of the mother, or was the result of a rape, or was economically inconvenient?);

- a single item may lack precision, may lack a sufficient range in values; (A question like "Are you in favour of abortion?" with yes/no response categories would be inadequate. Even with more response categories it would still be weak because the question does not identify conditions when a person might favour or not favour abortion);

- single items are also less reliable and more prone to random measurement error. If a question like the one above were repeated in a questionnaire, the respondent, having indicated opposition to abortion the first time, might well change her answer the second time, because she thinks: "Well, it depends on the situation, if the female was raped, and is 14 years old, I would be in favour of her right to have an abortion;"

- with multiple items it is possible to evaluate the reliability and validity of the index; with single indicators it is more difficult to gauge the amount of measurement error.

4. THURSTONE SCALING

Psychologist Louis Thurstone developed a method for constructing equal-appearing interval scales (1929). He argued that people can make comparative judgements about psychological phenomena: when pre-

sented with two statements, a person can typically indicate which of the statements he or she agrees with most.

A. STEPS IN CONSTRUCTING AN EQUAL-APPEARING THURSTONE SCALE

An equal-appearing **Thurstone scale** is constructed by having a number of potential items evaluated by a panel of judges; the best items are then selected for inclusion in the scale. The following processes are involved in the construction of such a scale.

STEP 1
SELECT INITIAL ITEMS.

Initially one proposes a number of items for possible inclusion in the final scale. The principles behind these items have been summarized by Edwards (1957) and cited in McIver and Carmines (1981, p. 19). They include the following guidelines:
- statements should refer to the present, not the past;
- avoid statements that ask matters of fact;
- questions should only be interpreted by respondents in one way;
- avoid statements with which almost everyone, or no one, would agree;
- range items across the attitude continuum;
- make the meaning of the item clear and simple;
- include only one idea in one item. Watch out for an item containing the word "and;"
- avoid the ambiguity caused by such universals as always, none, and never;
- avoid words that may sound judgemental such as "only," "merely," "just;"
- keep sentences simple.

STEP 2

GET JUDGES TO RESPOND TO THE ITEMS.

The degree of favourableness/unfavourableness of each item is rated by each judge (usually 100 judges); the items are sorted into 11 piles, pile 1 for the most favourable, through to pile 11 for the most unfavourable.

STEP 3

COMPUTE SUMMARY MEASURES FOR EACH ITEM.

For each item, the middle rating is identified (the *median* in statistical terms); lower median values indicate more favourable responses. In addition, the **interquartile range**—this range is a measure of how far apart the values are in the middle 50 percent of the judgements— is calculated. A large interquartile range indicates less agreement among the judges; a smaller range indicates more agreement.

STEP 4

CHOOSING THE FINAL ITEMS FOR THE SCALE.

Normally 20 to 22 items are then selected for the final scale. Items are selected to:
• represent all 11 categories, if possible;
• minimize the interquartile range of items selected (this indicates greater amounts of agreement among the judges).

STEP 5

PRESENT ITEMS TO THE RELEVANT RESPONDENTS.

The finalized scale is now ready for use. Respondents are asked to indicate their agreement or disagreement with each statement, and asked to answer other questions to reflect other variables in the study.

B. EVALUATION OF THE THURSTONE APPROACH

The selection of the panel of judges seems to require random selection procedures: if selection procedures are not random, one would be less confident that the selected items represent a consensus in the general population rather than a consensus among the judges that may not be generally shared. For example, if second-year college students were used as judges, it is probable that on some issues these judges would be systematically different from the general community population. Furthermore, there is no procedure for assessing the unidimensionality, or the validity of the scale.

The use of these techniques is time-consuming, requiring a two-stage research project. The first stage determines which items should go into the scale. It is only after completing this initial stage that one is then ready to move to the second stage—using the scale in the field. Other techniques, combined with the internal consistency approach to selecting items, permit the researcher to use proposed items in a questionnaire and then determine which ones will be used after the data are collected (see McIver & Carmines, 1981, p. 21).

5. LIKERT-BASED INDEXES

Wishing to simplify Thurstone scaling, Rensis Likert (1931) proposed that indexes could be constructed by summing respondents' answers to a number of related items. This type of question is widely used in social science research. In the original format, the respondent is asked to (1) strongly disagree, (2) disagree, (3) be undecided or neutral, (4) agree, or (5) strongly agree,

BOX 12.2

Likert Index Example: Job Satisfaction of Nurses

In the following items, circle a number to indicate the extent to which you agree or disagree with each statement.

16. I enjoy working with the types of patients I am presently working with.
Strongly Disagree   1 2 3 4 5 6 7 8 9   Strongly Agree

29. I would be satisfied if my child followed the same type of career as I have.
Strongly Disagree   1 2 3 4 5 6 7 8 9   Strongly Agree

30. I would quit my present job if I won $1,000,000 in a lottery.
Strongly Disagree   1 2 3 4 5 6 7 8 9   Strongly Agree

31. This is the best job that I have had.
Strongly Disagree   1 2 3 4 5 6 7 8 9   Strongly Agree

32. I would like to continue the kind of work I am doing until I retire.
Strongly Disagree   1 2 3 4 5 6 7 8 9   Strongly Agree

SOURCE: Clare McCabe, "Job Satisfaction: A Study of St. Martha Regional Nurses." St. Francis Xavier University, Sociology 300 Project, 1991. Cited with permission.

with a statement. Such items were, and continue to be, popular in measuring attitudes and perceptions. Box 12.2 illustrates some of these questions.

The reader will note that the items in Box 12.2 deviate somewhat from the original format. Given a preference to increase the variability in such items, the number of response categories has been increased from five to nine. This increase does not take more space on the questionnaire, nor more space when entered into a computer. Using more response categories (9-point rather than 5-point) should lead to slightly higher correlations between index items and prove to be somewhat better at reflecting true underlying values. (See the earlier discussion in Section D on the effects of reduced levels of measurement.)

A. TIPS FOR CONSTRUCTING A LIKERT-BASED INDEX

The following tips may be helpful in constructing such items for use in a ***Likert-based index***.

TIP 1

Avoid the word "and" in Likert items if such usage makes the item multidimensional. In such indexes we are attempting to measure a single variable, so it is important for us not to add a second dimension inadvertently. Suppose we asked a respondent to assess how well he or she gets along at home by making the following statement:

I get along well with my mother and father.
Strongly Disagree   1 2 3 4 5 6 7 8 9   Strongly Agree

What number is the respondent to circle if he or she gets along well with mother but fights continuously with father? The question has to be subdivided into two questions: one asking about relations with mother, and one asking about relations with father. Watch out for the word "and" in a Likert item. Most of the time, you will have to change the item.

TIP 2

Place the "Strongly Agree" on the right-hand side of the scale, with 9 indicating strong agreement. Some researchers prefer to vary the response categories, by, for example, reversing the side on which the agree/disagree labels are placed. This is done to prevent *response set*, a situation where the respondent tends to answer similarly to all items. While switching the side on which the agree/disagree categories are placed may reduce the tendency to respond in a set manner, it may also introduce additional errors in response. (Respondents may not notice that you have switched the agree/disagree categories.) This author's preference is to maintain a uniform presentation. Response sets are best avoided by wording some questions positively and others negatively.

TIP 3

Avoid negatives that may confuse respondent (statements such as: "I don't think the university administration is doing a bad job," will almost certainly confuse and slow down respondents).

TIP 4

Vary the "strength of wording" of questions to produce variation in response. Similarly, if there is uncertainty as to where responses will fall, use more than one item with different intensities in the wordings.

TIP 5

Before the first Likert-type item is presented, provide a brief explanation of how respondents are to indicate their answers.

Likert items result in an ordinal level of measurement. Typically such items are combined to form indexes by adding together the values on individual items (after having reversed the scores on the negative measures).

B. EVALUATION OF LIKERT-BASED INDEXES

We have assumed that the summation score reflects the true underlying variable. If an item does not correlate with this score, we assume that the item is not appropriate. It is, however, possible that the other items are in error. If index items are not well thought out, the chances are that the correlations between the items will generally be low and that this information may then be used to reject items.

> *To perform this analysis using SPSS see the RELIABILITY procedure in Appendix A.*

Likert-based indexes are widely used in the social sciences. Their popularity is due to these factors:

• they are easy to construct;

• there are well-developed techniques for assessing the validity of potential items;

• they are relatively easy for respondents to complete;

- they produce more reliable results than the Thurstone technique; and,

- they require fewer items than Thurstone scaled indexes to achieve the same level of reliability (Seiler & Hough, 1970, p. 171).

6. GUTTMAN SCALING

In the 1940s Louis Guttman developed a new index type. He wished to establish an index that could demonstrably reflect a single dimension. Items are viewed as ***scalable*** if one can demonstrate that there is a hierarchy among the items. This means that, when items are arranged in order of intensity, respondents should respond positively to all lower intensity items if they respond positively to an item of high intensity. Procedures are used to measure the extent to which items reflect a hierarchical structure.

Box 12.3 presents some possible items for a ***Guttman scale*** on attitudes toward capital punishment. There are five items, ranging from one on breaking and entering to one on the abuse and murder of a child. The idea here is that if you support the use of capital punishment for those convicted of breaking and entering, it is likely you will also agree to the other items. The items are designed to range from least serious to most serious. Given the five proposed items, we can propose that there will be six scale types: ranging from those who do not agree with capital punishment for any offences (type 0) through to those who agree that capital punishment should be used for all the offences noted (type 5).

Items may be rejected if they produce a lot of errors in response. An error would occur when a subject should have responded differently to an item of any given intensity. Table 12.3 shows the responses for 18 fictional respondents to the five questions. For each question we can count the number of errors and, on that basis, eliminate one or more of the questions.

The following steps would need to be included when developing a Guttman scale:

STEP 1

Develop wordings for questions that will range across the attitudinal continua that you wish to measure. The response categories may either be yes/no or agree/disagree. In the analysis, however, the questions will be dichotomized, or split into two categories.

STEP 2

These potential items are tested by administering them to a pre-test panel. An effort should be made to have items that range across the dimension being measured (i.e., they should not all be clustered at one end or in the middle of the continuum). Typically Likert-type responses are requested from members of the pre-test panel. Items upon which there is greatest agreement are retained for use in the scale to be used in the research project.

STEP 3

Administer the questions to a second pre-test panel.

STEP 4

Score the questions with *ys* and *ns* with the *ys* referring to support for the use of capital punishment. Score the responses and create a table similar to Table 12.3. Note that the right-hand column reports the total number of *yes* responses.

BOX 12.3

A Guttman Scale Illustration

Suppose you wished to develop a unidimensional scale on attitudes toward capital punishment. The following questions might be proposed, asking respondents to reply "yes" or "no" to each item.

1. People convicted of breaking and entering should be executed.

    Yes - - - - - - - - - - - - - 1( )
    No - - - - - - - - - - - - - 2( )

2. People who are convicted of income tax evasion should be executed.

    Yes - - - - - - - - - - - - - 1( )
    No - - - - - - - - - - - - - 2( )

3. People who have been convicted of selling drugs should be executed.

    Yes - - - - - - - - - - - - - 1( )
    No - - - - - - - - - - - - - 2( )

4. People who have been convicted of three violent crimes should be executed after the third offence.

    Yes - - - - - - - - - - - - - 1( )
    No - - - - - - - - - - - - - 2( )

5. People who are convicted of sexually abusing a child and then murdering the child should be executed.

    Yes - - - - - - - - - - - - - 1( )
    No - - - - - - - - - - - - - 2( )

Guttman Scale Response Patterns:

CRIME	0	1	2	3	4	5
Break and enter	No	Yes	Yes	Yes	Yes	Yes
Tax evasion	No	No	Yes	Yes	Yes	Yes
Drug sales	No	No	No	Yes	Yes	Yes
Three violence convictions	No	No	No	No	Yes	Yes
Child abuse and murder	No	No	No	No	No	Yes

STEP 5

Sort the cases by their total score (number of *yes* responses).

STEP 6

Draw scale response lines. Go through the sorted table and draw a line so as to minimize

TABLE 12.3   ILLUSTRATING GUTTMAN SCALE RESPONSE TYPES AND ERRORS FOR A DATA SET

CASE #	CRIME CATEGORIES					SCORE
	1	2	3	4	5	
1	n	n	n	n	n	0
2	n	n	n	n	n	0
3	n	n	n	y	n	1
4	n	n	n	n	y	1
5	n	n	n	n	y	1
6	n	n	y	n	y	2
7	n	n	n	y	y	2
8	n	n	y	y	n	2
9	n	n	y	y	y	3
10	n	n	y	y	y	3
11	n	y	n	y	y	3
12	n	y	y	n	y	3
13	n	n	y	y	y	3
14	n	y	y	y	y	4
15	n	y	y	y	y	4
16	y	n	y	y	y	4
17	y	y	y	y	y	5
18	y	y	y	y	y	5
y/n	3/15	6/12	10/10	12/6	14/4	
Errors	1	3	4	2	1	11

the number of errors in each of the scale types. (See Table 12.3.) Note that, for each question, we expect an error to have occurred when each case is not the same as the cases above the line. Similarly, we expect the opposite pattern below the line, and we count the number of error cases again.

STEP 7

Count the errors for each item and add these together for a total. Looking at the question that generated the most errors, question 3, note that the line for scale type was drawn after case 9: for the cases above case 9 we expect all respondents to answer *no*, but we get 3 error yes responses; below the line we expect all respondents to answer yes and note the one *no* response. When all the errors are added together, we note that a total of 11 have occurred.

STEP 8

Calculate the coefficient of reproducibility as follows:

Coefficient of reproducibility

$$= 1 - \frac{\text{Number of errors}}{(\text{No. of items}) \times (\text{No. of subjects})}$$

Coefficient of reproducibility

$$= 1 - \frac{11}{5 \times 18} = 1 - 0.12 = 0.88$$

STEP 9

Decide if you wish to withdraw any items from your proposed scale. Ordinarily you attempt to have a scale with a 0.90 coefficient of reproducibility.

STEP 10

Administer the completed scale in your research project.

A. EVALUATION OF GUTTMAN SCALES

Guttman scales do not seem to be as popular as they once were. Like Thurstone scales, they require the use of panels in setting up the scale and, therefore, are not easily used in studies that are under pressure to get completed. Second, Guttman scales result in respondents being assigned a score from a rather limited range. In the example shown above, each respondent would be classified into one of six categories. This assignment into categories would be regarded as an ordinal measurement.

7. SEMANTIC DIFFERENTIAL PROCEDURES

Osgood (1957) is most associated with the development of the semantic differential measurement technique. There are numerous index applications for this type of measurement technique. Originally, these measurement techniques were used to study subjective feelings toward objects or persons. For example, stereotyping behaviour, measuring how respondents view various out-groups, has been investigated using this

---

BOX 12.4

Semantic Differential

62. Circle a number to indicate where you think you fit on a continuum between the two opposites.

621	Shy	1	2	3	4	5	6	7	8	9	Outgoing
622	Passive	1	2	3	4	5	6	7	8	9	Dominant
623	Cautious	1	2	3	4	5	6	7	8	9	Daring
624	Bookworm	1	2	3	4	5	6	7	8	9	Social Butterfly
625	Quiet	1	2	3	4	5	6	7	8	9	Loud
626	Serious	1	2	3	4	5	6	7	8	9	Humorous
627	Conformist	1	2	3	4	5	6	7	8	9	Leader
628	Co-operative	1	2	3	4	5	6	7	8	9	Stubborn

SOURCE: Winston Jackson (1988:99)

approach. The format of such questions is shown in Box 12.4. These questions consist of a series of adjectives, indicating two extremes, placed at the margins of the page; the respondent is asked to indicate where, between the two extremes, he or she would place the group, individual, or object being evaluated. For example, respondents might be asked to indicate where a group would be placed on an honest/dishonest continuum, or on a hot/cold dimension. Respondents are encouraged to answer the questions quickly, letting their guards down, and thus revealing how they "see" various categories of individuals or objects.

There are a variety of traditional and non-traditional uses for such items. An examination of respondents' self-images is certainly possible; items for conducting such an examination appear on question 62 of Box 12.4. Such questions can be used to measure individual variables or be combined to create indexes.

8. MAGNITUDE ESTIMATION PROCEDURES

Magnitude estimation procedures are useful when comparative judgements are required. When these procedures are used, a respondent compares the magnitude of a series of stimuli to some fixed standard. These techniques emerged out of work done by S.S. Stevens (1966a, 1966b, 1969), who attempted to examine the relation between physical stimuli (e.g., the roughness of different sandpapers, and respondents' perception of their roughness). This powerful technique is useful when comparative judgements are required (Hamblin, 1971;

Hamblin, 1974; Jackson & Poushinsky, 1971; Lodge, 1981). The technique results in ratio level measurement and should be in the arsenal of the social researcher. Box 12.5 presents an illustration of it. This technique is best used in interview or in group-administered questionnaires. The instructions need to be reviewed carefully with the respondents, so it is necessary to have a researcher present when the instrument is completed.

Typically, one of two methods is used to do magnitude estimations. The first is to have respondents provide numerical estimates. If one were estimating the relative popularity of different students in a residence, for example, one might begin by having respondents compare the popularity of each student to that of a student the researcher has identified as being about average in popularity. The researcher would then assign this average student 100 units of popularity. The respondent would be asked to proceed through a list of students, indicating in each case, the amount of popularity each has, relative to that of the "average student." If the respondent thinks that Joan is two and a quarter times as popular as the average, a value of 225 would be assigned. Alternatively, if the respondent thinks that Joan has three-quarters the popularity of the "average student," then a value of 75 would be assigned.

A second approach is to have respondents draw different length lines to indicate their perceptions of the differences between stimulus objects. In this case, a standard line is given, and the respondent is asked to draw lines relative to the standard line. (Sample instructions for using the "line method" are presented in Box 12.6.)

BOX 12.5

Magnitude Estimation Training: Community Comparisons

We are now going to ask you to make some comparisons between this community and the one you lived in before moving here. We will ask you to draw lines to indicate how you feel about different things.

For example, we might ask you how much you like your neighbours here, compared to the ones you had in your last community. We will say you liked your neighbours in your last community this much:

_____

Now we would like you to draw a line indicating how much you like your present neighbours. If you like the present neighbours about half as much, then draw a line about half as long as the line above; if you like them more than your previous neighbours—say $2\frac{1}{2}$ times as much—then draw a line $2\frac{1}{2}$ times longer than the line above. Could you try it?

* * * * * *

Could you compare this community to the last one you lived in?

(Once again, we will draw lines to indicate the differences: if you think your present community is 1/2 as good as the previous one, draw a line one-half as long as the standard line; if it is $2\frac{1}{2}$ times as good, draw a line two-and-one-half times as long.)

If your last community was: _____

Could you now indicate how satisfied you are with your present community (compared to the last one you lived in) on the following dimensions?

CLIMATE

SCHOOLS

MEDICAL FACILITIES

COST OF LIVING

JOB SECURITY

HOUSING

JOB SATISFACTION

SOURCE: Jackson and Poushinski (1971).

A. TIPS FOR USING MAGNITUDE ESTIMATION PROCEDURES

Some tips for the utilization of magnitude estimations are:

TIP I

Only use magnitude estimations when a researcher is present to explain the method. The mailed questionnaire is not a suitable vehicle for using this technique.

TIP 2

Use magnitude estimations when comparative judgements are required.

TIP 3

Use a stimulus category somewhere near the middle of the range you intend to use as a standard. Avoid choosing a standard that is near the extreme high or low.

BOX 12.6

Sample Magnitude Estimation Instructions: Perceptions of Universities

Now we would like to have you rate the various local universities on a number of dimensions. The way you will do it will be to draw different lengths of line to indicate how each of the universities compare to one another. If you draw a line twice as long as the "standard" line, it means you think that a particular university is twice as good as average for the particular dimension being rated. For example, suppose you were asked to indicate how far each institution is from your home. You would then draw lines indicating the relative distances from your home. You might draw the following lines:

IF THE AVERAGE UNIVERSITY IS
_____ THIS FAR,

HOW FAR IS: (suppose you then drew the following lines)

Acadia _____

Dalhousie _____

Mount Allison _____

Mount St. Vincent _____

St. Francis Xavier _____

St. Mary's _____

We would interpret your lines to mean that you think that Acadia is about 11/2 times further than the average Nova Scotia university; Dalhousie, The Mount, and St. Mary's about average, while St. F.X. is about 1/3 as far as the average university.

Now we would like you to give us estimates on the following 25 aspects, using the technique that was described above.

* * * * *

How good are the residence accommodations?

Standard = _____

Acadia

Dalhousie

Mount Allison

Mount St. Vincent

St. Francis Xavier

St. Mary's

How good an academic reputation do you think each university has?

Standard = _____

Acadia

Dalhousie

Mount Allison

Mount St. Vincent

St. Francis Xavier

St. Mary's

SOURCE: Jackson (1973).

TIP 4

After the standard has been assigned, leave the respondent free to assign all other values.

TIP 5

Randomize the order of presentation and avoid starting with the extremes of the continuum.

TIP 6

Before the session begins, tell the respondent how to indicate a "zero" response or a "non-applicable" one.

TIP 7

Data derived from magnitude estimations will generally require three columns of space for each variable entered. When lines or numbers are used, the value "999" is used to indicate an item that has not been answered; "001" generally is used to indicate a zero response. Lines are generally measured in millimetres, while numerical estimates are entered directly without change.

B. EVALUATION OF MAGNITUDE ESTIMATIONS

The exciting part of this technique is its ability to provide ratio level measurement for perceptions about social phenomena. It is possible, for example, to measure: perceptions of the seriousness of different crimes (Sellin and Wolfgang, 1964); the status of occupations and people with different incomes and educations (Hamblin, 1971); the perceptions of those who have migrated (Jackson and Poushinsky, 1971); and the relative attractiveness of universities to high school students (Jackson, 1973).

In collecting data, respondents will sometimes use numbers incorrectly, rank ordering the stimuli rather than maintaining the proportionality between the stimulus items. One has to be careful to make certain that respondents understand the procedure. A further limitation is that a researcher must be present to train the respondents in the use of the technique and, hence, it is not applicable to mailed questionnaires, or phone interviews.

F. KEY TERMS

Concept	Index	Ordinal measurement
Conceptual hypothesis	Internal consistency approach	Ratio measurement
Construct validity	Internal validity	Reliability
Content validity	Interquartile range	Response set
Credibility	Likert-based index	Scalable
Criterion validity	Magnitude estimation procedures	Scale
Elite bias	Measurement	Split-half method
External validity	Measurement error	Thurstone scale
Face validity	Nominal measurement	True value
Guttman scale		Validity

G. KEY POINTS

If we are to test theories, we must find a way to measure our concepts. Measurement links abstract concepts to indicators. There are two key issues in this linkage: validity and reliability. The issue of *validity* raises concerns about whether a measure reflects the concept; the issue of *reliability* raises concerns about whether the measure consistently reflects the concept.

In *qualitative research* more emphasis is placed on the credibility of analysis. Such research attempts to describe and interpret social behaviour convincingly, in a way that would seem believable to those people engaging in the social behaviour as well as to other researchers.

Measurement error refers to the extent to which indicants fail to reflect the true underlying values of variables. Measurement error comes in two forms: systematic and random. Systematic error refers to biases which go in one direction, systematically distorting research outcomes; random error goes in either direction from the true underlying values of a variable.

Nominal measurement involves no underlying continuum; numerical values assigned have no meaning and values cannot be added, subtracted, or multiplied.

Ordinal measurement involves an underlying continuum; numerical values assigned are ordered, but intervals are not equal. When ordinal measures are combined, the values may be added, or subtracted, but not multiplied.

Ratio measurement involves an underlying continuum; numerical values assigned are ordered with equal intervals, and the zero point is aligned with true zero. When different ratio measures are combined, the values may be added, subtracted, multiplied, or divided.

There are three relevant *levels of measurement*: nominal, ordinal, and ratio. It is important to know the nature of the variable being measured (is it by nature nominal or ratio) so that appropriate indicators may be sought. Furthermore, the level of measurement achieved determines what forms of analysis are appropriate for analysing relationships among variables.

Researchers are encouraged to achieve *precise measurement* whenever possible. Reduced levels of measurement lead to underestimations of the strength of the relations between variables, giving undue emphasis to precisely measured variables at the expense of poorly measured variables.

When two or more items are combined to reflect a variable, we have created an index or scale. The rationale of using several indicators is that we gain precision and reflect the complexity of the variable more adequately. *Thurstone*, *Likert*, and *Guttman* devised different procedures for creating scales and indexes. The easiest index to create is a Likert-based one. It is the most widely used approach. In addition, researchers should be aware of the *semantic differential* and the *magnitude estimation* procedure for measuring variables.

H. EXERCISES

1. Would it be possible to have a valid measure which is not reliable? Could you have a reliable measure which is not valid?

2. Discuss sources of random and non-random measurement error in reactive research designs. To what extent are such errors due to:

(i) different perceptions of the question being posed;

(ii) differences in image management?

Is image management more likely to lead to random or non-random errors?

3. "In our culture, teenage males will over-estimate their weights; teenage females, however, slightly under-estimate their weights, but show less variability in their estimates of their true weight."

Discuss this quotation, making clear the differences between (i) true value, (ii) random error, and (iii) systematic error in social science measurement.

4. Develop and pilot test one of the following types of indexes or scales: Thurstone, Likert, Guttman, or Semantic Differential. Report fully on the methods you used to develop the scale/index.

I. RECOMMENDED READINGS

CARMINES, EDWARD G., AND RICHARD A. ZELLER (1979). *Reliability and Validity Assessment.* Beverly Hills: Sage Publications. This is an excellent introduction to the assessment of reliability and validity.

CORBIN, JULIET, AND ANSELM STRAUSS (1990). "Grounded Theory Research: Procedures, Canons, and Evaluative Criteria," *Qualitative Sociology,* 13(1), 3-21. This is an excellent article dealing with issues of reliability, validity, and appropriate evaluative criteria for qualitative research.

LODGE, MILTON (1981). *Magnitude Scaling: Quantitative Measurement of Opinions.* Beverly Hills: Sage Publications. Another in the Sage series; this introduction to magnitude estimation procedures neatly summarizes the alternative procedures and reviews the findings that have resulted.

MCIVER, JOHN P. AND EDWARD G. CARMINES (1981). *Unidimensional Scaling.* Beverly Hills: Sage Publications. This is an excellent introduction to scaling methods.

MILLER, DELBERT C. (1977). *Handbook of Research Design and Social Measurement,* Third Edition. New York: Longman. Reviews measurement procedures and reproduces the items contained in many currently used indexes and scales.

WALLACE, WALTER (1971). *The Logic of Science in Sociology.* Chicago: Aldine Atherton. Wallace does a good job of examining the relation between theoretical, conceptual, and operational levels of research.

QUESTIONNAIRE DEVELOPMENT

Questionnaires have many applications: they are used in interview projects, research assessing the effectiveness of different types of programs, experiments, and a host of other situations. A well-designed questionnaire does not impose on the patience of the respondent. It should be possible to move through the questionnaire rapidly, without becoming bored, and without having to reread questions because of ambiguity. An easy-to-complete questionnaire is more likely to be filled out successfully. For those doing a survey, Chapter 4 contains a discussion of how to administer different types of surveys. The present chapter focuses on the development of the questionnaire. We begin our consideration with some general issues, then pay attention to the phrasing of specific questions, and then deal with issues of layout and format.

A. GENERAL GUIDELINES FOR QUESTIONNAIRE DEVELOPMENT

The following list of rules for developing a questionnaire should be regarded as a guideline; there will be situations where it should not be followed in detail. Use these rules with intelligence and a good dose of common sense.

RULE 13.1

CONSULT THE RESPONDENT.

All surveys are something of an imposition on those who are asked to complete them. It is important, if you wish to have a high completion rate, not to impose on your respondents.

Above all, the respondent must be made to feel that he or she is being consulted and can express opinions freely. The questionnaire or interview schedule should be designed to be inclusive—designed to make all respondents feel that their opinions are both valued and acceptable.

RULE 13.2

KEEP IT SHORT.

Frequently projects involve a group of researchers and there may be considerable difficulty in keeping the questionnaire from becoming too long. Asking too many questions not only is an infringement on the respondent's time, but also creates additional work in data entry and error detection. To overcome this problem, it takes a careful negotiator to persuade a colleague that some proposed questions be left for a later study. One test when such difficulties arise is to request individuals to indicate precisely how the variable will be used in analysis. Such discussions force some careful thinking about the survey and the analysis that will follow. All too often a number of variables remain unanalyzed, either because they are considered to be poorly measured or because their relationship to the study is unclear.

There cannot be any strict rules for the length of a questionnaire. If the questions are easy to answer, and the respondents have a particular interest in the survey, it is possible to extend the length of the survey. It is always wise to use as few questions as possible, never asking questions merely for interest's sake. Table 13.1 suggests guidelines for maximum lengths for typical surveys.

The following table can only be approximate, since there can be enormous variations in the complexity of the questions,

TABLE 13.1
MAXIMUM NUMBER OF QUESTIONS FOR SURVEYS

TYPE OF SURVEY	MAXIMUM LENGTH
Phone survey	20 questions
Mailed survey	50 questions
Group-administered	70 questions
Interview	60 questions

the sophistication of the respondents, and in the respondents' interest in the survey.

Phone surveys have to be particularly easy to respond to. Each question must have simple response options, as the respondent will have difficulty trying to remember all the response categories if many are presented. The rule here is to keep the questionnaire simple and short.

Other surveys can involve more questions and greater complexity. Mailed surveys need to be kept somewhat shorter than the others because the researcher is not present to provide encouragement. Interviews can safely be extended to about 60 questions, and take as much as an hour to complete, but It should be remembered that many interviews will take much more time because of the tendency of respondents to stray from the topic. Questionnaires administered to an assembled collection of individuals can involve 70 or more questions. Here, as long as the questions are well designed, respondents can move through the instrument rapidly; because of subtle group pressure, most respondents will complete the form.

But no matter how the data are to be gathered, the researcher should strive for brevity and simplicity. There is no point in gathering data that you do not have the theoretical or analytical skills to process.

RULE 13.3
ACHIEVE PRECISE MEASUREMENT.

Generally, researchers should try to obtain the most precise measurement possible. Collect data in the rawest form: income to the dollar, precise occupation rather than a general category, and age to the nearest year rather than an age category that spans 10 years. This recommendation has to be moderated where other factors argue against precise measurement. You might avoid precision when it would entail asking for information that is too personal, require respondents to make distinctions beyond those they normally use, or when the methods needed to ensure such precision would be too cumbersome. Arguments in favour of precise measurement were presented in Chapter 12.

B. TYPES OF QUESTIONS ILLUSTRATED

This section will illustrate a variety of formats for typical questionnaire items. While it is not possible to anticipate all types of questions, the same principles can be applied to many questions. (Appendix J includes a sample questionnaire designed by students.)

1. PRE-CODED, SINGLE-CHOICE QUESTIONS

In *pre-coded, single-choice questions,* the respondent is asked to indicate with a check mark which category applies to him or her. Box 13.1 provides illustrations of such questions. In the first case, note that only the question is numbered; it will look too cluttered if the categories are also numbered. After the category label, a dashed line is used so that the respondent's eye moves laterally to the check-off category; the number beside the open/close parentheses is the value that will be used when the data are entered into the computer. To avoid a cluttered look, there should be no space between the number and the open/close parentheses.

The next items in Box 13.1 illustrate slightly more complex forms of the check-off question. Question 5 illustrates how to accommodate two columns of check-off categories; in this case, one for the mother's and one for the father's educational level. Once again, the computer codes are placed next to the categories, as this will facilitate data entry. Similar space saving can be achieved by splitting long category lists into two and placing them side by side.

The question on population size simply illustrates that when there are more than 9

BOX 13.1

The Simple Pre-Coded Question

4. What year are you in?

Freshman	– – – – – – – – 1( )
Sophomore	– – – – – – – 2( )
Junior	– – – – – – – – – – 3( )
Senior	– – – – – – – – – – 4( )

5.1/5.2 What is the highest education completed by your mother and father?

	Mother	Father
Grades 0 - 6	– – – – – – – – – – – – – 1( )	– – – – – – – – – 1( )
Grades 7 - 9	– – – – – – – – – – – – – 2( )	– – – – – – – – – 2( )
Grades 10 - 12	– – – – – – – – – – – – – 3( )	– – – – – – – – – 3( )
Some post-secondary	– – – – – – – – – – 4( )	– – – – – – – – – 4( )
University graduate	– – – – – – – – – – 5( )	– – – – – – – – – 5( )

11. What was the approximate population of your home area prior to attending university?

Rural area	– – – – – – – – 01( )
Small town under 999	– – – – – – 02( )
Between 1,000 - 4,999	– – – 03( )
Between 5,000 - 9,999	– – – 04( )
Between 10,000 - 19,999	– – – 05( )
Between 20,000 - 29,999	– – – 06( )
Between 30,000 - 49,999	– – – 07( )
Between 50,000 - 74,999	– – – 08( )
Between 75,000 - 99,999	– – – 09( )
Between 100,000 - 249,999	– – – 10( )
Between 250,000 - 999,999	– – – 11( )
Over 1,000,000	– – – – – – 12( )

categories, it is important to place the leading zero in the computer codes. If the leading zero is omitted, data entry errors will almost certainly occur. The particular population categories would, of course, have to be altered, depending on the target population.

Two points also need to be mentioned that are not illustrated in Box 13.1. Frequently, it is not possible to name all the possible responses that would be appropriate (religious affiliation, for example), and the researcher will have a final category that says:

> Other – – – – – – 12(   )
> please specify —————— .

The most obvious reason for using a "please specify" category is that there would not be sufficient room to list all possible religions. However, even more importantly, you do not wish to insult your respondent by not having included his or her religion. In actual fact, if the major religious groupings have been included, the person who specifies a category not included in the questionnaire will simply be coded as an "Other."

Finally, please note that the response categories provided should cover the full spectrum of possible responses and it should not be possible for a respondent to check off two of the categories. Note in Box 13.1 that the population categories are *mutually exclusive*—no category overlaps another one. A common error is illustrated in Example 1, Box 13.2.

Example 1 illustrates a situation where the researcher has failed to provide mutually exclusive categories; Example 2 corrects the error.

BOX 13.2

Two Versions of Population of My Home Town

Flawed Version: Not Mutually Exclusive Categories

Example 1. The population of the place I considered my home town when growing up was:

> Rural area – – – – – – – – – 1(   )
> town up to 5,000   – – – – – 2(   )
> 5,000 to 20,000   – – – – – – 3(   )
> 20,000 to 100,000   – – – – – 4(   )
> 100,000 to 1,000,000   – – – 5(   )
> 1,000,000 or over   – – – – – 6(   )

Better Version: Categories Are Mutually Exclusive

Example 2. The population of the place I considered my home town when growing up was:

> Rural area – – – – – – – – – 1(   )
> town under 5,000   – – – – – 2(   )
> 5,000 to 19,999   – – – – – – 3(   )
> 20,000 to 99,999 – – – – – – 4(   )
> 100,000 to 999,999   – – – – 5(   )
> 1,000,000 or over   – – – – – 6(   )

2. OPEN-ENDED QUESTIONS

An ***open-ended question*** asks the respondent to answer some question, or to offer some suggestion or opinion, but to do so without any pre-set categories being provided for the answer. There are at least six reasons for including some open-ended questions in a survey:

- such questions are used when there are too many possible responses (as in year of birth);

- open-ended questions are preferable if the researcher does not wish to impose response categories on the respondent;

- the researcher uses such questions when he or she wishes to create the sense that the respondent is really being consulted, by being asked to offer his or her opinions;

- the researcher wishes to provide a qualitative dimension to the study. Open-ended questions provide this dimension, along with material which may be used as a source of quotations for the final report;

- a pilot study is being done and the appropriate response categories have not been determined; and, finally

- such questions are used to provide a change in pace for the reader.

While open-ended data are not always analyzed when writing the final report on a project, they can provide insights to the researcher which might be missed if such questions were not asked.

Box 13.3 illustrates some variations in typical formats. Questions 20 and 22 are simple questions where the space for the response indicates that two numbers are expected. By providing two blanks, the respondent is being prompted to enter two numbers. The % symbol in question 20 also helps to indicate exactly what is expected. This helps to prevent frivolous replies, like writing in "average" in the case of question 20, which asks about the respondent's average in the final year of high school; or writing in "a long time ago" in the case of question 22, which asks about year of birth.

Question 21 illustrates a method of asking about occupation. The additional line (Brief Job Description) is included to ensure that the respondent provides sufficient detail to enable the researcher to attach an occupational rating code to the response. (See Appendix H for the Canadian Occupation Prestige Index.) If such specification is not requested, some respondents will simply indicate the employer (for example, writing in "CNR") and the researcher will not be able to attach an occupational rating to that kind of response. Where detail is required, the researcher must be careful to request it.

Questions 23 and 24 simply seek the opinion of the respondent on two issues. Typically, the responses that are given would either be listed (simply typed) or coded. If they are coded, the categories would be determined after the data have been collected and the responses examined.

RULE 13.4

MINIMIZE NUMBER OF OPEN-ENDED QUESTIONS.

Many researchers minimize the number of opinion-seeking, open-ended questions because they are time-consuming to code, tend

BOX 13.3

Sample Open-Ended Questions

20. Approximately, what was your average in your final year of high school?

_____ _____ %

21. What is (or was) your father's occupation? (e.g., supervisor, railway machine shop...supervises work of about 25 people.)

Job _____

Brief Job Description _____

_____

22. In what year were you born? 1 9 __ __ .

23. What is the one thing that you would like to see changed at the university?

_____

_____

24. In your opinion, what was the single best thing about attending university?

_____

_____

to generate responses which are inconsistent, and are more likely to be left blank. Indeed, respondents will frequently fail to complete a questionnaire that has too many such questions. Many respondents appear to feel that asking them to write a sentence or two is too much of an imposition.

Where a pilot study is conducted, and where the research team is uncertain about the appropriate response categories, it is a good idea to pose the question in an open-ended form, analyze the results, and then base the categories to be used in the final study on the those suggested in the pilot study (Schuman and Presser, 1981).

Placing an open-ended question at about the two-thirds mark of a long questionnaire may well provide the relief needed to sustain the respondent's interest and ensure completion of the questionnaire.

If both open-ended and fixed-choice questions are asked, it is advisable to place the open-ended version first so that the respondent is not influenced by the fixed-choice options (Sudman and Bradburn, 1983).

Michael D. Smith (no date) has explored the effectiveness of open versus precoded questions in revealing the incidence of physical abuse. Both formats were equally effective in detecting abuse; however it was noted that if questions about abuse were asked a second time, some 21 percent of the victims revealed their victimization on the second question. The findings suggest that it is a good idea to repeat a question a second time, using a variant of the question, as this may get respondents to reveal their abuse. Some may object that such persistent questioning may create an expectation (demand characteristic) that the respondent should make a positive response. However, if the question is properly worded this should not be a problem.

Use opinion-seeking, open-ended questions sparingly; do keep in mind, however, that they are an excellent vehicle for providing a change in pace for the respondent, or for exploring new issues in detail.

3. PRESENCE-ABSENCE QUESTIONS

Presence-absence questions request respondents to check off which items in a list do or do not apply to them. Box 13.4 provides examples of such questions. Of the two versions presented, the first one is preferable. In it, either a "yes" or a "no" is expected for each item. While this is a little more work for the respondent, the researcher can then be more confident that each item has been considered. In question 24, if an item is left blank, does that mean that the respondent is opposed to

capital punishment for that crime? Or did the respondent simply fail to consider that item?

In contrast to the questions presented in Box 13.1, where the respondent was asked to check one of a set number of answers, open/close parentheses are not used for the answer in Box 13.4. Instead respondents are asked to circle a 1 (Yes) or a 0 (No). The reader should also note that the computer codes used involve "1" for presence and "0" for absence. During analysis a "total experience" variable may be created by simply adding the variables together. A total score of "5," for example, would mean that the individual has had experience with disabled people in five of the settings identified in the question.

4. RANK-ORDERING QUESTIONS

Rank-ordering questions are those where a respondent is asked to indicate an ordering of response items, usually from most preferred to least preferred. Asking respondents to rank-order a list has to be done with great care. In this case, detailed instructions should be provided for the respondent. Box 13.5 includes an example of such a question.

First, note that the respondent is only asked to pick out the three most important items; in most cases, respondents will not be able to go beyond the top three meaningfully. These are difficult types of questions for respondents, and they should be kept as simple as possible.

Second, it should be noted that the instructions are embarrassingly explicit. While "rank-ordering" may be an obvious and

---

BOX 13.4

Flawed Version: Possible Ambiguity of Items Left Blank

24. On a guilty verdict, in which of the following situations would you support the use of capital punishment? (Check as many as appropriate.)

Manslaughter – – – – – – – _____ 1

Premeditated Murder – – – _____ 1

Rape – – – – – – – – – – – _____ 1

Murder of Police Officer – _____ 1

Murder of Prison Guard – – _____ 1

Better Format: Less Ambiguity about Items Left Blank

23. Have you ever had contact with disabled persons in any of these groups? (Circle to indicate "yes" or "no" for each group.)

	1 Yes	0 No
Community – – – – – – – –	1	0
Family – – – – – – – – – –	1	0
Relatives – – – – – – – – –	1	0
Elementary school class – –	1	0
Junior high school class – –	1	0
Senior high school class – –	1	0
University class – – – – – –	1	0
As co-worker – – – – – – –	1	0

---

simple idea for many people, the detailed instructions will minimize the number of respondents who will simply place a check mark beside three items, or check just one of the items.

Note that the respondents are given a short line on which they are to write their answers. Again, it is important to provide a different look for the item in order to cue the respondent that this is not a "check-one" question. Be assured that if you use a "check-one" format, a good number of questionnaires will be returned with one of the items checked.

BOX 13.5

Rank-Ordering Questions

31. Rank-order the three most important things you want in the job you make your life's work? (Place a 1 beside the most important one; a 2 beside the next important one; and a 3 beside the next most important one.)

Money – – – – – – – – – – – _____

Security – – – – – – – – – _____

Continued Interest – – – – _____

Power – – – – – – – – – – _____

Prestige – – – – – – – – – _____

Excitement – – – – – – – _____

TIP 13.1

One suggestion for coding these responses into the computer is to use the values provided by the respondents (i.e., 1=1, 2=2, and 3=3) and code all items left blank as a 4. In this way, means can be computed during analysis. (This is a situation where it seems to make sense to compute a mean using ordinal data.) In the few cases where respondents simply tick off three items, each one ticked can be given a 2. Of course, if the whole item is left blank, the researcher will be forced to assign the missing value code to each of the items.

Avoid over-using rank-ordering items in a questionnaire. They slow the respondent down and increase the risk of losing the respondent's cooperation.

5. LIKERT-TYPE QUESTIONS

Chapter 12 presented Likert questions under the discussion on index construction. The reader is referred to that chapter for a more extensive discussion of these items. But since they are used as stand-alone items, a brief comment will be made on them here. ***Likert-type questions*** are those which ask respondents to indicate the strength of their agreement or disagreement with a statement. This type of question is widely used in social science research. In the original format (Likert, 1932), respondents are asked to react to a statement by indicating whether they (1) strongly disagree, (2) disagree, (3) are undecided or neutral, (4) agree, or (5) strongly agree. Such items were, and continue to be, popular in measuring both matters of fact and attitudinal issues. (Box 13.6 illustrates some of these questions.)

The reader will note that the items in Box 13.6 deviate somewhat from the original format. Given a preference to increase the variability in such items, the number of response categories has been increased

BOX 13.6

Likert-Type Items

In the following items, circle a number to indicate the extent to which you agree or disagree with each statement:

52. I believe capital punishment is the most effective way to deter murder.

    Strongly Disagree   1 2 3 4 5 6 7· 8 9   Strongly Agree

53. I believe a murderer can be rehabilitated to become a responsible, functioning member of society.

    Strongly Disagree   1 2 3 4 5 6 7 8 9   Strongly Agree

54. I believe a life sentence is a satisfactory penalty for murder.

    Strongly Disagree   1 2 3 4 5 6 7 8 9   Strongly Agree

55. I would quit my present job if I won $1,000,000 through a lottery.

    Strongly Disagree   1 2 3 4 5 6 7 8 9   Strongly Agree

56. I would be satisfied if my child followed the same type of career as I have.

    Strongly Disagree   1 2 3 4 5 6 7 8 9   Strongly Agree

57. My mother would be upset if she knew I did drugs.

    Strongly Disagree   1 2 3 4 5 6 7 8 9   Strongly Agree

from five to nine. This increase does not take more space on the questionnaire, nor more space when coded into the computer.

The following tips may be helpful in constructing such items:

TIP I

Avoid the word "and" in such items if such usage makes the item multidimensional.

TIP 2

Place the "Strongly Agree" on the right-hand side of the scale, with 9 indicating strong agreement. Some researchers prefer to vary the response categories, such as reversing the side on which the agree/disagree labels are placed. This is done to prevent **response set**, a situation where the respondent tends to answer similarly to all items. While switching the side on which the agree/disagree categories are placed may reduce the tendency to respond in a set manner, it may also introduce additional errors in response. (Respondents may not notice that you have switched the agree/disagree categories.) My preference is to maintain a uniform presentation. Response sets are best avoided by wording some questions positively and others negatively.

TIP 3

Avoid negatives that may confuse respondent (statements such as: "I don't think the university administration is doing a bad job," will almost certainly confuse and slow down respondents).

TIP 4

Select a "strength of wording" to produce variation in response. For example, if you were asking patients about the quality of care given by nurses in a hospital you might ask several questions, varying the strength of the wording in each item. You might well suspect that nursing care will be rated high, so you might wish to strengthen the wording from:

VERSION 1: The nursing care I received at St. Martha's was good.

| Strongly Disagree | 1 2 3 4 5 6 7 8 9 | Strongly Agree |

to

VERSION 2: The nursing care I received at St. Martha's was perfect in every instance.

| Strongly Disagree | 1 2 3 4 5 6 7 8 9 | Strongly Agree |

The *strengthening* of the wording in version 2 will almost certainly produce more variation in response. Version 1 would be expected to produce 8s and 9s almost exclusively. (A further illustration is provided in Rule 13.7 below.)

TIP 5

If there is uncertainty about where responses will fall, use more than one item with different intensities in the wordings.

TIP 6

Before the first Likert-type item, provide a brief explanation of how respondents are to indicate their answers.

TIP 7

When respondents fail to answer a question, use the 0 value as a missing value code. (The 9, which is usually used for missing values, reflects a real value in the case of a 9-point Likert item.)

Likert items result in an ordinal level of measurement. Frequently such items are combined to form indexes by adding together the values on individual items (after having reversed the scores on the negative measures).

6. INDEX DEVELOPMENT

Indexes are constructed by combining several individual questions and represent an attempt to summarize, in one score, a measure of a variable. Indexes are constructed when we are dealing with a single-dimension variable, but in contexts where one question might not measure the variable adequately. Indexes can be constructed by combining a number of similarly formatted questions, or combinations of questions with different formats. In all cases, the indicators are combined, and possibly weighted, so that they add up to one index score. (See Chapter 12 for details on different methods of constructing indexes. Appendix A contains illustrations for index construction using SPSS.)

C. STEPS AND RULES FOR QUESTIONNAIRE DEVELOPMENT

This section will review the steps that will need to be taken in developing your questionnaire and will present rules to follow.

STEP 1

MAKE A LIST OF VARIABLES.

Questionnaires can be thought of as consisting of four major groupings of variables: background characteristics, the dependent variable(s), the independent variables, and the other types of variables: intervening, antecedent, and sources of spuriousness variables. Questions to measure variables in each of these groups will have to be developed. The first task is to create a list of variables; during this stage it is not necessary to worry about how the variables will be measured—a list is all that is required. The list may be derived by:

• applying relevant theoretical models and identifying variables that should apply;
• reviewing the literature, paying particular attention to which variables were measured by other researchers;
• examining other questionnaires for ideas as to which variables should be included;
• reviewing the causal models that have been developed for the current project; and finally
• thinking about which variables "make sense," given the topic of the research.

STEP 2

ANTICIPATE HOW DATA WILL BE ANALYZED.

After the list of variables is developed, it is important to discuss how the data will be ana-

lyzed when they are collected. Indeed, it is possible to set up proposed analysis tables showing what relationships are to be analyzed, and indicating what procedures will be used to examine each of them. It is critical to have some understanding of how the analysis is to proceed, since the methods used to examine relationships are constrained by the level of measurement attained in operationalizing each of the variables. This discussion may also include how the analysis will proceed, given different outcomes of preliminary runs on the data. Frequently important new variables will emerge as a result of this process. Table 13.2 indicates the types of procedures that would be appropriate given different levels of measurement of the variables involved in the study.

Suppose that you wished to do regression analyses on the data. In such cases, you would prefer to have ratio level measurement of all the variables. You might want to figure out how to use magnitude estimation procedures, or how to construct indexes that would meet, or be close to meeting, the standard for ratio measurement. On the other hand, if the nature of the dependent variable (nominal measurement) dictates a reliance on crosstabular analysis, then you would be content to get ordinal and nominal level measurements of your variables.

STEP 3

WRITE THE PROPOSED QUESTIONS ON INDEX CARDS.

During the development of a questionnaire it is a good idea to write proposed questions on index cards (usually 8 x 13 cm. cards are large enough). Using cards will facilitate both the quick editing of items and rearranging their location in the questionnaire.

TABLE 13.2   APPROPRIATE ANALYSIS PROCEDURES BY LEVELS OF MEASUREMENT

	INDEPENDENT VARIABLE		
Dependent	Nominal	Ordinal	Ratio
Nominal	CROSSTABS	CROSSTABS	CROSSTABS MEANS*
Ordinal	CROSSTABS	CROSSTABS NONPAR CORR	CROSSTABS NONPAR CORR
Ratio	MEANS ANOVA MANOVA DISCRIMINANT	MEANS ANOVA MANOVA DISCRIMINANT	CORRELATION PLOT PARTIAL CORR MANOVA REGRESSION

*In SPSS for this case, run the independent variable as though it were the dependent variable (i.e., name it first); the interpretation of the test of significance would be standard.

STEP 4

DOUBLE CHECK TO MAKE CERTAIN YOU HAVE ALL THE VARIABLES.

It is essential to ensure that all the variables which play a part in the hypotheses and models related to the project have been included. The list of variables must be checked and double checked. It is not unusual for a researcher to discover that some key variable has become lost in the shuffle. With checking completed, it is now time to begin drafting the questionnaire. Once again, there are some rules to keep in mind as this process begins.

STEP 5

REVIEW CONCEPTUAL DEFINITIONS.

When developing the wording for a particular question, it is important to review its conceptual definition. Knowing the conceptual de-finition provides an important guide as to what the question is to measure. To illustrate, suppose one is attempting to measure socio-economic status. And suppose that, in the conceptual definition of socio-economic status, reference is made to a hierarchical continuum of respect and prestige. Given this conceptual definition, the researcher might be led to adopt a measure particularly designed to reflect the relative amount of prestige an individual has. In this case one might opt to use an occupational prestige scale such as the one developed by Featherman and Stevens in the United States (1982), or Porter and Pineo in Canada (1967). While this procedure might yield a valid measure of the concept in general, the experienced researcher would realize that the measure may be weak on the "respect" aspect of the definition, and would also run into some serious difficulties if there were a number of housewives, or single stay-at-home parents in the sample—such individuals are not assigned scores in occupational prestige scales. One might therefore choose to measure the "respect and prestige" an individual has by getting a number of individuals to rate each individual compared to others. Perhaps the latter approach would yield the most valid measure of the concept, even though it would be rare for a research design (probably a study of a particular group) to allow for the practical use of this method.

Suppose, alternatively, that the proposed conceptual definition of socio-economic status stressed variations in access to scarce resources. In this case, one might attempt to reflect the variable by getting some indication of the individual's total income. Here the assumption is that an individual's total income would be a good reflection of that individual's ability to buy access to scarce items in the society.

The more general point is that the researcher must pay careful attention to conceptual definitions—they provide invaluable and crucial guides to valid measurement.

STEP 6

DEVELOP WORDING FOR QUESTIONS.

There are a few rules to keep in mind as you commence writing drafts of the questions to be included in your questionnaire.

RULE 13.5

WORDS MUST BE UNDERSTOOD.

The words used in questionnaires must be understood by all respondents. Err on the side of simplicity. If a survey is being done on high school students—play it safe—use words that a Grade Seven student can handle. Furthermore, the words selected should be those that have but one unambiguous meaning.

Showing off an impressive vocabulary has no place in a questionnaire that is intended to produce valid and reliable data.

RULE 13.6

PAY ATTENTION TO THE "AND" ALERT.

Individual questions should be unidimensional. Avoid the trap involved in a question such as:

I get along very well with my mother and father.

Strongly   1 2 3 4 5 6 7 8 9   Strongly
Disagree   Agree

The problem with the question, as worded, is that some respondents will not "get along" equally well with both mother and father. As a result, some respondents may indicate a 1 or a 2 if they do not get along well with both; others might indicate a 6 or 7 as a kind of average of the relationship they have with both their parents. The point is that two dimensions have been introduced—the relationship with mother *and* the relationship with father. Such questions should be divided into two separate questions. It is always useful to scan one's questions to eliminate such unwanted confusion: double check any question that has the word "and" in it.

RULE 13.7

VARY WORDING TO PRODUCE VARIABILITY.

It is important that the items in a questionnaire produce variability in response. If most respondents provide similar responses to a question, then the question will have little use during analysis. Try to ensure that the respondents will scatter themselves across the response continuum. A simple example will illustrate the point:

Mothers play an important role in our society.

Strongly
Disagree   1 2 3 4 5 6 7 8 9   Strongly
                                    Agree

Using common sense alone, one could anticipate that most respondents will be in strong agreement with this statement and will circle 8 or 9. If, indeed, respondents do not vary their responses much, the question will not prove useful in discriminating between respondents' views about the role of mothers. In this case, what one does to produce more variability in response, is to "strengthen" the wording of the item, so that more respondents will move toward the "disagree" end of the continuum: perhaps a statement such as, "Mothers play a more important role in society than fathers," or, "Mothers play the single most important role in our society." In both illustrations we have made it less likely that all respondents will remain at the "Strongly Agree" end of the continuum.

In dealing with a variable such as job satisfaction, a review of the literature will reveal that most respondents will report themselves to be relatively satisfied with their jobs. Knowing this, the researcher strives to identify items that will induce some respondents to report that they are less than fully satisfied— perhaps the researcher will ask if the respondent would like his or her child to have a job similar to their own; or ask if they think they are paid the "right amount" for the responsibilities that they have.

Similarly, questions which measure clients' satisfaction with services delivered, for example, the satisfaction of patients with services in a hospital, will need to ensure that the questions ferret out the slightest dissatisfaction. Otherwise it is likely that virtually everyone will rate the service as "good" or "excellent."

When one is phrasing questions so as to ensure that respondents vary in their scores, one is not attempting to distort reality—to show dissatisfaction when none is present—but rather one is attempting to develop measures that are highly sensitive. And, if one is attempting to understand what leads patients to be relatively more, or relatively less, satisfied with their treatment in a hospital, one would need highly sensitive measures, given the fact that respondents generally tend to respond positively. If all respondents simply reported that they were "satisfied," we would not be able to identify what factors influence levels of patient satisfaction.

RULE 13.8
AVOID COMPLEXITY.

Try to keep questions simple; avoid asking respondents to do difficult tasks. Where it is necessary, for example, to have respondents rank-order a list, it is usually best to ask them to rank-order the three most important items, rather than asking them to go through the whole list. In most cases, the slight reduction in discriminatory power will be offset by a higher response rate to the question.

RULE 13.9
USE EXISTING WORDINGS FOR COMPARATIVE ANALYSIS.

When a researcher wishes to compare data that he or she is generating to data reported by other researchers, it is important that the wording of questions be identical. Here one has to weigh the advantages of improving the wording of a question against the advantage of maintaining identical wordings to facilitate comparative analyses.

RULE 13.10

TAKE THE EDGE OFF SENSITIVE QUESTIONS.

Using a combination of experience and common sense, the survey researcher soon learns that there are some issues that respondents may be reluctant to report. Illegal activities, evaluating friends or neighbours, and indicating age or income can all be sensitive issues. By asking for the respondent's year of birth rather than age, the researcher makes the question sound scientific and more likely to be answered; if age is asked, the respondent may feel some invasion of privacy is occurring. Similarly with income. Here many researchers will ask respondents to indicate into which broad category of income they fall. Alternatively, if income is a key question, and if the question is located among those dealing with conditions of work, respondents will generally provide the information. However, if the income question is being used as a measure of socio-economic status, then other indicators, such as years of education or occupational prestige, might be considered preferable to income itself—simply to avoid prying unnecessarily into what may be perceived to be a highly personal matter.

RULE 13.11

AVOID ASKING RESPONDENTS TO SPECULATE ON WHY THEY ACT THE WAY THEY DO.

Generally we are not interested in polling respondents' opinions on whether certain relationships exist. For example, if you are studying the relationship between participation in student activities and levels of self-esteem, you would normally not ask respondents if they think there is a relationship between these two variables. Instead, the researcher would

get separate measures of the two variables (among others) and would then analyze the data to determine if there is any relationship.

RULE 13.12

BE PRECISE, HIGHLY SPECIFIC WHEN CHOOSING WORDINGS.

If you wish to measure, for example, how much people drink, ask questions which pinpoint the type of drink consumed and the time when it was consumed. Here the time period will have to be reasonable. It is silly to ask how many drinks someone has had in the past two years; few people could make a reasonable estimate without considerable thought. Box 13.7 illustrates some possibilities in asking about drinking patterns.

Question 1 suffers because of variations in what respondents consider light, moderate, or heavy drinking. Question 2 is better because it pins down a specific time period, but perhaps it goes overboard: you can become too specific. Question 3 hits a reasonable compromise, being specific and referring to a reasonable and recent time period.

STEP 7

PRE-TEST THE QUESTIONNAIRE.

It is important to have a few individuals complete the questionnaire or the interview before settling on the final wordings of the questions. Start by filling it out yourself. Make any necessary corrections, then try it on a few other people. Generally it is best to sit with the individuals completing the questionnaire. Before they begin, tell them exactly what you are doing (trying to remove any ambiguity in the questionnaire), and encourage them to ask for any clarifications. Perhaps, as they com-

BOX 13.7

Sample Alcohol Consumption Questions

Flawed Version: Fuzzy

1. How would you describe your drinking?

     Abstainer – – – – – – – – 0(   )
     Light – – – – – – – – – – – 1(   )
     Moderate – – – – – – – – 2(   )
     Heavy – – – – – – – – – – 3(   )

Flawed Version: Too Specific; Recall Problem

2. On Christmas Eve, 1993, how many beers did you have?

     ____ ____ beers

Better Version: Specific

3. In the past seven days, how many beers did you drink?

     None – – – – – – – – – – 0(   )
     1 to 3 beers – – – – – – – 1(   )
     4 to 7 beers – – – – – – – 2(   )
     8 to 12 beers – – – – – – 3(   )
     13 or more – – – – – – – 4(   )

plete the questionnaire, they may inquire: "When you ask about the size of my family, do you mean the family I was born into or the one I have with my husband? Also in that question, do you want me to include the parents in the count?" If so, clearly you will need to change your wording of the question. With experience, you will learn to be highly specific in your wording of questions. The goal is to minimize variations in respondents' understanding of each question. It is always a good idea to review your questionnaire and search for possible ambiguities. The goal, although impossible to achieve, is to have all respondents understand each and every question in an identical manner.

STEP 8

IF ADVISABLE, DO A PILOT STUDY.

It is recommendable to use a pilot study in a number of situations. A *pilot study* involves having a small sample of respondents complete the questionnaire or undergo the interview. Pilot studies are used to determine items to be included in indexes, and to determine, from open-ended questions, what categories should be used in a fixed-choice format. Further refinements in a questionnaire may be achieved through the use of a pilot study.

D. RULES FOR ORDERING QUESTIONS, FORMATTING, AND PRESENTATION

1. ORDERING QUESTIONS

RULE 13.13

INTRODUCE SURVEY TO RESPONDENTS.

Normally, questionnaires will contain a brief statement introducing the study to the respondent. It should be short (usually three or four lines is sufficient), and should inform the respondent about who is doing the study, who is sponsoring it, and what the study is about. These few lines should attempt to establish the legitimacy of the project. By identifying who is doing the study and who is sponsoring it, the idea is conveyed that the survey is important. Such identification also provides the respondent with some additional information which he or she can use to decide whether to fill out the questionnaire. The researcher should not identify the specific hypotheses of the study; to do so might well bias the responses. Finally, if the survey is anonymous, respondents should be assured that their anonymity will be protected. A good way to achieve the latter goal is simply to ask respondents not to write their names on the forms. (See Box 13.8 for sample wordings.)

BOX 13.8

Sample Introductory Questionnaire Statements

The following is a research project about attitudes toward some public issues. As all responses are confidential, please do not sign your name. Answer all questions as honestly as possible. Thank you for your co-operation.

* * * * *

This survey on the number of children female students would like to have and on their career plans is being conducted by nursing students. The information will be kept confidential and your name is not required.

* * * * *

The following questionnaire has been prepared by students from St. Mary's University to compare the future plans of high school students. Your cooperation in completing this study by responding to the following questions would be greatly appreciated. Please do not put your name on the questionnaire since all responses are confidential.

* * * * *

This is a survey being conducted by students. We would appreciate your cooperation in filling out this questionnaire to the best of your ability. Since your responses will remain anonymous, please do not write your name on the questionnaire.

In a mailed questionnaire, a letter describing the project and requesting the cooperation of the recipient is generally included. Ideally, this letter should be written on letterhead stationery and be signed by the head of the organization. One attempts to communicate the importance of the project by identifying its sponsors and by the professional appearance of the mailing. Normally, a stamped, return envelope is included for the convenience of the respondent.

RULE 13.14
EASE THEM INTO IT.

In deciding the order of questions, consideration should be given to starting with those questions that are easy to answer. It is important not to start by asking questions that may be regarded as "too personal." Background information questions are usually placed at the end of questionnaires (Dillman, 1978, p. 125; Erdos, 1983). However, when students are being surveyed, or in situations where there is little problem with refusals, it is possible to begin with items that reflect the respondent's place of birth, gender, and the size of the community in which the respondent lives. Perhaps then it will be possible to move to issues such as the respondent's year of birth. Whether one begins with background information or other questions, it is important that the respondent be able to move quickly through these first items, creating the impression that it will take only a few minutes to complete the whole questionnaire. Survey researchers are always concerned to do everything that they can to increase the proportion of people who will complete the form successfully. If obtaining the background information involves questions that may be considered highly personal, then it is best to place such items at the end of the questionnaire.

Another suggestion for question ordering is to begin with questions that the respondents will consider important. Respondents are more likely to complete a questionnaire if they view it as salient (Heberlein & Baumgartner, 1978, p. 457; Goyder and Leiper, 1985, pp. 60-65).

RULE 13.15
KEY AND REPEATED VARIABLES AT ONE-THIRD POINT.

In most projects there will be a few variables that are particularly important to the study. In most cases, there will be a major dependent variable. Ordinarily, it is a good idea to place key variables about one-third of the way through the questionnaire. One wants the respondent to be fresh, and paying maximum attention, when these key variables are presented.

If there are to be any "reliability checks" (repeated questions), then one needs as much separation as possible between the first and second presentation of such questions. The first presentation of any repeated questions should also be placed near the beginning of the questionnaire—after the respondent is warmed up—but before fatigue or boredom sets in.

RULE 13.16
GROUP QUESTIONS BY TYPE.

Some grouping by type of item is advisable. Minimize the amount of shifting between open-ended questions and pre-coded questions. If there are a number of Likert-type items, it is a good idea to group some of them together (Likert, 1932). The idea is to get the respondent used to a particular format in order to permit quick movement through the items. Continual shifting between types of questions will only slow the respondent down and increase the risk of error.

2. FORMATTING

BEGIN CONDITIONING RESPONDENTS.

The first questions begin a "conditioning" process. By always presenting the "check-one-of-the-following" questions in the same manner, the respondent soon gets the idea that questions presented in this manner are to be responded to by choosing one of the options provided by the researcher. Later, when a "fill-in-the-blank" question is asked, the researcher can draw attention to the fact that something else is required by varying the format. For example, if the respondent is to be asked to rank-order a list, or to choose the three most important items from a list, then a different look should be given to the question by varying the way in which the response categories are set up—perhaps a short line opposite each item rather than the open/close parentheses. (See Boxes 13.1 through 13.5 for illustrations; also see Appendix J.) The key point is that different formats should be used for different types of questions; this will help the respondent answer the questionnaire rapidly.

Note that the format in Box 13.1 requires the respondent to place a check mark in the appropriate space. Check marks are slightly easier than circling responses and so they are preferable. Any device to make the task easy for the respondent should be incorporated.

ANTICIPATE COMPUTER DATA ENTRY.

Virtually all surveys of any size will be analyzed using a computer. To simplify the entry of the data into the computer, it helps enormously if the values that are going to be entered into the computer are right on the questionnaire. Indeed, it is now quite common for researchers to avoid what was once referred to as "coding the data." By coding, reference is made to researchers going through the questionnaire and assigning values to each response category, recording this information on "code sheets," and then having the data entered into the computer off the code sheets. This process was expensive, time-consuming, and likely to introduce additional errors into the final data set. Where possible, avoid the whole coding process by placing the code values directly on the questionnaire. These numbers can then be used when the data are entered into the computer. They can be placed unobtrusively on the questionnaire and will not distract the respondent when completing the form.

Box 13.1 illustrates a set of questions where such numbers have been used. The reader should note that there are no blanks between the response category and the check-off space (usually open/close parentheses). Note, as well, that only question numbers are used, and that response categories are numbered beside the place where the respondent makes his or her check mark. As the reader will appreciate, when the data are entered into the computer, it is easy to enter the number immediately adjacent to the check mark made by the respondent.

Box 13.9 shows the formatting style favoured by Earl Babbie, by Don A. Dillman, Harvey Krahn, and by this author. Babbie does not appear to favour the use of code values, uses square brackets for the check-off responses, and places the response brackets before the category (Babbie, 1992, p. 155).

BOX 13.9

Four Format Styles Illustrated

1. Babbie Format Style for Fixed-Choice Responses:

    23. Have you ever smoked marijuana?

    [ ]   Yes
    [ ]   No

2. Dillman Format Style for Fixed-Choice Responses:

    Q-22 Your Sex (Circle number of your answer)

    1   MALE
    2   FEMALE

3. Krahn Format Style for Fixed-Choice Responses:

    54. In the past year, has any member of your immediate family (not counting yourself) been unemployed (out of work and looking for work)?

    No.   1
    Yes   2

4. Jackson Format Style for Fixed-Choice Responses:

    4. What year are you in?

    Freshman – – – – – – – – – 1( )
    Sophomore – – – – – – – – 2( )
    Junior – – – – – – – – – – – 3( )
    Senior – – – – – – – – – – – 4( )

SOURCES: Babbie (1992:155); Dillman (1978:134); Krahn (1991:51); Jackson (1988:87).

Dillman favours the use of capital letters to identify response categories, and, in mail surveys, places the code values to the left of the response categories. Dillman recommends placing the code values to the right of the categories in personal interview forms and telephone surveys (1978). Both Babbie's and Dillman's styles are acceptable.

Another formatting style is illustrated by questionnaires developed by the Population Research Laboratory at the University of Alberta. Harvey Krahn and his associates tend to include the actual computer code values on the questions, placing them to the right of the categories. Having respondents circle numbers placed to the right of the category ensures that right-handed respondents do not cover the category label with their hands. This formatting style is simple, uncluttered, and recommended.

My own preference is to include code values and place them to the right of the response categories, using a series of dashes "– – –" to carry the respondent's eye out to the check-off brackets. Note that no space is left between the code value and the brackets. (The intention is to make the numbers disappear as much as possible; when spaces are left between the number and the bracket, the number seems to gain prominence.) Because the numbers that will eventually be entered into the computer are right beside the check mark, data entry is simplified and less subject to error.

Some researchers place the computer screen column numbers on the questionnaire that each variable will occupy. These are placed on the extreme right-hand side of the questionnaire. The advantage of this is that errors can be avoided when entering the information into the computer. Certainly, in the case of interviews or phone questionnaires, it is advisable to include such codes. However, in cases where respondents are filling in the questionnaires themselves, such numbers add to the clutter on the questionnaire and should probably be avoided. (In Chapter 15 additional suggestions will be made to help reduce errors in data entry.)

RULE 13.19

VARY PLACEMENT OF RESPONSE CATEGORIES.

Box 13.1 also illustrates how the appearance of a questionnaire can be improved by varying the placement of the response categories for each question. While this might be an aesthetic rather than a scientific consideration, the appearance of a questionnaire where the response categories are all lined up on the right margin is not pleasing to the eye, nor is it easy to see where one question ends and another begins. The rule, then, is to vary the location of the response category sets.

RULE 13.20

CLEARLY INDICATE ANY BRANCHING.

Some questions are only to be answered by some respondents. In such cases, guide your reader clearly by using one of the techniques shown in Box 13.10. Note that those who responded positively to question 9 are directed to question 9.1.

3. PRESENTATION

RULE 13.21

GIVE QUESTIONNAIRE A DISTINCTIVE LOOK.

Besides paying attention to issues of layout, it is also important to give the questionnaire a distinctive appearance. The use of coloured paper is one way to achieve this. Another useful tip is to have the questionnaire prepared on 8-1/2" × 14" paper and then have it reduced to the standard 8-1/2" × 11" paper. When this is done, use small margins because a wide margin will show up after the reduction is made. While slightly smaller print will result from reducing the page size, this will permit more space between questions and greater flexibility when it comes to formatting each page of the questionnaire for optimal appearance.

RULE 13.22

DO NOT SQUEEZE TOO MUCH ONTO ONE PAGE.

Avoid trying to squeeze too much onto a single page: questionnaires should permit the respondent to move through each page rapidly. Squeezing material looks bad and discourages your respondent.

BOX 13.10

A Branching Question Illustrated

9. Have you consumed any beer in the past seven days?

Yes – – – – – – – 1(   )

No – – – – – – – 2(   )

> 9.1 If Yes: How much did you consume in the past week?
>
> Less than 3 pints   – –1(   )
>
> 4 to 9 pints   – – – – –2(   )
>
> 10 or more pints   – –3(   )

10. Have you ever been married?

Yes – – – – – – – 1(   )   [Answer questions 11-14]

No – – – – – – – 2(   )   [Go to question 15]

E. KEY TERMS

Likert-type questions

Open-ended question

Pilot study

Pre-coded single choice questions

Presence-absence questions

Questionnaires

Rank-ordering questions

Response set

F. KEY POINTS

A well-designed questionnaire is not only more likely to be answered. but is also more likely to generate usable information.

Open-ended questions are used when pre-coding is not a practical option, to provide a change of pace for the respondent, to give the respondent a greater feeling of control, and to provide a qualitative dimension to a research project.

Use nine categories for Likert-type questions.

In developing measures, pay close attention to the conceptual definition of the concept you wish to reflect. Use easily understood, unambiguous wordings.

Questions should measure one dimension; use indexes to get at multi-dimensional concepts.

G. EXERCISES

1. Develop a series of background information questions that would be appropriate for a study you would like to do. Be careful to obey as many of the rules for questionnaire construction as you can.

2. Using the questions developed in question 1:

(i) complete the questionnaire yourself. Decide what changes you would make, based on problems that emerged when you completed the questionnaire. Revise the questionnaire.

(ii) sit down with a fellow student and have him or her complete the revised questionnaire. What changes resulted from having another person complete the questions? Revise the questionnaire to remove any ambiguities.

3. Develop a series of items for an index that is of interest to you. Define the conceptual aspects of the index and suggest indicators.

H. RECOMMENDED READINGS

BRADBURN, NORMAN M., AND SEYMOUR SUDMAN (1980). *Improving Interview Method and Questionnaire Design*. San Francisco: Jossey-Bass Publishers.

DILLMAN, DON A. (1978). *Mail and Telephone Surveys*. New York: John Wiley & Sons. The Dillman book is an excellent presentation of many of the issues involved in doing mail or telephone surveys.

ERDOS, PAUL L. (1983). *Professional Mail Surveys*. Malabar, Florida: Robert E. Krieger Publishing Company. This book should be regarded as required reading for anyone considering doing a mail survey.

SUDMAN, SEYMOUR, AND NORMAN BRADBURN (1983). *Asking Questions*. San Francisco: Jossey-Bass Publishers.

## CHAPTER FOURTEEN

SAMPLING AND SAMPLE SIZE

A. THE RATIONALE OF SAMPLING

Social scientists, market researchers, political parties, and media people all need to describe elements of society accurately. One way to approach such problems is to take measures on the relevant variables for all people in the population. While this solution is possible if one is studying a few individuals (perhaps employees who work in a nursing home), when the concern is to understand how people from larger aggregations such as a community, region, or country feel about certain issues, then it is necessary to figure out ways to get a sense of their feelings without having everyone complete a questionnaire, or agree to be interviewed. In such cases, a sample that can reflect or represent the views of the larger population may be drawn.

Sampling is done to save time and money. If you can estimate who is going to win an election accurately with a sample of 1,500, why poll two million? And while common sense suggests that larger samples would be more accurate than smaller ones, this is not necessarily the case. The key issue is that a sample must be representative—it must reflect the population accurately. Box 14.1 reports a classic case of an inaccurate sample.

Box 14.1 illustrates a situation where a large sample failed to predict the winner of the 1936 American presidential election (Simon and Burstein, 1985, p. 108). This is a case where a huge sample (two million plus) did not do the job. The *Literary Digest* needed two key things:

BOX 14.1

Predicting the 1936 American Election

In 1920, 1924, 1928, and 1932 the New York-based *Literary Digest* conducted polls in an effort to predict the winner and the winning margin in the American presidential elections. The polls were accurate (within 1 percent in 1932), so the *Literary Digest* conducted its 1936 poll with considerable confidence. And on October 31, 1936 the magazine published results based on mailings to some 10 million Americans. The results are indicated in the table:

Literary Digest *Prediction of Results in 1936 American Presidential Elections*

CANDIDATE	NUMBER OF VOTES	PERCENTAGE OF VOTES
Landon	1,293,669	57.1
Roosevelt	972,897	42.9
TOTAL	2,266,566	100.0

Responses from over 10,000,000 ballots mailed out (under 23 percent response rate).

The poll suggested that Landon would win the November election easily. But it turned out that Roosevelt won by a substantial margin. So why, with a sample of over two million, did the *Literary Digest* miss the mark so badly?

The founder of the American Institute, George Gallup, predicted in July of 1936, some months before the *Literary Digest* began mailing out its ballots, that the *Literary Digest* poll would not be accurate. Gallup pointed to the flaw of using mailing lists based on telephone listings and listings of automobile owners. Gallup pointed out that such lists largely favoured the more economically prosperous; during the depression years, the new voters came largely from poorer groups (few of whom owned cars or telephones). Gallup also noted that those most likely to return their ballots would overrepresent the better educated and the higher socio-economic categories.

George Gallup thus challenged the sampling frame used by the *Literary Digest*. The *sampling frame* is the target population from which the researcher draws a sample. The sampling frame did not reflect American voters accurately; it favoured the more prosperous elements in society, and Roosevelt's strength was among the poorer elements of American society.

SOURCE: The information on the *Literary Digest* attempt to predict the 1936 American election was based on the presentation in Julian L. Simon and Paul Burstein, *Basic Research Methods in Social Science*, Third Edition. New York: Random House, 1985, pp. 107-110.

- a more representative sample of the general population, and;

- a situation where circumstances do not alter substantially between the time of data collection and the time of the election.

The lesson to be learned from the *Literary Digest* debacle is that, for reasons of both economy and accuracy, a well-selected small sample is to be preferred to a large, poorly selected sample.

Sampling is used in a great variety of research projects: choosing which children's stories will be subjected to a content analysis, choosing and then assigning subjects to different conditions in experimental designs, or deciding which constituencies are to be included in an voting study, all entail sampling decisions.

B. FUNDAMENTAL SAMPLING PROCEDURES

To begin our discussion, some terms need to be distinguished:

- *Population:* The population is the entire group that you wish to describe. In Box 14.1 the population would be the American electors of 1936. If you were studying residence students at a university, the population might be defined as "all students who reside in a university's dormitories during the week of March 22 to March 29". The terms "population" and "universe" are used interchangeably.

- **Sampling frame:** This is the list(s) from which you draw a sample. In Box 14.1 the sample frame included all those people listed as automobile owners plus all those who had a phone. Ideally, the sampling frame and the population are identical; in practice, however, it is often not possible to get a complete list of the population, so the sampling frame may not reflect the population perfectly. Almost any list will not be right up to date; some people will be left off, others perhaps listed twice. The goal is to get as accurate a sampling frame list as possible.

- **Sample:** The sample refers to those individuals (or units) selected for a study.

- **Response rate:** The response rate refers to the percentage of delivered questionnaires that are completed and returned.

There are two categories of sampling procedures: probability sampling procedures and non-probability sampling procedures.

1. PROBABILITY SAMPLING TECHNIQUES

Probability sampling procedures involve techniques for selecting sampling units so that each unit has a known chance of being included. It is important to appreciate that tests of statistical significance assume that sampling has been done using some form of probability sampling (see Chapter 8). If your study involves the use of such tests, be certain to meet the sampling assumption. The sampling units usually are individuals, but may also refer to other levels of analysis, such as communities or countries. The procedures for selecting each of the major types are listed below.

A. SIMPLE RANDOM SAMPLE

A simple random sample provides each unit (usually a person) in the population an equal chance of being selected for participation in a study. This procedure requires that a list of the potential respondents be available to the researcher. Such lists might include student lists, lists of eligible voters used for elections, lists of employees, lists of companies, and so forth. The following steps are necessary when selecting a **simple random sample**:

STEP I

Number the units on the list.

STEP 2

Computers are typically used to generate the random numbers used in sample selection. Alternatively one may use a table of random numbers to select the required number of units. (Sample size determination is discussed later in this chapter.) To use a table of random numbers, shut your eyes and stab a pencil into the table. The point where the pencil has struck is used as the starting point. From this point one reads the numbers systematically (perhaps reading down the column, continuing at the top of the next column and so forth), placing a check mark beside those cases whose number shows up on the random number table. This process continues until a sufficient number of cases for the study has been selected.

In experimental designs, a table of random numbers, or a computer-generated set of random numbers, may be used to assign subjects to treatment or control groups. To do this simply list the subjects, and then, using odd or even numbers from the table of random numbers or the computer, assign each subject to a condition (perhaps even numbers to control groups, odd ones to the treatment group). Thus the numbers might be odd, odd, odd, even, odd, even, even...the subjects would then be assigned, as shown in Table 14.1.

STEP 3

Additional replacement units should be selected, and kept on a separate list, so that when a sampling unit cannot be contacted or an individual or company does not participate, then that unit will be replaced by the first replacement unit. Replacements should be identified and numbered, since they will be used in the order in which they have been selected. R1, R2, etc. is a convenient way of noting them.

B. SYSTEMATIC SAMPLE

A *systematic sample* provides each unit (usually a person) in the population an equal chance of being selected for participation in a study by choosing every nth unit, starting randomly. The systematic sample provides a somewhat easier way of selecting cases from a list of potential respondents. In this case, names listed in phone books, directories, street maps, dormitory diagrams, student lists, or elector lists all might be sources from which one might draw a systematic sample. In the case of systematic samples, it is even possible to proceed with sampling when no list exists prior to sampling. For instance, one could choose students living in every fourth residence room and, so long as one numbers the rooms systematically, one could proceed without a list of the students.

The critical issue is that every person must have a known (usually equal) chance of being selected. The steps in selecting a systematic sample are as follows:

TABLE 14.1   USING TABLE OF RANDOM NUMBERS TO ASSIGN SUBJECTS TO TREATMENT AND CONTROL GROUPS

SUBJECT	ODD/EVEN FROM RANDOM NUMBER TABLE	EXPERIMENTAL CONDITION
Subject #1	Odd	Treatment
Subject #2	Odd	Treatment
Subject #3	Odd	Treatment
Subject #4	Even	Control
Subject #5	Odd	Treatment
Subject #6	Even	Control
Subject #7	Even	Control
...	...	...

STEP 1

Get a list, map, or diagram as appropriate.

STEP 2

Having determined the sample size required, plus the additional number for replacements (for the refusals, or for those with whom contact cannot be made), these two figures should be added together and will be regarded as the total sample requirement.

STEP 3

Divide the total sample requirement into the total number of units in the population being surveyed. This number should then be rounded to the nearest, but lower, round number. (E.g., if the number you get is 8.73, round it to the nearest, lower, whole number; in this case, 8.) This number represents what is known as the *skip interval*.

One caution that must be mentioned in the use of systematic samples is that if the list is ordered in some fashion there may be a problem; suppose you have a listing of couples, but with the name of the male always listed first. In such a case, if the skip interval was an even number, then all those selected would be females. If the list is patterned, as in the example above, a different sampling procedure will have to be used.

STEP 4

Using a table of random numbers, select a number between 1 and the value of the skip interval. The number selected becomes the starting case, the first one selected to participate in the survey. Suppose we were doing a survey of students living in campus dormitories and we have determined the skip interval to be 8 and the starting case to be 3. In this case,

we would develop a systematic procedure for numbering the dormitory rooms and for moving from floor to floor, dormitory to dormitory. We would begin with the 3rd door, then go to the 11th, 19th, and 27th rooms. In rooms with two student residents we would ask both to participate; otherwise students in double rooms would have less chance of being selected for the study. However, caution has to be exercised since, in some universities, students may select their roommates and, if this is the case, there would be a lack of independence in some of the units sampled. If this is a problem, the researcher would be well advised to obtain a list of all students in residence and then use a random sampling procedure.

When systematic samples are being selected from lists, it is a rather straightforward matter to go through the list, placing check marks beside cases that have been selected, perhaps marking every 5th one. Additional units should be selected for use as replacements.

C. STRATIFIED SAMPLE

There are times when a simple random or systematic sample would not provide an appropriate solution to sample selection. Suppose, for example, that you are doing a survey of attitudes toward capital punishment by members of different political parties. While it would be possible to do a random sample of individuals in the community, such a procedure might be somewhat wasteful, because the community might be made up predominantly of those who support one of the parties. As a result, a very large sample would be required to provide a sufficient number of respondents to allow generalizations about supporters of each of the parties. In situations such as the one described above, it is useful to draw a ***stratified sample***, a sample which will give supporters within each party an equal chance of selection, but will, at the same time, ensure that an equal number will be selected from each of the parties.

One might decide, for example, that you would like to have 150 respondents from each of the political parties. The steps in selecting a stratified sample are:

STEP 1

Determine the sample size required from each of the categories.

STEP 2

Develop a list for each of the categories from which you wish to draw your sample.

STEP 3

Using either a systematic or random sampling procedure, choose the cases for the sample, along with the required number of replacements.

Samples may be stratified by more than one variable. In order to achieve more precise estimates, we might also have stratified the above sample by gender and by socio-economic level. The procedures are identical: simply identify the stratification dimensions, then using an equal probability procedure, select respondents. Unless appropriate weighting procedures are used, the results of such surveys can only be used to compare the different sub-groups and do not represent the community in general. The reason they do not represent the community is that such samples overrepresent smaller categories and underrepresent the larger ones.

D. MULTI-STAGE AREA SAMPLE

When the task involves developing a sample to reflect a large unit such as a state, province, or country and no list of the population is available, then one develops a ***multi-stage area sample***. The key point is that at each stage of the sampling process, every individual (or unit) must have a known chance of being selected. In a simplified form, the procedures for a national survey may be summarized as follows:

STEP 1

Identify ***primary sampling units*** (these may be census tract areas, or other similar units, normally several hundred of them); these units are numbered, and a selection of units is made from them, using an equal probability technique.

STEP 2

Within the selected areas, identify the city blocks (in urban areas) or square miles (rural areas). From these choose, using an equal probability technique, an appropriate number of units.

STEP 3

Within the selected areas, number the housing units, and select the units that will be used randomly from among these.

STEP 4

For each household, list the people who fall within the desired sampling parameters (perhaps: adults, over the age of 18, who have lived in the community for one month or more). Table 4.3 gives an example of a sample form.

STEP 5

An equal probability procedure is then used to select respondents from a list of those who are eligible.

RULE 14.1

NO SAMPLING CHOICES ARE TO BE MADE BY DATA COLLECTION PERSONNEL.

All choices are to be made by probability procedures. When a selected participant is not available (moved away, not home after three call backs, or refuses to cooperate) then replacements are used, in the order selected. It is critical that interviewers not simply replace the unavailable respondent with the nearest, most convenient, replacement. This would bias the sample toward those who are at home, or are more cooperative. Whatever rules are established, these should be communicated clearly to those doing the data collection, and should also be made clear in any technical reports on the research project. (See Table 4.3 for a sample form that may be used.)

Box 14.2 presents the telephone introduction instructions for the 1993 Alberta Survey (see Kinzel, 1992). While the telephone number selected for dialling was randomly determined, the procedures favoured interviewing adult males, particularly those who happen to have answered the phone call from the interviewer. These procedures were followed to create a greater equality in the participation rates of male and female respondents.

BOX 14.2

The Alberta Survey

Telephone Introduction Sheet 1993

1. Hello, I'm calling (*long distance*) on behalf of the Population Research Lab at the University of Alberta. My name is ... (full name or Mrs. XXXXX)

2. I have dialed XXX-XXXX. Is this correct?

3. Your telephone number was selected at random by computer.

4. Just a moment of your time to explain why I'm calling.

5. The Lab at the University, is currently conducting an important study on current issues (*such as the family, health and well-being, AIDS, credit cards, crime, work, and social issues*).

6. In order to determine who is eligible for the study, please tell me how many women and men aged 18 or over live on a regular basis at this number?

   NUMBER OF WOMEN —— and
   NUMBER OF MEN ____

7. This total includes yourself as a member of this household over the age of 18?

Requesting an Interview with Person who Answers the Phone

8. I would like to interview you. I'm hoping that now is a good time for you. Your opinions are very important for the research that is being

done at the University of Alberta.

9. Before we start, I'd like to assure that your participation is voluntary and that any information you provide will be kept confidential and anonymous. As I mentioned there is a wide variety of questions. If any of them you do not wish to answer, please feel free to point these out to me and we'll go on to the next question. You of course have the right to terminate the interview at any time.

(OPTIONAL READ)

We do not need your name, so that no one will know your answers to these questions. If you have any questions about the survey, you can call the Study Supervisor in Edmonton at 492-2505 for further information.

Refusal

10. It is extremely important for this University study to have the highest number of people who have been selected, take part.

11. I can't replace this household with another one without destroying the randomness of the survey.

12. Do you think anyone else in the household could take part – (*either now or later*)? (do not pause) Could someone assist us with the study?

Requesting to Speak to Someone Else in the Home

13. We don't always interview the person who answers the telephone. In your

household it is one of the (*male/female*) members we need to talk to.

14. May I please speak to (*him/her*) (one of them who is free at the moment)?

15. Hello, I'm calling from the Population Research Lab at the University of Alberta. My name is … (full name or Mrs. XXXXX)

16. The Lab at the University, is currently conducting an important study on current issues (*such as the family, health and well-being, AIDS, credit cards, crime, work and social issues*).

Your telephone number was selected at random by computer.

I'm hoping that now is a good time for you. Your opinions are very important for the work that is being done at the University of Alberta.

17. Before we start, I'd like to assure you that your participation is voluntary and that any information you provide will be kept confidential and anonymous. As I mentioned there is a wide variety of questions. If any of them you do not wish to answer, please feel free to point these out to me and we'll go on to the next question. You of course have the right to terminate the interview at any time.

(OPTIONAL READ)

We do not need your name, so that no one will know your answers to these questions. If you have any questions about the survey, you can call the Study Supervisor in Edmonton at 492-2505 for further information.

SOURCE: Population Research Laboratory, Sociology Department, University of Alberta, Edmonton, Alberta T6G 2H4. Reprinted with permission.

2. NON-PROBABILITY SAMPLING TECHNIQUES

There are three additional **non-probability sampling techniques** that are commonly used by researchers. While these procedures do not provide potential respondents with a known chance of being asked to participate in a study, they are, nonetheless, important to know about.

A. QUOTA SAMPLE

In a **quota sample**, respondents are selected on the basis of meeting certain criteria. Here no list of potential respondents is required: the first respondent to meet the requirement(s) is asked to participate and sampling continues until all the categories have been filled—until the quota for each has been reached. Suppose one were asked to compare food preferences of the young versus the elderly. One might do a survey of supermarket customers, selecting the first 75 who meet the "young" criteria, and the first 75 who meet the criteria for inclusion in the comparison group. Note that this sampling procedure is the nonprobability twin of stratified sampling.

The steps in selecting a quota sample are as follows:

STEP 1

Define precisely the criteria for inclusion into each of the categories.

STEP 2

Select participants on a first-come-first-included basis until the quota for each category has been met.

B. CONVENIENCE SAMPLE

Convenience samples involve selection on the basis of ease or convenience. If you were to "poll" people entering a shopping mall on their attitudes toward an upcoming election, you would be selecting a convenience sample. Such samples may, however, involve particular categories of individuals. For example, by asking a couple of classes of Grade Ten students to complete questionnaires, you would obtain a convenience sample of the students present.

C. SNOWBALL SAMPLING

Snowball sampling is a name for a referral sampling procedure. As you complete one interview you ask if there is anyone else known to the respondent who might be appropriate for the study. This technique is frequently used in situations where one cannot get a list of the population who share some characteristic. Some examples where you might choose to use this sampling procedure are:

- a study of the marital adjustment of couples whose first child was born before the couple married; in this case, you would not easily find a list of this population, but through referrals, you could identify individuals who would be appropriate for your study;

- a study of prostitutes who are under 16;

- a study of people convicted of white-collar crimes;

- a study of pool hustlers.

Note that none of these procedures lead to independent nor randomly selected units. But, for some research problems, this type of sampling procedure is the only feasible one.

Convenience, quota, and snowball samples are reasonable approaches to sampling when one is investigating relationships among variables (say the relationship between participation and self-esteem) and one is interested in trying to understand the conditions under which there is, or is not, a relation between the major variables rather than generalizing to the entire population. Explanatory studies, in fact, frequently use nonprobability sampling procedures. However, when tests of significance are an important tool in one's research, it should be noted that such tests assume that probability sampling procedures have been used. Therefore, tests of significance are not appropriately used when quota, convenience, or snowball samples have been used.

C. SAMPLE SIZE DETERMINATION

A variety of factors influence the size of the sample that is appropriate for any study. No simple rule of thumb is possible in determining an appropriate sample size. So if someone tells you that samples should be 10 percent of the population, the advice is not sound. Sample size determination involves a series of trade-offs between precision, cost, and the numbers necessary to do the appropriate analyses. At the same time it is necessary to take into account the amount of variability in the factors studied and, sometimes, even the size of the population.

1. EIGHT STEPS IN DETERMINING SAMPLE SIZE

Sample size determination involves eight basic steps: some statistical, some prag-

matic. It is usually best to begin with the statistical ones, estimating the required sample size, and then modify this number to take practical considerations into account.

STEP 1

DECIDE ON THE CONFIDENCE LEVEL TO BE USED.

If you would like to be confident that your result will fall within a given range of precision 95 percent of the time, use the value 1.96. (Ninety five percent of the cases fall ± 1.96 standard deviation units from the mean). If you wish to be 99 percent confident, a larger sample will be required. (Here the appropriate value will be 2.58.) Most social science researchers use the 95 percent level in determining sample sizes. With this level you can be confident that your sample mean will be within a given precision 19 out of 20 times.

STEP 2

SELECT A MAJOR VARIABLE TO DETERMINE SAMPLE SIZE.

Normally you focus on the main dependent variable of the study in computing the required sample size. And, if the dependent variable is measured at the ratio level, it will be easier to determine sample size requirements. Such a variable might include percentage voting for a given party, or an attitude score. You will need to estimate the population standard deviation (sd pop) for this variable. This estimate can be made by examining results from other surveys, or, failing that, simply by using common sense, noting the mean and the range within which one expects to find two-thirds of the cases. (See illustration in Box 14.3.) Another suggestion for estimating an unknown population standard deviation is to approximate it by taking the range of values (exclud-

BOX 14.3

Estimating the Standard Deviation

Suppose you wished to estimate the standard deviation of a variable like the weight of male undergraduates. Try doing the following steps:

STEP 1: Estimate the average weight of male undergraduates. (***Estimate: 70 kilograms***.)

STEP 2: Within what weight range would you expect to find about two-thirds of the male students? (***Preliminary estimate: 9 kilograms***.)

STEP 3: Double the estimate in Step 2. (18 kilograms.) Does it make sense that

about 95 percent of all cases will fall within the range defined by the mean ± twice the estimate at Step 2? (I.e. 70 ± 18; range = 52 to 88 kilograms.) If the band is not wide enough, how much wider should it be? If it is too wide, how much narrower should it be? Suppose you decide that it should be slightly wider, arguing that about 95 percent of the cases will fall between 50 and 90 kilograms. Divide this range by 4 to get the estimated standard deviation. (***Standard deviation estimate: 10 kilograms***.)

ing extreme cases) and dividing this value by two. This method will generally provide a reasonable estimate. Finally, it must be acknowledged that in studies with a large number of variables involved, it is impossible to make claims, with any certainty, about the precision of all the variables. Most of them have unknown sampling distributions. Box 14.3 outlines the steps you should take to estimate the standard deviation of a variable.

STEP 3

DETERMINE THE MINIMUM PRECISION THAT WOULD BE ACCEPTABLE.

Do you want to be within three pounds of the true mean when estimating weight, within two percentage points in predicting a vote, or within three points on a scale with a maximum score of 75? The measure of precision

will have to be expressed in the same units as the standard deviation.

STEP 4

COMPUTE SAMPLE SIZE.

Compute the required sample using the following formula:

Required sample size =

$$\left[\frac{(\text{confidence limit}) \, (\text{sd pop})}{\text{Accuracy}} \right]^2$$

Suppose, for example, that you wished to determine the sample size required to estimate the average weight of male university graduates. You wish to be 95 percent confident (Z = 1.96), and be within 2 pounds of estimating the true weight. The estimated standard deviation of the population is 14.0 pounds. The values would be plugged into the equation, as in:

Required sample size =

$$\left[\frac{1.96(14.0)}{2.0} \right]^2 = 188$$

The indicated sample size is 188: if you use such a sample, you can be confident that your estimate of the population's average weight will be accurate to within two pounds 95 percent of the time.

STEP 5

COMPUTE SAMPLING FRACTION.

The *sampling fraction* is the sample size in relation to the population (see Monette, Sullivan and DeJong, 1990, p. 149). Thus, if you have a population of 800,000 and a sample of 188, the sampling fraction would be:

Sampling fraction = Sample size/Population
= 188/800,000
= 0.0002 (0.02 per cent: go to Step 7)

If the sampling fraction is less than 5 percent, go to Step 7. Alternatively, if the population was 1200 residence students, the sampling fraction would be:

Sampling fraction = 188/1200
= 0.157 (15.7 per cent: go to Step 6)

If the computed sampling fraction is more than 5 percent of the population, an adjustment may be made in your sample size. To compute the adjustment, go to Step 6.

STEP 6

SMALL POPULATION ADJUSTMENT.

Where the sampling fraction is greater than 5 per cent, the required sample size may be reduced according to the following formula:

Adjusted sample size
= n/(1 + (n/N))
= 188/(1 + (188/1200))
= 188/1.157
= 162

where: n = sample size estimated in Step 4.
N = estimated size of universe.

(See Monette, Sullivan, & Dejong, 1990.)

STEP 7

ARE THERE SUFFICIENT CASES FOR THE ANALYSIS?

The required sample size must now be scrutinized to ensure that it will provide a sufficient number of cases for the most complex analysis that is to be done. For example, if one intends to do a series of cross-tabulation tables with three categories in each of the independent and dependent variables, with a maximum of one control variable with two categories, then one is proposing a number of 18 cell tables ($3 \times 3 \times 2$). With 188 cases, the maximum expected frequencies would be just over 10 cases per cell ($188 \div 18 = 10.44$). This would hardly prove adequate and, therefore, one would want to increase the sample size, or else rethink the proposed types of analyses that are to be performed. Correlational techniques will place less stringent demands on one's sample so that, to the extent model testing can be done using those techniques, fewer cases will be required.

STEP 8

ADJUST SAMPLE SIZE FOR COST AND TIME FACTORS.

A final step is to adjust the sample to take time and cost into account. If one requires a sample of 3,000 but has only the resources to deal with 1,000, then one will have to do some rethinking on the precision that will be possible. If, on the other hand, one has sufficient resources to increase the sample size, then one usually does so, since some additional precision is likely to result.

2. SAMPLE SIZE AND ACCURACY

The relationship between sample size and precision of estimations is a simple one. To double precision, sample size must be quadrupled. In the illustration concerning the weights of graduating university males, if we wished to be within one pound of estimating the true value of the population, we would need a sample four times as large as the one proposed for a sample which would get us within two pounds. For example:

Required sample size =

$$\left[\frac{1.96(14.0) \text{ (sd pop)}}{1.0} \right]^2 = 753$$

The original sample size required was 188 or 1/4 of 753. "Precision" will be referred to in statistics texts as the confidence interval. In the above illustration, with a sample size of 753 we can be 95 percent confident that the true population mean weight is within one pound of the sample mean.

3. SAMPLE SIZE AND CONFIDENCE LIMITS

The relationship between precision and confidence limits means that to move from the 95 percent confidence limit to the 99 percent level, one may simply multiply the sample size by 1.73. Thus, in the illustra-

tion on graduating males, to be within two pounds of the average weight but to be 99 per cent confident, one would need to multiply the original sample size of 188 by a factor of 1.73. (188 x 1.73 = 325). A sample of 325 will be required to be 99 percent confident that the estimate will be within two pounds of the true population mean. Conversely, to move from the 99 percent confidence limit to the 95 percent limit, the sample size determined for the 99 percent level may be multiplied by 0.58.

4. THE IMPACT OF REFUSALS

While the evidence from studies examining different response rates under controlled conditions shows little variation in the descriptive accuracy independent of response rate, tests of significance assume probability sampling techniques and also assume that there is no systematic bias in who chooses to complete the form (Erdos, 1983, 146-47). Such tests also assume that any measurement error is random. As we cannot know what impact refusals and measurement error have on our data, researchers make every effort to get completed questionnaires from all respondents. It is not clear what conclusions one could legitimately arrive at if one had a response rate of 20 percent.

5. CONFIRMING REPRESENTATIVENESS

Steps, however, may be taken to confirm that one's sample is indeed representative of the population about which one is attempting to make generalizations. For example, one might compare the age, gender, and marital status distributions of one's sample, to known such distributions for the population from census data. If one's sample is not wholly representative, there are techniques for weighting results to get a better reflection of the population whose characteristics one is trying to estimate. Where, however, there has been a high non-participation rate, there is no guarantee that the sample will be representative for other variables, even if it is representative for those age or gender distributions that have been checked.

> *To perform a weighting of a sample, use the WEIGHT command in SPSS. This command is discussed in various SPSS manuals.*

D. KEY TERMS

Convenience sample

Multi-stage area sample

Non-probability sampling techniques

Population

Primary sampling units

Probability sampling procedures

Quota sample

Response rate

Sample

Sampling fraction

Sampling frame

Simple random sample

Skip interval

Snowball sampling

Stratified sample

Systematic sample

E. KEY POINTS

Sampling is used to save time and money. In reflecting characteristics of a population, well-selected small samples are both more economical and more accurate than large, poorly selected samples.

The two categories of sampling techniques are (i) probability and (ii) non-probability sampling. The former techniques include those sampling procedures where each unit in the sampling frame has a known chance of being selected: these include random, systematic, stratified, and multi-stage area samples. Non-probability sampling does not provide all members of the population with any known chance of being selected: non-probability sampling techniques include such approaches as quota, convenience, and snowball sampling.

Determining sample size requires the researcher to take into account the precision required, the variability in the phenomenon studied, the confidence level, the size of the population, the methods which will be used to analyze the data, and the time and resources available for data collection and analysis. A simple eight-step set of procedures is recommended for determining sample sizes for most studies.

F. EXERCISES

1. Suppose that you have census information indicating that the mean income of a population is $37,000 with a standard deviation of $21,000. You wish to draw a sample which will be within $2,000 of the true population mean 95 percent of the time. How large a sample would be required?

2. Assuming the same population values as in the above question, determine the sample size required to produce 99 percent confidence that you will be within $2,000 of the true mean.

3. If the most complex contingency table you wish to run in an analysis is a $2 \times 2 \times 2$ table, what sample size would produce a 20 expected in each cell (assuming breaks at the mid-point)?

4. Suppose you wish to sample the opinions of an organization that has 200 members; you wish to be 95 percent confident that you will be within 5 percent of estimating the true attitude of the membership. How large a sample size would you recommend? Show your computations for determining the sample size.

G. RECOMMENDED READINGS

COCHRAN, W.G. (1963). *Sampling Techniques*, 2nd ed. New York: John Wiley & Sons.

KISH, LESLIE (1965). *Survey Sampling*. New York: Wiley.

SLONIM, M.J. (1960). *Sampling in a Nutshell*. New York: Simon & Schuster.

SUDMAN, SEYMOUR (1976). *Applied Sampling*. New York: Academic Press.

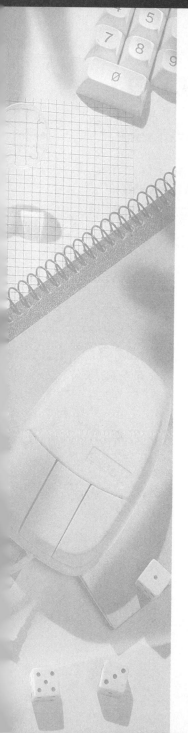

DATA ANALYSIS

The three Chapters in this section deal with aspects of data analysis. Chapter 15 presents various procedures for hand-analyzing data and then various computer concepts are introduced. Chapter 16 deals with the issue of examining three- and four-variable causal models, while Chapter 17 introduces three advanced techniques.

STARTING THE DATA ANALYSIS

Having collected the data, it is now time to analyze them. We will approach this task in two ways: we begin with a method of hand-tabulating the results; this section will be followed by a discussion of how computers may be used to analyze data.

A. ANALYZING DATA WITHOUT USING A COMPUTER

Some analyses that we do with a computer could also be done easily by hand. And sometimes it is even faster to analyze results manually if one does not have easy access to a computer. Chapters 7 and 8 presented a number of statistics that can readily be hand-computed, if the data set is small. The following section will provide a method of collecting and processing information from a field study.

1. FIELD STUDY DATA

We will work through a manual analysis of behaviour in a public elevator. These students were interested in whether passengers in an elevator would communicate (signal) the nervousness they felt because of the close proximity forced on people riding in an elevator. Three hypotheses were proposed in that study (Bonnar, 1992):

• females passengers would be more likely to signal than males;

• the more people present in the elevator, the higher the amount of signalling;

• the higher the status of the person, the lower the amount of signalling.

The data were collected on tally sheets such as the one described in Chapter 5 (see Figure 5.1). The student observers indicated on a tally sheet whether or not passengers in the elevator signalled (i.e., did the passengers exhibit any "nervous and/or unnecessary actions performed by people whose personal space is altered in some way" (Bonnar, 1992, p. 7). Signalling included such common behaviours as "staring at the elevator numbers, pushing the elevator buttons for no apparent reason, staring at the floor and subjects shifting their bodies in a nervous manner" (Bonnar, 1992, p. 8). Also entered on the tally sheet was the gender of each new passenger, the person's status (professor, student, other) and the number of people on the elevator.

Figure 15.1 illustrates how the ***tally sheet*** was set up. Note that each line on the tally sheets records the information for one subject. Column 1 records whether the passenger signalled in some way; column 2 records the gender of the passenger, column 3 records the number of passengers present during the observation; column 4 records the status of the passenger.

Having recorded the information on the sheets for 150 passengers, the task now is to analyze the results. The best way to do this is to set up a ***master table*** for the results, enter the observations into the master table, and then derive the results tables from the master table. By using a master table, you will only need to make one pass through the raw data. From the master table you can create any other required tables showing the relation between the independent variables and the dependent variable.

STEP 1

SET UP A MASTER TABLE.

A master table is generally set up on 11 1/2 by 14" paper. Using the paper so that the long side is across the top, arrange categories of the dependent variable on the left side of the sheet, with the categories "Signal Given" and "No Signal Given" as labels. Categories of the independent variables are arranged across the top of the master table. In this case we have three independent variables: gender, status, and number on the elevator. Each observation ends up in one—and only one—cell of the master table. Thus a female student, who is the fifth person entering the elevator, and pushes the button for the third floor three times would end up in one cell only.

STEP 2

TRANSFER DATA TO THE MASTER TABLE.

Once observations have been completed, the tally sheet data are transferred to the master table. Normally each observation is entered into the applicable cell with a short stroke; these are grouped together so that the fifth line entered into a cell is a line across the other four. Each group then reflects five observations falling into the cell. (See Figure 15.2). Later these can be counted and a total for each cell entered and circled at the bottom of the cell.

STEP 3

CREATE THE INDIVIDUAL TABLES.

To test the three hypotheses, three tables would be created, each showing the relation between signalling/non-signalling and each of gender (Table 15.1), status, and group size (Table 15.2). To determine the number of cases for each cell of the new table you simply add up the count in the appropriate cells of the master table. For example, to find out how many males versus females were seen signalling, one simply adds together the male cells (the first six cells) and then the female cells (next six cells). These two numbers would then be incorporated into the number of observations of males and females who signalled. Similar procedures are then followed to get the count on the number of males and females not signalling.

STEP 4

FORMAT THE TABLES.

Tables 15.1 and 15.2 show the format for two of the tables. Various features of these tables are to be noted:

FIGURE 15.1 TALLY SHEET FOR RECORDING OBSERVATIONS

	SIGNALLING		GENDER		STATUS			GROUP STATUS	
ID #	YES	NO	MALE	FEMALE	STUDENT	PROFESSOR	OTHER	4 OR FEWER	5 OR MORE
1	✓		✓		✓			✓	
2	✓			✓	✓			✓	
3		✓		✓	✓				✓
4	✓		✓			✓			✓
etc	✓			✓	✓				✓

FIGURE 15.2   MASTER TABLE FOR ELEVATOR STUDY

Number Present	FEMALE						MALE					
	4 OR FEWER			5 OR MORE			4 OR FEWER			5 OR MORE		
Status/ Signal	S	P	O	S	P	O	S	P	O	S	P	O
Signal given	⑳	㉑	③	④	②	①	⑱	⑨	①	⑮	①	—
No signal given	⑨	⑦	①	①	⑫	①	⑤	④	②	①	①	①

Status categories: S = Student
P = Professor
O = Other

SOURCE: Anne Marie Bonnar, "To Signal or Not to Signal: A Study of Personal Space and Behaviour." Antigonish: St. Francis Xavier University, First Year Paper for Sociology 100, March, 1992. (This project was jointly conducted by Anne Marie Bonnar and Erin Timmons.) Reprinted with permission.

• **Table title:** The title reports the name of the dependent variable followed by the independent variable. Any control variables would follow. Sometimes it is a good idea to report where and when the observations were made.

• **Lines to separate sections of the table:** Following the table title, draw two closely spaced lines to separate the table title from the body of the table. Single lines will be used to separate other sections of the table.

TABLE 15.1   SIGNALLING BEHAVIOUR BY GENDER

	GENDER					
	MALE		FEMALE		TOTAL	
SIGNALLING BEHAVIOUR	N	%	N	%	N	%
Signalling	44	75.9	51	55.4	95	63.3
Non-signalling	14	24.1	41	44.6	55	36.7
TOTALS	58	100.0	92	100.0	150	100.0

Chi-Square = 6.449
Degrees of freedom = 1
Probability = <0.05 (reject null hypothesis)

SOURCE: Adapted from Anne Marie Bonnar, "To Signal or Not to Signal: A Study of Personal Space and Behaviour." Antigonish: St. Francis Xavier University, First Year Paper for Sociology 100, March, 1992. (This project was jointly conducted by Anne Marie Bonnar and Erin Timmons.)

TABLE 15.2 SIGNALLING BEHAVIOUR BY NUMBER OF PEOPLE ON THE ELEVATOR

| | NUMBER OF PEOPLE | | | | | |
| | 4 OR FEWER | | 5 OR MORE | | TOTAL | |
SIGNALLING BEHAVIOUR	N	%	N	%	N	%
Signalling	72	72.0	23	46.0	95	63.3
Non-signalling	28	28.0	27	54.0	55	36.7
TOTALS	100	100.0	50	100.0	150	100.0

SOURCE: Adapted from Anne Marie Bonnar, "To Signal or Not to Signal: A Study of Personal Space and Behaviour." Antigonish: St. Francis Xavier University, First Year Paper for Sociology 100, March, 1992.(This project was jointly conducted by Anne Marie Bonnar and Erin Timmons.)

- **Independent variable across top of page:** Arrange categories of the independent variable across the top of the table, using easily understood category labels.

- **Dependent variable arranged on the vertical axis:** Note that the dependent variable is arranged along the side of the page. Once again, use labels that are easy to understand and that will communicate clearly to your reader what would be included in each category.

- **Calculated column percentages:** Note also that the percentages are calculated on each of the columns. The rule is to calculate percentages toward the independent variable (adding up to 100 percent on each category of the independent variable). For example, if we wished to calculate the appropriate percentages for looking at the relation between gender (independent variable) and signalling (dependent variable), we would calculate what percentage of males signal or do not signal. We would then do a similar calculation for the females. In this way, we can compare the percentage of males signalling with the percentage of females doing likewise. The reason you would not calculate the percentage toward the dependent variable is that we are not so much interested in the distribution of signalling by gender (we might have a different proportion of males and females in our sample and therefore more males might signal simply because there might have been more male passengers).

Occasionally tables are created where the percentages are run across the page: this is usually done to accommodate situations where there are a number of categories of the independent variable and, in order to have enough space, the table is turned sideways.

To calculate the percentage, divide the cell value by the marginal total (this is the column total if the dependent variable is arranged on the vertical axis) and multiply by 100. In Table 15.1 the first cell percentage would be calculated by $(44 \div 58) \times 100 = 75.9\%$. These percentages should be reported to an accuracy of one decimal point. The total should report the actual total—either 99.9, 100.0, or 100.1.

- **More complex tables:** More complex tables containing control variables may also be created from the master table. However, before constructing such tables, the material in Chapter 16 should be consulted in order to establish what model is being tested and how the results should be interpreted. For ease of interpretation, arrange the dependent variable along the vertical axis, with categories of the independent variables on the horizontal axis.

STEP 5

CALCULATE TESTS OF SIGNIFICANCE AND MEASURES OF ASSOCIATION.

Tests of significance and measures of association may be calculated manually. Chapter 8 provides examples of how such computations may be done. The results of these computations may be entered below the table, as shown in Table 15.1.

STEP 6

INTERPRET THE RESULTS.

In interpreting the results of the analysis, we typically focus on just one of the categories of the dependent variable; in the case of the elevator study, we would simply compare the percentage of males who are seen to signal in the elevator with the percentage of females who are seen to do likewise. In the case of Table 15.1, we would note that "while 75.9 percent of the males signal, 55.4 percent of the females signal." It is unnecessary to report the "Not Signal" categories since these are simply the remaining cases adding up to 100.0 percent. The writer of a report should also note whether the differences between the gender categories are statistically significant, whether the differences observed were in the direction predicted in the hypotheses, and report on any measures of the strength of the association.

A Chi-square test of significance could have been performed on this data using the procedures outlined in Chapter 8 (see Box 8.4).

2. EXPERIMENTAL DATA

Using the procedures outlined in Chapters 7 and 8, it should be possible for the researcher to analyze experimental data without using a computer. Suppose you do a between-subjects experiment: you could compute the dependent variable *means* and *standard deviations* for your treatment group and for your control group. (See Chapter 7 if you do not remember how to calculate means and standard deviations.)

Box 8.5 may be used as a model to calculate a between-subjects *t*-test. If you have a within-subject design, refer to Box 8.6. If you require a one-way analysis of variance, use Box 8.7 as a model. If you require an ANOVA you will probably find that it will save time to enter the values into a computer and have the machine, equipped with appropriate software such as SPSS, do the calculations.

> *To perform this analysis using SPSS see the ANOVA procedure in Appendix A.*

3. SURVEY AND NON-REACTIVE DATA

While survey and non-reactive data could be analyzed by recording the information on a master table (see above), generally the number of variables measured is substantial and it would usually be advisable to learn how to use a computer to process the information. However, if there are just a few variables measured, even with a large number of cases, it is possible to transfer the information to a master table and then derive cross-tabulation tables from it. But if you wanted to calculate means, standard deviations, or correlations among the variables, the chore of hand-computing the results would be onerous unless there were few cases in the study. In most situations, the use of computer technology is advised.

B. ANALYZING DATA USING A COMPUTER

The remaining sections of this chapter apply if a computer is to be used to assist in the analysis. While this process is relatively straightforward, there are a number of points to keep in mind so that data entry and error checking will proceed efficiently.

In most cases, the contemporary researcher will be working either on a personal computer (PC) or (MAC), or on a terminal which is connected to a "main frame" computer. The student need not understand much about computers in order to use them—just as you do not need to know much about engines in order to drive a car.

A simple analogy will introduce the reader to the computer. Think of entering a large, strange house. It is a little frightening at first, but after a while you will find that it can be fun exploring it. The first thing you will have to do is get inside. You will need a key, such as a secret password, in order to enter. Let us imagine that you have been provided with a password so you can get into the house. Looking down the hall you realize that there are many rooms in this house. The hall represents the computer's operating system; there are many procedures and utilities available to the user in the various rooms. Having entered the

house, you now have to decide which room to explore. The first room is marked Editor (here you can make, and modify files). The second room is marked Storage (you can save files here and get them later). A third door is marked SPSS (social science data is analyzed here). A fourth door is marked Word Processing (here reports are written and modified). A fifth door is marked Line Printer (here files get copied onto paper so that they will be available to the user). There are many other doors in the house, but these need not be explored immediately by the beginning social science student.

In this house, one starts off in the hall (the operating system) and from there one enters a room, does something, and then re-enters the hall. From there one either leaves the house or goes into another room to perform other tasks. The point is that it is from the operating system that one branches out to do other tasks and functions. The computer will provide a cue to inform you when it is in the operating system mode. These cues are called prompts. Symbols such as: "$", ">", or "?" are used. So if you get lost in the house try to get back to the operating system, back to the operating system prompt.

Before rules are given for the entry of the data into the computer two ideas need to be explored in a little more detail. These two are *files* and *editors*.

1. FILES

When data, or the text of a report, are entered into a computer they will be stored in a *file*. Computer files are just like those found in a filing cabinet, they contain information on some topic, and are arranged so that they can be retrieved easily. Many computers use a two-word naming convention for files. The first part consists of the file name, the second part the file type. The two parts are separated by a "." Typically, one is allowed eight character spaces for the file name, three for the file type. For the data collected in a study, one might use the name: JOAN.DAT. If Joan were involved in a number of studies, she would need to use unique names for each of them. However, she would always use the same file type label for data—perhaps use ".DAT". Later, we will need to know about other kinds of files and additional file types will be introduced. If a researcher is working on several studies, then the file names should refer to the subject of each one. The following names might be used to name the raw data files for five different studies:

ABORTION.DAT

ASPIRE.DAT

CAPPUN.DAT

ESTEEM.DAT

PRESTIGE.DAT

2. EDITORS

Computer systems will have one or more "editors"—simple word-processing programs—available to its users. Editor programs are used to manage the entry of information into a file. Normally there will be procedures to move quickly through a file, to append information, or to make changes in the text. There will be a flashing cursor on the screen which marks the position the machine is ready to work at. You will need to learn how to make use of the many features that are available on the editor you are using. And, after you have completed your work, you will need to know how to save your work permanently so that it will be available to you next time you sign on the computer. The operating system will have a simple command which will allow you to list all your files on the screen. You will learn how to call any file into the Editor so that you can look at it on the screen, perhaps make changes in it, and then print it on a line printer if you need a copy.

C. RULES FOR DATA ENTRY

Data entry is simply the process of transferring the information collected in a study to a computing device. We will assume that you have figured out how to use the Editor to create a file and that you are now ready to begin data entry. The following rules provide guidelines for data entry.

RULE 15.1

NUMBER QUESTIONNAIRES, FORMS, AND DATA SOURCES.

Questionnaires or data collection forms are numbered, normally beginning with 001 (or 0001 if there are more than 1,000 cases). This **ID number** is written on the front page of the instrument (usually top, right corner). This number will be entered into the computer and provides the only link between the particular form and the data that is entered into the computer file. If an error is found in the data, the original form can be located by using the ID number, then the information can be checked, and the error corrected. Keep the questionnaires or forms sorted by their ID number.

RULE 15.2

CODE ANY UNCODED QUESTIONS.

If there are questions which have not been pre-coded (such as occupational codes, or open-ended opinion questions), they should now be coded and the values written on the questionnaire (or form) in the margin next to the question. In the case of occupational prestige codes, they would be looked up and a value entered onto the questionnaire.

RULE 15.3

DO A COLUMN COUNT.

Using a blank copy of the questionnaire (or form), go through it, and, opposite each question, indicate where it will be entered onto the terminal screen. Typically, screen widths are 80 columns wide. This means that you can enter 80 digits across the screen before you run out of space.

The first three columns will be used for the ID number of the questionnaire, the fourth column will be used to identify the record number for the respondent. (This is required only for questionnaires which require more than 80 columns to enter the data: record #1 refers to the first line of data, record #2 the next set of data for the respondent, and so forth.) If a question can have values between zero and nine, then one column will be required to record the data; if the values range up to 99 then two columns will be required; if the values range up to 999, three columns will be required. On the right-hand margin of the questionnaire (or form) these values are recorded. The right-hand margin might look something like this:

> Variable Columns
>
> ID 1- 3
>
> Record # 4
>
> Blank 5
>
> Gender 6
>
> Yr. Birth 7- 8
>
> Income 9-14
>
> Occupation 15-16

In a short questionnaire the information for each variable will fit onto one 80-column line; each questionnaire will occupy one line of data. If more than one record (or line) is required, then a second record is used, with the first three columns being saved for a repeat of the ID number. The fourth column will contain a "2," meaning that it is the second record for the questionnaire. In the case of a questionnaire requiring two records, the data might be set in a way similar to the example below:

Note the first four columns. The first three contain the ID number (which has also been written on the questionnaire) and the fourth column refers to the record number. What we have here is respondent 001 first record; then the same respondent 001, second record; this is followed by respondent 002, first record, followed by respon-

```
0011476989232333 23222111222111 222456345644556666663339
0012453437676767221122211 1112299122876321453213345222
0021456338992212 21222113222112 2233411003344556654432211
0022234343445857463748 4985050595211222333423334444
```

dent 002, second record. It is not critical that the ID numbers be in sequence, but the case must be together—record one must be followed by record two for each case, even if the cases are not in order. The blanks in the data set are discussed below. (Incidentally, the reason we enter the ID number and then the record number is that most computer sorting routines will be able to sort your file with one simple command.)

RULE 15.4

ENTER DATA WITH THE HELP OF A PARTNER.

Inexperienced terminal operators will find that data entry will be much easier, and be done with fewer errors, if two people work together on entering the data. One person can read the numbers off the questionnaire, with the partner entering the values into the terminal.

RULE 15.5

LEAVE INTERNAL BLANKS TO MARK A NEW PAGE.

Errors can be identified more quickly if, after the end of each page in the questionnaire, a blank is left in the data. The column of blanks must always line up when the data are printed out; if the blanks do not line up then an error has been made and must be corrected. The first six lines of a data set are listed in the following example, showing how the blanks line up:

Note that the fourth line of data contains an error; by examining the listing it becomes apparent that the error is somewhere in the data entered from page two of the questionnaire (there are too many digits in the space reserved for page two). While the introduction of blanks to mark the end of pages is helpful in error detection, if the use of these blanks forces the use of an extra line of data for each respondent, then it is probably best not to include them in the data. The advantage of having them would be outweighed by the additional work involved in error-checking an additional line of data for each respondent.

RULE 15.6

SIMPLIFY MISSING VALUE CODES.

If respondents do not answer a question, or if the question is not applicable, a *missing value code* is used. These should be kept as simple and as consistent as possible. Where possible, use the values "9", "99", or "999" for one 1, two 1, and three 1 column variables respectively. Suppose a respondent is asked to indicate gender as either male or female and leaves the question blank. Instead of leaving the column blank, a "9" would be inserted into the appropriate column.

While it is possible to use alternate codes (question not answered or question not applicable) such as "8" for not answered, and "9" for not applicable, such discrimination

PAGE 1	PAGE 2	PAGE 3	PAGE 4
00112435445523	211212333448976999	123232111123212	23411112
00211231231234	322213222122232212	432235333211232	34532432
00314321234443	233445324433321212	332122341122233	23323222
00413444688822	1222221122321233219	234433221222321	34521211
00513335543221	223332221114124211	332111422111212	32121223
00614322345432	231143321122122121	112211222111231	22132454

should only be made where it is known that the information will be used later; if it is not going to be used, keep matters simple by using the single code "9" to cover both cases. In occupational codes, it may be necessary to provide special codes for "housewife" if values are not provided in the occupational code system being used. For the nine-point attitudinal scales, "0" is used for the missing value code.

A code must be entered for every question, even if it is not answered. The reason for this is that, when instructions are given to the computer, each question is identified with particular columns in the data; each question, therefore, must be in the identical position in all lines of data. (Actually most programs allow the use of a space or a comma to separate questions but, since error detection is easiest where questions occupy the identical columns in each question, we will use the same column method.)

RULE 15.7

DOCUMENT RESEARCH DECISIONS.

When data are being entered into the terminal, a number of decisions will be required. A questionnaire may have a lot of missing data and the person entering the data might decide that it would be better to discard the questionnaire. Set the questionnaire or form to one side and consult with fellow researchers as to whether that data should be used. Cases may arise where a respondent has checked two items on a question where only one was expected. Generally these discrepancies will be rare enough for it to be appropriate to "flip a coin" to decide which of the two will be taken. (One would not systematically take the highest placed item on

the list since that would systematically bias the results toward those items listed first.) When such a decision has been made, the decision should be marked clearly on the questionnaire and initialled by the person making the decision. With such documentation, it is then possible for others to check through the data and understand what coding decisions were made, and by whom.

RULE 15.8

CODE FOR INFORMATION NOT ON THE QUESTIONNAIRE.

Frequently there will be information that is not coded on the questionnaire that should be appended to the data. It is always recommended that provision be made to include a code to identify who collected the original information, who did the coding on the questionnaire, who did the data entry, and any other information that may be useful in the later data analysis or in error checking. The reason why it is helpful to code who did the coding is that if there are systematic differences between coders in dealing with different questions, then the cases dealt with by each coder can quickly be identified and compared. Appropriate corrections can then be made without too much fuss.

RULE 15.9

USE DOUBLE DATA ENTRY.

Where resources allow, it is recommended that data be entered twice, by different individuals. A computer program can then be used to compare the two files, flagging any differences between the files. This technique is extremely helpful in reducing data entry errors.

D. INITIAL STEPS IN CLEANING DATA ON A MAINFRAME COMPUTER

After the data have been entered into the computer and saved in a file, it is time to begin the systematic search for errors so that they can be corrected before analysis of the data begins. This process is referred to as *cleaning the data*.

STEP 1

SORT QUESTIONNAIRES (OR FORMS) BY ID NUMBERS.

During error correction it will be necessary to have all the questionnaires available: these should be sorted by ID number so that any particular questionnaire can be found quickly.

STEP 2

SORT FILE BY LINE TYPE.

When there are two or more lines of data (records) for each case, the first step will be to sort the data file into separate files, one for each line. The sort procedure, possibly called "Sort" or "SortMerge", will be available in the operating system of your computer. The objective is to create new files so that all the line ones are together in a file and all the line twos are a separate file and so forth. It is also useful to sort the cases within each file by ID number, as this will facilitate spotting errors of repeated data lines (data entered twice) or a missed line. If there are multiple lines per case, then the following procedures will have to be repeated for each line file.

STEP 3

LIST FILE ON PRINTER.

The file(s) being checked should be listed on a printer. The printout should be examined, and any irregularities circled. Check the following:
- All lines must end in the same column. If there are too few or too many columns in a line, it means that questions were either missed or entered twice. Mark discrepant lines so that they can be checked against the original questionnaire and the error(s) located. The file must be "rectangular" with no ragged edges.
- Any internal blanks must line up vertically. If end-of-page blanks have been used, one can quickly identify situations where there have been too many, or too few, entries made from a particular page on the questionnaire. Once again, mark any discrepancies.
- When there are two or more files to be checked, ensure that the file lengths are equal. If 165 questionnaires have been completed, there must be 165 lines in each of the files.
- Proofread ID numbers (columns one through three) to ensure that there are no repeated, or missing, ID numbers. Again, mark any errors. (Some cases may have been withdrawn so those ID values will be missing.)
- Finally, there must be no blank lines or partial lines left in the data set.

STEP 4

CHECK FOR NON-NUMERICS.

In cases where the file is not supposed to include any non-numerical data, checks should be run to catch any such non-numerical data. Simple programs can be written to accomplish this (one is included on the instructor's disk that goes with this text), or one can inspect the data visually to attempt to locate any such errors. The hardest such errors to detect are situations where an "O" has been entered rather than a "0"; or a "l" instead of a "1". If you do not detect such errors prior to submitting the job to SPSS, an SPSS warning will result if inappropriate non-numerics are present in the file.

STEP 5

CHECK FOR OUT-OF-RANGE VALUES.

Many of the errors in the data will have been removed by going through the first four procedures. However, two or more errors can lead to a situation where the file may be perfectly "rectangular" yet have questions coded into the wrong columns. Furthermore, slips may have been made in entering the data; for example, a "3" may have been entered when the value should have been a "2". Many such errors will show up if a frequency distribution is run on each column in the data set. For example, if, in column five, the legitimate entries include "1" for males, "2" for females, or "9" for no response, then any other value would be in error. Most computer installations will have utility programs for running such frequency distributions. (A program which performs this task is on the instructor's disk provided with this text.) The distribution should then be listed on the line printer. Once again, any discrepant values should be circled on the printout. A final alternative here would be to wait until the SPSS processing begins to identify out-of-range values and, then, with SELECT IF statements, identify the ID numbers of cases with incorrect values in them.

STEP 6

MAKE CORRECTIONS TO ELIMINATE OUT-OF-RANGE VALUES.

Looking at the printout, you will have certain columns that have been identified as containing out-of-range values. It will be necessary to identify the line(s) that have these incorrect values in them. Some Editor programs will permit the searching of particular columns for specified values. If you have access to an Editor with this facility you will be able to find the lines with the inappropriate values quickly. If such a program is not available, the chances are good that one of the quantitative social scientists will have a utility program for doing such searches. (One which does this is on the instructor's disk.) If all fails, get out a ruler, place it on the printout you got in Step 4 above, and scan the appropriate column for the out-of-range value. Mark the error. Having identified the questionnaire where the error has occurred, proofread the data, and make the necessary corrections. It is useful to proofread the questionnaire on a number of columns before and after the error to make certain that adjacent columns are correct.

STEP 7

MAKE CORRECTIONS TO FILES.

After the above errors have been identified, the files should be corrected by comparing the values that should be present (those in the original questionnaire) to those that are present in the data file. The questionnaires can be retrieved quickly, since they are in order; the ID numbers on the error lines identify which questionnaires have to be checked. A printout of the corrected files should then be made on the line printer.

STEP 8

MERGE DATA FILES TOGETHER.

Once all the files have been corrected, and you have confirmed that they all have the same number of lines, they should be merged together and sorted, so that the cases will be in order, and the line 1 of case 1 will be followed by the second line of case 1. The sorting should result in a file where the first four columns are as follows:

> 0011 ...
> 0012 ...
> 0013 ...
> 0021 ...
> 0022 ...
> 0023 ...
> 0031 ...
> 0032 ...
> 0033 ...

In the following example, there are three lines for each case. After confirming that the file is correctly sorted, that it contains the appropriate number of lines, and that there are no blank lines, the file should be saved. It is now ready for processing by SPSS. (See Appendix A.) Additional error-checking is possible once SPSS processing has commenced; however, the cleaner the data set prior to analysis, the fewer the delays you will encounter later.

E. KEY TERMS

Cleaning the data	ID number	Tally sheet
Data entry	Master table	
File	Missing value code	

F. KEY POINTS

Many analyses can be carried out without the assistance of a computer. Observational studies which collect information on a few variables (typically five or fewer) and not too many cases can be hand-tabulated readily.

Observational studies frequently proceed by recording information on *tally sheets*. This information may then be transferred to a *master table*. From the master table a number of individual tables which permit the testing of various null hypotheses may be calculated.

Typically, tables should include a title, place the independent variable on the horizontal axis, and place the dependent variable on the vertical axis. Percentages should be calculated for the vertical columns, and rounded to an accuracy of one decimal point. If applicable, the results of a test of significance should be included, noting the raw Chi-square, *t*, or *F* score, the degrees of freedom, and whether the results indicate a probability of less than or greater than 0.05.

In interpreting the results of contingency tables, the researcher compares the percentages of one category of the dependent variable for each category of the independent variable.

If mainframe or personal computers are used in data analysis, the user will have to become familiar with the *operating system* of the computer. *Editors* are programs to provide a way of entering information into the computer. This information is stored in *files*.

In entering data into the computer, one usually numbers the forms (questionnaires) and enters the information into the same columns for each variable, using 9s to indicate missing answers.

The following suggestions will also ease the preparation of data:

• for inexperienced computer operators, it is a good idea to work in teams, one person calling out the numbers to be entered, the other entering the information;

• leave a blank column at the end of each page of a form or questionnaire (this helps eliminate many errors by making them easier to detect);

• where coding decisions are made, they should be marked on the form and initialled by the coder;

• where more than one interviewer, coder, or data entry person is involved, it is a good idea to include, as supplementary information, a code identifying who performed each of these functions for each respondent. This will speed up checking for systematic differences between the decisions of different coders;

• to reduce data entry errors, it is recommended that data be entered twice and a computer program used to identify discrepancies between the two versions.

Initial cleaning of the data is commenced after data entry has been completed. The steps are:

• sort and create a file for each record type;

• list file(s) to be corrected on a printer, checking to ensure that there are no ragged edges and that internal blanks line up;

• check that the files to be merged are the same length;

• check that no cases are missed and that no cases are entered twice;

• check that no blank lines are included;

• use procedures to detect out-of-range values and non-numerics. These should be corrected before data processing begins.

G. EXERCISES

I. Using the information in Figure 15.2, set up a properly formatted table to test the null hypothesis for the relation between signalling and status of the subject. Hand-compute a test of significance for the relationship. What do you conclude about the null hypothesis?

2. The following figure shows a portion of the data for a study. Reviewing the section of the chapter dealing with error detection methods may help you locate some of the *eight* errors that can be found in scanning the data file. Two of the errors are hard to see; so if you only find six that is understandable.

The computer could find the others in a flash. Hint:
check for non-numerical entries. Good luck.

PARTIAL PRINTOUT FOR DATA

```
00112435445523    211212333448976999    123232111123212    23411112
00211231231234    322213222122232212    432235333211232    34530432
00314321234443    233445324433321212    332122341122233    23323222
00413444688822    122222112232123319    234433221222321    34521211
00513335543221    223332221114124211    332111422111212    321212
00513335543221    223332221114124211    332111422111212    32121223
00614322345432    231143321122122121    112211222111231    22132454
00812234342334    6545645646-0988777    793787987987423    98798777
00917879879877    878777778723442343    789987987777987    79879879
01018977772221    987798798778778987    798798777A97777    77788777
```

<EOF>

TESTING SIMPLE CAUSAL MODELS

In non-experimental research, how do we test whether a proposed explanation for some relationship has any merit? Suppose, for example, that you want to see if your data support the idea that heightened parental expectations among high SES parents explain the observed link between SES and the educational aspirations of youths. This chapter describes procedures for evaluating causal models such as the one suggested above. First, the type of model being dealt with must be determined: is it a source of spuriousness, an intervening variable, or a candidate variable model? (See Chapter 11 for a description of these models.) Second, the appropriate statistical procedures for the analysis must be determined. This determination will be based on the level of measurement of the variables involved in each of the relevant variables.

To establish a causal relationship, three conditions must be met:

• the variables must be *associated*;

• they must be in a plausible *causal sequence*; and,

• they *must not be spuriously connected*.

To show that two variables are *associated*, one has to demonstrate that they vary together. To argue that one variable is producing changes in another, one has to demonstrate that as one changes, so does the other. Empirical association is reflected through contingency table analysis (CROSSTABS), differences in means across categories (MEANS, T-TEST, ANOVA, MANOVA), and various correlational techniques (CORRELATION, REGRESSION).

To demonstrate a plausible *causal sequence* is largely a matter of theory or of common sense. What is meant here is not

only that the independent variable precedes the dependent variable in time, but that the ordering is believable. Usually, giving a little thought to the causal order will provide an answer. For example, it would be foolish to argue that the "size of your present community" influences the size of the "community in which you were born." The causal sequencing is wrong: the present cannot influence the past. The size of community one has chosen to live in may, of course, be influenced by the size of community in which one grew up.

To demonstrate that a relationship is not *spurious* is always a challenge, one which can never fully be met. (Recall that a spurious relation is one where some third factor is influencing both the independent and the dependent variables: thus their covariation may be the result of the common connection to the source of spuriousness.) A critic may always point to some potential **source of spuriousness** for the relation between the variables. The best the first-time researcher can hope to achieve is to deal with the more obvious potential sources of spuriousness. This chapter shows some techniques for testing three- and four-variable causal models.

A. THREE-VARIABLE CAUSAL MODELS

It turns out that identical analyses may be used to test different **three-variable causal models**. Such models generally attempt to explain or elaborate on some relationship that is known to exist, or that a research project expects to demonstrate. We will use some sample data to illustrate: suppose we have done a survey on 395 se-

TABLE 16.1 PERCENTAGE OF SENIOR HIGH SCHOOL STUDENTS WITH PLANS FOR FURTHER EDUCATION BY SOCIO-ECONOMIC STATUS (SES)

TYPE OF PLAN	LOW SES BACKGROUND		HIGH SES BACKGROUND		TOTAL	
	N	%	N	%	N	%
Some plans	144	73.1	176	88.9	320	81.0
No plans	53	26.9	22	11.1	75	19.0
TOTAL	197	100.0	198	100.0	395	100.0

$X^2 = 16.021$ df = 1   Significant at the .001 level.

nior high school students concerning their plans for education beyond the high school level. Table 16.1 presents the results.

Table 16.1 is a standard contingency table whose computations could be done with the CROSSTABS procedure. A shorter version of the table is also possible and will be used to illustrate the model testing to be presented below. The shorter version is illustrated in Table 16.2.

With the information provided it is possible to reconstruct the original table. As 73.1 percent of 197 low SES students plan on further education, it is possible to determine the number of students who fall into the category (0.731 x 197 = 144).

Similar calculations could be done to reconstruct Table 16.1.

The much simplified Table 16.2 is easy to read and focuses attention on the two percentage figures that are to be compared: while some 88.9 percent of the students with high socio-economic status backgrounds plan on some post-secondary education, 73.1 percent of those with low SES backgrounds have similar plans. Note that there is a 15.8 percentage point difference by SES categories in those planning on post-secondary education. We will use this table in discussing the first causal model, the intervening variable model.

TABLE 16.2 PERCENTAGE OF SENIOR HIGH SCHOOL STUDENTS WITH PLANS FOR FURTHER EDUCATION BY SOCIO-ECONOMIC STATUS (SES)

	LOW SES BACKGROUND	HIGH SES BACKGROUND
Percentage who have plans for further education	73.1	88.9
Number of cases	197	198

$X^2 = 16.021$ df = 1   Significant at the .001 level.

1. TESTING FOR INTERVENING VARIABLES

A. THE INTERVENING VARIABLE MODEL

In an intervening variable model the interest is in understanding the relationship between X and Y—understanding the mechanism by which X is connected to Y. Frequently the researcher will be testing a number of alternative explanations of how X influences Y. In the case of one intervening variable, the relationship could be diagrammed as follows:

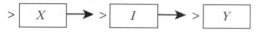

In this diagram, I is the ***intervening variable***, or the linking variable between X and Y. The hypothesis is that variations in X cause variations in I, which, in turn, influences Y. Typically, one would propose a number of possible intervening variables, so the following diagram would be more appropriate:

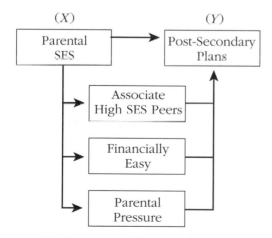

In this diagram, three alternative explanations are suggested for the connec-

tion between X and Y. The researcher would collect data that measure each of the variables involved and conduct the appropriate statistical tests to determine, which, if any, of the proposed alternative explanations, or intervening variables, explains the connection between X and Y.

Let us suppose, for example, that three alternative explanations are proposed for the relation between SES and likelihood of post-secondary educational plans:

(i) that high SES students associate with high SES peers who plan on post-secondary training;

(ii) high SES students perceive little financial difficulty in attaining a higher education and, therefore, are more likely to plan on such training than are low SES students; and

(iii) high SES parents are more likely to put pressure on their children to participate in post-secondary training.

How would we go about testing these three alternatives?

B. THE RATIONALE BEHIND THE TESTS

The thinking behind the test is as follows: if we have a *causal relationship* between X and Y (SES and Plans) and propose a link to explain how X influences Y, then X (SES) should not be able to influence Y (Plans) if we hold the linking variable constant. The argument is that X influences Y through I. A plumbing analogy may be helpful. Water can only flow from X to Y through a pipe. If you turn off a valve located between X and Y, then increasing the volume of water flowing into the pipe at point X will have no influence on Y, because the valve has been turned off; however if we open the valve, then changes in the pressure at X will influence the flow at Y. Keeping the analogy in mind, let us now see if we can "control" for the intervening variable.

The first explanation is that high SES students tend to associate more with other high SES students, and that this is the link between SES and educational plans. How can we analyze the data to see if the results are consistent with the model we wish to test? Using a contingency table analysis (CROSSTABS), we will run the relation between SES and plans, controlling for the intervening variable, association with high SES peers. We wish to see what happens when the control is applied. We wish to see whether the original 15.8 percentage-point difference in the relationship between SES and plans: (a) increases, (b) stays the same, (c) decreases/disappears, is (d) mixed.

C. JACKSON'S RULE OF THIRDS

According to *Jackson's rule of thirds*, if the original difference between the categories increases by one-third or more, we will interpret this as an *increase*, or a strengthening, of the original relationship; if

the difference remains within one-third of the original, we will interpreted this as an indication that the relationship has *remained the same*; if the difference decreases by more than one-third, we will interpret this as a *decrease/disappearance* of the relationship; finally, if the relationship is markedly different when different control categories are compared to one another (e.g., it disappears in one category, but stays the same in the other), the result is *mixed*.

To apply the rule of thirds to the case under examination, we must first decide where the cut-points are between the thirds. To do this we take the original difference of 15.8 and divide by 3; this yields a value of 5.3. Table 16.3 presents these values and shows how the differences would be interpreted.

D. USING CROSSTABS TO TEST FOR AN INTERVENING VARIABLE

But what are our expectations? If the model being tested is correct, we would expect the relationship between SES and plans to decrease/disappear when the relationship is run, controlling for the intervening variable. If SES influences plans through the linking

TABLE 16.3 APPLYING JACKSON'S RULE OF THIRDS

SAMPLE DATA RESULTS	INTERPRETATION
Original difference: 88.9 − 73.1 = 15.8 Determining thirds: 15.8 ÷ 3 = 5.3	
Outcomes:	
a. If new difference is greater than 21.1 (15.8 + 5.3 = 21.1)	Increased
b. If new difference is between 10.5 and 21.1 (15.8 ± 5.3)	Stayed the same
c. If new difference is less than 10.5	Decreased/Disappeared
d. If new differences vary markedly across categories of the control variable	Mixed

variable, then, if we hold the linking variable constant, there should be no relation between SES and plans. Differences in level of planning by SES category should decrease/disappear when the control is applied. All other outcomes are interpreted as not supportive of the model. Table 16.4 presents summary data for five possible outcomes.

To interpret the outcomes it is necessary to determine whether the original relationship has increased, stayed the same, decreased/disappeared, or is mixed. The beginning researcher should keep the interpretation of the data as simple as possible. Only when the difference decreases/disappears, do we have possible support for an intervening variable model. Let us look at the five outcomes and suggest an interpretation for each one.

OUTCOME I

According to the rule of thirds, the relationship has decreased/disappeared. The original difference has been reduced to one percentage point in the case of those whose best friends have high SES, and to two percentage points

TABLE 16.4 PERCENT OF SENIOR HIGH SCHOOL STUDENTS WITH PLANS FOR FURTHER EDUCATION BY SOCIO-ECONOMIC STATUS (SES), CONTROLLING FOR SES OF BEST FRIEND, WITH FIVE POSSIBLE OUTCOMES

PERCENT PLANNING FURTHER EDUCATION	BEST FRIEND HIGH SES		BEST FRIEND LOW SES*	
	LOW SES BACKGROUND	HIGH SES BACKGROUND	LOW SES BACKGROUND	HIGH SES BACKGROUND
1st outcome difference:	92.0	93.0	71.0	69.0
		1.0		−2.0
2nd outcome difference:	74.0	92.0	71.0	86.0
		18.0		15.0
3rd outcome difference:	85.0	92.0	68.0	76.0
		7.0		8.0
4th outcome difference:	74.0	96.0	61.0	82.0
		22.0		21.0
5th outcome difference:	90.0	92.0	60.0	82.0
		2.0		22.0

*The original difference, with no control for SES of Best Friend, is shown below:

	LOW SES BACKGROUND	HIGH SES BACKGROUND
Percent who have plans for further education:	73.1	88.9
Difference:		15.8

for those whose best friends are classified as low SES. This is the only outcome—one where the original relationship decreases/disappears—which we consider to be consistent with the intervening variable causal model.

OUTCOME 2

The relationship stays the same, so the intervening variable model is to be rejected.

OUTCOME 3

This outcome supports the intervening variable model: the difference decreases/disappears; the interpretation is that the independent variable influences the dependent variable through the tested intervening variable.

OUTCOME 4

This outcome would lead us to reject the intervening variable model; the relationship is strengthened, so this suggests that the proposed alternative explanation is having an independent influence on the dependent variable.

OUTCOME 5

This outcome would also lead us to reject the intervening variable model: the difference decreases/disappears in one of the control categories, but increases in the other, suggesting a conditional effect—the intervening variable is probably having an independent influence, but only at certain levels of the intervening variable. This is an example of a *mixed* result.

To perform this analysis using SPSS see the CROSSTABS procedure in Appendix A.

E. USING MEANS TO TEST FOR AN INTERVENING VARIABLE

The second explanation proposed for the connection between SES and plans is that high SES students plan on post-secondary education because they know their families can afford it. We will assume that plans are measured in terms of the number of years of post-secondary education planned on (ratio level measurement), permitting the use of the MEANS procedure.

The logic is identical to the previous procedure. We will examine the difference in the number of years planned between SES categories: we will then rerun that relationship, controlling for whether students believe they will have enough financial support to permit them to do some post-secondary training. Once again, we will apply the rule of thirds to provide a guideline for the interpretation of the data. Table 16.5 (bottom) indicates that there is a 1.40 year difference in the number of years of post-secondary education planned by SES categories. The question is: will this difference increase, stay the same, decrease, disappear, or be mixed when the control for perceived financial support is applied?

Table 16.5 shows different outcomes. Once again, we look at the control table, examine the difference between the levels of financial support high and low SES students believe they have available to them, and contrast this difference with the original difference of 1.40 years.

OUTCOME 1

For those students who perceive that no financial support will be available for higher education, the data indicate a 1.91 year difference between SES categories in total years of post-

TABLE 16.5   MEAN YEARS OF FURTHER EDUCATION PLANNED BY SOCIO-ECONOMIC STATUS (SES), CONTROLLING FOR PERCEIVED SUPPORT FOR HIGHER EDUCATION, WITH FIVE POSSIBLE OUTCOMES

MEAN YEARS OF FURTHER EDUCATION PLANNED	NO SUPPORT		SUPPORT*	
	LOW SES BACKGROUND	HIGH SES BACKGROUND	LOW SES BACKGROUND	HIGH SES BACKGROUND
1st outcome difference;	1.49	3.40	3.30	5.26
		1.91		1.96
2nd outcome difference:	2.23	3.66	2.55	3.98
		1.43		1.43
3rd outcome difference:	1.56	2.27	3.42	4.10
		0.71		0.68
4th outcome difference:	2.35	2.48	3.77	3.92
		0.13		0.15
5th outcome difference:	1.64	3.13	3.89	4.01
		1.49		0.12

*The original difference, with no control for financial support, is shown below:

POST-HIGH SCHOOL PLANS	LOW SES BACKGROUND	HIGH SES BACKGROUND
Mean number of years of further education planned:	2.47	3.87
Difference:		1.40

secondary education planned. Among those who perceive support, the difference between the categories is 1.96 years. By applying the rule of thirds we see that the difference in both SES categories has increased by more than one-third, and we therefore argue that the relationship has been intensified: we must reject the intervening variable model. The intensification suggests that the perception of financial support has an independent, positive impact on the level of post-secondary planning.

OUTCOME 2

In the second outcome, in both the "No Support" and "Support" categories, the difference between the low and high SES students remains almost the same as the original difference of 1.40. We therefore reject the intervening variable model.

OUTCOME 3

In the third outcome, the difference has been reduced by more than one-third, and we therefore conclude that there is some evidence to support the intervening variable model.

OUTCOME 4

In both the "Support" and "No Support" categories, the differences in years planned have decreased/disappeared (dropped by more than two-thirds); this outcome supports the intervening variable model.

OUTCOME 5

The final outcome suggests a mixed result. The difference decreases/disappears within the "Support" category, but remains the same within the "No Support" category. We reject the intervening variable model. The data here suggest that the financial support variable has a conditional impact on years of post-secondary education planned.

> *To perform this analysis using SPSS see the MEANS procedure in Appendix A.*

F. USING PARTIAL CORR TO TEST FOR AN INTERVENING VARIABLE

Partial correlations are measures of the strength of an association which take into account one or more additional variables. (Refer to Chapter 7 for a more detailed discussion.) Partial correlations measure how closely two variables are associated when the influence of other variables is adjusted for: a first-order partial is one that takes into account one additional variable, and a second-order partial takes into account two additional variables. By combining CORRELATIONS and PARTIAL CORR we can test for an intervening variable.

In this case, we wish to test whether parental influence intervenes between SES and plans. Using correlational techniques, we would first establish that there is an association between SES and plans. If there is an association we would then proceed with the analysis to test whether the data are consistent with an intervening variable model.

If the intervening variable model is correct, we should at least expect the following:

- that the correlation between adjacent variables will be greater than between non-adjacent categories ($r_{XY} < r_{XI}$ or r_{IY});.

- that if I is controlled, the relation between X and Y should disappear. This could be done with a partial correlation coefficient ($r_{XY.I} = 0$).

The model will be tested using two correlational techniques, CORRELATIONS and PARTIAL CORR. Table 16.6 presents the Pearson correlations between three variables: Parental pressure index (I), SES score (X), and years of future education planned (Y).

The first test is to see if the magnitude of the correlations are consistent with the model being tested. The prediction was that adjacent correlations would be higher than non-adjacent ones. The adjacent correlations are I-X and I-Y and the correlations are .31 and .46 respectively. The non-adjacent correlation is X-Y and the correlation is .22. So far, the data are consistent with the intervening variable model.

The next question is whether the partial correlation will be increased, stay the same, or decrease/disappear when I is controlled. For this analysis, a partial correlation would be computed. When this calculation is done, we find that (see Chapter 7 for the

TABLE 16.6	CORRELATIONS BETWEEN VARIABLES IN MODEL		
VARIABLES	PARENTAL PRESSURE (*I*)	SES SCORE (*X*)	YEARS OF EDUCATION (*Y*)
Parental pressure (*I*)	1.00		
SES score (*X*)	.31	1.00	
Years of education (*Y*)	.46	.22	1.00

formula) the partial ($r_{XY.I}$) is .10. By applying the rule of thirds, we see that the original relation between *X* and *Y* is .22 and, since the partial is about one-half of the original value, we note that the association has decreased/disappeared. We therefore find support for the model.

To perform this analysis using SPSS see the PARTIAL CORR procedure in Appendix A.

2. TESTING FOR SOURCES OF SPURIOUSNESS

A. THE SOURCE OF SPURIOUSNESS MODEL

The next major type of causal model is the source of spuriousness model. Here the researcher proposes that, while there is a statistically significant relation between the variables *X* and *Y*, this relationship may be a non-causal one, only existing because some third variable is influencing both *X* and *Y*. The argument is that the only reason *X* and *Y* are related to one another is that a third factor is influencing both of them.

Having observed a statistically significant relation, the researcher will want to ensure that the relationship is not spurious and, therefore, will run a number of spuriousness checks. The source of spuriousness model may be diagrammed as follows:

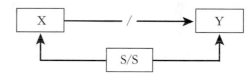

B. THE RATIONALE BEHIND THE TESTS

How do we go about testing a source of spuriousness model? The idea is this: if *X* and *Y* are spuriously associated, the reason they vary together is that a third variable (a source of spuriousness) is influencing both *X* and *Y*. Therefore, if we control for the source of spuriousness (S/S), there should no longer be any association between *X* and *Y*. This suggests that we need the same kind of analysis that we used for testing intervening variables. To test for a potential source of spuriousness, the steps are:

- test the original relation between *X* and *Y*; if this demonstrates a robust relationship (probably statistically significant) then;

- controlling for the source of spuriousness, rerun the relation between X and Y. As in the intervening variable model, we can then apply the Jackson's rule of thirds to determine if the relationship has increased, stayed the same, decreased/disappeared, or become mixed. In order to conclude that the original relation is spurious, the difference between the categories must decrease/disappear.

C. THE DILEMMA: THE MODELS ARE NOT EMPIRICALLY DISTINGUISHABLE

The difficulty is that it is possible for two researchers working with the same data and with the same three variables to establish two different causal models: one proposing that the variables are connected in an intervening variable model, the other proposing that the variables may be associated spuriously. They might then do the identical analysis but come to totally different conclusions. Let us suppose that when the control is applied, the original difference decreases/disappears: one researcher would conclude that the intervening variable model has found support in the data; the other would conclude that the relation is spurious. Both would be right.

Because the two models are not empirically distinguishable, the importance of precisely specifying models in advance becomes clear. If we develop the models after analysing the data, the interpretation of the data is little more than a flight of fancy.

D. USING MEANS TO TEST FOR SPURIOUSNESS

To illustrate a test for spuriousness, we will use the same variables as last time. Table 16.7 presents sample data showing how the analysis turned out for the relation between SES and plans.

The reader should note that there is a 1.40 year difference between the low and high SES students in the number of years of further education planned. Now suppose that we wanted to make certain that this relationship was not caused spuriously by the rural or urban backgrounds of these students. The type of home community (rural versus urban) may be influencing the SES level achieved by the families, and may also be influencing the educational plans of the students. It would therefore be the urban or rural location that is influencing both variables rather than the SES level that is influencing the students' plans.

Table 16.8 reports five different outcomes for this analysis. These should be examined carefully, the rule of thirds ap-

---

TABLE 16.7   NUMBER OF YEARS OF FURTHER EDUCATION PLANNED BY SENIOR HIGH SCHOOL STUDENTS, BY SOCIO-ECONOMIC STATUS (SES)

POST-HIGH SCHOOL PLANS	LOW SES BACKGROUND	HIGH SES BACKGROUND
Mean number of years of further education planned	2.47	3.87
Number of cases	197	198

TABLE 16.8 MEAN YEARS OF FURTHER EDUCATION PLANNED BY SOCIO-ECONOMIC STATUS (SES), CONTROLLING FOR RURAL AND URBAN BACKGROUNDS, WITH FIVE POSSIBLE OUTCOMES

MEAN YEARS OF FURTHER EDUCATION PLANNED	RURAL BACKGROUND		URBAN BACKGROUND*	
	LOW SES BACKGROUND	HIGH SES BACKGROUND	LOW SES BACKGROUND	HIGH SES BACKGROUND
1st outcome difference:	0.87	2.98	3.33	5.26
		2.11		1.93
2nd outcome difference:	2.27	3.67	2.58	3.96
		1.40		1.38
3rd outcome difference:	2.30	2.91	3.71	4.32
		0.61		0.61
4th outcome difference:	1.73	1.91	3.74	3.97
		0.18		0.23
5th outcome difference:	2.16	2.27	2.74	4.04
		0.11		1.30

*The original difference with no control for Urban/Rural backgrounds, is shown below:

POST-HIGH SCHOOL PLANS	LOW SES BACKGROUND	HIGH SES BACKGROUND
Mean number of years of further education planned:	2.47	3.87
Difference:	1.40	

plied, and a decision should be made as to which outcome lends support to the spuriousness model of the relationship between the variables. To apply this rule, simply divide the original difference by 3 (1.40 ÷ 3 = 0.47). Next, one has to compare the difference in years of future education planned by SES categories for each of the rural and urban categories.

OUTCOME 1

Here the differences (2.11 and 1.93) have both grown by more than a third and we therefore reject the source of spuriousness model. Perhaps the type of background has an independent influence on the number of additional years of education planned.

OUTCOME 2

The original difference between the number of years of education planned by low versus high SES students was 1.4 years. When the control for rural versus urban background is applied, the difference remains much the same and we therefore reject rural versus urban background as a source of spuriousness.

OUTCOME 3

The original difference in this result has been reduced to 0.61 for both categories. Since the difference has not decreased/disappeared, we find support for the source of spuriousness model.

OUTCOME 4

In this case, the original difference has been reduced to less than one-third of its original value and so we cannot reject the source of spuriousness model. Outcomes 3 and 4 both lend support to the spuriousness model.

OUTCOME 5

Here the result is mixed. The difference disappears among the rural students, but is only slightly reduced among the urban students. We reject the source of spuriousness model.

In order to do the analysis, we need a table showing the difference in additional years of education planned, by SES categories. Second, we will need to rerun this relationship, controlling for rural and urban backgrounds.

> *To perform this analysis using SPSS see the MEANS procedure in Appendix A.*

E. USING CROSSTABS TO TEST FOR A SOURCE OF SPURIOUSNESS

To use CROSSTABS in a test for a source of spuriousness, one runs the original relationship, then reruns the relationship controlling for the source of spuriousness. The rule of thirds would then be applied and, only if the difference decreases/disappears, do we consider the original relationship to be spurious.

> *To perform this analysis using SPSS see the CROSSTABS procedure in Appendix A.*

F. USING PARTIAL CORR TO TEST FOR SPURIOUSNESS

This test requires ratio level variables, and simply involves running the zero-order correlation, followed by a partial correlation controlling for the potential source of spuriousness. The analysis should be run and the data interpreted according to the rule of thirds. Only if the relationship decreases/disappears, do we consider the original relationship to be spurious.

> *To perform this analysis using SPSS see the PARTIAL CORR procedure in Appendix A.*

When procedures are being selected for evaluating causal models, and the researcher believes that the vast majority will only require one type of procedure, it will, in the interest of simplicity, sometimes be best to use the same procedure throughout rather than shift back and forth between techniques in a way that might confuse the reader. Normally this will mean some under-utilization of the data, since the procedure selected must meet the measurement requirements of the variable with the lowest level of measurement.

B. TESTING FOUR-VARIABLE CAUSAL MODELS

In *Causal Inferences in Nonexperimental Research* (1964), Hubert M. Blalock Jr. presented a number of ideas on testing causal models. These tests parallel the ideas presented in the earlier section of the chapter and should be seen as an extension of them. In the case of four-variable models, there may be two intervening variables (plus an independent and dependent variable). Figure 16.1 illustrates a four-variable model.

Suppose the model that you wish to examine is the one presented in Figure 16.1. This model suggests a specific causal ordering of the variables. Or, A→B→C→D. What could one do to test this model? Drawing on the work of Simon (1957) and on Driver and Massey's (1957) North American Indian data, Blalock suggests a number of properties that should hold true if the model is accurate:

- correlations between adjacent variables should be higher than between non-adjacent variables; if the model is correct, the following should hold:

$r_{AB} > r_{AC}, r_{AD}$

$r_{BC} > r_{BD}$

$r_{CD} > r_{AC}$

- the weakest correlation in a causal chain should be between the variables furthest apart causally; if the model is correct, the following should hold:

$r_{AD} < r_{AB}, r_{AC}$

$r_{AC} < r_{AB}$

$r_{BD} < r_{AB}, r_{BC}$

- the strength of relationships should diminish if intervening variables are controlled for; if the model is correct, the following partial correlation results should hold:

$r_{AC.B} = 0$

$r_{BD.C} = 0$

$r_{AD.BC} = 0$

As an illustration of the simplest model, we will show the steps necessary to test the model. First, we will examine the magnitude of the various correlations. Are they consistent with the four-variable model? Namely:

- are the correlations between causally adjacent variables higher than between non-adjacent variables?;

- do correlations drop when intervening variables are controlled?

FIGURE 16.1 FOUR-VARIABLE CAUSAL MODEL

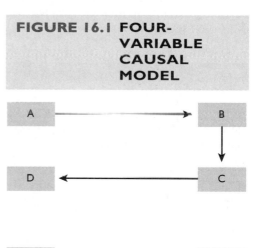

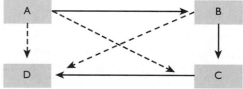

Suppose that we have the following correlation matrix between the variables A, B, C, and D.

CORRELATION MATRIX:

Variables	A	B	C
B	0.56		
C	0.21	0.61	
D	0.10	0.18	0.63

STEP 1

DOES THE CAUSAL ORDER MAKE SENSE?

The first step in assessing a causal model is to ensure that the causal ordering is plausible. The model should pass a commonsensical test, indicating that the variables are in a temporal sequence that is possible. For example, the first variable in the model should occur before other variables and should represent a possible cause of variation in variables that occur later in the model.

STEP 2

COMPARE THE CORRELATIONS.

Inspect the correlations to see if correlations between adjacent variables are higher than those between non-adjacent variables. In this case we note the following:

MODEL PREDICTS	OBSERVED CORRELATIONS	CON- CLUSIONS
$r_{AB} > r_{AC}, r_{AD}$	.56 .21 .10	Supports model
$r_{BC} > r_{BD}$	.61 .18	Supports model
$r_{CD} > r_{AC}$	.63 .21	Supports model

STEP 3

ELIMINATE CAUSAL LINKS NOT IMPLIED BY THE MODEL.

There are three causal links that are not implied by the model. These include the *AB* link, the *BD* link, and the *AD* link. (These are marked with hatched lines in Figure 16.1.) The first two are tested using first-order (one control) partial correlations and the last one is tested by means of a second-order partial correlation. The tests reveal the following:

MODEL PREDICTS	OBSERVED PARTIAL CORRELATION	CON- CLUSION
i) Testing AC link: $r_{AC.B} = 0*$	.10	Reduced by more than one-third: supports model**
ii) Testing BD link: $r_{BD.C} = 0$	$-.33$	Reduced by more than one-third: supports model
iii) Testing AD link: $r_{AD.BC} = 0$	.01	Reduced by more than one-third: supports model

* The formulas used to hand-compute the partials are as follows:

First-order:

$$r_{AC.B} = \frac{r_{AC} - (r_{AC})\,(r_{BC})}{\sqrt{1 - r_{AC}^2}\ \sqrt{1 - r_{BC}^2}}$$

Second-order:

$$r_{AD.BC} = \frac{r_{AD.B} - (r_{AC.B})\,(r_{CD.B})}{\sqrt{1 - r_{AC.B}^2}\ \sqrt{1 - r_{CD.B}^2}}$$

** The causal inference uses the *rule of thirds* introduced in this text; Hubert Blalock bears no responsibility on this point!

The evidence in this case is consistent with the proposed model. Had any of the results failed the test, then the interpretation would be that the evidence is not consistent with the proposed model.

While it is possible to test complex causal models using contingency tables, the procedure requires a large number of cases as additional control variables are added. Once again, however, the principle remains the same: observe what happens to the original relationship when the control variables are applied simultaneously. Does the original difference increase, stay the same, decrease/disappear, or is it mixed?

> *To perform this analysis using SPSS see the CORRELATION/PARTIAL CORR procedures in Appendix A.*

Chapter 17 will introduce some other basic techniques that are used when attempts are made to deal with multiple variables simultaneously.

C. KEY TERMS

Intervening variable

Jackson's rule of thirds

Partial correlations

Source of spuriousness

D. KEY POINTS

To *establish a causal relationship*, the researcher must demonstrate that:

(i) the variables are associated;

(ii) they are in a plausible causal sequence; and

(iii) they are not spuriously connected.

In *non-experimental research*, a variety of techniques are used to test for intervening and for source of spuriousness variables. These include the following SPSS procedures: CROSSTABS, MEANS, CORRELATIONS, and PARTIAL CORR.

The procedure for testing models includes:

(i) showing that the original relationship exists (*X* - *Y* relation);

(ii) re-running the relationship between *X* and *Y* controlling for either the proposed intervening variable or the source of spuriousness;

(iii) applying Jackson's rule of thirds to the result. Only if the original relationship decreases/disappears is there support for the proposed intervening or source of spuriousness model.

A logic similar to that employed when testing three-variable causal models may be used to test four-variable causal models.

In a causal chain the correlations between adjacent variables should be higher than the correlations between non-adjacent variables; the weakest correlation should be between the variables furthest apart in the chain.

E. EXERCISES

1. Working with a two-variable relationship that you think would be relatively strong, diagram four models (two intervening variables and two possible sources of spuriousness) which may explain the original two-variable relationship. Describe in detail how you would go about testing the four proposed models. What outcomes would lend support to each of your models and what kinds of evidence would lead you to reject them?

2. Compare the procedures used by a researcher using an experimental design to arrive at causal inferences with those used by a non-experimental researcher. Using the same three variables, illustrate an experimental and a non-experimental approach by outlining a possible design each might use in exploring the relationship between the same three variables. For the particular relationship you have explored, discuss the reasons why you prefer one of the designs.

F. RECOMMENDED READINGS

BLALOCK, HUBERT M. JR. (1964). *Causal Inferences in Nonexperimental Research*. Durham: The University of North Carolina Press. Undergraduates will find this book challenging but nonetheless rewarding to work through the methods for testing models with four or more variables.

FORCESE, DENNIS AND STEPHEN RICHER (1973). *Social Research Methods*. Englewood Cliffs, N.J.: Prentice-Hall Inc. This book has a fine section in it on interpreting three-variable relationships.

HYMAN, HERBERT (1955). *Survey Design and Analysis*. New York: The Free Press. Paul Lazarsfeld's foreword to Hyman's book contains the classic statement on interpreting three-variable causal models. Because most undergraduates find the terminology difficult to sort out, the Lazarsfeld approach is not followed by this author.

THREE MULTI-VARIATE TECHNIQUES

This chapter extends some of the techniques introduced in the previous chapters. The selection of the appropriate technique should be guided by a consideration of (i) the level of measurement attained in measuring the variables and (ii) what the analysis is attempting to reveal. We will begin our consideration of multi-variate analysis by exploring multiple regression analysis. An understanding of regression is helpful when examining the other approaches featured in this chapter: discriminant analysis, and multi-variate analysis of variance. An examination of these three basic multi-variate techniques reveals that they have much in common.

A. MULTIPLE REGRESSION: REGRESSION

1. THE RATIONALE

In *multiple regression analysis* we are attempting to predict variations in a dependent variable from two or more independent variables. As in correlational analysis (see Chapter 7), we are interested in both the equation that describes the relation as well as a measure of the strength of the association. We will only consider the simplest version of regression—that of an additive or linear relationship among the variables. Regression analysis assumes that the variables are normally distributed and that measurement is at the ratio level. Special procedures, however, do permit the inclusion of variables not achieving ratio measurement.

Regression analysis allows the researcher:

- to estimate the *relative importance* of independent variables in influencing a dependent variable;

- to identify a mathematical *equation* which describes the relation between the independent variables and the dependent variable.

For example, if you are trying to estimate the relative contribution of three variables when predicting the relative prestige of each employee of a company, a regression analysis might indicate that the length of time on the job accounts for 37 percent of the variation, that educational attainment accounts for 22 percent of the variation, and that income contributes another 14 percent of the variation in prestige. Taken together, the three variables account for 73 percent of the variation in prestige.

Alternatively, the relation between prestige and educational attainment could be analyzed by comparing the average prestige across categories of attainment (MEANS analysis). This would permit the researcher to show a significant relation between prestige and educational attainment, but would not enable the researcher to say that educational attainment is about one-half as important as length of time on the job. Because regression analysis provides this additional information, it is a powerful tool. Besides allowing the researcher to examine the relative importance of the various factors producing variation in a dependent variable, it also allows the researcher to express the relation in the form of an equation, and hence gives the researcher the ability to predict values for a dependent variable, given values for the independent variables.

Although regression analysis assumes ratio level measurement and normally distributed variables, researchers sometimes include ordinal and even nominal variables. However, the price one pays for reduced levels of measurement is almost certainly a weakened ability to predict variation in the dependent variable, as well as a greater instability in the coefficients associated with the independent variables. (See Box 12.2 for an example of the impact of reduced levels of measurement.)

2. THE LINEAR REGRESSION EQUATION

In Chapter 7 we examined the relationship between two variables using a correlation approach. The equation describing the relation between X (independent variable) and Y (dependent variable) consisted of an a value and a b coefficient as in:

$$Y = a + bx$$

To take into account two or more independent variables, this basic equation is extended as follows:

$$Y = a + b_1X_1 + b_2X_2 + \dots b_kX_k$$

In the equation the a is a constant and, if the values for each case were calculated and plotted, would represent the point where the regression line crosses the Y axis. The **b coefficients** refer to the slopes of the regression lines. If small increases in the X variable lead to large increases in the Y variable, the b value will be higher (see the relation between prestige and years of education shown in Figure 17.1); on the other hand, if it takes large increases in X to produce an increase in Y, the b value will be smaller (see the relation between prestige and annual income shown in Figure 17.2). In the two-variable case (as shown in Figure 17.1 and 17.2), the b value in the case of years of education is higher than the b value for the case of income predicting prestige. The reason is that the values for years of education have a small range from 0 to 20 years, while the range in the values for income is considerable, perhaps from $18,000 to $80,000. Thus, the b values will tend to be much lower. Even though the correlation between prestige and years of education and between prestige and income may be similar (let us say .90 in both cases), the b value for income will be much lower than the b value for years of education.

If standardized slopes are of interest, these will be referred to as β weights or **beta weights**. In this case, think of all the variables in the equation as being standardized—think of them as Z *scores*—so that it does not matter if the independent variables have different ranges (as in the case of income and years of education). Each independent variable is standardized (reassigned values so that each has a mean of zero and a standard deviation of one), which then allows us to compare the beta values directly. The β's represent the amount of change in Y (the dependent variable) that can be associated with a given change in one of the X's, when the influences of the other independent variables are held constant. Regression programs provide the researcher with both the b and the β (beta) coefficients (see Figure 17.16).

The strategy of multiple regression involves determining the slopes for each of the independent variables while simultaneously holding constant, or adjusting for,

FIGURE 17.1   PRESTIGE AND YEARS OF EDUCATION

Plot of Prestige with Years of Education
(a)

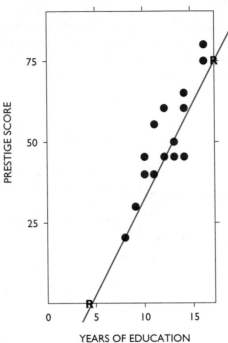

15 cases plotted

Regression statistics of prestige on education:

Correlation	0.89
R Squared	0.79
S.E. of Est	7.68
Significance	0.0000

Intercept (*a* value)	−21.64	Standard error	10.64
Slope (*b* value)	5.97	Standard error	0.86

Equation: Prestige = −21.64 + 5.97 (Education)

the other independent variables. The slopes (*b* coefficients) are determined so as to maximize our ability to predict variations in the dependent variable. Thus we may define a ***linear regression equation*** as one which describes a relationship between

FIGURE 17.1 PRESTIGE AND YEARS OF EDUCATION (CONTINUED)

Plot of Prestige with Years of Education (Standardized)
(b)

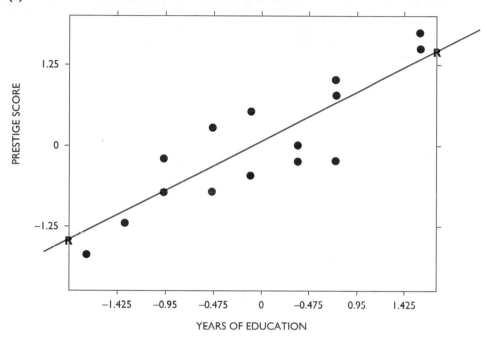

15 standardized cases plotted

Regression statistics of prestige on education:

Correlation	0.89		
R Squared	0.79		
S.E. of Est	0.48		
Significance	0.0000		
Intercept (*a* value)	0.0000	Standard error	0.47712
Slope (*b* value)	0.88804	Standard error	0.12752

Equation: Prestige = −21.64 + 5.97 (Education)

a number of independent variables and a dependent variable and which provides for the best linear (additive) weightings of the independent variables and a constant calculated so as to maximize the prediction of the dependent variable.

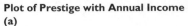

FIGURE 17.2 PRESTIGE AND INCOME

Plot of Prestige with Annual Income
(a)

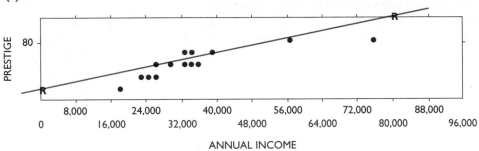

15 cases plotted

Regression statistics of prestige on income:

Correlation	0.87		
R Squared	0.75		
S.E. of Est	8.34		
Significance	0.0000		
Intercept (*a* value)	18.25	Standard error	5.67662
Slope (*b* value)	0.00097	Standard error	0.00016

Equation: Prestige = 18.25 = 0.00097 (Income)

3. THE STRENGTH OF THE ASSOCIATION, R^2

The R^2 is a measure of the amount of variation in the dependent variable that is explained by the combination of independent variables. Recall that when two variables are involved, the measure is r^2 (see Chapter 7). The two statistics are directly comparable and would yield identical results if, in a case where there are multiple independent variables, one simply took the values for each variable, plugged them into the equation, and then computed the "predicted value" for the dependent variable. If one then correlated the predicted and the observed values of the dependent variable, the problem is reduced to a simple two-variable correlation, and the r^2 would equal R^2. Both of these statistics vary from 0 to 1. The higher the value, the higher the explained variance; the higher the value, the higher the predictability of the dependent variable by the independent variables.

Regression analysis is an important technique for both applied and pure research. The applied researcher will be particularly interested in identifying those independent variables which combine:

- importance in influencing the dependent variable; and,

- being manipulatable through policy changes.

FIGURE 17.2 PRESTIGE AND INCOME (CONTINUED)

Plot of Prestige with Annual Income (Standardized)
(b)

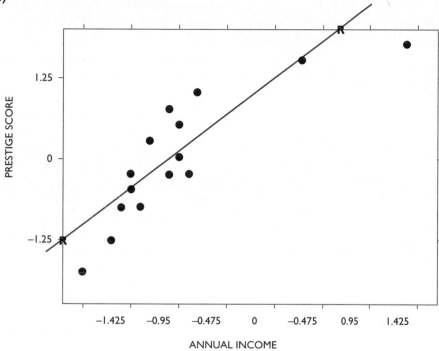

15 *standardized* cases plotted

Regression statistics of prestige on income:

Correlation	0.87		
R Squared	0.75		
S.E. of Est	0.5180		
Significance	0.0000		
Intercept (*a* value)	0.0000	Standard error	0.13374
Slope (*b* value)	0.86654	Standard error	0.13843

The applied researcher will be most concerned with the *b* coefficients for they will indicate how much change in the independent variable will be required for a unit change in the dependent variable. Pure researchers, on the other hand, will usually focus on the *β*s since, generally, the theorist will be more concerned with the relative impact of each independent variable on the dependent variable.

4. USING VARIABLES NOT MEETING THE MEASURE-MENT ASSUMPTION

Frequently researchers wish to include, along with ratio level variables, those variables measured at either the ordinal or nominal levels. It is possible to do this, although one must exercise greater caution in interpreting the results.

A. USING ORDINAL VARIABLES

The price one pays here is generally a weakened ability to predict variations in a dependent variable. In general, the fewer the categories in an ordinal variable, the lower its correlation with other variables. Thus, the more categories in the ordinal variable, the better; if regression analysis is anticipated, using nine-point Likert items rather than five- or seven-point categories is recommended. When ordinal variables are placed into competition with ratio level variables for explaining variance, the resulting equation will tend to underestimate the relative importance of the ordinal variables. (See Box 12.1 for more details on the effects of using fewer categories.)

B. USING PRESENCE-ABSENCE QUESTIONS

In the case of presence-absence questions, one really has an ordinal variable with two values. Normally such questions are coded so that "0" refers to the absence and "1" refers to the presence of the characteristic. Once again, these variables are at a disadvantage in explaining variation in the dependent variable. Indeed, with only two categories, these variables are at a particular disadvantage (when, for example, compared with another ordinal variable with

nine values, or a ratio variable). Once again, the coefficients are likely to underestimate the importance of such variables when they are in competition with variables measured at the ordinal or ratio levels.

C. USING DUMMY VARIABLES FOR NOMINAL VARIABLES

Suppose you have a religious affiliation variable (nominal) and wish to include it in a regression analysis. For purposes of illustration, suppose religion is coded into four categories: (i) Protestant, (ii) Catholic, (iii) Jew, and (iv) Other and None. The dummy-variable procedure involves creating three new variables (one fewer than the number of religious categories) and coding each of them into presence/absence variables. Thus we will have a "Protestant" variable, and it will be coded into presence (1) or absence (0), a "Catholic" variable using 1's for Catholics and 0's for non-Catholics, and a "Jewish" variable similarly coded 1 and 0 (see Table 17.1). These three new variables would then be entered into the regression analysis as independent variables along with the other relevant independent variables.

Another example of a dummy variable would be the inclusion of a gender variable into a regression analysis. In this case, either the males or the females would be assigned a value of 1, while those not assigned would be given a 0. Thus if females were assigned the value of 1, then the males would be given the value 0. In this case, only one new variable is needed to represent the two categories of gender (recall that we use one fewer dummy variable than categories of the original variable).

To summarize, then, the newly created *dummy variables* are placed into the regression analysis as independent variables.

TABLE 17.1 RECODING THE RELIGION VARIABLE INTO THREE DUMMY VARIABLES

CASE #	ORIGINAL CODING RELIGION VARIABLE	CODING FOR THREE NEW DUMMY VARIABLES		
		CATHOLIC	PROTESTANT	JEWISH
1	1 (Catholic)	1	0	0
2	2 (Protestant)	0	1	0
3	3 (Jewish)	0	0	1
4	3 (Jewish)	0	0	1
5	2 (Protestant)	0	1	0
6	1 (Catholic)	1	0	0
7	4 (Atheist)	0	0	0
8	9 (No answer)	0	0	0
9	4 (Mormon)	0	0	0
10	2 (Protestant)	0	1	0
...				
178	4 (Agnostic)	0	0	0

In each case, there will be one fewer dummy variable than there are categories of the original variable: in the case of the religion variable, there would be three variables to represent the four categories; in the case of gender, only the female variable would be included. The amount of variation explained by each of the new variables is represented by the beta weight associated with the variable. The reason the four categories are represented by three new variables is that the fourth category is taken into account by the combined values in the "absence" category of the three categories. In the case of the gender variable, with females scored as 1 and males as 0, the males are represented as those not scored as 1. A **dummy variable**, therefore, is one which is coded 1 for presence and 0 for absence of a characteristic and represents one category of an independent variable.

To perform this analysis using SPSS see the RECODE & REGRESSION procedures in Appendix A.

5. SOME TIPS FOR USING REGRESSION ANALYSIS

TIP 1

ENSURE THAT VARIABLES ARE THEORETICALLY INDEPENDENT OF ONE ANOTHER.

What this means is that you cannot use aspects of the dependent variable as independent variables. Ensure that you are including only meaningful potential causes of the dependent variable, *not alternate measures of it.*

WATCH OUT FOR HIGHLY CORRELATED INDEPENDENT VARIABLES.

The weighting which will be attached to the variables will be unstable if the independent variables are highly correlated with one another. The program will print out a warning if there is a problem in this area. The term *multicollinearity* is used to refer to the extent of the correlation among the independent variables. To achieve high predictability of a dependent variable, it is preferable to have the independent variables correlated with the dependent variable but not with one another. If you have a number of highly intercorrelated independent variables, it is usually advisable either:

• to develop an index out of them (if it makes sense to do so); or

• to select one of the measures and use it to represent the others.

TRY TO ACHIEVE RATIO LEVEL MEASUREMENT.

If you intend to use regression analysis, attempt to collect data in as raw a form as possible, at the ratio level if possible; if ordinal data are collected, use more categories, rather than fewer.

USE RAW DATA.

Do not use recoded variables (dummy variables are an exception) in regression analysis. For example, if you have a variable such as age coded as age-at-last-birthday, then use the raw age variable data (such as 24, 19, 37, 54, etc.) rather than recoded age categories that may

have used three categories to represent those under 30, those 30 to 49 years of age, and those 50 years of age or over.

USE THE BACKWARD SOLUTION IN THE REGRESSION PROCEDURE.

By using the **BACKWARD (stepwise) solution**, all the variables are included in the regression equation; then the least important variable is dropped, and the equation is recalculated. This procedure is repeated until only significant variables remain. The advantage of this format is that variables which are important when in combination with other variables will remain in the equation; in other formats they might never be included.

INTERPRET WEIGHTINGS WITH CARE.

Understand that the weightings are designed for the particular combination of independent variables in a particular sample and that they may not be reliable if applied to other samples. One has to be particularly cautious in situations where the independent variables are substantially correlated with one another. (In such situations, with another sample, it is quite likely that different variables will be selected as significant predictors of the dependent variable.)

MONITOR NUMBER OF CASES CAREFULLY.

By default (i.e., if you do not provide a specific instruction to the contrary) SPSS deletes a case if it has a missing value in any of the variables in the equation. Thus, if there are a lot of variables in an analysis, there is a danger of losing many cases. And, as the number of cases drops close to the number of variables, the R^2 will increase dramatically. To determine the number of cases used in the analysis, add one to the total degrees of freedom reported in the table.

If a large number of cases have been dropped, one should attempt to detect if there is a pattern to the missing cases. If one sub-category of respondents is more likely to respond to a question, one might wish to analyze the data these respondents provide separately from those sub-categories of respondents whose responses are less complete. However, if it appears that the missing values are random, consider using one or more of the following techniques:

• **Repeat analysis:** After an initial regression analysis (using the BACKWARD option) has identified the significant variables, rerun the analysis, naming only the significant variables, plus perhaps two or three that were dropped in the last few steps. This will preserve those cases which were dropped because of missing values in variables that are not in the final equation. Frequently, many fewer cases will be dropped if this procedure is followed.

• **Pairwise solution:** Try running the analysis using PAIRWISE treatment of missing cases. In this solution, the correlations are determined for all the pairs of variables for which data are available.

To perform this analysis using SPSS see the REGRESSION procedure in Appendix A.

• **Means solution:** A third approach is to try the MEANS treatment of missing values, which will substitute the mean of the variable for any missing cases.

To perform this analysis using SPSS see the REGRESSION procedure in Appendix A.

TIP 8

DEAL WITH INTERACTIONS AMONG INDEPENDENT VARIABLES.

If you have reason to suspect that the joint effect of two independent variables is important but that, individually, they may not be significant predictors of the dependent variable, there are two relatively easy approaches to this problem:

• Create a new variable by multiplying the values of the two variables suspected of interaction and include the new variable in the regression analysis along with the variables from which it was constructed. If the new variable is a significant predictor, it will remain in the equation when the analysis is done; if it is not, it will be dropped.

• Convert all the variables to log function variables (this converts the equation to a multiplicative power function) and by doing so any interactions will be taken into account in the weightings of the independent variables. In this form the equation is:

$$\log Y = \log a + \log X_1 + \log X_2 + \log X_k$$

The consequence of using log transformations is that each independent variable is raised to a power rather than multiplied by the value of the independent variable, as in the linear regression equation.

6. PRESENTING AND INTERPRETING REGRESSION RESULTS

Table 17.2 presents a sample of a regression results table. Note that both the *b* coefficients and the beta weights are reported. It is possible to hand-compute an estimate of the impact of each independent variables, by using the following formula (Hamblin, 1966):

% Variance explained by each variable

$$= \frac{\beta_1 \times R^2}{\sum \beta s} \times 100$$

This estimate represents the impact of each variable in the equation. However, if other variables were included, the percentages would change.

The regression equation is included in Table 17.2. This equation will help you identify where each if its elements are found in a printout; note that the *b* coefficients are used (not betas) along with the constant term.

Incidentally, Table 17.2 is based on some research examining possible gender discrepancies in faculty salaries. The question of the research was: given similar levels of qualification, tenure status, experience, age, and academic rank, are female faculty paid less than their male counterparts? The approach taken was to compute a regression equation based on the male faculty.

TABLE 17.2   MULTIPLE REGRESSION ANALYSIS FACULTY SALARIES

VARIABLE	B COEFFICIENT	BETA COEFFICIENT	PERCENT EXPLAINED
Qualifications	794	.038	3.1
Tenure status	1326	.065	5.3
Age in current year	94	.092	7.5
Length in rank	263	.153	12.5
Professional age	210	.172	14.0
Years at institution	264	.250	20.4
Academic rank	-4570	-.372	30.3
CONSTANT	38504	% EXPLAINED	93.1
Multiple R	.964		
R Square	.930		

The variables are:

Qualifications	Doctorate = 1; No doctorate = 0
Tenure status	Tenure = 1; No tenure = 0
Age	Age in 1987
Length in rank	Years in rank in 1987
Professional age	Years since highest degree earned
Years at institution	Years teaching at institution
Rank	Professor = 1; Associate = 2; Assistant = 3; Lecturer = 4

Salary = 38504 + 794(Qual) + 1326(Tenure) + 94(Age) + 263(Rank) + 210(ProAge) + 264(Years) − 4570(Rank).

These weightings were then applied to the female faculty, which gave us a predicted salary which, in turn, allowed us to compare actual salaries to predicted salaries for the female faculty. As is typical in most such studies, the females were found to be paid somewhat less than their male counterparts when adjusting for differences in levels of the independent variables.

To perform this analysis using SPSS see the REGRESSION procedure in Appendix A.

B. DISCRIMINANT FUNCTION ANALYSIS: DISCRIMINANT

1. THE RATIONALE

Discriminant function analysis has some similarity to regression analysis and this alternative is used in situations where:

- the measurement of the dependent variable is at the nominal level; or

- regression analysis is inappropriate because the assumption that the dependent variable is normally distributed is not met.

Discriminant function analysis attempts to predict the category of the dependent variable into which each case falls by using the combined information from the independent variables. For example, suppose you wished to predict whether or not a student will participate in some postsecondary education within five years of completing Grade 11. The independent variables include information on final Grade 11 average, information on socio-economic status of family, size of family, and the number of siblings who have engaged in postsecondary education. Based on a study of students who had completed Grade 11 a minimum of six years ago, discriminant analysis would then be used to predict whether each case would fall into the "participation" or "no participation" categories of post-secondary education.

Discriminant analysis is a valuable tool for the social researcher and has application in many situations. To illustrate some of these situations, let us consider applications that might be made of the technique in some of the social science disciplines:

- *Anthropology:* studies of the distribution of neolocal (newly married couple who have established their own residence), patrilocal (newly married couple residing with husband's family) and matrilocal (newly married couple residing with wife's family) residence patterns;

- *Education:* studies of rates of participation and non-participation in post-secondary education, of participation in a manual arts elective, or of the rates at which students drop out of school or stay in school;

- *Political Science:* attempts to determine whether individuals are voters or non-voters, vote switchers or non-switchers, and the distribution of voters who favour the left, the middle, and the right of the political spectrum;

- *Psychology:* classifying patients as mentally ill or mentally healthy, or to differentiate between leaders and non-leaders in group decision-making;

- *Sociology:* attempts to distinguish between delinquent and non-delinquent behaviour.

2. COMPARISON WITH MULTIPLE REGRESSION ANALYSIS

Like multiple regression analysis, discriminant analysis has an ability to deal with multiple independent variables simultaneously. So if your dependent variable has two, three, or four categories, and your independent variables are ratio variables, and you wish to assess the extent to which you can correctly classify category membership on the dependent measure, consider using discriminant function analysis. And, as with regression analysis, if you wish to use nominal or ordinal independent variables, it is possible to do so (using dummy-coded variables), so long as caution is exercised in interpreting the results.

The coefficients computed are based on a regression-like linear equation:

$$D = B_0 + B_1X_1 + B_2X_2 + ... + B_kX_k$$

The X values are the values of the independent variables and the B values are the coefficients associated with each independent variable, weighted to maximize the prediction of D, the categories of the dependent variable. The B values are weighted to maximize the ratio of the be-

tween-groups sum of squares to the within-groups sum of squares. The output for the analysis will display the discriminant function score for each case. The score for each case is derived by plugging in the observed values for each variable and multiplying it by the coefficient. Suppose the discriminant equation was as follows:

$$D = .013 + .003(X_1) + .004(X_2) + .078(X_3) + .056(X_4)$$

Table 17.3 displays the values for each variable, the coefficients, and the resulting discriminant score for the first case in the file.

Discriminant scores are calculated for each case and each case is then classified into one of the groups (participating or not participating in post-secondary education). The printed output will indicate the actual group each case belongs to and asterisks are used to indicate those cases that were misclassified.

3. PRESENTING AND INTERPRETING RESULTS

A basic statistic provided by discriminant analysis is the percentage of cases which can be classified correctly using information from the combination of independent variables.

TABLE 17.3 CALCULATING THE DISCRIMINANT SCORE, CASE 1

	VARIABLE	OBSERVED VALUE	COEFFICIENT	DISCRIMINANT SCORE
D	Dependent variable*	1		
	Constant	0.013	.013	
X1	Grade 11 average	72.6	.003	.218
X2	Family SES score	47.0	.004	.188
X3	Family size	3	.078	.234
X4	Siblings post-secondary	0	.056	.000
	Sum of values, Case # 1			.653

* Dependent variable is "Participating" or "Not Participating" in post-secondary education.

The statistic calculated is similar to that of **Lambda**, which was described in the section dealing with contingency table analysis (see Chapter 7). You may recall that Lambda computes the error reduction in estimating a dependent variable, given knowledge of an independent variable. In our example, using the computed discriminant function equation, we determine that 85.2 percent of the cases were correctly grouped according to the discriminant function analysis.

As with regression analysis, the computed coefficients are available in standardized and unstandardized forms. The unstandardized coefficients are used when calculating the discriminant scores for each case; when the researcher wishes to compare the relative impact of each variable, standardized coefficients are used (this is to take into account the different ranges of the variables). Indeed, if there were two categories in the dependent variable, we would have achieved similar results had we used regression analysis. The *b* coefficients in regression analysis will have a similar ratio to the *B* discriminant coefficients. However, where there are three or more categories in the dependent variable, the results are different.

Table 17.4 provides a sample of the way in which discriminant analyses may be presented.

To perform this analysis using SPSS see the DISCRIMINANT procedure in Appendix A.

C. MULTI-VARIATE ANALYSIS OF VARIANCE: MANOVA

1. THE RATIONALE

While regression analysis is appropriate in many situations, there are several situations where multi-variate analysis of variance (ANOVA or MANOVA) would be more appropriate than regression analysis. For example, as Kachigan (1986) points out, if you had predictor variables that have qualitative differences (three different countries for example), or if, rather than having a ratio variable measuring the amount of time spent watching TV, you had a variable that indicates whether someone watched TV or went to the movies, you again would probably opt for analysis of variance. In short, if an independent variable is made up of values which differ in *kind* rather than in *quantity*, you would opt for analysis of variance.

TABLE 17.4 DISCRIMINANT ANALYSIS, SAMPLE PRESENTATION

ACTUAL GROUP	NUMBER OF CASES	PREDICTED GROUP MEMBERSHIP	
		1	2
Participate (1)	261	221	40
Not participate (2)	83	11	72
TOTAL	344	232	112

Percent of "grouped" cases correctly classified: 293 out of 344 cases = 85.2%

A second situation which is better handled with analysis of variance is one where the relationship between the independent and the dependent variable changes over the continuum. Perhaps the relationship is non-linear and, once again, analysis of variance should be considered as an alternative to regression.

Multi-variate analysis of variance is useful for reasons other than the two cited earlier. It would be good to use such analysis in the following conditions:

- when the dependent variable is measured at the ratio level;

- when one or more of the treatment variables are measured at the ratio level and others are measured at the nominal or ordinal levels;

- if you have multiple dependent measures which you wish to examine simultaneously;

- in non-experimental designs you wish to examine whether there are significant interactions among independent variables.

In the above cases, you would consider using ***multi-variate analysis of variance (MANOVA)***. The ratio level treatment variables are called ***covariates***. Box 17.1 presents sample results. Note how MANOVA results combine standard analysis of variance results along with regression analysis. (See the discussion of analysis of variance in Chapter 8.)

BOX 17.1

MANOVA Analysis, Sample Presentation: Analyzing Egalitarianism
Analysis of Variance

SOURCE OF VARIATION	SUMS OF SQUARES	MEAN SQUARE	DF	F	SIG. OF F
Within cells [error]	11539.00	69.10	167		
Regression	127.71	63.85	2	.92	.399
COUNTRY [A]	932.68	466.34	2	6.75	.002
GENDER [B]	2.18	2.18	1	.03	.859
COUNTRY by GENDER [A × B]	87.92	43.96	2	.64	.531

Regression analysis for within cells error term

Dependent variable   EGALITARIANISM

Covariate	Beta	T-Value	Sig. of T
SES	-.024	-.311	.756
FAMSIZE	.100	1.290	.199

The variables are as follows:

- Dependent variable:
  EGALITARIANISM

- Independent variables:
  COUNTRY (Canada, New Zealand, Australia)
  GENDER (Males, Female)

- Covariates:
  SES (Occupational Prestige Rating)
  FAMSIZE (Number of Children in family)

1. Understanding the Values in the Summary Table

(i) The degrees of freedom are calculated as follows:

- Regression: df = number of covariates in analysis [in this case: 2]

- main effect (A): df = 1 less than number of levels in that factor. [In this case: 3 – 1 = 2]

- main effect (B): df = 1 less than number of levels in that factor. [In this case: 2 – 1 = 1]

- interaction effect (A x B): df = product of the dfs making up the interaction. [In this case: 2 × 1 = 2]

- error term: df = total number of cases minus the product of number of levels of A and B. [In this case, 173 – (3 × 2) = 167.]

(ii) To compute the mean square for an effect, divide the sum of squares for the effect by its df. [For the effect of COUNTRY: 932.68 ÷ 2 = 466.34.]

(iii) To compute the F value for each effect, divide the mean square by the mean square error term. [The F for COUNTRY: 466.34 ÷ 69.10 = 6.75.]

2. Interpreting the Results

You will want to examine two issues as you begin to interpret your results. First you will want to know if your treatment (or independent) variables had significant effect; if there are covariates, is the regression effect significant? If there are significant treatment effects, you will want to see if there is any interaction between the treatments.

A. MAIN EFFECTS To decide if a treatment or covariate was statistically significant, you will need to examine the "significance of F" column to see if the value is less than .05. [If this value is not shown, you will need to compare the F value to the values found in Appendix E using the appropriate degrees of freedom. If the value you obtained is larger than the one reported in Appendix E, you have a statistically significant effect. To use Appendix E you will need values for the required degrees of freedom: use the smaller value across the top of the table, and the larger one on the vertical axis.]

B. INTERACTION EFFECTS If you have a significant main effect, you will then want to inspect your results for any interactions between the effects. Your job is simple if there is no significant interaction effect: you simply report that none was present. It is more complicated with an interaction: in this case, the effect of a treatment is not independent of the other treatment. It may be that under the high condition of Treatment A, we find that treatment B does not enhance the impact on the dependent variable. Here you will need to indicate the conditions under which the interaction occurs. You

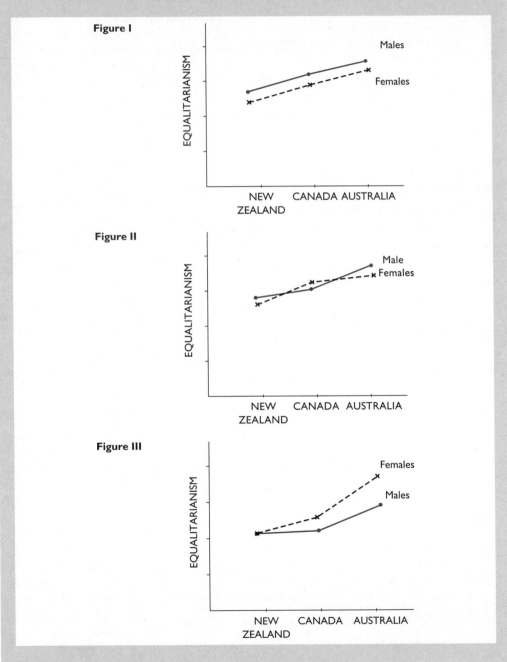

Figure I

Figure II

Figure III

might, for example, create a plot of the relationship between the variables, such as one of the ones shown in Figures I, II, or III.

- **Figure I:** This figure illustrates a situation where there is a significant main effect of COUNTRY on EGALITARIANISM. But the plot of the means of egalitarianism by GENDER categories indicates that, since in each country the males remain about the same distance above the mean scores for the females, there is no interaction between GENDER and COUNTRY.

- **Figure II:** Like the previous figure, this one features a significant main effect

(COUNTRY) and shows a weak but not significant interaction of GENDER by COUNTRY. [This is the data from those reported in Figure I above.]

- **Figure III:** This figure indicates a significant GENDER by COUNTRY interaction, as well as a significant main effect (COUNTRY). In this case, there appears to be no difference between the egalitarian scores of genders in New Zealand, but the gap between the genders in egalitarianism increases as one moves from the Canadian data to the Australian data.

Some aspects of analysis of variance were also discussed in Chapters 7 and 8.

2. COMPARISON WITH MULTIPLE REGRESSION ANALYSIS

While the strength of regression analysis lies in its ability to take many variables into account simultaneously and determine the mathematical equation that best describes the relationship between independent variables and the dependent variable, the strength of analysis of variance lies in its ability to assess interactions among variables and estimate the extent to which the results of a study might be due to random sampling fluctuations. Hence, analysis of variance is most associated with tests of significance (see Chapter 8), while regression analysis focuses on predictive equations. Regression analysis uses analysis of variance as a test of significance for the influence of the independent variables in the equation.

It is possible to analyze a data set using both analysis of variance and re-

gression techniques. The regression analysis would simply use dummy-coded variables so as to match the categorization used in the analysis of variance. The key difference between the two techniques is shown in Box 17.2.

While the residuals in regression analysis are measured in terms of deviations from the regression line (see Chapter 7), the residuals in analysis of variance are measured as deviations from group means. As Iversen and Norpoth point out:

If the regression line passes through all group means, the residual sum of squares will turn out the same for the regression analysis as for analysis of variance. But if the relationship between X and Y is not linear, then the regression line will not pass through all group means, and as a result, the regression residual sum of squares will exceed the analysis of variance residual sum of squares. (1976, p. 91)

BOX 17.2

Comparing the Correlation Coefficient and Analysis of Variance

A. Correlation Coefficient

The correlation coefficient is calculated by using the following formula:

$$r^2 = 1 - \frac{\text{Variations around regression}}{\text{Variations around mean of Y}}$$

In the case of the correlation coefficient, the sum of the squared deviations in the numerator refer to deviations from predicted values; the denominator uses sum of squared deviations from the mean of Y. The denominator measures within category variation. Note that the correlation coefficient refers to the ratio of the two types of variation measured subtracted from 1.

B. Analysis of Variance (F Score)

The *F* Score is calculated by using the following formula:

$$F = \frac{\text{Variation within category + Variation between categories}}{\text{Variation within category}}$$

In the case of analysis of variance, treatment effects are reflected by the sum of squared deviations between treatment categories; random error refers to the sum of squared deviations within treatment categories. The *F* represents the ratio between the two types of deviations.

Note that in both cases we use the sum of squared deviations from relevant means. For both statistics, the denominator reflects variations within a category. The numerators are different: for the correlation coefficient, the value reflects deviations from predicted values. In the case of analysis of variance, the numerator reflects variations between categories.

Thus, if there is a substantial difference in the residual sums of squares between analysis of variance and regression analysis, this would indicate a non-linear relationship between the variables. If there is not much difference in the residual sums of squares, this would lead us to conclude that the relationship is indeed linear.

While generally seen as the technique associated with experimental and quasi-experimental designs, analysis of variance can also be used in a variety of non-experimental situations, particularly those where there are a limited number of independent variables. In all cases, however, the dependent variable should be measured at the ratio level.

To perform this analysis using SPSS see the MANOVA procedure in Appendix A.

Table 17.5 summarizes some of the characteristics of each of the techniques considered in this chapter.

Table 17.6 identifies the SPSS techniques and their associated levels of measurement. This table should be consulted when deciding which form of analysis would be most appropriate for your project.

TABLE 17.5 CHARACTERISTICS OF THREE MULTI-VARIATE TECHNIQUES

TECHNIQUE/ SPSS PROCEDURE	MEASUREMENT/ DISTRIBUTION ASSUMPTIONS	MAJOR STRENGTH	MAJOR WEAKNESS	TYPICALLY USED USED FOR
Multiple Regression REGRESSION	Ratio level on all variables; uses dummy variables for nominal independent variables; assumes normal distribution of of all variables	Dealing with multiple variables simultaneously, with modest number of cases; predictive equations	Instability of weightings from study to study if independent variables share much common variance	Non-experimental designs; particularly used in survey research and in non-reactive research designs
Discriminant Function Analysis DISCRIMINANT	Nominal dependent; ratio independent variables; like regression, can use dummy independent variables; normal distribution of independent variables; population covariance matrices must be equal	Does regression-type analysis using a nominal dependent variable; provides a measure of predictive accuracy of model	Like regression, an instability of weightings assigned if the independent variables share much common variance	Non-experimental designs
Multi-variate Analysis of Variance MANOVA	Ratio level dependent variable; handles treatment/control variables measured at all measurement levels	Handles a great variety of analysis of variance problems; deals well with interactions among variables	Not designed to handle large numbers of variables simultaneously	Experimental, quasi-experimental, and non-experimental designs

TABLE 17.6 SPSS PROCEDURES FOR MULTI-VARIATE ANALYSIS

Dependent	INDEPENDENT VARIABLE		
	Nominal	Ordinal	Ratio
Nominal	CROSSTABS	CROSSTABS	CROSSTABS MEANS*
Ordinal	CROSSTABS	CROSSTABS NONPAR CORR	CROSSTABS NONPAR CORR
Ratio	MEANS ANOVA MANOVA DISCRIMINANT	MEANS ANOVA MANOVA DISCRIMINANT	CORRELATION PLOT PARTIAL CORR MANOVA REGRESSION

* In SPSS for this case, run the independent variable as though it were the dependent variable (i.e., name it first). The interpretation of the test of significance would be standard.

D. KEY TERMS

b coefficient

BACKWARD (stepwise) solution

Beta weight

Covariates

Discriminant function analysis

Dummy variable

Lambda

Linear regression equation

Multicollinearity

Multi-variate analysis of variance (ANOVA or MANOVA)

Multiple regression analysis

R^2

E. KEY POINTS

Selection of appropriate multi-variate technique should be based on the level of measurement achieved on relevant variables and on what the analysis is attempting to reveal.

Multiple regression provides the researcher with:

(i) estimates of the relative importance of the independent variables in bringing about changes in the dependent variable; and

(ii) an equation which describes the relationship.

Dummy-coded independent variables may be used to include nominal variables in multiple regression analysis.

Beta weights refer to the weightings of standardized variables; *b* coefficients refer to the weightings of non-standardized variables.

Discriminant function analysis is used in situations where the dependent variable is measured at the nominal or ordinal level. This procedure provides weightings maximizing the likelihood of correctly predicting the category of the dependent variable each case will fall into.

Multi-variate analysis of variance is used in examining relations between a ratio level dependent variable and independent variables measured at any level. MANOVA techniques also permit the researcher to examine multiple dependent variables simultaneously. While this technique is used particularly in evaluating experimental data it also has many applications in examining non-experimental data.

F. EXERCISES

1. Suppose you wish to predict whether or not a convict will re-offend (be reconvicted of a crime). You have non-experimental data on age, intelligence, size of community, a scale score on employability (likelihood of getting a permanent job). Of the methods outlined in this chapter, which one would seem to be most appropriate for this problem? Provide the rationale for your choice.

2. Suppose you are examining variations in IQ test scores using socio-economic status and region of country as independent variables; and suppose in addition that you suspect that there is an interaction between region of country and socio-economic status. What factors would you need to take into account in deciding which method of analysis you would use? How might you deal with the suspected interaction between the two independent variables?

G. RECOMMENDED READINGS

HEDDERSON, JOHN (1987). *SPSS Made Simple.* Belmont, California: Wadsworth Publishing Company. As the title suggests, Hedderson's book offers straightforward information on many of the SPSS procedures.

IVERSEN, GUDMUND R., AND HELMUT NORPOTH (1976). *Analysis of Variance.* Beverly Hills: Sage Publications. This is a fine introduction to analysis of variance emphasizing the link between regression and analysis of variance techniques.

KACHIGAN, SAM KASH (1986). *Statistical Analysis: An Interdisciplinary Introduction to Univariate & Multivariate Methods.* New York: Radius Press. This text includes a fuller discussion of the techniques included in this chapter.

NETER, JOHN, WILLIAM WASSERMAN, AND MICHAEL KUTNER (1985). *Applied Linear Statistical Models.* Homewood, Illinois: Irwin. This is a more advanced presentation which is, however, excellent in explaining the principles of regression and analysis of variance techniques.

THE RESEARCH REPORT

However well designed and well executed a research project is, its impact will depend, above all, on the quality of the written report. This chapter will present some suggestions for the organization and presentation of a research report.

A. WORD PROCESSORS AND THE RESEARCH REPORT

When the time comes to prepare a research report, you will be greatly assisted if you have access to a word processor. While it is beyond the scope of this text to provide details for using word processors, most word processors will:

- be able to move material from place to place in the manuscript, or add and delete material, with automatic adjustments in page breaks,

- allow the user to search for particular combinations of letters, providing for a quick movement to a desired location in the file;

- search and replace words or expressions with other words or expressions;

- provide a spelling checker to locate and correct misspelled words;

- provide codes for signalling the printer which font to use and when to use italics, bolding, underlining.

In general, it is much easier to edit a document using a word processor, as the machine can automatically reformat the material when changes are made. And, in conducting research projects, word processors have made it easier to record field notes, edit them, and incorporate selected items into the final report without having to re-enter the information into a machine.

B. GENERAL ORIENTATION

1. AUDIENCE

Reports are written for a variety of audiences, and this should be taken into account when preparing one. If a report is intended for a professional journal, then it should be organized in a manner similar to material found in the journal to which the report is to be submitted. If the audience is a non-technical one, then the report should avoid the use of technical terminology.

Most often, it is best to write for the general audience, to assume no prior knowledge of the project, and to convey ideas clearly and simply. The student who is submitting a paper for a course requirement is well advised to write not for the professor, but rather in a manner that any intelligent person would be able to follow. One hint is to write for your "Aunt Martha" or your "Uncle John," not for your professor. Your aunt and uncle have no knowledge of your research project, are not social scientists, in fact never went to university, but they are very smart, and if you explain things clearly they will understand your project. A side benefit of this is that your professor will also be able to figure it out!

Why would writing for an aunt or uncle be helpful? There is a tendency when preparing a report to use too many computer terms, to use technical jargon, and to fail to explain either the logic behind your research design or the logic behind the inferences you have made from your data. If you write for Aunt Martha, you will be less likely to fall into some of these traps. And, in the process, you will probably write a better report, whether it is intended for a journal, a term paper, or for the president of your company.

If you know your audience, you will also know what questions will come to their minds and you will be able to address issues of concern to them. Above all, explain your points clearly and fully: do not assume specialized knowledge on the part of your reader.

2. STYLE

Edit your material carefully. Read it slowly, perhaps out loud, and eliminate redundant words, sentences, and paragraphs. Editing should shorten the document considerably. Do not sacrifice readability and brevity for the sake of saving a nice turn-of-phrase. Keep it short.

It is a good idea to provide headings and subheadings to help guide your reader through the material. Footnotes should be used where technical details that would detract from the flow of the main text are nonetheless required. For purposes of editing, it is easier to place footnotes at the end of the paper.

Tables should include sufficient information to permit the reader to read tables rather than text. Conversely, a reader should be able to get the main points of your findings without studying your tables in detail. Generally, it is preferable to locate tables and figures on separate sheets and place them on the page following the first reference to them in the text. In manuscript

preparation, tables are also placed on separate sheets so that the editor may move the material to the nearest convenient spot in the text.

3. AVOIDING PLAGIARISM

In writing papers you must scrupulously avoid plagiarism. ***Plagiarism*** is the unacknowledged borrowing of other authors' ideas or words. Most academic disciplines have now adopted the method of referencing used by the American Psychological Association. This method requires you to identify the source from which the material has been taken in the body of the text and to include the complete bibliographic information in the list of references at the end of the paper. This is the referencing method used throughout this text.

A. SHORT QUOTATIONS

Where fewer than forty words are being directly quoted, the material should be enclosed in quotation marks, and, after the quotation, reference is made to the name of the author, year of publication, and the page number. For example: "The difference between mores and folkways lies in the nature of the reaction the violation of the norm produces, and not in the content of the rule" (Teevan, 1989, p. 19).

B. LONG QUOTATIONS

Where more than forty words are directly quoted, the material is indented an additional five spaces on both the right- and left-side of the page, and the material is single spaced, with a reference to the author's name, date, and page at the end of the quotation.

C. PARAPHRASED MATERIAL

When using paraphrased material by borrowing ideas that you are not quoting directly, you are nonetheless required to cite your source. Once again, you include the author's name, and the year of publication, but not the page number.

D. MULTIPLE AUTHORS' REFERENCES

Where there is more than one author, the first reference includes all the names; subsequent references to their work uses only the first author's name, followed by "et al."

E. REFERENCE LIST

At the end of the paper, provide a reference list that includes all references cited in alphabetical order. Note how books and articles are cited. Additional examples may be noted in the bibliography which is included at the end of this text.

> Breton, R. (1989). "Quebec Sociology: Agendas from Society or from Sociologists?" *Canadian Review of Sociology and Anthropology*, 26(3), 557-570.
>
> Rosenthal, Robert (1966). *Experimenter Effects in Behavioral Research*. New York: Century.

4. AVOIDING SEXIST LANGUAGE

In the last few years, there has been an increasing awareness of sexist language. We will briefly look at some of the major pitfalls in gender references.

A. THE PRONOUN PROBLEM

The ***pronoun problem*** encourages stereotypic thinking by referring to doctors and managers as *he*, nurses as *she*. There are a number of solutions to the pronoun problem. To illustrate, suppose we have the following sentence:

> *"A doctor has to be especially careful otherwise he can be sued for malpractice." (The problem is characterizing the doctor as a he.)*

This sentence can be changed in any one of the following ways:

- "A doctor has to be especially careful otherwise he or she can be sued for malpractice." (A somewhat awkward solution, but all right if not used too frequently.)

- "Doctors have to be especially careful, otherwise they can be sued for malpractice." (This is a common solution, converting to the plural form avoids the use of *he or she*.)

- "If not especially careful, doctors can be sued for malpractice." (The last sentence avoids the pronoun all together by reconstructing the sentence.)

B. THE MAN PROBLEM

Traditionally, many words and expressions in the English language used *man* or *men* to refer to persons of either gender. In a manner similar to the pronoun problem, such usage may unintentionally suggest, for example, that a *foreman* should be a male. Table 18.1 includes a few examples and some alternative forms that could be considered.

TABLE 18.1 NEUTRALIZING GENDER TERMS

TRADITIONAL USAGE	ALTERNATIVE FORMS
Chairman	Chair, chairperson, coordinator, leader, moderator, presiding officer
Clergyman	Cleric, member of the clergy
Fisherman	Fisher
Foreman	Boss, supervisor
Mailman	Letter carrier, postal worker
Mankind	Human beings, humanity, people
Manmade	Artificial, manufactured, synthetic
Manpower	Personnel, workers
Salesman	Sales agent, salesperson
To man	Operate, to staff
Workman	Employee, labourer, worker

SOURCE: Modified version of a similar listing found in Diana Hacker (1990). *A Canadian Writer's Reference*. Scarborough: Nelson Canada, p. 103.

C. THE NON-PARALLEL CONSTRUCTION PROBLEM

Frequently language may put one gender at a disadvantage. For example, the male may be referred to more formally than the female, suggesting a power or importance differential. More generally, non-parallel constructions can result in confusion or misrepresentation by violating the principle that parts of a sentence that are parallel in meaning should be parallel in structure. Table 18.2 provides some illustrations of non-parallel gender references and more appropriate, parallel forms.

TABLE 18.2 NON-PARALLEL AND PARALLEL GENDER REFERENCES

INAPPROPRIATE USAGE (Non-Parallel)	ALTERNATIVE FORMS (Parallel)
Mr. Chrétien and Kim	Mr. Chrétien and Ms. Campbell
Jean Chrétien and Ms. Campbell	Jean Chrétien and Kim Campbell
Man and wife	Husband and wife
Men and ladies	Men and women
Men's and ladies' teams	Men's and women's teams
Males and women	Males and females

C. ORGANIZATION

A paper should be organized into sections. An effort should be made to cover the material discussed under each of the following headings.

1. INTRODUCTION

The introduction should inform your reader what the project is about, indicate what general approach has been used to solve the problem it tackles, and suggest what critical problems the project raises. Raise interesting questions and unresolved issues that you propose to answer in your research.

2. REVIEW OF THE LITERATURE

The *review of the literature* tries to provide an overview of the "state of scientific knowledge" in your area of study. Consider reviewing the theoretical models that are appropriate and the empirical findings that bear on the particular relationships you will be examining or, if such material is not available, then give the reader some sense of what variables have been related to the major dependent variable in your study. The review should highlight those areas where there are inconsistencies in the conclusions of other studies and indicate which of these inconsistencies you intend to address. Generally, it is best not to present summaries of articles, but rather focus on what the consensus is on the relation between particular variables and the dependent variable. For example, suppose that you were examining factors related to "po-

litical conservatism." It would be useful for your reader to know whether there is any agreement in the scientific literature on whether "conservatism" is related to such variables as: age, sex, rural/urban backgrounds, and socioeconomic status. Where there are inconsistencies, have you any observations as to why they emerged? Different regions, different measurement or analytic procedures, or systematic variations in the compositions of the populations studied might all account for the variations between studies. If inconsistencies are present, these can be noted, and you can heighten your reader's interest in your project by proposing to answer some of the questions that have been raised.

Chapter 9 contains a discussion of how a review of literature can be developed and presented. The reader is referred to that chapter for additional suggestions.

3. HYPOTHESES AND RESEARCH DESIGN

The Review of Literature section should lead into a section defining what hypotheses, questions, or relationships are to be examined. These should be precisely stated and connected to the literature of the discipline. It is almost always best to diagram the causal models that are being evaluated in the research. Not only does this permit the presentation of hypotheses clearly but, by drawing in causal arrows and "greater than" and "less than" symbols, additional precision is achieved. Figure 18.1 presents the diagrams used by Michelle Broussard (1991) in her study of unwanted intimacy.

The rationale given for the design selected should state the advantages the chosen design has over alternative designs.

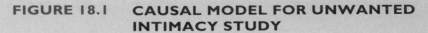

FIGURE 18.1   CAUSAL MODEL FOR UNWANTED INTIMACY STUDY

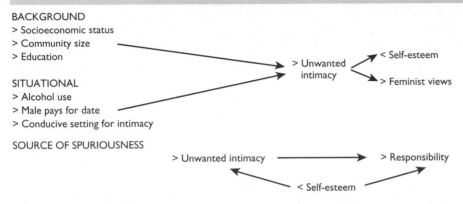

SOURCE: Adapted from Michelle Broussard (1991). "Unwanted Intimacy in Female University Students." Antigonish: St. Francis Xavier University, Research Methods Paper. (This project was jointly conducted by Michelle Broussard, Suzanne Hawco, Marybeth Ryan and Gertrude Morris.) Cited with permission.

What designs have typically been used by other investigators looking at similar relationships?

4. DATA COLLECTION PROCEDURES

Having determined the questions and the design, the next step is to describe the measurement, sample selection, and data collection procedures. In describing a questionnaire it is not necessary to discuss each question. Rather focus attention on non-standard items and, if possible, include a copy of the questionnaire in an Appendix to the report. Any comments on problems in data collection should be mentioned at this point in the report.

5. DESCRIPTION OF THE SAMPLE

The reader should be introduced to the results by reporting some of the background characteristics of the individuals involved in the study: sex distribution, rural/urban location, and average age all might be reported if judged to be relevant by the researcher. If efforts are to be made to assure the representativeness of the sample, this is the stage in the report that such material would be introduced appropriately. If you know from census material, for example, that 54.0 percent of the region's population above 15 is female, and your sample is 59.0 percent female, this fact should be noted. In experimental studies a detailed description of the method of randomization used should be included.

6. DESCRIPTION OF INDEXES, MEASUREMENT PROCEDURES

A description and evaluation of indexes constructed and a preliminary report on the mean results should be made at this point.

If you have used a previously used index, comparisons may be made between the mean results of your study and those of other researchers. Details for the measurement of other key variables should also be included. If the study involves repeated measures, what steps were taken to assure that the measurement process itself was not contaminating the results?

7. PRESENTING BASIC RESULTS

The variations in the dependent variable should be explored at this point. Any basic runs leading up to an exploration of the formal hypotheses of the study should be presented. Where possible, use **summary tables** to compress the results of many analyses into one table. Remember to focus on the relationships being explored when reporting findings. If you are using tests of significance, report whether the findings are statistically significant; if a particular relationship is not statistically significant, is there a trend in the data? It is misleading simply to report "significant" findings. As noted earlier, relationships which are not statistically significant may well have substantive significance. In small sample studies, it is particularly important to report on whether the data trend is in the direction predicted by the various research hypotheses. Generally, SPSS output is not in an appropriate form for presentation. Tables placed in a final report will need to be reformatted and their format should conform to those shown throughout this book or be modelled on those presented in journal articles or books. While it is possible to control the SPSS output format, the beginning researcher will probably find it easier to re-type the tables. In some cases, if the report is being prepared with a word processor, it will be possible to read parts of the .OUT file into the report, modify it, and thus avoid having to re-enter the various numbers.

8. ORGANIZING SUMMARY TABLES

A challenge for the researcher is to compress information into as few tables as possible. Well-designed summary tables can add a lot to your report without sacrificing anything. Let us look at some formats for reporting single-variable information, contingency table, differences of means, and correlations into summary tables.

A. SUMMARIZING UNIVARIATE STATISTICS

Table 18.3 presents one way of compressing the information on a number of variables into a single table. Note that nominal variables can simply have the frequencies listed for each category. These kinds of listings are useful in summarizing descriptive characteristics of the cohort studied. Ratio variables can be summarized by including the mean values and standard deviations.

B. SUMMARIZING CONTINGENCY TABLES

Table 18.4 shows one method for reporting a series of contingency table results (CROSSTABS procedure in SPSS). Note that only the percentage of smokers is reported, along with the number of cases in the column, the Chi-Square probability, and whether the results have a trend in the pre-

TABLE 18.3   SUMMARIZING UNIVARIATE STATISTICS

A. NOMINAL/ ORDINAL VARIABLES	NUMBER	PERCENTAGE
Gender:		
Male	82	48.0
Female	89	52.0
Status:		
Student	26	15.2
Retired	2	1.2
Unemployed, looking for work	13	7.6
Unemployed, not looking for work	4	2.3
Employed part-time	19	11.1
Employed full-time	107	62.6
Size of home community:		
Under 5,000	17	9.0
5,000 – 19,999	24	12.7
20,000 – 99,999	16	8.5
100,000 – 999,999	108	57.1
1,000,000 or more	24	12.7

B. RATIO VARIABLES	MEAN	STANDARD DEVIATION	NUMBER OF CASES
Age	29.6	14.7	183
Income	$43,257.	16,419.	77
Seniority	8.87	3.76	104
Number of children	1.37	1.06	78

dicted direction (+) or in the opposite direction (–).

C. SUMMARIZING MEAN VALUES FOR A DEPENDENT VARIABLE

Table 18.5 provides an illustration of how you can compress a number of analyses of ratio variables into one table. The analysis by Annette Fougere compares the academic performance of Grade 12 students who did or did not regularly eat breakfast. Note that this Figure 18.6 includes the mean grade performance, standard deviations, number of cases, probability level, and an indication of whether the data have a trend in the predicted direction (+) or in the opposite one (–).

D. SUMMARIZING CORRELATIONS

Table 18.6 shows a correlation matrix for variables related to first-year university performance. Note that a report on many relationships can be compressed into such a table. By using asterisks it is also possible to indicate which of the correlations are statistically significant.

TABLE 18.4 **SUMMARIZING CONTINGENCY TABLES: RESPONDENTS' SMOKING BEHAVIOUR BY SELECTED INDEPENDENT VARIABLES**

INDEPENDENT VARIABLES	PERCENTAGE OF SMOKERS	NUMBER OF CASES: COLUMN TOTAL	PROBABILITY (CHI-SQUARE)	TREND
Residence:				
On campus	19.8	101	0.93283	?
Off campus	20.4	54		
SES of father:				
Low SES	22.2	54	0.61304	+
Mid to high SES	18.8	101		
Respondent's age:				
9 or younger	19.7	76	0.93597	+
20 or older	20.3	79		
Level of self-esteem:				
Low	19.5	77	0.87237	−
High	20.5	78		
Level of stress:				
Little	19.4	67	0.90052	−
Much	18.6	86		
Home community:				
Under 30,000	17.8	118	0.22068	−
30,00 or more	27.0	37		
Gender:				
Male	17.6	68	0.51734	+
Female	21.8	87		
Type of program:				
Arts	23.3	60	0.48859	+
Science	18.7	91		
Exercise/Week:				
Less than 3 times	29.6	71	0.00613	+
3 or more times	11.9	84		
Father smokes:				
Yes	29.3	41	0.08363	+
No	16.7	114		
Mother smokes:				
Yes	45.5	33	0.00004	+
No	13.1	122		

SOURCE: Adapted from Michelle Lee (1992). "Smoking Behaviours." Antigonish: St. Francis Xavier University, Research Methods Paper. Cited with permission.

TABLE 18.5   COMPRESSING MEANS: GRADE PERFORMANCE OF GRADE 12 STUDENTS.

INDEPENDENT VARIABLES		MEAN	STANDARD DEVIATION	NUMBER OF CASES	TEST OF SIGNIFICANCE	TREND
Eats breakfast:	No	68.9	12.7	46	0.0003	+
	Yes	76.3	10.0	95		
Breakfast eaten	No	69.5	9.9	39	0.0049	+
in last 7 days	Yes	75.4	11.5	106		
Breakfast maker	Others	72.7	14.4	42	0.2731	–
	Self	75.1	10.0	85		
Lunch maker	Others	73.8	11.7	105	0.8412	*
	Self	74.3	11.6	29		
Supper maker	Others	74.1	11.6	117	0.6416	*
	Self	72.9	10.6	27		
Gender	Male	71.4	11.7	85	0.0026	+
	Female	77.2	10.0	58		
Community size	≤5000	73.7	11.9	103	0.8024	–
	>5000	74.2	10.2	42		
Career:	university plans	78.2	9.0	92	0.0000	+
	non-university	66.2	11.1	53		
Extracurricular	No	70.9	12.0	70	0.0015	–
activities	Yes	76.8	9.9	74		
After school job	No	73.4	11.8	88	0.5825	–
	Yes	74.5	10.8	57		

+ trend predicted correctly   – trend predicted incorrectly   * trend not predicted

SOURCE: Adapted from Annette Fougere (1992). "Effects of Eating Breakfast on Grade Performance." Antigonish: St. Francis Xavier University, Research Methods Paper. Cited with permission.

9. USING GRAPHS, CHARTS

Where feasible, it is a good idea to present data using graphs and charts to make a greater visual impact on the reader. Figures 18.2 and 18.3 show some alternative forms of reporting information. Figure 18.2 uses a bar graph to show for each gender the relationship between age at first sexual intercourse and country of origin. Respondents'

countries of origin are grouped into two categories: respondents from Canada and New Zealand are grouped together and compared to respondents from Australia.

Figure 18.3 uses a plot to show the relation between prestige and income. The visual information conveys much about the strength of the association between the two variables. To the seasoned researcher, the correlation of .87 between the two variables

TABLE 18.6 CORRELATIONS BETWEEN FIRST YEAR UNIVERSITY AVERAGE, AVERAGE HIGH SCHOOL GRADE, AND ENGLISH HIGH SCHOOL GRADE (N = 3617)

CORRELATIONS	FIRST YEAR UNIVERSITY AVERAGE	AVERAGE HIGH SCHOOL GRADE	ENGLISH HIGH SCHOOL GRADE
First year university average	1.000		
Average high school grade	.573	1.000	
English high school grade	.464	0.662	1.000

SOURCE: Winston Jackson.

FIGURE 18.2 AGE OF FIRST SEXUAL INTERCOURSE BY COUNTRY

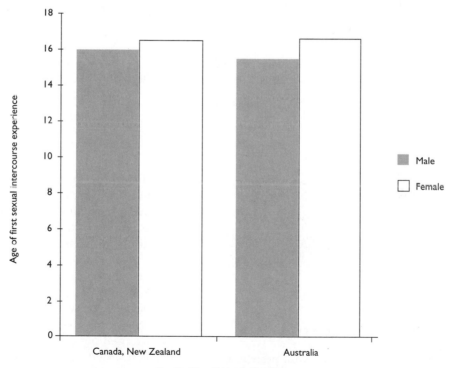

Canada, New Zealand, Australia

FIGURE 18.3 SAMPLE PLOT

Prestige rating by income

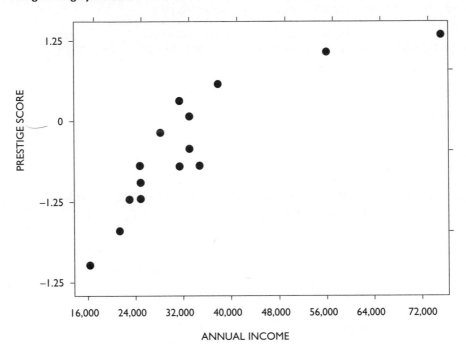

Correlation = .867
(Fictitious data)

reveals much, but for most readers the plot of the information reveals much more.

To perform this analysis using SPSS see the PLOT procedure in Appendix A.

10. EVALUATING HYPOTHESES, MODELS

The reader should now be well prepared, and anticipating, the results of the hypothesis/model testing. If diagrams described the original relationships, they should be employed once again when the findings are reported. If you are testing a theory and have derived a hypothesis, then you should report the finding of the test, even if the relationship is not statistically significant. In cases where you are investigating alternative explanations for some relationship you have initially assumed to be statistically significant, you would only continue to test the alternative explanations if the relationship turned out to be statistically significant. You would, of course, include the intervening variable model in your report; however, if no relationship has emerged, you would not proceed with an evaluation of the alternative explanations—you have no relationship to explain. All you would do is note in your report that the alternative explanations will not be explored, since the original relationship was not sufficiently strong. If it turns out that the primary relationship is not statistically significant, it is then appropriate to explore the relationship of independent variables to the dependent variable. If you are forced to this "fall back" position, and have not established the various hypotheses in advance, then you should indicate that your explorations are being conducted without the guidance of hypotheses. The reader is then alerted to the fact that you are on a hunting expedition. Hunting is fine so long as the reader is alerted.

11. DISCUSSION

At this point an effort should be made to tie the whole project together. References should be made to the review of literature section once again, showing how the results of your research fit into the general picture. Such references will also help tie the paper together, reminding the reader of the problems that the project raised initially. In what areas does your research support the general view, in what areas does it not? Where there are discrepancies, what are some of the possible explanations? This discussion should provide the reader with a sense of what has been learned, and what remains problematic.

12. CONCLUSION

The final section should try to briefly state what the central problem was and what conclusions have been identified. This section may also include suggestions for how the current project might have been improved, and what other issues the researcher identifies as worthy of further exploration.

D. KEY TERMS

Plagiarism   Review of literature   Summary tables
Pronoun problem

E. KEY POINTS

The use of a word processor is highly recommended when preparing a research report.

Research reports are written for different audiences. Be sensitive to your audience so that your organization and language is suitable for your intended audience.

Strive to write crisply, clearly, and briefly.

Be certain to cite sources for your quotations and ideas properly.

Avoid the use of stereotypic gender references: where this may be a problem, consider pluralizing the noun or reconstructing the sentence to avoid the use of the pronoun entirely.

Where appropriate, use diagrams to communicate research hypotheses effectively.

Tables and charts should contain sufficient infor-mation to permit the reader to reconstruct the original tables from which the tables have been con-structed. Use summary tables to condense many tables efficiently into a few tables.

Use graphs, charts, and plots to simplify the pre-sentation of your results.

F. RECOMMENDED READINGS

HACKER, DIANA (1990). *A Canadian Writer's Reference.* Scarborough: Nelson Canada. This handy reference manual deals with how to write more effectively. The manual covers basic grammar, punc-tuation, effective sentences, and alternative citation styles.

HODGES, JOHN C., MARY E. WHITTEN, JUDY BROWN, AND JANE FLICK (1994). *Harbrace College Handbook: for Canadian Writers,* Fourth Edition. Toronto: Harcourt Brace, Canada. This is a comprehensive guide to grammar and style in-cluding a section on the research paper.

PARROTT III, LES (1994). *How to Write Psychology Papers.* New York: HarperCollins. A short and use-ful guide to manuscript preparation for the psy-chology student.

STRUNK, WILLIAM, AND E. B. WHITE (1959). *The Elements of Style.* Galt, Ontario: Brett-MacMillan Ltd. Originally published by Strunk in 1935, this short manual is a classic in the art of clear writing.

APPENDICES

Appendix A contains information on using SPSS. The remaining appendices contain tables and other information necessary for understanding different aspects of social science research. The Appendices are as follows:

ANALYZING DATA WITH SPSS^X AND SPSS/PC+

A. INTRODUCING SPSS^x AND SPSS/PC+

The Statistical Package for the Social Sciences (SPSS) was developed in the 1960s and has gone through a series of embellishments over the years. It contains a number of statistical and data manipulation procedures. The most recent version which is used on mainframe computers is known as SPSS^x. In addition, various versions of SPSS/PC+ are available for personal computers. There are additional versions that feature such items as advanced statistics packages, Data Entry II, graphics, a student version, and a version designed to work with Microsoft's Windows. Versions of SPSS are undoubtedly the most popular, and widely available, statistical packages used by social scientists.

This primer on the use of SPSS provides only the most basic information covering the techniques used in the text. A number of manuals are available from SPSS which detail the many additional features and options that are available for the various commands. Some of these manuals are listed at the end of Appendix A and you may wish to consult them as you develop your facility in working with SPSS. As much as possible, identical commands are used for the SPSS^x and the SPSS/PC+ versions. One fundamental difference between the two version is that SPSS/PC+ commands end with a "." To help distinguish the two sets of commands there will be a light green background for SPSS^x commands, and a thick rule around SPSS/PC+commands.

As used in this text, SPSS refers to all versions of the package; when a specific version is referred to, it is identified as either SPSS^x or SPSS/PC+. This elementary presentation of SPSS begins by describing one convention for identifying the various files used in using SPSS.

1. TYPES OF FILES USED IN SPSS

Typically, the contemporary user of SPSS will either be working on a terminal connected to a mainframe computer (using SPSS^x) or will be using a personal computer equipped with a version of SPSS/PC+. In the former case, the researcher enters raw data into a computer terminal, saves the file of data, and then creates job control files to submit instructions to SPSS. In the latter case, all the work is done on the personal computer. In both cases, however, five types of files will be used. A brief examination of Figure A1 shows how the files are related to one another.

As discussed in Chapter 15, in many computer installations files are made up of a *filename* and a *filetype* separated by a period, such as: data.DAT. The filename can be up to eight characters in length while the filetype is limited to three characters. In this presentation the filename is printed

FIGURE A1 FILE TYPES USED IN SPSS

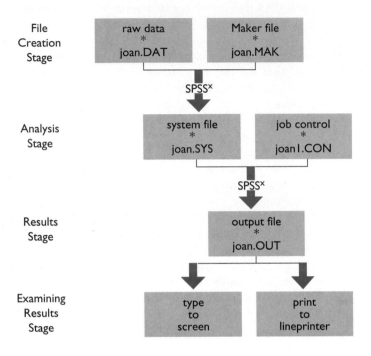

The convention is that the file types (the part following the " . " are printed in UPPER CASE, indicating that they always remain the same. The file names preceding the " ." in lower case, are names assigned by the researcher. Each project should use distinctive file names, which will help keep the files from different projects identified. The file types are:

joan.DAT	.DAT	= raw data file
joan.MAK	.MAK	= SPSS˟ system MAKER file
joan.SYS	.SYS	= SPSS˟ system file
joan.OUT	.OUT	= results sent to OUTPUT file
joan1.CON	.CON	= job control file containing analysis instructions.

in lower case, indicating that it is to be named by the researcher. For convenience, filetypes will always remain the same (these are in UPPER case). There is no requirement that the filenames be the same for each type of file, nor that filetypes use the conventions used here. But whatever naming convention you choose, keep it simple to avoid confusion.

A. SPSS SYSTEM MAKER FILES: EMILY.MAK.

This file type is referred to as a maker file (.MAK) because it creates an SPSS system file. This file contains all the instructions concerning where the data are located, what the names of the variables are, how the variables are labelled, and what values have been assigned in cases where the data are missing. There will be one *maker* file for each project. This file should be retained permanently along with the raw data file in case you wish to transfer the data to a different SPSS version or to an entirely different system. The details for creating such a file are presented later in this appendix.

B. DATA FILES: EMILY.DAT.

This file contains the raw data for your study. It will contain no blank lines, and the records will be sorted so that where there are two lines of data for each respondent/subject, the file will contain the first line of case one and then the second line of case one; this would then be followed by subsequent cases, ensuring that the cases always follow the same pattern and that there are no missing lines of data, or blank lines. Care in the preparation and entry of data is critical because if an error occurs, wrong data may be read. Chapter 15 outlines the procedures for preparing the data for submission to SPSS. The emily.DAT file will be read into SPSS when the emily.MAK file is submitted to the computer.

C. SPSS SYSTEM FILES: EMILY.SYS.

The convention used here is that .SYS files are SPSS system files. These files combine all of the data, and all of the variable names, labels, and other information included in the .MAK file. Once created and confirmed as correct, the .SYS files are used throughout the project analysis. Consistently labelling such files as .SYS files will ensure that they are immediately recognizable. They can only be altered by issuing commands contained in an SPSS job. System files should be retained permanently, along with at least one backup copy of each file.

System files can be updated to include any new variables which have been computed. It is especially important, therefore, to retain any files that have been used to update system files. Should errors in the raw data be discovered after analysis has started, it is then possible to make the changes in the raw data, resubmit the .MAK job, recreate the .SYS file with the new information contained in it, and then resubmit any jobs which have been used to update and modify the .SYS file. Much time will be saved if any files updating the .SYS file are retained until the project is completed. After the project is completed, however, only three files need to be retained: the .DAT, .MAK, and the .SYS files. All others may be deleted.

D. JOB CONTROL FILES: EMILY1.CON.

Control (.CON) files include the procedures to be used in an analysis. For bigger jobs, or jobs which update the system file, it is a good idea to retain these files under separate names, such as: emily1.CON, emily2.CON, emily3.CON, and so on. Generally these files contain just a few lines so that they will not take up too much space in the computer. They are retained so that if it becomes necessary to resubmit the analysis, the contents of the files will not have to be reentered. As a hint, control jobs of the form, emily0.CON, may be used for jobs which do not need to be retained (such as listing some cases, printing the dictionary, or running a frequency distribution before recoding a variable). To save time, the FILE HANDLE and GET FILE commands can be retained and the procedures can be modified from run to run.

E. OUTPUT OF RESULTS FILES: EMILY.OUT.

The .OUT file is the output file which contains the results of an SPSS analysis. The researcher examines this file, determines whether the run is error-free and has produced the intended analyses, and, if everything is correct, prints the file on the computer's printer. It is generally advisable to use the same name for .OUT files. Not only will you be able to remember the name of the file, but you will avoid building up a number of unnecessary files in your directory. But realize that once you run another job, the new results will be printed over the previous one, so that you will need to print any results you wish to retain before you run another job. In cases where the printer is broken, you can continue to analyze data but remember that the .OUT files will have to be given different names, so that they will not be over-written. After the printer is operating again, you will want to print and then purge all of these .OUT files since they use a lot of space.

F. BACKUP FILES: DATA.BAK, SYSTEM.BAK, MAKER.BAK.

A sixth type of file, not identified on Figure A1, is a .BAK file. This is the backup file. Once again, the name assigned is arbitrary. It is a good idea to

back up your raw data, SPSS system, and SPSS system maker files using totally different names. In case you then happen to delete all your .DAT files,
you will still have your data stored under another name. The three critical files
are your raw data, system, and system maker files. Names such as data.BAK,
system.BAK, and maker.BAK may be used. They should also be backed up
on tape or on diskettes and removed from the computer location. That way,
short of a nuclear attack, no disasters should destroy the files that have
taken so much time to create.

2. CREATING AND SAVING A SIMPLE SPSS^X OR SPSS/PC+ SYSTEM FILE: THE .MAK FILE

In order to create an SPSS system file, a maker file will be used. We will use
the file extension .MAK to refer to such files. Such files should be saved
permanently since they are time-consuming to develop. Another option
available from SPSS is the Data Entry package which allows the researcher
to create and save a system file which has error-checking and variable definition procedures contained within it. If this package is available to you, use
it; if not, the following steps will be required in creating and saving a SPSS
system file.

The commands required to create an SPSS system file which combines
the raw data with the instructions for how the variables are to be named and
labelled are illustrated below. The reader should note, however, that SPSS
can deal with more complex data sets and one of the SPSS basic manuals
should be consulted if your data do not fit into the type described below
(*SPSS^x User's Guide*, 1988; *SPSS/PC+ Base System User's Guide*, 1992). We will
assume that we have a data file of 150 observations, and 25 variables. In
such cases, we will want to keep the raw data on a separate file, which
will then be combined with a set of data definition commands in order to
create an SPSS system file.

SPSS commands are broken into two parts: a *command name*, which
starts in column 1, followed by *specifications*. To indicate the continuation
of a line, indent it. Each of the commands will be discussed briefly. Only the
basic commands are treated here; for additional information, consult an
SPSS manual.

SPSS^x Version of a MAKER File

TITLE Maker File For Survey of
  Graduates, your name
FILE HANDLE file specifications for raw
  data file
FILE HANDLE file specifications for new
system file
DATA LIST FILE=data RECORDS=2
    /1 id 1-3 v1 TO v4 5-8 v5 9-10
       v6 TO v22 11-45
    /2 name 5-33 (A) v23 35-37 (1)
VARIABLE LABELS id "dentification
Number"
    v1 "Sex of Respondent"
    v2 "Size of Home Community"
    v3 "Religious Affiliation"
    v4 "Ethnic Origin"
    v5 "Year of Birth"
    ...etc
    name "Name of School"
VALUE LABELS v1 1 "Male" 2 "Female"/
    v2 1 "Rural Area" 2 "Under 1,000"
       3 "1,000 to 4,999"
       4 "5,000 to 49,999"
       5 "50,000 to 99,999"
       6 "Over 100,000"/
    v3 1 "Roman Catholic" 2 "Anglican"
       3 "United" 4 "Baptist"
       5 "Presbyterian"
       6 "Other Protestant" 7 "Jewish"
       8 "Buddhist" 9 "Muslim"
       10 "None" 11 "Other"/
MISSING VALUES v1,v6,v29 TO v34 (9)/
    v16,v19 (0,98,99)/
    v17,v18,v20 TO v22 (0)/
FREQUENCIES VARIABLES = v1,v2,v17
SAVE OUTFILE = system
FINISH

SPSS/PC+ Version of a MAKER File

TITLE Maker File For Survey of
  Graduates, your name.
DATA LIST FILE='data.DAT'
    / id 1-3, v1 TO v4 5-8, v5 9-10,
      v6 TO v22 11-45
    / name 5-33 (A) v23 35-37 (1).
VARIABLE LABELS id "Identification
Number"
    /v1 "Sex of Respondent"
    /v2 "Size of Home Community"
    /v3 "Religious Affiliation"
    /v4 "Ethnic Origin"
    /v5 "Year of Birth"
    ...etc
    /name "Name of School".
VALUE LABELS v1 1 "Male" 2 "Female"
    /v2 1 "Rural Area" 2 "Under 1,000"
       3 "1,000 to 4,999"
       4 "5,000 to 49,999"
       5 "50,000 to 99,999"
       6 "Over 100,000"
    /v3 1 "Roman Catholic" 2 "Anglican"
       3 "United" 4 "Baptist"
       5 "Presbyterian"
       6 "Other Protestant" 7 "Jewish"
       8 "Buddhist" 9 "Muslim"
       10 "None" 11 "Other".
MISSING VALUES v1,v6,v29 TO v34 (9)
    /v16,v19 (0,98,99)
    /v17,v18,v20 TO v22 (0).
FREQUENCIES VARIABLES = v1,v2,v17.
SAVE OUTFILE = 'EMILY.SYS'.
FINISH.

A. TITLE

The TITLE command should be included so that a label will be placed at the top of each page of output. It is a good idea to include the researcher's name in the text of the title. The text of the title can include up to 60 characters and might look like:

TITLE A Study of Sibling Rivalry, Charlie McMullin

B. FILE HANDLE (PC+ USERS SKIP THIS SECTION)

File handles provide SPSS^x information as to where raw data, or system files, are located. The format for these commands varies for each type of computer and operating system. Two common ones will be listed here but these may not work on your particular installation. For a DEC/VAX system, the following is used to identify raw data and system, files respectively:

```
FILE HANDLE data/NAME='joan.DAT'
FILE HANDLE system/NAME='joan.SYS'
```

The convention that is being followed uses lower-case letters to refer to those added by the researcher (SPSS works with either upper or lower case). For an IBM/CMS system, the following command lines would identify the raw data and system files:

```
FILE HANDLE data/NAME='joan data a'
FILE HANDLE system/NAME='joan sys a'
```

Researchers will need to consult with their computer centre to find out how to do the file handles if the above commands do not work. Any file you wish to access, or create, in a run must be identified by a FILE HANDLE command. Normally, after the researcher has created the system file and is analyzing data, only one file handle will be required—the one which identifies the system file.

C. SET

This command sets various output options. Two of them are particularly useful. If you require typewriter-width output, rather than computer printer-width paper, use the WIDTH=80 option; if you wish to start a new page with each analysis, use the LENGTH=59 option. These commands are as follows:

SPSS^x	**SPSS/PC+**
SET WIDTH=80	SET WIDTH=80.
SET LENGTH=59	SET LENGTH=59.

D. DATA LIST

The DATA LIST command is the most complex one that will be encountered in creating a system file. Do this one carefully, and double check it, for this is the one most likely to produce errors. A simple DATA LIST might look like:

SPSS^x
DATA LIST FILE=data RECORDS=2
/1 id 1-3, v1 TO v4 6-9 v5 10-11,
   v6 TO v22 13-46, v23 48-50
/2 name 5-33 (A) v24 35-37 (1)

SPSS/PC+
DATA LIST FILE='emily.DAT'
/ id 1-3, v1 TO v4 6-9 v5 10-11,
   v6 TO v22 13-46, v23 48-50
/ name 5-33 (A) v24 35-37 (1).

FILE=	is used to identify the file where the raw data are located. This file is fully identified on the FILE HANDLE in SPSS^x or is the name of the raw data file if using SPSS/PC+, as in: FILE = 'emily.DAT'.
RECORDS=	indicates how many lines of data there are for each case. In the above example there are two lines, or records, per case. Variable names and the column locations of the data are then identified. In SPSS/PC+ each new record is identified by including a / mark.
/1	identifies, in SPSS^x, that what follows are the variable names and column locations for information on the first line (record) of data; in SPSS/PC+ only the / is used.
id	is the identification number of the case, and is always included; 'id' becomes the first variable name in the study. Variable names may be up to eight characters in length and must begin with an alphabetical character. For studies involving many variables, it is best to simply use the question numbers printed on the questionnaire (or data-recording form) to name variables. In the illustration, the variables are named ID followed by v1, v2 ... v22. The advantages of using sequential numbers are: • if you have many variables it will be difficult to remember special variable names; • variables named after question numbers can be quickly identified; and, • time can be saved because variables can be named by using the **TO** convention, which has the computer assign variable names, as in: v1 TO v4. Researchers analyzing few variables may wish to assign variable names such as "FAED, MAED, AGE, INCOME" to refer to father's education, mother's education, age of respondent, and income of respondent.
Column #s	are indicated in the information that follows the variable name. The ID data are located in columns 1 through 3, indicated by "1-3." Where there are a series of variables with the same field lengths (i.e., all 1, or all 2, or all 3 columns

long), time can be saved by naming a series of variables, followed by the columns that contain the data, as in:

v1 TO v4 6-9 [4 1-column variables in sequence]

v12 TO v14 10-15 [3 2-column variables in sequence]

This series identifies four variables (v1, v2, v3, and v4) and the four columns (6, 7, 8, and 9) where the data are found for them. It should be noted that not all columns need to be read—you can skip any columns that you will not be using.

/2 | signals the beginning of the second record. A variable called NAME is located in columns 5-33. In SPSS/PC+ only the / is used to indicate the beginning of the next record.

(A) | indicates an alphabetic variable and might refer to the names of schools, names of people, or even whether responses to a set of true/false questions have been coded as T or F. Generally, however, yes/no or true/false questions are best coded numerically as it will be somewhat easier to analyze the data later.

(1) | indicates the number of decimals that you wish to force into your data. This number is in parentheses following column location. Suppose when you recorded the occupational prestige scores you entered 636 for a prestige score of 63.6; by placing the (1) after the column numbers, you would force one decimal place into the data, resulting in a value of 63.6.

E. VARIABLE LABELS

Although optional, it is useful to label variables, since they will be printed on many of the analyses that will be used in data analysis. Each label may be up to 40 characters in length. The following format uses double quotation marks (") to signal the beginning and the end of a label. The double quotation mark is recommended because this then permits the researcher to use apostrophes in variable labels, as in, "Father's Education". Note that if a single apostrophe had been used, SPSS would not properly interpret the label, since the 's' would signal the end of the label. The recommended format for VARIABLE LABELS is as follows:

SPSS^x

VARIABLE LABELS id "Identification
    Number"
    v1 "Sex"
    v2 "Program of Study"
    v3 "Education of Respondent's
        Father"

SPSS/PC+

VARIABLE LABELS id "Identification
    Number"
    /v1 "Sex"
    /v2 "Program of Study"
    /v3 "Education of Respondent's
        Father".

F. VALUE LABELS

Labels assist the researcher to understand the results of various analyses because with them included, labels are placed on the various categories within a variable. Once again, these are optional. Each label may be up to 20 characters in length. Value labels can be appended to multiple variables simultaneously, by listing the variables to which the same labels should be appended. It is useful in 9-point Likert-type items to label the extremes. Note that a slash is placed between the labels for each variable (this omission is a common error). The labels may be illustrated as follows:

SPSS^x

```
VALUE LABELS v1 1 "Male" 2 "Female"/
    v2 1 "Arts" 2 "Science"
        3 "Business Admin." 4 "Nursing"
        5 "Physical Ed."/
    v7 TO v14 1 "Strongly Disagree"
        9 "Strongly Agree"/
```

SPSS/PC+

```
VALUE LABELS v1 1 "Male" 2 "Female"
    /v2 1 "Arts" 2 "Science"
        3 "Business Admin." 4 "Nursing"
        5 "Physical Ed."
    /v7 TO v14 1 "Strongly Disagree"
        9 "Strongly Agree".
```

G. MISSING VALUES

Most variables require a code for missing values. As discussed in Chapter 15, it is best to use 9s to reflect missing values. Up to three values may be designated as missing values. A missing value is used when a respondent has not answered a question or when a question does not apply to the respondent. When new variables are created using SPSS commands, the program will assign missing values where the information is incomplete for any case. Multiple variables can be assigned missing values simply by listing all the variables to which the same missing values apply, as in:

SPSS^x

```
MISSING VALUES v1, v7 to v10, v21 (9)/
    v16,v19 (998, 999)/
    v3 to v6,v11 to v15,v17,v18,v20 (0)/
```

SPSS/PC+

```
MISSING VALUES v1, v7 to v10, v21 (9)
    /v16,v19 (998,999)
    /v3 to v6,v11 to v15,v17,v18,v20 (0).
```

H. FREQUENCIES

Some procedure is included here to activate the file. Any number of procedures could be used at this point. In this case, the following command might be used:

SPSS^x
FREQUENCIES VARIABLES= v1, v56

SPSS/PC+
FREQUENCIES VARIABLES= v1, v56.

3. ERROR-CHECKING A
NEW SYSTEM FILE USING SPSS^X AND SPSS/PC+

Having entered the above commands into a file called emily.MAK, the time has come to save the file and then to submit it to SPSS for processing. Depending on how SPSS has been set up, in DEC/VAX systems, at the operating system prompt, the command is likely to be something like:

>SPSS emily.MAK

Your terminal will now freeze until the job has been completed, at which point the prompt will reappear. Now you examine the results by listing emily.OUT on your terminal. If there are errors (almost a certainty the first time!), try to spot them on the screen, and note them. If you cannot figure out the errors, you can print the results on the printer. After you figure out what has gone wrong, put your emily.MAK file into the editor, make the necessary corrections, and resubmit the job to SPSS. One error which is often confusing for the beginning student of SPSS is one which tells you that an end-of-file marker has been encountered in the middle of a case. This is an error in your .DAT file. Double check your file for the following:

• make certain that there are no blank lines in your .DAT file. The most common error is to leave blank lines at the top or bottom of the file—SPSS will treat these lines as data. Also, check to make certain there are no blank lines anywhere in the middle of the file.

• where you have more than one line of data for each case, look for cases sorted improperly; if you are missing one line anywhere in the file, it will throw everything off. Similarly, if you had corrected a line by reentering it, but then failed to delete the old line, you would have two similar lines. This error would produce scrambled data from this point onward.

When the message at the bottom of the .OUT file indicates that there are no SPSS errors, you have not, however, entirely finished the error-checking. A little time spent on some final checks will help to ensure that when you begin analysis you will be working with a file that is substantially error-free. The following steps are recommended:

STEP 1. Check the printout section showing the data list command. There will be a listing of the variable names and the record number and column location of each variable. Go through the list carefully and check it against the codes on your questionnaire. For example, if question 27 is named v27 and should be located on RECORD 1, column 26-27, be certain that v27 is listed on your printout as being located in that position (see Box A1 which provides a sample listing).

STEP 2. Run a job which lists all the variables for the last case in the system file. Proofread the last case, comparing what is in the system file to the raw data input form (questionnaire, data-recording form). Assuming that you have 150 cases in the file, the following command would list the variable names and the value for each case in the last case in the file:

*SPSS*ˣ

LIST VARIABLES = ALL/CASES = 150
   TO EOF

SPSS/PC+

LIST VARIABLES = ALL/CASES = 150
   TO EOF.

BOX A1   SAMPLE OUTPUT OF A .MAK FILE

A. SPSSˣ Version

TITLE system file creation nursing project

FILE HANDLE data/NAME='g2wj94.DAT' ❶

FILE HANDLE system/NAME='eval.SYS' ❷

DATA LIST FILE=data RECORDS=3
   /1   id   1-3   v1   5-6   v2   7   v3.1   8   v3.2   9   v4   10   v5.1   11   v5.2   12
         v6   13-14   v7.1   15-17   v7.2   18   v8.1   19   v8.2   20   v9   21   v10.1   ❸

...

   /2   v19.1   5   v19.2   6   v20   7   v21   8   v22   9   v23.1   10   v23.2   11
         v24.1   TO   v24.2   12-13   v25.1   TO   v25.4   14-17   v25.5   TO   v25.6   19-20   ❹

...

   /3   v49   5   v50   6   v51   7   v52   8   v52.1   9   v52a   10   v53.1   TO   v53.4   11-14 ──❺

SPSS Output: ❻

Variable	Rec	Start	End	Format
ID	1	1	3	F3.0 ──❼
V1	1	⑤	⑥	F2.0
V2	1	7	7	F1.0 ❽
V3.1	1	8	8	F1.0

BOX A1   SAMPLE OUTPUT OF A .MAK FILE (continued)

V3.2	1	9	9	F1.0
V4	1	10	10	F1.0
...				
V19.1	2	5	5	F1.0
V19.2	2	6	6	F1.0
V20	2	7	7	F1.0
V21	2	8	8	F1.0
...				
V49	3	5	5	F1.0
V50	3	6	6	F1.0
V51	3	7	7	F1.0
...				
V57	3	19	19	F1.0

VARIABLES LABELS

    id   "Identification Number"
    v1   "Year of Graduation"
    v2   "Marital Status"
    v3.1   "Children"
    v3.2   "Number of Children"
    v4   "Home Prior to ST.F.X."
    ...

VALUE LABELS

    v2 1 'single' 2 'married' 3 'separated' 4 'divorced' 5 'widowed' ①————————⑨
    v3.1, V7.1, V8.1, V23.1, V24.1, V34, v35 1 'yes' 2 'no'/
    v4 1 'cape breton island' 2 'mainland ns' 3 'other atlantic prov' 4 'other can province'
         5 'outside canada'/
    ...

MISSING VALUES

    v8.1, v11, v14.01 TO v14.10, v22, v23.1, v39, v51, v52.1
    v52a, v54, v3.2, v4, v9, v32a v32.1 TO v32.4, v33.1 TO v33.3
    v8.2, v17.2, v18.2 (9)/
    v3.1, v17.1, v18.1, v53.1 TO v53.4 (0) ①————————⑩
    v1, v6, v10.1 TO v10.8 (00)/
    v7.1, v12.1, v12.2 (000)/

BOX A1 SAMPLE OUTPUT OF A .MAK FILE (continued)

FREQUENCIES VARIABLES= v57

SAVE OUTFILE= system

FINISH

B. SPSS/PC+ Version

TITLE system file creation nursing project.

DATA LIST FILE='g2wj94.DAT'
```
    / id 1-3 v1 5-6 v2 7 v3.1 8 v3.2 9 v4 10 v5.1 11 v5.2 12
    v6 13-14 v7.1 15-17 v7.2 18 v8.1 19 v8.2 20 v9 21 v10.1 TO v10.8 23-38
...
    / v19.1 5 v19.2 6 v20 7 v21 8 v22 9 v23.1 10 v23.2 11
    v24.1 TO v24.2 12-13 v25.1 TO v25.4 14-17 v25.5 TO v25.6 19-20
...
    / v49 5 v50 6 v51 7 v52 8 v52.1 9 v52a 10 v53.1 TO v53.4 11-14 v54 15
    v55 17 v56 18 v57 19.
```

SPSS Output:

Variable	Rec	Start	End	Format
ID	1	1	3	F3.0
V1	1	5	6	F2.0
V2	1	7	7	F1.0
V3.1	1	8	8	F1.0
V3.2	1	9	9	F1.0
V4	1	10	10	F1.0
...				
V19.1	2	5	5	F1.0
V19.2	2	6	6	F1.0
V20	2	7	7	F1.0
V21	2	8	8	F1.0
...				
V49	3	5	5	F1.0
V50	3	6	6	F1.0
V51	3	7	7	F1.0
...				
V57	3	19	19	F1.0

BOX A1 SAMPLE OUTPUT OF A .MAK FILE (continued)

VARIABLES LABELS

id   "Identification Number"
/v1   "Year of Graduation"
/v2   "Marital Status"
/v3.1 "Children"
/v3.2 "Number of Children"
/v4   "Home Prior to ST.F.X.".
...
                                ⑰

VALUE LABELS

v2 1 'single' 2 'married' 3 'separated' 4 'divorced' 5 'widowed'
/v3.1, V7.1, V8.1, V23.1, V24.1, V34, v35 1 'yes' 2 'no'
/v4 1 'cape breton island' 2 'mainland ns' 3 'other atlantic prov' 4 'other can province'
      5 'outside canada'.
...

MISSING VALUES

v8.1, v11, v14.01 TO v14.10, v22, v23.1, v39, v51, v52.1
v52a, v54, v3.2, v4, v9, v32a, v32.1 TO v32.4, v33.1 TO v33.3
v8.2, v17.2, v18.2 (9)
/v3.1, v17.1, v18.1, v53.1 TO v53.4 (0)
/v1, v6, v10.1 TO v10.8 (00)
/v7.1, v12.1, v12.2 (000).
                                 ⑱

FREQUENCIES VARIABLES= v57.

SAVE OUTFILE= 'eval.SYS'.

FINISH.

NOTES

① this is a VAX/VMS file handle indicating where raw data file is located
② this will be the file name of the system file
③ variables and columns, first record
④ second record; note slash at beginning
⑤ third record; note slash at beginning
⑥ record number
⑦ field three characters wide
⑧ field starts in column 5, ends in column 6
⑨ note slash after each value label is computed

⑩ note slash after each group of variables
⑪ variables and columns, first record
⑫ second record, note slash at beginning
⑬ third record, note slash at beginning
⑭ record number
⑮ field three characters wide
⑯ field starts in column 5, ends in column 6
⑰ note slash between end of one label and start of another
⑱ note slash between each group of variables

If the values for each variable are not the same as on the original input form, then there is a problem either in the .DAT or the .MAK file. If the data are correct for a number of variables and then are off, the error probably is in the DATA LIST command in the .MAK file. If the values are incorrect starting with variable 1, then there is a good chance that there is an inconsistency in the .DAT file. The file may have a repeated line in it, or a missing line, or a blank line (top, bottom, or middle of file). Make corrections and resubmit the job to check for errors. Recycle the process until the last case is being read properly.

STEP 3. It is a good idea at this point to run the frequency distribution on all nominal and ordinal variables, and a procedure to compute the means on all ratio level variables; in addition, it is useful to have a listing made of the names and labels placed on all variables. The following SPSS commands added to the end of the .MAK file will produce the required information:

```
SPSSx
FREQUENCIES VARIABLES= v1 TO v6,
   v19, v21, v30 TO v39
DESCRIPTIVES VARIABLES= v7 TO
   v18,v20,v22 TO v29
DISPLAY DICTIONARY
FINISH
```

```
SPSS/PC+
FREQUENCIES VARIABLES = v1 TO
   v6, v19, v21, v30 TO v39.
DESCRIPTIVES VARIABLES= v7 TO
   v18,v20,v22 TO v29.
DISPLAY.
FINISH.
```

STEP 4. This output file will be a large one but it should be checked carefully. This is your last opportunity to correct errors easily. Check the frequency distributions for any out-of-range values. Make certain that the MISSING values are noted. (If the 9s, for example, have not been flagged as MISSING, note which variables have been missed so that you can make changes in the .MAK file.) For ratio-level variables, the DESCRIPTIVES procedure will show the means, and the minimum and maximum values for each variable will be shown on the printout. Check these to make certain that the appropriate range is noted. There are two common errors that can be noted here: zeros which should have been coded as MISSING; or values that are too high but not identified as MISSING. For example, in occupational codes, "98" may have been used to identify a housewife, and should be flagged as a MISSING value (these can be switched later if necessary). Finally, the dictionary of variables and labels should be checked carefully for completeness and for any spelling errors.

STEP 5. All the changes should now be made in the .DAT file. The .MAK file should be submitted once again but the FREQUENCIES, DESCRIPTIVES, and DISPLAY DICTIONARY commands may be removed and replaced by "contingency checking" procedures. These checks apply where branching questions have been used or where other combinations of responses are not possible. Two simple illustrations will demonstrate "contingency checks." Figure 13.10 (Chapter 13) illustrated a branching question which asked respondents to indicate whether they had consumed any beer in the past seven days; those who responded with a "yes" were then asked to indicate how much they had consumed. Only those who responded "yes" were to answer the question which followed. Those who responded "no" were to be consistently recorded as a "0" or as a MISSING value (9) on the amount consumed. Suppose we decided to record them all as 9s and we wanted to check to make certain that the coding was done consistently. We could then use the SPSS procedure, CROSSTABS, to see whether there was inconsistency in the data, as in:

SPSS^x
CROSSTABS TABLES = v9.1 BY v9

SPSS/PC+
CROSSTABS TABLES = v9.1 BY v9.

Similar checks may be done with the gender variable where some questions may only apply to one gender. Suppose, for example, that the following questions should always have 9s (MISSING values) for males: v12, v23, v24, and v30. The following CROSSTABS procedure would show the relationships between gender (v3) and each of the other variables:

SPSS^x
CROSSTABS TABLES =
   v12,v23,v24,v30 BY v3

SPSS/PC+
CROSSTABS TABLES =
   v12,v23,v24,v30 BY v3.

The various contingency check procedures should be added to the bottom of the .MAK file and then submitted to SPSS for processing.

STEP 6. The results of this run should be inspected and if any inconsistencies appear, they should then be identified in the next run. Let us suppose that errors have shown up and we now need to identify the cases where the errors are found. To find these cases, the SELECT IF procedure may be used, as in:

SPSS^x
TEMPORARY
SELECT IF (v9 EQ 2 AND v9.1 NE 9)
LIST VARIABLES = id, v9, v9.1
FREQUENCIES VARIABLES = v9, v9.1

SPSS/PC+
PROCESS IF (v9 EQ 2 AND v9.1 NE 9).
LIST VARIABLES= id, v9, v9.1
FREQUENCIES VARIABLES= v9, v9.1.

These commands should be added into the .MAK file immediately before the FINISH command and the job should be submitted to SPSS.

STEP 7. Inspect the output of the analysis. It should indicate the ID (identification number) of cases which are inconsistent. The questionnaires with the errors should be pulled out and checked to see whether the problem was an error in recording gender, or in the questions to which gender has been related. The errors should be corrected in the .DAT file.

STEP 8. The stage has now finally arrived to create and save the SPSS system file. The contingency check procedures should be removed from the .MAK file, and two additional commands should be added:

*SPSS*ˣ

DISPLAY DICTIONARY
SAVE OUTFILE = system
FINISH

SPSS/PC+

DISPLAY.
SAVE OUTFILE = 'dani.SYS'.
FINISH.

Submit the .MAK file to SPSS for processing. The results of this successful run should be printed and retained as a permanent record. On the last page of the output, note the message informing you that the system file has been saved. You are now ready to begin analyzing your data.

Should additional errors in the data appear during data processing, you should immediately determine the ID number of the case (through the SELECT IF procedure) and correct both the raw data file and the system file. The system file w'ould be corrected and saved. Suppose you discovered during data analysis that a university student had earned $50,000 in the previous summer. Through a SELECT IF, you identify that the respondent's ID is 132. You would then check the questionnaire to see if a coding error has been made. Suppose you discover that indeed an additional "0" had been added to v27 (income) and that it should be $5,000, rather than $50,000. At this stage, the system file could be updated by the following commands:

*SPSS*ˣ

IF (id EQ 132) v27 = 5000
SAVE OUTFILE = system
FINISH

SPSS/PC+

IF (id EQ 132) v27 = 5000.
SAVE OUTFILE = 'dani.SYS'.
FINISH.

If the corrected variable has been used in the creation of permanent indexes or variables, the runs performing those tasks would have to be resubmitted so that the error would be removed. It is a good idea to record the dates, and the details of such corrections made to the raw data and system files.

4. USING SPSS^X AND SPSS/PC+ SYSTEM FILES

Having created an SPSS^x system file, we will now review basic procedures for using such files.

A. GET FILE

System files are accessed by creating an emily0.CON file which includes commands to identify the system file, retrieve it, and list the procedures that are to be run, as in:

SPSS^x

TITLE Project, Danielle Keating
FILE HANDLE system/NAME='dan.SYS'
GET FILE system
... any analysis procedures ...
FINISH

SPSS/PC+

GET FILE 'dani.sys'.
... any analysis procedures ...
FINISH.

In the SPSS^x version, the first three lines retrieve the system file. These lines are followed by any number of procedures that may be requested. The file is ended with the FINISH command which tells SPSS that the run is concluded. In SPSS/PC+, it only takes one line to identify and access the system file.

B. LIST

Frequently the researcher will want to list some variables for some, or all, of the cases. Any time new variables are created, it is a good idea to list a few cases, and the variables involved in the computation, so that manual checks of a few of the computations can be made to ensure that there are no errors. (Hint: if you list 12 or fewer variables, and are printing your results on computer-width paper, the output is easy to read.) The command to LIST is:

SPSS^x

LIST VARIABLES = id,v1,v17/CASES = 50

SPSS/PC+

LIST VARIABLES = id,v1,v17/CASES = 50.

The above command would list the first 50 cases for the three variables identified.

C. SORT CASES

The researcher may wish to sort cases on one or more variables. Suppose we had a list of employee names, departments, and salaries. And suppose we wish to sort them alphabetically by department, and then list the salaries. The following commands would do the task:

SPSS^x	SPSS/PC+
SORT CASES BY dept,name LIST VARIABLES= dept,name,salary	SORT CASES BY dept,name. LIST VARIABLES= dept,name,salary.

The above commands would reorder all the cases in the file, sorted alphabetically within each department, and provide a complete listing of the cases.

D. SELECT IF

This procedure provides a method for selecting cases that meet designated criteria. Suppose you wished to list women earning over $50,000. Here the following commands would produce the list:

SPSS^x	SPSS/PC+
SELECT IF (sex EQ 2 AND income GE 50000) LIST VARIABLES = name,income	SELECT IF (sex EQ 2 AND income GE 50000). LIST VARIABLES = name,income.

In the above case, the commands select and then list the names of females earning $50,000 or more. There are eight key words that should be understood. All of them may be used in SELECT IF statements and in other similar commands that will be introduced later. They are:

EQ   equal to

NE   not equal to

LT   less than

LE   less than or equal to

GT   greater than

GE   greater than or equal to

AND   both conditions must be met

OR   either condition is met

If a file is going to be saved at the end of a run, and a SELECT IF has been used, caution must be exercised since any cases not selected will disappear when the new file is saved. SPSS^x provides a method of avoiding this problem by providing a command, called TEMPORARY, which, when placed before a SELECT IF command, will be in effect for only one procedure. The researcher must be extremely careful if a SAVE OUTFILE is used in the same run where a SELECT IF has been used. The importance of always having a backup system file cannot be overemphasized.

E. SAVE OUTFILE

Anytime a file has been modified, and the researcher wishes to permanently retain the changes in the system file, then the file should be updated by using the appropriate command, as in:

SPSS^x
SAVE OUTFILE = system
FINISH

SPSS/PC+
SAVE OUTFILE = 'dani.SYS'.
FINISH.

5. TIPS FOR USING SPSS

Suggestions to increase your efficiency in running SPSS jobs are listed below:

A. NAME DEPENDENT VARIABLE FIRST

It will always be correct to name the dependent variable first when using any of the procedures in this appendix. In some cases this will not be *necessary* (CORRELATIONS, for example), but naming the dependent variable first is an easy rule which will not be incorrect for any of the procedures presented in this text.

B. USE VARIABLE LISTS

Preparing SPSS command files may be speeded up by using variable lists. Remember, SPSS allows you to use the **TO** convention to refer to all the variables located between the two identified variables, as in:

v14 TO v23, v27 TO v34, v45, v55

In this case, all the variables between v14 and v23 would be included along with v14 and v23 as well as the other ones identified on the command line. It is also worth remembering that new variables that are created are saved in the order in which they were created. Sometimes knowing this will allow you to list out a series of variables using the TO convention, which otherwise would require the listing of each variable separately.

C. USE QUESTION NUMBERS IN NAMING VARIABLES

In projects with a large number of variables, it is advisable to employ question numbers in naming variables. With multiple sectioned questions, use a decimal after the variable name to indicate the sub-divisions of the question. For example, Figure A2 illustrates a question where respondents have been asked to check off which consumer products they own. The variable names attached to such an item would be v23.1 TO v23.4. Note that there would be no variable known as v23 in this file.

D. KEEP A RECORD —NUMBER .CON FILES

It is important while analyzing project data to maintain a record of what jobs were run, but especially those which involved creating new variables or modifying old ones. One simple way to do this is to number your .CON jobs: as in, emily1.CON; emily2.CON; emily3.CON. Later, if you cannot remember exactly which variables went into an index, you can examine the .CON jobs to see how you did it. If you wish to add some cases to the file it is a simple task to then rerun the .CON jobs. Moreover, if part way through the analysis you discover an error in the data, you can correct it, and then rerun the .CON jobs that would have been influenced by the error in the data. Keeping careful track of jobs can save a lot of time.

In SPSS/PC+ you can run interactively, which is fine so long as you are not modifying the system file. If you plan on modifying the system file,

---

FIGURE A2 ASSIGNING VARIABLES NAMES TO SUB-DIVIDED VARIABLES

23. Place a check mark to indicate whether or not each of the following items are available to you in your household.

	Yes 1	No 0
.1 colour television	_____	_____
.2 VCR	_____	_____
.3 personal computer	_____	_____
.4 video camera	_____	_____

[The variable names would be V23.1, V23.2, V23.3, V23.4]

use an emily1.CON file to retain a record of what you have done. Within this file you can start the processing at any point in the file: this allows you to maintain a record of what you have done. Once you access your system file, simply put emily1.CON into the REVIEW editor and add commands to the end of the file. Once you have added the commands, move the cursor back to the line where you wish processing to begin and use the F10 key to commence processing.

B. BASIC PROCEDURES: PRESENTATION AND INTERPRETATION

Typically researchers begin the analysis of a project with a description of the sample so that the reader of the report will understand who has been studied. Basic variables such as the age, gender, and background of the respondents are normally presented. The most frequently used procedures and options are highlighted in the following sections detailing SPSS commands. Information on additional procedures and options are available in various SPSS manuals (see a partial listing of these at the end of the Appendix). The command structure used here will work for both SPSS^x and SPSS/PC+. But do remember that when working with SPSS/PC+ you will need to end each procedure with a period mark '.'.

1. FREQUENCIES: HOW MANY CASES IN EACH CATEGORY?

CHAPTER REFERENCE: Chapter 7

APPROPRIATE MEASUREMENT LEVELS:

• nominal, ordinal

BRIEF DESCRIPTION: Nominal and ordinal variables are examined using the FREQUENCIES procedure. This procedure provides a count of the number of cases falling into each category. This procedure is also used to check the distribution of a variable before recoding it. FREQUENCIES will also produce Barcharts and Histograms. To automatically produce either Barcharts (variables with fewer than 12 categories) or Histograms (12 or more categories) use the HBAR subcommand. Various statistics are available on request.

BASIC COMMAND STRUCTURE:

SPSS*
**FREQUENCIES VARIABLES= v1
v7 TO v10 v22**

SPSS/PC+
**FREQUENCIES VARIABLES= v1
v7 TO v10 v22.**

FREQUENCIES SPSS command
VARIABLES =   indicates the variable(s) which is (are) to be processed using the
                       FREQUENCIES procedure

ADDITIONAL COMMAND FORMATS:

SPSS*
**FREQUENCIES VARIABLES= v1
v7 TO v10 v22
/STATISTICS= DEFAULT
MEDIAN MODE SUM ALL
/HBAR**

SPSS/PC+
**FREQUENCIES VARIABLES= v1
v7 TO v10 v22
/STATISTICS= DEFAULT
MEDIAN MODE SUM ALL
/HBAR.**

SAMPLE OUTPUT AND NOTES: FREQUENCIES: Often it is possible to present nominal/ordinal data in a summary table. Table 18.4 (Chapter 18) illustrates such a table for nominal/ordinal data, generated using the FREQUENCIES procedure. It is useful in summary tables to report both the numbers and the percentages.

Box A2 shows what the output will look like from a FREQUENCIES procedure. The specially marked items draw attention to key points on the output.

BOX A2   SAMPLE OUTPUT USING FREQUENCIES PROCEDURE

SPSS*
FREQUENCIES VARIABLES= v58

SPSS/PC+
FREQUENCIES VARIABLES= v58.

BOX A2 SAMPLE OUTPUT USING FREQUENCIES PROCEDURE (continued)

V58   SIZE OF HOME COMMUNITY

Value Label	Value	Frequency	Percent	Valid Percent	Cum Percent
UNDER 1,000	1	18	9.7	10.3	10.3
1,000-4,999	2	20	10.8	11.5	21.8
5,000-9,999	3	17	9.1	9.8	31.6
10,000-19,999	4	15	8.1	8.6	40.2
20,000-49,999	5	29	15.6	16.7	56.9
50,000-99,999	6	21	11.3	12.1	69.0
100,000-499,999	7	10	5.4	5.7	74.7
500,000-999,999	8	7	3.8	4.0	78.7
1,000,000 & OVER	9	37	19.9	21.3	100.0
	0	12	6.5	MISSING	
	TOTAL	186	100.0	100.0	

Valid Cases   174   Missing Cases   12

SPSS^x

FREQUENCIES VARIABLES= v58
    /STATISTICS= MODE MEDIAN
    /HBAR

SPSS/PC+

FREQUENCIES VARIABLES= v58
    /STATISTICS= MODE MEDIAN
    /HBAR.

V58   SIZE OF HOME COMMUNITY

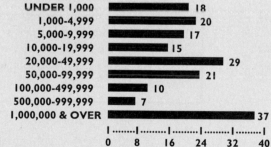

Median   5.000   Mode   9.000

Valid Cases   174   Missing Cases   12

NOTES

1 does not include MISSING cases

2 cumulative percentage: useful when recoding variable to determine mid-point, or thirds

2. DESCRIPTIVES: COMPUTING THE MEAN, MEDIAN AND MODE

CHAPTER REFERENCES: Chapter 7

APPROPRIATE MEASUREMENT LEVELS:

• ratio

BRIEF DESCRIPTION: The DESCRIPTIVES procedure computes means and standard deviations and is appropriately used for ratio-level variables. The output will provide the mean, standard deviation, the minimum, and the maximum value for the variable(s) identified on the variable list. In addition, the number of valid (non-missing) cases is reported.

BASIC COMMAND STRUCTURE:

SPSSˣ DESCRIPTIVES VARIABLES= v3, v6, v17	**SPSS/PC+** DESCRIPTIVES VARIABLES= v3, v6, v17.

OPTIONAL COMMANDS:

SPSSˣ **DESCRIPTIVES VARIABLES= v3, v6, v17** **/SAVE** [provides a Z scored (standardized) variable for each of the variables named on variable list; the new variable will have a Z prefixed to it, as in: zv3, zv6, zv17]	**SPSS/PC+** **DESCRIPTIVES VARIABLES= v3, v6, v17** **/OPTIONS= 3.** [provides a Z scored (standardized) variable for each of the variables named on variable list; the new variable will have a Z prefixed to it, as in: zv3, zv6, zv17]

OPTIONAL STATISTICS:

/STATISTICS= ALL [Provides a variety of statistics]

SAMPLE OUTPUT AND NOTES: DESCRIPTIVES   The most commonly used form of the command is simply:

SPSS^x

DESCRIPTIVES VARIABLES= v3, v6, v17

SPSS/PC+

DESCRIPTIVES VARIABLES= v3, v6, v17.

The above command would, by default, report the means, standard deviations, and the minimum and maximum values. Usually this is all we want. An important facility, however, is OPTIONS 3 which generates standardized values (Z scores) for the variables named. These values are stored in new variables whose names are the same as the old ones except that each is prefixed with a Z. Once created, these variables are available to the researcher for immediate use. The commands are different in SPSS/PC+ and in SPSS^x (see Box A3 for sample job). An SPSS manual should be consulted to identify other less frequently used options associated with the DESCRIPTIVES command. Box A3 shows sample output from the DESCRIPTIVES procedure.

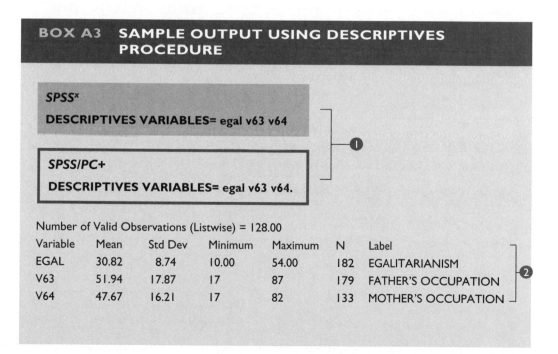

BOX A3   SAMPLE OUTPUT USING DESCRIPTIVES PROCEDURE

SPSS^x

DESCRIPTIVES VARIABLES= egal v63 v64

SPSS/PC+

DESCRIPTIVES VARIABLES= egal v63 v64.

Number of Valid Observations (Listwise) = 128.00

Variable	Mean	Std Dev	Minimum	Maximum	N	Label
EGAL	30.82	8.74	10.00	54.00	182	EGALITARIANISM
V63	51.94	17.87	17	87	179	FATHER'S OCCUPATION
V64	47.67	16.21	17	82	133	MOTHER'S OCCUPATION

BOX A3 SAMPLE OUTPUT USING DESCRIPTIVES PROCEDURE (continued)

SPSS^x

DESCRIPTIVES VARIABLES= egal v63 v64
  /SAVE
  /STATISTICS=SUM DEFAULT

❸

SPSS/PC+

DESCRIPTIVES VARIABLES= egal v63 v64.
  /OPTIONS= 3
  /STATISTICS= 12 13.

Number of Valid Observations (Listwise) = 128.00

Variable	Mean	Std Dev	Minimum	Maximum	Sum	N	Label
EGAL	30.82	8.74	10.00	54.00	5609.00	182	EGALITAR
V63	51.94	17.87	17	87	9297.00	179	FATHERS
V64	47.67	16.21	17	82	6340.00	133	MOTHERS

The following z-score variables have been saved on your active file:

From Variable	To Z-score	Weighted Valid N
EGAL	ZEGAL	182
V63	ZV63	179
V64	ZV64	133

DESCRIPTIVES VARIABLES= zegal zv63 zv64.

Number of Valid Observations (Listwise) = 128.00

❹

Variable	Mean	Std Dev	Minimum	Maximum	N	Label
ZEGAL	–.00	1.00	–2.38296	2.65339	182	ZSCORE: EGAL
ZV63	–.00	1.00	–1.95521	1.96209	179	ZSCORE: FATH
ZV64	.00	1.00	–1.89148	2.11731	133	ZSCORE: MOTH

NOTES

❶ basic command

❷ sample output

❸ commands to generate Z-score variables

❹ new Z-score variables available for immediate use: note the means and the standard deviations of the new Z-score variables

C. MULTI-VARIATE PROCEDURES: PRESENTATION AND INTERPRETATION

The procedures described in this section are used for examining the relationships between variables. The reader may wish to review Figure A3 which indicates the appropriate analysis procedure for given levels of measurement in the independent and dependent variables. In each case only the basic procedure and the most commonly used options and statistics will be presented. For full details of SPSS procedures, consult the appropriate SPSS manual listed at the end of the Appendix.

1. ANOVA: ANALYSIS OF VARIANCE

CHAPTER REFERENCES: Chapter 7, 8, 17.

APPROPRIATE MEASUREMENT LEVELS:

- Dependent variable: ratio

- Independent variables: nominal (ratio variables may be included as covariates).

BRIEF DESCRIPTION: Experimental researchers use analysis of variance (ANOVA) when their design has more than one independent variable or has more than two treatment levels. (T-Tests may be used when there are two

FIGURE A3 SPSS PROCEDURES FOR MULTI-VARIATE ANALYSIS

| DEPENDENT | INDEPENDENT VARIABLE | | |
	Nominal	Ordinal	Ratio
Nominal	CROSSTABS	CROSSTABS	CROSSTABS MEANS[1]
Ordinal	CROSSTABS	CROSSTABS NONPAR CORR	CROSSTABS NONPAR CORR
Ratio	MEANS ANOVA MANOVA DISCRIMINANT T-TEST	MEANS ANOVA MANOVA DISCRIMINANT T-TEST	CORRELATION PLOT PARTIAL CORR MANOVA REGRESSION

[1] In SPSS for this case, run the independent variable as though it were the dependent variable (i.e., name it first); the interpretation of the test of significance would be standard.

treatment levels and one independent variable.) The inclusion of additional complexity is relatively simple and provides an opportunity to explore the interaction of treatment variables (where effects change for different combinations of treatment variables) in influencing the dependent variable.

BASIC COMMAND STRUCTURE:

SPSS^x
ANOVA egal BY country(0,2)
v50(1,2)

SPSS/PC+
ANOVA egal BY country(0,2)
v50(1,2).

ANOVA	the SPSS command name
egal	the dependent variable [can be a list of dependent variables]
BY	separates dependent variable(s) from treatment variables
country	name of first treatment (independent) variable
(0,2)	lowest and highest values of treatment values; in this case the implied values include 0, 1, and 2; ANOVA assumes that there are no blank categories, so you will have to RECODE values if there are no values in one of the categories implied by the range indicated.
v50	name of the second treatment (or independent) variable

SAMPLE OUTPUT AND NOTES: ANOVA Note that the variations which are compared in an analysis of variance are composed of two elements: random error and possible treatment effects. The test which is done compares the ratio in the following way:

$$F = \frac{\text{random error + possible treatment effects}}{\text{random error}}$$

The interpretation of the results of an ANOVA test is split between a concern for:

- the main effect of treatment variable A: (Box A4 indicates that COUNTRY has a statistically significant main effect on egalitarianism);

- the main effect of treatment variable B: (Box A4 indicates that v50 (gender) does not have a statistically significant main effect on egalitarianism);

- an interaction of the treatment variables (A × B): (the interaction between COUNTRY and v50 is not statistically significant);

- an error term (within groups): this is the "residual source of variation."

BOX A4 SAMPLE OUTPUT USING ANOVA PROCEDURE

SPSS^x

ANOVA egal BY country(0,2) v50(1,2)

SPSS/PC+

ANOVA egal BY country(0,2) v50(1,2).

ANALYSIS OF VARIANCE

		EGAL	EGALITARIANISM		
	BY	COUNTRY	NAME OF COUNTRY		
		V50	GENDER		

Source of Variation	Sum of Squares	DF	Mean Square	F	Signif of F
Main Effects	1449.436	3	483.145	6.947	.000
COUNTRY	1449.393	2	724.697	10.421	.000
V50	12.652	1	12.652	.182	.670
2-way Interactions	125.990	2	62.995	.906	.406
COUNTRY V50	125.990	2	62.995	.906	.406
Explained	1575.426	5	315.085	4.531	.001
Residual	12239.591	176	69.543		
Total	13815.016	181	76.326		

186 Cases were processed.

4 Cases (2.2 PCT) were missing.

NOTES

❶ degrees of freedom

❷ probability levels for each test

❸ variables tested for interaction

2. CORRELATIONS: CORRELATIONAL ANALYSIS

CHAPTER REFERENCES: Chapter 7

APPROPRIATE MEASUREMENT LEVELS:

- Dependent variable: ratio

- Independent variables: ratio

BRIEF DESCRIPTION: Where variables are measured at the ratio level, then various correlational techniques are appropriate. As discussed in Chapter 7, a correlation, or r, measures the strength of an association between two variables. The values can range from +1.00 to -1.00. Typically, they are reported to two decimal places, as in .56. Explained variance is the square of the correlation coefficient or r^2.

BASIC COMMAND STRUCTURE:

SPSS^x

CORRELATIONS v17,v19,v22 to v24

[provides a correlation matrix for all variables named]

SPSS/PC+

CORRELATIONS v17,v19,v22 to v24.

[provides a correlation matrix for all variables named]

CORRELATIONS	name of the SPSS command
v17 etc.	names of variables

ADDITIONAL COMMAND OPTIONS:

CORRELATIONS v17 **WITH** v19 TO v24

WITH [instead of a matrix for the correlations between all variables, the WITH option will provide the correlation between the variable named before the WITH option to the rest of the variables named after the WITH option; in this case v17 will be correlated with v19 to v24]

OPTIONAL STATISTICS:

SPSS^x:

CORRELATIONS v10 v12 v15 /PRINT=ONETAIL SIG

[produces a one-tailed test of significance and displays the number of cases and the significance level]

CORRELATIONS v10 v12 v15 /PRINT=TWOTAIL SIG

[produces a two-tailed test and displays the number of cases and the significance level]

SPSS/PC+:

CORRELATIONS v10 v12 v15.

[produces a two-tailed test]

CORRELATIONS v10 v12 v15 /OPTIONS=3,5.

[produces a one-tailed test and displays the number of cases and the significance level]

SAMPLE OUTPUT AND NOTES: Box A5 includes a summary table of correlations. The CORRELATIONS procedure also may be used along with the PARTIAL CORR procedure to test for intervening and for sources of spuriousness variables. Box A6 illustrates the command structure that could be used to test such causal models.

BOX A5 SAMPLE OUTPUT USING CORRELATIONS PROCEDURE

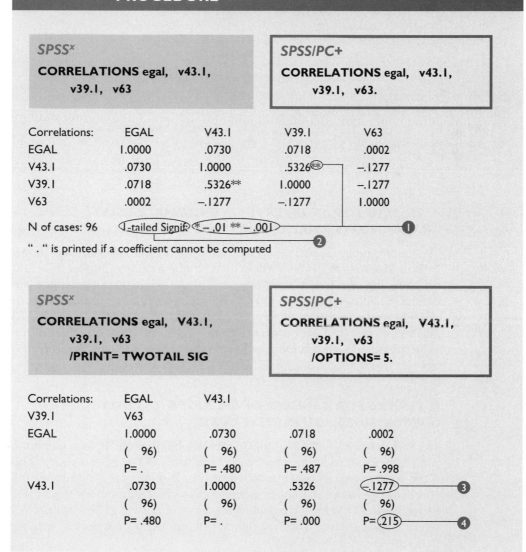

SPSS^x

CORRELATIONS egal, v43.1, v39.1, v63

SPSS/PC+

CORRELATIONS egal, v43.1, v39.1, v63.

Correlations:	EGAL	V43.1	V39.1	V63
EGAL	1.0000	.0730	.0718	.0002
V43.1	.0730	1.0000	.5326⊛⊛	−.1277
V39.1	.0718	.5326**	1.0000	−.1277
V63	.0002	−.1277	−.1277	1.0000

N of cases: 96   1-tailed Signif: * − .01 ** − .001   ❶

" . " is printed if a coefficient cannot be computed   ❷

SPSS^x

CORRELATIONS egal, V43.1, v39.1, v63
/PRINT= TWOTAIL SIG

SPSS/PC+

CORRELATIONS egal, V43.1, v39.1, v63
/OPTIONS= 5.

Correlations:	EGAL	V43.1		
V39.1	V63			
EGAL	1.0000	.0730	.0718	.0002
	(96)	(96)	(96)	(96)
	P= .	P= .480	P= .487	P= .998
V43.1	.0730	1.0000	.5326	−.1277 ❸
	(96)	(96)	(96)	(96)
	P= .480	P= .	P= .000	P= .215 ❹

BOX A5   SAMPLE OUTPUT USING CORRELATIONS PROCEDURE (continued)

V39.1	.0718	.5326	1.0000	−.1277	
	(96)	(96)	(96)	(96)	— ⑤
	P= .487	P= .000	P= .	P= .215	
V63	.0002	−.1277	−.1277	1.0000	
	(96)	(96)	(96)	(96)	
	P= .998	P= .215	P= .215	P= .	

(Coefficient / (Cases) / (2-tailed Significance)) ————————————— ②

" . " is printed if a coefficient cannot be computed

NOTES

① significance levels indicated by number of asterisks

② indicates whether the test was one- or two-tailed

③ correlation coefficient

④ two-tailed significance

⑤ number of cases

A. TESTING FOR AN INTERVENING VARIABLE USING CORRELATIONS AND PARTIAL CORR

The computations for testing this model can be done in SPSS and are shown in Box A6. *Jackson's rule of thirds* may be applied (see Chapter 16). And for each, the question is what happens to the original relationship when control variables are applied. Box A6 indicates that the correlation between v63 and v64 is .45; when "famsize" is controlled, the correlation between v63 and v64 is .44. Since the partial correlation remains within one-third of the value of the original relationship, this would lead us to argue that the control variable does not intervene between the two variables.

B. TESTING FOR A SOURCE OF SPURIOUSNESS USING CORRELATIONS AND PARTIAL CORR

The computations for testing this model can be done in SPSS by using the same commands as in the intervening variable model discussed above. And if the results were to come out as shown in Box A6, we would reject the source of spuriousness model. Remember, to find support for the source of spuriousness model, the partial correlation would have to be less than .30, which would indicate that the original relation had been reduced by more than one-third (.45 × .33 = .30).

BOX A6 SAMPLE OUTPUT USING CORRELATIONS AND PARTIAL CORR WITH A CONTROL VARIABLE

Note: the following run was performed using SPSS[x]. The PARTIAL CORR command is not currently available in the base package of SPSS/PC+ (version 5.0). The partial correlation may be hand-computed quickly (see Chapter 16).

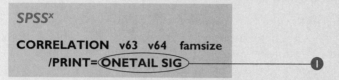

SPSS[x]

CORRELATION v63 v64 famsize
  /PRINT=ONETAIL SIG ────────────── ❶

- - Correlation Coefficients - -

	V63	V64	FAMSIZE
V63	1.0000	.4459	-.0474
	(179)	(131)	(176)
	P= .	P= .000	P= .266
V64	.4459	1.0000	-.0047
	(131)	(133)	(130)
	P= .000	P= .	P= .479
FAMSIZE	-.0474	-.0047	1.0000
	(176)	(130)	(181)
	P= .266	P= .479	P= .

(Coefficient / (Cases) / 1-tailed sig)
" . " is printed if a coefficient cannot be computed

                                              ❷
PARTIAL CORR v63 WITH **v64** BY famsize(1) ──────────── ❸
                                        ❹
        - - - - P A R T I A L   C O R R E L A T I O N   C O E F F I C I E N T S - - -
CONTROLLING FOR.. FAMSIZE
              V64
V63   .4403
              (125)
              P= .000

(COEFFICIENT / (D.F.) / SIGNIFICANCE)
" . " IS PRINTED IF A COEFFICIENT CANNOT BE COMPUTED.

NOTES

❶ requests one-tailed test and significance levels

❷ placed before the control variable

❸ indicates one control variable, requesting a

first-order partial

❹ placed between the dependent and the independent variable

3. CROSSTABS: CONTINGENCY TABLES

CHAPTER REFERENCES: Chapter 7, 8

APPROPRIATE MEASUREMENT LEVELS:

- Dependent variable: nominal, ordinal

- Independent variables: nominal (possibly recoded into fewer categories), ordinal (recoded version), ratio (recoded version)

BRIEF DESCRIPTION: CROSSTABS is a procedure used to examine the association between a nominal or ordinal dependent variable and a nominal, ordinal, or ratio independent variable. In the latter two cases, the variables would be recoded prior to the analysis being run.

BASIC COMMAND STRUCTURE:

SPSS^x	*SPSS/PC+*
CROSSTABS TABLES= depend	**CROSSTABS TABLES= depend**
BY independ	**BY independ**
/CELL= COUNT COLUMN	**/CELL= COUNT COLUMN**
/STATISTICS= CHISQ	**/STATISTICS= CHISQ.**

CROSSTABS	the SPSS command
TABLES=	specifies table format for output
depend	the name of the dependent variable (may be a dependent variable list if more than one is desired)
BY	separates the dependent list from the independent variable list
independ	the name of the independent variable (may also be a list)
/CELL = COUNT COLUMN	computes column percentages and cell counts
/STATISTICS	= CHISQ displays Chi-Square values
	= LAMBDA displays Lambda values
	= GAMMA displays Gamma values
	= ALL provides all available statistics

ADDITIONAL COMMANDS:

CROSSTABS TABLES= v4 BY v6, v18 TO v22 v7 v8 BY v10 V11

[note that additional tables can be requested by adding a slash and naming new variables]

SAMPLE OUTPUT AND NOTES: Box A7 presents the results from a simple CROSSTABS analysis. Note where the Chi-square value is printed and the probability is identified. Usually CROSSTABS results are reformatted when prepared for presentation in a paper. See Table A1 below for suggestions on how to reformat a CROSSTABS table for presentation in a paper.

Table A1 presents the relationship between respondent's country and illegal drug use. Since we are attempting to assess the impact of the independent variable on the dependent one, we are interested in the percentage of drug users in each category of the independent variable. Thus we might describe the findings as indicating that "while 38.4 percent of the respondents from Canada and New Zealand report having used illegal drugs, some 60.3 percent of those from Australia report such usage." In short, we compare percentages in each column. Usually it will be sufficient to use one row (in this case, just the row for those reporting illegal drug use).

For analysis involving three or more variables simultaneously, the procedures are the same, with the control variable added after an additional "BY", as shown in Box A8.

Where control variables are utilized, it is necessary to minimize the number of categories in the independent and in the control variables. Generally, there should be no more than two or three categories within these variables. There are two major reasons for this limitation: first, the number of cases in each cell will become too small if there are many categories in either the independent or the control variable; second, the interpretation of the table is very difficult if simplicity is not maintained. Chapter 16 discusses interpretations of three variable contingency tables.

TABLE A1 ILLEGAL DRUG USE BY COUNTRY OF RESPONDENT

ILLEGAL DRUG USE	COUNTRY					
	CANADA AND NEW ZEALAND		AUSTRALIA		TOTAL	
	N	%	N	%	N	%
Have Used	48	38.4	35	60.3	83	45.4
Have Not Used	77	61.6	23	39.7	100	54.6
TOTAL	125	100.0	58	100.0	183	100.0

Chi-Square = 7.69793
Degrees of Freedom = 1
Significance = .0055
Number of Missing Observations = 3

BOX A7   SAMPLE OUTPUT USING CROSSTABS PROCEDURE

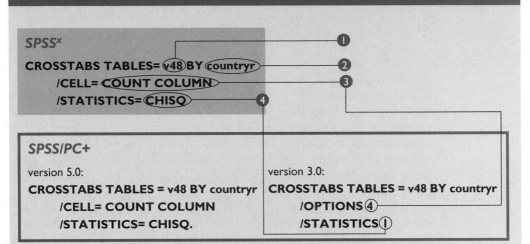

SPSSˣ

CROSSTABS TABLES= v48 BY countryr   ①

 /CELL= COUNT COLUMN   ②

 /STATISTICS= CHISQ   ④   ③

SPSS/PC+

version 5.0:
CROSSTABS TABLES = v48 BY countryr
 /CELL= COUNT COLUMN
 /STATISTICS= CHISQ.

version 3.0:
CROSSTABS TABLES = v48 BY countryr
 /OPTIONS ④
 /STATISTICS ①

SPSS/PC+ OUTPUT:

Crosstabulation: V48   ILLEGAL DRUG USE

  By COUNTRYR   Canada, New Zealand, Australia

COUNTRYR	Count Col Pct	Canada, New Zeal 1.00	Australia 2.00	Row Total
V48 YES	1	48	35	83
		38.4	60.3	45.4
NO	2	77	23	100
		61.6	39.7	54.6
	Column	125	58	183
	Total	68.3	31.7	100.0

⑤   ⑥

Chi-Square	D.F.	Significance	Min E.F.	Cells with E.F.< 5
6.83798	1	.0089	26.306	None
7.69796	1	.0055	(Before Yates Correction)	

⑦
⑧

Number of Missing Observations = 3

NOTES

① dependent variable
② independent variable
③ requests column percentages and cell counts
④ requests Chi-square
⑤ dependent variable categories

⑥ compare these percentages when interpreting the table: note difference (60.3 − 38.4 = 21.9)
⑦ significance (two-tailed)
⑧ Chi-square value

The command structure to test for an intervening variable or to test for a source of spuriousness variable is shown in Box A8. Note that the same procedure is used to test for sources of spuriousness variables.

Box A8 shows sample results from such an analysis. See Chapter 16 for a discussion of interpreting the results of the analysis. Remember that to apply *Jackson's rule of thirds,* it is necessary to compare the original difference

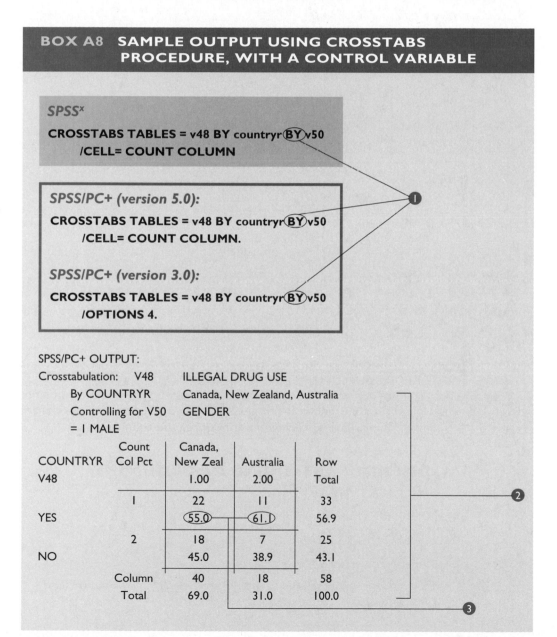

BOX A8   SAMPLE OUTPUT USING CROSSTABS PROCEDURE, WITH A CONTROL VARIABLE

SPSS^x

CROSSTABS TABLES = v48 BY countryr BY v50
/CELL= COUNT COLUMN

SPSS/PC+ (version 5.0):

CROSSTABS TABLES = v48 BY countryr BY v50
/CELL= COUNT COLUMN.

SPSS/PC+ (version 3.0):

CROSSTABS TABLES = v48 BY countryr BY v50
/OPTIONS 4.

SPSS/PC+ OUTPUT:
Crosstabulation: V48   ILLEGAL DRUG USE
       By COUNTRYR   Canada, New Zealand, Australia
       Controlling for V50   GENDER
       = I MALE

COUNTRYR V48	Count Col Pct	Canada, New Zeal 1.00	Australia 2.00	Row Total
I YES		22 55.0	11 61.1	33 56.9
2 NO		18 45.0	7 38.9	25 43.1
	Column Total	40 69.0	18 31.0	58 100.0

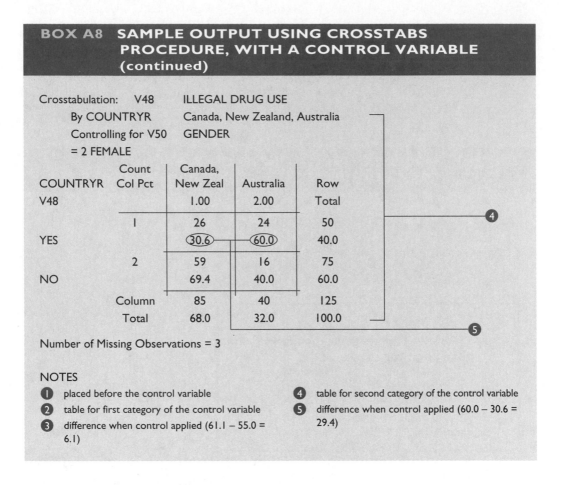

BOX A8   SAMPLE OUTPUT USING CROSSTABS PROCEDURE, WITH A CONTROL VARIABLE (continued)

Crosstabulation: V48   ILLEGAL DRUG USE
    By COUNTRYR   Canada, New Zealand, Australia
    Controlling for V50   GENDER
    = 2 FEMALE

COUNTRYR V48	Count Col Pct	Canada, New Zeal 1.00	Australia 2.00	Row Total
YES	1	26 30.6	24 60.0	50 40.0
NO	2	59 69.4	16 40.0	75 60.0
	Column Total	85 68.0	40 32.0	125 100.0

Number of Missing Observations = 3

NOTES

① placed before the control variable

② table for first category of the control variable

③ difference when control applied (61.1 − 55.0 = 6.1)

④ table for second category of the control variable

⑤ difference when control applied (60.0 − 30.6 = 29.4)

in the percentages between the categories of the independent variable, and to rerun the relation controlling for the intervening (or source of spuriousness) variable. Only if the original difference is reduced by more than one-third do we have any evidence supporting the proposed model.

4. DISCRIMINANT: DOING DISCRIMINANT FUNCTION ANALYSIS

CHAPTER REFERENCES: Chapter 7, 17

APPROPRIATE MEASUREMENT LEVELS:

- Dependent variable: nominal

- Independent variables: ratio (dummy variables may, however, be used for ordinal and nominal independent variables)

BRIEF DESCRIPTION: Discriminant function analysis is a procedure for examining the relationship between a nominal dependent variable and ratio independent variables. The basic idea behind discriminant function analysis is to correctly classify the dependent variable in each case. It can also be used to predict which category a case will fall into when measures of the dependent variable are missing. The statistic *Lambda* was discussed in Chapter 7 and the reader should recall that this statistic measures the proportionate reduction in error that is achieved when a variable is added to an analysis. Lambda is used in discriminant function analysis to measure the success in correctly classifying cases. Similar to regression analysis, standardized weightings are provided which permit the researcher to assess the relative impact of independent variables on the dependent one. Also like regression analysis it is possible to employ *dummy* independent variables (see examples of how to construct these in the Regression Analysis section of this Appendix) which provides a method of incorporating nominal independent variables into the analysis.

BASIC COMMAND STRUCTURE:

SPSS^x	SPSS/PC+ (Professional Statistics, Version 5.0)
DISCRIMINANT GROUPS=v12(1,2) /VARIABLES= v5,ses,v58,egal /STATISTICS= MEANS, TABLE	**DISCRIMINANT GROUPS= v12(1,2)** /VARIABLES= v5,ses,v58,egal /STATISTICS= 13.

DISCRIMINANT	the SPSS command name
GROUPS=	identifies the dependent variable name (v12); the values in parentheses represent the lowest and highest value to be analyzed;
VARIABLES=	lists the independent variables; note that if *dummy* variables are to be included they should be developed prior to initiating the discriminant command (see Regression Analysis section below for how to create dummy variables);
STATISTICS=	MEANS requests SPSS to list the total and group means for all the independent variables; TABLE requests a table showing the percentage of cases correctly classified; if all additional statistics are desired, replace TABLE with ALL and a variety of additional analyses will be presented.

SAMPLE OUTPUT AND NOTES: Box A9 presents sample output from a discriminant analysis of suicidal thoughts (v12) among respondents in the international survey. Selected for independent variables were v5 (a measure of how often a respondent feels depressed), SES (socio-economic status: the higher score of the mother's and father's occupational prestige scores), v58 (size of home community), and EGAL (an index measuring egalitarianism).

The output shown in Box A9 shows how many cases were used in the analysis, the number of cases who reported that they had thought about committing suicide (60), and the number who reported that they had not had such thoughts (108). The mean scores for each independent variable were then reported for each category of suicidal thoughts. Note that those who scored higher on depression were more likely to be in the *yes* category of suicidal thoughts (mean of 4.42 compared to 2.94). Note also that those

BOX A9   SAMPLE OUTPUT USING DISCRIMINANT PRODCEDURE

Note: The DISCRIMINANT command is not available in the base package of SPSS/PC+ (version 5.0). It is available in *SPSS/PC+ Professional Statistics, Version 5.0*.

SPSS^x.
DISCRIMINANT GROUPS= v12(1,2)
    /VARIABLES= v5, ses, v58, egal
    /STATISTICS= TABLE

SPSS/PC+ (Professional Statistics, Version 5.0)
DISCRIMINANT GROUPS= v12(1,2)
    /VARIABLES= v5, ses, v58, egal
    /STATISTICS= 13.

--------DISCRIMINANT ANALYSIS--------
ON GROUPS DEFINED BY V12   THOUGHTS ABOUT SUICIDE
  186   (UNWEIGHTED) CASES WERE PROCESSED.
   18   OF THESE WERE EXCLUDED FROM THE ANALYSIS.
    0   HAD MISSING OR OUT-OF-RANGE GROUP CODES.
   16   HAD AT LEAST ONE MISSING DISCRIMINATING VARIABLE.
    2   HAD BOTH.
  168   (UNWEIGHTED) CASES WILL BE USED IN THE ANALYSIS.

BOX A9 SAMPLE OUTPUT USING DISCRIMINANT PRDCEDURE (continued)

NUMBER OF CASES BY GROUP

NUMBER OF CASES

V12	UNWEIGHTED	WEIGHTED	LABEL
1	60	60.0	YES
2	108	108.0	NO
TOTAL	168	168.0	

- - - - - - - - D I S C R I M I N A N T   A N A L Y S I S - - - - - - - -

ON GROUPS DEFINED BY V12   THOUGHTS ABOUT SUICIDE

ANALYSIS NUMBER   1

DIRECT METHOD: ALL VARIABLES PASSING THE TOLERANCE TEST ARE ENTERED.
MINIMUM TOLERANCE LEVEL...0.00100

CANONICAL DISCRIMINANT FUNCTIONS
MAXIMUM NUMBER OF FUNCTIONS..1
MINIMUM CUMULATIVE PERCENT OF VARIANCE...............100.00
MAXIMUM SIGNIFICANCE OF WILKS' LAMBDA....................1.0000

CANONICAL DISCRIMINANT FUNCTIONS

		PCT OF	CUM	CANONICAL	AFTER	WILKS'			
FCN	EIGENVALUE	VARIANCE	PCT	CORR	FCN	LAMBDA	CHISQUARE	DF	SIG
					: 0	0.8138	33.783	4	0.0000
1*	0.2287	100.00	100.00	0.4315	:				

* MARKS THE 1 CANONICAL DISCRIMINANT FUNCTIONS REMAINING IN THE ANALYSIS.

STANDARDIZED CANONICAL DISCRIMINANT FUNCTION COEFFICIENTS

	FUNC 1
V5	0.85423
SES	0.30254
V58	0.10224
EGAL	0.30739

STRUCTURE MATRIX:
POOLED WITHIN-GROUPS CORRELATIONS BETWEEN DISCRIMINATING VARIABLES
AND CANONICAL DISCRIMINANT FUNCTIONS (VARIABLES ORDERED BY SIZE OF COR-
RELATION WITHIN FUNCTION)

BOX A9 SAMPLE OUTPUT USING DISCRIMINANT PRDCEDURE (continued)

	FUNC I
V5	0.90978
EGAL	0.41694
SES	0.28258
V58	0.08986

CANONICAL DISCRIMINANT FUNCTIONS EVALUATED AT GROUP MEANS (GROUP CENTROIDS)

GROUP	FUNC I
I	0.63784
2	-0.35436

CLASSIFICATION RESULTS -

ACTUAL GROUP		NO. OF CASES	PREDICTED I	GROUP MEMBERSHIP 2
GROUP	I	60	36	24
YES			60.0%	40.0%
GROUP	2	108	32	76
NO			29.6%	70.4%

PERCENT OF "GROUPED" CASES CORRECTLY CLASSIFIED: 66.67% ——————————— ④

CLASSIFICATION PROCESSING SUMMARY

 186 CASES WERE PROCESSED.

  0 CASES WERE EXCLUDED FOR MISSING OR OUT-OF-RANGE GROUP CODES.

  18 CASES HAD AT LEAST ONE MISSING DISCRIMINATING VARIABLE.

 168 CASES WERE USED FOR PRINTED OUTPUT.

NOTES

① the dependent variable: thoughts about suicide, where: 1=yes and 2=no

② 60 reported thoughts of suicide, 108 did not

③ these values reflect the relative importance of the independent variables; of the four independent variables, V5 (feeling of depression) is the most important predictor of suicidal thoughts

④ note the percentage of respondents correctly classified when information about the four independent variables is used

with suicidal thoughts had higher mean scores on SES, size of community, and egalitarianism.

The last presentation on the output shows the percent of cases correctly classified. It is reported that 66.67 percent of the cases were correctly classified using the four independent variables. But how might we have fared if we had just randomly assigned cases to the suicidal thought or non-suicidal thought categories? To compute the number of correct classifications we would have made using random assignment, the following steps may be taken:

- compute the proportion of cases that fall into each category: in this case, $60 \div 168 = .36$; $108 \div 168 = .64$

- square the proportions and add them together and then multiply by 100: $(.36^2 + .64^2) \times 100 = 53.9 \%$

- proportion of errors in random assignment: $1 - .54 = .46$

- proportion of errors using discriminant analysis-based classifications: $1 - .67 = .33$

- the percent error reduction using the model, compared to random assignment, may be calculated by comparing the proportion of errors in the model compared to random assignment divided by the proportion of errors using the model, multiplied by 100: $((.46 - .33) \div .46) \times 100 = 28.3\%$.

The results indicate that we were able to improve our classification of people into the thought-of-suicide category versus the have-not-thought-of-suicide category by 28.3 percent by using the information on the four independent variables. But how important were each of the independent variables?

There are two basic ways of estimating the relative importance of variables in correctly estimating into which category of the dependent variable a case will fall:

1. Use the DISCRIMINANT procedure including all variables on the first run, then continue to repeat the analysis but exclude a different independent variable each time until you have an analysis excluding each independent variable. The contribution of each independent variable may then be judged by comparing the percentage of correct assignment using the variable compared to when it is not used, as in:

Contribution = (percent correct with variable included) – (percent correct without variable included)

The variable which produces the greatest drop in correct assignments is the most important factor, the one with the second greatest drop is the second most important variable, and so forth.

2. Examine the *standardized discriminant function coefficients*. These co-efficients are similar to the beta weights in regression analysis in that they are standardized (so that differences in the range and variability of values in a variable do not influence the coefficient; if it helps, think of these as Z scores where each variable has a mean of 0 and a standard deviation of 1). The larger the coefficient, the more importance the variable has in predicting into which group the individual will fall.

The table called "Canonical Discriminant Functions" should be examined. First, it should be noted that the total amount of the variation explained by the combination of variables can be determined by squaring the *canonical correlation*. In our example, the canonical correlation is .4315 which means that together the four independent variables account for 18.6 percent of the variance in suicidal thoughts ($.4315^2$ = .1862 × 100 = 18.6%).

The *eigenvalue* (.2287) represents the ratio of the between-groups variance to the within-groups variance. The higher this value, the greater the ability of the independent variables to discriminate between categories of the dependent variable.

The *lambda* value, like the canonical correlation, varies from 0 to 1.0 and is an inverse measure of the discriminating power of the model being tested. That is, the lower the value, the higher the discriminating ability of the model to distinguish between categories of the dependent variable.

A *Chi-Square* value is reported along with the degrees of freedom (DF) and the probability of the difference occurring on a chance basis (SIG). In our illustration, the significance level is .0000.

The number of functions which the DISCRIMINANT procedure will calculate is one less than the number of categories in the dependent variable. Thus, as is the case in the example we are using, when there are two categories in the dependent variable, one function will be computed; if we had three categories, two functions would be calculated.

As in regression analysis, if there is a high correlation among the independent variables (multicollinearity), say above .7, then it is a good idea to either drop one of the highly correlated variables or multiply them together to provide a composite measure of the two variables.

5. MANOVA: DOING MULTI-VARIATE ANALYSIS OF VARIANCE

CHAPTER REFERENCES: Chapter 7, 8, 17

APPROPRIATE MEASUREMENT LEVELS:

- Dependent variable: ratio
- Independent variables: nominal, ordinal, ratio

BRIEF DESCRIPTION: While regression analysis is appropriate in many situations, there are several situations where analysis of variance (ANOVA or MANOVA) would be more appropriate. For example, as Kachigan (1986) points out, if you had predictor variables that have qualitative differences (three different countries for example); or if rather than having a ratio variable measuring the amount of time spent watching T.V., we have a variable that indicates whether the person watched T.V. or went to the movies, we again would probably opt for analysis of variance. In short, if an independent variable is made up of values which differ in *kind* rather than in *quantity*, we would opt for analysis of variance.

A second situation which is better handled with analysis of variance is one where the relationship between the independent and the dependent variable changes over the continuum. Perhaps the relationship is nonlinear and once again analysis of variance should be considered as an alternative to regression.

BASIC COMMAND STRUCTURE:

SPSS^x	*SPSS/PC+*
MANOVA egal BY country(0,2) v50(1,2) WITH ses famsize	**MANOVA egal BY country(0,2) v50(1,2) WITH ses famsize.**

MANOVA	the SPSS command name
egal	the dependent variable [can be a list of dependent variables]
BY	separates dependent variable(s) from treatment variables
country	name of first treatment (independent) variable
(0,2)	lowest and highest values of treatment values; in this case the implied values include 0, 1, and 2; ANOVA assumes that there are no blank categories, so you will have to RECODE values if there are no values in one of the categories implied by the range indicated.
v50	name of the second treatment (or independent) variable
WITH	signals that a *covariate* is about to be named
ses	first covariate variable
famsize	second covariate

SAMPLE OUTPUT AND NOTES: See the discussion for ANOVA. Both ANOVA and MANOVA are included because MANOVA is not included in the *Base System* (Version 5.0) of SPSS/PC+. If you are working with a system having both ANOVA and MANOVA, you are advised to work simply with MANOVA since it does everything ANOVA does and it also has a number of

BOX A10   SAMPLE OUTPUT USING MANOVA PROCEDURE

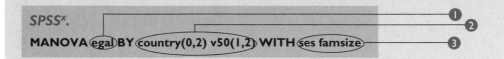

SPSS^x.

MANOVA egal **BY** country(0,2) v50(1,2) **WITH** ses famsize

SPSS/PC+ (Advanced Statistics, Version 5.0)
MANOVA egal **BY** country(0,2) v50(1,2) **WITH** ses famsize.

******ANALYSIS OF VARIANCE******

175 cases accepted.
  0 cases rejected because of out-of-range factor values.
 11 cases rejected because of missing data.
  6 non-empty cells.
  1 design will be processed.

******ANALYSIS OF VARIANCE—DESIGN 1******

Tests of Significance for EGAL using UNIQUE sums of squares

Source of Variation	SS	DF	MS	F	Sig of F
WITHIN CELLS	11539.00	167	69.10		
REGRESSION	127.71	2	63.85	.92	.399
COUNTRY	932.68	2	466.34	6.75	.002
V50	2.18	1	2.18	.03	.859
COUNTRY BY V50	87.92	2	43.96	.64	.531

Correlations between Covariates and Predicted Dependent Variable

	COVARIATE	
VARIABLE	SES	FAMSIZE
EGAL	−.315	.973

Averaged Squared Correlations between Covariates and Predicted Dependent Variable

VARIABLE	AVER. R-SQ
SES	.099
FAMSIZE	.948

Regression analysis for WITHIN CELLS error term
— Individual Univariate .9500 confidence intervals
Dependent variable .. EGAL EGALITARIANISM

BOX A10 SAMPLE OUTPUT USING MANOVA PROCEDURE (continued)

COVARIATE	B	Beta	Std. Err.	t-Value	Sig. of t
SES	−.01134	−.02406	.036	−.311	.756
FAMSIZE	.57236	.09969	.444	1.290	.199

COVARIATE Lower -95% CL- Upper		
SES	−.083	.061
FAMSIZE	−.303	1.448

NOTES

1. dependent variable
2. independent variables
3. covariates

4. note only the main effect of country is significant; interaction not significant

additional facilities, such as working simultaneously with multiple dependent variables (see Box 10).

The following conditions typically would recommend the use of multivariate analysis of variance (MANOVA):

• you are using an experimental design;

• the dependent variable is measured at the ratio level;

• one or more of the treatment variables are measured at the ratio level and others at the nominal or ordinal levels;

• you have multiple dependent measures which you wish to examine simultaneously;

• in nonexperimental designs you wish to examine whether there are significant interactions among independent variables.

6. MEANS: COMPARING MEANS

CHAPTER REFERENCES: Chapter 7, 8

APPROPRIATE MEASUREMENT LEVELS:

• Dependent variable: interval/ratio

• Independent variables: nominal, ordinal, ratio (recoded)

BRIEF DESCRIPTION: The MEANS procedure is used to compare the mean values of a dependent variable across categories on an independent variable. The test of significance associated with the test is a one-way analysis of variance.

BASIC COMMAND STRUCTURE:

SPSS^x

MEANS TABLES=depend BY
  independ
      /STATISTICS= ANOVA

MEANS	the SPSS command name
TABLES=	specifies a tables format for the output
depend	the name(s) of the dependent variable(s)
BY	separates the dependent variable(s) from the independent variable(s)
independ	the name(s) of the independent variable(s)
/STATISTICS= ANOVA	requests a one-way analysis of variance of the relation between the independent and the dependent variable

ADDITIONAL COMMANDS:

MEANS TABLES= *income BY sex BY control*

first BY	separates the dependent from the independent variable
second BY	separates the original relation (income & sex) from the control variable; in this case the mean income will be computed for each gender for each category of the control variable]
control	the name of the control variable

SPSS/PC+
MEANS TABLES=depend BY
  independ
      /STATISTICS= 1.

/STATISTICS= 1.	requests a one-way analysis of variance of the relation between the independent and the dependent variable

SAMPLE OUTPUT AND NOTES: Box A11 presents the results resulting from the use of the MEANS procedure. Note that the average values for all respondents on the egalitarianism index are presented for each country.

When you have a dependent variable measured at the ratio level, and either a nominal or ordinal independent variable, then it is appropriate to compute the mean values of the dependent variable for each category of the independent variable. Table A2 on page A-55 presents the kind of data that would be appropriate for this kind of analysis. Note that the dependent variable (income) is ratio level one, while the independent variable is nominal (gender).

These categories of the table should be carefully labelled. The means, standard deviations of the dependent variable, and the number of cases are normally reported in columns across the table. (See Table A2 for an example.)

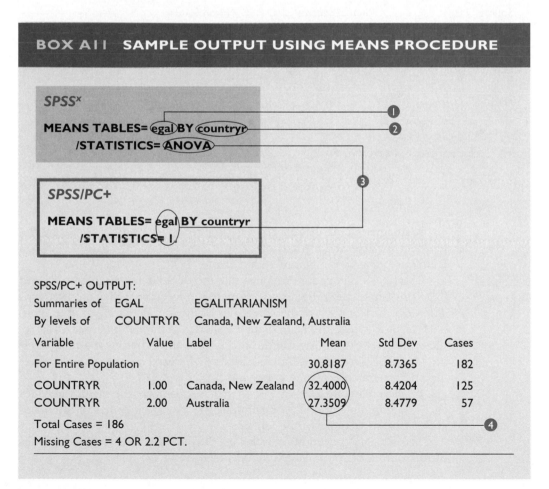

BOX A11   SAMPLE OUTPUT USING MEANS PROCEDURE

SPSS^x

MEANS TABLES= egal BY countryr
      /STATISTICS= ANOVA

SPSS/PC+

MEANS TABLES= egal BY countryr
      /STATISTICS= 1

SPSS/PC+ OUTPUT:

Summaries of   EGAL   EGALITARIANISM
By levels of   COUNTRYR   Canada, New Zealand, Australia

Variable	Value	Label	Mean	Std Dev	Cases
For Entire Population			30.8187	8.7365	182
COUNTRYR	1.00	Canada, New Zealand	32.4000	8.4204	125
COUNTRYR	2.00	Australia	27.3509	8.4779	57

Total Cases = 186
Missing Cases = 4 OR 2.2 PCT.

BOX A11   SAMPLE OUTPUT USING MEANS PROCEDURE (continued)

Summaries of   EGAL   EGALITARIANISM
By levels of   COUNTRYR   Canada, New Zealand, Australia

Value	Label	Mean	Std Dev	Sum of Sq	Cases
1.00	Canada, New Zealand	32.4000	8.4204	8792.0000	125
2.00	Australia	27.3509	8.4779	4024.9825	57
Within Groups Total		30.8187	8.4383	12816.9825	182

Criterion Variable EGAL

Analysis of Variance

Source	Sum of Squares	D.F.	Mean Square	F	Sig.
Between Groups	998.0340	1	998.0340	14.0163	.0002 — ⑤
Within Groups	12816.9825	180	71.2055		

Eta = .2688   Eta Squared = .0722

NOTES

① dependent variable

② independent variable

③ requests a one-way analysis of variance

④ mean values for egalitarianism for each country category

⑤ test of significance results: reject the null hypothesis

A summary table may be used to report the relation between one dependent variable and a series of independent variables. A sample of such a table is presented in Figure 18.6 (Chapter 18).

The MEANS procedure requires that the dependent variable be named first. This causes the program to compute the mean value for the first variable (income) for each of the categories of the independent variable (gender). In cases where there are many categories in the independent variable, these will have to be regrouped into two or three before the analysis is run (RECODE procedure). Variable lists may be used so that multiple tables may be generated with one command.

In interpreting the outcome of an analysis, compare the mean values for each category. In Table A2, for example, the average incomes of the males are compared to those of the females.

The MEANS procedure may be used to test for intervening variables or for sources of spuriousness models (see Box A12).

TABLE A2   MEAN INCOME BY SEX

SEX	MEAN INCOME	NUMBER OF CASES
Male	37,052	142
Female	34,706	37
COMBINED MEAN	$36,567	179

If appropriate, test of significance values entered here.

BOX A12   SAMPLE OUTPUT USING MEANS WITH A CONTROL VARIABLE

SPSS^x

MEANS TABLES = egal BY countryr BY v53R, v50

SPSS/PC+

MEANS TABLES = egal BY countryr BY v53R, v50.

Display # 1

Summaries of	EGAL	EGALITARIANISM
By levels of	COUNTRYR	Canada, New Zealand, Australia
	V53R	Religion Recoded

Variable	Value	Label	Mean	Std Dev	Cases
For Entire Population			30.8621	8.8372	174
COUNTRYR	1.00	Canada, New Zealand	32.4167	8.5431	120
V53R	1.00	Catholic	31.4242	8.6060	66
V53R	2.00	Non-Catholic	33.6296	8.3853	54
COUNTRYR	2.00	Australia	27.4074	8.5683	54
V53R	1.00	Catholic	20.4000	9.8133	5
V53R	2.00	Non-Catholic	28.1224	8.2098	49

Total Cases = 186

Missing Cases = 12 OR   6.5 PCT.

BOX A12   SAMPLE OUTPUT USING MEANS WITH A CONTROL VARIABLE (continued)

Display # 2

Summaries of   EGAL   EGALITARIANISM

By levels of   COUNTRYR   Canada, New Zealand, Australia

                V50   GENDER ——————————————————— ④

Variable	Value	Label	Mean	Std Dev	Cases
For Entire Population			30.8187	8.7365	182
COUNTRYR	1.00	Canada, New Zealand	32.4000	8.4204	125
V50	1	MALE	31.7143	9.8161	42
V50	2	FEMALE	32.7470	7.6602	83
COUNTRYR	2.00	Australia	27.3509	8.4779	57
V50	1	MALE	28.5294	10.8519	17
V50	2	FEMALE	26.8500	7.3504	40

Total Cases =   186

Missing Cases = 4 OR   2.2 PCT.

NOTES

① difference between countries, Catholics only (31.4 – 20.4 = 11.0)

② difference between countries, without control variable (32.4 – 27.4 = 5.0)

③ difference between countries, non-Catholics only (33.6 – 28.1 = 5.5)

④ control for gender in this table

Note that to test whether the relation between egalitarianism and country is spurious, caused by the number of each gender who happened to be in the sample, we first compare the original mean difference between the countries 32.4000 – 27.3509 = 5.0491. (see Box A11) Second, we now see whether the difference holds up when we control for the gender of the respondents: Display 2 indicates that among the males respondents the difference is 3.1849 (31.7143 – 28.5294 = 3.1849) while for the females the difference in egalitarian scores is 5.897 (32.7470 – 26.8500 = 5.897). Using *Jackson's rule of thirds*, we note that among both the male and female respondents the difference "remained the same."

a. original difference: 5.0491

b. determining thirds: 5.0491 ÷ 3 = 1.6830

c. to have decreased or disappeared, new value must be:

5.0491 − 1.6830 = 3.3661

d. observed difference, males:

31.7143 − 28.5294 = **3.1849**: falls into "stays the same" category

e. observed difference, females:

32.7470 − 26.8500 = **5.897**: falls into "stays the same" category

f. conclusion:

gender is not spuriously causing the link between egalitarianism and country

Note that to test whether the relation between egalitarianism and country is to be explained by the intervening variable of religion, we compare what happens to the original mean difference between the countries (32.4167 for Canada and New Zealand, and 27.4074 for Australia, producing a difference of 5.0 in the mean scores [32.4147 − 27.4074 = 5.0073]. What happens when we control for the religious affiliation of the respondents? How would you interpret the findings when the control for religion is applied?

7. NONPAR CORR: SPEARMAN CORRELATIONS

CHAPTER REFERENCES: Chapter 7

APPROPRIATE MEASUREMENT LEVELS:

- Dependent variable: ordinal

- Independent variables: ordinal

BRIEF DESCRIPTION: Spearman correlations are used when ordinal-level measurement has been attained. They may be reported and interpreted in the same manner as Pearson correlations. Like Pearson correlations, they vary from -1.00 to +1.00 and measure the strength of an association.

BASIC COMMAND STRUCTURE

> **SPSS^x:**
>
> **NONPAR CORR VARIABLES=**
>   **v23 v24**
>   **/PRINT= TWOTAIL**

NONPAR CORR	the name of the SPSS^x command
v23,v24	the names of the variables to determine Spearman's rho correlations
/PRINT= TWOTAIL	requests that a two-tailed test of significance be reported (default is a one-tailed test)

> *SPSS/PC+*
>
> **RANK VARIABLES= v23**
>   **v24/RANK.**
> **CORRELATIONS VARIABLES=**
>   **rv23 rv24**
>   **/OPTION 5.**

RANK	an SPSS/PC+ command to rank-order values
/RANK	retains new variables with an R prefixed to them and these are available for use immediately
CORRELATIONS	the CORRELATIONS procedure is used to measure the association between the newly created ranked variables (Spearman Correlation)
rv23 rv24	the names of the new variables to be correlated
/OPTION 5	displays number of cases and probability

SAMPLE OUTPUT AND NOTES: Box A13 presents the procedures and sample output showing how to calculate Spearman's rho using SPSS[x] and SPSS/PC+.

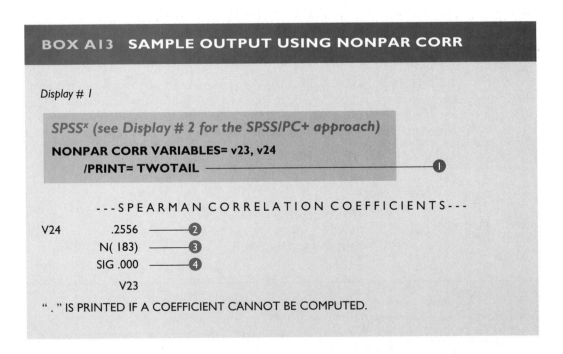

BOX A13   SAMPLE OUTPUT USING NONPAR CORR

Display # 1

SPSS[x] (see Display # 2 for the SPSS/PC+ approach)
NONPAR CORR VARIABLES= v23, v24
       /PRINT= TWOTAIL ───────────────── ①

---SPEARMAN CORRELATION COEFFICIENTS---

V24   .2556 ─────── ②
           N(183) ───── ③
           SIG .000 ───── ④

           V23

" . " IS PRINTED IF A COEFFICIENT CANNOT BE COMPUTED.

BOX A13 SAMPLE OUTPUT USING NONPAR CORR (continued)

Display # 2

Note: In SPSS/PC+ to compute *Spearman's rho*, the following procedure is suggested. Use the RANK command to create a new rank-ordered version of the variable and then use the CORRE-LATION procedure to calculate Spearman's rho.

SPSS/PC+

RANK VARIABLES= V23, V24/RANK.
CORRELATIONS VARIABLES= rv23, rv24
　　　/OPTION=⑤. ───────────────────── ⑤

From variable	New variable	Label
V23	RV23	RANK of V23
V24	RV24	RANK of V24

Correlations: RV23　　RV24

RV23	1.0000	.2559 ───── ⑥
	(183)	(183) ───── ⑦
	P= .	P= .000　⑧
RV24	.2559	1.0000
	(183)	(183)
	P= .000	P= .

(Coefficient / (Cases) / 1-tailed Significance)

" . " is printed if a coefficient cannot be computed

NOTES

① requests two-tailed test

② Spearman correlation coefficient

③ number of cases

④ significance (reject null hypothesis)

⑤ request to display number of cases and proba-bilities

⑥ Spearman correlation equivalent

⑦ number of cases

⑧ significance, one-tailed (reject null hypothesis)

8. PLOT: THE PLOT THICKENS

CHAPTER REFERENCES: Chapter 7

APPROPRIATE MEASUREMENT LEVELS:

- Dependent variable: ratio

- Independent variables: ratio

BRIEF DESCRIPTION: The PLOT procedure enables the researcher to produce a scatterplot of the relation between two variables. The researcher may also designate various labels to be placed on the output as well as specifying the scale for each dimension of the plot.

BASIC COMMAND STRUCTURE:

*SPSS*ˣ
PLOT
   /SYMBOLS='*'
   /TITLE="PRESTIGE RATING BY EDUCATION"
   /VERTICAL='PRESTIGE SCORE'
   /HORIZONTAL='YEARS OF EDUCATION'
   /PLOT=prestige WITH ed

PLOT
   /SYMBOLS='*'
   /TITLE="PRESTIGE RATING BY EDUCATION"
   /VERTICAL='PRESTIGE SCORE'
   /HORIZONTAL='YEARS OF EDUCATION'
   /PLOT=prestige WITH ed.

PLOT	SPSS command name
/SYMBOLS='*'	specifies the plot symbols to be used, in this case, the asterisk; the default symbols are numbers: the number 'I' is used for each point; if two or more plot points are the same, then the number used will reflect the number of points falling on the plot point
/TITLE='...'	specifies the title to be placed on the display
/VERTICAL='...'	label to be placed on the vertical dimension of the table (default is the variable label)
/HORIZONTAL='...'	label to be placed on the horizontal dimension of the table (default is the variable label)
/PLOT=prestige	plot instruction, 'prestige' is the name of the dependent variable which will be placed on the vertical dimension of the table
WITH ed	WITH separates the dependent variable from the independent variable; 'ed' is the independent variable and will be plotted on the horizontal dimension of the display

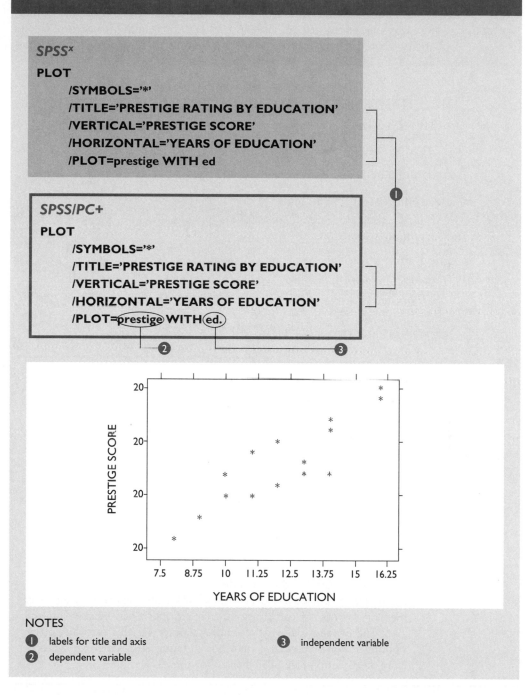

BOX A14 SAMPLE OUTPUT USING PLOT

SPSS^x

PLOT
    /SYMBOLS='*'
    /TITLE='PRESTIGE RATING BY EDUCATION'
    /VERTICAL='PRESTIGE SCORE'
    /HORIZONTAL='YEARS OF EDUCATION'
    /PLOT=prestige WITH ed

SPSS/PC+

PLOT
    /SYMBOLS='*'
    /TITLE='PRESTIGE RATING BY EDUCATION'
    /VERTICAL='PRESTIGE SCORE'
    /HORIZONTAL='YEARS OF EDUCATION'
    /PLOT=prestige WITH ed.

NOTES

❶ labels for title and axis

❷ dependent variable

❸ independent variable

SAMPLE OUTPUT AND NOTES: As in other procedures, the dependent variable is named first in the PLOT command. This results in a plot of the relationship between two variables, with the dependent variable on the vertical axis. Various options are available to permit the researcher to control the intervals printed along the two dimensions and to print various statistics. Consult an SPSS manual for more elaborate graphics.

9. REGRESSION: DOING MULTIPLE REGRESSION ANALYSIS

CHAPTER REFERENCES: Chapter 7, 17

APPROPRIATE MEASUREMENT LEVELS:

- Dependent variable: ratio

- Independent variables: ratio (nominal measurement involves the use of dummy variables)

BRIEF DESCRIPTION:The REGRESSION procedure does various forms of multiple regression analyses. This type of analysis allows the researcher to determine an equation to describe the relation between a dependent variable and multiple independent variables.

BASIC COMMAND STRUCTURE:

SPSS^x
REGRESSION DESCRIPTIVES
/VARIABLES= prestige income educ ex
/DEPENDENT= prestige
/BACKWARD

SPSS/PC+
REGRESSION DESCRIPTIVES
/VARIABLES= prestige income educ ex
/DEPENDENT= prestige
/BACKWARD.

REGRESSION	SPSS command name
DESCRIPTIVES	provides the means, standard deviations, and the correlation matrix for the variables
VARIABLES=	lists all the variables to be used in the analysis
/DEPENDENT=	indicates the name of the dependent variable
/BACKWARD.	requests SPSS to place all independent variables into the equation and drop them out in order of least significance, recalculating a new equation at each step. The process stops when only significant variables remain; other options provide alternative methods of entering or deleting variables from the equation (see SPSS manual for these)

SAMPLE OUTPUT AND NOTES: Box A15 presents a regression analysis of 15 fictional cases, examining the relation between prestige and three independent variables: income, years of experience, and educational attainment. In examining the output, note that the means, standard deviations, and the correlations between variables are presented (the DESCRIPTIVES sub-command requested this information). Given that we have requested the BACKWARD solution, note that all the independent variables are entered into the equation at Step 1, then the variable which is not statistically significant is removed, and the equations are recomputed and shown at Step 2. If we had more non-significant variables, the process would have continued until only statistically significant variables remained. Note that the R Square (explained variance) value, the *b* coefficients (labelled B) and beta weights are all reported on the output as well as the test of significance (labelled Sig T).

BOX A15   SAMPLE OUTPUT USING REGRESSION PROCEDURE

SPSS^x

REGRESSION DESCRIPTIVES
    /VARIABLES=prestige income **TO** ex — ①
    /DEPENDENT=prestige — ②
    /BACKWARD — ③

SPSS/PC+

REGRESSION DESCRIPTIVES
/VARIABLES= prestige income **TO** ex
/DEPENDENT= prestige
/BACKWARD.

****MULTIPLE REGRESSION****

	Mean	Std Devia	Label
INCOME	33866.667	14367.581	ANNUAL INCOME
ED	12.200	2.396	YEARS OF EDUCATION
PRESTIGE	51.133	16.097	PRESTIGE SCORE
EX	3.067	2.344	YEARS WORKING FOR COMPANY

BOX A15 SAMPLE OUTPUT USING REGRESSION PROCEDURE (continued)

Correlation:

	INCOME	ED	PRESTIGE	EX
INCOME	1.000	.842	.867	.664
ED	.842	1.000	.888	.442
PRESTIGE	.867	.888	1.000	.479
EX	.664	.442	.479	1.000

****MULTIPLE REGRESSION****

[Step 1]

Equation Number 1   Dependent Variable..   PRESTIGE   PRESTIGE SCORE

Variable(s) Entered on Step Number

   1..   EX   YEARS WORKING FOR COMPANY

   2..   ED   YEARS OF EDUCATION

   3..   INCOME   ANNUAL INCOME

Multiple R   .91609

R Square   (83922)————4

Adjusted R Square   .79537

Standard Error   7.28184

Analysis of Variance   5

	DF	Sum of Squares	Mean Square
Regression	3	3044.45649	1014.81883
Residual	11	583.27684	53.02517

F = 19.13844   Signif F = .0001

———————————— Variables in the Equation ————————————

Variable	B	SE B	Beta	T	Sig T
EX	-.44225	1.15886	-.06440	-.382	.7100
ED	3.48355	1.57231	.51860	2.216	.0487
INCOME	5.294729E-04	3.14360E-04	.47258	1.684	.1203
(Constant)	-7.94121	12.54358		-.633	.5396

End Block Number 1   All requested variables entered.

BOX A15 SAMPLE OUTPUT USING REGRESSION PROCEDURE (continued)

****MULTIPLE REGRESSION****

[Step 2]

Equation Number 1   Dependent Variable..   PRESTIGE   PRESTIGE SCORE
Beginning Block Number 2. Method: Backward
Variable(s) Removed on Step Number
     4.. EX   YEARS WORKING FOR COMPANY

Multiple R   .91493
R Square   .83709
Adjusted R Square   .80994
Standard Error   7.01783

Analysis of Variance

	DF	Sum of Squares	Mean Square
Regression	2	3036.73385	1518.36692
Residual	12	590.99949	49.24996

F = 30.82981   Signif F = .0000 ──────────────────────── ⑥

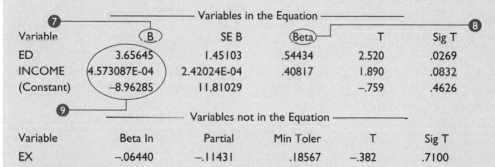

──────── Variables in the Equation ────────
⑦   ⑧

Variable	B	SE B	Beta	T	Sig T
ED	3.65645	1.45103	.54434	2.520	.0269
INCOME	4.573087E-04	2.42024E-04	.40817	1.890	.0832
(Constant)	−8.96285	11.81029		−.759	.4626

⑨

──────── Variables not in the Equation ────────

Variable	Beta In	Partial	Min Toler	T	Sig T
EX	−.06440	−.11431	.18567	−.382	.7100

End Block Number 2   POUT = .100 Limits reached.

NOTES

① list of all variables to be used

② dependent variable

③ requests all variables to be included and then dropped, one at a time, if they are not significant

④ 83.9 percent of the variation is explained

⑤ degrees of freedom (to determine the number of cases used in the analysis add DFs plus 1, as in 3 + 11 + 1 = 15)

⑥ indicates that a significant amount of variation in prestige is explained by the two remaining variables, ed and income

⑦ the *b* coefficient (not standardized; use this value if writing the equation)

⑧ the beta weight (standardized; use this value to judge the relative importance of predictors)

⑨ final equation after variable ex has been dropped

Table A3 presents an example of a regression results table. Note that along with the *b* coefficients and the beta weights, the percentage contribution of each independent variable is presented, using the following formula (Hamblin, 1971):

$$\begin{array}{c}\text{\% Variance Explained} \\ \text{by Each Variable}\end{array} = \frac{\text{\ss}_1 \times R^2}{\sum \text{\ss's}} \times 100$$

where:

$\text{\ss}_1$ is the beta weight for the variable

R^2 is the R Square (explained variance) for the equation

$\sum \text{\ss's}$ is the sum of the beta weights (ignoring + and − signs)

TABLE A3   **SIMPLIFIED TABLE SUMMARIZING RESULTS OF STATISTICALLY SIGNIFICANT VARIABLES IN PREDICTING VARIATIONS IN PRESTIGE RATING, FICTIONAL DATA**

Multiple Regression Analysis
Dependent Variable = Prestige Rating

Multiple R	.91493		
R Square	.83709		

	DF	Sum of Squares	Mean Square
Regression	2	3036.73385	1518.36692
Residual	12	590.99949	49.24996

F = 30.82981   Signif F = .0000

------------------ Variables in the Equation ------------------

Variable	B	SE B	Beta	T	Sig T	Percent Contribution
ED	3.65645	1.45103	.54434	2.520	.0269	47.8
INCOME	4.573087E-04	2.42024E-04	.40817	1.890	.0832	35.9
(Constant)	−8.96285	11.81029		−.759	.4626	____
				Total Variance Explained		83.7
				Variance Unexplained		16.3

------------- Variables not in the Equation -------------

Variable	Beta In	Partial	Min Toler	T	Sig T
EX	−.06440	−.11431	.18567	−.382	.7100

This estimate is "rough" because the betas represent the particular variables in the equation and would change if other variables were included. The calculation is shown in Table A4.

The pure researcher has greater interest in the beta weights, for these provide a basis for directly comparing the impact of the different independent variables on the dependent one. Applied researchers are more concerned with *b* coefficients, especially those which can be changed through policy alterations. They provide the basis for understanding how much change in the dependent variable may be produced for each change in the independent variable. Variables can be grouped for presentation so as to illuminate the degree to which different variable types influence the dependent variable (for example, how much of the variation in the dependent variable is due to socio-economic variables in comparison to the variety of experience variables).

A second method for estimating the relative importance of variables is to calculate a *part correlation coefficient*. This coefficient is calculated for each independent variable and represents the difference in the R^2 when the variable is included versus when it is not included. The variables may then be ordered in terms of the unique contribution of each independent variable. The SPSS commands for calculating the part correlation coefficients are presented in the manuals for both SPSS^x and SPSS/PC+.

In presenting the results of a regression analysis, most researchers present the final table after the non-significant variables had been dropped. But you will want to:

- indicate the names of variables that remained

- indicate the names of variables that were dropped

- point out total variation explained (R^2 value)

- note the percentage contribution of each of the statistically significant variables

- discuss the implications of the findings

TABLE A4   CALCULATING THE PERCENTAGE CONTRIBUTION OF EACH INDEPENDENT VARIABLE

VARIABLE	BETA	CALCULATION	PERCENT CONTRIBUTION
ED	.54434	((.54434 * .83709) / .95251) * 100 =	47.8
INCOME	.40817	((.40817 * .83709) / .95251) * 100 =	35.9
		Total Variance Explained	83.7
		Variance Unexplained	16.3

- present, in addition, the formula describing the relationship. In the case presented above, the formula would be as follows: Prestige = –8.96 + 3.66(ED) + .000457(INCOME)
- note that the formula uses *b* coefficients, the *a* value is the constant

i. Dummy Variable Analysis

There may be times when a researcher wishes to use a nominal variable within a regression analysis. This can be done by using dummy variables. Suppose we had three religious categories: Protestant, Catholic, and Jewish. To submit religion as a variable, we would create two new variables (one less than the number of categories) and enter each of these into the regression analysis. These variables are coded as 1 for presence, 0 for absence. These are best created using the RECODE procedure, as in:

```
SPSSˣ
RECODE religion (1=1)(ELSE=0)
  INTO prot
RECODE religion (2=1)(ELSE=0)
  INTO cath
VARIABLE LABELS prot
    "DUMMY VARIABLE
    PROTESTANT"
    /cath "DUMMY VARIABLE
    CATHOLIC"
VARIABLE LABELS prot TO cath
    1 "PRESENCE" 0 "ABSENCE"
```

```
SPSS PC+
COMPUTE prot=religion.
COMPUTE cath=religion.
RECODE prot (1=1)(ELSE=0).
RECODE cath (2=1)(ELSE=0).
VARIABLE LABELS
    /prot "DUMMY VARIABLE
    PROTESTANT"
    /cath "DUMMY VARIABLE
    CATHOLIC".
VARIABLE LABELS prot TO cath
    1 "PRESENCE" 0 "ABSENCE".
```

The third religious category, Jewish, is taken into account in the residual category of the two remaining categories. One has to be cautious in interpreting the results when dummy variables are used. These variables are at some disadvantage in explaining variance since they have only two values, 0 and 1. In short, we may somewhat underestimate the importance of the variable religion in such an analysis.

ii. Some Cautions

CAUTION 1. Ensure Variables are Theoretically Independent from one Another.
What this means is that one cannot use aspects of the dependent variable as independent variables. Include only meaningful potential causes of the dependent variable, not alternate measures of it.

CAUTION 2. Watch Out for Highly Correlated Independent Variables.
The weightings which will be attached to the variables will be unstable if the independent variables are strongly correlated with one another. The program will print out a warning if there is a problem in this area.

CAUTION 3. *Interpret Weightings with Care.*
Understand that the weightings are for the particular combination of independent variables for a particular sample and these weightings may not apply reliably to other samples.

CAUTION 4. Monitor the Number of Cases Carefully.
By default, SPSS will delete a case if it has a missing value in any of the variables in the equation. Thus, if there are several variables in an analysis, there is a danger of losing many cases. And, as the number of cases drops closer to the number of variables, the R^2 will increase dramatically. *To determine the number of cases used in the analysis, add 1 to the total degrees of freedom reported in the table.* If a large number of cases have been dropped, try running the analysis using PAIRWISE treatment of missing cases; and if there are still many missing try MEANS (this will substitute the mean of the variable for any missing cases). Either one of these commands can follow the DEPENDENT specification, as in:

REGRESSION DESCRIPTIVES
    /VARIABLES= depend, v1,v2
    /DEPENDENT= depend
    /MISSING = PAIRWISE
    /BACKWARD

or

REGRESSION DESCRIPTIVES
    /VARIABLES= depend, v1,v2
    /DEPENDENT= depend
    /MISSING= MEANS
    /BACKWARD

An additional possibility, after an initial narrowing down of the variables has been done, is to resubmit the analysis, naming only the significant variables, plus perhaps two or three that were dropped in the last few steps. This preserves those cases which were dropped because of missing values in variables that are not in the final equation.

10. T-TEST: COMPARING MEANS

CHAPTER REFERENCES: Chapter 7, 8

APPROPRIATE MEASUREMENT LEVELS:

- Dependent variable: ratio

- Independent variables: nominal, ordinal (recoded), ratio (recoded)

BRIEF DESCRIPTION: The T-TEST procedure tests whether the difference in the means between two groups is statistically significant.

BASIC COMMAND STRUCTURE:

SPSS^x
T-TEST PAIRS=time1 time2

SPSS/PC+
T-TEST PAIRS=time1 time2.

T-TEST	the SPSS command name
PAIRS=	specifies a within-subject design
time1 time2	specifies the variable names reflecting the time 1 and time 2 measures on the variable

---

SPSS^x
T-TEST GROUPS=tire (1,2) /
   VARIABLES= time

SPSS/PC+
T-TEST GROUPS=tire (1,2) /
   VARIABLES= time.

T-TEST	the SPSS command name
GROUPS=	specifies a between-subjects design
tire (1,2)	specifies which treatment group the subject falls into (identified as either a 1 or a 2)
/VARIABLES=time	identifies the variable which is to be used in comparing the mean scores for the two groups

---

SAMPLE OUTPUT AND NOTES: Box A16 shows sample output from two T-TEST analyses. The first shows the command format and results from a within-subject design, the second shows how to set up a job to do a between-subjects analysis.

The presentation of basic commands for examining relationships includes the minimum instructions. The SPSS package contains a broad range of options, statistics, file management, and analysis procedures. The chances are that most analyses you wish to do are possible within SPSS. After you have mastered the basic procedures, you will be ready to begin exploring SPSS in greater detail.

BOX A16   SAMPLE OUTPUT USING T-TEST PROCEDURE

Output #1 SPSS/PC+ job
TITLE t-test on within-subject race times differences.
DATA LIST /time1 11-14 time2 36-39.
BEGIN DATA.

James	13.1	James	13.0
Peter	12.8	Peter	12.9
Margaret	13.5	Margaret	13.4
Jeremy	13.4	Jeremy	13.2
Stefan	13.5	Stefan	13.5
Don	13.6	Don	13.3
Paul	13.5	Paul	13.3
Tom	12.8	Tom	12.7
Linda	12.9	Linda	12.9
Melanie	13.5	Melanie	13.4

END DATA.
T-TEST PAIRS = TIME1 TIME2.
FINISH.

SPSS^x

T-TEST PAIRS=time1 time2

SPSS/PC+

T-TEST PAIRS=time1 time2.

Paired samples t-test: TIME1
TIME2

Variable	Number of Cases	Mean	Standard Deviation	Standard Error
TIME1	10	13.2600	.324	.102
TIME2	10	13.1600	.267	.085

(Difference) Mean	Standard Deviation	Standard Error	Corr.	2-Tail Prob.	t Value	Degrees of Freedom	2-Tail Prob.
.1000	.115	.037	.941	.000	2.74	9	.023

BOX A16 SAMPLE OUTPUT USING T-TEST PROCEDURE (continued)

Output #2 SPSS/PC+ job

TITLE t-test on race between-subjects design.

DATA LIST /time1 11-14 tire 16.

BEGIN DATA.

James	21.4	1
Peter	16.2	1
Margaret	18.0	1
Jeremy	16.1	1
Stefan	15.9	1
Don	20.3	1
Paul	17.1	1
Tom	21.4	1
Linda	17.7	1
Melanie	19.8	1
James	20.7	2
Peter	19.0	2
Margaret	16.4	2
Jeremy	16.7	2
Stefan	21.6	2
Don	20.1	2
Paul	14.4	2
Tom	16.3	2
Linda	15.7	2
Melanie	19.7	2

END DATA.

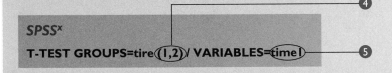

SPSS^x

T-TEST GROUPS=tire (1,2) / VARIABLES=time1

SPSS/PC+

T-TEST GROUPS=tire (1,2) / VARIABLES=time1.

BOX A16   SAMPLE OUTPUT USING T-TEST PROCEDURE (continued)

Independent samples of TIRE

Group 1: TIRE EQ 1   Group 2: TIRE EQ 2

t-test for: TIME1

	Number of Cases	Mean	Standard Deviation	Standard Error
Group 1	10	18.3900	2.168	.685
Group 2	10	18.0600	2.447	.774

		Pooled Variance Estimate			Separate Variance Estimate		
F Value	2-Tail Prob.	t Value	Degrees of Freedom	2-Tail Prob.	t Value	Degrees of Freedom	2-Tail Prob.
1.27	.724	(.32)	18	.753	.32	17.74	(.753)——7

6

NOTES

1 average lap times using different tires

2 test of significance results: reject the null hypothesis

3 correlation between time1 and time2 speeds

4 identifies which tire used: 1 = standard 2 = new tire

5 dependent variable, lap time

6 test of significance on variances

7 t-test of significance: accept null hypothesis

D. CREATING NEW VARIABLES

SPSS provides a number of ways to create or change variables. Three such techniques are examined below.

1. RECODE

The RECODE procedure is used to temporarily change a variable during analysis or to create a new variable. Suppose we have three 9-point Likert-type items we wish to reverse score (ie., change the 9s into 1s, 8s into 2s, etc.) The command looks like this:

RECODE v33,v37,v38 (9=1)(8=2)(7=3)(6=4)(5=5)(4=6)(3=7)(2=8)(1=9)

Suppose alternatively that we wished to regroup the values in one or more variables, and to create new versions of the variables to be saved permanently. In SPSS^x, the following could be done:

```
SPSSˣ
RECODE v21,v22 (1,2,3 = 1)(4,5 = 2)
  (6,7,8,9 = 3) INTO v21r,v22r
VARIABLE LABELS v21r
  "Recoded Version v21"
  /v22r "Recoded Version v22"
VALUE LABELS v21r, v22r
  1 "low score"
  2 "medium score"
  3 "high score"/
... any analysis procedures here ...
SAVE OUTFILE = system
FINISH
```

This time two new variables have been created, and will be saved permanently if the file is saved at the end of the run. Note that the new variable names simply have an "R" appended to the original name. It is a good idea to maintain the original name in the new name so that the researcher will know that it is a recoded version of the original variable. Variable labels may be attached as indicated.

Since the **INTO** sub-command is not available in SPSS/PC+, using the above procedure would require a slight variation on the command such as:

```
SPSS/PC+
COMPUTE v21r = v21.
COMPUTE v22r = v22.
RECODE v21r,v22r (1,2,3 = 1)
  (4,5 = 2)(6,7,8,9 = 3).
VARIABLE LABELS v21r
  "Recoded Version v21"
  /v22r "Recoded Version v22".
VALUE LABELS v21r, v22r
  1 "low score"
  2 "medium score"
  3 "high score"/.
... any analysis procedures here ...
SAVE OUTFILE = 'dani.SYS'.
FINISH.
```

Assume we have a variable, MAED, indicating mother's education and we wish to divide our sample into those with low, medium, and high levels of education. We create and save the new variable with the following SPSS^x commands:

```
SPSSˣ
RECODE
  maed (LOWEST THRU 8 = 1)
  (9,10,11,12 = 2)
  (13 THRU HIGHEST = 3)
  INTO maedr
VARIABLE LABELS maedr
  "Education of Mother, Recoded"
VALUE LABELS maedr
  1 "8 years or less"
  2 "9 to 12 years"
  3 "13 or more years"
... any analysis procedures here...
SAVE OUTFILE = system
FINISH
```

Note the use of terms LOWEST, HIGHEST, and THRU. If there is a residual category, the keyword ELSE may be used to assign values, as in:

RECODE maed (13 THRU 22 = 2)(ELSE = 1)

RECODE maed (13 THRU 22 = 13)(ELSE=COPY)

ELSE=COPY	retains the original values for those not recoded in the previous statement
ELSE = 1	to be used with caution because all values not previously identified will be set to a value of 1, including all those coded as missing values.

```
SPSS/PC+
COMPUTE maedr = maed.
RECODE maedr
  (LOWEST THRU 8 = 1)
  (9,10,11,12 = 2)
  (13 THRU HIGHEST = 3).
VARIABLE LABELS maedr
  "Education of Mother, Recoded".
VALUE LABELS maedr
  1 "8 years or less"
  2 "9 to 12 years"
  3 "13 or more years".
... any analysis procedures here...
SAVE OUTFILE = 'dani.SYS'.
FINISH.
```

RECODE is a quick way to create new variables or to regroup the values in a variable. Survey researchers in particular have many occasions to use this procedure.

2. COMPUTE

COMPUTE allows the researcher to create new variables by performing mathematical operations on variables. The general form of a COMPUTE command is:

```
SPSSˣ
COMPUTE newvar = (v16 + v22) / 2
```

```
SPSS/PC+
COMPUTE newvar = (v16 + v22) / 2.
```

The above operation creates a new variable, newvar, representing the addition of values in two variables divided by 2. Computations within parentheses are performed first and are used to control the order of the mathematical operations. Make certain that there are an equal number of open and closed parentheses. SPSS employs the following symbols to indicate basic functions:

+ Addition	/ Division
− Subtraction	** Exponentiation
* Multiplication	

Many other functions are available to the researcher in SPSS; three commonly used ones include:

RND(var)	rounds to whole number
SUM(var list)	sums values in variable list
MEAN(var list)	mean of values

The following illustrates the use of the above procedures:

SPSS^x
COMPUTE wages = RND(salary)
COMPUTE total = SUM (v12, v13, v14, v15, v16)
COMPUTE scale = MEAN(v17, v18, v21)

SPSS/PC+
COMPUTE wages = RND(salary).
COMPUTE total = SUM (v12, v13, v14, v15, v16).
COMPUTE scale = MEAN (v17, v18, v21).

The difference between the SUM and the MEAN functions is that the former simply adds together the values found in the designated variables (returning a SYSTEM MISSING value in cases where any of the values are missing); the latter computes the mean of the designated variables.

Whenever new variables are created, they can be given LABELS. It is also useful to document complex computations so that the researcher can return to the data set at a later date and find out how various computations were performed. An easy way to save such information is through the DOCUMENT command in SPSS^x. (This command is not available in the version of SPSS/PC+ currently available.) The following show the commands necessary to create and to retrieve DOCUMENT statements:

DOCUMENT The variable known as 'total' was created in the following way: COMPUTE total = SUM (v12, v13, v14, v15, v16)

To retrieve DOCUMENTS in a later run include:

DISPLAY DOCUMENTS

3. IF

A third way new variables can be created (among several available in SPSS) is through IF statements. The simple form of the command is as follows:

```
SPSSˣ
COMPUTE newvar = 0
IF (v15 LT 25) newvar = 1
```

```
SPSS/PC+
COMPUTE newvar = 0.
IF (v15 LT 25) newvar = 1.
```

Here the new variable is set to 0 initially and then whenever v15 has a value of less than 25, NEWVAR is set to 1.

More complex uses of the IF statement are illustrated in the following example. Suppose we are studying poverty in a community, have survey data on 300 people over the age of 18, and wish to create a variable identifying different types of poverty, taking into account age group and income levels. The following represents one way of creating the new variable:

```
SPSSˣ
COMPUTE poortype = 0
IF (age LT 25 AND income LT
   12000) poortype = 1
IF (age GE 25 AND age LT 65
   AND income LT 15000)
   poortype = 2
IF (age GE 65 AND income LT
   12000) poortype = 3
VARIABLE LABELS poortype
   "Type of Poor"
VALUE LABELS poortype
   0 "all ages, non-poor"
   1 "under 25 under $12 K"
   2 "25-64, under $15 K"
   3 "over 64, under $12 K"/
```

```
SSPSS/PC+
COMPUTE poortype = 0.
IF (age LT 25 AND income LT
   12000) poortype = 1.
IF (age GE 25 AND age LT 65
   AND income LT 15000)
   poortype = 2.
IF (age GE 65 AND income LT
   12000) poortype = 3.
VARIABLE LABELS poortype
   "Type of Poor".
VALUE LABELS poortype
   0 "all ages, non-poor"
   1 "under 25 under $12 K"
   2 "25-64, under $15 K"
   3 "over 64, under $12 K".
```

The above set combines age and income levels to create a new variable called POORTYPE, which identifies the non-poor (those with incomes over $12,000 for the young and old, and over $15,000 for the middle-aged respondents) and three categories of the poor: the young, incomes under $12,000; the middle-aged with incomes under $15,000; and the seniors with incomes under $12,000.

Consult SPSS manuals for other methods of creating new variables or for transforming old ones. Having understood how new variables may be created, and saved, it is now time to examine how indexes are constructed.

E. CREATING INDEXES

Indexes combine two or more indicators to reflect complex variables such as socio-economic status, job satisfaction, or an attitude toward some social issue. Frequently, the researcher constructs subindexes which may be treated alone or combined with other subindexes to form a composite measure. For example, a researcher measuring attitudes toward abortion might construct a subindex for "soft reasons" (economically inconvenient, preference for having a baby later, etc.) and "hard reasons" (pregnancy as a result of rape, severely handicapped, etc.). These subindexes might also be combined to form an overall index. In each case, however, the researcher will have to ensure that appropriate items are included in each subindex.

In the sections below, the RELIABILITY procedure for evaluating index items is presented followed by a demonstration of how Z scores may be used in creating composite measures. Chapter 12 presented a discussion of item analysis and introduced the principles of index construction. This section demonstrates the commands to be used in SPSS to create and evaluate indexes.

1. RELIABILITY: ASSESSING INTERNAL CONSISTENCY

CHAPTER REFERENCE: Chapter 12

MEASUREMENT LEVELS:

- ratio (however, ordinal Likert-type items are typically used)

BRIEF DESCRIPTION: The RELIABILITY procedure evaluates which items should go into an index. RELIABILITY examines the components of a proposed additive index providing a variety of diagnostics for each item. The procedure does not actually compute the index, but rather provides an assessment of each item; the actual index would be constructed with a COMPUTE command. Of particular note for the beginning social researcher is that RELIABILITY computes item means and standard deviations, inter-item correlations, a series of item-total comparisons, and *Cronbach's Alpha* for index reliability.

BASIC COMMAND STRUCTURE:

SPSSˣ

RELIABILITY VARIABLES= v29
  v30r to v33r
    /SCALE (sexatt)=v29 v30r TO
    v33r
    /STATISTICS DESC CORR
    /SUMMARY= MEANS, CORR,
    TOTAL

SPSS/PC+ (Professional Statistics,
Version 5.0)

RELIABILITY /VARIABLES=v29
  v30r to v33r
    /SCALE (sexatt)=v29 v30r to
    v33r
    /STATISTICS= DESC CORR
    /SUMMARY= MEANS CORR
    TOTAL.

RELIABILITY	SPSS command name
VARIABLES=	lists all variables involved in proposed indexes
/SCALE (sexatt)=	SCALE is the sub-command, followed by the name of the proposed scale in parentheses; this is followed by the list of variables proposed for the index
/STATISTICS=	identifies statistics requested; see manual for other available statistics or use =ALL which will generate all available ones
/SUMMARY=	summary statistics requested on this line

SAMPLE OUTPUT AND NOTES: The RELIABILITY procedure in SPSS uses the internal consistency approach to reliability. The method that is used to calculate the Standardized Alpha involves the number of items going into the index and the average inter-item correlation among the items, as in:

$$\text{Alpha} = \frac{N \text{ (average inter-item correlation)}}{1 + \text{(average inter-item correlation } (N - 1))}$$

where **N** is the number of items proposed for the index being tested, and **average inter-item correlation** is the average of the correlations between the items: this value is printed when the SUMMARY options MEANS is selected.

The Standardized Alpha for the index evaluated in Box A17 would be as follows:

$$\text{Alpha} = \frac{5 \, (.3507)}{1 + (.3507 \, (5 - 1))}$$

$$\text{Alpha} = 1.7535 \div 2.4028$$

$$\text{Alpha} = .7298$$

Cronbach's alpha varies with the average inter-item correlation, taking into account the number of items that make up the index. If there is an increase in either the inter-item correlation or the number of items, alpha increases. For example, with 2 items and a .4 mean correlation, the alpha value would be .572; with 8 items and a .4 mean inter-item correlation, the alpha would be .842. With .6 inter-item correlations, the alpha for 2 versus 8 items would be .750 and .924 respectively. See Appendix G for a table which summarizes the relation between items and inter-item correlations.

In examining Box A17, note that we are examining five 9-point Likert-type liberal gender attitude items, known as v29, v30, v31, v32, and v33. Note that v30 to v33 are inverse measures (the higher the score, the *less* liberal the attitude). Let us go through the steps to evaluate these items. We will proceed by creating a james.CON file to access the .SYS and do the following:

STEP 1 Reverse score any items that are negative (in this case: v30 to v33) using the RECODE procedure.

STEP 2 Indexes are evaluated by naming all the variables that are relevant and then specifying one or more indexes that the researcher wishes to evaluate. The command structure is as follows:

RELIABILITY VARIABLES=v29 v30r TO
* v33r*
* /SCALE (sexatt)=v29 v30r TO v33r*
* /STATISTICS= DESC CORR*
* /SUMMARY= MEANS, CORR, TOTAL*

STEP 3 Examine the results. As a rule of thumb, you have an acceptable index if:

* the *correlation matrix* indicates that the correlations between the items are positive (all are positive; they vary from .13 to .56).

* the *mean inter-item correlations* should be above .25 (in the case we are examining the value is .3507); note here, however, that if you were using items based on Likert items with fewer than 9 points you might wish to accept slightly lower mean inter-item correlations, perhaps as low as .20.

* examine the *item-total statistics*; this part of the analysis examines the individual items, comparing each to the total score for the index being evaluated; the *corrected item-total correlation* presents the correlation between the item and the total index score with the effects of the individual item removed. Generally you would expect each of these items to be above .25.

* at the bottom of the table two alphas are reported; earlier the calculation for the standardized item alpha was demonstrated; we attempt to get as high an

BOX A17   SAMPLE OUTPUT USING RELIABILITY PROCEDURE

*SPSS*ˣ

RECODE v30, v31, v32, v 33 (9=1) (8=2) (7=3) (6=4) (5=5) (4=6) (3=7) (2=8) (1=9) INTO
    v30r, v31r, v32r, v33r

LIST VARIABLES= id, v30, v30r/CASES=10

ID	V30	V30R
1	5	5.00
2	1	9.00
3	1	9.00
4	1	9.00
5	7	3.00
6	6	4.00
7	1	9.00
8	6	4.00
9	2	8.00
10	9	1.00

Number of cases read: 10   Number of cases listed: 10

*SPSS*ˣ

  ❶ **RELIABILITY VARIABLES= v29 v30r to v33r**
        /SCALE (sexatt)= v29 v30r to v33r   ❷
        /STATISTICS= DESC CORR
        /SUMMARY= MEANS CORR TOTAL

SPSS/PC+ (Professional Statistics, Version 5.0)

RELIABILITY /VARIABLES= v29 v30r to v33r
      /SCALE (sexatt)= v29 v30r to v33r
      /STATISTICS= DESC CORR
      /SUMMARY= MEANS CORR TOTAL.

BOX A1.7   SAMPLE OUTPUT USING RELIABILITY PROCEDURE (continued)

SPSS^X OUTPUT:

****** METHOD 2 (COVARIANCE MATRIX) WILL BE USED FOR THIS ANALYSIS ******

RELIABILITY ANALYSIS – SCALE (SEXATT)

1.	V29	HUSBAND'S NAME TAKEN BY WIFE
2.	V30R	MEN BETTER EMOTIONALLY FOR POLITICS (R)
3.	V31R	MEN RESPONSIBLE TO PROVIDE FOR FAMILIES (R)
4.	V32R	MEN MAKE BETTER ENGINEERS (R)
5.	V33R	MOTHER'S PLACE IS IN HOME (R)

		MEAN	STD DEV	CASES
1.	V29	4.4341	2.4435	182.0
2.	V30R	7.2143	2.2773	182.0
3.	V31R	6.7253	2.4430	182.0
4.	V32R	7.6209	1.9845	182.0
5.	V33R	5.4341	2.8291	182.0

CORRELATION MATRIX

	V29	V30R	V31R	V32R	V33R
V29	1.0000				
V30R	.1331	1.0000			
V31R	.3135	.3185	1.0000		
V32R	.1629	.5046	.4422	1.0000	
V33R	.3043	.3740	.5569	.3975	1.0000

③

OF CASES = 182.0

ITEM MEANS	MEAN	MINIMUM	MAXIMUM	RANGE	MAX/MIN	VARIANCE
	6.2857	4.4341	7.6209	3.1868	1.7187	1.7480

INTER-ITEM CORRELATIONS	MEAN	MINIMUM	MAXIMUM	RANGE	MAX/MIN	VARIANCE
	.3507	.1331	.5569	.4238	4.1837	.0173

④

BOX A1-7   SAMPLE OUTPUT USING RELIABILITY PROCEDURE (continued)

ITEM-TOTAL STATISTICS

	SCALE MEAN IF ITEM DELETED	SCALE VARIANCE IF ITEM DELETED	CORRECTED ITEM-TOTAL CORRELATION	SQUARED MULTIPLE CORRELATION	ALPHA IF ITEM DELETED
V29	26.9945	52.4696	.3110	.1227	.7464
V30R	24.2143	49.8599	.4479	.2908	.6947
V31R	24.7033	44.2098	.5932	.3880	.6367
V32R	23.8077	50.6203	.5274	.3508	.6714
V33R	25.9945	40.2596	.5901	.3773	.6358

⑤ ⑥

RELIABILITY COEFFICIENTS   5 ITEMS
ALPHA = .7268   STANDARDIZED ITEM ALPHA = .7298

SPSSˣ

COMPUTE trad = v30r + v31r + v32r + v33r
VARIABLE LABELS trad "Traditional Gender Role Attitudes"
SAVE OUTFILE= system

SPSS/PC+

COMPUTE trad = v30r + v31r + v32r + v33r.
VARIABLE LABELS trad "Traditional Gender Role Attitudes".
SAVE OUTFILE= 'dani.SYS'.

⑦

NOTES

① name of index
② list of potential items (variables) for index
③ note: all should be positive
④ average of correlations in matrix above (excluding the 1.0s)
⑤ correlations between the item and the total score with item value subtracted out (to avoid part-whole correlation problem)
⑥ what the Alpha value would be if the item were dropped; V29 is a candidate for dropping, the researcher would have to decide if the increase in Alpha is worth achieving by moving to a four-item index
⑦ computing the index for use later; save outfile if you wish to retain it permanently in your system file

alpha as possible when constructing an index. The alpha reported in Box A17 is .7268.

- the *alpha if item deleted column* reports on what the alpha would be if the item were deleted; in Box A17 we note that if we dropped v29 the alpha would be .7464; for all other cases the alpha would be lowered if the item were deleted. Our decision will be to drop v29 when the final index is calculated using the COMPUTE procedure.

STEP 4 If two or more items are to be removed from the final index, it will be necessary to resubmit another RELIABILITY job. If one or no items need to be eliminated, then one can go immediately to Step 5.

STEP 5 Having decided which items are to be included in the index, a new job should be run adding the items together using a COMPUTE command. The system file should be updated, saving the new index scores with a SAVE OUTFILE command, as in:

SPSS^x **COMPUTE sexatt= v30r + v31r + v32r + v33r** **VARIABLE LABELS sexatt "Sex Role Attitude"** **... any analysis ...** **SAVE OUTFILE=system** **FINISH**

SPSS/PC+ **COMPUTE sexatt= v30r + v31r + v32r + v33r.** **VARIABLE LABELS sexatt "Sex Role Attitude".** **... any analysis ...** **SAVE OUTFILE= 'Paula.SYS'.** **FINISH.**

There are many other options available within the RELIABILITY procedure. It is possible to compute split-half coefficients and various coefficients proposed by Louis Guttman. Consult the *SPSS^x User's Guide* for additional models and options. (The RELIABILITY procedure is available in the Professional Statistics option of Version 5.0 of SPSS/PC+.)

2. USING Z SCORES TO CREATE AN INDEX

CHAPTER REFERENCES: Chapter 7, 12

MEASUREMENT LEVELS:

- ratio

BRIEF DESCRIPTION: Z scores are used to standardize variables so that each variable will have a mean of 0 and a standard deviation of 1.

BASIC COMMAND STRUCTURE:

SPSSˣ

DESCRIPTIVES VARIABLES=
   income, educa
     /SAVE

DESCRIPTIVES	SPSS command
income, educa	the names of the variables
/SAVE	requests SPSS to create a standardized variable, with a Z prefixed to the variable's name, as in: ZINCOME, ZEDUCA

SPSS/PC+

DESCRIPTIVES VARIABLES=
   income, educa
     /OPTIONS 3.   requests SPSS to create a standardized variable, with a Z prefixed to the variable's name, as in: ZINCOME, ZEDUCA

SAMPLE SPSS COMMANDS AND NOTES: The researcher may wish to add items together to construct an index. Suppose we had two items: annual income and years of education. Given the vastly different ranges in these two variables, we will standardize them first and then add them together. This may be done using the DESCRIPTIVES procedure's OPTIONS 3, which computes Z scores and stores them in a new variable whose name is the original one prefixed with a Z (e.g., "educa" becomes "Zeduca"). The following job could be run which would create our socio-economic index and save it for future runs:

```
SPSSˣ

TITLE Creating the SES index
FILE HANDLE
   system/NAME='norm.SYS'
GET FILE system
DESCRIPTIVES VARIABLE=
   income, educa
      /OPTIONS= SAVE
COMPUTE ses = Zincome + Zeduca
VARIABLE LABELS ses
   "Socioeconomic Index"
... any analysis procedures ...
SAVE OUTFILE = system
FINISH
```

```
SPSS/PC+

TITLE Creating the SES index.
GET FILE 'Marlies.SYS'.
DESCRIPTIVES VARIABLE=
   income, educa
      /OPTIONS= 3.
COMPUTE ses = Zincome +
   Zeduca.
VARIABLE LABELS ses
   "Socioeconomic Index".
... any analysis procedures ...
SAVE OUTFILE = 'Marlies.SYS'.
FINISH.
```

Items may be weighted differently by simply altering the COMPUTE statement. Suppose, for example, you wish to have income contribute two-thirds and education one-third of the index. The following would accomplish this weighting:

```
SPSSˣ

COMPUTE ses2 = (zincome * .67)
   + (zeduca * .33)
VARIABLE LABELS ses2
   "Weighted Socioeconomic Index"
```

```
SPSS/PC+

COMPUTE ses2 = (zincome * .67)
   + (zeduca * .33).
VARIABLE LABELS ses2
   "Weighted Socioeconomic Index".
```

3. COMPUTING AN SES INDEX USING IF STATEMENTS

Another illustration of an SES index which identifies for a respondent the higher of the mother's or father's occupational prestige rating. Assuming that information has been collected on both the mother's and father's occupations and that the prestige scores for the occupations have been entered into the computer, our task is to develop a new variable which will use the higher of the mother's or father's occupational prestige rating to reflect the SES level of the family unit. The challenge here is to have SPSS compute the index. Box A18 shows how the new variable could be created using SPSS.

BOX A18 SAMPLE OUTPUT USING IF STATEMENT TO CREATE AN SES INDEX

SPSS^x version used in this Box

DESCRIPTIVES VARIABLES= v63, v64

Number of valid observations (listwise) = 131.00

Variable	Mean	Std Dev	Minimum	Maximum	Valid N	Label
V63	51.94	17.87	17	87	179	FATHER'S OCCUPATION
V64	47.67	16.21	17	82	133	MOTHER'S OCCUPATION

MISSING VALUES v63, v64 ()/ ———————————————— ❶

DESCRIPTIVES VARIABLES= v63, v64

❷ Number of valid observations (listwise) = 186.00

Variable	Mean	Std Dev	Minimum	Maximum	Valid N	Label
V63	53.71	19.69	17	99	186	FATHER'S OCCUPATION
V64	62.07	26.66	17	99	186	MOTHER'S OCCUPATION

IF (v64 GE v63 AND v64 LT 98) ses=v64 ⌐

IF (v63 GE v64 AND v63 LT 98) ses=V63 |

IF (v64 GE 98 AND v63 LT 98) ses=V63 ❸

IF (v63 GE 98 AND v64 LT 98) ses=V64 ⌐

LIST VARIABLES= id, v63, v64, ses/CASES=25

ID	V63	V64	SES
1	45	98	45.00
2	66	37	66.00
3	42	27	42.00
4	28	98	28.00
5	40	46	46.00
6	50	68	68.00
7	51	65	65.00
8	33	42	42.00
9	78	36	78.00
10	87	65	87.00
11	38	98	38.00
12	36	98	36.00
13	52	98	52.00

❹

BOX A18   SAMPLE OUTPUT USING IF STATEMENT TO CREATE AN SES INDEX (continued)

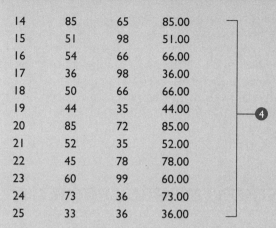

14	85	65	85.00
15	51	98	51.00
16	54	66	66.00
17	36	98	36.00
18	50	66	66.00
19	44	35	44.00
20	85	72	85.00
21	52	35	52.00
22	45	78	78.00
23	60	99	60.00
24	73	36	73.00
25	33	36	36.00

DESCRIPTIVES VARIABLES= v63 v64 ses

Number of valid observations (listwise) = 181.00

Variable	Mean	Std Dev	Minimum	Maximum	Valid N	Label
V63	53.71	19.69	17	99	186	FATHER'S OCCUPATION
V64	62.07	26.66	17	99	186	MOTHER'S OCCUPATION
SES	54.60	17.48	17.00	87.00	181	FAMILY OCC. PRESTIGE

MISSING VALUES v63, v64 (98,99)/ ────────── ⑤

DESCRIPTIVES VARIABLES= v63, v64

Number of valid observations (listwise) = 131.00

Variable	Mean	Std Dev	Minimum	Maximum	Valid N	Label
V63	51.94	17.87	17	87	179	FATHER'S OCCUPATION
V64	47.67	16.21	17	82	133	MOTHER'S OCCUPATION

NOTES

① removes MISSING VALUES from listed variables

② now we have more cases and higher means because the 98s and 99s are treated as non-missing

③ these IF statements choose the higher of the mother's and father's occupational prestige and create a new variable, ses, with the higher value

④ confirming that the procedure is working properly

⑤ putting MISSING VALUES back on

⑥ note that values are reset to original ones

Examine Box A18 carefully. Because "housewife" (coded as 98) and those who did not answer the question (coded as 99) were both identified as MISSING VALUES, it was necessary to remove the missing values identifiers before the index could be created (see Note 1 in Box A18). Through the use of IF statements, SPSS was then instructed to use the higher of the mother's or father's occupational prestige score to determine the value for the new variable, SES (see Note 2 in Box A21). It is crucial in creating more complex variables to do a listing of a number of cases to be certain that the values are being properly assigned to the new variable (see Note 3). After the IF statements have been completed, it is necessary to have SPSS do some procedure before the MISSING VALUES for v63 and v64 are reassigned (see Note 4).

F. STEPS IN ANALYZING DATA FOR A PROJECT

Assuming that you have a corrected version of your system file prepared and you wish to proceed with the data analysis for a project, remember that to access the file you need the following lines:

SPSS^x

TITLE smoking project, Danielle Keating
FILE HANDLE system/ NAME= 'dani.SYS'
GET FILE system

SPSS/PC+

GET FILE 'dani.SYS'.

Remember that if you modify a file with a **COMPUTE**, **IF**, or **RECODE** statement, and you wish to save the changes for your next session, just include the following line at the end of your job:

SPSS^x

SAVE OUTFILE=system
FINISH

SPSS/PC+

SAVE OUTFILE='jeremy.SYS'.
FINISH.

When doing your runs, be careful to use a different number for each of your job control (.CON) jobs. The reason for this is that if you have errors in your data and it becomes necessary to rerun a job after corrections have been made, you can then quickly resubmit your jobs. Jobs should look like the following:

jeremy0.CON   jeremy1.CON   jeremy2.CON

If you are running SPSS^x and you encounter a "disk capacity exceeded" error, you will have to delete any .OUT files before you submit a new job. In order to save computer paper and to save computer time, it is a good idea to run several smaller jobs rather than one enormous one. Let us now go through the steps in analyzing a data set.

STEP 1. Be certain to have the questionnaire or the recording form on which you have recorded the column numbers for each variable, and printouts of your **FREQUENCIES** and **DESCRIPTIVES** with you. If you have not run these analyses, run them.

STEP 2. If you need to construct any indexes, this should be done at this point. Review the procedures for creating indexes; if you are using **RELIABILITY**, do the run, determine the items that are to go into the index and then do a **COMPUTE** to create the index. Add **VARIABLE LABELS** (and **VALUE LABELS**, if appropriate). Retain the new infirmation by using a **SAVE OUTFILE** command at the end of the job..

STEP 3. Examine your causal models. Select the appropriate procedures for testing the models. Do the runs to test the various relationships indicated by the model. Note that you may need to **RECODE** some variables. If most of the relationships are examined using one method (say **MEANS**), you should probably do all of them using that procedure, even though a few could be examined using correlations. Enter the commands to do the basic runs and, if recoding of variables has been done, retain the recodes for future use by updating your system file with a **SAVE OUTFILE** command at the end of the job.

STEP 4. If you have any intervening or sources of spuriousness models, these should be processed. Review Chapter 16 for suggestions on interpreting results.

STEP 5. After you have assembled the computer output, you will want to consider how you will present the results. (See various summary tables in Chapter 18 for possible ways of setting up your tables for presentation. Note that it is helpful, particularly in small sample studies, to indicate whether the trends in various relationships go in the directions predicted.

STEP 6. Write your report in sections, following the outline suggested in Chapter 18.

G. WHEN YOU GET ERRORS AND WARNINGS

Expect errors and warning messages when you run SPSS jobs. Some of these errors will lead to the termination of the job, other less serious ones (warnings) will simply lead SPSS to ignore an instruction. SPSS has error-checking routines which will identify the error immediately following the line on which the error occurs.

Figure A4 presents a listing of some of the more common errors and warnings and what procedures might be taken to solve them. But before you examine that figure, we will review some basic strategies in error detection.

FIGURE A4 COMMON SPSS ERRORS AND WARNINGS AND HOW TO FIX THEM

SPSS ERROR/WARNING	DOUBLE CHECK THIS
Error – Unexpected end of file encountered	Check *data file* (.DAT file) for blank lines, or missorted cases
Error – Variable name not recognized	i) if this happens on the first and subsequent variables mentioned, make certain system file was accessed (check for correct file names, file handles); ii) check the spelling of the variable name.
Error – Unrecognized commands due to incorrectly spelled words	A common error is a misspelled command such as STTSTICS for STATISTICS
Warning – The (ADD) VALUE LABELS command. Be certain to include the values for each category	Correct: VALUE LABELS rv43 1 "No" 2 "Yes" Incorrect: VALUE LABELS rv43 "No" 2 "Yes"
Warning – Incorrectly enclosed literal	Correct: VARIABLE LABEL v43 "Place of Birth" Incorrect: VARIABLE LABEL v43 "Place of Birth"

Error – Text: Dependent. In regression analysis, this warning occurs if you fail to include the slash before the dependent variable is identified: the machine will try to read DEPENDENT as a variable if the / is omitted; if / missed other consequent errors may result, such as the machine attempting to do a BACKWARD solution but with no dependent variable identified.	Correct:
	REGRESSION VARIABLES= v34 v12 V56
	   /DEPENDENT= v34
	   /BACKWARD
	
	Incorrect:
	REGRESSION VARIABLES= v34 v12 V56
	   DEPENDENT=v34/
	   BACKWARD

TIP 1. Expect Errors.

The first thing to realize is that you will make errors. Even after many years of using SPSS you will continue to make them. SPSS errors are just part of your life as a data analyst.

TIP 2. Examine Errors and Warning Messages Carefully.

The errors and warnings will be listed on the output immediately after the problem has been encountered. To assist the researcher, the characters or symbols creating the problem will be quoted. A key point is to examine carefully the description SPSS provides of the error which will assist you in identifying your mistake.

TIP 3. Make Certain SPSS is Accessing Necessary Files.

A common error a new user will encounter is that SPSS is not able to access the file(s) required. This means that you have an error on your FILE HANDLE or GET FILE command lines (SPSS^x) or you failed to properly identify a file or the path to it if using SPSS/PC+. In SPSS the computer will do an error search and identify all the problems it has with the instructions. Of course if the machine has not been able to find your system file, every variable you mention will produce an error since the machine has not found a file containing the named variables. So the first thing to do when you get an error at the beginning of a job is to check to see that the machine was able to access the necessary files for the task.

TIP 4. Fix First Errors First.

When correcting errors in a set of commands, begin with the first errors identified. Often when you fix an error at the beginning, you will eliminate at least some of the subsequent errors. For example, if you do a COMPUTE to create a new variable known as TOTALS, but on all your subsequent commands you refer to the variable as TOTAL, each time the machine encounters TOTAL it will give you an error. If you change the name of the variable on the COMPUTE statement to TOTAL and resubmit the job, all the subsequent references to TOTAL will be correct. Sometimes it is a good idea to resubmit a job after you have fixed the first few errors to see how many have been eliminated. Proceed then by again fixing the first errors that show up and then continue to resubmit the job until you get an error-free run.

TIP 5. Stuck? Re-enter the Command Line.

Sometimes you can stare at a error line and cannot see what is wrong with it. Perhaps you used an O rather than a 0, as in v1O when you meant v10. SPSS does not have a variable called v1O but it is hard to see the difference on some monitors. Do not waste a lot of time—just re-enter the command line.

TIP 6. Examine Results on Screen Before Sending to a Printer.

Sometimes you may inadvertently do something very silly and produce an enormous, meaningless, output file. Suppose, for example, that you are running CROSSTABS and you are examining the relationship between two variables with a control for occupational prestige of the respondent. In error you failed to use the recoded version of the occupational prestige variable and you therefore produced a monster output file because for each occupational code (there may be 70 or 80 distinct numbers) the computer generated a table showing the relationship between your main variables. If you look at the results on the screen before you print, you will avoid wasting computer paper on foolish output.

TIP 7. Double Check Variable List.

When the output reflects an inappropriate analysis, check the list of variables submitted. A common mistake is to RECODE a variable for use in an analysis but then use the original form of the variable rather than the recoded one when the variable is mentioned on the command line. This mistake will not generate an error or a warning but it will generate a lot of useless output.

TIP 8. Check for a Premature FINISH command.

If part of your job is run but is terminated before all the expected output is completed, check to make certain that you have not left a FINISH command in the middle of your job. Often when previously used .CON jobs are modified and resubmitted, we forget to take out the old FINISH command. SPSS will ignore any commands after the FINISH command.

H. SPSS MANUALS

There are many manuals currently available for SPSS[x] and SPSS/PC+. The major ones of particular relevance to this text are listed below. They are available in the United States from SPSS Inc., Publication Sales, 444 N. Michigan Ave., Chicago, Illinois 60611. In Canada the distributor of SPSS publications is Prentice Hall Canada Inc., 1870 Birchmount Road, Scarborough, Ontario, M1P 2J7. The following SPSS manuals may be useful to the student:

NORUSIS, MARIJA J. (1986). *The SPSS Guide to Data Analysis.*

NORUSIS, MARIJA J. AND SPSS INC (1992). *SPSS/PC+ Base System User's Guide, Version 5.0.*

NORUSIS, MARIJA J. AND SPSS INC (1992). *SPSS/PC+ Advanced Statistics, Version 5.0.*

NORUSIS, MARIJA J.AND SPSS INC (1992). *SPSS/PC+ Professional Statistics, Version 5.0.*

SPSS INC. (1988). *SPSS^x User's Guide*, Third Edition.

AREAS UNDER THE NORMAL CURVE

Fractional parts of the total area (10,000) under the normal curve, corresponding to distances between the mean and ordinates which are Z standard-deviation units from the mean.

Z	.00	.01	.02	.03	.04	.05	.06	.07	.08	.09
0.0	0000	0040	0080	0120	0159	0199	0239	0279	0319	0359
0.1	0398	0438	0478	0517	0557	0596	0636	0675	0714	0753
0.2	0793	0832	0871	0910	0948	0987	1026	1064	1103	1141
0.3	1179	1217	1255	1293	1331	1368	1406	1443	1480	1517
0.4	1554	1591	1628	1664	1700	1736	1772	1808	1844	1879
0.5	1915	1950	1985	2019	2054	2088	2123	2157	2190	2224
0.6	2257	2291	2324	2357	2389	2422	2454	2486	2518	2549
0.7	2580	2612	2642	2673	2704	2734	2764	2794	2823	2852
0.8	2881	2910	2939	2967	2995	3023	3051	3078	3106	3133
0.9	3159	3186	3212	3238	3264	3289	3315	3340	3365	3389
1.0	3413	3438	3461	3485	3508	3531	3554	3577	3599	3621
1.1	3643	3665	3686	3718	3729	3749	3770	3790	3810	3830
1.2	3849	3869	3888	3907	3925	3944	3962	3980	3997	4015
1.3	4032	4049	4066	4083	4099	4115	4131	4147	4162	4177
1.4	4192	4207	4222	4236	4251	4265	4279	4292	4306	4319
1.5	4332	4345	4357	4370	4382	4394	4406	4418	4430	4441
1.6	4452	4463	4474	4485	4495	4505	4515	4525	4535	4545
1.7	4554	4564	4573	4582	4591	4599	4608	4616	4625	4633
1.8	4641	4649	4656	4664	4671	4678	4686	4693	4699	4706
1.9	4713	4719	4726	4732	4738	4744	4750	4758	4762	4767
2.0	4773	4778	4783	4788	4793	4798	4803	4808	4812	4817
2.1	4821	4826	4830	4834	4838	4842	4846	4850	4854	4857
2.2	4861	4865	4868	4871	4875	4878	4881	4884	4887	4890
2.3	4893	4896	4898	4901	4904	4906	4909	4911	4913	4916
2.4	4918	4920	4922	4925	4927	4929	4931	4932	4934	4936

Z	.00	.01	.02	.03	.04	.05	.06	.07	.08	.09
2.5	4938	4940	4941	4943	4945	4946	4948	4949	4951	4952
2.6	4953	4955	4956	4957	4959	4960	4961	4962	4963	4964
2.7	4965	4966	4967	4968	4969	4970	4971	4972	4973	4974
2.8	4974	4975	4976	4977	4977	4978	4979	4980	4980	4981
2.9	4981	4982	4983	4984	4984	4984	4985	4985	4986	4986
3.0	4986.5	4987	4987	4988	4988	4988	4989	4989	4989	4990
3.1	4990.0	4991	4991	4991	4992	4992	4992	4992	4993	4993
3.2	4993.129									
3.3	4995.166									
3.4	4996.631									
3.5	4997.674									
3.6	4998.409									
3.7	4998.922									
3.8	4999.277									
3.9	4999.519									
4.0	4999.683									
4.5	4999.966									
5.0	4999.997133									

SOURCE: Harold O. Rugg: *Statistical Methods Applied to Education, pp. 889–90. Copyright © 1917, renewed 1945 by Houghton Mifflin Company, Boston, U.S.A. Used by permission.*

CHI-SQUARE VALUES

Probability

df	.30	.20	.10	.05	.02	.01	.001
1	1.074	1.642	2.706	3.841	5.412	6.635	10.827
2	2.408	3.219	4.605	5.991	7.824	9.210	13.815
3	3.665	4.642	6.251	7.815	9.837	11.341	16.268
4	4.878	5.989	7.779	9.488	11.668	13.277	18.465
5	6.064	7.289	9.236	11.070	13.388	15.086	20.517
6	7.231	8.558	10.645	12.592	15.033	16.812	22.457
7	8.383	9.803	12.017	14.067	16.622	18.475	24.322
8	9.524	11.030	13.362	15.507	18.168	20.090	26.125
9	10.656	12.242	14.684	16.919	19.679	21.666	27.877
10	11.781	13.442	15.987	18.307	21.161	23.209	29.588
11	12.899	14.631	17.275	19.675	22.618	24.725	31.264
12	14.011	15.812	18.549	21.026	24.054	26.217	32.909
13	15.119	16.985	19.812	22.362	25.472	27.688	34.528
14	16.222	18.151	21.064	23.685	26.873	29.141	36.123
15	17.322	19.311	22.307	24.996	28.259	30.578	37.697
16	18.418	20.465	23.542	26.296	29.633	32.000	39.252
17	19.511	21.615	24.769	27.587	30.995	33.409	40.790
18	20.601	22.760	25.989	28.869	32.346	34.805	42.312
19	21.689	23.900	27.204	30.144	33.687	36.191	43.820
20	22.775	25.038	28.412	31.410	35.020	37.566	45.315
21	23.858	26.171	29.615	32.671	36.343	38.932	46.797
22	24.939	27.301	30.813	33.924	37.659	40.289	48.268
23	26.018	28.429	32.007	35.172	38.968	41.638	49.728
24	27.096	29.553	33.196	36.415	40.270	42.980	51.179
25	28.172	30.675	34.382	37.652	41.566	44.314	52.620

Probability

df	.30	.20	.10	.05	.02	.01	.001
26	29.246	31.795	35.563	38.885	42.856	45.642	54.052
27	30.319	32.912	36.741	40.113	44.140	46.963	55.476
28	31.391	34.027	37.916	41.337	45.419	48.278	56.893
29	33.530	36.250	40.256	43.773	47.962	50.892	59.703
30	14.953	16.306	18.493	20.599	23.364	25.508	29.336

For large values of df, the expression $\sqrt{2x^2} - \sqrt{2df - 1}$ may be used as a normal deviate with unit variance, remembering that the probability for x^2 corresponds with that of a single tail of the normal curve. A slightly more complex transformation, which gives far better approximations for relatively small values of v, is

$$Z = \left[\sqrt[3]{x^2} - \sqrt[3]{v}\,(1 - 2/9v) \right] \sqrt[3]{v}\, \sqrt{2/9v}$$

(See A.C. Acock and G.R. Stavig: "Normal Deviate Approximations of x^2," *Perceptual and Motor Skills*, vol. 42, p. 220, 1976.)

SOURCE: Appendix C is taken from Table 10 of R.A. Fisher and F. Yates, *Statistical Tables for Biological, Agricultural and Medical Research*, (6th ed. 1974) published by Longman Group UK Ltd., London (previously published by Oliver and Boyd Ltd., Edinburgh) and by permission of the authors and publishers.

THE *T* DISTRIBUTION

Level of significance for one-tailed test

	.10	.05	.025	.01	.005	.0005

df

Level of significance for two-tailed test

	.20	.10	.05	.02	.01	.001
1	3.078	6.314	12.706	31.821	63.657	636.619
2	1.886	2.920	4.303	6.965	9.925	31.598
3	1.638	2.353	3.182	4.541	5.841	12.941
4	1.533	2.132	2.776	3.747	4.604	8.610
5	1.476	2.015	2.571	3.365	4.032	6.859
6	1.440	1.943	2.447	3.143	3.707	5.959
7	1.415	1.895	2.365	2.998	3.499	5.405
8	1.397	1.860	2.306	2.896	3.355	5.041
9	1.383	1.833	2.262	2.821	3.250	4.781
10	1.372	1.812	2.228	2.764	3.169	4.587
11	1.363	1.796	2.201	2.718	3.106	4.437
12	1.356	1.782	2.179	2.681	3.055	4.318
13	1.350	1.771	2.160	2.650	3.012	4.221
14	1.345	1.761	2.145	2.624	2.977	4.140
15	1.341	1.753	2.131	2.602	2.947	4.073
16	1.337	1.746	2.120	2.583	2.921	4.015
17	1.333	1.740	2.110	2.567	2.898	3.965
18	1.330	1.734	2.101	2.552	2.878	3.922
19	1.328	1.729	2.093	2.539	2.861	3.883
20	1.325	1.725	2.086	2.528	2.845	3.850

Level of significance for one-tailed test

	.10	.05	.025	.01	.005	.0005

df

Level of significance for two-tailed test

	.20	.10	.05	.02	.01	.001
21	1.323	1.721	2.080	2.518	2.831	3.819
22	1.321	1.717	2.074	2.508	2.819	3.792
23	1.319	1.714	2.069	2.500	2.807	3.767
24	1.318	1.711	2.064	2.492	2.797	3.745
25	1.316	1.708	2.060	2.485	2.787	3.725
26	1.315	1.706	2.056	2.479	2.779	3.707
27	1.314	1.703	2.052	2.473	2.771	3.690
28	1.313	1.701	2.048	2.467	2.763	3.674
29	1.311	1.699	2.045	2.462	2.756	3.659
30	1.310	1.697	2.042	2.457	2.750	3.646
40	1.303	1.684	2.021	2.423	2.704	3.551
60	1.296	1.671	2.000	2.390	2.660	3.460
120	1.289	1.658	1.980	2.358	2.617	3.373
∞	1.282	1.645	1.960	2.326	2.576	3.291

SOURCE: Appendix D is abridged from Table III of R.A. Fisher and F. Yates, *Statistical Tables for Biological, Agricultural and Medical Research* (1948 ed.), published by Oliver & Boyd, Ltd., Edinburgh and London, by permission of the authors and publishers.

THE *F* DISTRIBUTION

$p = .05$

$n_2 \backslash n_1$	1	2	3	4	5	6	8	12	24	∞
1	161.4	199.5	215.7	224.6	230.2	234.0	238.9	243.9	249.0	254.3
2	18.51	19.00	19.16	19.25	19.30	19.33	19.37	19.41	19.45	19.50
3	10.13	9.55	9.28	9.12	9.01	8.94	8.84	8.74	8.64	8.53
4	7.71	6.94	6.59	6.39	6.26	6.16	6.04	5.91	5.77	5.63
5	6.61	5.79	5.41	5.19	5.05	4.95	4.82	4.68	4.53	4.36
6	5.99	5.14	4.76	4.53	4.39	4.28	4.15	4.00	3.84	3.67
7	5.59	4.74	4.35	4.12	3.97	3.87	3.73	3.57	3.41	3.23
8	5.32	4.46	4.07	3.84	3.69	3.58	3.44	3.28	3.12	2.93
9	5.12	4.26	3.86	3.63	3.48	3.37	3.23	3.07	2.90	2.71
10	4.96	4.10	3.71	3.48	3.33	3.22	3.07	2.91	2.74	2.54
11	4.84	3.98	3.59	3.36	3.20	3.09	2.95	2.79	2.61	2.40
12	4.75	3.88	3.49	3.26	3.11	3.00	2.85	2.69	2.50	2.30
13	4.67	3.80	3.41	3.18	3.02	2.92	2.77	2.60	2.42	2.21
14	4.60	3.74	3.34	3.11	2.96	2.85	2.70	2.53	2.35	2.13
15	4.54	3.68	3.29	3.06	2.90	2.79	2.64	2.48	2.29	2.07
16	4.49	3.63	3.24	3.01	2.85	2.74	2.59	2.42	2.24	2.01
17	4.45	3.59	3.20	2.96	2.81	2.70	2.55	2.38	2.19	1.96
18	4.41	3.55	3.16	2.93	2.77	2.66	2.51	2.34	2.15	1.92
19	4.38	3.52	3.13	2.90	2.74	2.63	2.48	2.31	2.11	1.88
20	4.35	3.49	3.10	2.87	2.71	2.60	2.45	2.28	2.08	1.84
21	4.32	3.47	3.07	2.84	2.68	2.57	2.42	2.25	2.05	1.81
22	4.30	3.44	3.05	2.82	2.66	2.55	2.40	2.23	2.03	1.78
23	4.28	3.42	3.03	2.80	2.64	2.53	2.38	2.20	2.00	1.76
24	4.26	3.40	3.01	2.78	2.62	2.51	2.36	2.18	1.98	1.73
25	4.24	3.38	2.99	2.76	2.60	2.49	2.34	2.16	1.96	1.71

$p = .05$

$n_2 \backslash n_1$	1	2	3	4	5	6	8	12	24	∞
26	4.22	3.37	2.98	2.74	2.59	2.47	2.32	2.15	1.95	1.69
27	4.21	3.35	2.96	2.73	2.57	2.46	2.30	2.13	1.93	1.67
28	4.20	3.34	2.95	2.71	2.56	2.44	2.29	2.12	1.91	1.65
29	4.18	3.33	2.93	2.70	2.54	2.43	2.28	2.10	1.90	1.64
30	4.17	3.32	2.92	2.69	2.53	2.42	2.27	2.09	1.89	1.62
40	4.08	3.23	2.84	2.61	2.45	2.34	2.18	2.00	1.79	1.51
60	4.00	3.15	2.76	2.52	2.37	2.25	2.10	1.92	1.70	1.39
120	3.92	3.07	2.68	2.45	2.29	2.17	2.02	1.83	1.61	1.25
∞	3.84	2.99	2.60	2.37	2.21	2.09	1.94	1.75	1.52	1.00

Values of n_1 and n_2 represent the degrees of freedom associated with the larger and smaller estimates of variance respectively.

SOURCE: Appendix E is taken from Table V of R.A. Fisher and F. Yates, *Statistical Tables for Biological, Agricultural and Medical Research* (6th ed. 1974), published by Longman Group UK Ltd., London (previously published by Oliver and Boyd Ltd., Edinburgh) and by permission of the authors and publishers.

Appendix E continued

$p = .01$

$n_2 \backslash n_1$	1	2	3	4	5	6	8	12	24	∞
1	4052	4999	5403	5625	5764	5859	5981	6106	6234	6366
2	98.49	99.01	99.17	99.25	99.30	99.33	99.36	99.42	99.46	99.50
3	34.12	30.81	29.46	28.71	28.24	27.91	27.49	27.05	26.60	26.12
4	21.20	18.00	16.69	15.98	15.52	15.21	14.80	14.37	13.93	13.46
5	16.26	13.27	12.06	11.39	10.97	10.67	10.27	9.89	9.47	9.02
6	13.74	10.92	9.78	9.15	8.75	8.47	8.10	7.72	7.31	6.88
7	12.25	9.55	8.45	7.85	7.46	7.19	6.84	6.47	6.07	5.65
8	11.26	8.65	7.59	7.01	6.63	6.37	6.03	5.67	5.28	4.86
9	10.56	8.02	6.99	6.42	6.06	5.80	5.47	5.11	4.73	4.31
10	10.04	7.56	6.55	5.99	5.64	5.39	5.06	4.71	4.33	3.91
11	9.65	7.20	6.22	5.67	5.32	5.07	4.74	4.40	4.02	3.60
12	9.33	6.93	5.95	5.41	5.06	4.82	4.50	4.16	3.78	3.36
13	9.07	6.70	5.74	5.20	4.86	4.62	4.30	3.96	3.59	3.16
14	8.86	6.51	5.56	5.03	4.69	4.46	4.14	3.80	3.43	3.00
15	8.68	6.36	5.42	4.89	4.56	4.32	4.00	3.67	3.29	2.87

p = .01

n_2\\n_1	1	2	3	4	5	6	8	12	24	∝
16	8.53	6.23	5.29	4.77	4.44	4.20	3.89	3.55	3.18	2.75
17	8.40	6.11	5.18	4.67	4.34	4.10	3.79	3.45	3.08	2.65
18	8.28	6.01	5.09	4.58	4.25	4.01	3.71	3.37	3.00	2.57
19	8.18	5.93	5.01	4.50	4.17	3.94	3.63	3.30	2.92	2.49
20	8.10	5.85	4.94	4.43	4.10	3.87	3.56	3.23	2.86	2.42
21	8.02	5.78	4.87	4.37	4.04	3.81	3.51	3.17	2.80	2.36
22	7.94	5.72	4.82	4.31	3.99	3.76	3.45	3.12	2.75	2.31
23	7.88	5.66	4.76	4.26	3.94	3.71	3.41	3.07	2.70	2.26
24	7.82	5.61	4.72	4.22	3.90	3.67	3.36	3.03	2.66	2.21
25	7.77	5.57	4.68	4.18	3.86	3.63	3.32	2.99	2.62	2.17
26	7.72	5.53	4.64	4.14	3.82	3.59	3.29	2.96	2.58	2.13
27	7.68	5.49	4.60	4.11	3.78	3.56	3.26	2.93	2.55	2.10
28	7.64	5.45	4.57	4.07	3.75	3.53	3.23	2.90	2.52	2.06
29	7.60	5.42	4.54	4.04	3.73	3.50	3.20	2.87	2.49	2.03
30	7.56	5.39	4.51	4.02	3.70	3.47	3.17	2.84	2.47	2.01
40	7.31	5.18	4.31	3.83	3.51	3.29	2.99	2.66	2.29	1.80
60	7.08	4.98	4.13	3.65	3.34	3.12	2.82	2.50	2.12	1.60
120	6.85	4.79	3.95	3.48	3.17	2.96	2.66	2.34	1.95	1.38
∝	6.64	4.60	3.78	3.32	3.02	2.80	2.51	2.18	1.79	1.00

Values of n_1 and n_2 represent the degrees of freedom associated with the larger and smaller estimates of variance respectively.

Appendix E continued

p = .001

n_2\\n_1	1	2	3	4	5	6	8	12	24	00
1	405284	500000	540379	562500	576405	585937	598144	610667	623497	636619
2	998.5	999.0	999.2	999.2	999.3	999.3	999.4	999.4	999.5	999.5
3	167.5	148.5	141.1	137.1	134.6	132.8	130.6	128.3	125.9	123.5
4	74.14	61.25	56.18	53.44	51.71	50.53	49.00	47.41	45.77	44.05
5	47.04	36.61	33.20	31.09	29.75	28.84	27.64	26.42	25.14	23.78

p = .001

n_2＼n_1	1	2	3	4	5	6	8	12	24	00
6	35.51	27.00	23.70	21.90	20.81	20.03	19.03	17.99	16.89	15.75
7	29.22	21.69	18.77	17.19	16.21	15.52	14.63	13.71	12.73	11.69
8	25.42	18.49	15.83	14.39	13.49	12.86	12.04	11.19	10.30	9.34
9	22.86	16.39	13.90	12.56	11.71	11.13	10.37	9.57	8.72	7.81
10	21.04	14.91	12.55	11.28	10.48	9.92	9.20	8.45	7.64	6.76
11	19.69	13.81	11.56	10.35	9.58	9.05	8.35	7.63	6.85	6.00
12	18.64	12.97	10.80	9.63	8.89	8.38	7.71	7.00	6.25	5.42
13	17.81	12.31	10.21	9.07	8.35	7.86	7.21	6.52	5.78	4.97
14	17.14	11.78	9.73	8.62	7.92	7.43	6.80	6.13	5.41	4.60
15	16.59	11.34	9.34	8.25	7.57	7.09	6.47	5.81	5.10	4.31
16	16.12	10.97	9.00	7.94	7.27	6.81	6.19	5.55	4.85	4.06
17	15.72	10.66	8.73	7.68	7.02	6.56	5.96	5.32	4.63	3.85
18	15.38	10.39	8.49	7.46	6.81	6.35	5.76	5.13	4.45	3.67
19	15.08	10.16	8.28	7.26	6.61	6.18	5.59	4.97	4.29	3.52
20	14.82	9.95	8.10	7.10	6.46	6.02	5.44	4.82	4.15	3.38
21	14.59	9.77	7.94	6.95	6.32	5.88	5.31	4.70	4.03	3.26
22	14.38	9.61	7.80	6.81	6.19	5.76	5.19	4.58	3.92	3.15
23	14.19	9.47	7.67	6.69	6.08	5.65	5.09	4.48	3.82	3.05
24	14.03	9.34	7.55	6.59	5.98	5.55	4.99	4.39	3.74	2.97
25	13.88	9.22	7.45	6.49	5.88	5.46	4.91	4.31	3.66	2.89
26	13.74	9.12	7.36	6.41	5.80	5.38	4.83	4.24	3.59	2.82
27	13.61	9.02	7.27	6.33	5.73	5.31	4.76	4.17	3.52	2.75
28	13.50	8.93	7.19	6.25	5.66	5.24	4.69	4.11	3.46	2.70
29	13.39	8.85	7.12	6.19	5.59	5.18	4.64	4.05	3.41	2.64
30	13.29	8.77	7.05	6.12	5.53	5.12	4.58	4.00	3.36	2.59
40	12.61	8.25	6.60	5.70	5.13	4.73	4.21	3.64	3.01	2.23
60	11.97	7.76	6.17	5.31	4.76	4.37	3.87	3.31	2.69	1.90
120	11.38	7.31	5.79	4.95	4.42	4.04	3.55	3.02	2.40	1.56
∝	10.83	6.91	5.42	4.62	4.10	3.74	3.27	2.74	2.13	1.00

Values of n_1 and n_2 represent the degrees of freedom associated with the larger and smaller estimates of variance respectively.

TABLE OF RANDOM NUMBERS

10	09	73	25	33	76	52	01	35	86	34	67	35	48	76
37	54	20	48	05	64	89	47	42	96	24	80	52	40	37
08	42	26	89	53	19	64	50	93	03	23	20	90	25	60
99	01	90	25	29	09	37	67	07	15	38	31	13	11	65
12	80	79	99	70	80	15	73	61	47	64	03	23	66	53
66	06	57	47	17	34	07	27	68	50	36	69	73	61	70
31	06	01	08	05	45	57	18	24	06	35	30	34	26	14
85	26	97	76	02	02	05	16	56	92	68	66	57	48	18
63	57	33	21	35	05	32	54	70	48	90	55	35	75	48
73	79	64	57	53	03	52	96	47	78	35	80	83	42	82
98	52	01	77	67	14	90	56	86	07	22	10	94	05	58
11	80	50	54	31	39	80	82	77	32	50	72	56	82	48
83	45	29	96	34	06	28	89	80	83	13	74	67	00	78
88	68	54	02	00	86	50	75	84	01	36	76	66	79	51
99	59	46	73	48	87	51	76	49	69	91	82	60	89	28
65	48	11	76	74	17	46	85	09	50	58	04	77	69	74
80	12	43	56	35	17	72	70	80	15	45	31	82	23	74
74	35	09	98	17	77	40	27	72	14	43	23	60	02	10
69	91	62	68	03	66	25	22	91	48	36	93	68	72	03
09	89	32	05	05	14	22	56	85	14	46	42	75	67	88
91	49	91	45	23	68	47	92	76	86	46	16	28	35	54
80	33	69	45	98	26	94	03	68	58	70	29	73	41	35
44	10	48	19	49	85	15	74	79	54	32	97	92	65	75
12	55	07	37	42	11	10	00	20	40	12	86	07	46	97
63	60	64	93	29	16	50	53	44	84	40	21	95	25	63

61	19	69	04	46	26	45	74	77	74	51	92	43	37	29
15	47	44	52	66	95	27	07	99	53	59	36	78	38	48
94	55	72	85	73	67	89	75	43	87	54	62	24	44	31
42	48	11	62	13	97	34	40	87	21	16	86	84	87	67
23	52	37	83	17	73	20	88	98	37	68	93	59	14	16
04	49	35	24	94	75	24	63	38	24	45	86	25	10	25
00	54	99	76	54	64	05	18	81	59	96	11	96	38	96
35	96	31	53	07	26	89	80	93	54	33	35	13	54	62
59	80	80	83	91	45	42	72	68	42	83	60	94	97	00
46	05	88	52	36	01	39	09	22	86	77	28	14	40	77
32	17	90	05	97	87	37	92	52	41	05	56	70	70	07
69	23	46	14	06	20	11	74	52	04	15	95	66	00	00
19	56	54	14	30	01	75	87	53	79	40	41	92	15	85
45	15	51	49	38	19	47	60	72	46	43	66	79	45	43
94	86	43	19	94	36	16	81	08	51	34	88	88	15	53
98	08	62	48	26	45	24	02	84	04	44	99	90	88	96
33	18	51	62	32	41	94	15	09	49	89	43	54	85	81
80	95	10	04	06	96	38	27	07	74	20	15	12	33	87
79	75	24	91	40	71	96	12	82	96	69	86	10	25	91
18	63	33	25	37	98	14	50	65	71	31	01	02	46	74
74	02	94	39	02	77	55	73	22	70	97	79	01	71	19
54	17	84	56	11	80	99	33	71	43	05	33	51	29	69
11	66	44	98	83	52	07	98	48	27	59	38	17	15	39
48	32	47	79	28	31	24	96	47	10	02	29	53	68	70
69	07	49	41	38	87	63	79	19	76	35	58	40	44	01
09	18	82	00	97	32	82	53	95	27	04	22	08	63	04
90	04	58	54	97	51	98	15	06	54	94	93	88	19	97
73	18	95	02	07	47	67	72	52	69	62	29	06	44	64
75	76	87	64	90	20	97	18	17	49	90	42	91	22	72
54	01	64	40	56	66	28	13	10	03	00	68	22	73	98
08	35	86	99	10	78	54	24	27	85	13	66	15	88	73
28	30	60	32	64	81	33	31	05	91	40	51	00	78	93
53	84	08	62	33	81	59	41	36	28	51	21	59	02	90
91	75	75	37	41	61	61	36	22	69	50	26	39	02	12
89	41	59	26	94	00	39	75	83	91	12	60	71	76	46

77	51	30	38	20	86	83	42	99	01	68	41	48	27	74
19	50	23	71	74	69	97	92	02	88	55	21	02	97	73
21	81	85	93	13	93	27	88	17	57	05	68	67	31	56
51	47	46	64	99	68	10	72	36	21	94	04	99	13	45
99	55	96	83	31	62	53	52	41	70	69	77	71	28	30
33	71	34	80	07	93	58	47	28	69	51	92	66	47	21
85	27	48	68	93	11	30	32	92	70	28	83	43	41	37
84	13	38	96	40	44	03	55	21	66	73	85	27	00	91
56	73	21	62	34	17	39	59	61	31	10	12	39	16	22
65	13	85	68	06	87	64	88	52	61	34	31	36	58	61
38	00	10	21	76	81	71	91	17	11	71	60	29	29	37
37	40	29	63	97	01	30	47	75	86	56	27	11	00	86
97	12	54	03	48	87	08	33	14	17	21	81	53	92	50
21	82	64	11	34	47	14	33	40	72	64	63	88	59	02
73	13	54	27	42	95	71	90	90	35	85	79	47	42	96
07	63	87	79	29	03	06	11	80	72	96	20	74	41	56
60	52	88	34	41	07	95	41	98	14	59	17	52	06	95
83	59	63	56	55	06	95	89	29	83	05	12	80	97	19
10	85	06	27	46	99	59	91	05	07	13	49	90	63	19
39	82	09	89	52	43	62	26	31	47	64	42	18	08	14
59	58	00	64	78	75	56	97	88	00	88	83	55	44	86
38	50	80	73	41	23	79	34	87	63	90	82	29	70	22
30	69	27	06	68	94	68	81	61	27	56	19	68	00	91
65	44	39	56	59	18	28	82	74	37	49	63	22	40	41
27	26	75	02	64	13	19	27	22	94	07	47	74	46	06
91	30	70	69	91	19	07	22	42	10	36	69	95	37	28
68	43	49	46	88	84	47	31	36	22	62	12	69	84	08
48	90	81	58	77	54	74	52	45	91	35	70	00	47	54
06	91	34	51	97	42	67	27	86	01	11	88	30	95	28
10	45	51	60	19	14	21	03	37	12	91	34	23	78	21
12	88	39	73	43	65	02	76	11	84	04	28	50	13	92
21	77	83	09	76	38	80	73	69	61	31	64	94	20	96
19	52	35	95	15	65	12	25	96	59	86	28	36	82	58
67	24	55	26	70	35	58	31	65	63	79	24	68	66	86
60	58	44	73	77	07	50	03	79	92	45	13	42	65	29

53	85	34	13	77	36	06	69	48	50	58	83	87	38	59
24	63	73	87	36	74	38	48	93	42	52	62	30	79	92
83	08	01	24	51	38	99	22	28	15	07	75	95	17	77
16	44	42	43	34	36	15	19	90	73	27	49	37	09	39
60	79	01	81	57	57	17	86	57	62	11	16	17	85	76
03	99	11	04	61	93	71	61	68	94	66	08	32	46	53
38	55	59	55	54	32	88	65	97	80	08	35	56	08	60
17	54	67	37	04	92	05	24	62	15	55	12	12	92	81
32	64	35	28	61	95	81	90	68	31	00	91	19	89	36
69	57	26	87	77	39	51	03	59	05	14	06	04	06	19
24	12	26	65	91	27	69	90	64	94	14	84	54	66	72
61	19	63	02	31	92	96	26	17	73	41	83	95	53	82
30	53	22	17	04	10	27	41	22	02	39	68	52	33	09
03	78	89	75	99	75	86	72	07	17	74	41	65	31	66
48	22	86	33	79	85	78	34	76	19	53	15	26	74	33
60	36	59	46	53	35	07	53	39	49	42	61	42	92	97
83	79	94	24	02	56	62	33	44	42	34	99	44	13	74
32	96	00	74	05	36	40	98	32	32	99	38	54	16	00
19	32	25	38	45	57	62	05	26	06	66	49	76	86	46
11	22	09	47	47	07	39	93	74	08	48	50	92	39	29
31	75	15	72	60	68	98	00	53	39	15	47	04	83	55
88	49	29	93	82	14	45	40	45	04	20	09	49	89	77
30	93	44	77	44	07	48	18	38	28	73	78	80	65	33
22	88	84	88	93	27	49	99	87	48	60	53	04	51	28
78	21	21	69	93	35	90	29	13	86	44	37	21	54	86
41	84	98	45	47	46	85	05	23	26	34	67	75	83	00
46	35	23	30	49	69	24	89	34	60	45	30	50	75	21
11	08	79	62	94	14	01	33	17	92	59	74	76	72	77
52	70	10	83	37	56	30	38	73	15	16	52	06	96	76
57	27	53	68	98	81	30	44	85	85	68	65	22	73	76
20	85	77	31	56	70	28	42	43	26	79	37	59	52	20
15	63	38	49	24	90	41	59	36	14	33	52	12	66	65
92	69	44	82	97	39	90	40	21	15	59	58	94	90	67
77	61	31	90	19	88	15	20	00	80	20	55	49	14	09
38	68	83	24	86	45	13	46	35	45	59	40	47	20	59

25	16	30	18	89	70	01	41	50	21	41	29	06	73	12
65	25	10	76	29	37	23	93	32	95	05	87	00	11	19
36	81	54	36	25	18	63	73	75	09	82	44	49	90	05
64	39	71	16	92	05	32	78	21	62	20	24	78	17	59
04	51	52	56	24	95	09	66	79	46	48	46	08	55	58
83	76	16	08	73	43	25	38	41	45	60	83	32	59	83
14	38	70	63	45	80	85	40	92	79	43	52	90	63	18
51	32	19	22	46	80	08	87	70	74	88	72	25	67	36
72	47	20	00	08	80	89	01	80	02	94	81	33	19	00
05	46	65	53	06	93	12	81	84	64	74	45	79	05	61
39	52	87	24	84	82	47	42	55	93	48	54	53	52	47
81	61	61	87	11	53	34	24	42	76	75	12	21	17	24
07	58	61	61	20	82	64	12	28	20	92	90	41	31	41
90	76	70	42	35	13	57	41	72	00	69	90	26	37	42
40	18	82	81	93	29	59	38	86	27	94	97	21	15	98
34	41	48	21	57	86	88	75	50	87	19	15	20	00	23
63	43	97	53	63	44	98	91	68	22	36	02	40	09	67
67	04	90	90	70	93	39	94	55	47	94	45	87	42	84
79	49	50	41	46	52	16	29	02	86	54	15	83	42	43
91	70	43	05	52	04	73	72	10	31	75	05	19	30	29

SOURCE: Reprinted from pages 1–3 of *A Million Random Digits with 100,000 Normal Deviates* by RAND Corporation (New York: The Free Press, 1955). Copyright 1955 and 1983 by the RAND Corporation. Used by permission.

CRONBACH'S STANDARDIZED ALPHAS FOR VARIOUS INTER-ITEM CORRELATIONS

# Items	.10	.20	.30	.40	.50	.60	.70	.80	.90
				Mean Inter-Item Correlation					
2	.182	.333	.462	.571	.667	.750	.824	.889	.947
3	.250	.429	.562	.667	.750	.818	.875	.923	.964
4	.308	.500	.632	.727	.800	.857	.903	.941	.973
5	.357	.556	.682	.769	.833	.882	.921	.952	.978
6	.400	.600	.720	.800	.857	.900	.933	.960	.982
7	.438	.636	.750	.824	.875	.913	.942	.966	.984
8	.471	.667	.774	.842	.889	.923	.949	.970	.986
9	.500	.692	.794	.857	.900	.931	.955	.973	.988
10	.526	.714	.811	.870	.909	.937	.959	.976	.989
11	.550	.733	.825	.880	.917	.943	.962	.978	.990
12	.571	.750	.837	.889	.923	.947	.966	.980	.991
13	.591	.765	.848	.897	.929	.951	.968	.981	.992
14	.609	.778	.857	.903	.933	.955	.970	.982	.992
15	.625	.789	.865	.909	.938	.957	.972	.984	.993
16	.640	.800	.873	.914	.941	.960	.974	.985	.993

PINEO AND PORTER'S CANADIAN OCCUPATIONAL PRESTIGE INDEX

National N=793

OCCUPATION	SCORE
Professional	
Accountant	63.4
Architect	78.1
Biologist	72.6
Catholic Priest	72.8
Chemist	73.5
Civil Engineer	73.1
County Court Judge	82.5
Druggist	69.3
Economist	62.2
High School Teacher	66.1
Lawyer	82.3
Mathematician	72.7
Mine Safety Analyst	57.1
Mining Engineer	68.8
Physician	87.2
Physicist	77.6
Protestant Minister	67.8
Psychologist	74.9
Public Grade School Teacher	59.6
University Professor	84.6
Veterinarian	66.7
Semi-Professional	
Airline Pilot	66.1
Author	64.8
Ballet Dancer	49.1

OCCUPATION	SCORE
Chiropractor	68.4
Commercial Artist	57.2
Computer Programmer	53.8
Disc Jockey	38.0
Draughtsman	60.0
Funeral Director	54.9
Journalist	60.9
Medical or Dental Technician	67.5
Musician	52.1
Musician in a Symphony Orchestra	56.0
Physiotherapist	72.1
Playground Director	42.8
Professional Athlete	54.1
Professionally Trained Forester	60.1
Professionally Trained Librarian	58.1
Registered Nurse	64.7
Research Technician	66.9
Sculptor	56.9
Social Worker	55.1
Surveyor	62.0
T.V. Announcer	57.6
T.V. Cameraman	48.3
T.V. Director	62.1
T.V. Star	65.6
YMCA Director	58.2

Proprietors, Managers and Officials, Large

Administrative Officer in Federal Civil Service	68.8
Advertising Executive	56.5
Bank Manager	70.9
Building Contractor	56.5
Colonel in the Army	70.8
Department Head in City Government	71.3
General Manager of a Manufacturing Plant	69.1
Mayor of a Large City	79.9
Member of Canadian Cabinet	83.3
Member of Canadian House of Commons	84.8
Member of Canadian Senate	86.1
Merchandise Buyer for a Department Store	51.1
Owner of a Manufacturing Plant	69.4
Provincial Premier	89.9
Wholesale Distributor	47.9

Proprietors, Managers and Officials, Small

Advertising Copy Writer	48.9
Beauty Operator	35.2
Construction Foreman	51.1
Driving Instructor	41.6
Foreman in a Factory	50.9
Government Purchasing Agent	56.8
Insurance Claims Investigator	51.1
Job Counsellor	58.3
Livestock Buyer	39.6
Lunchroom Operator	31.6
Manager of a Real Estate Office	58.3
Manager of a Supermarket	52.5

Member of a City Council	62.9
Motel Owner	51.6
Owner of a Food Store	47.8
Public Relations Man	60.5
Railroad Ticket Agent	35.7
Sawmill Operator	37.0
Service Station Manager	41.5
Ship's Pilot	59.6
Superintendent of a Construction Job	53.9
Trade Union Business Agent	49.2
Travel Agent	46.6

Clerical and Sales

Air Hostess	57.0
Bank Teller	42.3
Bill Collector	29.4
Bookkeeper	49.4
Cashier in a Supermarket	31.1
Clerk in an Office	35.6
File Clerk	32.7
IBM Keypunch Operator	47.7
Insurance Agent	47.3
Manufacturer's Representative	52.1
Post Office Clerk	37.2
Real Estate Agent	47.1
Receptionist	38.7
Sales Clerk in a Store	26.5
Shipping Clerk	30.9
Stenographer	46.0
Stockroom Attendant	25.8
Telephone Operator	38.1
Telephone Solicitor	26.7
Travelling Salesman	40.2
Truck Dispatcher	32.2
Typist	41.9
Used Car Salesman	31.2

Skilled

Airplane Mechanic	50.3
Baker	38.9
Bricklayer	36.2
Butcher in a Store	34.8
Coal Miner	27.6
Cook in a Restaurant	29.7
Custom Seamstress	33.4
Diamond Driller	44.5
Electrician	50.2
House Carpenter	38.9
House Painter	29.9
Locomotive Engineer	48.9
Machine Set-up Man in a Factory	42.1
Mucking Machine Operator	31.5
Plumber	42.6
Power Crane Operator	40.2
Power Lineman	40.9
Pumphouse Engineer	38.9
Railroad Brakeman	37.1
Railroad Conductor	45.3
Saw Sharpener	20.7
Sheet Metal Worker	35.9
T.V. Repairman	37.2
Tool and Die Maker	42.5
Typesetter	42.2
Welder	41.8

Semi-Skilled

Aircraft Worker	43.7
Apprentice to a Master Craftsman	33.9
Assembly Line Worker	28.2
Automobile Repairman	38.1
Automobile Worker	35.9
Barber	39.3
Book Binder	35.2
Bus Driver	35.9

Cod Fisherman	23.4
Firefighter	43.5
Fruit Packer in a Cannery	23.2
Logger	24.9
Longshoreman	26.1
Loom Operator	33.3
Machine Operator in a Factory	34.9
Newspaper Pressman	43.0
Oil Field Worker	35.3
Oiler in a Ship	27.6
Paper Making Machine Tender	31.6
Policeman	51.6
Private in the Army	28.4
Production Worker in the Electronics Industry	50.8
Professional Babysitter	25.9
Quarry Worker	26.7
Sewing Machine Operator	28.2
Steam Boiler Fireman	32.8
Steam Roller Operator	32.2
Steel Mill Worker	34.3
Textile Mill Worker	28.8
Timber Cruiser	40.3
Trailer Truck Driver	32.8
Troller	23.6
Worker in a Meat Packing Plant	25.2

Unskilled

Carpenter's Helper	23.1
Construction Labourer	26.5
Elevator Operator in a Building	20.1
Filling Station Attendant	23.3
Garbage Collector	14.8
Hospital Attendant	34.9
Housekeeper in a Private Home	28.8
Janitor	17.3
Laundress	19.3

Mailman	36.1
Museum Attendant	30.4
Newspaper Peddler	14.8
Railroad Sectionhand	27.3
Taxicab Driver	25.1
Waitress in a Restaurant	19.9
Warehouse Hand	21.3
Whistle Punk	18.4
Worker in a Dry Cleaning or Laundry Plant	20.8

Farmer

Commercial Farmer	42.0
Dairy Farmer	44.2
Farm Labourer	21.5
Farm Owner and Operator	44.1
Hog Farmer	33.0
Part Time Farmer	25.1

Not in Labour Force

Archaeopotrist	63.7
Biologer	64.2
Occupation of my family's main wage earner	50.9
Occupation of my father when I was 16	42.5
Someone who lives off inherited wealth	45.8
Someone who lives off property holdings	48.7
Someone who lives off stocks and bonds	56.9
Someone who lives on relief	7.3

SOURCE: This table represents a portion (national scores only) of Peter C. Pineo and John Porter (1967), "Occupational Prestige in Canada," *The Canadian Review of Sociology and Anthropology*, 4(1), pp. 36–40.

SSHRC: ETHICAL GUIDELINES— RESEARCH WITH HUMAN SUBJECTS

While recognizing the vital importance of research to human progress, the Council affirms that the welfare and integrity of the individual or particular collective must prevail over the advancement of knowledge and the researcher's use of human subjects for that purpose. The Council is not itself vested with any authority to decide when an individual's rights may be superseded by the need for research but, as a trustee of public funds, the Council has a responsibility to ensure that the activities it supports respect the rights of the public it serves.

The guidelines are offered to assist the researcher and the institutional ethics review committee in avoiding any adverse effects of research involving human subjects.

INSTITUTIONAL ETHICS REVIEW COMMITTEES

1. Research projects involving human subjects must be approved by the ethics review committee of the institution employing the principal investigator before being submitted to Council, or shortly thereafter.

2. The review committee should include representatives from inside and outside the department and discipline in ques-

tion, and the institution should keep the Council informed of disciplinary affiliation of the members. The Council may sometimes require names.

3. If the review committee makes an exception to these guidelines, an explanation must be provided.

4. Any dissent within a review committee must be made known to the Council.

5. The Council is concerned that monitoring procedures be established by review committees; it leaves them to propose their own approaches and to inform the Council. But special attention must be paid to research on children or captive and dependent populations, and to projects involving deception or an element of risk. With regard to children, review committees should seek expert advice, whenever necessary, on potential short- and long-term risks. Unforeseen damage must be remedied without delay or the research terminated.

6. Institutional review committee approval should not be advertised as an inducement to potential subjects; however, the researcher has the right to inform them of such approval.

DEFINITION OF "HUMAN SUBJECT"

7. The term "subject" signifies any person who is a source of raw or unformulated data and who is not acting as, or assisting, the principal investigator.

RIGHTS OF THE INDIVIDUAL

8. Certain individual or collective "rights" must be maintained. These include the right to know the precise nature and purpose of the research, so that consent may be given or withheld advisedly; the right to know of the risks and benefits; the right to assurance that privacy will not be invaded and that information disclosed will remain confidential; the right of cultural groups to accurate and respectful description of their heritage and customs and to the discreet use of information on their lives and aspirations.

INFORMED CONSENT

9. Information given to subjects should respect their levels of comprehension. A description should be provided of the purpose, usefulness, expected benefits, methods, effects, risks (including risks to physical and psychological well-being and jeopardy to social position), and possible alternative procedures. Subjects should always be told of factors which might lead them to refuse to participate. In exceptional circumstances, the guidelines on deception should be applied.

10. Participants should be apprised of their rights to inquire about the research and have recourse to a resource person outside the research group.

11. There should be no coercion, constraint or undue inducement (see special guidelines for captive and dependent populations).

12. Participants should understand that they may withdraw at any time, just as investigators may terminate their research in the interest of the subjects, the project or themselves.

13. Informed consent of parents or guardian and, where practical, of children should be obtained in research involving children (see special guidelines concerning research on children).

14. Participants should be informed of the degree of confidentiality that will be maintained in the study.

15. Informed consent should be obtained in writing. Where this is not practical, the procedures used in obtaining consent should be on record.

16. Written consent should set out:
    a) purpose of the research;
    b) benefits envisaged;
    c) any inconveniences;
    d) tasks to be performed;
    e) rights of the subject, e.g. the right to withdraw at any time without penalty, the right to confidentiality of personal information;
    f) risks involved;
    g) the name(s) of the person(s), group(s) or institution(s) eliciting or receiving the consent.

17. The wording of the consent form should be as similar as possible to the oral description given to the subject. The form should provide for hearing any subsequent complaint.

DECEPTION

18. Deception is a situation in which subjects have essential information withheld and/or are intentionally misled about procedures and purposes.

19. Deception should never be permitted when there is risk of harm to the subject or when it is not possible to advise subjects subsequently as to the reasons why the deception was necessary.

20. The researcher must satisfy the review committee that:
    a) significant scientific advance could result; and that
    b) no other methodology would suffice.

21. Nothing must be withheld which might have caused subjects to refuse to participate.

RISK AND BENEFIT

22. Greater consideration must be given to the risks to physical, psychological, humane, proprietary and cultural values than to the potential contribution of the research to knowledge. The more incalculable the risk, the more cautious should be the researcher and the review committee in proceeding.

23. Where procedures involve risk, the researcher should have previously carried them out successfully, at least under supervision, without detriment to the subjects. For a new procedure, the investigator must convince the review committee that adequate precautions will be taken, and monitor preliminary work to ensure appropriateness. The results should be available to the committee.

24. Except where there is clear foreseeable benefit to the participant, such as in therapeutic research, the researcher has no right to attempt to make long-term changes in a person's behaviour or attitudes. Where the researcher plans to induce short-term behavioural changes, permission to proceed should depend upon reversibility.

25. The researchers must guard against risks to non-participants (third-party risks).

26. The onus is on the researcher to avoid or minimize risks to subjects, both in carrying out the research and in publication of results.

PRIVACY

27. The right to privacy extends to all information on a person's physical and mental condition, personal circumstances and social relationships, which is not in the public domain. It gives to the individual or collective the freedom to decide when, where, in what circumstances and to what extent their personal attitudes, opinions, habits, eccentricities, doubts and fears are to be published.

28. If there is to be a probing of private personality or private affairs the intention should be explicit. Where there is an implication of protection of privacy, the protection should be more generous than the promise.

29. Informed consent should be obtained from those to be observed or studied in private settings.

30. Since concepts of privacy vary from culture to culture, the question of invasion of privacy should be looked at from the point of view of those being studied.

31. If confidentiality or anonymity cannot be guaranteed, participants should be made aware of possible consequences.

32. There should be a clear understanding between investigator and subjects as to what extent information they divulge will be kept confidential in the original use of data and their deposit for future use.

33. Unless there is an explicit statement by the researcher to the contrary, to which the subject agrees, personal information given by the subject will be confidential and the researcher will explain steps to be taken to ensure confidentiality and anonymity.

34. Steps should be taken to guard against indirect or unwitting disclosure of identity of subjects by association or by combination of information.

35. The researcher has an obligation to third parties.

36. Obtaining access to institutional records should respect the individual's rights to confidentiality and anonymity.

RESEARCH ON CAPTIVE AND DEPENDENT POPULATIONS

37. "Captive and dependent populations" are individuals or groups in a relationship where a power differential could operate to their disadvantage as subjects: for example, students, minors, prisoners, employees, military personnel, minority groups, incapacitated people and the socially-deprived. Review committees should be especially alert to ensure that consent obtained is not obtained by subtle pressures on the captive subject. Such pressures may invalidate the consent.

38. In addition to consent of the subjects themselves, informed consent of the authorities should be obtained.

39. Where consent of the subjects themselves cannot be obtained, it must be sought from someone in authority, together with written consent from a person who may act as an independent advocate.

40. Captive subjects should always have the right and power to veto others' consent.

RESEARCH ON CHILDREN

41. Informed consent of parents or guardians should be obtained before using minors. In school, camp, or other group settings, consent of the principal, director or other appropriate authority must also be obtained. Where a child is a ward of the state or of an agency, such as the Children's Aid Society, informed consent of the agency director, as well as of the person having custody, must be obtained.

42. Children should be given individually the opportunity to refuse to participate or to withdraw.

RESEARCH IN THE HUMANITIES

43. Research ethics are involved wherever an investigator intervenes in the lives of others. Historical and/or biographical investigation may pose problems of confidentiality or invasion of privacy if living persons are likely to be affected by the publication of private materials.

44. Researchers should be careful, in purchasing and taking out of the country original manuscripts, that they are not depriving another country of what may be a national treasure.

45. Those writing history, biography or artistic criticism should be aware that private papers, photographs or artistic productions are protected by copyright, regardless of whether such material resides in an archive, gallery or museum. One cannot legally consult, cite, reproduce, publish, refer to or distribute such documents or articles without permission, either from the author or heirs or from the person or institution given copyright ownership.

ACQUISITION AND USE OF CULTURAL PROPERTIES

46. Acquisitions should be for the purpose of scholarship and not for personal gain, private collection or sale.

47. Legal requirements of the country of origin must be observed.

48. Where there is doubt as to legal ownership, the researcher acquires an object at risk and must immediately inform the authorities of the country concerned. If the acquisition is not approved, the researcher should return the object to those authorities.

49. The researcher should not accept or otherwise acquire objects unless proper storage, protection and preservation of the objects can be provided.

50. Materials should be catalogued, with a description of their provenance, and this catalogue made part of the public record.

51. After a reasonable time, objects or documents should be made accessible to other scholars with legitimate research interests.

52. If objects or documents are to be de-accessioned or discarded, they should be offered to public authorities or educational institutions in the country or district of origin. If the offer is refused or cannot be made, they should be offered to educational institutions in Canada where they could be put to proper use or preserved. Such objects or documents should never be traded or sold to individuals or to dealers, but always remain in the public domain.

53. All copies or reproductions of documents and objects, whether collected for exhibition or distribution, should be clearly marked.

54. Material should not be publicly exhibited, discussed or published in a way which causes embarrassment to individuals, groups or countries associated with it.

55. Objects or documents should not be exhibited in ways likely to damage them.

RESEARCH ON OTHER CULTURES, COUNTRIES AND ETHNIC GROUPS

56. Research on cultures, countries and ethnic groups different from one's own requires a different ethic. Researchers in the field have to give an account of themselves acceptable to the people among whom they are working, and in accord with the role the subjects will

observe. To gain the subjects' trust and cooperation, researchers may tell them that they have come to learn about their way of life, languages, customs and beliefs. But the problems of communicating what uses will be made of the information may be unsurmountable.

57. This communication gap may make informed consent impossible, especially as the people under study may be unable to estimate the risks to their wellbeing and reputations, and potential damage to their descendants. To add to the problem in fieldwork, individual consent may not be feasible, and there may not be any person with authority to give collective consent. Absence of informed consent places additional responsibility and restrictions on researchers. Researchers must satisfy the review committee concerning the safeguards in the methodology.

58. Subjects may be paid for their time and this remuneration may take into consideration the inconvenience of participation. In anthropological field work, reciprocity is normal in some regions for certain persons, in the form of gifts, loans, transportation and other services.

59. If dangers can be foreseen but not forestalled it is questionable whether research should be undertaken. Intentions and risks must not be concealed to obtain cooperation.

60. In some societies, privacy and confidentiality may apply to unexpected kinds of activity. Certain ceremonies may be the privilege of a particular class or group: men may not view ceremonies of women, or youths may not be a party to deliberations of elders.

Concepts of privacy must be viewed from the perspective of the research subject or the subject's culture.

61. When researchers outside their own culture are operating from a position of advantage, they have particular responsibility to subjects as regards publication. Margaret Mead sums these up: "There is first of all the responsibility to individuals who, if identified, must not thereby be exposed to legal sanctions, to ridicule or to danger. Second there is the responsibility to the group as a whole. Where customs are portrayed that contrast with the ethical standards of those who govern them or with the missionized or educated members of their own society, these must be represented in such a way that full justice is done to the cultural framework within which a given practice, however apparently abhorrent, occurs. Finally, there is the responsibility of the anthropologist for the way in which his findings are interpreted and articulated into the ongoing understanding of human behaviour in the human sciences of his day."*

* Mead, Margaret, 'Research with Human Beings: A Model Derived from Anthropological Field Practice.' In *Ethical Aspects of Experimentation with Human Subjects*, edited by Paul E. Freund, pp. 361–387. Cambridge: Daedelus, Spring 1969.

Source: "SSHRC: Ethical Guidelines for Research with Human Subjects." *SSHRC Granting Programs, Detailed Guide*, August 1993, pp. 66–70.

SAMPLE QUESTIONNAIRE

The following questionnaire has been prepared by St. Francis Xavier University students in Atlantic Canada. The focus of the questionnaire is a crosscultural study of students' attitudes and behaviors. Please do not put your name on the questionnaire since all responses are confidential. Thank you for your cooperation.

1. Do you have regular access to:

	Yes	No
A stereo	____	____
Color T.V.	____	____
Walkman	____	____
VCR	____	____
Personal computer	____	____

2. How often do you:

	Never								Every day
Listen to music	1	2	3	4	5	6	7	8	9
Watch T.V.	1	2	3	4	5	6	7	8	9
Listen to radio	1	2	3	4	5	6	7	8	9
Read the newspaper	1	2	3	4	5	6	7	8	9
Read books for leisure	1	2	3	4	5	6	7	8	9
Watch rock videos	1	2	3	4	5	6	7	8	9
Watch home movies	1	2	3	4	5	6	7	8	9

3. What things are important to you?

	Not Important								Very Important
Acceptance by God	1	2	3	4	5	6	7	8	9
Being loved	1	2	3	4	5	6	7	8	9
Success in what you do	1	2	3	4	5	6	7	8	9
Freedom	1	2	3	4	5	6	7	8	9

	Not Important					**Very Important**			
A rewarding career - - - - - - -	1	2	3	4	5	6	7	8	9
A comfortable life - - - - - - - -	1	2	3	4	5	6	7	8	9
A good education - - - - - - - -	1	2	3	4	5	6	7	8	9
Popularity - - - - - - - - - - - - -	1	2	3	4	5	6	7	8	9
Family life - - - - - - - - - - - - -	1	2	3	4	5	6	7	8	9

4. How much pleasure do you derive from...

	Very little							**A Lot**	
Friendships - - - - - - - - -	1	2	3	4	5	6	7	8	9
Family - - - - - - - - - - - -	1	2	3	4	5	6	7	8	9
Girl/boy friend - - - - - - -	1	2	3	4	5	6	7	8	9
Dating - - - - - - - - - - - -	1	2	3	4	5	6	7	8	9
Sports - - - - - - - - - - - -	1	2	3	4	5	6	7	8	9
Being by yourself - - - - -	1	2	3	4	5	6	7	8	9
Listening to music - - - -	1	2	3	4	5	6	7	8	9
Watching T.V. - - - - - - -	1	2	3	4	5	6	7	8	9

Please circle a number to best indicate your rating of the following:

5. I feel depressed.

Never   1   2   3   4   5   6   7   8   **Often**

6. I worry about dating/relationship problems.

Never   1   2   3   4   5   6   7   8   **Often**

7. I worry about money.

Never   1   2   3   4   5   6   7   8   **Often**

8. I feel lonely.

Never   1   2   3   4   5   6   7   8   **Often**

9. I worry about the way I look.

Never   1   2   3   4   5   6   7   8   **Often**

10. I feel bored.

Never   1   2   3   4   5   6   7   8   **Often**

11. I worry about getting a job after graduation.

Never   1   2   3   4   5   6   7   8   **Often**

12. Have you ever had any thoughts of committing suicide?

Yes - - - - - - - - 1( )
No - - - - - - - - - 2( )

13. Have you ever actually attempted suicide?

Yes - - - - - - - - 1( )
No - - - - - - - - - 2( )

14. I think the following problems affect my country...

	Not at all							Greatly	
Crime - - - - - - - - - - - - - - 1	2	3	4	5	6	7	8	9
Pollution - - - - - - - - - - - 1	2	3	4	5	6	7	8	9
Unemployment - - - - - - 1	2	3	4	5	6	7	8	9
The economy - - - - - - - - 1	2	3	4	5	6	7	8	9
AIDS - - - - - - - - - - - - - 1	2	3	4	5	6	7	8	9
Racial discrimination - - - 1	2	3	4	5	6	7	8	9
Threat of nuclear war - - 1	2	3	4	5	6	7	8	9
Family breakdown - - - - 1	2	3	4	5	6	7	8	9
Quality of education - - - 1	2	3	4	5	6	7	8	9

15. I am very involved in student politics.

Not Involved   1   2   3   4   5   6   7   8   9   **Very Involved**

16 How satisfied are you with the courses you are taking?

Unsatisfied   1   2   3   4   5   6   7   8   9   **Very Satisfied**

17. My government should increase its provision for foreign aid.

Strongly Disagree   1   2   3   4   5   6   7   8   9   **Strongly Agree**

18 Quotas in job hiring should be used to increase the numbers of visible minorities in good jobs.

Strongly Disagree   1   2   3   4   5   6   7   8   9   **Strongly Agree**

19. My government should create definite sanctions against the regime in South Africa.

Strongly Disagree   1   2   3   4   5   6   7   8   9   **Strongly Agree**

20. Visible minorities in this country are not given an equal chance in education compared to the majority.

Strongly Disagree   1   2   3   4   5   6   7   8   9   **Strongly Agree**

21. The immigration policies of this government are too strict.

   Strongly Disagree   1   2   3   4   5   6   7   8   9   **Strongly Agree**

22. Abortion should be entirely the personal choice of the woman involved.

   Strongly Disagree   1   2   3   4   5   6   7   8   9   **Strongly Agree**

23. There is nothing wrong with being homosexual.

   Strongly Disagree   1   2   3   4   5   6   7   8   9   **Strongly Agree**

24. The government does not pay enough to welfare recipients.

   Strongly Disagree   1   2   3   4   5   6   7   8   9   **Strongly Agree**

25. During your childhood, household tasks (doing dishes, laundry, cleaning) were performed by:

	Never						Always		
Your mother - - - - - - - -	0	1	2	3	4	5	6	7	8
Your father - - - - - - - - -	0	1	2	3	4	5	6	7	8
Your sister(s) - - - - - - - -	0	1	2	3	4	5	6	7	8
Your brother(s) - - - - - - -		0	1	2	3	4	5	6	7	8
Yourself - - - - - - - - - - -	0	1	2	3	4	5	6	7	8

26. Was your mother usually employed outside the home when your age was:

	1 Yes	0 No
0–5 years - - - - - - - - - -	_____	_____
6–13 years - - - - - - - - -	_____	_____
14–18 years - - - - - - - -	_____	_____
19+ years - - - - - - - - - -	_____	_____

27. Between the ages of 5–12 years, which parent was most often involved in the following activities:

	Mother	Father
Reading to/with children - - - - - - - -	_____	_____
Helping with homework - - - - - - - - -	_____	_____
Playing indoors - - - - - - - - - - - - - -	_____	_____
Playing outdoors - - - - - - - - - - - - -	_____	_____

28. If there is a military draft, both men and women should be included in it.

   Strongly Disagree   1   2   3   4   5   6   7   8   9   **Strongly Agree**

29. *A woman should not take her husband's name at marriage.*
   Strongly Disagree   1   2   3   4   5   6   7   8   9   *Strongly Agree*

30. *Men are better-suited emotionally than women for politics.*
   Strongly Disagree   1   2   3   4   5   6   7   8   9   *Strongly Agree*

31. *It is the responsibility of a man to provide for his family.*
   Strongly Disagree   1   2   3   4   5   6   7   8   9   *Strongly Agree*

32. *Men make better engineers than women.*
   Strongly Disagree   1   2   3   4   5   6   7   8   9   *Strongly Agree*

33. *When children are young, a mother's place is in the home.*
   Strongly Disagree   1   2   3   4   5   6   7   8   9   *Strongly Agree*

34. *What is the total number of children you would like to have?* _____ *children.*

35. *Who is (or was) the major influence in determining your desired career goals in life? (check one only)*

   Father - - - - - - - - - - - - - - -   1(   )
   Mother - - - - - - - - - - - - - -   2(   )
   Brothers/sisters - - - - - - - - -   3(   )
   Friend - - - - - - - - - - - - - - -   4(   )
   Teachers - - - - - - - - - - - -   5(   )
   Guidance Counsellors - - - -   6(   )
   Professionals - - - - - - - - - -   7(   )
   Others - - - - - - - - - - - - - - -   8(   )
   Please specify _____

36. *Do you have a specific career in mind after graduation?*
              Yes - - - - - - - - 1(   )
              No - - - - - - - - - 2(   )

37. *What do you think are the chances you will realize your career expectations?*
   Very poor   1   2   3   4   5   6   7   8   9   *Very good*

38. What are the three most important things you expect of a job you want to make your life's work? (Place a 1 beside the most important; a 2 beside the next most important and a 3 beside the next important one.)

Money - - - - - - - - - - - - - - _____

Security - - - - - - - - - - - - - - _____

Continued interest - - - - - - - _____

Power - - - - - - - - - - - - - - _____

Prestige - - - - - - - - - - - - - _____

Freedom of behavior - - - - - _____

Excitement - - - - - - - - - - _____

39. Have you ever dated?

Yes - - - - - - - - 1(   )

No - - - - - - - - - 2(   )

39.1 If yes, at what age did you begin dating? _____ _____ .

40. What type of relationship are you presently involved in?

I am married - - - - - - - - - - - - - - - - - - - 1(   )

I am living with someone - - - - - - - - - - - - 2(   )

I am engaged to be married - - - - - - - - - - 3(   )

I date one person regularly (go steady) - - - 4(   )

I date more than one person - - - - - - - - - - 5(   )

I date occasionally - - - - - - - - - - - - - - - - 6(   )

I have never dated - - - - - - - - - - - - - - - - 7(   )

41. Have you ever been in love?

Yes - - - - - - - - 1(   )

No - - - - - - - - 2(   )

41.1 If yes, how many times have you felt that you were in love?

Once - - - - - - - - - - - - - - - - 1(   )

2–3 times - - - - - - - - - - - - - 2(   )

4–6 times - - - - - - - - - - - - - 3(   )

7–8 times - - - - - - - - - - - - - 4(   )

9 or more times - - - - - - - - - 5(   )

42. If you have been dating someone for a month, and you feel affection towards that person, how far do you believe it is proper to go sexually?

Kissing - - - - - - - - - - - - - - 1(   )
Petting - - - - - - - - - - - - - - 2(   )
Foreplay - - - - - - - - - - - - - 3(   )
Intercourse - - - - - - - - - - 4(   )
All of the above - - - - - - - - 5(   )
None of the above- - - - - - - 6(   )

43. Have you ever engaged in sexual intercourse?

Yes - - - - - - - - 1(   )
No - - - - - - - - - 2(   )

> **43.1   If yes, at what age did you first engage in sexual intercourse?**
> _____ _____ *years of age.*

44. How many sexual partners have you had in the past six months?

None - - - - - - - - - - - - - - - 1(   )
1–2 partners - - - - - - - - - - - 2(   )
3–4 partners - - - - - - - - - - - 3(   )
5–6 partners - - - - - - - - - - – 4(   )
7 or more partners- - - - - - - 5(   )

45. How often do you or your partner use contraceptive or birth control methods?
Never   1   2   3   4   5   6   7   8   9   *often*

46. Men should be allowed more freedom than women in engaging in intercourse before marriage.
Strongly Disagree   1   2   3   4   5   6   7   8   9   **Strongly Agree**

We are providing the following information so you can better estimate your alcohol consumption for the following questions:

1 drink = 1 bottle of beer = 1.5 oz. of spirit (rye, rum, etc.)
1 drink = 5 oz. wine
Most mixed drinks, and also highballs (rum & coke) have 1 oz. of liquor.

47. Have you ever used alcohol?

Yes - - - - - - - - 1(   ) ⌐
No - - - - - - - - 2(   ) │→

47.1 If yes, how many drinks of alcohol do you have per week, on the average?

1-3 drinks - - - - - - - - - - - - - - 1(   )
4-7 drinks - - - - - - - - - - - - - - 2(   )
8-12 drinks - - - - - - - - - - - - - 3(   )
13 or more drinks - - - - - - - - - 4(   )

47.2 Do you drink alone?

Never - - - - - - - - - - - - - - - - - 0(   )
Rarely - - - - - - - - - - - - - - - - - 1(   )
Occasionally - - - - - - - - - - - - 2(   )
Frequently - - - - - - - - - - - - - - 3(   )

48. Have you ever used illegal drugs?

Yes - - - - - - - - 1(   ) ⌐
No - - - - - - - - 2(   ) │→

48.1 If yes, which of these have you ever used?

	Yes	No
Barbituates (i.e., seconal, amytal, phenobarb) - -	_____	_____
Opiates, (i.e., heroin, morphine opium) - - - - - -	_____	_____
Stimulants (i.e., pep pills, speed, uppers) - - - - -	_____	_____
Tranquillizers (i.e., librium, valium, PCP) - - - - - -	_____	_____
LSD -		_____
Downers -	_____	_____
Marijuana -	_____	_____

48.2 How often do you use drugs?

Never - - - - - - - - - - - - - - - - - 0(   )
1-2 times a week - - - - - - - - - 1(   )
3-4 times a week - - - - - - - - - 2(   )
5-6 times a week - - - - - - - - - 3(   )
7 or more times a week - - - - - 4(   )

48.3 Do you do drugs when alone?

Never - - - - - - - - - - - - - - - - - 0(   )
Rarely - - - - - - - - - - - - - - - - - 1(   )
Occasionally - - - - - - - - - - - - 2(   )
Frequently - - - - - - - - - - - - - - 3(   )

49. If you drink or do drugs, you do so

	Yes	No
To feel like "part of the crowd" - - - - - - - - - -	_____	_____
To relieve frustration/relax - - - - - - - - - - - -	_____	_____
For kicks, thrills, fun - - - - - - - - - - - - - - -	_____	_____
To say awake while studying/working - - - - -	_____	_____

Background Information:

50. Gender:

I am:
Male - - - - - - - 1(   )
Female - - - - - - 2(   )

51. I am presently enrolled in the following type of program:

University, diploma program - - 1(   )
College program - - - - - - - - - - 2(   )
Technical school - - - - - - - - - - 3(   )
Vocational school - - - - - - - - - 4(   )
Other - - - - - - - - - - - - - - - - 5(   )

If other, please specify _____

52. How many years have you been a student at this institution?

One year - - - - - - - - - - - - - 1(   )
Two years - - - - - - - - - - - 2(   )
Three years - - - - - - - - - - - 3(   )
Four years - - - - - - - - - - - - 4(   )
Five years - - - - - - - - - - - - 5(   )
Other - - - - - - - - - - - - - - 6(   )

Please specify _____

53. What is your religious affiliation?

Roman Catholic- - - - - - - - - 01( )	Other Protestant - - - - - - - - 06( )
Anglican (Episcopalian) - - - 02( )	Jewish - - - - - - - - - - - - - - - 07( )
United - - - - - - - - - - - - - - 03( )	Buddhist - - - - - - - - - - - - - 08( )
Baptist - - - - - - - - - - - - - - 04( )	Muslim - - - - - - - - - - - - - - 09( )
Presbyterian - - - - - - - - - - 05( )	Other - - - - - - - - - - - - - - - 10( )

Please specify _____

54. How often do you attend church services?

	At University	At Home
More than once a week	1( )	1( )
Once every week	2( )	2( )
2 to 3 times a month	3( )	3( )
Once a month	4( )	4( )
7 to 10 times a year	5( )	5( )
2 to 6 times a year	6( )	6( )
Once a year	7( )	7( )
Never	8( )	8( )

55. What type(s) of organizations do you belong to while attending this institution?

	Yes	No
Volunteer	_____	_____
Church	_____	_____
Athletic	_____	_____

56. Please indicate the sources of funding for your university education.

	Yes	No
Vacation savings	_____	_____
Parents	_____	_____
Spouse	_____	_____
Student loan	_____	_____
Bursaries		
Scholarships	_____	_____
Part-time earnings	_____	_____
Other	_____	_____

Please specify _____

57. As a student, do you work part-time while attending this institution?

Yes -------- 1( )
No -------- 2( )

57.1 How many hours a week do you work? _____ hours.

58. Approximately, what was the population of your hometown or city before coming to university?

Rural area under 1,000 - - - - 1(   )
1,000-4,999 - - - - - - - - - - 2(   )
5,000-9,999 - - - - - - - - - - 3(   )
10,000-19,999 - - - - - - - - - 4(   )
20,000-49,999 - - - - - - - - - 5(   )
50,000-99,999 - - - - - - - - - 6(   )
100,000-499,999 - - - - - - - 7(   )
500,000-999,999 - - - - - - - 8(   )
1,000,000 and over - - - - - - 9(   )

59. Do you consider yourself to be a member of an ethnic minority group in your country of origin?

Yes - - - - - - - - 1(   )
No - - - - - - - - 2(   )

59.1 If yes, please specify _____ .

60. Where do you live while attending school?

Residence - - - - - - - - - - - - - 1(   )
Apartment/house/boarding - - - 2(   )
With both parents - - - - - - - - 3(   )
With one parent - - - - - - - - - 4(   )
Other - - - - - - - - - - - - - - - - 5(   )

If other, please specify _____

60.1   If you live in residence or an apartment, what type of room do you have?

Single room - - - - - - - - - - - - - 1(   )
Double room - - - - - - - - - - - - 2(   )
Other - - - - - - - - - - - - - - - - - 3(   )

Please specify _____

61. What is your parents' marital status?

Single - 1(   )
Living with someone but not married - - - - - 2(   )
Married - 3(   )
Divorced - 4(   )
Separated - 5(   )
Remarried - 6(   )
Widow/widower - - - - - - - - - - - - - - - - - - 7(   )

62. What is the highest education completed by your parents?

	Mother	Father
No education - - - - - - - - - -	1( )	1( )
1–3 years - - - - - - - - - - - - -	2( )	2( )
4–8 years - - - - - - - - - - - - -	3( )	3( )
9–12 years - - - - - - - - - - -	4( )	4( )
13–15 years - - - - - - - - - - -	5( )	5( )
16 years + - - - - - - - - - - - -	6( )	6( )

63. What is (or was) the occupation of your father? (e.g., social worker)

Job _____

Brief Job Description _____

_____

64. What is (or was) the occupation of your mother (e.g., school principal, homemaker)

Job _____

Brief Job Description _____

_____

65. How many brothers do you have? _____

66. How many sisters do you have? _____

67. I was the _____ child in a family of _____ children.
(e.g., 1st, 2nd, 3rd, etc.)

Thank you

GLOSSARY

ADVOCACY RESEARCH   Social research which advocates social changes or which advances the personal or collective agendas of its practitioners.

ALTERNATIVE HYPOTHESIS   See research hypothesis.

ANALYSIS OF VARIANCE   Analysis of variance (ANOVA) is a procedure for deciding if a ratio level dependent variable is significantly associated with a nominal or ordinal independent variable.

ANALYTIC FILES   Files relating to a specific topic or relationship explored in a field study.

ANDROCENTRICITY   Refers to a presentation given exclusively from a male perspective.

ANECDOTAL EVIDENCE   Evidence for a generalization based on one incident which serves to illustrate why or how some relationship exists.

ANTECEDENT VARIABLE MODEL   A causal model which proposes a variable which causes variation in an independent variable which, in turn, influences the dependent variable in the model. Thus the antecedent variable is one which precedes both the main independent and dependent variables.

APPEAL TO AUTHORITY   Using the opinion of a person on a topic when the person's expertise falls outside the topic area.

APPLIED RESEARCH   Research that focuses on figuring out how to bring about specific changes in society.

AXIOMATIC DERIVATION   Refers to a method of logically deriving new statements of relationship from a given set of assumptions and propositions.

BACKWARD (STEPWISE) SOLUTION   In this procedure, all the variables are initially included in the regression equation; then the least important variable is dropped, and the equation is recalculated. This procedure is repeated until only significant variables remain.

BASELINE MEASURE   A measure taken once stability has been achieved in the dependent variable at the beginning of a set of observations.

B COEFFICIENT   A coefficient that is associated with regression analysis and that is an unstandardized measure of the influence of an independent variable on the dependent variable. If small increases in the X variable lead to large increases in the Y variable, the b value will be higher; on the other hand, if it takes large increases in X to produce an increase in Y, the b value will be smaller.

BETA WEIGHT   A beta weight is associated with regression analysis and is a standardized measure of the relative influence of an independent variable on the dependent variable when the influences of other independent variables are held constant.

BETWEEN-SUBJECTS DESIGNS   Experimental designs where each group of experimental subjects is exposed to either the control group treatment or the experimental group treatment.

BIAS   A preference—or predisposition—to favour a particular conclusion.

BI-MODAL DISTRIBUTION   A distribution with two peaks.

BLOCKING   Refers to experiments where subjects have been grouped together on some variable that needs to be controlled, and subjects are then randomly assigned to treatment and control groups.

BOURGEOISIE   In the conflict perspective, the owners of the means of production (factories, farms, businesses, etc.) are referred to as the bourgeoisie and they seek to exploit workers.

CANDIDATE VARIABLE MODEL   A model which proposes several independent variables as possible causes of variation in a dependent variable.

CAUSAL EXPLANATION   An explanation in which an event, or sequence of events, is explained by making reference to preceding, influencing events.

CAUSAL MODEL   A graphic representation of proposed causal connections between variables.

CHI-SQUARE TEST   A test of statistical significance associated with contingency table analysis, where the dependent variable is a nominal one.

CLEANING THE DATA Refers to the systematic search for errors in a data set so that they can be corrected before analysis of the data begins.

COEFFICIENT OF RELIABILITY A measure of agreement between the coders on the categorization of the items being analyzed. The proportion of times there is agreement is reflected in the coefficient.

COMPARATIVE STUDIES Studies that typically involve cross-cultural or historical analyses of social behaviour. Such studies look at the similarities and differences between cultures, or within the same culture, over time.

CONCEPT A general idea referring to a characteristic of an individual, a group, or a nation.

CONCEPTUAL HYPOTHESIS A statement of the relationship between two or more conceptual variables.

CONCEPTUAL LEVEL Defines the variables that are to be used in the research.

CONCEPTUAL VARIABLE An idea which has a dimension that can vary.

CONDITIONAL VARIABLE A variable that accounts for a change in the relationship between an independent variable and a dependent variable when the general conditions change.

CONFLICT THEORY/PERSPECTIVE This perspective argues that society is fundamentally characterized by conflict between interest groups; in the Marxist version, for example, owners of the means of production (factories, farms, businesses, etc.), the bourgeoisie, seek to exploit workers, the proletarians, whose labour is undervalued and underpaid.

CONFOUNDING VARIABLE A variable which may unintentionally obscure or enhance a relationship. Such variables may influence the outcome of an experiment systematically.

CONSEQUENTIALIST This view of research ethics stresses that ethical judgements about a research project should be made in terms of its consequences for the subject, for the academic discipline, and for society.

CONSTRUCT VALIDITY Measures have construct validity when a theoretically derived hypothesis turns out as predicted.

CONTENT ANALYSIS Any technique for making inferences by objectively and systematically coding information.

CONTENT VALIDITY Refers to the extent to which the measure reflects the dimension(s) implied by the concept.

CONTINGENCY TABLE A table that cross-classifies variables so that the relationship between a nominal-level dependent variable can be related to an independent variable.

CONTROL BY CONSTANCY A type of control used in within-subject designs where the same subject experiences different levels of the treatment; hence the subject acts as his/her own control.

CONTROL GROUP DESIGN An experimental design in which the researcher uses randomized assignment to groups (or precision matching) to adjust for known and unknown variations between the two groups.

CONTROLLED OBSERVATIONS Observations in which confounding factors are minimized or taken into account.

CONTROL VARIABLE A variable which is taken into account in exploring the relation between an independent and a dependent variable. There are three basic types of control variables: the intervening variable, the conditional variable, and the source of spuriousness (or confounding) variable.

CONVENIENCE SAMPLE A non-probability sampling procedure that involves selection on the basis of ease or convenience.

CORRELATION ANALYSIS A procedure for measuring how closely two ratio level variables co-vary together.

CORRELATION COEFFICIENT (R) A measure of the strength of association between two variables; a correlation may vary from +1 to –1.

COUNTERBALANCING Counterbalancing in experimental designs involves introducing, changing, maintaining, and then returning to the first level of the experimental treatment to control for effects of learning on the subject's performance.

COVARIATES Ratio level treatment variables.

COVERT ENTRY Entry into a group by a researcher without the knowledge of the group.

COVERT OBSERVATIONAL STUDIES Studies where the researcher records observations without the subjects being aware that they are being observed.

CREDIBILITY In qualitative research a study "is credible when it presents such faithful descriptions or interpretations of a human experience that the people having that experience would immediately recognize it from those descriptions or interpretations as their own. A study is also credible when other people (other researchers or readers) can recognize the experience when confronted with it after having only read about it in a study" (Sandelowski, 1986, p. 30).

CRITERION VALIDITY Refers to the extent to which a measure is able to predict accurately.

CRITICAL APPROACH This approach views human behaviour as fundamentally characterized by different groups attempting to enhance their interests at the expense of less powerful groups. The fundamental goal of the critical approach is to bring about a truly egalitarian society—one where there is an equality of opportunity *and* an equality of result.

CURVILINEAR RELATIONSHIP A relationship where the plot between the variables goes in one direction and then switches to another one.

DATA ENTRY The process of transferring the information collected in a study to a computing device.

DATA MASSAGING The practice of playing with the data until the analysis producing the strongest association is identified and retained. In massaging the data, the bias will usually be to find evidence supporting expected or preferred outcomes.

DEBRIEFING Refers to researchers explaining studies to subjects after the data have been collected, noting any deception, why it was necessary, and reassuring subjects that their participation was appreciated and helpful.

DEDUCTIVE EXPLANATION An explanation in which the phenomenon to be explained is shown to be a logically necessary consequence of the explanatory premises. As in: if A = B, and B = C, then A = C.

DEFINITION OF THE SITUATION A concept developed by W. I. Thomas. The symbolic interactionists argue that how things are perceived is critical. Each social situation is interpreted; the interpretation may or may not be correct but, nonetheless, people act on their interpretations.

DEHOAXING Refers to the process of a researcher informing subjects in a study about what was really going on in an experiment, particularly informing them of any deception that was used.

DEMAND CHARACTERISTIC A distortion introduced when people respond in terms of how they think they are expected to respond.

DEONTOLOGICAL This view of research ethics proposes absolute moral strictures that must never be violated.

DEPENDENT VARIABLE A variable thought to be influenced by other variables; it is the "effect" in a cause-effect relationship.

DESCRIPTIVE RESEARCH Research that emphasizes the accurate portrayal of a population. A study which is primarily descriptive has as its major concern the accurate description of some aspect of society. Descriptive research is about *what* and how many of *what*.

DESCRIPTIVE STATISTICS A branch of statistics that provides various tools, conventions, and procedures for describing variables or the relation between variables. (Means, standard deviations, normal distributions, and Z scores are used to describe individual variables; crosstabulations, means across categories, and correlations are some of the procedures used to describe relationships between variables.)

DISCRIMINANT FUNCTION ANALYSIS A mode of analysis used in situations where the dependent variable is measured at the nominal or ordinal level and the researcher wishes to examine the impact of several independent variables simultaneously. This procedure provides weightings maximizing the likelihood of correctly predicting the category of the dependent variable each case will fall into.

DOUBLE BLIND An experimental design where neither experimenters nor subjects are aware of the experimental condition that is being applied to the subjects.

DOUBLE STANDARD If a researcher uses different means of measuring identical behaviours, attitudes, or situations for each gender, that researcher would be guilty of using a double standard.

DUMMY VARIABLE A variable which is coded 1 for presence and 0 for absence of a characteristic and represents one category of an independent variable. Dummy variables are used in multiple regression and in discriminant analysis to enable the researcher to incorporate nominal variables.

EMPATHETIC EXPLANATION An explanation in which the experience of coming to see or coming to understand is stressed.

ETHNOMETHODOLOGY A methodology that typically involves a detailed examination of a single event or case; ethnomethodology is associated with the interpretive approach.

EXCHANGE THEORY/PERSPECTIVE The basic premise of this theory is that social actors interact with one another so that both profit by the exchange.

EXPECTANCY Refers to an anticipation of particular research results; this may lead to a distortion of results in the direction of expectations.

EXPERIMENTER EFFECT   Refers to a tendency to produce findings which are consistent with the experimenter's expectations.

EXPLANATORY RESEARCH   Research that seeks to provide answers to why questions.

EXTERNAL VALIDITY   A measure of the extent to which results may be extrapolated from the particular study to other groups in general.

EXTINCTION   Refers to the cessation of a behaviour which was once displayed.

FACE VALIDITY   Refers to an evaluation of an indicator which, on inspection, appears to reflect the concept you wish to measure.

FALSE DILEMMA   A dilemma that occurs when the researcher argues that something is caused by either A or by B: then, having provided some evidence that B is not responsible, the researcher falsely concludes that A must be the cause.

FAMILISM   A special case of gender insensitivity which involves treating the family as the unit of analysis when, in fact, it is individuals within the family unit that engage in a particular activity or hold a certain attitude. Familism is also a problem when we assume that some phenomenon has an equal impact on all members of the family when, in fact, it may affect different family members in different ways.

FEMINIST PERSPECTIVES   The basic premise of feminist theory is that one cannot adequately understand human societies without paying attention to the universal role of patriarchy, a term which refers to the domination of social groups by males who have greater power and privilege than women and children.

FIELD EXPERIMENTS   Experiments where the researcher intervenes in a natural setting and which, in contrast to to most participant observation studies, can be simple and quickly completed.

FIELD NOTES   Notes that attempt to capture the essence of the group being studied: included are descriptions of events and people as well as the interpretations of the researcher and the participants.

FIELD STUDIES   Field studies include those investigations where the researcher observes and records the behaviour of individuals or groups in their natural settings.

FILE   The name for a data set, or the text of a report, entered into a computer.

FOLK WISDOM   Maxims passed down from generation to generation. They are an important source of ideas for the social researcher; such ideas should not, however, be accepted as true until tested in some rigorous scientific fashion.

FORMAL THEORY   According to theorists such as Homans, a formal theory contains a set of concepts and a set of propositions, each stating a relationship between some of the concepts. Furthermore, the propositions must form a deductive system. Also some of the propositions must be contingent—that is, they must be amenable to some form of empirical test.

FUNCTIONAL EXPLANATION   An explanation in which the presence of some phenomenon is explained in terms of the role it plays in maintaining some system.

FUNCTIONALIST THEORY   A theory which emphasizes the interrelationships of parts and how they complement one another; functionalists believe that there is a tendency for societies to move toward balance and harmony. Functionalists ask about how different items contribute to balance, to the maintenance of the social system.

GAMMA   A measure of the strength of association between ordinal-level variables.

GENDER INSENSITIVITY   A disregard of the differential impacts of research conclusions or of social policy on men and on women.

GENERALIZATION   A statement which attempts to describe a pattern of behaviour or a relationship which is, on average, correct.

GROUNDED THEORY   Refers to the idea that the conclusions of a participant observation study should be grounded in the data—that is, based on direct and careful observations of everyday life within the group.

GUERILLA RAIDERS SYNDROME   Researchers suffering from this syndrome typically do not do original research. Instead they fashion a career out of attacking a particular theoretical or methodological approach.

GUTTMAN SCALE   An index that can demonstrably reflect a single dimension. Items are viewed as scalable if one can demonstrate that there is a hierarchy among them. This means that when items are arranged in order of intensity, respondents should respond positively to all lower intensity items if they respond positively to an item of high intensity.

HAWTHORNE EFFECT   Refers to any variability in a dependent variable that is not the direct result of variations in the treatment variable (see also: source of spuriousness, confounding variable).

HISTORY In the context of experimental design, history refers to concurrent events that, along with the experimental manipulation, may be influencing variation in the dependent variable.

INADVERTENT REINFORCEMENT Describes a process whereby we may unintentionally reinforce undesired behaviour.

INDEPENDENT VARIABLE A "cause" in a cause-effect relationship. It is a variable which has been selected as a possible influence on variations in a dependent variable.

IN-DEPTH INTERVIEWS Personal interviews where probing is used to explore issues in detail.

INDEX A combined score based on two or more indicators.

INDIVIDUALLY-DELIVERED QUESTIONNAIRES Questionnaires handed to the respondent by a researcher.

INFERENTIAL STATISTICS The branch of statistics that deals with making extrapolations from a sample to the population from which it was drawn.

INFORMED CONSENT The right of a potential respondent to be informed as to the nature of the study, the kinds of issues that will be explored, how the respondent was selected, and who is sponsoring the research. Where studies are done involving children, the infirm, or incompetent adults, the organization or individual responsible for the prospective respondent should provide consent in writing.

INFORMED OPINION An opinion based on evidence which has been collected under controlled circumstances.

INSTRUMENT DECAY A deterioration in the measurement instrument over the course of measurements in a study.

INTERNAL CONSISTENCY APPROACH TO RELIABILITY Assessing reliability by comparing an individual item's correlation to the total index score: if an item is consistent with the total score it will correlate with it.

INTERNAL VALIDITY A study has internal validity when the researcher has demonstrated that the treatment in fact produced the changes in the dependent variable.

INTERPRETIVE APPROACH The interpretive approach relies mainly on field studies, with an emphasis on participant observation studies (joining a group and participating in it), in-depth interviews with people, and on ethnomethodology (often a detailed examination of a single event or case). Each of these studies typically involves a few cases which are described in detail. A key question for researchers who favour this approach is: does the explanation offered make sense to the people whose behaviour is being explained? Communication of the results of such studies usually emphasizes verbal descriptions rather than numerical analyses.

INTERQUARTILE RANGE A measure of how far apart the values are in the middle 50 percent of a distribution.

INTERVENING VARIABLE A variable that links an independent variable to a dependent variable. An intervening variable represents an explanation of how the independent variable influences the dependent variable.

INTERVIEW PANELS Groups with which at least one follow-up interview is conducted.

INTERVIEW SCHEDULES Schedules that outline the major questions that are to be raised. The interviewer has autonomy in exploring questions in detail.

JACKSON'S RULE OF THIRDS A rule to be used in interpreting three-variable relationships. If the original difference between the categories increases by one-third or more, we will interpret this as an *increase*, or a strengthening, of the original relationship; if the difference remains within one-third of the original, we will interpreted this as an indication that the relationship has *remained the same*; if the difference decreases by more than one-third, we will interpret this as a *decrease/disappearance* of the relationship; finally, if the relationship is markedly different when different control categories are compared to one another (e.g., it disappears in one category, but stays the same in the other), the result is *mixed*.

KEY CHARACTER FILES Files established on key players in the organization or group being observed. Here items are drawn from the master file which provide clues as to the personality and manner of operation of each individual.

LAMBDA A statistic measuring the *proportionate reduction in error* that occurs in estimating a dependent variable given knowledge of the independent variable.

LEPTOKURTIC DISTRIBUTION A distribution with little variability—with a small standard deviation relative to the magnitude of the values—and that is sharply peaked.

LIKERT ITEMS   Questions that ask respondents to categorize a statement by indicating whether they strongly disagree, disagree, are undecided or neutral, agree, or strongly agree with the statement.

LINEAR REGRESSION EQUATION   An equation that describes a relationship between a number of independent variables and a dependent variable and which provides for the best linear (additive) weightings of the independent variables and a constant calculated so as to maximize the prediction of the dependent variable.

LOOKING GLASS SELF   The idea that our perception of self is reflected in how others see us—we come to see ourselves as others see us.

MACROVARIABLES   Properties or characteristics of societies, as opposed to qualities of individuals.

MAGNITUDE ESTIMATION PROCEDURES   Procedures that are useful when comparative judgments are required. When using magnitude estimation procedures, a respondent estimates the magnitude of a series of stimuli compared to some fixed standard.

MASTER FIELD FILE   A file made up of the complete journal of field notes.

MASTER TABLE   A table that records all collected information so that required tables can be derived from it without going back to tally sheets.

MATURATION   Refers to any changes that occur in an individual subject over the course of an experiment which may, along with the experimental manipulation, influence the outcome of the experiment.

MEAN   The mean (more formally known as the *arithmetic mean*; less formally known as the *average*) is computed by summing the values of a variable and dividing the result by the total number of cases.

MEASUREMENT   The process of linking abstract concepts to empirical indicants.

MEASUREMENT ERROR   A measure of the extent to which indicants fail to reflect the true underlying values of variables.

MEASURES OF CENTRAL TENDENCY   Measures that use one number to typify a set of values.

MEDIAN   The mid-point of a distribution.

MICROVARIABLES   Properties or characteristics of individuals as opposed to societal properties.

MISSING EVIDENCE   Refers to the idea that evidence necessary for the argument to be true may be missing.

MISSING VALUE CODE   A value assigned to a variable for those cases where the information is absent or not applicable.

MODE   The most frequently occurring response to a nominal variable.

MORTALITY   A process in which subjects select themselves out of a study.

MULTICOLLINEARITY   A measure of the extent of the correlation among independent variables.

MULTIPLE REGRESSION ANALYSIS   Identifies an equation to predict variations in a dependent variable from two or more independent variables.

MULTI-STAGE AREA SAMPLE   When sampling involves an attempt to reflect a large unit such as a state, province, or country and no list of the population is available, then one develops a sample by stages. At each stage of the sampling process, every individual (or unit) must have a known chance of being selected.

MULTI-VARIATE ANALYSIS OF VARIANCE   Multivariate analysis of variance (MANOVA) is used in examining relations between a ratio level dependent variable and independent variables measured at any level. MANOVA techniques also permit the researcher to examine multiple dependent variables simultaneously.

MULTI-VARIATE MODELS   Models which involve numerous variables.

MUTUALLY EXCLUSIVE CATEGORIES   Categories whose boundaries are established in such a way that no category overlaps with another one.

NATURAL SETTING EXPERIMENTS   Experiments where everyday situations can be manipulated, allowing for the researcher to observe reactions of people to the intervention.

NOMINAL MEASUREMENT   A quantitative measure where the numbers are arbitrarily assigned to categories of the variable.

NON-PROBABILITY SAMPLING TECHNIQUES   Techniques that do not provide potential respondents with a known chance of being asked to participate in a study. Convenience , quota, and referral (snowball) sampling are examples of nonprobability sampling techniques.

NON-REACTIVE STUDIES   involve indirect data collection—where there is no opportunity for the person being studied to react to the observations.

NORMAL DISTRIBUTION A distribution that approximates a bell-shaped curve, where there will be few cases on the extremes with most clustered at the mean of the distribution.

NULL HYPOTHESIS A hypothesis stating that there will be no relation between the variables.

OBJECTIVE A term referring to observations which are free from bias.

ONE-TAILED TEST A term referring to situations where we are predicting which particular tail of the normal distribution the result will fall into if the null hypothesis is to be rejected.

OPEN-ENDED QUESTION A question that asks a respondent to answer some question, or to offer some suggestion or opinion, but to do so without any pre-set categories being provided for the answer.

OPERANT CONDITIONING THEORY A term referring to the process by which our behaviour is developed, sustained, and modified by the consequences that our behaviour produces.

OPERATIONALIZATION The selection of indicators (measures) to reflect conceptual variables, and the implementation of a research project.

OPERATIONAL LEVEL Consists of the measurement of variables as well as the collection and analysis of data.

ORDINAL MEASUREMENT Ordinal measurement involves an underlying continuum in which the numerical values are ordered so that small numbers refer to lower levels on the continuum, and large numbers to higher points; however, the distances between the assigned numbers and the underlying continuum are not in a one-to-one relation with each other.

OVERGENERALIZATION A statement which claims to refer to all people but is based on evidence which does not represent all people.

OVERSPECIFICITY The use of single sex terms when members of both sexes are involved: for example "the doctor...he".

PANEL STUDIES Studies that monitor specific organizations or individuals over time.

PARTIAL CORRELATION A correlation that measures the strength of association between two ratio level variables while simultaneously controlling for the effects of one or more additional variables.

PARTIAL THEORY Explains an assumed or known relationship by specifying a testable causal model.

PARTICIPANT OBSERVATION STUDIES Participant observation studies ordinarily involve an intensive examination of some culture, community, organization or group. Normally, such studies involve having the researcher join the group for an extended period.

PATH MODEL A graphic representation of a complex set of proposed interrelationships among variables.

PATRIARCHY A term used to refer to the domination of social groups by males who have greater power and privilege than women and children.

PERCENTAGE Represents a proportion multiplied by 100. Thus a percentage represents *how many* for every 100 of something.

PHONE SURVEY A survey that relies on information reported by the respondent over the telephone.

PILOT STUDY In survey research such a study would involve having a small sample of respondents complete a questionnaire or undergo an interview. Pilot studies are used to determine items to be included in indexes, and to determine, from open-ended questions, what categories should be used in a fixed choice format.

PLAGIARISM The unacknowledged borrowing of other authors' ideas or words.

PLATYKURTIC DISTRIBUTION A distribution with a great deal of variability which will tend to be flat and wide.

POINT-IN-TIME DATA Data that measure variables at a particular point in time rather than changes over time.

POPULATION That collection of individuals, communities, or nations about which one wishes to make a general statement.

POSITIVIST APPROACH The approach to knowledge largely adopted in the physical sciences. In the early development of the social sciences some theorists attempted to model the new disciplines on the physical sciences. The French scholars Auguste Comte (1798-1857) and Emile Durkheim (1858-1917) were leaders in encouraging positivist approaches to understanding social behaviour.

PRECISE COMMUNICATION Refers to information that is unambiguous.

PRE-CODED, SINGLE CHOICE QUESTIONS Questions that ask the respondent to indicate which category applies to him or to her.

PREDICTION   When this term is used in connection with a regression analysis, it refers to the extent to which variation in a dependent variable can be accurately estimated with knowledge of the independent variables.

PRESENCE-ABSENCE QUESTIONS   Questions that request respondents to check off which items in a list do or do not apply to them.

PRIMARY SAMPLING UNITS   These units may be census tract areas, or other similar units, normally several hundred of them; these units are numbered, and a selection of at least 30 units is made from them, using an equal probability technique.

PROBABILISTIC EXPLANATION   An explanation in which it is argued that a particular case will be similar to others in the same general category.

PROBABILITY SAMPLING PROCEDURES   Techniques for selecting sampling units so that each has a known chance of being included.

PROLETARIANS   In the conflict perspective, these are the workers whose labour is undervalued and underpaid.

PRONOUN PROBLEM   Encourages stereotypic thinking by referring, for example, to doctors and managers as *he*, and nurses as *she*.

PROPORTION   Represents that part of 1 which is represented by a category; for example, how many females there are in a population compared to the total population. Proportions always begin with a decimal point.

PROPORTIONATE REDUCTION IN ERROR   Associated with the statistic *Lambda,* which measures the reduction in error in estimating variation in a dependent variable given knowledge of an independent variable. If two variables are strongly associated, then errors in predicting variations in the dependent variable will be considerably reduced if information on the independent variable is taken into account.

PROVINCIALISM   The tendency to see things as one's culture sees them.

PROXEMICS   The study of the norms surrounding personal space and the conditions under which such space will or will not be violated.

PURE RESEARCH   Research which focuses on understanding social relationships.

QUALITATIVE RESEARCH   Research that uses concepts and classifications so as to attempt to interpret human behaviour in a way that reflects not only the analyst's view but also the views of the people whose behaviour is being described; the emphasis is on verbal descriptions as opposed to numerical descriptions.

QUALITY CONTROL MONITORING SYSTEM   Refers to procedures used to ensure that interviewers are following established procedures for selecting respondents, asking questions, and entering the data.

QUANTITATIVE RESEARCH   Research seeking to quantify, or reflect with numbers, observations about human behaviour.

QUASI-EXPERIMENTAL DESIGN   A design in which it has not been possible to do any or all of the following: (i) randomly assign subjects to a treatment or control group; or (ii) control the timing or nature of the treatment. The quasi-experiment comes as close as possible to experimental design in order to measure the impact of a treatment.

QUESTIONNAIRE   A document made up of a series of set questions which either provides spaces for answers or a number of fixed alternatives from which the respondent makes a choice.

QUOTA SAMPLE   A sample in which respondents are selected on the basis of meeting certain criteria: the first respondent to meet the requirement(s) is asked to participate and sampling continues until all the categories have been filled—until the quota for each has been reached.

R^2 A measure of the amount of variation in the dependent variable is explained by an independent variable.

R A measure of the amount of variation in the dependent variable that is explained by the combination of independent variables (regression analysis).

RANDOM ERROR   Inconsistencies which enter into the coding process but which have no pattern in the errors.

RANDOM SAMPLE   A sample that provides each unit (usually a person) in the population with an equal chance of being selected for participation in a study.

RANDOM VARIABLE   A variable that varies without control but is taken into account by the way groups are set up in an experiment.

RANGE   Indicates the gap between the lowest and highest value in a distribution.

RANK-ORDERING QUESTIONS   Questions where a respondent is asked to indicate an ordering of response items, usually from most preferred to least preferred.

RATE A measure of the frequency of some phenomenon for a standard sized unit (such as incidence per 1,000 or per 100,000).

RATIO MEASUREMENT A quantitative measurement where intervals are equal and there is a true zero point.

RATIOS are used to compare rates or other measures across categories.

REGRESSION ANALYSIS A method for analysing the relation between a ratio level dependent variable and independent variables. This form of analysis provides weightings that may be used in an equation to describe the relationship; standardized weightings provide a means of estimating the relative impact of independent variables on the dependent variable.

REGRESSION LINE A straight line describing the relation between an independent and a dependent variable drawn so that the vertical deviations of the points above the line equal the vertical deviations below the line.

RELIABILITY Refers to the extent to which, on repeated measures, an indicator will yield similar readings.

RELIABLE KNOWLEDGE Knowledge you can count on, knowledge which allows you to predict outcomes.

REPLACEMENT OF TERMS The replacement of general theoretical concepts by specific instances of these concepts.

RESEARCH BIAS Systematic distortions in research outcomes.

RESEARCHER AFFECT A process whereby the researcher, having fallen in love with a particular explanation for some relationship, or view of the world, may inadvertently engage in procedures which lead to conclusions supporting the preferred explanation.

RESEARCH HYPOTHESIS A statement of a relation between variables.

RESIDUALS When we allow one variable to explain all the variation that it can in another variable, what is left unexplained (deviations from the regression line) are the residuals.

RESPONSE BIAS Response bias is exhibited if respondents who wish to appear consistent give the same responses to questions as they did the first time; others might want to help the researchers, and, suspecting that the study is meant to demonstrate how good something is, respond by being more positive after the experimental stimulus has been given.

RESPONSE RATE The percentage of delivered questionnaires that are completed and returned.

RESPONSE SET A situation where a respondent tends to answer similarly to all items.

REVIEW OF THE LITERATURE A section of a paper which tries to provide an overview of the "state of scientific knowledge" on the topic being researched.

ROLE MODELLING Emulating someone else's attitudes and behaviours.

SALIENCE OF THE TOPIC The degree of interest in the topic of the researcher by the respondent; the greater the salience of the topic to respondents, the greater the response rate.

SAMPLE A segment selected from a population that is interpreted to represent that population.

SAMPLING FRACTION The sample size in relation to the population.

SAMPLING FRAME The list from which you draw a sample.

SCALABLE ITEMS Items among which there is a hierarchy: this means that when items are arranged from low intensity to high intensity, if a person responds positively to an item at the high end, the or she is expected to respond positively to all lower intensity items.

SCALE A complex combination of indicators in which the pattern of the responses is taken into account.

SECONDARY DATA Information collected by persons other than the researcher.

SELECTED EVIDENCE Selected evidence is used when the researcher chooses to report those studies that support a particular point of view, ignoring the evidence that runs counter to what the researcher is attempting to demonstrate.

SELECTION Refers to subjects selecting themselves into a study.

SEMANTIC DIFFERENTIAl Items are used to study subjective feelings toward objects, or persons.

SEXUAL DICHOTOMISM Treating the sexes as discrete social. as well as biological, cohorts rather than two cohorts with shared characteristics.

SIGNIFICANT OTHERS Those who help define the world for individuals by serving as models for attitudes and behaviour.

SIMPLE RANDOM SAMPLE A sample that provides each unit (usually a person) in the population with an equal chance of being selected for participation in a study.

SKIP INTERVAL An interval determined by dividing the total sample requirement into the total number of units in the population being surveyed; this number should then be rounded to the nearest, but lower, round number.

SNOWBALL SAMPLING A name for a referral sampling procedure. As you complete one interview you ask if there is anyone else known to the respondent who might be appropriate for the study.

SOURCE OF SPURIOUSNESS VARIABLE A variable viewed as possibly influencing both the independent and the dependent variable in such a way that it accounts for the relationship between them.

SPEARMAN CORRELATION This statistic is used to measure the strength of association between two ordinal level variables.

SPLIT-HALF METHOD This method for testing reliability involves randomly splitting index items into two groups, computing the indexes, and then correlating the resulting scores. Internal reliability would be indicated by a high correlation between the two indexes.

STANDARD DEVIATION A measure that reflects the average amount of deviation from the mean value of the variable.

STANDARD ERROR OF THE MEANS A measure of variability in the means of repeated samples.

STATISTICAL REGRESSION Statistical regression is demonstrated when a sample is selected on the basis of extreme scores and retesting shows a tendency toward less extreme scores.

STRATIFIED SAMPLE A sample that will give individuals within designated categories an equal chance of selection.

STRUCTURED INTERVIEWS Face-to-face interviews where questions are read to the respondents. Such interviews ordinarily will provide for in-depth probes on some of the questions.

SUMMARY TABLES Tables that compress the results of many analyses into one table.

SURVEYS A method of collecting information by having respondents complete a questionnaire.

SYMBOLIC INTERACTIONIST THEORY Symbolic interactionist theory pays attention particularly to how one's self-concept is formed. People develop a sense of self that is influenced by how others see them and by how others react to them.

SYSTEMATIC ERRORS Errors that distort the data in one particular direction.

SYSTEMATIC SAMPLE A sample that provides each unit (usually a person) in the population an equal chance of being selected for participation in a study by choosing every nth unit, starting randomly.

TALLY SHEETS Sheets used to record information during the data collection phase of observational studies.

TEST OF SIGNIFICANCE A test reporting the probability that an observed association or difference is the result of sampling fluctuations, and not reflective of some "real" difference in the population from which the sample has been taken.

THEORETICAL LEVEL The most abstract, general conceptualization of the research problem in a research project.

TREATMENT LEVEL A term referring to the number of different categories of a variable that will be exposed to the subject in an experiment. A study, for example, with three treatment levels might compare the effects of seeing a short, medium, or long film.

TREATMENT VARIABLE A variable whose effect on some dependent variable is being assessed in an experiment.

TRIANGULATION The use of a variety of techniques to test research questions.

TRUE VALUE The underlying exact quantity of a variable at any given time.

T-TEST A test of significance frequently used to compare two groups on a ratio-level dependent variable. The test determines if the differences in the means may be regarded as statistically significant. This test is usually used with small samples.

TWO-TAILED TEST A term that refers to situations in which we have not predicted into which particular tail of the normal distribution the result will fall into if the null hypothesis is to be rejected.

TYPE I ERROR The error that results when we reject a null hypotheses that should be accepted.

TYPE II ERROR The error that results when we accept a null hypothesis that should be rejected.

UNILINEAL MODEL A model where the same patterns of development are followed by all societies.

UNIT OF ANALYSIS The basic type of object under investigation: usually researchers define the unit and deal with only one unit at a time. This unit may be a speech, or a paragraph from the speech; it may be a number of individuals or a number of groups. The information collected describes the unit under investigation.

VALIDITY   The term validity refers to the extent to which a measurement reflects a concept. A valid measurement reflects neither more nor less than what is implied by the conceptual definition.

VARIABLES   Those concepts which we intend to measure.

VARIANCE   The average amount of deviation from the mean value of the variable; it is the standard deviation squared.

VERIFIABLE   A term referring to information which can be confirmed by tests conducted by others.

VERSTEHEN   A German word meaning the empathetic understanding of behaviour.

WITHIN-SUBJECT DESIGN   An experimental design exposing one subject to different experimental treatments. Since the subject is the same person, background characteristics, attitudes, and intelligence are all perfectly controlled.

Z SCORE   A measure expressing an observation's location relative to the mean (in standard deviation units) within a normal distribution.

BIBLIOGRAPHY

ABRAHAMSON, MARK (1983). *Social Research Methods*. Englewood Cliffs, N.J.: Prentice-Hall, Inc.

ABRAHAMSSON, BENGT (1970). "Homans on Exchange: Hedonism Revisited," *American Journal of Sociology*, 76(2).

ALLPORT, GORDON W. (1954). *The Nature of Prejudice*. Cambridge, Mass.: Addison-Wesley.

ANDERSON, NELS (1961). *The Hobo*. Chicago: Phoenix Edition, [1923].

ARNOLD, STEPHEN, AND DOUGLAS J. TIGERT (1974). "Canadians and Americans: A Comparative Perspective," *International Journal of Comparative Sociology*, 15, 68-83.

ASHER, HERBERT B. (1976). *Causal Modelling*. Beverly Hills: Sage Publications.

BABBIE, EARL (1990). *Survey Research Methods*, Second Edition. Belmont: Wadsworth Publishing Company.

———— (1992). *The Practice of Social Research*, Sixth Edition. Belmont: Wadsworth Publishing Company.

BAER, DOUG, EDWARD GRABB, AND WILLIAM A. JOHNSTON (1990). "The Values of Canadians and Americans: a Critical Analysis and Reassessment," *Social Forces*, 68(3), 693-713.

BAILEY, KENNETH D. (1970). "Evaluating Axiomatic Theories," in Edgar F. Borgatta and George W. Bohrnstedt, *Sociological Methodology 1970*. San Francisco: Jossey-Bass Inc.

BARON, STEPHEN W. (1989). "The Canadian West Coast Punk Subculture: A Field Study," *Canadian Journal of Sociology*, 14(3), 289-316.

BART, P., AND L. FRANKEL (1986). *The Student Sociologist's Handbook*, Fourth Edition. New York: Random House.

BECKER, HOWARD S. (1953). "Becoming a Marijuana User," *American Journal of Sociology*, (November), 235-242.

BECKER, HOWARD S., BLANCHE GEER, EVERETT C. HUGHES, AND ANSELM L. STRAUSS (1961). *Boys in White*. Chicago: The University of Chicago Press.

BEGLEY, SHARON 1993 "The Meaning of Junk," *Newsweek*, (March 23), 62-64.

BENJAMIN, LUDY T. JR. (1988). *A History of Psychology*. New York: McGraw-Hill Book Company.

BERGER, PETER L., AND THOMAS LUCKMAN (1966). *The Social Construction of Reality*. Garden City, New York: Doubleday.

BERREMAN, GERALD D. (1973). "Behind Many Masks: Ethnography and Impression Management in a Himalayan Village," in Donald P. Warwick,

and Samuel Osherson, *Comparative Research Methods*. Englewood Cliffs, N.J.: Prentice-Hall, Inc., 268-312.

BESHERS, JAMES M. (1958). "On 'A Critique of Tests of Significance in Survey Research,'" *American Sociological Review*, (23 April).

BLALOCK, HUBERT M. JR. (1964). *Causal Inference in Nonexperimental Research*. Chapel Hill: The University of North Carolina Press.

———— (1969). *Theory Construction*. Englewood Cliffs, New Jersey: Prentice-Hall, Inc.

———— (1974). *Measurement in the Social Sciences*. Chicago: Aldine Publishing Company.

———— (1979). *Social Statistics*. Toronto: McGraw-Hill Book Company.

———— (1984). *Basic Dilemmas in the Social Sciences*. Beverly Hills: Sage Publications.

BLAU, PETER (1964). *Exchange and Power in Social Life*. New York: John Wiley & Sons, Inc.

BLISHEN, B.R. (1968). "A Socioeconomic Index for Occupations in Canada," *Canadian Review of Sociology and Anthropology*, (February), 41-53.

BLISHEN, B.R., AND H. MCROBERTS (1976). "A Revised Socioeconomic Index for Occupations in Canada," *Canadian Review of Sociology and Anthropology*, 13(1), 71-79.

BLUMER, HERBERT (1951). "Collective Behavior," in A.M. Lee (ed.), *Principles of Sociology*. New York: Barnes and Noble, 167-222.

BOHRNSTEDT, G.W. (1969). "A Quick Method for Determining the Reliability and Validity of Multiple-Item Scales," *American Sociological Review*, 34, 542-548.

BONNAR, ANNE MARIE (1992), "To Signal or Not to Signal: A Study of Personal Space and Behaviour," Antigonish: St. Francis Xavier University, Sociology 100 paper.

BOTTOMORE, T.B., AND MAXIM-ILIEN RUBEL (1988). *Karl Marx: Selected Writings in Sociology and Social Philosophy*. London: Penguin Books.

BRADBURN, NORMAN M., AND SEYMOUR SUDMAN (1980). *Improving Interview Method and Questionnaire Design*. San Francisco: Jossey-Bass Publishers.

BRAITHWAITE, R. W. (1960). *Scientific Explanation*. New York: Harper Torchbooks.

BRENNAN, ANDREA (1985). "Participation and Self-Esteem: A Test of Six Alternative Explanations," *Adolescence*, 20(78), 445-466.

BROUSSARD, MICHELLE (1991). "Unwanted Intimacy in Female University Students," Antigonish: St. Francis Xavier University, Research Methods Paper.

BURGESS, ROBERT G. (1984). *In the Field: An Introduction to Field Research*. London: George Allen & Unwin.

CAMPBELL, DONALD T., AND JULIAN C. STANLEY (1966). *Experimental and Quasi-Experimental Designs for*

Research. Chicago: Rand McNally & Company.

CARMINES, EDWARD G., AND RICHARD A. ZELLER (1979). *Reliability and Validity Assessment*. Beverly Hills: Sage Publications.

CHEYN, EFIAN (1972). "The Effect of Spatial and Interpersonal Variables on the Invasion of Group Controlled Territories," *Sociometry*, 477-488.

CLAIRMONT, DONALD H., AND WINSTON JACKSON (1980). "Segmentation and the Low Income Blue Collar Worker: A Canadian Test of Segmentation Theory," Halifax: Institute of Public Affairs, Dalhousie University.

COCHRAN, W.G. (1963). *Sampling Techniques*, Second Edition. New York: John Wiley & Sons.

COLLINS, RANDALL (1975). *Conflict Sociology: Toward an Explanatory Science*. New York: Academic Press.

COMTE, AUGUST (1875). *System of Positive Polity*. London: Burt Franklin, [1851].

CORBIN, JULIET, AND ANSELM STRAUSS (1990). "Grounded Theory Research: Procedures, Canons, and Evaluative Criteria," *Qualitative Sociology*, 13(1), 3-21.

COSER, LEWIS A. (1956). *The Functions of Social Conflict*. London: Free Press of Glencoe.

COSTNER, R.L., AND R.K. LEIK (1964). "Deductions from 'Axiomatic Theory,'" *American Sociological Review*, 29 (December), 819-835.

CRAWFORD, CRAIG, AND JAMES CURTIS (1979). "English Canadian-American Differences in Value Orientations," *Studies*

in Comparative International Development, 14, 23-44.

CURTIS, JAMES (1971). "Voluntary Association Joining: A Cross-National Comparative Note," *American Sociological Review*, 36 (October), 872-880.

CURTIS, JAMES, RONALD D. LAMBERT, STEVEN D. BROWN, AND BARRY J.KAY (1989). "Affiliation with Voluntary Associations: Canadian-American Comparisons," *Canadian Journal of Sociology*, 14(2), 143-161.

CURTIS, JAMES, AND LORNE TEPPERMAN (1990). *Images of Canada*. Scarborough, Ontario: Prentice-Hall Canada Inc.

DAHRENDORF, RALF (1958). "Out of Utopia: Toward a Reorientation of Sociological Analysis," *American Journal of Sociology*, 64.

DAVIDOFF, HENRY (1953). *A World Treasury of Proverbs*. London: Cassell & Company.

DESROCHES, FREDERICK J. (1990). "Tearoom Trade: A Research Update," *Qualitative Sociology*, 13(1), 39-61.

DEUTSCHER, IRWIN (1966). "Words and Deeds: Social Action and Social Policy," *Social Problems*, 13, 235-254.

DILLMAN, DON A. (1972). "Increasing Mail Questionnaire Response in Large Samples of the General Public," *Public Opinion Quarterly*, 36, 254-257.

———— (1978). *Mail and Telephone Surveys: The Total Design Method*. New York: John Wiley & Sons.

DILLMAN, DON A., JAMES A. CHRISTENSON, EDWIN H. CAR-PENTER, AND RALPH M. BROOKS (1974). "Increasing

Mail Questionnaire Response," *American Sociological Review,* 39(5), 744-756.

DRIVER, H.E., AND W.C. MASSEY (1957). *Comparative Studies of North American Indians.* Philadelphia: The American Philosophical Society.

DURKHEIM, EMILE (1938). *The Rules of Sociological Method.* New York: The Free Press, [1895].

———— (1951). *Suicide: A Study of Sociology.* Translated by J. Spaulding and G. Simpson. New York: The Free Press, [1897].

———— (1965). *The Elementary Forms of the Religious Life.* New York: The Free Press, [1912].

EASTHOPE, GARY (1974). *History of Social Research Methods.* London: Longman Group Limited.

EICHLER, MARGRIT (1988). *Nonsexist Research Methods.* Boston: Allen & Unwin.

EICHNER, KLAUS, AND WERNER HABERMEHL (1981). "Predicting Response Rates to Mailed Questionnaires," *American Sociological Review,* 46, 361-363.

ERDOS, PAUL L. (1983). *Professional Mail Surveys.* Malabar, Florida: Robert E. Krieger Publishing Company.

ERIKSON, KAI T. (1967). "A Comment on Disguised Observation in Sociology," *Social Problems,* 14, 366-373.

ETZIONI, A. (1968). "A Model of Significant Research.," *International Journal of Psychiatry,* 6, 279-280.

FAY, BRIAN (1987). *Critical Social Science: Liberation and its Limits.* Ithaca, N.Y.: Cornell University Press.

FEATHERMAN, DAVID L., AND GILLIAN STEVENS (1982). "A Revised Index of Occupational Status: Application in Analysis of Sex Differences in Attainment," Chapter 7 in *Social Structure and Behavior: Essays in Honor of William Hamilton Sewell.* New York: Academic Press.

FESTINGER, L., H.W. RIECKEN, AND S. SCHACHTER (1956). *When Prophecy Fails.* New York: Harper & Row.

FISHER, DOUG (1993). "Fed up with too many questions, Canadians are hanging up on pollsters," *Montreal Gazette,* September 24, A8.

FORCESE, DENNIS P., AND JOHN DEVRIES (1977). "Occupation and Electoral Success in Canada: The 1974 Federal Election," *Canadian Review of Sociology and Anthropology,* 14(3), 331-340.

FORCESE, DENNIS P., AND STEPHEN RICHER (1973). *Social Research Methods.* Englewood Cliffs, N.J.: Prentice-Hall.

———— (eds.) (1970). *Stages of Social Research: Contemporary Perspectives.* Englewood Cliffs, N.J.: Prentice-Hall.

FOUGERE, ANNETTE (1992). "Effects of Eating Breakfast on Grade Performance," Antigonish: St. Francis Xavier University, Research Methods Paper.

GALTUNG, JOHAN (1967). *Theory and Methods of Social Research.* New York: Columbia University Press.

GIBBS, JACK P. (1972). *Sociological Theory Construction.* Hinsdale, Illinois: The Dryden Press, Inc.

GIBBS, J.P., AND W.T. MARTIN (1964). *Status Integration and*

Suicide: A Sociological Study. Eugene Oregon: University of Oregon Press.

GLASER, BARNEY G., AND ANSELM STRAUSS (1967). *The Discovery of Grounded Theory.* Chicago: Aldine Press.

GOFFMAN, ERVING (1962). *Asylums.* Chicago: Aldine.

GOLD, DAVID (1958). "Comment on 'A Critique of Tests of Significance,'" *American Sociological Review,* 23 (February), 85-86.

GORTNER, SUSAN R., AND PHYLLIS R. Schultz (1988). "Approaches to Nursing Science Methods," *Image,* 20(1), 22-24.

GOYDER, JOHN C. (1982). "Further Evidence on Factors Affecting Response Rates to Mailed Questionnaires," *American Sociological Review,* 47(August), 550-553.

———— (1985a). "Nonresponse on Surveys: A Canada-United States Comparison," *Canadian Journal of Sociology,* 10 (Summer), 231-251.

———— (1985b). "Face-to-Face Interviews and Mailed Questionnaires: The Net Difference in Response Rate," *Public Opinion Quarterly,* 49, 234-252.

GOYDER, JOHN, AND JEAN MCKENZIE LEIPER (1985c). "The Decline in Survey Response: A Social Values Interpretation," *Sociology,* 19(1), 55-71.

GRAYSON, J. PAUL (1983). "Male Hegemony and the English Canadian Novel," *Canadian Review of Sociology and Anthropology,* 20(1), 1-21.

GROVES, ROBERT M., AND ROBERT L. KAHN (1979). *Surveys by Telephone: A*

National Comparison with Personal Interviews. New York: Academic Press.

GUBA, E. G., AND Y.S. LINCOLN (1981). *Effective Evaluation.* San Francisco: Jossey-Bass.

GUTTMAN, LOUIS (1950). "The Basis for Scalogram Analysis," in S.A. Stouffer, L. Buttman, E.A. Suchman, P.F. Lazarfeld, S.A. Star, and J.A. Clausen, *Measurement and Prediction.* Princeton, N.J.: Princeton University Press.

HABERMAS, JURGEN (1984). *The Theory of Communicative Action,* Vol.1. Boston: Beacon Press.

HACKER, DIANA (1990). *A Canadian Writer's Reference.* Scarborough: Nelson Canada.

HAMBLIN, ROBERT L. (1971). "Mathematical Experimentation and Sociological Theory: A Critical Analysis," *Sociometry,* 34, 423-452.

————— (1971). "Ratio Measurement for the Social Sciences," *Social Forces,* 50, 191-206.

————— (1974). "Social Attitudes: Magnitude Measurement and Theory," in H. M. Blalock, Jr., *Measurement in the Social Sciences.* Chicago: Aldine Publishing Company: 61-120.

HEBERLEIN, THOMAS A., AND ROBERT BAUMGARTNER (1978). "Factors Affecting Response Rates to Mailed Questionnaires," *American Sociological Review,* 43.

HEDDERSON, JOHN (1987). *SPSS^x Made Simple.* Belmont, California: Wadsworth Publishing Company.

HEISE, DAVID R., AND GEORGE W. BOHRNSTEDT (1970). "Validity, Invalidity, and

Reliability," in Edgar F. Borgatta and George W. Bohrnstedt, *Sociological Methodology 1970.* San Francisco: Jossey-Bass Inc.

HENRY, FRANCES, AND EFFIE GINZBERG (1990). "Racial Discrimination in Employment," in James Curtis and Lorne Tepperman, *Images of Canada.* Scarborough, Ontario: Prentice-Hall Canada Inc., 302-309.

HENSHEL, RICHARD L. (1971). "Sociology and Prediction," *The American Sociologist,* 6, 213-220.

————— (1976). *On the Future of Prediction.* Indianapolis: The Bobbs-Merrill Company, Inc.

HENWOOD, MALENA (1992). "Unwanted Intimacy," Antigonish: St. Francis Xavier University. Research Methods Report.

HODGES, JOHN C., MARY E. WHITTEN, JUDY BROWN, AND JANE FLICK (1994). *Harbrace College Handbook: for Canadian Writers,* Fourth Edition. Toronto: Harcourt Brace, Canada.

HOLDEN, CONSTANCE (1979). "Ethics in Social Science Research," *Science,* 206 (November), 537 540.

HOLSTI, OLE R. (1969). *Content Analysis for the Social Sciences and Humanities.* Don Mills: Addison-Wesley Publishing Company.

HOMAN, ROGER (1991). *The Ethics of Social Research.* London: Longman.

HOMANS, GEORGE C. (1964). "Bringing Men Back In," *American Sociological Review,* 29, 809-818.

————— (1961). *Social Behavior: Its Elementary Forms.* New York: Harcourt, Brace and World.

HOROWITZ, IRVING LOUIS (1973). "The Hemispheric Connection: A Critique and Corrective to the Entrepreneurial Thesis of Development with Special Emphasis on the Canadian Case," *Queen's Quarterly,* 80 (Autumn), 327-359.

HOROWITZ, IRVING LOUIS, AND LEE RAINWATER (1970). "Jounalistic Moralizers," *TransAction,* 7(7), 5-7.

HUBER, PETER W. (1991). *Galileo's Revenge: Junkyard Science in the Courtroom.* New York: Basic Books.

HUMPHREYS, LAUD (1970). *Tearoom Trade.* Chicago: Aldine Press.

HUNTER, ALFRED A. (1985). "Doing it with Numbers," *The Canadian Review of Sociology and Anthropology,* 22(5), 643-672.

HYMAN, HERBERT (1955). *Survey Design and Analysis.* New York: Free Press.

IVERSEN, GUDMUND R., AND HELMUT NORPOTH (1976). *Analysis of Variance.* Beverly Hills: Sage Publications.

JACKSON, WINSTON (1973). *University Preferences and Perceptions of Pictou County Students.* Antigonish: St Francis Xavier University.

————— (1988). *Research Methods: Rules for Survey Design and Analysis.* Scarborough: Prentice-Hall Canada Inc.

JACKSON, WINSTON, AND NICHOLAS W. POUSHINSKY (1971). *Migration to Northern Mining Communities: Structural and Social Psychological*

Dimensions. Winnipeg: Center for Settlement Studies, University of Manitoba.

JOHNSON, RONALD W., AND JOHN G. ADAIR (1970). "The Effects of Systematic Recording Error vs. Experimenter Bias on Latency of Word Association," *Journal of Experimental Research in Personality,* 4, 270-275.

JOHNSON, RONALD W., AND BRENDA J. RYAN (1976). "Observer Recorder Error as Affected by Different Tasks and Different Expectancy Inducements," *Journal of Research in Personality,* 10, 201-214.

KACHIGAN, SAM KASH (1986). *Statistical Analysis: An Interdisciplinary Introduction to Univariate & Multivariate Methods.* New York: Radius Press.

KAUFMAN, H. (1967). "The Price of Obedience and the Price of Knowledge," *American Psychologist,* 22, 321-322.

KISH, LESLIE (1965). *Survey Sampling.* New York: Wiley.

KINZEL, CLIFF (1992). "The Alberta Survey 1992: Sampling Report," The University of Alberta: Population Research Laboratory.

KNOKE, DAVID, AND PETER J. BURKE (1980). *Log-Linear Models.* Beverly Hills: Sage Publications.

KRAHN, HARVEY (1991). "Sociological Methods of Research," in Lorne Tepperman and R. Jack Richardson, *The Social World: An Introduction to Sociology.* Toronto: McGraw-Hill Ryerson Limited, 34-66.

LAPIERE, RICHARD T. (1934). "Attitudes vs. Actions," *Social Forces,* 13, 230-237.

LASTRUCCI, CARLO L. (1967). *The Scientific Approach.* Cambridge, Massachusettes: Schenkman Publishing, Inc.

LECOMPTE, MARGARET D., AND JUDITH PREISSLE GOETZ (1982). "Problems of Reliability and Validity in Ethnographic Research," *Review of Educational Research,* 52(1), 31-60.

LEE, MICHELLE (1992). "Smoking Behaviours." Antigonish: St. Francis Xavier University, Research Methods Paper.

LEVIN, JACK, AND JAMES ALAN FOX (1991). *Elementary Statistics in Social Research,* Fifth Edition. New York: HarperCollins Publishers Inc.

LI, PETER S., AND B. SINGH BO-LARIA (1993). *Contemporary Sociology: Critical Perspectives.* Toronto: Copp Clark Pitman Ltd.

LIEBOW, ELLIOT M. (1967). *Tally's Corner. A Study of Negro Streetcorner Men.* Boston: Little, Brown and Company.

LIKERT, RENSIS (1931). "A Technique for the Measurement of Attitudes," *Archives of Psychology.* New York: Columbia University Press.

LODGE, MILTON (1981). *Magnitude Scaling: Quantitative Measurement of Opinions.* Beverly Hills: Sage Publications.

LOFLAND, JOHN (1971). *Analyzing Social Settings.* Belmont: Wadsworth Publishing Company, Inc.

MACDONALD LARA (1991). "Attitudes Toward the Elderly," Antigonish: St. Francis Xavier University, Research Methods Report.

MALINOWSKI, BRONISLAW (1954). *Magic, Science and Religion.* New York: Doubleday, [1925].

MANIS, JEROME G., AND BERNARD N. MELTZER (Eds.) (1978). *Symbolic Interaction: A Reader in Social Psychology,* Third Edition. Boston: Allyn and Bacon.

MARTIN, DAVID W. (1991). *Doing Psychology Experiments.* Pacific Grove: Brooks/Cole Publishing Company, Third Edition.

MARX, KARL (1977). *Capital.* New York: Vintage Books, [1867].

MCGINNIS, ROBERT (1958). "Randomization and Inference in Sociological Research," *American Sociological Review,* 23 (October), 408-414.

MCIVER, JOHN P., AND ED-WARD G. CARMINES (1981). *Unidimensional Scaling.* Beverly Hills: Sage Publications.

MEAD, GEORGE H. (1934). *Mind, Self, and Society.* Chicago: University of Chicago Press.

MEAD, MARGARET (1935). *Sex and Temperament in Three Primitive Societies.* New York: Morrow.

———— (1966). *An Anthropologist at Work: Writings of Ruth Benedict.* New York: Harcourt Brace Jovanovich.

MILGRAM, STANLEY (1963). "Behavioural Study of Obedience," *Journal of Abnormal and Social Psychology,* 67, 371-378.

———— (1964). "Issues in the Study of Obedience," *American Psychologist,* 19, 848-852.

———— (1968). "Reply to Critics.," *International Journal of Psychiatry,* 6, 294-295.

MILL, JOHN STUART (1925). *A System of Logic,* Eighth Edition. London: Lognmans, Green and Co.

MILLER, DELBERT C. (1977). *Handbook of Research Design and Social Measurement,* Third Edition. New York: Longman.

MILLS, C. WRIGHT (1959). *The Sociological Imagination.* New York: Oxford University Press.

MINER, HORACE (1939). *St. Denis: A French-Canadian Parish.* Chicago: University of Chicago Press.

MITCHELL, MARK, AND JANINA JOLLEY (1992). *Research Design Explained,* Second Edition. Orlando: Harcourt Brace Jovanovitch College Publishers.

MONETTE, DUANE R., THOMAS J. SULLIVAN, AND CORNELL R. DEJONG (1990). *Applied Social Research: Tool for the Human Services,* Second Edition. Fort Worth: Holt, Rinehart and Winston, Inc.

MORRISON, E. DENTON, AND RAMON E. HENKEL, EDS. (1970). *The Significance Tests Controversy.* Chicago: Aldine Press.

MURDOCK, GEORGE P. (1960). *Social Structure.* New York: Macmillan.

NACHMIAS, DAVID, AND CHAVA NACHMIAS (1981). *Research Methods in the Social Sciences,* Second Edition. New York: St. Martin's Press.

NAGEL, ERNEST (1961). *The Structure of Science: Problems in the Logic of Scientific Explanations.* New York: Harcourt, Brace & World, Inc.

NETER, JOHN, WILLIAM WASSERMAN, AND MICHAEL KUTNER (1985). *Applied Linear Statistical Models.* Homewood, Illinois: Irwin.

NEUMAN, W. LAWRENCE (1991). *Social Research Methods.* Needham Heights, Massachusetts: Allyn and Bacon.

NORUSIS, MARIJA J., (1985). *The SPSS Guide to Data Analysis.* Chicago: SPSS Inc.

NORUSIS, MARIJA J., AND SPSS INC. (1992). *SPSS/PC+ Base System User's Guide, Version 5.0.* Chicago: SPSS Inc.

———— (1992). *SPSS/PC+ Advanced Statistics, Version 5.0.* Chicago: SPSS Inc.

———— (1992). *SPSS/PC+ Professional Statistics, Version 5.0.* Chicago: SPSS Inc.

O'CALLAGHAN, TERRANCE (1991). "Alcohol Consumption and Its Correlates at St. F.X.U." Antigonish: St. Francis Xavier University, Research Methods Paper.

ORNE, MARTIN T. (1962). "On the Social Psychology of the Psychological Experiment: With Particular Reference to Demand Characteristics and Their Implications," *American Psychologist,* 17, 776-83.

PALYS, TED (1992). *Research Decisions: Quantitative and Qualitative Perspectives.* Toronto: Harcourt Brace Jovanovitch Canada Inc.

PARROTT III, LES (1994). *How to Write Psychology Papers.* New York: HarperCollins.

PATTEN, S.C. (1977a). "The Case that Milgram Makes," *Philosophical Review,* 88, 350-364.

———— (1977b). "Milgram's Shocking Experiments.," *Philosophy,* 52, 425-440.

PILIAVIN, J.A., AND I.M. PILIAVIN (1972). "Effect of Blood on Reactions to a Victim," *Journal of Personality and Social Psychology,* 23, 353-361.

PINEO, PETER C., AND JOHN PORTER (1967). "Occupational Prestige in Canada," *Canadian Review of Sociology and Anthropology,* 24-40.

PLATT, JOHN R. (1964). "Strong Inference," *Science,* 146(3642), 347-353.

POSTERSKI, DONALD, AND REGINALD BIBBY (1987). *Canada's Youth "Ready for Today": a Comprehensive Survey of 15-24 Year Olds.* Ottawa: The Canadian Youth Foundation.

PSATHAS, GEORGE (1973). *Phenomenological Sociology: Issues and Applications.* New York: Wiley.

RAINWATER, LEE, AND DAVID J. PITTMAN (1967). "Ethical Problems in Studying a Politically Sensitive and Deviant Community," *Social Problems,* 14, 357-366.

REYNOLDS, PAUL DAVIDSON (1982). *Ethics and Social Science Research.* Englewood Cliffs: Prentice-Hall Inc.

RING, K., K. WALLSTON, AND M. COREY (1970). "Mode of Debriefing as a Factor Affecting Subjective Reaction to a Milgram-Type Obedience Experiment: An Ethical Inquiry," *Representative Research in Social Psychiatry,* 1(1), 67-88.

ROETHLISBERGER, F.J., AND W.J. DICKSON (1939). *Management and the Worker.*

Cambridge, Mass.: Harvard University Press.

ROSENTHAL, ROBERT (1966). *Experimenter Effects in Behavioral Research.* New York: Century.

———— (1979). "The 'File Drawer Problem' and Tolerance for Null Results," *Psychological Bulletin,* 86(3), 638-641.

ROSENTHAL, ROBERT, AND K.L. FODE (1963). "The Effect of Experimenter Bias on the Performance of the Albino Rat," *Behavioral Science,* 8, 183-189.

ROSENTHAL, ROBERT, AND RALPH L. ROSNOW (1991). *Essentials of Behavioural Research: Methods and Data Analysis,* Second Edition. New York: McGraw-Hill, Inc.

SANDELOWSKI, MARGARETE (1986). "The Problem of Rigor in Qualitative Research," *Advances in Nursing Science,* 8(3), 27-37.

SCHATZMAN, LEONARD, AND ANSELEM L. STRAUSS (1973). *Field Research: Strategies for a Natural Sociology.* Englewood Cliffs: Prentice-Hall, Inc.

SCHUESSLER, KARL F. (1982). *Measuring Social Life Feelings.* San Francisco: Jossey-Bass Publishers.

SCHUMAN, HOWARD, AND STANLEY PRESSER (1981). *Questions and Answers in Attitude Surveys.* New York: The Academic Press, Inc.

SCHUTZ, A. (1954). "Concept and Theory Formation in the Social Sciences," *Journal of Philosophy,* 51(9), 257-273.

SCHWARTZ, HOWARD, AND JERRY JACOBS (1979). *Qualitative Sociology: A Method to the Madness.* New York: The Free Press.

SEILER, LAUREN H., AND RICHARD L. HOUGH (1970). "Empirical Comparisons of the Thurstone and Likert Techniques," in Gene F. Summers (Ed.), *Attitude Measurement.* Chicago: Rand McNally & Company, 1970, 159-173.

SELLIN, J.T., AND M.E. WOLF-GANG (1964). *The Measurement of Delinquency.* New York: John Wiley.

SELVIN, HANAN C., AND ALAN STUART (1966). "Data Dredging Procedures in Survey Analysis," *Journal of the American Statistical Association,* 61, 20-23.

SELVIN, HANAN C. (1957). "A Critique of Tests of Significance in Survey Research," *American Sociological Review,* 22 (October), 519-527.

SHEPPARD, ROBERT (1993). "Yes, no, undecided or just hangs up?," *Globe and Mail,* August 23, A11.

SHIELDS, STEPHANIE A. (1988). "Functionalism, Darwinism, and the Psychology of Women: A Study in Social Myth," in Ludy T. Benjamin, Jr., (1988) *A History of Psychology.* New York: McGraw-Hill Book Company.

SILVERSTEIN, BRETT, LAUREN PERDUE, BARBARA PETERSON, AND EILEEN KELLY (1986). "The Role of the Mass Media in Promoting a Thin Standard of Bodily Attractiveness for Women," *Sex Roles,* 14(9/10), 519-532.

SIMON, HERBERT A. (1957). *Models of Man.* New York: John Wiley & Sons.

SIMON, JULIAN L., AND PAUL BURSTEIN (1885). *Basic Research Methods in Social Science,* Third Edition. New York: Random House.

SKIDMORE, WILLIAM (1975). *Theoretical Thinking in Sociology.* London: Cambridge University Press.

SKIPPER, JAMES K., ANTHONY L. GUENTHER, AND GILBERT NASS (1967). "The Sacredness of .05: A Note Concerning the Uses of Statistical Levels of Significance in Social Science," *American Sociologist,* 2, 16-18.

SLONIM, M. J. (1966). *Sampling in a Nutshell.* New York: Simon and Schuster.

SMITH, DOROTHY E. (1987). *The Everyday World as Problematic: a Feminist Sociology.* Toronto: University of Toronto Press.

SMITH, MICHAEL D. (no date). "Effects of Question Format on the Reporting of Woman Abuse: A Telephone Survey Experiment." Toronto: Institute for Social Research, York University.

SPSS INC. (1988). *SPSS^x User's Guide,* Third Edition. Chicago, SPSS Inc.

STERLING, T.D. (1959). "Publication Decisions and Their Possible Effects on Inferences Drawn from Tests of Significance—or Vice Versa," *Journal of the American Statistical Association,* 54, 30-34.

STEVENS, S.S. (1951). "Mathematics, Measurement, and Psychophysics," in S.S. Stevens (ed.), *Handbook of Experimental Psychology.* New York: Wiley.

———— (1957) "On the Psychophysical Law," *Psychological Review,* 64, 153-181.

———— (1966a). "A Metric for the Social Consensus," *Science,* 151, 530-41.

———— (1966b). "Matching Functions Between Loudness and Ten other Continua," *Perception and Psychophysics*, 1, 5-8.

STRUNK, WILLIAM, AND E. B. WHITE (1959). *The Elements of Style*. Galt, Ontario: Brett-MacMillan Ltd.

SUDMAN, SEYMOUR (1967). *Reducing the Cost of Surveys*. Chicago: Aldine Publishing Company.

———— (1976). *Applied Sampling*. New York: Academic Press.

SUDMAN, SEYMOUR, AND NORMAN BRADBURN (1983). *Asking Questions*. San Francisco: Jossey-Bass Publishers.

SUMMERS, GENE F. (Ed.) (1970). *Attitude Measurement*. Chicago: Rand McNally & Company.

SYKES, GRESHAM M. (1968). *The Society of Captives*. New York: Atheneum.

TANNER, JULIAN, AND HARVEY KRAHN (1991). "Part-Time Work and Deviance Among High School Seniors," *Canadian Journal of Sociology*, 16(3), 281-302.

TAWNEY, R.H. (1926). *Religion and the Rise of Capitalism*. Harcourt, Brace and Company, Inc.

TEEVAN, JAMES J. (1992). *Introduction to Sociology: A Canadian Focus*, Fourth Edition. Scarborough: Prentice-Hall Canada Inc.

TEPPERMAN, LORNE, AND R. JACK RICHARDSON (1991). *The Social World: An Introduction to Sociology*. Toronto: McGraw-Hill Ryerson Limited.

THIBAUT, JOHN W., AND HAROLD H. KELLEY (1959). *The Social Psychology of Groups*. New York: Wiley.

THURSTONE, L. L. (1929). "Fechner's Law and the Method of Equal-Appearing Intervals," *Journal of Experimental Psychology*, 12, 214-224.

TURNER, JONATHAN H. (1991). *The Structure of Sociological Theory*, Fifth Edition. Belmont, California: Wadsworth Publishing Company.

VON HOFFMAN, NICHOLAS (1970). "Sociological Snoopers," *TransAction*, 7(7), 4-6.

WALLACE RUTH A., AND ALISON WOLF (1991). *Contemporary Sociological Theory: Continuing the Classical Tradition*, Third Edition. Englewood Cliffs, New Jersey: Prentice Hall.

WALLACE, WALTER (1971). *The Logic of Science in Sociology*. Chicago: Aldine Atherton.

WARWICK, DONALD P. (1973b). "Tearoom Trade: Means & Ends in Social Research," *Hastings Center Studies*, 1(1), 27-38.

WARWICK, DONALD P., AND SAMUEL OSHERSON (1973a). *Comparative Research Methods*. Englewood Cliffs, N.J.: Prentice-Hall, Inc.

WAX, SYDNEY LAWRENCE (1948). "A Survey of Restrictive Advertising and Discrimination by Summer Resorts in the Province of Ontario, *Information and Comment*, 7, 10-13.

WEBB, EUGENE J., DONALD T. CAMPBELL, RICHARD SCHWARTZ, AND LEE SECHREST (1966). *Unobtrusive Measures: Nonreactive Research in the Social Sciences*. Chicago: Rank McNally.

WEBER, MAX (1904). *The Protestant Ethic and the Spirit of Capitalism*. New York: Charles Scribner & Sons.

———— (1964). *Sociology of Religion*. Boston: Beacon Press.

WEINBERG, EVE (1971). *Community Surveys with Local Talent*. Chicago: National Opinion Research Center.

WEITZ, ROSE (1990). "Living with the Stigma of AIDS," *Qualitative Sociology*, 13(1), 23-38.

WHYTE, WILLIAM FOOTE (1955). *Street Corner Society: The Social Structure of an Italian Slum*, Second Edition. Chicago: University of Chicago Press.

WRIGHT, EDWARD F., WINSTON JACKSON, SCOTT D. CHRISTIE, GREGORY R. MCGUIRE, AND RICHARD D. WRIGHT (1991). "The Home-Course Disadvantage in Golf Championships: Further Evidence for the Undermining Effect of Supportive Audiences on Performance Under Pressure," *Journal of Sport Behavior*, 14(1), 51-60.

WRIGHT, EDWARD F., DANIEL VOYER, RICHARD D. WRIGHT, AND CHRIS RONEY (1994). "Supporting Audiences and Performance Under Pressure: The Home-Ice Disadvantage in Hockey Championships," *Journal of Sport Behavior* (in press).

ZETTERBERG, HANS L. (1965). *On Theory and Verification in Sociology*. Totowa, New Jersey: The Bedminster Press.

INDEX